ANIMALS IN RELIGION

For my human family: David, Rhys, Cara, Bronwen, Ron, Mary and Bernadette.

A special heart-felt 'thank you' to Dianne Aitken, who read every word of this text; your passion for animals continues to inspire me.

For my non-human family, who live out the sacred everyday: Primo, Rosa, Pigeon, Leaf, Ms Chip, Mani, Bern, Laurie and my fish community.

And to God, Creator of all. Thank you for blessing us with feathered, furred and finned brethren.

ANIMALS IN RELIGION

Devotion, Symbol and Ritual

BARBARA ALLEN

REAKTION BOOKS

Published by Reaktion Books Ltd
Unit 32, Waterside
44–48 Wharf Road
London N1 7UX, UK

www.reaktionbooks.co.uk

First published 2016
Copyright © Barbara Allen 2016

proudly supported by
voiceless
the animal protection institute
www.voiceless.org.au

While Voiceless has provided financial assistance in connection with this Project, it does not necessarily endorse the views expressed nor does it guarantee the accuracy, completeness or legality of the material provided

All rights reserved
No part of this publication may be reproduced, stored in a retrieval system, or transmitted, in any form or by any means, electronic, mechanical, photocopying, recording or otherwise, without the prior permission of the publishers

Printed and bound in Great Britain
by TJ International, Padstow, Cornwall

A catalogue record for this book is available from the British Library

ISBN 978 1 78023 569 1

Contents

Introduction *7*

ONE
Animals in Tribal and First Peoples' Religions *13*

TWO
Animals in Ancient Egyptian Religion and Mythology *88*

THREE
Animals in Celtic and Viking Myth and Ritual *120*

FOUR
Animals in Judaism *132*

FIVE
Animals in Christianity *183*

SIX
Animals in Islam *242*

SEVEN
Animals in Hinduism *289*

EIGHT
Animals in Jainism *340*

NINE

Animals in Buddhism *361*

TEN

Animals in Religion in China and Japan *408*

Conclusion *457*

REFERENCES *463*
BIBLIOGRAPHY *531*
ACKNOWLEDGEMENTS *537*
PHOTO ACKNOWLEDGEMENTS *539*
INDEX *543*

Introduction

I think I could turn and live with animals . . .
They do not lie awake in the dark and weep for their sins,
They do not make me sick discussing their duty to God . . .
Not one kneels to another, nor to his kind that lived
thousands of years ago.
                       Walt Whitman[1]

How we understand God in relation to animals will influence how we treat them.
                       Jay McDaniel[2]

In the past, religions and mythologies of different cultures have been key to the way we recognize and come to partly know the 'other'. Religious traditions have either acknowledged or ignored the ways in which non-human animals dwell in this divinely created world. As organized religion is on the decline in the West, will this be a sign of hope, or hindrance, for non-human species? During the last two centuries, since the bursting through of the Enlightenment, animals have been, for the most part, left off the pages in Judaism, Christianity and Islam. Animals are prominent in Hinduism and Buddhism, but is this focus as positive as is often thought?

Different religions assign animals particular roles or status, from being pivotal in the creation of the world or introducing humans to essential life skills (such as the acquisition and use of fire), to having been created solely for humans' use. Animals have been accorded both the high status of gods, and the lowly rank of 'beasts of burden'. While these are the extremes, with many shades in between, animals have always been present within religions,

Bison in the great hall of polychromes, Cave of Altamira, Spain.

some with major roles, others with more of a 'walk-on' part; but they are there.

Animals (more correctly, non-human animals, for we are all animals) have had their images painted and scratched on to cave walls and rock faces for thousands of years. Encounters elicit images. From the Chauvet-Pont-d'Arc Cave in Ardèche, southern France, the second-oldest known cave art,[3] to Lascaux and many other sites around the world, cave paintings and petrographs portray relationships between humans and animals. Relationship can arise from awe (size of the creature), fear (size and nature), but also from love or a fondness for that which is 'other' yet 'the same'. Common themes in these cave paintings are large wild animals, such as bison, horses, lions, bears and deer. Usually the images are of those most suitable for hunting by humans. In Chauvet, among the hundreds of animal paintings, there are both herbivores and predatory animals.

There are a number of theories concerning the cave paintings. Some hypothesize that the paintings were a form of hunting magic or that to paint or scratch them into rock was a way to attract more game. Another theory suggests that they were drawn by palaeolithic shamans, who entered the dark cave and, while in a trance state, painted the images of their visions. There is one painting of a figure that is half-human, half-bison and wearing animal garb, so the shaman idea might be feasible, but we have to exercise caution; we do not know.

In some caves, evidence has been found of what could constitute elements of worship. There is a collection of at least thirty bear skulls found placed in a circle around a fallen stone,[4] which has become known as the 'bear altar'. Theories abound: is this evidence of an ancient bear cult, or were the skulls just arranged in such a fashion? There are also paw prints of cave bears and large, round depressions believed to have been 'bear nests', where they slept. Other sites have uncovered remains of bones and skulls, particularly of bears, which seem to have been part of a ritual of worship.[5] These caves don't appear to have been utilized for ongoing habitation and are often located in areas that are not easily accessible.

In caves and on rocks, artwork testifies to something; the images acknowledge the presence of animals, many of them dealing with the nature of the hunt, but it is hard to determine with any certainty what other activities were involved. Whatever the reasons might be, we do know that humans were with the animals. Were these cave paintings a way to communicate with others, or did they serve a religious or ceremonial purpose? Were these animals part of a worship ritual? What we do know is that animal deities preceded anthropomorphic ones, and that these prehistoric paintings in European caves centre more on animals than on humans. The first subject matter was animals, and they were painted using their blood.

People danced in imitation of the animals that shared their land: to show affinity, respect, reverence and/or mastery. One of the earliest hunter-gatherer-fisher sites in Britain is at Star Carr in North Wales, where twenty sets of deer antlers have been discovered, dating to about 9000 BCE.[6] Archaeologists are convinced these antlers are masks, not trophies, because holes had been drilled through the skull bone at the base of each set, which would have enabled the dancer or shaman to tie the horns on to his head. Acknowledgement needs to be made of these finds and their significance, yet these are not the focus of this work.

What does it mean to acknowledge the arrival of non-human animals before human animals? For some, it has led to recognizing that animal wisdom is older than the wisdom of human animals. Among First Peoples (indigenous) religions, and in many pagan/Wicca practices, animal wisdom is drawn on and honoured, partly because it takes precedence, having arrived first: 'Animals . . . are beings who still remember the original instructions given them by an ancient universe.'[7] 'Since we are the youngest children of Creation, our accumulated wisdom is young, too, and so I search outside of the tiny and fragile box of humankind's insight and understanding for the older wisdom, the more ancient and enduring healing.'[8]

Our fascination with other animal species continues to rise. Note the proliferation of nature programmes, the rise in pet ownership,[9] and the popularity of eco-friendly holidays or volunteer programmes. Cards in shops feature photographs of animals; emails circle the world with photographs of animals heading positive, motivational quotes. Some of this is, putting it bluntly, sentimental sludge. Is this fascination with the 'other' evident in religious traditions?

Religious traditions have considered the paths in which non-human animals partake of, and reside in, this divinely created world. These views filter through the culture of the time and are carried forward into the future. Within this work, I will discuss religions that are still practised, in some shape and form, with one exception. One chapter is devoted to a religion or mythology that is no longer practised, but continues to attract a strong following of admirers: the religion and mythology of ancient Egypt. The strong presence of animals in ancient Egypt's spiritual life merits such a chapter. I have not covered every religion, for there is not room. I have not written a separate chapter about paganism and the rise of the Wicca (White Witch) movement, though pagan practices will be touched on in relevant chapters. Though animal power may be drawn on in shamanic practices in New Age/Wicca rituals, there does not appear to be a clear, central, commonly accepted body of beliefs.

My initial outline was to cover key topics within each chapter: 'Solo', 'Birthing', 'Together', 'Departed'. In some cases, this was achieved; in others, these categories were not a correct fit, so were either discarded, or absorbed under a slightly different title. I would, however, ask you to keep those categories in mind as you read this text.

I am a person of story; we all are, for our own narratives inform who we are and what we believe. Religions, before being collated, condensed and regimented into doctrine and creeds, are first and foremost story. Theo-logy: 'God-word'. 'In the beginning was the Word . . .'; therefore this work draws on the rich bounty of story, religious narrative and myth. Religious or spiritual narrative is usually twofold: the divine and the mortal intersect. The mortal includes our non-human kin, so religious narrative includes them, even if it isn't always clearly stated. Tom Regan reminds us that 'Animals not only have biologies; they also have biographies.' Who are we to say they have no part in sacred narrative? We do not have to be exclusive, for many religious texts include writings or stories about animals.

On a recent trip, I brought back a small statue of a cow. The cow is sitting cross-legged in a meditation pose, dressed in a black and white kimono. This is not what is usually thought of as 'the sacred cow', but perhaps it is appropriate to ponder its significance as we venture forth to consider the cow (and other animals) in the realm of the sacred. Do religions consider the cow (and other creatures) as sacred, or only as creatures created by the divine to serve humans? Are animals able to experience something of the divine? Are animals spiritual beings? Do animals possess souls? How do religions acknowledge Creation?

Within the religious/scriptural texts themselves, there are differences. Sometimes animals are cursed, sometimes they are agents of God, as in the story of Balaam's donkey,[10] which includes the donkey as both prophetic and as a beast of burden.[11] In Genesis we move swiftly, from everything being blessed and pronounced as 'good' in the opening verses, to humans being granted dominion over other creatures; from a vegetarian diet in the Garden, to permission to consume flesh, following the Flood. Sometimes animals serve as divine agents of blessing: Elijah is fed by ravens; Daniel is not eaten in the lion's den; and there are stories of saints having food brought to them by animals.

Within other religions, one finds different interpretations of texts as well; some of these differences led to heated debates, even to internal division. For example, in Buddhism there are differences of opinion concerning whether one is permitted to eat meat if it has been placed in an alms bowl as an offering for a monk. Should there be total abstinence from meat consumption or can the monk eat it if he knows that meat was not specially prepared for him?

In considering how religions view animals, it is important to note that these beliefs and opinions are fluid; there has been much change throughout the centuries. Modern-day environmental issues are being examined by many religions, and the topic of animals informs some of these discussions. Some seekers are going back to their own traditions, asking their own questions. Sometimes this search is due to their own bond with an animal. Perhaps the questions are asked because their animal companion has died and they want to know if their loved one will go to heaven. Tricky theological questions are raised. (Did God create everything? Do animals have souls? Do animals go to heaven? Is God/Allah/ Jehovah 'good'?) In many instances, the questions are being asked outside the places of worship, away from the church/synagogue/temple.

A favourable outcome would be that an understanding or a recognition of the role and presence of non-human animals in religions is grasped, which could lead to a deeper respect for our four-legged, finned and feathered brethren. Respect should lead to a reassessment of the practical (ethics). From the living out of the principle of ahimsa (non-violence) in Jainism, Buddhism and Hinduism, to the laws that relate to *tz'ar ba'alei chayim* (avoiding the suffering/ pain of living creatures), we acknowledge the Jain guiding principle of *Parasparopagraho Jivanam*: the interdependence of life. From the Jain notion of 'reverence for life', to the pronouncement in Genesis 1 that 'it was good,' we may come to a realization that the *mysterium* resides in all living beings, and that all have value. Such an exploration is good for the human animal as well: 'When we regard creatures as "things", "commodities", or "products" then we have denied them their "essence" or their "soul"; we have "de-sacralized" them. When we "de-sacralize" animals, we rob them of their holy qualities, and, in the process, de-humanize ourselves.'[12]

ONE

Animals in Tribal and First Peoples' Religions

> In the beginning of all things, wisdom and knowledge were with the animals; for Tirawa, the One Above, did not speak directly to man. He sent certain animals to tell men that he showed himself through the beasts, and that from them . . . man should learn. Tirawa spoke to man through his works.[1]
> Chief Letakots-Lesa, Pawnee Tribe

Myth and Religion: Ensouled Narratives

LONG AGO HUBERT HOWE BANCROFT WROTE: 'Language is thought incarnate; mythology soul incarnate. The one is the instrument of thought, the other the essence of thought. In mythology, language assumes personality and independence.'[2]

'In his traditional world the Native American lives in the presence of stories. The storyteller is one whose spirit is indispensable to the people. He is magician, artist and creator. And, above all, he is a holy man. His is sacred business.'[3] Stories are predicated upon belief. The primary object of the story is the realization of wonder and delight.

At the beginning of this work, it is necessary to define the difference between mythology and religion. Religion contains ritual, ethics, beliefs and a belief in the reality of an unseen world, a sense of the holy/sacred/'the other'. There are many definitions of the term 'religion', most referring to a unified set of beliefs and/or rituals related to the sacred or holy. Ninian Smart's definition is both broad and succinct, touching on the relationship between myth and religion: religion is 'a set of institutionalized rituals with a tradition and expressing and/or evoking sacral sentiments directed at a divine or trans-divine focus seen in the context of the human phenomenological environment and

Tsimshian (Pacific Northwest Coast) painted wooden dish in the form of a fish.

at least partially described by myths or by myths and doctrines'.[4] Religion contains a philosophy, customs and rituals, ethics and stories, which usually include teaching tales or parables and myths.

Both religion and mythology contain story. The Greek word *mythos* means 'saying', 'word' or 'story'. Many of these narratives embody belief systems that try to make sense of the world, set within a particular culture. Sometimes the narratives deal with natural phenomena, for example, explaining the origins of thunder. Thunder can be Yahweh venting his anger; it can be a particular god dropping dishes in heaven, or it can be Thunderbird searching for prey across his vast hunting grounds. While not all myth embodies belief in deities that are worshipped, or worthy of worship, many myths do address what it means to live on this earth, and what human beings' relationship with other creatures might entail. For example, in Maori mythology, the kiwi bird represents the soul of Tane-Mahuta (god of the forests) and lives deep in the heart of the forest.[5] It is rarely seen, like the heart, but it remains vital for the forest, as the heart does for the body.

Myths differ; the myths found within the stories of Genesis 1 and 2 have more in common with First Peoples' myths than those found within the narratives of ancient Rome and Greece.[6] In the myths and legends of ancient Greece and Rome, jealousies and personality traits of particular gods and goddesses are highlighted. These are not myths designed to awaken a sense of wonder and awe at the universe, its deity/deities and the earth's inhabitants; these stories do not invite one to grapple with or to question humanity's role in the world, within an ethical framework. One exception, however, is the myth concerning the Titan god Epimetheus and his brother Prometheus; this story highlights what supposedly sets humans apart from other creatures. The brothers had been entrusted with the task of populating the world and providing their creations with natural gifts. Prometheus created human beings; Epimetheus created animals and birds. Epimetheus squandered many powerful gifts upon the animals, such as blessing birds with flight and granting speed to horses. Finally, none of these types of gifts remained for humankind, so Prometheus invented a new attribute called 'intelligence', which he gave to humans, as well as the gift of fire, which he stole from Zeus, in order that humans would be armed against wild beasts.

Both mythology and religion are grounded in narrative; stories are told about deities, of beings interacting on a single plane, of animals and humans changing form, of different species speaking the same language, or at least being understood by the other. Religion and mythology (pertaining to First Peoples and tribal groups, as well as to other religions) both try to answer the question about *why* the world came into being (and some try to answer the scientific *how* question as well). Origins of the world, or stories about the structure of the universe, are described. The everyday world is played out on the wider

Akkadian stone cylinder seal (*c.* 2250–2150 BCE) and impression: bull-man fighting a lion and a nude man fighting a water buffalo.

canvas of the invisible world above which is the abode of deities or divine ancestors, and in the underworld, where the dead reside, along with certain spirits. Creation stories address the origins of human beings and of animals, and usually consider the relationship between the two, but not always.

Myths are sacred; they help to explain the cosmic and social order as well as speak of the relationship between humans and gods. Creation myths explain the basic structure of the universe and the origins of humans, animals and death. Some of these myths can only be told at certain times of the year. There are ritual myths, which accompany sacred ceremonies; these are usually in the form of re-enactments. There are also entertainment myths that often involve the figure of the 'trickster'. Heroes and tricksters, both agents of change, can be either human or animal. In North America, the culture heroes, like the early creator divinities, are commonly represented in myths as animals. In African mythology, which, in common with other tribal and First Peoples', is to speak of many mythologies, reflecting the understandings and priorities of various social groups, tribes and races, there are differences, but also common elements. Despite the size of the continent and the more than 2,000 languages spoken, there is the glue of commonality, which includes the myth of the cosmic egg, the chameleon or trickster culture hero and the introduction of death through garbled or broken messages. Animals are more prominent in African myths than just about anywhere else other than North America, with great importance placed on the theriomorphic gods of spider, dog, chameleon, monkey and hare.

> Myth develops as humanity begins to emerge from the realm of animals. Like technology, myth is a compensation for our relative lack of instinct and specialized abilities. Through cosmic dramas, myth organizes our experience, helping us to orient ourselves as human beings in a world that seems alien in so many ways.[7]

Perhaps 'spirituality' is a more fitting word to use, at least for Native American First Peoples, because the word religion is 'a word that most Native Americans agree does not fit their personal experience with the Great Medicine (or the Great Mystery), which is without scripture or edifice'.[8]

Banyang mask and costume of Basinjom, a bird-trickster figure, Cameroon.

This bronze bird is a hand-held percussion instrument, known as a 'clapper', that is sounded by beating the bird's beak with a baton. Clappers were used in an annual festival to commemorate Benin's expansion past the Niger River. In Benin birds were believed to possess supernatural powers – to be mediators between the earthly/human heavenly/spiritual realms.

Did the Native Americans believe in a supreme being, a 'Great Spirit'? This term refers to a supreme being often known as 'the Changer'. 'He was called *Dokibatl, Doquebuth, Xelas, Mikamatt* and other names difficult for white people to pronounce and to spell. This being changed the world of the ancients into the world of the Indian; he was the creator and transformer, but apparently he was not worshipped.'[9] In some stories it is not clear whether the Great Spirit was the chief of the sky spirits, or a powerful spirit, the Supreme Being. The Great Spirit can be a blending of indigenous concepts with the Christian idea of God.[10]

In North America, as in other countries, different regions have their own myths, which usually take into account the topography of the land. The Pacific Northwest peoples are coastal cultures;[11] totem poles portray each clan's mythical founder, such as Raven and Thunderbird. On the Plains, the main animal myth centres around the buffalo and the receiving of the sacred pipe from the White Buffalo Girl.[12] In the Southwest are the Pueblo peoples, whose myths are 'emergence' myths, which are deeply embedded in agriculture.[13] And in the Southeast Woodlands, forests and lakes are part of the landscape;[14] the myths of the tribes in this region include forest spirits.[15]

Native Americans believe that all creatures are under the control of a guardian spirit, a Master or Mistress of the Animals. This figure is either understood literally (as the father or mother of every animal in a particular species) or figuratively (as the species' collective spirit, made up of the souls of the individuals).

In the mythology of the Karuk (Karok) people of the Klamath River, in northwest California, as it is for many tribes in western North America, the world was once occupied by a species called *Ikxareyavs*, 'First People', who had magical powers. At a certain time, they realized that human beings were coming into existence, so the First People announced their own transformations: into rocks, mountains, disembodied spirits and into species of plants and animals. This is how Deer became the species of deer, Bear the species of bear, and so on. At the same time, it was ordained how human beings were to live: 'the most important of the *Ikxareyavs* is Coyote the trickster – who, before his transformation, lays down the law. Humans will eat salmon and acorns, but life will not be too easy and death will always come, to keep the world from overcrowding.'[16]

Many Native American myths are about transformation; not only do they narrate tales about change, they can also be agents of change, because they may transform the listener. Surely this is also a feature of religion, and this is where there is a blurring of categories between mythology and religion, especially in the Native American systems of belief and ritual: 'Most Indian languages lack a word for "myth", using simply "story".'[17] In religious language, 'transformation' can be known as 'resurrection'. Resurrection is about change, new life, and many of these First People stories relate tales of extraordinary change, of physical, emotional and spiritual renewal.

The relationship between humans and animals was fundamental to all aspects of Native American life. For most, survival without animals would have been impossible. Hunters needed to gain an intimate knowledge of animal behaviour, anatomy, feeding patterns, breeding habits and migratory cycles. This body of practical knowledge was underpinned by a rich repository of myth, legend, songs and ritual that placed the hunter's action in context. Hunting was more than merely gathering food; it was a ritual act with rules and deep spiritual significance, for animals played a vital role in the spiritual life of Native American communities. Animals had been present at Creation and were thought to embody certain aspects of that mythical time. All animals were believed to possess souls. Some, particularly the buffalo, bear and eagle, were thought to have powerful spirits that could either aid people or harm them; therefore, they were revered as holy or sacred beings.

Africans have regarded themselves as part of the environment, which, of course, includes animals. Together they share the earth and its resources, as well as similar experiences, such as birth, procreation and death. This interconnectedness extends to all forms of life, according all life forms reverence and respect. Attributes that in the West are traditionally viewed as belonging to humans alone, such as consciousness and will, are thought to be found in other animals. Such a belief underlies the premise that humans and other forms of life can communicate with each other.

Fear was a strong element in the mythology of pre-Columbian Central and South America, deeply embedded within the Aztec calendar. There was a confrontation between the deities, a struggle for supremacy. This resulted in the destruction of successive world eras or 'suns'. The Aztecs believed that there were four eras, or 'suns', before the present one. The first was ruled by Tezcatlipoca,[18] 'Lord of the Smoking Mirror', the foremost of the Mexican pantheon and a terrifying solar deity. He originated in the Olmec and Toltec past, his cult brought to central Mexico by the Toltec around the tenth century CE. As the supreme Aztec god he was the patron deity of royalty, and was believed to possess an animal presence in the form of a great jaguar. Because of this association with a large cat, jaguars (and ocelots) were venerated as the divine protectors of royalty. Because it was believed to rear its young in caves, the jaguar symbolized life, death and the underworld.[19] Even today in South American hunting and gathering societies, the jaguar is the spirit ally of shamans. This first era was brought to an end after 676 years when Quetzalcoatl knocked Tezcatlipoca into the water, and then jaguars consumed the earth.

The second era in the Aztec calendar was ruled over by Quetzalcoatl,[20] the plumed serpent, god of the west. As the wind god, he was the balancing adversary of Tezcatlipoca. His origins were as the principal fertility and creator god of the older Toltec civilization.[21] This era ended with hurricanes, and humans were transformed into monkeys. The third was ruled by Tlaloc, god of the south. This era ceased dramatically in a shower of fire, with humans transformed into birds. The fourth era, or 'Sun', was ruled over by Chalchihuitlicue, goddess of the east and of water. This period concluded with a flood, with humans being changed into fish.[22]

In the First Peoples' imagination, there is no division between the animal and human spheres; each can inhabit the other's skin, shifting appearances at will. Some of today's shamans (or medicine men) still claim to understand the language of animals. When a television interviewer laughed at Lame Deer's suggestion that he could understand birds, he replied: 'In your Good Book a lady talks to a snake. I, at least, speak to eagles.'[23]

Animals are thought to clothe themselves in various disguises when they wish to trade or communicate with people:

> It was, and still is in many places, a widely held belief that the part of the animal we see is not the real part but only a disguise, an outfit it wears when it comes to visit our world. Once home again, it removes that costume and changes back into its true form.[24]

Totemism: 'One Flesh'

In an effort to merge the human and animal realms, marriages between the two can be imagined as a natural outcome. All cultures across the continent depict bear spouses, and in addition to the buffalo (in the Southwest and Plains) and the whale (in the Northwest), the dog husband is also popular. Intermarriage is one of the components in totemism:

> In the most restrictive sense, [totemism] refers to tracing by a tribe of its lineage to an animal ancestor, which married a human being and retains an honored position. Tribal totem animals constantly revisit their descendants to offer guidance, in ceremonies, in dreams, and in shamanic trances . . . In a broader sense, totemism can refer to any conception of continuity between the human and animal worlds.[25]

Totemism does not just encompass a descendant of a particular animal species, but is a belief system that ensures that bond is present and actual, as well as genetic. As in marriage, 'totemism involves a merging of formerly divergent beings, which become, in a sense, "one flesh".'[26]

The etymology of 'totem', from the Ojibwa *ototeman*, is a phrase that expresses membership in an exogamous group:[27] 'he is a relative of mine.'[28] In totemic societies the animal is not a symbolic conveyer

Totem pole with Eagle, Raven and Bear, unknown Haida artist, *c.* 1878.

A Salish canoe with a stylized wolf-head bow, Canada, c. 1910. Some believe that the hunting skill of the wolf will aid fishermen on the waters.

of identity, the animal is a relative, is kin. Totemic beliefs eventually developed into formal creeds or beliefs. Totemic culture has as its core a set of myths or stories about Creation.

Myths, ancestors and mythic beings are made visible in every aspect of Pacific Northwest Coast life; they are carved and painted on huge wooden buildings that house entire families, on the monumental poles that display the owners' history and status, on canoes, spoons and on ceremonial regalia, such as masks, robes and rattles.

The Northwest Coast Native American societies were structured according to a system of clans, arranged within an elaborate hierarchy. Each clan traced its origin to an animal spirit, or totem. Prominent clans would proclaim their status and lineage by erecting tall carved poles outside their communal houses. These totem poles were decorated with the animal crests of the families who dwelled within. Every clan traced its lineage back to an encounter in mythical time with a particular animal spirit who had endowed the groups with his power and bestowed on them his image.[29] For example, in southeast Alaska, Tlingit society was composed of two divisions: the Raven and the Eagle (in the south the Eagle was replaced by the Wolf). Each division had subdivisions, with different animal crests. One myth credits the making of the clans to Raven. After Raven had stolen the box that contained the sun, he offered it to the people in exchange for food. The people did not believe Raven, so he opened the lid of the box.

With a great roar the sun burst through. The advent of daylight transformed the living beings into the forms they have today. Those who were wearing animals skins became those animals (otters, beavers, seals) and those who were naked remained as human beings, with the clan crests being selected in memory of their transformed companions.[30] Important crest animals included the raven, the killer whale, the grizzly bear, the octopus and the frog. For a variety of reasons, both practical and spiritual, hunters would avoid killing these animals (the raven, for example, was highly regarded in its role as a creator-hero).

Different rituals were observed when a person had died, or when it was time to honour that death. For the Tlingit of the North Pacific coast, Tlingit bowls with clan crests were used to 'feed' the deceased during ceremonies.

Myths, ancestors and mythic beings are also given physical expression through specific ritual performances involving songs and dancers wearing masks. Many masks have a dual role: they may simply represent crests but when worn in a ceremony they may represent mythic beings. They depict the art of transformation, some split open, while others are rotated to reveal changes on the top or bottom. In the guise of their lineage animals, performers would mimic the call and movements of their particular ancestral creatures. They would wear masks, some quite elaborate, depicting the different birds, animals and imaginary beings.

For the indigenous people of Australia, Dreamtime began with the deeds of totemic ancestors. Due to the complexities of oral tradition, there is no single, orthodox version of aboriginal myths. The common source for all the myths is its creation period, better known as 'Dreamtime'. Dreamtime, or Dreaming, has two aspects: it refers to both a period of time and to a state of being.[31] As a period of time, Dreamtime gives accounts of the primordial epoch, when the aboriginal ancestors travelled across Australia, shaping the landscape. Kangaroos, wallabies, lizards, snakes and birds, as well as humans, left caves, rocks and creeks to mark the places where they camped and hunted, or where battles had taken place.[32] These landmarks are regarded as sacred and are imbued with the ancestor's power or energy. As a state of being, Dreamtime is drawn on in the present day, for participants in certain rituals become, for a brief time, the ancestors whose journeys they recreate.

There are two main types of ritual, the first being a public re-enactment of an episode from the Dreamtime. The second involves clan animal

Dreamtime: carved baobab nut with incised design of kangaroos, birds and snakes, before 1900.

ancestors in another way, for this ritual is known as an 'increase' ritual.[33] This ceremony involves a small number of people, and it takes place at a sacred site. The purpose of the ceremony is to release the ancestor's power and propagate the animal species with which the ancestor is linked. Each clan has an ancestral spirit, who is associated with a particular animal, as its guardian ancestor.

In these Dreamtime tales, humans and animals may change from one to another, or share the form and nature of both. In that dream world, humans dreamed of kinship with everything that surrounded them, and the stories provided a satisfying account of the origin of natural life. There was a 'oneness' with humans and all aspects of nature. The Rainbow Serpent was symbolic of rain, water and the products of rain, all vitally important to tribes that ventured into the vast desert regions of the Australian interior. Many tribes believed that, if it were not for the Rainbow Serpent, life would cease to exist. The extent to which the Rainbow Serpent entered into fertility rites is indicated by the frequency of its appearance in sacred designs and drawings. The Serpent who brought rain was the life-giving force in religious rites. The Serpent cleared the land by uprooting trees and causing rivers to flow to the sea;[34] he/she also symbolized the storms and floods that caused the rivers to rise. In Arnhem Land he/she protected sacred lore by sending floods to drown those who offended it,[35] or who broke the taboos. The close association of the Rainbow Serpent with totemic ancestors and their beneficent role in providing water is an indication that reptiles were not regarded with revulsion, but were treated with respect.

In Africa a totem belongs to a clan, a group of people who are related to each other through a common ancestor, the ancestor often being an animal:

> Camara Laye reports that he could swim in the river with his brothers and cousins, because their totem was the crocodile, so the crocodiles would do them no harm. Were they not themselves the crocodiles' cousins? . . . A human woman living on her own was visited regularly by a lion, who did her no harm; on the contrary, he brought her meat. When she had a son, the lion took the boy and trained him in bushlore so he became a hunter, the ancestor of the Lions' clan.[36]

A daughter can be given to an animal in marriage, as happens in many of the tales, because the animal will be as good a husband, if not better, than a human one. Animal wives, too, are faithful to their human husbands until the desire to go back home to the forest becomes too strong.[37]

The Haida version of the story of the Bear Mother is about a woman lured away by a handsome stranger, who later reveals himself to be a Bear. This story is about the interrelationship of humans and animals, as well as defining the social order, reminding the listener of the importance of maintaining the clan system: 'Both the Bear and the woman are of the Raven clan and are thus from the same lineage. When they marry and have children, they do so knowing that they have broken the law forbidding marriage between members of the same clan.'[38] Note that the taboo is not about marriage between different species, but about marrying within the same clan. 'We know what the animals do, what are the needs of the beaver, the bear, the salmon, and other creatures, because long ago men married them and acquired this knowledge.'[39]

In some cultures, particular animals are raised as family. In Papua New Guinea, villagers have a special relationship with pigs. Pigs, say the Enga men of the Western Highlands, are our hearts.[40] Highlanders in the Nondugl area insist that pigs are so central to their social and religious life that they will never sell them. The piglets among the Siuai of Bougainville's Great Buin Plain share their owners' food and are baptized and given ritual names.[41] When ill, they receive medications and the women chew up tubers for them to eat. 'While the men "own" their pigs, it is the women who take care of them, allowing them to share their sleeping quarters, even nursing orphaned piglets.'[42] In West Irian, wild piglets are sometimes captured. They are raised as family, provided with names and addressed in kinship terms: 'When grown, the animals are killed and eaten, but not by the households that have been rearing them, for, as Tor people say, "Who would eat his own son or brother?"'[43]

Finally, it is important, before examining creation myths, to remember that myths are not told for enjoyment, or for education (this may happen, but these outcomes are of secondary importance). Myths are told in order to be believed. They tell of a living religion, giving concrete form to a set of beliefs and traditions that link people living today with ancestors from centuries past. 'Myth in its living, primitive form is not merely a story told but a reality lived.'[44]

Creation Stories: Animals as Midwives and Messengers

For the Bushman, the Creator made the earth and the plants, then thought up the many different kinds of animals that were to live in this world:

> Striking a huge baobab tree, He caused the animals to walk into the light of day for the first time. As each one appeared through a great rent in the tree's roots, He named it and gave it a place to live. Even though He was assisted by Mantis who was a super-being and the Creator's helper, the animals took a long time to come out of the tree and be named. Last of all came man. By then, there was only one role left in the great scheme of things, so the Creator and Mantis assigned this place to the Bushman – that of Hunter-Gatherer. The Bushman fulfilled his designated role faithfully, living in close harmony with the animals, birds and the plants upon the earth.[45]

For the Khoikhoi of southwestern Africa, their culture hero-trickster, their first man, is Heitsi-Eibib, whose mother, a cow, conceived him miraculously by eating a special grass.[46] Heitsi-Eibib gave order to nature, for at the beginning of Creation the creatures had not assumed their specific qualities: lions built nests in trees, fish lived in the desert, mice ate snakes. Heitsi-Eibib took each animal in turn and gave it the nature it was to have forever. The only one that escaped was Hare, because he ran from him. Because of this, Heitsi-Eibib gave Hare the attributes of fear and the ability to run.[47]

Many tribes have supreme creator beings who have retreated to the sky and associate with humans only by way of intermediaries. For the Shilluk people of the Nilotic tribes in Africa, 'Juck is such a god, and Nyikang, son of a crocodile mother, is the intermediary. It was he who turned animals into the Shillucks.'[48] For the Pygmies, their sky god Khonvum has a strong association with earth, and with the animals, for he once lived on earth as an animal master. This relationship continues through intermediary animal spirits.[49]

There are myths to explain the creation of the unwanted animals, those seen as annoying or dangerous. Mwuetsi, a moon god sacred to the Makoni tribe of Zimbabwe, married the evening star maiden, Morongo, and together they produced animals and human children. He was then advised to cease procreation as he was soon to die, but Mwuetsi ignored this advice, the result being the production of dangerous and less pleasant animals and insects, including a snake, which bit him and was the source of his death.[50]

Most Native American peoples attribute the conception, if not the making, of the universe to a supreme divinity or 'Great Spirit'. Some view this supreme divinity as both the creator of the world and the spirit that presides over and pervades all living beings.

This spirit is known by different names in the various regions: as Gitchi Manitou to the Algonquians of the Northeast Woodlands, as Wakan Tanka (*Wakan* means 'sacred' or 'sacred power') to the Lakota of the Plains, as Napi (Old Man) to the Montana Blackfeet and as Tirawa to the Pawnee. In most creation stories the active deities include animal figures, including those not well regarded in the West; for example, Spider is said to have woven a web that eventually formed the earth.[51] In Native American spirituality, some elders insist that all animals are good, yet certain animals and birds have negative connotations within particular tribes; for example, bats are disliked by the

Ceremonial 'Crooked Beak of Heaven' mask depicting a man-eating bird, Kwakwaka'wakw, Pacific Northwest Coast.

Algonquins, but revered by the Taino; owls are liked by some, yet feared by others.[52]

Common to many cultures and their associated myths and religions, certain birds, such as the Native American Thunderbird, and the southern African Lightning Bird, symbolize the upper world, while large serpents represent chaotic energy within the underworld. These cosmic birds dominate the heavenly realm, while the serpents rule the watery underworld. In Central American and Mexican mythology, the serpent represented time and the green quetzal bird (of Mayan origin), symbolized the hope of release from time's bondage. Both were combined in a hybrid, as the feathered serpent god Quetzalcoatl.[53]

Some animals found in common in myths of different cultures include the great turtle, who bears the world upon his back (his body the tripartite universe, for his upper shell represents the upper world, his body the earth, and the lower shell the underworld). The turtle is sometimes depicted in the 'Earth Diver' myth, bearing mud from the primeval waters; this mud expands to become land for creatures to inhabit.

In Pacific Northwest cosmology, the universe is shared by humans, animals (including birds and sea creatures) and mythic beings. The universe consists of a number of realms, whose names and natures differ from nation to nation: the sky world, the underwater or water world, the mortal or land/forest world and the spirit/ghost world. In the underwater and sky worlds, beings have the external appearance of animals, birds, sea or other creatures and, like humans, live in houses and in villages.

Much of the mythology of the sky world is associated with ancestral beings who descended from the sky and transformed into humans to found lineages. Therefore, many crests are creatures from the sky world, such as Raven and Eagle. Sky beings are noted for their ability to cross boundaries (birds dive into the ocean to take fish; birds sit in trees and observe humans and learn their habits and rituals). Raven is both real and supernatural; he is a great trickster, but he is also respected for stealing the sun from the chief of the sun and giving it to the world. The Thunderbird is found in many Native American traditions. This immense mythical creature, whose wings make thunder and whose eyes and beak generate lightning, was primarily associated with the rain that brings fertility. Worshipped as a creator of new life, it was thought to inhabit craggy mountain peaks from where it surveyed its hunting grounds. It was believed that it hunted whales and carried them off inland to devour them. In many Plains cultures, the Thunderbird was regarded as second in rank only to the Great Spirit deity.

The mortal world is home to humans and animals. One myth with a lesson is that of the frog. In a Nisga'a (an indigenous people of Canada) version, three boys are playing in the forest, and they build a fire to keep warm. A small frog tries to jump past them, but twice the boys toss the frog back. On the third time the boys throw the frog into the fire where it burns to death. Volcano Woman, the mother of the frog, soon realizes that one of her children is missing, and when she finds out what has happened, she tells the villagers that they must punish the boys. The villagers ignore her, so she causes a nearby mountain to erupt, covering the village with lava and killing most of the inhabitants.[54] This is a reminder that all life is precious.

The undersea world has its own sky realm, with birds, sun, moon and stars, as well as a spirit world with its own unique beings. There are various great sea monsters who rule the ocean.

In indigenous Southeast Asian religious beliefs, the upper world of sun and sky, of birds and ancestors is matched by the lower world of water, which is home to reptilian creatures such as snakes, crocodiles and serpents. Birds are the symbols and messengers of the heavens, and symbolize the upper world of the ancestors who have the ability to take on avian form and are envoys between the human and ancestral worlds, while various reptiles are associated with the waters of the nether world. Images of reptiles are placed in the front ladders, doors and lintels so that only benign beings would enter the house. Reptilian creatures not only protect the house but safeguard its ongoing prosperity. The heavy doors of houses, shrines and granaries are decorated with crocodile, lizard and serpent images, hoping that this will secure wealth and life-sustaining crops of rice, millet and corn. The lizard is associated with the earth goddess Boraspati ni Tano, the supreme symbol of fertility.[55]

Several African myths tell of a time when the sky and the earth were connected by a rope. The Fajulu of Sudan and Madi of Uganda both hold the hyena as responsible for the severing of the rope, narrating that the hyena bit off the cow-skin rope that once joined the earth to heaven.[56] The cutting of the rope, according to the Nuer myth of the Sudan, is the origin of death: when the rope was joined to the sky, humans climbed into the sky when they were old and returned to earth young again; but the hyena and the weaver bird severed the rope on their return and since that time humans have died.[57]

For many First Peoples, numerous myths focus on the blurred boundaries between these worlds and the constant interaction between the inhabitants of two or more domains. These events took place long ago, when the membrane separating the realms was thin and permeable. At different times in the past, animals or mythic beings crossed over to the mortal world and changed the nature of the universe. Some married humans, and some animals shed their skin, fur or feathers to transform into human beings, becoming the founding ancestors of a lineage, clan or nation. Some humans had encounters with the spirit world that equipped them with special powers.

There is no beginning moment of Creation, for Creation is happening now and we are part of it.[58] Some refuse to even acknowledge the notion of time, or at least the conventional notion of time. Because of this, there is no date of Creation, no single event that has equal significance for all, and spiritual beliefs are different for each cultural group. There are many versions of creation stories, as one would expect in an oral tradition, and creation is sacred because life is viewed as sacred.[59]

The *Popol Vuh*, a sacred myth-historical book of the K'iché (Quiché) Maya people in Guatemala's western highlands, was written by anonymous members of the K'iché Maya nobility, prior to the arrival of Spanish conquerors in 1524.[60] It is the most important text in the native languages of the Americas. It begins with the deeds of the Mayan gods in the darkness of the primeval sea, concluding with the magnificence of the Mayan lords who founded the K'iché' kingdom. Originally written in Mayan hieroglyphs, it was translated into the Roman alphabet in the sixteenth century. One of its great features is its creation narrative. Animals are created, then humans. The first humans, made out of mud, dissolve in water; the second group are created from wood, but have no souls or minds (but from these wooden figures monkeys are created). Finally, humans are perfected, created from corn that had been gathered by the animals. What stands out in this creation narrative is the assumption that animals are unable to praise their creator (or perhaps it would be better to assume that the gods do not understand their languages), which is the reason given for their use/domination by humans. In the second attempt at creating human beings, we note a reversal of evolutionary theory, with monkeys being formed from human beings:[61]

> Now Heart-of-Sky plans the creatures of the forest –
>   birds, deer, jaguars and snakes.
> And each is given his home.
> 'You the deer, sleep here along the rivers.
> You the birds, your nests are in the trees.
> Multiply and scatter', he tells them.[62]

In the creation narrative, there is no one to praise the creator, or Heart-of-Sky:

> Then Heart-of-Sky says to the animals,
> 'Speak, pray to us.'
> But the creatures can only squawk.
> The creatures only howl.
> They do not speak like humans.
> They do not praise Heart-of-Sky.
> And so the animals are humbled.
> They will serve those who will worship Heart-of-Sky.[63]

Then comes the first attempt at creating human beings, but, being made of mud, they disintegrate. After that, humans are crafted from wood, but, because they have no mind or soul, they are thought to be unsatisfactory and are destroyed by a flood:

> There is a terrible flood and the earth is blackened.
> The creatures of the forest come into the homes of
>   the doll-people.
> 'You have chased us from our homes so now we will take yours',
>   they growl.
> And their dogs and turkeys cry out, 'You have abused us
>   so now we shall eat you!'[64]

The wooden figures flee into the woods:

> The wooden people scatter into the forest.
> Their faces are crushed, and they are turned into monkeys.
> And this is why monkeys look like humans.
> They are what is left of what came before, an experiment
>   in human design.[65]

Many stories suggest that people and animals have existed since the beginning of time.[66] In many origin tales, people, animals and a semi-divine trickster all live together at the beginning of time. Common to most of these myths is an understanding that humans were created as companions, not as masters, of all other creatures.

For the Ashanti people in West Africa, the culture hero-trickster Anansi (or Ananse), the Spider, acts as the sky god Nyame's connection to human beings.[67] The Ashanti people tell how Anansi created the first people, into whom the sky god Nyame (Nyankopon) breathed life.[68] The Abure people believe that Nyame created the hot sun, but Anansi acted in the interests of human beings by persuading Nyame to send rain down to cool them off.[69]

One of the most prevalent creation myths among Native Americans is the 'earth diver' or 'mud diver' myth,[70] in which the world rose from the primal waters with the magical help of birds or animals. These primal days are seen as a time when people and animals shared thoughts and language, when creatures like Raven and Coyote walked the earth and made natural features, animals and people. There are a number of versions, yet the majority recount the tale of a lowly creature who descends to the bottom of the primeval sea or waters to retrieve some mud that will be used to expand the earth. Some versions have Loon, Beaver and Otter, who fail, but Muskrat who succeeds. In the Munsee version, Turtle, Duck and Bull Frog all try, but have no success. Little

Muskrat offers to dive, and succeeds, clutching some mud in his paws, but he dies during his journey back to the others.[71] Within this myth a key religious concept, that of sacrifice, enters the picture. Perhaps the tale is also one of 'quest' or pilgrimage.

In the Cheyenne version, Maheo, the creator, is floating on the water. He gathers all the birds that swim and asks them to dive to the bottom of the sea to find the clay he will use to fashion the world. Many try, but fail. Finally the coot, or mud hen, dives and reappears with mud from the ocean bottom in its beak: 'the mud coot places the mud lovingly in Creator's hands, in service to Creation.' Maheo places the dust on the water's surface and the dust expands to form the continents.[72]

In another version of the Cheyenne account, Maheo could not carry back the amount of mud, so old Grandmother Turtle carried it. On her back the mud continued to grow, becoming the first land. In a number of different cultures, the world is viewed as resting on the back of a turtle.[73]

In a Cherokee diver tale, the Cherokee believe that the creator formed the earth as a floating island in a sea of water. In the beginning, the animals were born above it, but became curious to see what was below the water. The Beaver's Grandchild dived and grabbed hold of a beautiful arch and pulled it to the surface. This was the opening for the people's earth. The animals knew that the earth was too wet, that they needed a dry place. The birds were sent out to scout, but came back with no good news. They sent out Buzzard, but he too returned, saying there was nowhere that was safe:

> The animals sang to Grandfather Buzzard, for he held all their hope.
> Grandfather Buzzard pulled his strength into his mighty wings. He flew to the place where the Cherokee now are. He flew hard and fast down to the wet land, beating his wings as the animals sang. He slapped the air with his powerful feathers.
> The wet earth dried. The animals sang. Grandfather Buzzard felt their courage fill his muscles, and he let the wind from his powerful wings fill the air. The air warmed and the land grew hard and firm. The animals sang their thanks. Grandfather Buzzard perched on this newly made hard, dry land. It was safe. It was good. It was fine. It was as it should be. The animals then called up the people.

> The Cherokee people came to this fine land, singing, 'We thank you, thank you, Grandfather Buzzard, animals, birds, reptiles, insects, and your songs of hope.'
> The power of the animals was never forgotten.[74]

In a creation myth of the Yoruba, from West Africa, Olodumare, the Almighty, decided to create the world. The earth was a watery wasteland. Olodumare sent the arch-divinity, Orishanla, with some soil and a hen. The hen was to help scatter the soil after Orishanla had thrown it onto a particular spot. After the hen had scattered the soil, Olodumare sent a chameleon to inspect the proceedings.[75] This myth has echoes of the Genesis flood narrative, for the chameleon made two trips: the first time to report that the earth was still wet, and on the second occasion to proclaim that the earth was now wide and dry. This myth is also similar to the diver myths.

While the Great Spirit reigns over all creation, the day to day running of the world is usually left in the hands of powerful deities and culture heroes. The origins of the stars and planets, seasons, death, fire and the sun are often ascribed to these figures, colourful personalities such as Raven, Glooskap, Coyote and Great Hare. Glooskap, a legendary benevolent hero of the Wabanaki peoples, was responsible for creating life as well as protecting it from evil and destruction. The gift of fire is attributed to Coyote, yet for the Cherokees, Water Spider is credited with the theft of fire; having spun a bowl from her web, she steals an ember from the sycamore tree in which Thunder God had hidden fire. Here we see both positive and negative aspects in the one story. It is interesting to note that some of these figures are also tricksters, especially Coyote. Their contributions may be positive in one story, yet negative in another.

In several creation myths, there is terrible cruelty. In the myth of the Sea Mother an orphan girl named Nuliajuk was teased by her peers.[76] One day when the community was on kayaks searching for fish, she was pushed overboard by the other children. Just as she was going under the water, she seized the edge of the kayak with her fingers. The children took hold of their knives and severed her fingers. As she sank to the bottom of the sea, where she became an ocean spirit, her fingers turned into floating sea mammals. The seals, walruses and whales were all born from her cut flesh, and all became obedient to her will. These are violent animistic aspects in which parts of Nuliajuk become creatures of value to the Inuit. Nuliajuk's anger made her a fierce enemy; storms and heavy seas rose at her command. She also governed the land animals, the animals the Inuit also depended on for food and clothing. 'A word from her, and land and sea animals alike would forsake their normal haunts, leaving the community which had displeased her to starve.'[77] Ceremonies are held in her honour. If she causes famine, the *angakok*, or conjurer (shaman), goes on a spirit journey to her house and arranges her thick hair (because she has no fingers, she cannot plait her hair); she is grateful to the *angakok* so she sends seals and other animals to the hunters.[78]

In a Maori origin myth, Maui goes fishing with his brothers. He chants a spell that causes the fish to become placid and the waves to subside. A large fish lay still on the surface of the water, with the canoe high and dry on its back. Maui had fished up the North Island of New Zealand, traditionally known for this reason as Te Ika-a-Maui (The Fish of Maui),[79] for the shape of the island resembles a fish. Maui goes off to make an offering to the gods, and forbids his brothers to injure the fish, saying that he will prepare it on his return. The brothers promise, but as soon as he is out of sight, they begin to cut up the fish and eat it:

> The fish writhed and twisted, but the brothers never let up. They sliced, they hacked, they chopped, until the entire surface of the fish had become jagged and mutilated.
>
> Thus, through the greed and disobedience of the brothers, were formed the cliffs, valleys, plains and mountain ranges of the North Island. If they had listened to their brother's words, the island would have been smooth and level to this day – as smooth and level as Maui's fish had been.[80]

Some African creation myths also highlight the cruelty of humans. In a creation myth from the Yao,[81] humans violate the sacred harmony of the world and force God to retreat to the sky: 'At first there were no people. Only Mulungu and the decent peaceful beasts in the world.' One day Mulungu's son caught two human beings in his fish trap. They grew and the animals watched to see what the people would do. They made fire, and it roared through the forest, forcing the animals to flee. The people caught a buffalo and killed it and roasted it in the fire and ate it. The next day they did the same thing. Every day they set fires and killed some animal and ate it. 'They are burning up everything!' said Mulungu. 'They are killing my people!' All the animals ran into the forest, away from the humans. Mulungu sought Spider's help; Spider spun a rope for Mulungu and Mulungu climbed the rope and went to live in the sky; thus the gods were driven off the face of the earth because of human cruelty.[82]

In another African tale, which is not a creation myth but one concerning marrying another species, the man, a hunter, wishes to become an animal because of the cruelty of the human race.[83] In these examples gods leave the earth because of cruelty; people wish to transform themselves and live amongst gentler creatures.

The Cahto (Kato) were a small group of Athapaskan peoples who inhabited parts of northern California. Like many First Peoples, they revered all creation. The Cahto believed that every creature had a name, and a need to be known by that particular name.[84] The Cahto appear to have had a special bond with dogs; the dogs were given names, kept indoors at night and, like their human companions, buried after they died.[85] Dogs were so essential to the Cahto's thoughts and actions they became an integral component of their belief system. The Cahto believed that when the Creator created the world out of nothing, he had a companion with him; Dog was this fellow-traveller:

It could not have been imagined without the company of dog.
 'We have made it good, my dog', the Great Traveller said,
 they say.[86]

Some myths narrate the creation of humans and of different tribes. One creation story, according to the Native American Washoe people, involves Coyote and Bear. Bear wanted to make the Washoe people, and he sat by Lake Tahoe, creating them from the clay. They were strong, with big shoulders, made in Bear's own image. He then put them in the sun to dry, but he left them in the sun for too long and they were too dark. He made more, but he did not leave them in the sun for long enough, so they were too light. Coyote teased Bear relentlessly, causing Bear to become so discouraged that he let the people walk away, and they became neighbouring tribes, which explains the variety of skin tones in the region. The third time, Bear knew the right length of time to leave them in the sun, so these were the Washoe people. Coyote, miffed because he had not been allowed to help, tripped Bear, who knocked the Washoe people, breaking them into pieces. Some of the pieces of the legs were lost, and even though Bear patched everything together, those legs were never found, which explains why many of the Washoe people have short legs today.[87]

This is interesting on several levels, perhaps the most important element being that, according to the Washoe people, Coyote is not a 'power animal', because power animals need to be trusted in order to be invoked and worked with as allies. The Coyote spirit is viewed as being untrustworthy, like the animal itself. Bear, on the other hand, could be trusted and had originally created humans 'in Bear's own image'.

There are three main types of trickster tales: stories in which the trickster is benevolent, tales in which the trickster learns by doing or from his mistakes and the third, where the trickster acts on destructive childish impulses in order to teach children the terrible results of such actions.

In the animal tales of the Pueblos, Coyote is many things, a scapegoat, a trickster, a fool, but also a creator:

> Coyote is also a hero figure and creator, a demi god not unlike the Greek Gods in whom were combined divine attributes and human lust and greed. In some myths, Coyote is the one who got fire and daylight for man and taught him how to be a hunter. Coyote is also thought to have curative powers.

Chief Shake's Bear Paw Rattle, Tlingit, Nanya.aayi clan, Wrangell, Alaska, 1800s.

According to Crow Indian mythology, the Sun-Coyote created the earth and made living creatures for it.[88]

In the story 'The Great Reformation', the Great Spirit lets the animals choose new names, for the world would soon change and a new kind of people (humans) would be created. Each of the animals wanted to have the most powerful and most respected name, so they all wished to be first in line the next day, when the Great Spirit would allow them to choose their names. Coyote wanted a new name, for his own had become synonymous with 'trickster'. Unfortunately, he overslept, so all the other names had been taken:

> 'Do not despair, noble Coyote, for it was my will that you missed all the great names. I have saved a special distinction for you. You will become the chief of all the tribes and protector of the new people that are to come', said Great Spirit . . . 'It is to you that I give magical powers to defeat the beasts and teach the people the ways of the world. With this power you can change into anything you can think of and do all kinds of magical things that you never imagined.'[89]

In the northwest interior of North America, Coyote is believed to have created the animals and people, and to work in conjunction with the Great Spirit much of the time. He is the most important and most popular character in the Northwest, because he was put on earth to make it a good place to be. Coyote has been around from the beginning and has lived many lives over the millennia. Time means nothing to Coyote, for he exists outside it.

One myth has Coyote forming the heavens. He frees a large number of animals who had been captured by a hag. Coyote unlocks their chains and throws the golden locks into the heavens, where they become stars, and those stars form the shape of every single animal the hag had captured. When Coyote howls, the stars come to life.[90]

> When the Great Spirit in his wisdom saw fit to bring the people into the world Coyote helped them to survive. He showed them how to use language and how to build their villages, and when they were hungry, Coyote even led the salmon up the river so the people could eat. While the people were still young

and finding their way through the world, they would often call out to Coyote when they needed help, but as time passed, he heard fewer prayers in his name. The people had learned what they needed and began to spread out from their place of birth into the valleys and onto the distant plains.[91] . . . Generations passed, and more of the white-faced visitors came, and more of the people died. Those created in the image of the Great Spirit still cling to their bits of land and await the coming of Coyote and the Great One to return the earth to balance.[92]

In an Inuit myth, animals played a role in the creation of human beings. In ancient times a girl refused to marry, for no one pleased her enough. Her father became angry and married her to one of his dogs.[93] The couple went to live on an island, and the woman gave birth to ten children: two were Inuit,[94] two were dogs, two were *erkileks* (dogs with men's heads), two were *qavdlunat* (white men), and two were *qavdlunatsait* (white men with warlike dispositions).[95] The woman placed the four white men into a boot and let it float out to sea, and it eventually was washed ashore on the land of the white man. There the four remained, becoming the ancestors of all white men.[96]

In another creation myth, from the coastal Chukchi, Raven, more commonly portrayed as a trickster, creates the world. After he had formed the world, Raven came to a group of trees and chopped them with his axe. Chips of wood flew in the air and those from the oak trees became seals, pine chips became walruses and the black birch wood chips became whales. Other chips settled on land and became polar bears, reindeer and foxes.[97] Much revered, Raven, however, was seldom trusted. For the Inuit, Raven is the only clear manifestation of a personified creator.[98] He created dry land, various species of plants and animals, as well as man and woman. He also instructed them on how to care for children, how to use animals, how to make fire and other essential survival skills.

Animals are the bringers of fire feature in popular myths. We have already noted Raven's role in this; Coyote has also been credited as the acquirer of fire. In some traditions, Coyote is thought to have brought back fire for humans to use. Some stories tell of Coyote making a ladder to the sky and stealing fire to bring back to earth; some versions have Fox accompanying him and Fox's tail becoming singed (the telltale black mark on his tail to this day). Another story has Coyote bringing back fire from the moon, as well as knowledge about the making of arrowheads, the drying of salmon and the weaving of baskets and mats.[99]

In Africa a number of different animals are credited as the bearers of fire: the Pygmies attribute its arrival to a dog or to the chimpanzees, the Ila people of Zambia believe it to be the work of a mason wasp who was bringing fire from the High God to the earth, and the bushmen say that fire was stolen from Ostrich by the Praying Mantis (a creature widely regarded by Africans as sacred).[100] Another myth links fire with the jaguar and the human. In this myth the jaguar, who possessed the gift of fire and the use of arms (bow and arrow), adopted a human as his son and hunting companion. In the jaguar's home, the human saw fire and cooked meat for the first time. The jaguar's wife bared her claws and snarled at the human when her husband was out, so the jaguar taught the human how to defend himself with a bow and arrow. Later, the human killed the jaguar's wife, stole weapons and cooked meat and went back to his village. On seeing his gifts, some of the men went to the jaguar's house and stole fire, cooked meat, bows and arrows. The jaguar was incensed at his adopted son's ingratitude 'and now eats its food raw and hunts with its claws and fangs, whereas humans eat grilled meat and hunt with bows and arrows'.[101]

This was a universe open to transformation: 'In primordial times the world order was inverted, and it was . . . jaguars who owned fire and hunted with bows and arrows. The myths recount how these first relationships were overturned and the current order established.'[102] Rules and rituals, often thought to be passed on from mythic ancestors, were to be observed in order to prevent disaster. Myths are a way to stabilize a culture, a way to warn of the consequences when one departs from set codes of conduct.

The Siberian origin myth of the elk stealing the sun has similarities with the myth of Raven stealing the sun; the difference being that in the Evenk Siberian tale, the mighty elk wants to keep the sun for himself (causing the hero, Main, to retrieve it), whereas Raven brings the sun back and restores light to the world. The succession of day and night is attributed to the elk, with the episode repeated each evening, for Main was turned into a spirit and he keeps guard over the sun. Every evening he pursues the elk through the darkness of night, captures the sun and returns it to the people the next morning.[103] This myth highlights the importance of sharing, as well as the predictability and stability of the universe's cycle of day and night.

Another Siberian creation myth contains an extinct animal, the mammoth, whose remains are often discovered in the ground. In this myth the mammoth is viewed as one of the masters of the lower world, having played a role in the creation of the topography of the landscape: 'It used its tusks to draw up mud from the water and make the land. Wherever the mammoth walked, it created rivers in its wake; and wherever it lay down, it created lakes.'[104]

Some creation myths, as we have already noted in the mud-diver stories, contain the notion of sacrifice. In Micronesia, in the Gilbert Islands, the primordial deity Nareau is said to have persuaded an eel to separate the sky and earth. In nearby Nauru, there is a similar myth. The primordial Spider, Areop-Enap, found a clam shell and asked a shellfish to prise it open. The shellfish could only open it a little, so Areop-Enap asked a caterpillar to assist. The caterpillar managed to do so, but the effort had been so laborious, that the caterpillar had produced salty sweat, which formed in the base of the clam shell. The work had been too much for the poor caterpillar, who died from exhaustion. The top part of the clam shell became the sky, the dead caterpillar became the sun, the sweat became the sea, and the shellfish, the moon.[105] The creature who died helping to create the world is now part of the body of creation, in this case, the sun; the caterpillar's by-product, sweat, becomes the sea.

The Iban, one of the Dayak peoples of Borneo,[106] believe that the world was created by two spirits, Ara and Irik, who floated above the primeval waters in the form of birds. They swooped down and gathered two eggs from the waters, Ara forming the sky from one of the eggs and Irik forming the earth from the other. After compressing the earth, which produced rivers and streams, and creating trees and plants, they created humans. After several attempts to bring them to life, their bird cries ended up giving the lifeless figures life.[107] Another creation myth of the Dayak concerns the powerful serpent; primeval times are described as 'when everything was still enclosed in the mouth of the coiled Watersnake'.[108]

Sometimes the creation myth arises from a human failing. In one Inuit story of the first narwhal, a great horned whale, a greedy mother disappears into the sea, where she is changed into a narwhal, her heavy plaited hair becoming a long, spiralling horn. It is said that from her, all narwhals are descended.

Muluku was the paramount deity of the Macouas of Zambezi. After he created humans, he equipped them with knowledge and skills.

However, after Muluku had left them, they threw down their tools, ate their food raw and slept in the open. When Muluku returned, he was enraged. He summoned two monkeys, then equipped them as he had done the humans. 'These clever animals began to do and use everything as Muluku had intended, so he cut off their tails and made them human, turning the original people into monkeys.'[109]

We may think again of the moon god Mwuetsi, whose excessive procreation gave birth to the snake that killed him.[110]

In a story about the union of Wolverine and Muskrat, the First People are born. From this animal union springs both interrelatedness and interdependence. Their first child was White Man, father of all the white people. After a while a second child was born. This child was to be Indian, father of all Indian people. A third baby was born; this child would be Eskimo (Inuit), father of all Eskimo (Inuit). Then, a fourth child was born; this baby was to be Iroquois. Finally a fifth baby was born, and this baby would be Black, the father of all black people. They remained with their parents until they were adults; they had been taught the ways of the animals and were now to go to different places. The mother 'directed them to go to the animals whenever they were in need. The animals, she said, would have everything – and they would always share with her children.'[111]

In Maori mythology, every living creature descends from Ranginui (Rangi, the sky father) and Papatuanuku (Papa, the earth mother). They had a number of sons, including Tane-Mahuta (god of the forests) and Tangaroa (god of the sea). All land-based animals, including humans, trace their descent from Tane, and all the creatures of the sea, reptiles and insects trace their descent from Tangaroa.[112] This means that all are related, and is why Maori believe that all creatures are brothers and sisters:

> Most animals are, in fact, our older siblings as most were created long before humans arrived. This shared whakapapa (genealogy) makes humans' relationship with the animal kingdom rather complex. While humans respect these creatures they also have a desire to dominate them. Humans are willing to respect animals yet they would not hesitate to eat them either.[113]

Flood Myths

Some myths describe floods, similar to the deluge in the Judaeo-Christian tradition, visited upon the earth by vengeful deities. The Caddo people of the southeastern plains of America tell of a mythical time when the waters on earth had dried up. The people went crazy due to thirst and accused the river animals and fish of causing the drought. They collected the dead turtles and fish from the riverbeds and then they cut them into pieces and threw them around. This foolish action incurred the anger of a sky spirit, who came down to earth and punished them by causing a flood. Then the spirit led a small group of people to the summit of a high mountain. When the flood had receded, these people were joined by other people whom the great flood had turned into alligators.[114]

In an Inuit version of the flood narrative, eagles came to help save the people. They shed their feathers on the waters, as a sign of peace to the Chief of the Heavens; other birds followed their example. Soon the waters were covered with downy bird feathers. The water began to lessen, until finally it receded. Ever after, the people knew the power of the feathers of the eagle, and their feathers have been regarded ever since as a sign of peace. In times of war, or during disputes, when the chief holds the feather in his hand and blows it into the air, then it is a promise of peace.[115]

In another flood account, the Great Spirit, who lived on the snowy summit of Takhoma, became angry with the people and the animals of the world. He decided to get rid of them, but to keep the good animals and a good man and his family. The man was instructed to shoot arrows into a cloud until there was a long rope of arrows reaching from the cloud on top of the mountain down to the ground. Then he was told to tell the good animals and then his own family to climb the rope. As they were climbing the arrow rope, the man looked back and saw the bad animals and the bad people following, so he broke the rope. All the bad animals and people tumbled back down the mountain. When the good man, his family and the good animals were safe in the cloud, the Great Spirit sent a flood. Later, after the flood, and when the earth was dry, the good man, his family and the good animals descended from the cloud. There were no bad animals or snakes left, and there have been none on Takhoma to this day.[116]

Another form of creation myth is known as the emergence myth. In these narratives beings, usually humans, emerge from the ground, or from several levels underground. This form of myth is common to the Hopi and Pueblo peoples. In one Hopi emergence myth, the Hopi people had come into the Fourth World. They were told to migrate to the four directions before they would come to the right place to settle. In one of the migration tales, the Hopi people were accompanied by Kokopelli (Kokopilau), an insect person (a grasshopper or locust). He was also a trickster of sorts. He encountered an eagle who would not let them through unless they passed a test, which Kokopelli, through trickery, accomplished. The eagle was impressed by Kokopelli's power, and the future ritual use of eagle feathers on prayer sticks was instituted: 'You have my permission to lead your people into this new land. You may also use my feathers for your prayer sticks whenever you wish to speak with the Creator. As I am the one who flies the highest and closest to the Sun, your prayers will be taken up to the Creator quickly.' So it was that ever since then, the Eagle's feathers have been placed on the *pahos*, or prayer sticks, of the Hopi people.[117]

Animals as Participants and Kin in the Cosmos

In most First Peoples' understanding of the cosmos, there is no separation between the spiritual and the material, between the real and the supernatural, or between the animate and the inanimate. There was (and is) fluidity of boundaries; there is a 'crossing over' between animal and human. Gods take on animal form, or are therianthropic in presentation.[118] Everything is endowed with spirit power, or 'medicine', and this understanding means that everything is part of the sacred unity. The earth is holy, as is every living being. Animals are seen as kin to humans and have the same spiritual value as humans. As with humans, they must be acknowledged and treated with respect when they have died or been killed. All inhabitants are viewed as family, with the animals called 'brother' and 'sister'. When one speaks of 'Brother Bear', this address referred to a familial relation. The Sioux categorize these relationships in terms of motion, rather than as species, with 'the creeping people', 'the standing people', 'the flying people', and 'the swimming people'. Human beings refer to the earth as Mother, for the earth is the source and provider of and for all life, therefore all inhabitants are related, all are kin. There is a primordial connectedness with animals and with the earth.

In First Peoples culture the heroes are generally animals or natural elements, such as the moon and stars, not people. The animals tend to be the bearers of culture, teaching humans how to weave (spider), how to build places of shelter (beaver, nesting birds), and how to write (spider). Animals are respected as equals; therefore many of the myths and tales have animals speaking, and sharing their wisdom with humans. Pijoan puts it succinctly: 'Every animal is a spiritual powerholder in native American mythology.'[119]

The spirit world and the natural world are close; in Christianity the word for certain special or holy places is 'thin' (that is, permeable). This notion is part of the First Peoples' belief system; this closeness means that certain beings can pass between the two, and that the spirits are present, or nearby, to call upon when needed. Just as spirits and certain human beings can pass back and forth between the natural and the spirit worlds, so too can humans pass between their human and animal forms:

> In the very earliest times, when both people and animals lived on earth, a person could become an animal if he wanted to and an animal could become a human being. Sometimes they were people and sometimes they were animals and there was no difference. All spoke the same language.[120]

Each tribe has its own attitude towards animals and forms a closeness to some in particular. The way a certain animal is viewed by one tribe does not mean every tribe will see that animal in that way; these are not universal understandings.

The Cree believe they were given spoken language by animals. The very first Cree speaker and storyteller was Wichikapache, the Cree trickster. In the Swampy Cree world,

> Wichikapache is considered the first human being; since he was born 'out of' animals, the first interspecies communication was this metamorphosis . . . In one version of Wichikapache's birth, an owl and hare say to him, 'All right, we gave birth to you, now start wandering. Get out there, see many things, return and tell us about them.' From that point on, Wichikapache will wander endlessly.[121]

On these wanderings Wichikapache discovers he is able, sometimes at whim and sometimes mysteriously even to him, to switch forms: to a crow and back again, to a turtle to a crow and back to a turtle again, and then perhaps back to human form . . . Each time such a metamorphosis takes place Wichikapache remembers something about what it is like to be each animal . . . This knowledge, in one way or another, sinks into his intuition; and these metamorphoses are a basis for his (and every Cree who later hears Wichikapache tales) empathy with animals. Sometimes animals indeed instruct Wichikapache in how to speak properly with them . . . Early in his wanderings, Wichikapache mates with other species as well. From this union, other animal persons appear on earth. Some are humans.[122]

In the mythology of the Dogon people of Mali, the jackal is the first-born from the union of the sky-god Amma with the Earth. From his mother, the jackal learned to speak, and 'as the first possessor of the Word, the jackal is the god of diviners who will reveal the Creator's will.'[123] The jackal speaks to people by dancing, leaving tracks for the shamans to interpret, and is therefore a very important power animal.

In some First Peoples stories, there is no clear boundary between animal beings and human beings. The storyteller would act out the parts and, using certain gestures and movements, the audience could 'see' the animal form inside the human form. Shapeshifting was common, and within the human community it was the role of the shaman to enter the animal realm or spirit world to bring back guidance or advice for his or her community or tribe.

In ancient times it was believed that the animals were the people of the country; they were like humans. Everyone understood their language, they would put on fur and skin and take it off like a coat. Animals and birds and fish were all the same in this respect. Some believed that the world was inhabited by a race of animal people before humans came. The animal people in the myths of the Pacific Northwest were giants. Mosquito, Spider and Ant were larger than our cows. Eagle and Beaver, Fox and Coyote could reason and talk. They lived in the way humans now do; they fished and hunted, dug roots and cooked them, lived in lodges, used sweat lodges and had chiefs.[124]

Different tribes had different heroes, but seemingly all of them believed that the world was once inhabited by mythological beings and that, in the days long past, some Changer came to transform the ancient world into the world that we know today.[125] Among the interior tribes of Washington and Oregon, the Changer was Coyote. Coyote is the chief character in the myths of the Pacific Northwest and over the western half of North America. In the myths of other regions other characters play major roles; in Washington and British Columbia, for example, the character is Raven.

Among most of the Puget Sound and Pacific Coast First Peoples, Coyote is believed to have transformed the creatures of the mythological age into animals, birds, fish, stars, rocks and trees, in preparation for the race of human beings he was planning to create. In the Columbia River Basin, Coyote was the greatest of these ancients. He had supernatural power, which he used for the good of the lesser animal people, but, being a trickster, he also was foolish at times. At the end of this mythical period of the animal people, 'the world turned over', 'the world turned inside out', or 'the world changed'.[126] Human beings were created, the animals shrank to their present size and became more numerous. In some traditions Coyote destroyed the power of the monsters and the evil beings and then changed the ancients into Native Americans. He divided them into groups and settled them in different places, giving each group a different name and a different language. These good ancients became the ancestors of all the First Peoples.

In some tales about Coyote, he is an animal, for his tail or snout is mentioned. In others, he is a man, old and ugly, or young and handsome. 'In a Sanopoil myth, Coyote is described as tall and strong: "... perhaps a chief of some kind"; his hair was worn in long braids, "his forelocks were carefully combed back, and the few strands of hair in front of his ears were covered with beads".'[127]

A guardian spirit was an individual spirit that gave a Native American some special power, guided and protected him, and came to his aid when in need. This guardian spirit was usually in the form of an animal or a bird and was the soul of that particular creature. The particular traits of the animal or bird would give the person that power, for example, swimming skills if the guardian spirit were an otter, or the ability to hunt if the guardian spirit was a cougar. For the Algonquin, an animal *manitou* or 'spirit' was sought at puberty; the Inuit sought a *tuunraq* ('helping spirit'). In Central America and

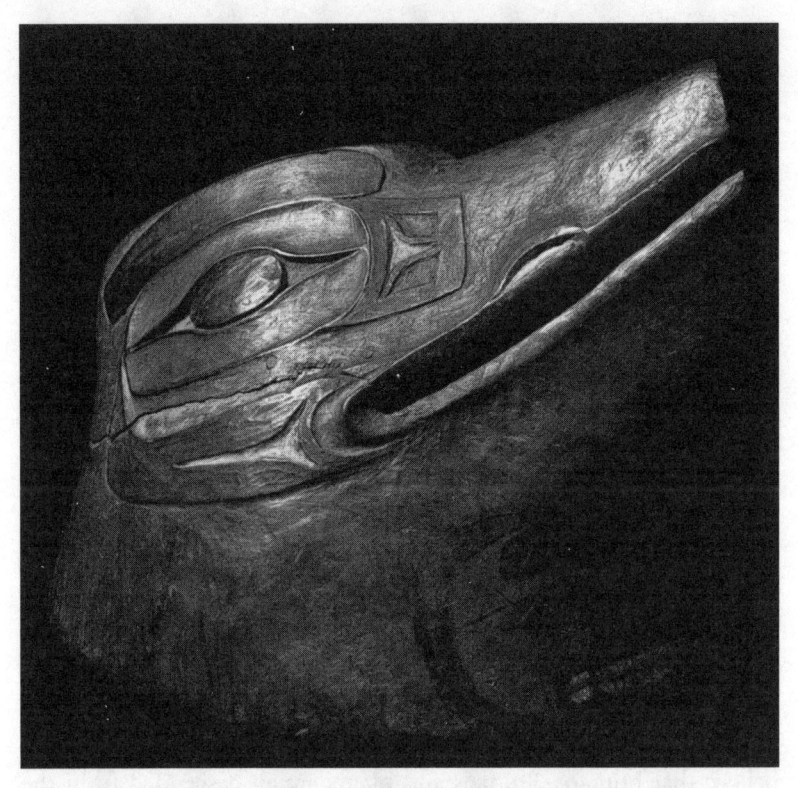

Tlingit painted wood and leather helmet, Alaska, late 18th century.

Mexico it was common to believe that each person had his own personal totem animal, known as his *nagual* (or *nahual*), who lived and died with him.[128] The *nagual* was a personal guardian spirit, believed to reside in an animal, such as a deer, jaguar or bird. Powerful individuals were thought to have the power to transform themselves into the shape of their particular *nagual* and acquire supernatural abilities, but for most the *nagual* was only to be met in their dreams.[129] Among the Tlingit of southeast Alaska, a young man may hang a river otter's tongue around his neck, for the spirit of the otter is thought to reside in the tongue and can provide the owner with an understanding of the language spoken by all animals.[130] In some tribes, no one dares to reveal the source of his special power unless death is imminent:

> A long time ago a dreadful sickness spread throughout the Umpqua tribe. Many people died. The medicine men said all should leave the village and go up to the top of the Big Mountains where they would be nearer to the Great Spirit,

who would be able to hear their prayers and their cries, so the people moved to the mountains. Then Teola, the chief's daughter became ill. One night they thought she would die.

Then a strange thing happened. A deer, white as snow, came out of the dark forest beyond the fire. Unafraid, it walked across the meadow to the people near Teola's tepee. Silent, wondering, the men watched the deer walk round the tepee three times. Each time it looked in at the dying girl.

The third time, the white deer entered the tepee, and the girl stretched out her hand toward it. The deer came close to her, kissed her lips, and then walked off into the darkness.

As soon as the white deer had gone, Teola rose from her bed and walked among her people. 'I am well! I am well!' she called to them. 'The angel of the Great White Spirit has kissed away my sickness!'

Since that time . . . the Umpqua have never killed a white deer. The white deer is sacred, to be protected and loved.[131]

In Southeast Asian myths, all things in the world have one source, or are otherwise closely connected to each other. The Dayak of Borneo believe that humans, animals and plants are all descended from the same spirit and are therefore all related. Also widespread is the belief that any form of life can readily change into another. In the Philippines, the Bagobo of Mindanao believe that monkeys once looked and behaved like humans, only taking on their current form after the god Pamalak Bagobo created a separate human race.[132]

In some areas of Indonesia, ancestors are depicted upon mythical animal mounts. The most striking equestrian image in all Southeast Asia is the great wooden steed, *ja heda* or *jara heda*, of the people of

Nagé wooden horse figurine depicting tribal ancestors, Flores Strait, 19th century.

Sculpture of naga *(snake) couple, probably a snake god and goddess, in the Chennakesava Temple, Belur, in South India.* Nagas *are objects of great reverence in many parts of South India; the female goddesses are believed to aid fertility in women and protect their families, while the male gods are believed to bring prosperity.*

central Flores, an area known for its horsemanship.[133] On the back of these creatures, often three metres in length, the ancestral rulers are seated. This spirit guardian, said to be an amalgam of the horse and the *naga* serpent, is thought to confer wealth and power, and has the ability to fly through the different realms of the cosmos.[134] These images are placed under the eaves, in front of the entrance to the clan temple in the central Flores village.

The whale has been a very important member of the Maori family, and has been revered for generations:

> When the earliest explorers left their homelands to travel to Aotearoa they made sure to bring everything that was important to them. Amongst these treasured possessions was the mauri or life forces of the various creatures, places and objects.
>
> Ruawharo is said to have brought the mauri of the whales on board the Takitimu canoe. The mauri was in the form of special rocks taken from a sacred pool in Hawaiki. When he

arrived here he placed the rocks at various points and thus established a sacred life-force for the local whale population.[135]

The Soul of the Animal

The word 'animal' comes from the Latin *anima* (breath, spirit, current of air) and *animalis* (having breath). The term is used to identify living, animate or 'ensouled' (endowed with soul, spirit or breath) beings. We cannot speak of an animal without realizing that the term includes and acknowledges its soul, or spirit.

For the Arctic people, animals and humans are equal, for all have the same kind of soul or life essence, known as *inu*. All have *inua* or 'in-dwelling beings'. The word comes from the same root as 'Inuit' ('the people'), and it means 'his (or her) man', the person within each animal. In Alaska the Yupik people made remarkable shamanic masks of birds, sea mammals and fish, showing the *inua* as a human face. Just as humans reincarnated their ancestors from one generation to another, so slaughtered animals kept returning to clothe and feed them: 'Every time a hunter killed to eat, he took a life belonging to another soul, his equal – yet such was the generosity of these spirits that they submitted willingly to being killed over and over again through the generations. The least man could do in return was to show gratitude for the animals' bounty.'[136]

> One thinks of *Inusia*, the soul – that small Eskimo-shape that lives within a bubble in the lower part of the body and does the breathing. It is the soul that gives beauty and purpose; it is what makes one a man and another a caribou or bear. When the hair is cut, part of the soul is cut away too, and when a man sleeps, *Inusia* hangs upside down by one big toe, almost ready to fall – death and sleep being very close.[137]

When an animal dies, its *inua* (soul) is not destroyed. It transmigrates to another animal. Certain rites have to be observed in order to appease the animal's *inua*: 'When . . . the Netsilingmiut people killed a seal, they would leave a small piece of freshwater ice for the dead seal's *inua*. Seals are believed to be always thirsty because they swim in salt water, so the freshwater is a welcome offering.'[138] For other peoples, when a seal is killed, fresh water is poured into its mouth so that its soul will not be thirsty, and it will tell other seals of the respect shown to it.

Paradoxically, we worship what we both love and fear. Is this a little like the Roman god Janus, facing opposite ways? Responding to a question about belief, a shaman told Danish explorer and ethnologist Knud Rasmussen, 'We do not believe, we fear.'[139] A sense of awe inspires both responses. From our beginnings, when humans first had contact with large and powerful beasts, such as mammoths, bears, bison and elk, worship grew out of a sense of need, for we sought to pacify that which we feared. That need gradually evolved into a ritual of thanksgiving for the gift of food and skins, which the humans depended on for survival. Mystery and awe can stem from the kill, for a hunter may struggle to atone for the taking of an animal's life, especially if he recognizes the animal as kin. An Inuit man spoke of this to Rasmussen:

> The greatest peril of life lies in the fact that human food consists entirely of souls. All the creatures that we have to kill and eat, all those that we have to strike down and destroy to make clothes for ourselves, have souls, like we have, souls that do not perish with the body, and which must therefore be propitiated lest they should revenge themselves on us for taking away their bodies.[140]

The bodies of the animals, as for humans, were temporary; they were clothing for immortal souls. 'This notion was especially vivid for peoples accustomed to dressing in animal hides.'[141]

In many festivals and rites, the dead animal was or is honoured. In the western Arctic, the Yupik of southwest Alaska were renowned for the Bladder Festival, held annually for a period of weeks between November and January.[142] The Bladder Festival lasted for up to fifteen days. The bladders of all the seals and walruses killed in the previous

Inuit flying or swimming bear amulet, ivory, Middle Dorset culture (c. 300 BCE–600 CE).

hunting season were welcomed into the men's communal house as honoured guests. They were greeted with dancing and feasting, and were then inflated and hung from the rafters:

> From this point on a whole range of taboos and ritual requirements came into play, all designed to avoid giving offence to the seals' souls, which were thought to be contained in the bladders. There had to be someone in the house constantly, and a lamp kept alight. Loud noises were forbidden, and sharp implements could not be used, bringing all work to an end. Sexual activity was also banned.[143]

The bladders remained there for several days, with different social activities taking place each night. On the penultimate day of the festival, the men would go down to the sea and cut holes in the ice. That evening the entire village, plus neighbouring communities, would gather for festivities that lasted until dawn, then the bladders were returned to the sea with great ceremony, where, it was believed, they would be reborn as new seals. To help them on their way, they were offered gifts, including miniature spearheads and miniature paddles, in order to help the reincarnated animals with their own hunting.[144] As the inflated bladders are pushed through holes in the ice, the animals' souls return to the spirit world.

The underlying strength of the Bladder Festival ritual for the Yupik is rooted in a myth that narrates the origin of this rite. Once a boy had been sent by a shaman to live with the seals, so that he could learn their ways. During this time he was harpooned by a hunter and taken back to the village in his seal form. When the bladders of his companion seals had been returned to the sea, he was found, now in human form, naked and shivering, crying because he could not go with his seal companions. From him the villagers learned how to honour the seals, which resulted in what was understood to be consent between hunter and the hunted.[145]

The human soul, dwelling within an animal's body, learned particular skills and gained insight into what it meant to be a certain animal. In a myth told by Naukatjik, an Inuit woman had a miscarriage and fed it to a dog, as she didn't want anyone to know about it. It lived as a dog, but had a human soul, and changed to different animals, from a dog, to a seal, to a wolf, to a caribou, to a walrus, eventually returning to the one it liked most, the seal. One day it allowed itself to be caught by the man whose wife had had the miscarriage. When it was time to cut up the seal, the soul slipped into the woman's body and she became pregnant. Her son grew up to be a skilful hunter.[146]

Hunting and Agriculture: Respect and Ritual

In Inca astronomy, the skies were important for animal husbandry: the star group known as Orqo-Cilay (the Multicoloured Llama) was thought to protect the royal llama flocks from harm. The Milky Way and its adjacent 'dark cloud' constellations were given names that included Yacana (the Llama) and Yutu-yutu (the Tinamou, a partridge-like bird). According to myth, when the celestial llama disappears at midnight it is believed to be drinking water from the earth and thereby preventing flooding. Llamas were among the most prized sacrificial animals and were offered on mountain tops at the new moon. Black llamas were starved during October in order to make them weep, pleading the deities for rain.[147]

In the Quechua-speaking Andean village of Misminay, animal constellations, as for the earlier Incas, exerted a profound influence on their mythology. The 'dark cloud' constellations, such as the Adult Llama, Baby Llama, Fox, Toad, Tinamou and Serpent, are referred to collectively as Pachatira, reflecting their association with Pachamama, the earth mother, and hence with fertility. When alpha and beta Centaurii ('the eyes of the llama') rise before dawn in late November and December, earthly llamas give birth.[148]

'Dark cloud' constellations are also important for their relationship with the rainy season; the constellation of the Serpent is visible in the sky during the rainy season, but it is 'below ground' (below the horizon) during the dry season. In Quechua thought, rainbows are multicoloured serpents that emerge from the ground following a rain shower.[149]

The beliefs of certain indigenous groups are embedded in animism; all things are believed to have a living essence. This is important when considering hunting practices of First Peoples. Courtesies shown to freshly killed animals were thought to promote their reincarnation as new animals of the same species. Humans have to kill creatures like themselves,[150] so hunting practice is based upon respect and reciprocity. It was believed that the hunter would only succeed if the animal chose

Peruvian llama figure, *c.* 1500 CE.

to give its life as a gift in return for moral and respectful behaviour on the part of the whole community. The hunter had to earn his right to his prey by uttering prayers of praise and flattery; he was to give thanks and to deal respectfully with the carcass, acknowledging the living soul that remained within the dead body. In a number of rites, or acts of respect, the hunter affirmed that he was taking the life of his spiritual equal. Animals were of enormous significance in many First People communities, such as the Inuit, because there were few vegetable food sources.

Spirit songs were essential among whale hunters and Inupiat hunters would always open the skull of a freshly killed animal to release its spirit. Their spring whaling festival, or Nalukataq, is held after the whale hunt as a thanksgiving for its success and to ask for continued good fortune with next year's hunt. It is held to appease the spirits of killed whales, similar to the Bladder Festival in this respect.

Sacred whaling rituals and ceremonies have long empowered chiefly families in their quest to capture the mighty whale. Private whalers' shrines, secreted in remote locations, were places of ritual cleansing, prayer and other rites, in order to encourage the whale to submit to the hunter. The skulls of deceased whalers placed in the shrines were thought to provide guidance, while carved whale sculptures manifested the spirit of the whale. Whale hunting among the Inuit was associated with a myth in which the trickster Raven harpooned a nameless, whale-like sea beast; after it died its body changed into the land inhabited by the whale hunters.[151] The Inuit therefore regarded both the whale and their homeland as sacred.

The Desana of eastern Colombia (northwestern Amazon) believe that the destinies of the animal species of the tropical rainforest are in the hands of Vai-mashe, the Master of the Animals. He is the eternal guardian of the game mammals, birds and fish that the Desana depend upon for their sustenance, and the Master of the Animals 'is also the guardian for all animal species, regardless of their immediate usefulness or disposition toward human beings'.[152] He can metamorphose into a number of different forms, and he punishes humans for their transgressions against their animal kin.[153]

Vai-mashe replenishes his precious stores of animal essences and populations with the life-nourishing souls of Desana Indians when they die. He negotiates with his spiritual counterpart in human society, the shaman, the terms of exchange between human souls and the impending animal births. The shaman pleads for a good season of game; in return he promises a certain number of souls of people after they have died. These souls 'will replenish the energy of the animals the Master of the Animals gives to the hunters'.[154]

In the forests of northern Cameroon, the animals belong to the Bedimo, the Ancestral Spirit; the hunter must pray to his

Joe David, Nuu-chah-nulth artist, sculpture of the moon to honour sacred whaling rituals.

Ekoi (Nigeria and Cameroon) wood and skin mask.

ancestors so that they may release the game from their 'stables'. Some hunters have to pray to the Game-Lord of a particular species to ask permission for hunting it.[155]

In San (or Bushmen, of the Kalahari desert) mythology the eland, the largest species of antelope, is the 'master animal'. The eland is not only a major source of food, but also a representation of the sacred, and therefore central in ritual. For the San, the praying mantis is the incarnation of the creator god Cagn (Kaggen). Mantis changes into other forms, animal and human, one of his favourite being that of the eland.[156] The eland is said to have been the first thing created by Mantis. In San initiation rituals, San boys have to kill an eland with a bow and arrow as their initiation into manhood. The marks made on the bodies of the young men to signify the change from boy to man are made with eland fat. San girls, undergoing initiation rites, are called elands, and the dance performed following a girl's first menstruation is known as the Eland Bull Dance.[157] The eland is also involved in the marriage rite: a man intending to marry must present his future mother-in-law with an eland's heart, and at the wedding ceremony the bride is smeared with eland fat.[158] As is common among many First Peoples, the San believe that the eland willingly offers itself as food, for the hunter frees it for its spiritual journey so that it can return again as food for humans. The eland is also thought to be responsible for the fertility and prosperity of the group, through its own death and consumption. It is treated with great reverence; after it has been shot with a poisoned arrow, the San hunter enters into a mystic spiritual union with the dying animal (the poison may take up to a day to cause the eland's death) and certain rites and taboos are observed by the hunter.[159] The San believe that after death a hunter becomes an eland.

In hunting societies, if the animal slain is not thanked properly, repercussions could include the withholding of future prey, because its spirit will tell other animals.[160] For the Cherokee, if a hunter does not show respect for the animal he has killed, he will be haunted by one of the guardians of the hunted, but if respect is shown, and he 'prays before and after killing an animal, the deer, the wolf, the fox, and the opossum will guard his feet against frostbite'.[161]

A story from the Sioux, 'Greedy Brothers', narrates the dreadful consequences that can occur when the death of an animal is not respected. Four brothers went hunting for buffalo. 'They killed a strong buffalo out on the plains, and stood as four when the dead buffalo lifted its head and told them that they could eat of its meat, but that they must leave the skin, head, hooves, and tail in place.'[162] They agreed to this; but during the night three of the four brothers went back and took the skin, fur, tail, hooves and head of the buffalo. The youngest brother saw this and waited until they had fallen asleep. He then returned all the parts of the buffalo. He joined them together and said a prayer of respect. 'When he looked up, there in front of him stood the buffalo. The fine, strong, whole buffalo lifted his nose in the air and bellowed. The youngest brother remained kneeling, watching the buffalo as it trotted away to greet the rising sun.'[163] When he returned to his brothers to tell them of this wonder, they were not there. He went to pack up their belongings and discovered a rattlesnake in each of their bedrolls, but not in his. Then he knew that his brothers had been turned into rattlesnakes because of their disrespect for the buffalo. They joined and became one big snake and burrowed into the ground. 'The people do not bother this snake, and they are very respectful of the game they kill. When respect is given, respect is received.'[164]

It is common to apologize to the animal the hunter has brought down:

To the Dead Deer

I am sorry I had to kill thee, Little Brother;
But I had need of thy meat.
My children were hungry and crying for food.
Forgive me, Little Brother.

I will do honor to thy courage, thy strength and thy beauty.
See, I will hang thine horns on this tree.
I will decorate them with red streamers.
Each time I pass, I will remember thee and do honor
  to thy spirit.
I am sorry I had to kill thee.
Forgive me, Little Brother.
See, I smoke to thy memory.
I burn tobacco.[165]

When the animal dies, the hunter performs a brief ceremony to ensure that its soul is returned to the non-earthly world to rejoin the society of animals, in readiness for being sent out again as possible prey. Festivals and elaborate ceremonies are held as propitiation, to honour the deceased animal and to influence the appearance of animals on earth:

> After the [Chippewa] hunter had killed the bear, the head, liberally decorated with ribbons and beadwork, was laid out, with the hide, on a mat. A slice of the tongue was hung up for four days. The body was not chopped up but, to show the respect with which it was held, carefully disjoined with a knife. At the feast, although other food was provided, everyone ate some bear meat. Food bears eat, including maple syrup and berries, was laid next to the body. If it was a male, a nicely braided man's costume was placed next to the hide; if a female, a woman's costume. The speaker talked to the bear village, calling attention to the fine treatment accorded this visitor and promising the other bears would be similarly and respectfully welcomed. The bones were gathered up and buried, never left lying about.[166]

The relationship between hunter and hunted was imagined by Arctic people in a number of ways. Some saw the two as master and servant, father and son, as friends, or even as lovers: 'Among the Mistassini Cree of Canada's James Bay coast, the hunter felt for the caribou he stalked much as he would for a human girl he was wooing. The beaver too was regarded as a lover, but one much more coy in her ways.'[167] Hunters do not outwit and slaughter an animal; they court it, and prove their spiritual worthiness in order to receive it. Through this we can begin to understand the myths of intermarriage, for animals were family, or kin. All of these relationships highlight the hunters' deep identification with the animals they hunted and killed. The different ways of imagining the relationship acknowledged that, though the animals inhabited a separate plane of existence (which could be crossed, particularly with shamanistic practices), the animals, like humans, had individual identities.

Once satisfied about the hunter's integrity, the animal gives him or herself and the negotiation proceeds. In return for meat, fur and bone, the hunter loads the animal's spirit with gifts. The animal is given a proper send-off and this ensures that others will return once they learn of the hunter's generosity.

There are many taboos and different rites to observe. In Native American cultures, after killing a bear, its eyes are sewn up to prevent the bear from pursuing the hunter. For the Western Apache, it was considered a grave offence against the Deer Spirit to boil a deer's stomach or to eat its tongue.[168] The Cherokee believed that when a hunter shot a deer, the Chief Deer Spirit would ask the dying deer if he had heard the hunter pray for pardon. If the hunter had not done so, the Chief Deer would track the hunter and cripple him with rheumatism.[169] If the hunters did not know the appropriate prayer, they would build a fire on the path behind them to prevent themselves from being pursued.

When summoning buffalo, the Apache would begin their preparations for hunting by praying that the guardian spirit of the buffalo would ensure a plentiful supply of animals. The sacred pipe was lit. People would then sing and dance in honour of the buffalo, mimicking the animal's horns by putting their hands to their heads. When the herds were scarce, the Apache observed a special hunting ritual, conducted by the community's shaman. The shaman would scatter dung and pollen on a piece of ground while the people prayed, then the shaman would sing four songs and imitate the sound of the buffalo.[170] At the end of a successful hunt, butchering had to be conducted according to a strict procedure, lest the buffalo's soul be offended and its companions avoid future hunters: 'First, the hide was cut along the right shoulder. The foreleg and shoulder were then severed. A piece of fatty meat was cut from the back and thrown towards the east as an offering to the animal's spirit.'[171] The remainder of the buffalo was used for food and clothing, with reverence shown in dealing with every aspect of the carcass: 'The feet, in particular, were treated with great respect, for fear of incurring the wrath of the spirit and being trampled by the herd's hooves on the next hunt.'[172]

After animals were killed, there were taboos about playing with the food or joking about the dead creature. In an Ainu myth, Chikap Kamuy, the god of owls, instructed a young water owl to visit the Country of Heaven to enquire about the famine and ask why the gods in the Country of Heaven had not sent deer and fish. Several days later, the owl returned:

> 'The reason', he said, 'why the god of the deer and the god of the fish in the Country of Heaven are sending no deer and no fish is that when men took deer they beat them over the head with a stick, flayed them, and without more ado threw the head away into the woods; and when they caught fish, they hit them over the head with a piece of rotten wood. The deer, weeping bitterly, went to the god of the deer, and the fish with the rotten stick in their mouths went to the god of the fish. These two gods, very angry . . . agreed to send no more deer, no more fish. But if men would promise to treat the deer they take with courtesy, and the fish they catch with courtesy, the gods will send them deer and fish.'
>
> So I [Chikap] visited men in their dreams when they were asleep and taught them never again to do such things. Then they saw that it was bad to do as they had done. They decked out the heads of the deer daintily, and made offerings before them. Henceforward the fish came happy and proud to the god of fish . . . and the deer came happy to make reports to the god of deer. The gods of deer and fish were pleased, and sent plenty of fish, plenty of deer.[173]

Animals were believed to ignore a hunter if he did not promise to offer their spirit the appropriate death rite. Among the Alaskan Inuit, the whale's soul was thought to reside in its head. The soul had to be returned to the sea, with the head intact, otherwise the soul could not return to its place of origin and be reborn.[174] Other large animals, such as the caribou or wolf, had to be ritually butchered to allow their spirits to escape from their lodgings in their neck.[175] If people performed the correct rites, then the animals would help them by allowing themselves to be hunted. If people killed and butchered an animal 'kindly' and 'correctly', with sharp clean weapons and following the set rituals, then it was believed that the animal would not resent its death and other animals would return on hearing the good report about that particular hunter.

Careful disposal of bones was another important way of honouring an animal that had been killed. The bones were often rearranged into complete skeletons, with great care being taken not to mislay a single bone. This was to ensure that, though the animal had been consumed, it would still be reborn. Bear bones were treated with particular respect:

> The bears were believed to have once been people who decided to separate from the killers of animals and start their own group. The people who continued to hunt eventually killed off all the game and were starving. The Bear People came out of the forests and offered themselves as food, having the magic to turn their bodies back into bears if hunters left the skin and bones behind untouched.[176]

These practices have been incorporated into non-hunting societies up to the present day, with Sax making this observation: 'The custom of saying grace before meals derives from the practice among tribal hunters of asking to be pardoned by animals they have killed.'[177]

Shamans and Shamanic Practice: Entry to the Animal World

Much of the religious tradition of the First Peoples was passed on by female or male shamans. Shamanism is a religious phenomenon involving the disciplines and the practices of shamans, who are intermediaries with the spirit world. The word 'shaman' was originally a term given to tribal specialists, medicine men or exorcists by the Tungus of Siberia, from where it was extended to similar individuals among First Peoples of North America.[178] Shamanism is native to Siberia and Central Asia, to the First Peoples of North America, particularly the Navajo, and to South America and parts of Asia. Shamans have also existed in the context of Shinto in Japan, their duties relating primarily to village rituals. Traditional native practices and the power of shamans decreased with increased contact with Europeans.

Direct contact with the world of the gods and spirits is of great importance in most First Peoples communities. The path into the animal world is not always easy to follow and often it demands a vision. It is achieved primarily through the 'vision quest', a process of fasting and prayer in a remote place. During this time, a person hopes to gain a vision of a guardian spirit, which generally appears in the form of an animal or bird. The most powerful to whom such a visionary experience occurs will go on to become a shaman. Shamans are primarily concerned with healing and with locating game. These shamans could call upon a *tuunsaq*, or helping spirit, in times of crisis.

This spirit often took the shape of a land animal, into whose shape the shaman would change him/herself. According to Leakey, a dying eland is thought to be a metaphor for a shaman entering a trance state and entering the spirit world: 'An eland struggling to die and a shaman entering into trance behave in the same way. Like the eland about to

Wooden grouse rattle, Makah, Pacific Northwest, 19th century.

Nw-chah-nulth or Makah buxic (bird rattle), c. 1890. This rattle may represent a type of gull and may have been used during the Wolf Ritual or other ceremonies. It is painted with lines and dashes to represent feathers.

die, the shaman shakes violently, sweats superabundantly, bleeds from the nose, and ultimately collapses unconscious.'[179]

Shamans were deemed capable of travelling to the invisible world of the spirits to rescue lost souls and to bargain for game. They were the individuals who received the visions and dreams, who were able to induce a trance, shed their skins and step into the animal realm. They were known by different names, each telling something of their power: Elik (Inuit) 'the one who has eyes', and Makunaima (Caribbean), 'the one who works in the dark'.[180] The shaman is the master/mistress of the spirits, and he/she has the ability to climb behind the masks the other living creatures present to humans.

> Many traditions have held that the shaman is actually a separate species with family in all the animal 'houses'. It is because of this that he is able to travel between them with such ease, demanding that each obey his wishes. For not only does each species possess its own traditions with its own origin myths and culture heroes, but it also has its shamans who travel into the 'other houses' to barter and battle with their opposite members.[181]

Animals and fish that figure in shamanic objects include land otters, bears, mountain goats and other animals.[182] Carved headdresses, rattles, whistles, bowls, boxes and amulets are all part of the shaman's regalia. Visible representations of the spirits are found in the shaman's medicine bundle, a collection of objects of spiritual significance used in healing rituals. Symbols of the spirits are also depicted on clothing and on ritual and personal items. The frog is often associated with the shaman, for it is a creature that moves freely between the separate realms of land and water and understands the world of the deep forest.[183]

Shamans summon their spirit helpers by singing, dancing and drumming, until the spirits enter their bodies and speak through them in sacred language. This message is delivered in another language, a secret one that spirits and animals are thought to use in their own worlds: 'This is the language of transformations and Magic Words, the language of the unconscious and the underworld, the one that shamans speak to one another, and refer to as the "Language of the Birds".'[184] According to a tale from eastern Greenland, at one time ravens, not humans, had the power of speech. One day a shaman worked his magic, and wrested from the raven knowledge of words and how to use them. From that day onwards, people could speak, and ravens could only caw.[185]

While others may not understand the language, bonds between humans and nature were reaffirmed and integrated through rituals, using dance, song and dress. 'The ceremonial life of the tribal person was a constant dialogue, with interspecies communication both ordering and transforming it.'[186] Every tribal person, shaman or not, knew that the real power of a being lies not in its physical or external form, but in its secret, inner form, and that was the purpose of the ritual, to reach that hidden world; 'to record that meeting was the purpose of myth'.[187] The shaman is seen to be able to link the different worlds, as a mediator between human and animal cultures, and the one who seeks to restore balance whenever it is disturbed.

Shamans wore the skins, tail, claws and heads of animals they had encountered in their vision quests. The shaman would dance, shaking the animal amulets to invoke the souls they represented, and would then call upon one or more animal spirits to restore the health of the person who consulted them. In South America the shamans who are able to transform into jaguars are the most feared and respected of all. They dress in jaguar skins, wear necklaces of jaguar teeth and may growl like the jaguar in ceremonies where they divine the future and cure illnesses. In the northwest Amazon, several of the drugs used in the ceremonies used to be called the 'jaguar's drug', or the 'jaguar's sperm', sometimes kept in a hollow jaguar bone.[188]

Some believe that a deceased shaman's soul changes into his or her alter ego, the jaguar.[189]

Among the Pima, the shaman, called *ma:kai*, is recruited by animal spirits and specializes in diagnosing and curing what is known as 'staying sickness'.[190] An eagle's feather is used to wave smoke over a patient's body: 'The shaman keeps secret his spirit helpers, summoned by night-long diagnostic sessions called *doajida* in which shamans sing to them. After the songs, the shamans make difficult diagnoses with help from their spirit aids.'[191] An important phase of the initiation for a shaman was the acquisition of spirit helpers. Many of these were animal spirits that possessed similar qualities and attributes of the animals themselves: a bear spirit helper was fierce, a fish swift and capable of swimming underwater for long periods of time. In some traditions, shamans could impart bodily form to their spirit helpers: 'Among the Siberian Yakut, shamans would anoint the amulets that contained the power of their spirit helpers with the blood of reindeer and believed that this created living animals to voyage on their behalf to the world of the spirits.'[192]

The shaman could also use an amulet to transform him/herself temporarily into the shape of that particular animal and call upon its spiritual power in this manner. Smallpox was once a great killer in Siberia. The shamans of the Even people believed that the spirit of the disease took on the form of a red-headed Russian woman. When the smallpox attacked, she became a red bull that charged head down at the shaman.[193]

The Canadian Inuit tell of a woman named Uvavnuk who discovered her destiny to be a shaman. She was struck by a blazing meteor, but before she lost consciousness she saw the spirit of the meteor had two bodies that were joined: one side was a polar bear, the other a human. The polar bear spirit that features in the story concerning Uvavnuk appears in many initiations of Inuit shamans. Often they have to endure a psychic dismemberment akin to being torn limb by limb and then being eaten alive by the spirit-bear.[194]

A legend from Greenland recounts how a shaman named Tugtutsiak held a seance at a time of famine. Feeding the people being a common task for shamans in times of poor or failed hunting, he summoned his polar bear and walrus helpers. 'Both animals could immediately be heard clamouring outside the house where the seance was being held. The bear seized the shaman and threw him bodily to the walrus, who passed him back to the bear. Between them the animals carried him far from his village.'[195] He found himself at the bottom of the sea. Tugtutsiak was required to propitiate the Sea Mother for human sins and try to persuade her to release the sea mammals. When he had finished his mission, the animal spirits transported him home safely.[196]

For Native Americans, good health has traditionally depended on behaving correctly by respecting the spirits of nature. In an Iroquois myth about the first medicine man (shaman), the animals and the birds of the forest brought back from the dead a warrior whose behaviour had earned their friendship. After the warrior had been killed and scalped by his enemy, Fox, Bear and Oriole tried to bring him back to life. They searched high and low for his scalp, eventually finding it in a distant camp, but it was too dry and shrunken to put back on his head. All the animals gathered leaves and herbs and tree bark, and Eagle used the dew she had collected for many years, to soften the scalp. Together they succeeded in bringing him back to life. Fox, Bear and Oriole revealed to the warrior the secrets of the medicines they had used to revive him. He went on to become the first medicine man.[197]

Significant Rituals

It is worth exploring in some detail several important rituals, which should aid a deeper understanding of the spiritual connection between First Peoples and their animal kin. I have limited the description to three rituals: the Salmon Ritual (the Northwest coast), Bear Medicine (the Forest and Plains peoples) and the giving of the sacred pipe (Plains people).

Story of the Salmon

No fish was as important as the salmon which, during the summer months, makes spawning runs up every inlet of the Northwest Coast. The five types of salmon were all viewed as five distinct clans of salmon 'people'.[198] For most of the year, these salmon people looked human and lived in underwater communities, but every spring, the salmon clans would leave their underwater lodges, replace their human clothes with salmon scales and swim to their spawning grounds, where they allowed themselves to be caught as fish. The First Peoples of the

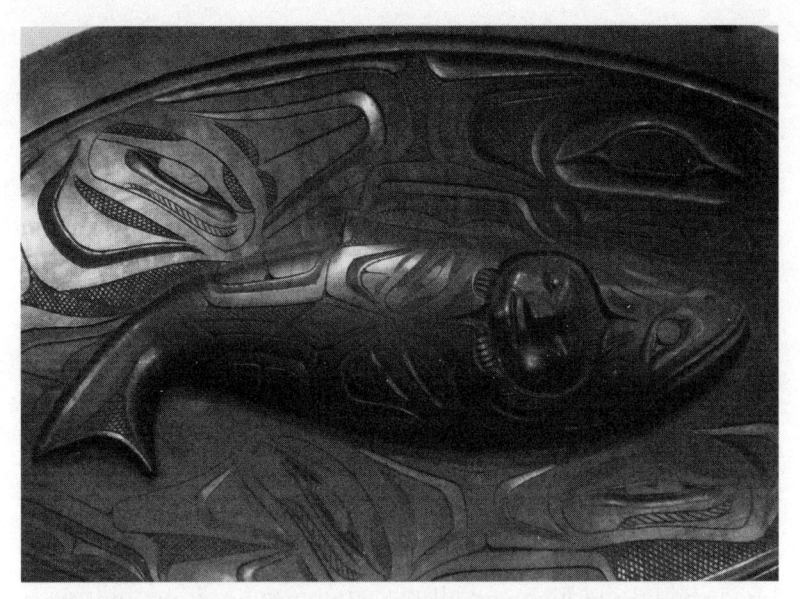

Qwa.a qíihlaa (platter) attributed to John Cross, Haida, *c.* 1885, carved argillite. A Haida story tells of a young man, unfairly chastised by his tribe, who went to live with the Salmon People. One day, a salmon was caught with the young man inside it; he then grew to life size, and taught his tribe to treat salmon with respect.

Northwest Coast acknowledged the generosity of the salmon people in salmon-welcoming ceremonies, performed by the Tsimshian, and some communities, such as the Nootka, would reverently return the bones of the first salmon catch back to the water.[199] These bones would become salmon people. The annual salmon runs were a constant reminder of the cyclical flow of life and death:

> The Great Spirit appeared to our people and spoke as he placed the Little Salmon in the water. He commanded them to go out to the great waters to prepare themselves to take care of the generations that are to follow.
>
> He placed the moon in the heavens, changing the years into seasons – each kind of salmon choosing its part of the season to gather and travel to the headwaters to spawn to restock its line and to give up its life for people and for all of the things that feed upon the salmon for survival.
>
> After introducing the salmon to our people, the Great Spirit told our people to watch for the changing seasons. After the north wind and snow of winters, in April the first Spring Salmon came.

> In the cycle of life to this day, the Little Salmon still fulfil the commandment God gave them. They appear to the people, give up their lives for mankind – feeding the people.[200]

In the tale 'Coyote and the Salmon', Coyote, as trickster, wishes to eat salmon, but at the time there were no salmon in the Klamath Reservation. Two Indian girls in the area feasted on salmon all the time, so Coyote wished to see how they came by the fish. He made a salmon out of bark and deer marrow, and put it over a fire to roast. The girls saw this and wondered where he had got the salmon, because only they knew where to obtain it. After pretending to eat his fake fish, Coyote turned aside, making the girls think he was asleep. They of course rushed to their salmon supply, took out a salmon and went back to their fire. Coyote followed them, and when they had left, he lifted the top of the trap to get a salmon; but he lifted the lid too high and all the salmon jumped out and swam down the Klamath River, and that is how salmon came to be in the Klamath River.[201]

On one level this tale is about warning against the dangers of selfishness and greed, yet there are other messages here. On another level the story reminds us of the time when the first salmon weir or fish trap was built on the Klamath River. Symbolically, there were no fish in the river, because one could not see them.[202] When the fish trap was invented, it suddenly seemed that the fish appeared out of nowhere, into the trap. The tale captures the surprise of realizing how many fish are within the river.

Perhaps the deeper message is that one should only take what one needs from nature. A similar lesson is taught in the Glooskap stories of Grandmother Woodchuck's game bag, where Glooskap, also known as the Creator, hunts all the animals at once, to his own disadvantage, and places them all in a single game bag. Here, all the salmon are placed in a single fish trap, which suggests that there are not an unlimited number of salmon in the world.[203] One of the casualties of Coyote's greed is that it affects the 'whole world'. Pritchard suggests that Coyote did not know how to operate the fish trap; the religious implication here is that Coyote had not prayed to the Creator: 'if we don't pray, we won't receive the instructions and will do harm to Mother Earth. This is perhaps the oldest teaching of all.'[204]

Coyote taught the Indians that salmon must always be kept clean. 'If you do not keep them clean after you have caught them,' Coyote said, 'they will be ashamed and not come up the river any more. And you must never cook any more than you can eat. If you cook three salmon when you are able to eat only half of one, the salmon will be ashamed and will refuse to enter the river.'[205]

Once we treat that first salmon with respect, it'll go back and tell the Salmon People it was treated with great respect by our tribe, and then it'll bring the rest of the people from the Salmon Village to us to be caught.[206]

An important ritual was the catching of the season's first salmon. A fire (representing creation) was lit inside a sweat lodge, which symbolizes the cosmos. The first fish was cooked over the fire, eaten and its remains disposed of with great ceremony. Different tribes honoured the salmon in a variety of ways: 'The first caught salmon is placed on a bed of ferns and cedar boughs, while a special song welcomes it: "yubec ti? A?" (Here is King Salmon!) After sharing morsels of the cooked fish, all the bones are reverently returned to the water to tell the salmon people to return again.'[207]

The First Salmon Ceremony celebrates the enduring kinship between Native Americans and the salmon in the Pacific Northwest. There are small differences in the ceremonies, but each community recognizes the Salmon People as relatives and honours them to ensure their return. The danger is that the salmon runs have declined and in some places are critically threatened. For the First People, they were promised salmon in the treaties of 1854–5, but the loss of salmon is not only an economic and legal problem, it strikes at the heart of their religion:

We are children of the salmon. We came from a village beneath the sea. Those who decided to live on land had to be responsible for taking care of the water. The salmon, our relatives, come back to us and feed us; so we have that connection of always taking care of each other.[208]

The First Salmon of the Season is mentioned in one of the tales about Coyote. In the story 'The Hungry Woman and the Great River

Rock', a hungry woman breaks the ancient traditions of her tribe. She catches the first salmon of the season and takes it home to feed her children, rather than having the salmon honoured in a special ceremony. The spirits are angry at this lack of respect and send storms. The woman is picked up by the wind, dropped into the waters and disappears. From the waters a giant boulder emerges where she has been dropped. The people do not understand what has happened, so they call upon the spirit of Coyote to explain. Coyote appears before the people:

> 'You have called me here to explain what has just occurred', said Coyote. 'The woman, Ka-eel, caught the first salmon of the season, but instead of following the tradition of prayers to the spirits with the rest of the village, she greedily took the fish home and fed her family alone. This is a grave offense to the spirits of the salmon and the river, and a price had to be paid. Ka-eel now sits in the center of the river, changed into the giant boulder, and for all of eternity, she will watch over the salmon as they make their way up the river.'[209]

Respect for the salmon was shown by observing certain rituals, and uttering particular prayers concerning the belief in the immortality of the salmon and the conscious will of the fish, which allowed itself to be caught for the benefit of humans. Now, with the demise of the once great salmon runs, and with mismanagement of the waters combined with a lack of respect for the salmon: 'The poor things come up here with their noses bent this way and that,' lamented Indian elder Flora Thompson, 'and covered with oil and scratches'.[210]

From this brief description, it is easy to see the religious or spiritual significance of the salmon and the pivotal role it has played (and still plays, especially in relation to environmental issues and over-fishing of salmon runs). When one acknowledges another species as kin, rituals are performed, respect is shown. What happens when one's kin is viewed as commodity, a product with dollar signs on its scales (or on its pelt, antlers or claws)? What name does one give to a spiritual crisis such as this, when those of one's own species (perhaps even within the tribe, and certainly outside it) do not 'see' the fish/animal in this light? I would suggest that conflict such as this gives rise to existential tension, an internal struggle to define what constitutes boundaries of sacredness.

Bear Medicine

Bear Medicine was seen as powerful, drawn on for vision quests and dreams, helping the person to find a way to protect them from harm. Bear Medicine was viewed by some First Peoples as the most powerful of all medicines and was drawn on for healings. For the Pueblo Bear Clan (usually consisting of women), a healing ceremony would take four days to perform. On the fourth day of the ceremony:

> the sick one is taken to the inner chamber of the healing house. The healing ones have their sand paintings placed on the floor along with their paraphernalia – bowls of healing cornmeal, fetishes . . . and bear paws . . .
>
> The Healing ones sit singing behind the altar as the patient is brought in and placed next to the wall, in front of the sand painting. The Wisest Healer of the men is called *Masewi*, or the leader, and he sits to the left of the patient – the side of the spirit world. The Follower is called *Oyoyewi*, and he is the taker-away of pain and illness. He sits on the right hand of the patient, whose close relatives stay at the end of the room praying quietly.
>
> The healing ones sing and ask the spirits of the animals *tcaianyi* (Bear, Mountain Lion, Badger, Wolf, Eagle, and Shrew), to come into the chamber, traveling over the road of sacred cornmeal that has been prepared and laid out in front of the patient. The healing ones work only with sacred spirit power received from these animals. Next, one of the powerful healing women brings in a bowl of water, and the other healing ones place it near the altar. Then *Masewi* pours six dippers of water, and the animals are called to come and take from it.
>
> The healing ones sing. *Masewi* takes powdered herbs from his bearskin bag and puts them into the water. The family leaves quietly, and only the strongest healing ones are left inside to work with the healing herbs. It is believed that people cured in this manner will have a bear come into their dreams and warn them of danger, or tell them of a better path to take in their lives. In fact, the bear is a guardian, and the sacred *ma-cinyi* (skin of bear's forelegs) and bear claw necklaces bring vision to those in need.[211]

There is a myth concerning a boy of the Pawnee tribe who imitated the ways of a bear. As he grew older, he would go into the forest to pray and sing and perform smoke rituals to the Bear. While he was part of a war party, he was slain by the Sioux. Afterwards several bears came to his body and recognized him as the human who had done them many good turns. They used their bear medicine and brought him back to life. He stayed with them, learning a lot from the bears, for the bears are one of the wisest animals. At last it was time for him to return to his tribe. He was given a bear-skin cap to hide his hairless scalp (for he had been scalped by the Sioux). When he arrived home, he told his family what had happened. He took the bears presents of Indian tobacco, clay, buffalo meat and beads. The male bear said: 'As my fur has touched you, you will be great; as my hands have touched your hands, you will be fearless; and as my mouth touches your mouth, you will be wise.' And with that the bears departed. True to his word, the animal made Bear-man the greatest warrior of his tribe and he was the originator of the Bear dance, famous among the Pawnee.[212]

'There was a family that belonged to the Cherokee clan called the Ani'-Tsa'guhi. They had a son who would leave home for days.'[213] He was going deep into the forest and having plenty to eat, but he was also changing. He spoke with the elders and told them they could come with him and live there, but they must fast for seven days first. On the seventh day, all the Ani'-Tsa'guhi people left and went into the woods. When people from other villages heard about this, they went to see them. They noticed that the Ani'-Tsa'guhi people had started to change; they now had hair all over their bodies:

> 'We shall be called the *yanu* [bears] forever. If you should be hungry, come into the woods, kill us, and eat our flesh. You need not be afraid, for we shall live always.' The Ani'-Tsa'guhi taught the other people the song with which to call them. The people were sad and looked down. When they looked up again, they saw a drove of bears going into the forest.
>
> The people who hunt bears were told by the Ani'-Tsa'guhi how to prepare the meat of the bear when they skinned it. They were told to take a hide of the bear and the bones and place them under a pile of leaves. The people could take the meat, but they must leave the hide and the bones buried. The people did this, and when they turned to say a final prayer, they saw

'Sea Bear': Chilkat wool tunic, intended for a member of a bear clan, Canada.

a bear rise up out of the leaves and go back into the forest. They then knew that this was great magic, for they had the meat of the bear and the bear had regained his life to live again. The people who hunt remembered to sing the songs.[214]

White Buffalo Calf Woman and the Sacred Pipe

The smoking of the sacred pipe is one of the most widespread and ancient rituals among the people of the Plains. Communal smoking is an act that confirms and strengthens bonds linking family, tribe and the universe. The decorations on the actual pipe reflect the caretaker's personal spirits and visions, and symbolize creation. The Lakota tale of the White Buffalo Calf Woman tells of the giving of the sacred pipe.

She places it on a chip of buffalo dung. As the buffalo is sacred, the chip is keeping the pipe from touching the earth. In Black Elk's version of this tale,[215] the following speech is quoted:

> She held the pipe before the chief and said, 'Behold this and always love it! It is *lila wakan*, very sacred, and you must treat it as such. No impure man should ever be allowed to see it, for within this bundle there is a sacred pipe. With this you will, during the winters to come, send your voices to *Wakan-Tanka* [Great Mystery], your Father and Grandfather.'
>
> ... The woman laid the pipe on a buffalo chip. Again she spoke, and said: 'With this sacred pipe you will walk upon the Earth, for the Earth is your Grandmother and Mother, *Maka*, and she is sacred. Every step that is taken upon her should be as a prayer. The bowl of this pipe is of red stone; it is the Earth. Carved in the stone and facing the center is this buffalo calf who represents all the four-leggeds who live upon your Mother. The stem of the pipe is of wood, and this represents all that grows upon the Earth. And these twelve feathers which hang here where the stem fits into the bowl are from *Wanbli Gleska*, Spotted Eagle, and they represent the eagle and all the wingeds of the air. All these peoples and all the things of the universe are joined to you who smoke the pipe – all send their voices to Wakan-Tanka, the Great Spirit. When you pray with this pipe, you pray for and with everything!'[216]

As White Buffalo Calf Woman walked away, she first became a young red and brown buffalo calf and then a black buffalo. She bowed to the four quarters of the universe, then disappeared over the hill.

It was thought that, along with the sacred pipe, White Buffalo Calf Woman also imparted to the Sioux seven rites that are central to their religion. These included the vision quest, the rites of purification that took place in the sweat lodge, funeral rites that ensured the soul of the deceased returned to the Great Spirit, puberty rites for girls and the Sun Dance.[217]

Parted: The Afterlife – Soul Bearers and Sharers in Another Existence

Most accounts of the origin of death accept the logic that space is limited on earth and that death was introduced so that there would not be overcrowding (and that there would be sufficient food for the living). Myths describing the afterlife are few, because most First Peoples were and are generally more focused on the present world than with what might follow. The afterlife of animals was perceived as being happy. Dead animals lived in soul villages and ranged over extensive plains that resembled the earthly ones. It was thought that the afterlife would include more game: some hunting societies, such as the Peoples of the Plains and the Great Lakes, used the image of the 'Happy Hunting Ground' to express their concept of an afterlife as a reward for good conduct. The Happy Hunting Ground is referenced in the legend of 'The Recluse':

> As he heard the last beat of the Thunder Bird's wings dying slowly, slowly, faintly, faintly, among the crags, he knew that the bird, too, was dying, for its soul was leaving its monster black body, and presently that soul appeared in the sky. He could see it arching overhead, before it took its long journey to the Happy Hunting Grounds, for the soul of the Thunder Bird was a radiant half-circle of glorious color spanning from peak to peak.[218]

In an African Khoikhoi myth, the Moon sent an insect to humans, telling the insect to proclaim this message to them concerning the nature of death: 'As I die and dying live, so shall you also die and dying live.'[219] The insect began his journey and was overtaken by a hare, who said that he would deliver the message, as he was faster. When he reached the humans he jumbled the message, 'I am sent by the Moon to tell you, "As I die and wholly perish, in the same way you also shall die and come to an end."'[220] Once the Moon realized the incorrect message, he scolded the hare and struck it on the nose with a piece of wood. Since that day the hare's nose has been split, and humans have believed the hare's message.[221]

There are a number of variants concerning garbled communication. A myth from the Mende people of the west coast of Africa tells of the

Thunderbird head-dress and ceremonial blanket with eagle feathers, Nuu-chah-nulth people, worn during the winter ceremonial season of indigenous families on Canada's Vancouver Island, 1920s.

Creator sending two messengers to humans: the first, a dog, to tell humans that they will live forever, the second, a toad, to inform them that they will die. Owing to a series of events, the slower messenger, the toad, arrives first.[222]

In the myths of the Ibo people of Nigeria, Chuku ('Great Spirit', also known as Chineke, 'Maker') created the universe. Chuku wanted human beings to live forever and sent Sheep to tell them that if anyone died, they should lay the corpse on the ground and cover it with ashes to bring it back to life. Unfortunately Sheep mixed up the message, saying that corpses should be burned to ash and then buried. This is the reason why human beings die and why the Earth is populated with ghosts and other spirits.[223]

In another myth about the origins of death, the mistake benefits an animal. Holawaka, a mythical bird sent by the creator to the Ethiopian Galla people, was instructed to tell them that when they were getting old they should throw off their skins and then they would rejuvenate themselves. On the way to deliver this message, Holawaka met a snake eating a dead animal. Holawaka offered to tell the snake his important message in exchange for a piece of meat. The snake agreed to do so if Holawaka agreed to change the message in favour of the snake. The change was made, the new message stated that humans would die, but the snake would always rejuvenate itself through the shedding of its skin.[224]

In a myth told by the Shoshoni people of the Western Plains, death also comes about through deception. Coyote thought it was a bad idea to bring people back from the dead, because there would be too many people on the earth. Wolf agreed, but he decided, in secret, that Coyote's son would be the first to die. Grieving Coyote regretted his original words, but it was too late, for death had now become part of life.[225]

The Caddo people of Arkansas also believe that death would have been temporary if Coyote had not decided that it should be final. In this tale, Coyote had also come to this decision in order to protect those living from scarcity. In the beginning there was no death, so the earth ran out of room. The chiefs held a council and one man said that people should die, but only for a while and then they would come back to life. Coyote disagreed, saying that the world was not big enough to hold everyone forever; there was not enough food. The medicine men built a grass house facing east, placing a black and white eagle feather on top of it. When anyone died, the feather would become bloody and fall over; then the medicine men would sit in the house and sing the spirit of the person back to life. After a while, the first feather grew bloody and fell. The medicine men gathered and, after several days, a whirlwind blew in from the west, circled the house and entered it from the east. When it was in the house, the dead man emerged alive. Everyone was delighted, with the exception of Coyote. The next time the feather grew bloody and fell from the roof, Coyote closed the door. The whirlwind, unable to enter the house, swept by. From that time on death became final. When Coyote saw what he had done, he was scared and since then has been on the run. When anyone hears the wind whistle, they say that it is a spirit, wandering the earth until it locates the spirit land.[226]

Another amazing attribute of Coyote is his inability to be destroyed; he has the power of resurrection. This is demonstrated in the tale 'Coyote Rattles some Bones'. Coyote comes across a graveyard and he sings: 'Dead Brothers, hear my song. Come back to this world and tell me your story. I have not seen anyone in a long time, and I need to be entertained.' Coyote continues to sing his tune into the night sky when suddenly all the bones began to rattle. Then a voice comes from the darkness: 'Why do you disturb us, Coyote? What is so important that you have called the dead back to their bones?'[227]

Coyote learns that he has disturbed a moose graveyard. He is chased by one of them and finally asks for peace, saying, 'I will fix you and bring you back to life so that you might once again roam the forests and eat all the greens you want.'[228] Coyote indeed brings them back to life, giving them new skins, thick fur, strong legs and antlers. In fact, Coyote carves so many antlers from the stone of the mountain that he creates the Okanagan Valley. The moose are so happy that they decide to reward Coyote, who is short, with round eyes and a pushed-in nose. The moose chief changes all this and also gives him a new coat of fur.[229]

As mentioned earlier, myths of First Peoples dealing with the cycle of life and death are a means of coming to terms with the fact that death happens to all. One Aboriginal myth treats death as the consequence of human misdeeds; all are subject to death with the exception of the moon and the crab, which casts off its old shell to replace it with a new one. In a myth of the Ugandan Banyoro people, death for humans also came about due to a human's behaviour, although in this case it was punishment for grieving. Ruhanga, the fertility god, had provided everything for humans to enjoy, indeed, people would live forever. But there was an old woman who grieved when her dog died. When Ruhanga came to know of her sadness he angrily declared that if life could not be appreciated, then humans would not live forever.[230]

According to a myth common to the Worora peoples of the western Kimberley, Widjingara was the first person to die. His wife, the Black-Headed Python, shaved off her hair and rubbed ashes over her body and head.[231] When Widjingara returned from the dead, his wife was upset, for she had shaved her head and blackened her body with ash. Widjingara was angry at his wife's outburst, so he transformed himself into the native cat (Dasyurus), an Australian marsupial. Now the option of rejuvenation has been lost forever and the python has always appeared to be in mourning. It was Worora custom, until stopped by missionaries in the early twentieth century, to place the deceased on a burial platform. During the time the body was on the burial platform, the native cat was often seen prowling around the corpse; the cat was thought to be the living manifestation of Widjingara.[232]

Debates also occurred between different animals concerning the best way to die. The Murrin-Patha (Murinbata) people of the northeastern Victoria River District in Australia tell of Crow and Crab arguing over the best way to die.[233] Crab descends into a hole in the ground. Crab casts off her old shell and waits for the new one to grow. Crow becomes impatient and asks her to hurry up, saying there must be a quicker way to die. Eventually she ascends, with her new shell, but Crow decides that method takes too long – he knows a much quicker way. Having said this, he rolls back his eyes, falls backwards and dies. Crab cannot revive him, for he has, indeed, died. The Murrin-Patha people compare the two different types of death in dances, with each dancer choosing to dance the method of death that suits them best.[234]

In many First Peoples beliefs, animals also inhabited the world of the human afterlife. The souls of dogs would often pass down the same road as human souls and would continue to be devoted to their masters.[235] Some believed that the Great Hare presided over the next world. In some cultures, fearsome animals guarded the river leading to the other world. The Iroquois believed that a fierce dog stood at the far end of the bridge leading to the land of the dead. The Senel people of California thought that a dangerous buffalo bull stood in the path of every deceased soul. Those who had lived a good life were allowed to pass, but others fell victim to this fierce beast. The Ojibway people of the Great Lakes believed that a huge serpent served as the bridge spanning the river. The serpent was harmless to other animals, but would threaten shamans in search of spirit helpers.

Some believe that an animal that regularly changes its skin will live forever. This is quite an important notion, especially in reference to the snake. The indigenous people of the Guianas believe that snake spirits can be good or evil, can help or harm. One Guiana song has these words:

> You will always be young like snakes if you change your skins, or you shall die. Kururumanni [Creator] came down to earth to see what the Arawaks were doing. They were bad, very bad, and he destroyed them by taking away their everlasting life.

They could no longer change their skins. This great virtue he blessed upon the snakes, lizards, and cockroaches.[236]

Other animals are associated with death. Some First Peoples view a particular animal or bird, such as the hornbill, as the one to help bear souls to the other side or to another existence. Birds, like angels, are of the air rather than the earth, of the spirit rather than of the body. They are able to move between the two worlds and are therefore messengers from the gods and frequently associated with prophecy.

Huitzilopochtli, often identified with the Toltec Quetzalcoatl,[237] was the Aztec god of sun and war, and was known as the 'Hummingbird of the South'. He was particularly honoured, for he was believed to have led the Aztecs to their new city site. He is depicted in art with hummingbird feathers on his left leg and a serpent-shaped spear thrower. Hummingbirds were seen as the souls of fallen warriors, who accompanied their patron's solar image as it made its way each day across the sky. Aztecs believed that warriors who lost their lives in battle (the highest and most honourable death for an Aztec), or on the sacrificial altar (Huitzilopochtli required a constant supply of fresh hearts cut out of live bodies), formed part of the sun for four years and then lived forever inside the bodies of hummingbirds.[238]

In Aztec mythology, Xolotl (which means 'the animal'), the dog-god, is a soul companion to the deity Quetzalcoatl. Xolotl journeys to the land of the dead and brings back human bones, which are crafted to create a new humanity.[239] Xolotl and Quetzalcoatl carry the dual identity of the evening and morning star. Xolotl supports Quetzalcoatl during his nightly journey through the underworld so that he may emerge renewed as the morning star.[240]

Owls are often associated with death. When Soo-koo'-me, the Great Horned Owl hoots, it means someone is dying. He is himself the ghost of dead people.[241] The Maori honour the proud white heron, which carries the souls along Te Ara Whaiti-a-Maui (The Narrow Path of Maui), the path to the underworld, in Rarohenga. 'Maori know this as a very special place called Te Muriwaihou and it is the first stage in the souls' journey to the world of darkness. The birds leave the souls there to be cleansed and prepared for the next stage.'[242]

Since ancient times Southeast Asians have buried their dead with extraordinary care and great ceremony. The most vivid image is of the boat that is to transport the soul into the afterlife. Often the boat is in

Wakash bird mask, Alaska, 1890s.

the form of a hornbill, or a dragon or serpent. In Borneo, the hornbill is a messenger of the deities. The carved boats of the Ngaju of central Borneo that are used in mortuary rites to transport souls to the afterworld are known as *banama tingang*, 'the hornbill boat'.[243] These creatures are thought to be able to move between the earth and the sky, between the different stages of existence. If we note the presence of animals that can shed their skins, or winged creatures that can fly between different realms, then we see the importance of metamorphosis and the concept of resurrection.

Bats, being winged creatures, travel between different realms, are often considered sacred and have come to be associated with death. 'When spirits are expected to pass on rather than return, bats appear as demons or, at best, souls unable to find peace.'[244] In Africa, Swahili-speaking people believe that after death the spirit hovers near the body in the form of a bat. People in Uganda or Zimbabwe believe that bats flying in the evening are actually departed spirits coming to visit the living.[245]

The gifts animals bequeath to humans can vary. One of these gifts is grief. In the story of 'Coyote and his Beautiful Daughter', her death brings Coyote much grief. Coyote was left on top of the mountain and for days he remained there, weeping for his daughter:

> 'This sorrow I feel is great. From this day forward, I will pass on these feelings to humans, and when they lose a loved one, they, too, will know the sorrow of Coyote.' It is said that every time a person dies, Coyote can be heard howling his sorrowful tune to the spirits.[246]

In the story 'The End', the Great Spirit comes to take Coyote back from the earth, for his work is finished for the moment. The Great Spirit is in disguise (as is Coyote) so for a while Coyote does not recognize his master. This story is very much coined in the genre of a quest narrative; once he has recognized the Great Spirit, Coyote becomes aware of the nature of the visit. The Great Spirit says:

> 'I have watched you for some time now wandering this existence looking for purpose. You were placed on this earth at the very beginning and have done many great things. But lately, you have become listless and have become something of a nuisance to the people of this land. They have taken your lessons and are surviving in this world . . . we will leave this world to the people and only come back to wipe the earth clean and start again.'
>
> . . . The Great Spirit built a house of ice and stone on the highest mountain. Coyote's only companion for his long slumber would be a small fire that would burn throughout eternity until he would reawaken.

It has long been said that every time Coyote turns in his sleep, summer blossoms, and winter's chill descends when he rolls over to the other side of his bed. So it is in this state that Coyote remains to this day, sleeping in front of the fire, waiting for the Great Spirit to call upon him to make his glorious return to earth when the people need him once more.[247]

Carved *manda* in the form of a beaver, with a set of potlatch rings, by the Haida artist Jim Hart, 1993–5. Traditionally a *manda* was a large wooden crest figure used to support the burial box of an important chief.

Conclusion

Within the world of First Peoples, it is easy to acknowledge a spiritual connection between human beings and animals on their sacred space, earth. Religion and mythology governed their relations and established an abiding bond of family, of kin. The majority of First Peoples' creation narratives speak of animals playing an active role in the creation of human beings and of their surroundings. This spiritual, continuous bond formed, for the most part, an unspoken covenant, for these things of great importance were 'known'; they were part of one's very being, essence or soul. Some believed that animals had given humans language, and other skills, to assist them in their daily lives. Prayers of thanks were said over killed animals, thanking them for the gifts of food, clothing and shelter. During the seasons, certain rituals and prayers were observed, sometimes with great ceremony, and during the dark days and nights of winter stories were told and re-enacted through dance and music. Animals were a necessary element for survival,[248] sometimes feared (due to their size or ferociousness, or a fear that they would not return the following season) but also, for the most part, respected.

Kwakwaka'wakw wood and leather mask of Kolus, Pacific Northwest, 1920s.

Animals were such a key component of First Peoples' psyche that particular animals were addressed as 'Brother' or 'Sister'. Not only were animals' actions and behaviours observed (and not purely as a means of assistance in hunting or fishing), but the belief that animals (and shamans) could shape-shift, or transform themselves into other creatures' bodies, allowed for a deeper level of respect and reverence to be shown to all. This commonality meant that the antics of tricksters, such as Coyote and Raven, were acknowledged, accepted and forgiven. Because of the close bond of kinship, these tricks were also acknowledged as being part of human life as well.

Having said this, we must be careful not to romanticize. First Peoples' relations with animals have not always been characterized by altruistic intent; European settlement and the new settlers' demand for buffalo meat, hides and land meant that money, greed and force changed this for many tribes. The accompanying sense of alienation, with its deep, dark scars of substance abuse and depression, lie outside the scope of this work, belonging more to the fields of sociology and anthropology, yet I would suggest that many of these present-day problems have come to the surface due to a breakdown in familial relations with their animal kin. This tearing apart has led many to be set adrift from their spiritual clan. Separation of First Peoples and their animal kin can shatter a spiritual heart. Such a break forces one into exile: physically, emotionally and spiritually. Because of the connection to nature, for most First Peoples spiritual exile is also environmental exile.

Not maintaining good relations with animals can have dire consequences. In a Cherokee myth, the animals are driven from the forest because of the expansion of the human population. As a result, the animals turn against humans, who had formerly lived in harmony with them. A council was held, and every animal devised a disease with which they could afflict human beings.[249]

Perhaps we humans have demanded too much of our animal kin. Wulbari, the main god of the West African Krachi tribe, grew tired of living near to humans, for they constantly pestered him with their demands. He eventually withdrew from them and founded a court consisting only of animals, including the spider/trickster Anansi.[250]

To be apart from spiritual kin leads to dis-ease; what was once embraced and worn with ease has altered, like an item of clothing that no longer fits. It is time for mending, time for story, mask, dance and prayer.

TWO

Animals in Ancient Egyptian Religion and Mythology

WHEN THE GREEK HISTORIAN Herodotus visited the Nile Valley in the fifth century BCE,[1] he was filled with astonishment at what he saw, particularly with the cults of the various gods and goddesses and their animal counterparts. He witnessed numerous rites, leading him to conclude that the Egyptians 'were beyond measure religious, more than any other nation'.[2]

When we think of animals in religion, Egyptian gods may spring to mind. These are the names we are familiar with, the stuff of legend: Anubis, Bastet and Horus. How many of us, having had a run-in with our felines, have chastised them with these words, or something similar: 'You have never forgotten that cats were once worshipped . . . just reminding you, this isn't Egypt!' Although the focus of this book is on the role of animals in religions that are still observed today, or on animals that are still key in cultural ritual memory (for example, many creation myths still play significant roles in some societies), Egypt remains outside these categories, yet it begs to be acknowledged, even by way of a short chapter, because of the presence of animals in the lives, mythology and religion of the ancient Egyptians. One cannot understand Egyptian civilization without looking at the role of animals in religion, for in ancient Egypt the animal world was almost as important as the human world.

Food, Taboos and Pets

More than five thousand years ago a wide range of animal life was known to ancient Egyptians. Humans looked to the animals around them to express or to personify a particular belief. In Predynastic times the gods would very likely have been tribal fetishes that took the form

Late Period statuette of Bastet, Egypt, c. 600 BCE.

of animals;³ many of them then made the transition into the form of a god.

Ancient Egyptian religion was a vast and largely unsystematic collection of diverse ideological beliefs that developed in different parts of the country in prehistoric times (before 3000 BCE). There were no attempts to introduce a uniform system for the whole country, so there were local variations and different rituals, customs and deities. The fluctuating fortunes of various cities also had a direct bearing to play on the standing of local deities. If there was a common, unifying belief in all regions, it was that of the divinity of the pharaoh (king).

The importance of animals to the ancient Egyptians is one of the defining features of their culture and religion. Animals and birds are depicted in tombs and on papyrus; they are featured in folk tales and in many myths. Their forms are sculptured on weapons of war and on amulets to aid their protection. Animals are prominent in hieroglyphic script. Hieroglyphs, developed during the Early Dynastic Period

(3100–2686 BCE), were used for the writing of sacred and religious texts; therefore it was the language of gods, and the script itself was revered and feared. The carved hieroglyph of an animal or bird was thought to capture its spirit or reflect its essence. Sometimes a sign representing a dangerous creature, such as a snake or a crocodile, would have been rendered harmless, its power stopped by severing the head or transfixing it with a knife.

Living animals brought the Egyptians closer to their gods. This was partly due to their physical appearance and what the animals could do that the humans were unable to; humans were unable to run like a cheetah or to fly like a bird; therefore, the ancient Egyptians perceived that animals were closer to gods than humans were.

Egyptians explored foreign lands and saw exotica, including bears, leopards, giraffes and monkeys. Some were brought back to Egypt or were used as trade or tribute by foreigners, but only animals indigenous to the Nile Valley, the marshy Delta region and the desert fringes were chosen to represent a deity.[4] These exotic creatures may not have merited the status of gods, but they were invested with a certain power. Leopard skins, for example, were prized for their dazzling golden colour and were imported in large numbers. Wearing a garment of leopard skin was thought to transfer the power of the animal to the wearer of its skin. When the Egyptians were depicted wearing leopard-skin garments, the animal's paws were carefully arranged so that they covered the wearer's arms and legs, with the leopard's head on the wearer's chest. The Egyptian word for 'strength' is written with two leopard head hieroglyphs.[5]

In the region, domestication of certain animals – cattle, sheep, goats and pigs – as sources of food was achieved as early as the eighth millennium BCE. Fish and fowl were also used. Pigs and certain fish, however, were deemed to be unclean, or taboo, on religious grounds. The food most frequently prohibited in the most detailed surviving example of a calendar of unlucky and lucky days (in this case, the Cairo Calendar) is fish.[6] Fish appears to have been considered unclean, perhaps because it caused the breath to smell: 'The word for a "stink" (*henes*) was written with the hieroglyphic sign of a *Petrocephalus bane* fish. The ancient Egyptians also made use of the *Barbus bynni* fish to write the word *bwt* ("abomination"), and the *Mormyrus kannume* oxyrhynchus fish was used to write the word *hat* ("corpse").'[7] Another reason for the taboo could be due to Plutarch's version of the myth of

Osiris: in his rendition, Osiris's penis ends up in the river Nile and is eaten by three types of fish, one being the oxyrhynchus (*Mormyrus*).[8]

Another reason for the negative associations with fish could be because of the sea, which was regarded as a place of chaos, unable to be subdued. It is thought that the king and the priests were forbidden to eat fish because of its association with Seth, the god of chaos and barrenness. On the Twenty-fifth Dynasty Victory Stela of Piye, it states that most of the Delta princes were forbidden from entering the palace because they were uncircumcised and because they ate fish which, according to the inscription, was an 'abomination to the palace'.[9] There were, however, areas of ancient Egypt where fish was consumed, so what was taboo in one region, was not in another.

The pig is connected with the evil god Seth. In mythology, Seth once took the form of a black pig in order to attack his nephew Horus, so eating the flesh of pigs became taboo, especially for priests, though it had been consumed in earlier times.[10]

Certain animals were kept as pets, including dogs, cats, monkeys and gazelles. Dogs were popular in Egypt as pets, guardians and hunters for the elite. Hounds often appear with leashes and collars in tomb scenes and sculptures, alongside their owners. Cats kept away rats, mice and snakes, and accompanied their masters when they went fishing and fowling in the marshes. It was only from the time of the Middle Kingdom that they are depicted in art sitting near their masters' chairs, as pets.[11] Young gazelles were captured to become pets, perhaps valued for their timidity and grace. Gazelles, surviving in a hot desert climate, signified order over chaos. Pet gazelles have been found buried alongside their owners, sometimes with funerary offerings of their own.[12]

Animals and Deities

The division between animal and human did not exist; even the category 'animal' did not exist.[13] 'Living beings' included gods, people and animals. A theological treatise recorded under Shabako (716–702 BCE), but perhaps composed as early as the third millennium BCE, describes the heart and tongue of the creator-god Ptah being present in 'all gods, all people, all cattle, all worms, all that lives'.[14]

The role played by animals in Egyptian religion has been misunderstood. Herodotus states that all animals were held to be sacred, which was not true. Animals themselves were not the gods;[15] rather, they were manifestations of gods or goddesses in animal form. This could be in inanimate form (as statues or two-dimensional representations of the deities) or via live animals. It was believed that a portion of the god's soul entered the animal and in its lifetime was that god on earth. Generally the actual animal was not regarded as an incarnation of the god himself; however, there were exceptions, such as the Apis bull. Animal forms were used in art to represent the characteristics of gods and goddesses. An animal was chosen to act as a god's image for the period of its natural life because of its special external characteristics, such as the unusual markings on the hide of the Apis bull. It was unique, and when it died it was buried as befitted its high religious status, and a successor was then found. 'The role of animals in Egyptian religion was quite different from, and had nothing to do with, zoolatry (animal worship).'[16] There were exceptions to the rule; this account, though probably fictitious, gives us an insight on how other nations perceived the value of animals in Egyptian society:

> In the second century AD, the Macedonian rhetorician Polyaenus gave an account of the battle of Pelusium, in the eastern Delta, in 525 BC. The stratagem of the Persian conquerer Cambyses was to shield his soldiers from missiles by putting rows of animals, cats among them, in the front rank. The Egyptians were afraid that they might injure or kill their gods and duly lost the battle.[17]

Different animals were revered as manifestations of deities. Many cats, baboons, crocodiles, ibises and other creatures were kept on temple estates, to be mummified and presented as votive offerings to the gods by pilgrims. Cult images of the same deity could be anthropomorphic (imitating human beings) as well as zoomorphic (imitating animals).

When a certain animal was chosen as the vehicle for the deity (for example, the bull), this did not mean that conditions improved for that species, for economic exploitation continued; the species as a whole was not accorded a higher status. Having said this, there may have been benefits for that particular animal's immediate family, for 'relatives of the animal chosen as the god's cult image (e.g. the mother of the Apis-bull and his offspring) may have been given special treatment.'[18]

Upper and Lower Egypt

The country had no embracing name and was known as 'The Two Lands'. The fertile area, with its thick black silt deposits was also known as Kemet (Black Land) and the desert region, with its cliffs that glowed pink at dawn, Deshret (Red land). The ancient gods Horus and Seth each came to be associated with a region, Horus presiding over Lower Egypt and Seth over Upper Egypt.[19] Nekhbet, the vulture goddess of Nekheb, and Wadjet, the cobra goddess of Buto, were Egypt's protective goddesses and were associated with kingship.

Thebes (modern Luxor) was the prime religious centre for more than a millennium. It was the site of the largest surviving temple complexes in the ancient world. Its principal god, Amun (Amun-Ra), may have originated elsewhere and supplanted the falcon god Mont (Montu) of Armant.[20]

In the Early Dynastic Period, during the first and second dynasties (as early as 3100 BCE), hieroglyphic writing was developed and Upper and Lower Egypt unified, with a capital at Memphis. This was the first great nation-state of history, and its kingship was associated with the falcon god Horus. By the end of the Second Dynasty, north and south were again separate, coming together by about 2800 BCE with a new religion centred on the god Atum or Ra (also Re), at Heliopolis. This began the time known as the Old Kingdom, in which the first pyramids were built.

It was during the Old Kingdom that an Egyptian pantheon began to take form. Particular versions would develop at several major cult centres; the main one being at Heliopolis, but other areas included Thebes, Memphis and Heracleopolis. In the Old Kingdom early Egyptian civilization reached a very high level. Temples were erected to the great gods Ptah, Ra, Hathor and Horus, whose incarnation the king was thought to be.

Egyptian mythology was dominated by the idea of sacred kingship and the themes of death and the afterlife/rebirth. There was tension between light and darkness, between the solar deities and the gods of earth and of the underworld. Stories of encounters between deities and ordinary people are rare, and there is little interest in the creation of humans.

Balance and order were very important concepts, embodied in the principle of *maat*, which translates as 'truth', 'order', 'justice' or

Head of a calcite figure of a cow, *c.* 1450 BCE. This carved head came from a statue of the goddess Hathor in her animal manifestation. The hole in the forehead was for the attachment of a gold sun disc between two precious metal horns. Although it was found in the 11th Dynasty temple at Deir el-Bahari, its original home would have been the sanctuary of the 18th Dynasty shrine to the goddess in Queen Hatshepsut's temple.

'balance'. The idea of *maat* as universal order or harmony governed Egyptian society; to maintain *maat* was the reigning king's focus. Temples were built to make offerings to the gods and to placate them, thereby maintaining *maat*. Enemies, and nature (especially wild animals) were to be controlled, for they represented *isfet*, chaos. Chaos, epitomized by the desert, included foreign lands, foreign people and wild animals; anything that was outside the Egyptian border, outside the reign of *maat*, was *isfet*. The principle of *maat* was represented by a goddess, Maat, a woman with an ostrich feather on her head.[21] Deadly animals were an essential part of this world view. Ancient Egyptians believed that certain gods manifested themselves in the form of deadly creatures (such as the scorpion, crocodile or snake) and they would make offerings to them to ensure protection for themselves, or in order to receive a particular blessing. One example is the protective goddess of childbirth, Taweret, who is portrayed as a hippopotamus with additional characteristics of a lion and a crocodile. This threatening combination would protect the mother and child.

Creation Myths

Creation myths are central to Egyptian mythology. In the Pyramid Texts, originating in Heliopolis,[22] Egyptian Creation starts from the concept of the primeval waters.[23] Before the gods came into being there was only a dark, watery abyss, called the Nun, whose chaotic energies contained the potential forms of all living things. In some areas, especially in Hermopolis, this is personified as Nun, the father of gods. Nun contained the essential energy of the dark and formless chaos out of which Creation emerged. The destructive forces of evil were embodied in the serpent Apep (or Apophis). Later, the serpent remained a danger even to the gods, because each evening the sun god in his journey through the hours of the night had to face the onslaught of the giant serpent.

Land rose out of the waters of the Nun, which provided a place for the first deity. He sometimes took the form of a bird (a falcon, heron or yellow wagtail) that perched on the mound of earth.[24] In some myths it was the god Thoth in his ibis form who laid the egg on the primeval mound formed by the Ogdoad (the Hermopolitan pantheon of eight). Another story held that it was the primeval or celestial goose, the 'Great Cackler', who broke the silence of the universe, and who laid the egg. Inside the egg was the sun god Ra, who would create the world.[25] Ancient traditions of Egypt transferred from centre to centre. At the temple of the sun god in Heliopolis, the Benu bird was said to be the first deity. Depicted as a heron, this shining bird was believed to be a manifestation of the creator sun god, and brought the first light out of darkness. 'When it landed on the primeval mound, it gave a cry that was the first sound.'[26] Another variation of the myth states that the Benu bird was a yellow wagtail. One of the explanations for the variances is the age of the text: in the Pyramid Texts, the Benu bird appears as a yellow wagtail, but by the time of the Book of the

Dead, the Benu bird was represented as a grey heron with a straight beak and a two-feathered crest.[27] The most sacred object in the temple at Heliopolis was the Benben stone on which alighted the Benu bird, Ra himself.

From the primeval waters arose the god Atum, later Atum-Ra, the light of the rising sun. The visible form of the invisible god Atum was Khepri,[28] the scarab, symbol of the rebirth of the sun that looked down from the sky as the god Ra. Another version of Ra's birth is that a lotus flower opened and revealed a scarab beetle. The beetle turned into a boy who wept and his tears became humankind.[29]

In ancient Egypt the forces of chaos were personified as eight divinities known as the Ogdoad. This consisted of four deity couples, representing primordial chaotic forces: forces of the invisible, of infinity, of darkness and of primal waters. They were imagined as snakes and frogs and other creatures of the primeval slime. Sometimes the Ogdoad was depicted as baboons greeting the first sunrise.[30] The Ogdoad was worshipped at Khemenu, where it was claimed the sun rose for the first time. The Ogdoad had come together to form the cosmic egg from which the sun god was hatched.

The Egyptians possessed four main creator deities: Amun, Atum, Khnum and Ptah, each of which was the focus of an important cult. Amun, one of the Ogdoad, was worshipped as a fertility god at Thebes in Upper Egypt. In the second millennium BCE Amun became a national god and his name was fused with that of the supreme solar deity, Ra. A snake form of Amun was the earliest being in the primeval waters and it fertilized the cosmic egg formed by the other members of the Ogdoad.[31] Atum, a creator deity worshipped at Heliopolis, emerged from the primeval chaos in the form of a serpent, but was later shown in human form.

In Esna, south of Thebes, the story of the creation of humans makes use of a universally popular motif: creation from clay. Here the creator is Khnum. As the ram-headed god (the word for 'ram' being equivalent to the word for *ba*, 'soul'),[32] Khnum was the soul of the high god, Amun.

The principal cult centre of Khnum was on the southern island of Elephantine. Khnum was thought to control the annual rising of the Nile. On his potter's wheel he shaped gods, humans and animals, and put the breath of life into their bodies. Heqet, the kind goddess of fertility and childbirth, was his companion. Women prayed to her during labour and midwives were called the 'servants of Heqet'.[33] She was in the form of a frog, so the frog is associated with rebirth in the afterlife. Frog amulets have been found within mummy wrappings.

The most detailed Egyptian account of Creation concerns the deities known as the Nine Gods of Heliopolis, or the Ennead (from the Greek *ennea*, 'nine').[34] One of the Nine was Nut, the sky goddess. She sometimes took on the form of a cow, patterned with stars. She was said to swallow the sun every evening and was sometimes accused of wanting to swallow all her children. In these instances, Nut was represented as a sow, with her piglets on her belly; in one tradition it is thought that she devoured her young every morning, for the piglets were believed to be the stars. A different interpretation of this portrays her in a more positive light, for each night she swallowed her piglets, the stars, to protect them until they could be reborn at night. Mother Sows were sacred to the sky goddess Nut.

Several animals could be regarded as manifestations of the same deity: Amun of Thebes as a ram or a goose, for example, or Thoth of Hermopolis as a baboon or an ibis. The same animal species could be associated with deities at different localities.

The Sun God

At dawn the sun was likened to a scarab beetle rolling the sun before him just as he would roll a ball of dung. The Egyptians believed that the ball pushed by the beetle contained an egg; therefore, the beetle was renewed by its own substance. The scarab beetle, Khepri, became identified with Atum, the creator and sun god, representing the new-born sun. Unlike other sacred animals, the scarab beetle was never mummified and entombed but it appears again and again on amulets and sculptures. It was common on funerary amulets, a sign of the deceased being reborn into a new life.

During the Fifth Dynasty of the Old Kingdom, Atum was displaced by the ancient sun god Ra. As the centre of the sun cult in later times, Ra became Ra-Harakhte (Ra-Horus of the Great Horizon), the personification of the midday sun, and was usually depicted as a human with the head of a falcon surmounted by a sun disc. The rising sun was Ra as Khepri, the scarab. The evening sun was Ra-Atum. In most periods the sun god was the principal god of Egypt.

The falcon was viewed as god of the sky. Some authorities believe that the cult surrounding the falcon began in Libya.[35] The falcon was connected with Ra, Horus and Seker. It may have had cults in many parts of Egypt and come together over a period of time.

Heroism is tied to the themes of sacred kingship in relation to the sun's journey across the sky and the idea of the king's, and later any individual's, passage after death to the underworld. The god's timeless enemies, led by the giant serpent Apep, sought to bar his passage through the sky and underworld. Throughout the night, the sun god has to contend with Apep, but in his last hours he himself enters a great snake, from which he emerges, rejuvenated, to be reborn at dawn. The ichneumon, or mongoose, can successfully fight snakes and rats, and this accounts for its association with the sun god Ra, who needed protection from such creatures during his nocturnal journey. It is shown in a number of tombs at Saqqara, which date from the Old Kingdom.[36]

The sun god Ra was also said to have taken on the form of a cat to defeat the evil snake. In other accounts, the cat was seen as the feline Sekhmet, lion goddess and protector of pharaohs. Sekhmet was thought to have protected the deceased king as he travelled through the underworld on his mighty journey.

A picture accompanying Spell 17 in the Book of the Dead shows a cat killing the sun god's foe, the serpent. A successful outcome of this ensued that the sun reappeared the following morning and that stability reigned. The cat is usually depicted trampling on the serpent with one paw, while another paw is raised, often holding a knife that will be used to sever the serpent's head.[37]

Scarab, New Kingdom, Egypt, c. 16th–11th century BCE.

The king was gifted with special knowledge; according to one text, the king, as the principal priest, 'knows' eight things about the sunrise, among them the 'speech which the Eastern Souls pronounce'. The Eastern Souls were baboons, animals that characteristically bark at sunrise.[38]

From the time of his accession, an Egyptian king played the part of a god. The king identified himself with Horus, the only son of Osiris, Egypt's first god-king. He was a manifestation of the sky god Horus and the son of the sun god Ra. The myth of Horus justified the sacred kingship. The falcon was the symbol of the sovereign god Horus, so it has an ancient connection with the king. The names of the earliest kings of Egypt were written in rectangular blocks known as serekhs. These serekhs always had a falcon perched on top of them, for the king was under the protection of Horus.[39] The falcon is also seen in other artwork, some pictures depicting the king in battle with a falcon hovering protectively above him.

The high god of Egypt was a creator god, usually associated with the sun. In Memphis, the first capital, he probably began as the falcon-headed sky and sun god Horus, the source of earthly kingship: 'Soon, however, he emerged as Ptah, the god of the primeval mound (Tatenen), who created by thinking things "in his heart" and then naming them with speech.'[40] His wife was the lioness goddess Sekhmet.

A text on one of the golden shrines of Tutankhamun (1336–1327 BCE), and which also appears on walls of later royal tombs, tells of the sun god Ra, who saw that human beings were beginning to plot against him. He summoned the Divine Eye, in the form of the goddess Hathor, who then was changed into Sekhmet, the fierce lioness, in order to destroy humankind. Ra decided, after some killing, that he should save a remnant of humanity, so he had many jars of beer dyed red and poured onto the ground to resemble blood, in order to distract Sekhmet from her orgy of killing. This worked, but plague and death had come into existence. Ra was still very weary and sad; Nut, the sky goddess, became a cow and carried Ra up into the firmament, where he created the stars and the fields of paradise.[41] Lion-headed Sekhmet was the defender of the divine order, called upon to chastise humans when required.

The power of the god-king was being threatened by the late third millennium BCE by an increase in the influence of the priests and the noble class. The Old Kingdom came to an end and the country broke

ANIMALS IN RELIGION

Limestone statue of a Horus-falcon, Egypt, 30 BCE–641 CE.

into two kingdoms. These were reunited, heralding the beginnings of the Middle Kingdom during which, under new rulers based in Thebes, an assimilation of gods took place. Amun came to the fore as the sun god. He was represented with a ram's head.[42]

Egypt was invaded about 1700 BCE by the Hyksos, but with their defeat in 1580 BCE at the hands of a Theban dynasty, the New Kingdom was established.

As well as the protective falcon god Horus, there were other animals associated with the king, notably the cobra. The ancient Egyptian name for the symbol of a rearing cobra posed to attack its prey is the uraeus. It was part of the king's regalia, worn on the forehead as a symbol of divinity and power. It was also a symbol of power: 'Religious texts describe the king's uraeus spitting fiery venom at his enemies.'[43]

Sometimes the king is shown wearing both a uraeus and the head of a vulture: these represent the 'Two Ladies', Wadjet and Nekhbet, the

100

cobra and vulture goddesses of Lower and Upper Egypt, respectively, who guard the king.

The vulture is associated with the queen and the symbol was part of her headdress. This linked her with the Theban goddess Mut, wife of the supreme god Amun. *Mut* meant 'mother', so the vulture was associated with rebirth and protection, but was also a reminder of fear and the need to pay respect to the queen (for vultures are not kindly creatures). The vulture goddess, Nekhbet, was connected with death. She had a cult centre of her own on the right bank of the Nile at the city of Nekheb, and she remained the protective goddess of Upper Egypt throughout the country's long history.

Other Gods

The moon god, Thoth, could be shown as a baboon, an ibis, or as a man with the head of an ibis. Perhaps the long curve of the neck reminded the Egyptians of the moon, or perhaps, as the god of writing, the finger of the scribe is the beak of the ibis-headed god.[44] Thoth was strongly connected with secret knowledge and magic. Thoth was also the god of wisdom, inventor of speech, patron of scribes, the Divine Recorder (a synthesis of a number of gods from a number of regions). In some myths Thoth is associated with creating the world. The ancient moon god Asten was in the form of a baboon, a form in which Thoth is frequently depicted.

The most important religious centre dedicated to Thoth was at Hermopolis, where many mummified baboons have been found. As the sacred animal of Thoth, the baboon usually wore a headdress with a full moon nestled within a crescent moon. Despite this association with the moon, Thoth was often depicted on his two front paws, worshipping the rising sun, and this is the way Thoth is commonly depicted on the bases of obelisks. The earthly form of the baboon came from neighbouring countries. Baboons tend to sit on their hind legs with their arms in the air in the morning, seated towards the sun, drying their fur; ancient Egyptians thought they were praying to the sun god Ra. These supposedly pious actions endeared them to the Egyptians and, as a result, baboons were treated with great reverence. When they died, the baboons at the temple in Hermopolis were carried to a special cemetery in the desert. Inside the cemetery were thousands of gifts offered to mummified baboons by pilgrims. Over one thousand mummified baboons have been found, embalmed with incredible skill.

Crocodiles were the biggest threat to people living on the banks of the Nile, therefore there was an ongoing need to placate them. An account of a friendly encounter concerns Menes and the crocodile god Sobek (Sebek):

> Menes, the first king of Egypt, was hunting when he fell into a swamp. His dogs failed to help him, but a friendly crocodile ferried the monarch to safety on its back. At the place where

Late Period stone figure of Taweret, Egypt, *c.* 600 BCE.

he arrived in safety, Menes founded the city of Crocopolis, where the crocodile-god Sebek was worshipped.⁴⁵

Perhaps this accounts for the association of crocodiles with kings, for they were frequently agents of divine retribution. Sobek was represented either as the reptile itself or as a man with the head of a crocodile. Sobek was worshipped in the ancient oasis of Faiyum and at the temple of Kom Ombo. He was associated with the might of the pharaoh, and in the form of Sobek-Ra he was worshipped as a manifestation of the solar deity. His consort was Hathor.

The Greek historian Herodotus reported that Egyptians in some districts killed and ate crocodiles, but in other regions the crocodile was considered to be sacred. In Crocopolis priests would place a live crocodile in a temple, and golden ornaments would be placed in its ears and bracelets on its legs. Pilgrims would bring the holy crocodile special offerings to eat, and after death it would be embalmed and placed in a coffin. Herodotus, who visited the labyrinthine temple containing the remains of crocodiles and kings at Crocopolis, wrote, 'though the pyramids were greater than words can tell . . . this maze surpasses even the pyramids.'⁴⁶ The crocodiles often died young, or perhaps they were killed before they became too large and dangerous to worship.

Crocodiles were the objects of terror for another reason. Many of the paintings from the Book of the Dead depict the monster Ammit waiting to eat those found wanting, as the soul was weighed on the scales. Ammit had the head of a crocodile, the forepart of a lion, and the hind legs of a hippopotamus.

The goddesses of Egyptian mythology were often more formidable than the male deities, visiting war and destruction on those who angered them. Neith, the Great Mother, was a creator deity who was also associated with war and hunting. When she spat into the Nun, the chaos serpent Apep was born from her spittle. She was also the mother of the crocodile god Sobek.

Another goddess, Taweret, helped the dead to be reborn in the Nun. She could appear as a fearsome beast, part hippopotamus, part lion, part crocodile. Since Seth could take hippopotamus form, Taweret was often regarded as his consort. Taweret, as the goddess who looked after women and children, used her power to protect them from harm. Her common form is that of the hippopotamus.

Hathor was among the most complex of Egyptian deities. Like Taweret, she protected women and children and was connected with death and rebirth. In cow form she nursed the infant Horus. The cow is associated with the goddesses Isis and Hathor, because cows are depicted as loving mothers. Sometimes the goddess is portrayed in human form, with a cow-horn headdress known as a sistrum. Starting in the New Kingdom, one or more cats appeared quite often on Hathor-headed sistra associated with the goddess Nebethetepet, one of whose characteristics was sexual energy. Perhaps the linking of the cat with this goddess was due to the animal's fertility.[47]

One of the most interesting gods was Seth, the god of chaos. Egyptians represented Seth as a mythical beast, part wild ass and part pig or anteater. His domain was the desert and most desert animals were associated with him. A number of different myths are told concerning Seth and the allies of Horus:

> Seth kept trying to disturb the body of Osiris, taking the guise of various animals. On one occasion he turned himself into a panther, but Thoth recited magic spells against him, whereupon Seth fell to the ground. Anubis tied him up, branded his fur and then skinned him. Seth's followers tried to march to his rescue, but Anubis beheaded them all. Seth recovered from his injuries and gathered new followers in the desert hills, but Isis came against him. Seth turned himself into a bull, but Isis took the form of a dog with a knife at the end of her tail and pursued him. The goddess Hathor turned into a venomous snake and bit Seth's followers. Their blood stained the hills red.[48]

The identity of the symbolic creature of the god Seth has been the subject of debate for more than a hundred years. The Seth animal has the muscular body of a canine predator, and its raised tail and ears suggest aggression, but its unnatural snout and square-tipped ears and arrow-like tail prevent it from being identified with any known dog.[49] In this form, Seth symbolizes chaos and violence. The animal may have belonged to a species that is now extinct, but it is more likely to have been fabricated 'to produce a disconcerting appearance for a deity associated with trouble and barrenness'.[50]

Feline Goddesses

Cats were sacred to the people of the Delta from Predynastic times. The image of a cat-headed woman or goddess sometimes appears in the Book of the Dead as an usherette in scenes of judgement of the deceased. She is usually nameless but may be Mafdet, the female panther deity, who was viewed as a protector of the dead.[51] Representations of Mafdet may have paved the way for Bastet, the most famous deity of this type.

Bastet was less threatening than Sekhmet, the lion-headed goddess. Bastet was originally a lioness goddess of love, sex and fertility, but from the middle of the second millennium BCE she began to be shown as a cat.[52] The temple cult of Bastet was established at Bubastis, which became a place of stability in a period of uncertainty and disunity during the first quarter of the first millennium BCE. The female cat was now firmly associated with the goddess Bastet.[53] Bastet was a goddess without a real name, for *Bastet* means 'She of the City of Bast'.[54] Early representations of Bastet show a woman with the head of a lioness and a uraeus on her forehead, holding a long sceptre in one hand, and an ankh ('life') sign in the other.[55] During the Ptolemaic Period the cat's popularity reached its peak. It was the most Egyptian of all the animals associated with the gods.[56]

The great fertility festival held each year at her temple in Bubastis, when mummified cats were purchased by pilgrims to bring as offerings to Bastet, became one of the largest and most popular in the country. These occasions included a ceremonial procession in which an image of the deity would be brought out and presented to the ordinary people. The goddess began to be linked with other localities, in particular, Memphis (perhaps through assimilation with the lioness Sekhmet), Heliopolis and Heracleopolis.

Priests would bury mummified cat offerings in catacombs in the temple so that the goddess would always look after them. Did the priests deliberately kill them? Evidence seems to point to this practice, suggesting that they were deliberately killed in order to be mummified for offerings. A common cause of death was a dislocation of the cervical vertebrae, which would have happened if strangled.[57] These drastic measures were undertaken in order to please the gods. Many of the mummified cats died young. From an investigation of cat mummies at the British Museum in London, it appears that the majority

Bastet, the cat goddess, Late Period or Ptolemaic Period (*c.* 664–630 BCE), bronze with precious metal inlays.

of them died at two to four months, or between nine and twelve months.[58] There are two theories for these premature killings. The first theory is that pilgrims who visited temples during annual religious festivals may have wished to pay for the mummification and burial of a cat as a visible expression of their piety. Very young cats would have been more suitable for the small containers in which they were buried. Deaths may also have been the result of culls in a temple cattery necessary to reduce the numbers of male cats, once they had reached sexual maturity (normally around eight to fourteen months), to an acceptable level.

The cat cemeteries in the vicinity of the temple of the goddess Bastet at Bubastis may have been among the earliest large animal necropolises and date from 900 BCE. Several other sites have yielded large numbers of mummified cats, including Saqqara and Istabl Antar, which were close to the temples of the local deities Sekhmet, Bastet and Pakhet. Most of the cats came from catteries attached to these temples and had been cared for by the temple personnel. It is easy to understand why extensive cat cemeteries appeared wherever the local goddess manifested herself as a lioness, since ultimately all these goddesses were regarded as aspects of the same deity. The name of the lioness goddess Pakhet, whose cult was established at Istabl Antar, near Beni Hasan in Middle Egypt, was derived from *pakh* ('to scratch') and literally means 'She Who Scratches'.[59]

It was characteristic of Egyptian thinking that concepts consisted of two opposites: the Nile Valley and the desert, Upper and Lower Egypt, the white and the red crowns,[60] and many others. The goddesses Sekhmet and Bastet began to be paired as opposites, complementing each other, as early as 1850 BCE, although at that stage the main manifestation of each was still the lioness. Eventually they began to be seen as aspects of the same goddess, one threatening and dangerous, the other protective, peaceful and maternal.[61]

It may be that the link between cat and lioness came about due to the physical similarity and patterns of behaviour. Sometimes it is hard to distinguish between the two in Egyptian art. Apart from her traditional representation as a lioness, or a lioness-headed woman, the goddess Bastet could now be represented as a cat or cat-headed woman. Sekhmet (Powerful One) was always viewed as a terrifying lioness goddess. Contagious diseases were said to be her messengers, and her priests served as doctors.

Mummified cat, Egypt, c. 30 BCE–641 CE.

Some statuettes feature both forms of Bastet, as a woman with the head of a lioness, accompanied by a small figure of a cat: 'A fragment of such a piece shows the seated goddess, almost certainly the warlike lioness-headed Sekhmet, with her feet resting on the backs of prostrate bound captives, while a cat is perched rather nonchalantly on their legs.'[62]

In one myth, the Eye of Ra quarrelled with her father and went south into the distant Nubian Desert. Thoth disguised himself as a baboon and went after her. He found her in the form of the cat goddess and prevented her from attacking him by telling her a story. He talked about Egypt, making her homesick. But she saw through his ploy and became angry, turning from a cat goddess to the raging lioness goddess. Thoth soothed her with more stories, and they eventually travelled home together.[63] In this myth the Eye of Ra takes on two contrasting feline manifestations: first as Bastet, and then as Sekhmet.

Herodotus, writing in the mid-fifth century BCE, says that anybody who intentionally killed a sacred animal in Egypt was put to death. An accidental killing was punished by whatever penalty the priests deemed appropriate. Diodorus recounts an incident he witnessed, probably in 59 BCE during the reign of Ptolemy XII Auletes, when a visiting member of a Roman delegation accidentally killed a cat. Neither the king's intervention nor delicate diplomatic considerations could save the man from being lynched by an angry crowd.[64]

The Underworld

The death of the good god Osiris was due to his brother, Seth. There are different myths concerning the circumstances. One states that he was drowned in the river Nile by Seth, who had taken on the form of a crocodile or hippopotamus. In another version, Seth took the form of a bull and trampled Osiris to death. The foreleg that trampled him was cut off by Horus and thrown into the sky, where it became part of the constellation known as the Great Bear.[65] A later tradition states that Seth became a small insect and gave Osiris a fatal bite on his foot. Isis, the consort of Osiris, watched over him in the form of a sparrow-hawk, fanning the breath of life into him with her wings.

Osiris, the first son of Earth and Sky, was perhaps the most important of the Egyptian deities. The king died as Osiris and was resurrected as his son, Horus. The dying god was resurrected and became the king of the underworld. He was the basis for the Egyptian practice of mummification and afterlife belief in general.

The Egyptian underworld was imagined as an elaborate landscape with rivers, islands, deserts and lakes of fire. To find a way through it, and to placate the gods and demons, the soul had to be a hero-magician. From the late third millennium BCE people of rank and wealth had spells inscribed on their coffins. Later these spells were developed into the texts now known as the Book of the Dead.

On reaching the throne room of Osiris, the god of the dead and the afterlife (as well as of rebirth and fertility), a dead person had to declare him/herself innocent of varying crimes before 42 judges of the underworld. The heart (the conscience) of the dead person was weighed on a pair of scales against the feather of the goddess Maat, the personification of justice and truth. A female monster, the Devourer of the Dead, also known as Ammit, squatted by the scales, ready to consume the deceased if their heart weighed more than the feather. Ammit was terrifying, for she could condemn her victims to a second, final death. Ammit was composed of three of the most aggressive creatures: she had the head of a crocodile, the body of a lion or leopard, and the

Painted statuette of Anubis, guardian of the dead, Egypt,
Ptolemaic Dynasty (330–305 BCE).

hindquarters of a hippopotamus. If the person's heart was judged heavier than the feather of justice, the heart was thrown to the monster to devour and the person was denied an afterlife. Because of the tremendous power she had over life and death, Ammit was sometimes called 'Fate'.[66] It was thought that this dreadful fate could be avoided by use of a spell that would stop the heart from declaring its owner's crimes.

If the deceased passed judgement, they became spirits with the power to move among the gods, due to the element of *ba*. The *ba* was a spiritual aspect of an individual, one of the elements of the Egyptian 'soul', usually depicted as a bird with a human head. The *ba* of a deceased person was able to move through the underworld and revisit the earth by day, for the *ba's* wings let it leave the tomb and revisit the places the deceased had loved in life.[67] The deceased may even be involved in heroic deeds, such as doing battle with the chaos serpent, Apep.

Clearly associated with Osiris is the jackal- or dog-headed god Anubis (Anpu) who, in his earliest form, devoured the dead. Anubis was the guardian of the body and soul of the deceased. Jackals lived in the desert, where the Egyptians buried their dead, so they came to be associated with cemeteries. Later, as funerary practices developed, Anubis became known as the god who discovered the process of mummification that preserves the body for eternity, and became the embalmer and the protector of graves. Statues of Anubis were often placed in tombs, for they served as watchdogs, ready to hear the sounds of intruders. The tombs in the Valley of the Kings each had a seal with a guardian jackal figure on it.[68] As a man with a jackal's head, Anubis stands in the Great Hall of Judgement next to the scales, guarding the deceased from Ammit, serving Osiris as a judge of the dead. Anubis was sometimes depicted lying on the chest containing the inner organs of the deceased.

Sometimes other animals are mentioned as playing a role in the underworld. The cat, for example, is described in one papyrus as 'mistress of the embalming house', perhaps because the original role of the cat was to accompany and serve the sun god in the underworld.[69]

In human mummification, canopic jars were used to hold the internal organs that were removed from the body before mummification. From the Eighteenth Dynasty onwards the stoppers of the stone vessels were each shaped like the head of one of the minor funerary deities known as the Four Sons of Horus. These were the baboon-headed Hapi (Hapy, guardian of the lungs), the human-headed Imsety

(Imset, guardian of the liver), the jackal-headed Duamutef (protector of the stomach) and the falcon-headed Qebehsenuef (protector of the lower intestines).[70] It was the task of these four deities to protect the internal organs of the deceased. In the Pyramid Texts of the Old Kingdom, the Four Sons of Horus were described as the 'friends of the king', because they were said to assist him in his ascent into the sky.[71] In funerary art they were depicted as small mummified human figures with their respective heads. The ancient Egyptians believed that the deceased would need his or her organs in order to be reborn in the afterlife.

The Eye of Horus (Wedjat, literally 'the eye which is sound or whole') was a funerary amulet in the shape of an eye that was probably used more often on mummies than any other amulet. It was first found in the late Old Kingdom and continued in use until the Roman Period. The amulet was placed over the incision for the removal of the internal organs, which was usually on the left side of the abdomen. In one myth, Horus, as a sky god, took the form of a falcon whose right eye was the sun and whose left eye was the moon. During a terrible combat Seth damaged one or both of the eyes of Horus. In another version, Seth, in the form of a black boar, tore out and swallowed (or ripped to pieces) the Moon Eye of Horus. The moon god Thoth searched for it, found the various pieces and made it whole again. In another version of the myth of Osiris, his son Horus offered his healed eye to his dead father, and it was so powerful a charm that it brought Osiris back to life.[72]

Temples and Centres of Worship

In 1600 BCE the centre of power in ancient Egypt shifted to Thebes (now Luxor and Karnak). The city was thought to have been built on the primeval mound, hence its sacred nature. Priests of Thebes insisted that all other gods were derived from the great god of Thebes, Amun, who until then had only been of local importance. Amun's first appearance in the world was as the head and skin of a ram, a creature viewed as a symbol of fertility. Ram-headed sphinxes lined the way to the great temple of Amun at Thebes.

In the first millennium BCE animal cults became an increasingly prominent feature of Egyptian religious activity, with this trend reaching its peak during the Ptolemaic and Roman periods. At the height of the popularity of animal cults during the Late Period, a large area of the necropolis of Saqqara was occupied by underground cemeteries for the mummified remains of sacred animals. The mummy galleries, known since the eighteenth century, were dedicated to particular species. There were catacombs for ibises, falcons and baboons; some galleries still contain several million mummies. The larger mummies were buried in pottery jars or miniature coffins; smaller ones, such as snakes, mongooses or beetles, encased in reliquary boxes made of bronze or wood.

The animals were bred on temple estates and mummified after death. Each of the groups of sacred animals had its own personnel of priests, feeders and embalmers. In the case of baboons, their canine teeth were removed to decrease the risk of being bitten. X-rays have revealed that their time kept in captivity in small enclosures, with little activity, resulted in long fingernails. Arthritis and stress fractures in their bones are also evident. However, other fractures that could be set had apparently been mended, so it is thought that this is evidence of accomplished early veterinary practices.

Pilgrims paid for the embalming of sacred animals as expressions of their devotion to particular gods. Most numerous were mummies of cats (associated with the goddess Bastet) and ibises (representative of the god Thoth). Birds, especially geese, were important in ritual. The remains of sacrificed geese have been discovered beneath the foundations of various temples, and within burial chambers as sustenance for the deceased in the afterlife. Birds raised in temple enclosures for religious purposes were sacred, and stealing them was considered a great crime.[73]

The Apis Bull

The most sacred animal in Egyptian religion and mythology was the bull. The bull was the cult of more than one god, for he was a symbol of strength, virility and the generative power of the male. Apis is the most famous of the bulls. Two others were Mnevis and Buchis. Mnevis was worshipped at Heliopolis, but it is believed that a bull cult existed there in Predynastic times.[74] The cult centre for Buchis was at Hermonthis, close to Thebes, but he was a latecomer and there is no

Apis, 26th Dynasty (*c.* 664–630 BCE) or later, bronze statue.

mention of him before the Thirteenth Dynasty. The bull was also associated with ithyphallic god Min, and in Ptolemaic times worship was accorded to the Golden Bull of Canopus in the Delta.[75]

Ptah, the creator god of Memphis, was in some traditions incarnate in a black bull brought to life by a moonbeam. Apis was a fertility god and the fertility aspect was emphasized by the association of Osiris at Memphis with the Apis bull, for Osiris was also a fertility god.[76]

The sacred bull was given divine honours for 25 years, which included being housed in a special enclosure, living a luxurious existence. After 25 years the bull was killed, before he started to show weakness due to his age. The dead bull was mourned for sixty days before being embalmed and then buried with elaborate burial rites.

Burials of sacred bulls have been found at several sites in Egypt. They were usually interred in large stone tombs. The most elaborate burials of the Apis bulls were at Saqqara, in a huge sarcophagus within the extensive underground complex known as the Serapeum (the necropolis of the Apis bulls).[77] The Serapeum, built in the Eighteenth Dynasty, was discovered in 1851 and contained 64 mummified bulls. Their trappings included jewellery, amulets and even *ushabti* (*shabti*) figures.[78] The embalming of the Apis bull was a heavily ritualized process based closely on the procedures for human mummification. Stone tables on which mummification was carried out have been found at Memphis. Similar treatment was accorded to the bulls at Buchis. Tombs dating to the Ptolemaic and Roman periods were uncovered at Armant during a 1930s excavation. Cult objects were also found, including funerary stelae, offering tables and ritual vessels.

It was thought that at the moment of death, the new Apis was being born. A search was then undertaken throughout Egypt until one was found and its identification confirmed by special markings that the priests identified. The Apis bull was black, with white patches on its forehead and back and a scarab shape under its tongue.[79]

Amun as a ram protecting King Taharqa, 25th Dynasty (760–656 BCE), granite, from Kawa in Nubia. Worship of Amun, imported into Nubia by the Egyptians, was carried on with great zeal by the royal family. King Taharqa built several temples in honour of Amun. This statue symbolizes the god's protection of the king.

The ram-headed Amun, Khnum and the ancient ram of Mendes were represented by a real ram who enjoyed a cult like that of the Apis bulls. Other centres of ram worship were Hermopolis, Lycopolis and Busiris. With the exception of Amun, these ram-headed gods date back to the beginning of recorded history. Khnum, an ancient god, was self-created and in some traditions the maker of earth, water and the underworld. The Egyptians had two types of sheep: in the Old Kingdom the sheep were of a heavy build with long, twisted horns, but in later periods this breed was replaced by sheep with slender bodies and inward-curving horns. Khnum is depicted with the earlier, twisted horns, whereas Amun has the inward-curving horns.

Mummies and Cemeteries

More than four million mummified animals have been found in Egypt. This highlights the complete immersion of ancient Egyptians in the natural world, as well as the importance of animals in Egyptian religion. The animals would live forever in the afterlife if properly preserved, but they had to remain intact in order to live on. The number of mummified animals also tells us something of Egypt's changing history.

In the Old Kingdom, hieroglyphs on tomb walls and on coffins depicted the deceased hunting hippos and fishing on the Nile, representing activities they would do in the next life. The needs in the afterlife were seen to be identical with those in this life. Pets were preserved for the elite, for their bond would endure in the afterlife. Other animals were mummified, representing particular deities. Meat, comprising usually choice cuts, was also mummified for use in the next life and placed in the tombs of the royal or the elite.[80] The ox had an extremely important role both in the everyday life of the Egyptians and in their afterlife: 'Many tomb scenes depict the ceremonies surrounding the slaughter of an ox and the offering of choice cuts to the blessed dead. Offering lists from all periods usually begin with the wish for a thousand portions of beef.'[81] Goats were a common source of food, but not usually listed in the offering or on the lists on tomb walls. Their absence may be because they were an everyday food and not a delicacy.

Small amulets showing cats, in bone or green faience, were found in the cemeteries in the El-Badari area of Upper Egypt, and dated to the end of the Old Kingdom. Worn on the body, they would have provided protection against potential hazards.[82] Some of the earliest representations of the cat in popular religion were on a piece of tomb equipment known as magic knives, which were made during the Middle Kingdom. Many of the decorations featured fantastic beings intended to provide protection for the deceased against scorpions and poisonous snakes, and against illnesses and accidents, as well as from dangers in the afterlife.

The increase in the popularity of cats in late Egypt was reflected in the large numbers of bronze statuettes of cats. Some may have held the remains of a cat in the hollow left after casting, some were buried in cemeteries, and small statuettes have been found among the bandages of real animals. Others may have been fixed to small caskets that contained the cat's body. The majority of these were intended to be dedicated in a shrine.

The complex religious ideas expressed in texts and decorations in Egyptian temples were for the minority: the priests. Before 600 BCE, the majority of the people were not allowed beyond the temple's gateway. In the temples the king, and the priests on his behalf, communicated with the gods. From 600 BCE onwards, however, more and more people had access to the cult of the gods. Now the public visited temples and took religion into their own hands. Animal mummies are a window into Egypt and how it changed and evolved.

The idea of the gift of a statuette of a deity to the deity itself was common in Late Period Egypt. It was now becoming commonplace to present a small monument to a temple, perhaps as an expression of gratitude to the god for past favours. At one time it was only kings who provided temples with their cult images, such as statues, or renewed the existing ones. Gradually this royal prerogative was modified and became available to ordinary folk.

Large animal cemeteries were a feature of the first millennium BCE. By the time of the Late and Graeco-Roman periods, there was a more widespread recognition of cults with animal images, and cats were mummified after their deaths in huge numbers. The large numbers of animals made it impossible to bury them in individual tombs:

> It is impossible to estimate the numbers of animals involved with any accuracy but hundreds of thousands, possibly millions, are indicated. An idea may be gleaned from the example of a

single shipment of cat remains, weighing about nineteen tons and thought to have contained some 18,000 mummified cats, which was sent to England to be processed to make fertilizer towards the end of the nineteenth century.[83]

The chosen method of burial depended on local conditions: communal brick-lined graves at Bubastis (Tell-Basta), in specially prepared rock-cut galleries at Dendera (ancient Iunet or Tantere), in reused tombs in Saqqara, or in large pottery jars at Bubastis and Abydos (ancient Abdju).[84]

Mass burials, and the sheer numbers involved, seem to point to religious change for everyone. It was believed that the animal would take one's prayer to the god in the afterworld and the god would listen to the prayer forever. Yet these developments were mostly political; growth of the 'sacred animal industry' associated with temples and cemeteries meant that the state became involved. The state benefited from the sale of priestly offices, taxation of the institutions connected with the cults and donations from pious worshippers.[85]

Animal cults cemented Egyptian identity. Persian rule in Egypt had ended in 332 BCE. Under Greek rule Egyptians were allowed to keep their practices and customs, as was the case under Roman rule. Many Egyptian deities acquired new forms under Hellenistic and Roman rule.[86] Animal cults became a way to unify the Egyptian population under foreign pressure, a visible expression of Egyptian nationalism. However, with the loss of Egyptian independence to Rome in 30 BCE the more formal aspects of Egyptian religion started losing ground and the process accelerated when Christianity reached the country.

Conclusion

Animals were extremely important in ancient Egyptian beliefs. They were central to creation myths, considered to be manifestations of many gods, and at the centre of practices of worship. We cannot assess ancient Egypt without them: from the sun god and the king himself, to funerary practices, their presence is everywhere. While it is interesting to note the inclusion of pets and other animals in tombs, there remains an underlying sense of disquiet. These pets were killed in order to accompany their owners in the afterlife; the many cats and other animals associated with particular cult centres were killed as offerings or as agents of protection. Many live animals were certainly kept in cramped conditions in temple enclosures and killed prematurely. Five thousand years ago early worship practices involved priests mummifying the hearts of falcons and offering prayers; the temple was off limits to the general public. Two thousand years later the temples had become sites of mass production, with thousands of animals paying the price of the temples' accessibility to the common people, the pilgrims. As the role of the priest changed, and weakened, the animal cults increased in popularity, with disturbing consequences.

With the exception of the family of the chosen Apis bull, were animals treated any better because of their association with the divine? There is no evidence that they were. There is a disturbing absence of any ethical framework concerning animals, or even of a general interest in animal welfare, which one may have expected to find, considering the popularity of animals in Egyptian religion and culture. This chasm, which seems unable to be bridged, leads to my final questions. Were animals respected and valued for themselves, or only because of their links with a particular deity? Did the individual animal inspire admiration, or merely association? How does one marry Herodotus's observations concerning mourning practices when a family cat dies, with the thousands of mummified cats, slaughtered at an early age because of increasing numbers? Perhaps our felines today are more fortunate.

THREE
Animals in Celtic and Viking Myth and Ritual

A NIMALS HOLD A PROMINENT PLACE in both Celtic and Viking mythology and ritual. Information comes to us mainly in the form of stories, which for the Celts are contained in the tradition of the bards. At times we may assume we 'know' something, when it has, in fact, been information that has entered our psyche through film or other forms of media. Imagination and fantasy, plus a selective interest in both Celts and Vikings (for example, modern-day adherents of Wicca), may prevent one from 'seeing' the role animals played in the lives of the Celts and Vikings; hence the necessity for a short examination of the role of animals in their mythology, religion and ritual.

Celts

The exact origin of the Celts is uncertain. A warlike people, they dominated much of Europe. The Greeks knew them as the Keltoi, the Romans as the Galli or Gauls. By about 500 BCE they controlled what we know as southern Germany, Austria, Switzerland and Hungary, also claiming parts of Spain, southern Italy and the Balkans. The Celts continued through northern Europe, reaching the British Isles by 400 BCE. By the end of the third century BCE, however, they were in decline. Although the Celts had no written language until about the fifth century CE, they had a strong oral tradition.[1]

Druids were the mysterious religious or priestly caste who performed a multifunctional role within Celtic society as priests, teachers and diviners. Druids were involved in educating the young in the oral traditions,[2] as well as officiating at religious rites, which included sacrifice. Much remains unknown about them, for their knowledge was deliberately not recorded but transmitted orally and consequently died

The Woodwrae Stone, a Pictish stone carved with animal decorations, 8th or 9th century. The Picts are thought to have been ethno-linguistically Celtic.

with them.³ What information we do have has come mainly from secondary sources.⁴

The Celts believed that with the correct knowledge and techniques it was possible to divine the future. The most common form of augury involved animals:

> It was said that the druids could look at birds in flight and make prophecies based on the way they flew or the shape of their talons. The druids were able to look into the future by cracking open the bones of certain creatures, usually dogs, cats or 'red' pigs, and chewing the marrow or bloody flesh. In some

rituals, a druid ate the flesh of a sacrificed animal, then slipped into a deep sleep, during which his totem ancestor or animal would appear to answer his questions about the future.[5]

Sacrifice played a part in the selection and installation of the High King of Ireland at Tara. A ritual known as the 'Bull-Sleep' began with the slaughter of a white bull. A druid consumed some of the bull's blood and flesh, and then went to sleep wrapped in the bull's hide. The dreams he had during this ritual indicated whether he had made the right choice in regards to the new king.[6]

The most important deity, and probably the oldest, for his origins may lie in the horned god of Palaeolithic cave painting,[7] is Cernunnos, the 'Horned One', the Celtic lord of animals (both domestic and wild), sometimes known as the god of the hunt. He is often depicted with animals, usually deer or horses, attesting to his power over animals, for he is a god associated with agriculture and pastoral concerns. His head is adorned with antlers, perhaps symbolic of annual renewal or fertility, and he is often depicted with a ram-headed serpent in attendance. 'The Celts equated Cerunnos with Dis Pater, the god of the dead, and with the Wild Hunt during which the hounds of Hell collected the souls of the dying to take them to the underworld.'[8] Most Celtic deities are local, but Cernunnos is found throughout Celtic myth and this bears witness to his importance and prominence. The earliest recorded depiction of Cernunnos is on a rock carving of an antlered god in northern Italy, dating from the fourth century BCE. On a relief at Rheims, Cernunnos is seated, Buddha-like, with Mercury and Apollo on either side, and at his feet a stag and bull.[9] The animals are being fed grain from a large bag.

Two British representations are noteworthy. A stone relief from southwest England shows the god with two large ram-headed serpents forming his legs. The serpent, a widespread symbol of fertility and regrowth, is connected with the underworld. Cernunnos also appears on a silver coin, shown with a wheel between his horns. The wheel, a symbol of the sun, suggests fertility and the rebirth of the earth in the spring.[10]

In the Celtic world several animals were highly regarded in mythology and ritual: the boar, the deer and the horse. Celts regarded the boar as a sacred and prophetic beast. The boar and its bristles were believed to possess magical qualities. In one Celtic legend, Fion steps on a boar bristle and dies after breaking a prohibition against hunting boar. The skin of a boar was endowed with healing properties by the Celts: when placed over an injury, all wounds disappeared. Druids called themselves 'boars' in order to align themselves with the boar's knowledge and magical properties.[11] In a similar way, Ceridwen, the Celtic goddess of inspiration, would often transform herself into a sow to speak to her people, and therefore the Druids were referred to as piglets, and the goddess as the snow-white sow.

There is evidence that boars were ritually sacrificed, perhaps as offerings to hunting deities. Moccus (*moccus* is a Latinized form of the Gaulish word for 'pig' or 'swine'[12]) is a Celtic swine god, worshipped in Britain and on the Continent. Under Roman occupation he was identified as Mercury and may have been a protector of boar hunters.

Boars have a prominent role in the Fenian stories in which they are often linked with the supernatural. In the tale of Diarmaid and Gráinne, Diarmaid's foster brother takes the form of a boar, but Diarmaid is wounded by the boar and dies. Celts connected the boar with battle and leadership. To dream of a boar, or to have a vision of one, indicated war. Their fierceness meant that they were of great symbolic significance to the Celts. Bronze boars have been found all over the Celtic world. They also appear on coins. Warriors on a panel of the Gundestrup Cauldron are shown with boar-shaped helmet crests.[13] There are many myths featuring boars, such as Twrch Trwyth in the Welsh tale of Culhwch and Olwen.[14] In a Celtic legend, the swine of Manannan, the Irish sea god, would reappear after having

Cernunnos, from the Gundestrup Cauldron, silver, *c.* 200 BCE–300 CE.

been consumed. In a similar myth, in the Otherworld pigs could be slaughtered and cooked in a cauldron, only to come back to life the next day, to be eaten again.

Even in the afterlife, boars were prominent. On their hunting expeditions, Finn and the Fianna (Ireland's elite warrior group) often pursued magic boars that led them to the Otherworld.[15] Pigs were also placed in Welsh and Celtic graves as food and to ensure the safe passage of the soul in the afterlife.

Another animal that features widely in Celtic mythology is the deer. The account of the search for the Holy Grail begins with the knights of King Arthur following a white stag into the forest. Deer also drew the chariot of Flidais, goddess of the chase, and, like the boar, were connected to the afterlife, for deer were revered as conveyers of souls to the spirit world.

In Celtic Britain and Gaul the horse goddess Epona, the Divine Horse, was associated with water, fertility and death, and was also known as a war and mother goddess. Horse sacrifice was widespread in the belief that the horses 'would become soul-mounts for their masters' symbolic ride of death'.[16] Epona had the unique honour among Gaulish divinities of being given a festival by the Romans.[17] She was always portrayed mounted or close to her equine familiars. The horse was a vital totem in Celtic culture, with more than three hundred monuments to Epona discovered in Gaul alone.[18]

There are other animals of importance, including ravens. One of the Morrigna, the trio of goddesses associated with war and death, was Badb, who sometimes took the form of a raven or crow. She was also responsible for cleansing the battlefield of carrion, which may be one of the reasons for her crow form. The story of Bendigeidfran, 'Bran the Blessed' (*bran* means 'raven'), in the Second Branch of the *Mabinogi*, the earliest prose literature in Britain, may have some association with the tradition that the kingdom will be safe as long as ravens are kept at the Tower of London.[19] Other birds and animals are associated with healing. Cliodna, an Otherworld queen, had three birds whose song restored health.

Animals feature in Celt funerals, which were often elaborate affairs, especially for the nobles. Graves have been found that contain the remains of dogs, hares, birds and even whole teams of horses, complete with cart. The dead were thought to arrive at the Otherworld equipped with objects and creatures that had been useful to them in the mortal

Relief of the Gaulish horse goddess Epona from Thessaloniki, 4th century CE.

world (a practice common in other cultures, the best-known being the tombs of the ancient Egyptians). Perhaps the burial of animals with their owners demonstrates that they too were expected to have an existence after death. Military victories had their own rituals, which included the winners sacrificing any living creatures they had captured to their gods.[20]

Dogs, particularly hounds, are among the animals most often connected with the Otherworld in Celtic myth. In the Welsh Otherworld, Annwn, a land of hunting and feasting, was ruled by King Arawn who sometimes emerged into the mortal world on hunting expeditions with his magical hounds. These dogs were said to be shining white with red ears, often viewed as harbingers of death. Dog skeletons have been found at many sites, which suggests that they were involved in ritual sacrifice, possibly associated with the afterlife/Otherworld. For the Celts, dogs were also believed to have magical healing qualities; depictions of dogs are commonly found at Celtic healing sanctuaries. No fewer than nine canine images were found at a sanctuary at Lydney in Gloucestershire, placed as offerings to the Celtic deity Nodens, god of health and healing.[21] A symbol commonly associated with Nodens was that of his companion, a deerhound, whose lick was thought to cure the sick. In France, visitors to the sacred healing springs at the source of the river Seine would sometimes offer up images of a person carrying a pet dog to the Celtic river goddess Sequana.[22]

Within Celtic mythology there are many tales of shape transformation, sometimes concerning trials demanded by deities.[23]

As is the case in many cultures, popular Celtic deities were often incorporated into the successive religion or beliefs of the region. The Celtic goddess Brigid (Bride, Brigit) was so popular that she was appropriated by Christianity and is now viewed as a Christian saint. Brigid was closely associated with livestock and domesticated animals, including dairy cows; in some accounts her cows produced a whole lake of milk three times a day. Her festival on 1 February was known by the early Celts as Imbolc (*i mbolc* meant 'in the belly' in Old Irish; *oimelc* was 'ewes' milk' in Gaelic), its name referring to the lactation of ewes, which heralded the coming of spring. This was one of the four great Celtic seasonal festivals. Brigid had two oxen named Fea and Feimhean, who gave their names to plains in County Carlow and Tipperary, respectively. She was also the guardian of Twrch Trwyth (Torc Triath), king of the wild boar, who gave his name to Treithirne, a plain in West Tipperary. These three totem animals used to raise a warning cry if Ireland was in danger. Legend has it that, as a child, Brigid was unable to eat ordinary food, so she was reared on the milk of a special white-eared cow. White animals with red ears are frequently found in Celtic mythology as beasts of the Otherworld, as already seen in reference to dogs. In popular belief, Brigid continues to protect flocks.

Vikings

The terms 'Norse' and 'Viking' are often used interchangeably for the peoples from Scandinavia who, between the eighth century and the eleventh, travelled as far as Italy, Spain and southern France, Kiev and Constantinople, raiding and, in many cases, colonizing. They conquered much of the British Isles and went on to colonize Iceland, where their mythology, which we tend to think of as Norse mythology, was recorded after most of Europe had become Christian.

In a region where the land was divided by mountains, fjords and lakes, there were many cults, some widespread and others more localized. Recurring themes suggest the preoccupations of a people living under harsh climatic conditions, at the mercy of the seasons. Gods and heroes of myths could be terrifying, commanding the elements with one hand and dispatching monsters of the deep with the other.[24] Hunting cults, in which creatures such as the bear were worshipped, gave way to earth and then to sky and warrior deities. One of the

Henry Fuseli (Johann Heinrich Füssli), *Thor Battering the Midgard Serpent*, c. 1788, oil on canvas.

earliest recurring myths of Scandinavia, portrayed in many rock carvings, is that of the wheeled chariot of the sun travelling across the heavens, drawn by horned beasts, or by horses.

The creation myths of the people of the north, as they were known in the earliest periods, told of an earth formed from a great emptiness known as Ginnungagap. In the beginning layers of ice and sparks of fire came together to form a primeval androgynous giant, Ymir, from whose body giants and the first male and female humans were formed. 'The giant was fed by a primeval cow which licked the salty ice-blocks until the Sons of Bor emerged – three creator gods,'[25] who slew Ymir. These creator gods were the offspring of the primeval cow, Auðumbla, and Ymir drank the four rivers of milk that poured from her.

The three major gods of the Vikings/Norse are Odin, Thor and Freyr (or Frey). Cosmology in the Viking Age includes a belief in the World Tree, Yggdrasil. The earth is represented as a circle of land surrounded by ocean. In the ocean lies the World Serpent, Jörmungandr, who bit his own tail, thus forming a firm belt to hold the world together, while in the centre of the land is the mighty ash tree. The tree's roots go down into the underworld, as well as to the source or spring of hidden wisdom. A squirrel runs up and down the trunk of the tree, carrying messages between the eagle at the top and the serpent gnawing its roots. A hart feeds on its branches and from its horns flow large rivers. A goat grazes next to the tree, producing mead for the warriors in Odin's hall. Yggdrasil probably means 'Horse of Ygg', one of Odin's names.[26]

Odin's power came not only from his defeats in battle, but also from his supernatural abilities to take various forms, including that of an eagle.[27] The eagle was both Odin's magic form and the guardian of the World Tree and enemy of the serpent. It presided over sacrifice and battle. This eagle could suddenly assume other forms, such as a wild beast, a dragon or a fish, and journey to distant lands.[28] Odin had gained these powers by hanging from the World Tree, Yggdrasil, core of the universe. The serpent at its base and the eagle at its top, together with the god Heimdallr, guarded Asgard, the world of the warlike Æsir god tribe.

Odin, ruler of Asgard, was said to summon kings and heroes who had died in battle to his Hall of the Slain, Valhalla, where they spent their time feasting and fighting, ready to defend Asgard. The boar Saehrimnir was killed every evening, served to the heroes in Valhalla, and reborn the next day.

Odin was an accomplished shape-shifter, sending out his spirit in bird or animal form. This gave him the ability to journey to the realm of the dead, having some affinity with the shamans of the northern Eurasian peoples. His constant companions were wolves and ravens. Two ravens, Huginn and Muninn, would bring him news of battles and tidings from distant lands. The sight of a raven was taken to be a good omen of Odin's protection, giving magical powers on the battlefield.

Thor, the thunder god, was known for his enormous appetite, even devouring the goats that drew his chariot, then collecting their bones and restoring them to life by the power of his hammer. His most deadly enemy was Jörmungandr, whom he once pulled up from the seabed using an ox-head as bait.[29] This was one of the most popular myths of the Viking period and has been found depicted on carved stones of the Viking age, including the tenth-century Gosforth Cross.

In the last great battle, known as Ragnarok, the monsters break loose and the wolf Fenir devours Odin. Thor slays the World Serpent, which emerges from the waves, blowing poison and causing floods, but is destroyed by its poison.

In Norse mythology Freyr, god of fertility and plenty, and his sister Freyja of the Vanir rode in a chariot drawn by the boar Gollinborsti,

'Odin Rides to Hel', from 'Baldr's Dreams' in an English translation of the *Poetic Edda*, c. 1900.

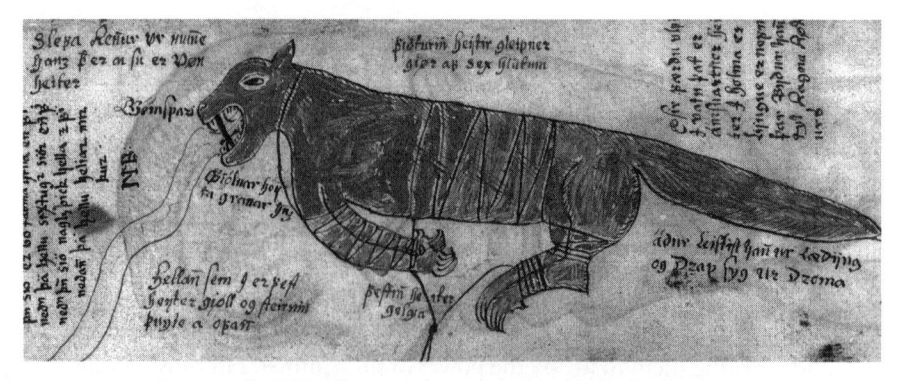

Fenrir, in the Edda Oblongata (AM 738 4to), an Icelandic manuscript from *c.* 1680 that contains a copy of the *Prose Edda*.

a golden boar that raced through the sky and the underworld.[30] The symbol of the boar was also used as a protective charm in battle, appearing on warriors' helmets. Sometimes the golden boar was known as the Swine of Battle. Horses also were dedicated to Freyr, and it is said that he kept some in his temple.[31]

The chief goddess of the Vanir was Freyja, who also had the boar as one of her symbols and was linked with the horse cult, although her chariot was drawn by cats.[32] She also transformed herself into the shape of a bird, mainly to assist in her travel.

Loki, who plays an important part in Northern myths, is portrayed as a trickster. It is never clear whether Loki is a god or a giant, but to some extent he is a creator figure, for he himself gave birth to Sleipnir, a powerful eight-legged horse that Odin rode between the worlds, and Jörmungandr, who became the World Serpent. Loki also fathered the fierce wolf Fenrir, who grew up among the gods in Asgard and broke through every chain until the dwarves fashioned a magical one that held him. The chain was made from intangible elements, including a fish's breath, a mountain's roots and the stealth of a moving cat. Loki could also assume other forms, including that of a horse, a fly and a falcon.

The female battle-spirits were known as the Valkyries, the choosers of the slain, sent out by Odin to decide the course of battle and to conduct the noble slain to Valhalla. In much of the Viking literature they are portrayed as noblewomen on horseback, but sometimes they are seen as riding on wolves, accompanied by their companions, the ravens, birds of prey.

There are also several myths concerning the slaying of a dragon, the most popular being that of Fafnir, slain by Sigurd.[33] One interesting part of this story describes how Sigurd burned his finger when he was roasting the dragon's heart. He put his finger into his mouth to soothe it and was then able to understand the speech of birds, which ended up saving his life.[34]

Conclusion

Although this is a short account, it has been important to demonstrate that animals have played key roles in both Celtic and Viking mythologies, from keepers of ancient wisdom, as means of divination, for sacrifice, as modes of celestial travel, to the more bizarre aspect of being able to provide a magical, never-depleted food supply for the gods. The power of particular key animals is more recognizable, and more frequent, in the Celtic tradition, but the importance of animals is still detectable within Norse myths. It is interesting to note that the pig or boar, an animal viewed as unclean in several religions, is accorded deep respect and honoured within both Celtic and Viking beliefs.

FOUR

Animals in Judaism

The Lord is good to all,
and his compassion is over all that he has made.

Psalm 145:9

Creation: Animals as God's Handiwork

JUDAISM IS ONE OF THE WORLD'S oldest surviving religions, originating more than 3,500 years ago.[1] It is a practical faith, one that has at its heart, in both laws and ethics, reverence for life.

In Judaism, as in other monotheistic religions, animals are not sacred beings or creatures to be worshipped. They have been created by God and are products of the Creator's handiwork. As such they are worthy of respect, but not of worship. Nature, as God's creation, is to be revered, but, unlike in pantheism, the individual elements of nature are not worshipped. (God is *in* nature, in that God created everything and his imprint is on all creation, but the object itself is not God.) In Judaism the universe itself is not divine, yet God's works of creation point to aspects of the Divine, such as God's goodness.

Within Judaism there are different traditions, from the ultra-orthodox to the adherents of the mystical Kabbala. These traditions, for the most part, agree on the goodness of animals, for all creatures have been created by God, but they differ in their interpretations concerning the use of animals for food, the question of whether animals possess souls, and whether there is transmigration or reincarnation. Animals are to be respected because they have been created by God, each with its own purpose: 'There is nothing superfluous in the universe. Even flies, gnats, and mosquitoes are part of creation and, as such, serve a divinely-appointed purpose.'[2]

In 1732 Rabbi Tzvi Hirsch Kaidanover wrote: 'All creatures are the handiwork of the Holy One, and all are needed for the world. Therefore, a person should not kill any creature unnecessarily, even something that is harmful to people such as snakes and spiders, if they are not chasing him to harm him.'³ In Judaism creation is to be loved, because creation, which includes all creatures, is the work of a loving, holy God. This idea is echoed in many Jewish writings, including the following:

> Love of all creatures is also love of God, for whoever loves the One, loves all the works that He has made. When one loves God, it is impossible not to love His creatures. [The converse is also true.] If one hates the creatures, it is impossible to love God Who created them.⁴

Not only did God create other creatures, but God loves His creation, and, as with humans, God is in relationship with them as well:

> When a man goes into a synagogue and stands behind a column and prays in a whisper, God still hears his prayer. It is the same with all his creatures. Can there be a closer God than this? He is as close to his creatures as the ear is to the mouth.⁵

In the Hasidic tradition, the Baal Shem Tov spoke of God being covered with a garment of the physical world, and of the kinship of 'man and the worm and all small creatures',⁶ creation being an aspect of God's love. This is the key of Jewish mysticism, the bond of love, and it is the root of the Jewish ethic of compassion for all creatures.⁷

Jewish Texts

Several types of Jewish texts will be considered in determining various views concerning animals: the biblical texts (the Torah, the Psalms, the Prophets), as well as the Mishnah and the Talmud. The Mishnah and the Talmud were composed during the first five hundred years of the Common Era (CE). The Babylonian and Palestinian Talmuds ('teaching') contain rabbinical discussions and laws, including the Mishnah and the Gemara. The Talmud contains the doctrine of *bal tashchit*: 'thou shalt not destroy.' This rabbinical teaching was formulated in order to prevent waste and destruction. This doctrine encapsulates the work of protection, of caring for the world and of not destroying God's handiwork. A slight, yet significant text, *Perek Shirah*, will be examined as well.

Perek Shirah (or *Pereq Shira*, Hebrew for 'Chapter of Song' or 'The Song of the Universe') contains biblical verses sung to God by nature, insects, birds and animals. It is divided into five or six sections, corresponding to the physical creation: plants and trees, insects, fish, birds and land animals. Traditionally the work was thought to have been composed by either David or Solomon. Legend states that David was boasting that no one had recited more praises to God than he had; after all, he had written the Psalms! A frog overheard him and told David not to be so proud, because he had sung more songs to God than David had. David then went on to pen *Perek Shirah*. According to another legend, it was Solomon, David's son, who wrote this work as it was believed that he understood the language of birds and animals. Others suggest it was compiled by the great sages of the Mishnah,[8] or that it originated among the Hekhalot mystics of the fourth or fifth centuries CE.[9]

This chapter includes stories, for the Aggadah (Aramaic for 'story') contains moral and theological ideas. The rabbis of the Mishnaic and Talmudic periods (the first six centuries CE) did not write moral or theological treatises; instead, they told stories as a way to express basic religious concepts, with aggadic literature forming sermons and Midrash. For the most part, Aggadah does not deal with legal and ritual matters: instead we encounter ethics, theology, history, folklore and legend. The Aggadah has been criticized by Jewish rationalists 'who feared it would encourage anthropomorphism'.[10] Aggadah does not have the binding force of the Halakha, the legal tradition of Judaism.

Midrash is a homilectic method of biblical interpretation, in which the text is explained differently from its literal meaning.[11] It is also the name given to a number of collections of biblical commentaries compiled from Oral Torah. Midrash often makes fantastic claims about biblical characters and events; therefore, midrashic teachings are not treated literally.

Types of Blessings

Before we proceed to a closer examination of the texts themselves, it is worth considering the Jewish notion of 'blessing'. Blessings are an essential component of Judaism and are present in many aspects of daily life. On seeing beauties of nature, one blesses God: 'Blessed is the Eternal our God, Ruler of the universe, whose world is filled with beauty.'[12]

The Talmud states that two different blessings are to be pronounced upon animals, one for 'beautiful' animals and one for 'unusual' animals: 'The Rabbis taught: One who sees an elephant, monkey or *kifof* (a type of monkey) says, "Blessed is He who makes his creations unusual" (*meshaneh habriyos*). One who sees beautiful trees and beautiful creatures says, "Blessed is He that has such in His world".'[13] Note that the blessing is reserved for the Creator, *not* for the animal.

Both these blessings are quite complex. While the blessing to be recited upon seeing unusual animals is generally understood to apply when seeing any unusual creature, there is also another view that states it should only be said when seeing an elephant or a monkey. Rabbi Menachem Meiri (1249–1306) gave this explanation: 'Since they are similar to man in a few ways, one blesses upon them "Blessed is He who makes his creatures unusual".'[14] Meiri's suggestion that the monkey and the elephant have similarities to human beings is an unusual observation, especially for its time. Another interpretation by some Jewish scholars is that at the time of the Flood, people were transformed into elephants and monkeys.[15]

The frequency of the blessings differs. The blessing when seeing unusual creatures can be pronounced as long as one has not seen them within the last thirty days. The blessing on seeing beautiful creatures can only be said once, that being the first time you see the animal. The reason for this difference is unclear.

There are separate blessings to be said for each type of food, but there is not a separate one for flesh foods: if an animal has been slaughtered, then that act cannot be blessed. The same applies to clothing: there is a blessing that is said over new items of clothing, but no blessings are said over furs or animal skins, the idea being that you cannot bless God for an act of creation that has then been destroyed.

In the Apocrypha, as in other passages of Scripture, animals are viewed as having the ability to pray and therefore being able to bless their Creator:

Bless the Lord, you whales and all that swim in the waters;
sing praise to him and highly exalt him forever.
Bless the Lord, all birds of the air;
sing praise to him and highly exalt him forever.
Bless the Lord, all wild animals and cattle;
sing praise to him and highly exalt him forever.[16]

Before Humanity: Dreams, Visions and Gods

Many religions believe that there was a time before humans, when animals walked the earth and were part of it before humans were created, or before humans evolved. In Judaism, in the first creation account, animals were created before humans, but were not part of a pantheon of gods deliberating over the fate of mortals. In Genesis 1 the world is formed, then non-human animals are created:

> And God said, 'Let the waters bring forth swarms of living creatures, and let birds fly above the earth across the dome of the sky'. So God created the great sea monsters and every living creature that moves, or every kind, with which the waters swarm, and every winged bird of every kind. And God saw that it was good... And God said, 'Let the earth bring forth living creatures of every kind: cattle and creeping things and wild animals of the earth of every kind'. And it was so. God made the wild animals of the earth of every kind, and the cattle of every kind, and everything that creeps upon the ground of every kind. And God saw that it was good. (Genesis 1:20–21, 24–5, NRSV)

This passage of Scripture is pivotal in the thought and beliefs of the Judaeo-Christian world, because in this creation account, all of creation is pronounced 'good', testimony to God's greatness and to God's goodness; the Creator made no mistakes. Although this is not a hierarchical view of creation (the birds and animals are not superior to humans by virtue of having been created first), the order can be used to keep humans humble:

> Why was man created on the last day?
> So that if he is overcome by pride it might be said:

'In the creation of the world
the mosquito came before you.'[17]

Fantastic beasts play a role as well.[18] According to rabbinic legend, on the sixth day of Creation, just before the beginning of the Sabbath, miraculous things were created, including the mouth of Balaam's ass who spoke, Aaron's rod, which turned into a serpent, and the ravens who would feed Elijah.[19] The Leviathan, the biblical sea monster of enormous dimension and king of all sea creatures, comes into this category of the miraculous. In legend, God killed the female of the species to prevent the pair from breeding and destroying the world. Its skin was used for the clothing of Adam and Eve. God will eventually have the Leviathan killed in the age of the Messiah, by either the angel Gabriel or by the gigantic Behemoth (when they will kill each other). At the great Messianic banquet for the righteous, the flesh of the Leviathan will be eaten and its skin stretched out to form an enormous marquee.[20] Leviathan has never been identified. Perhaps it was an Egyptian crocodile, a flying sea snake, an extinct primeval creature or a creation of human imagination.[21]

The Behemoth (Hebrew for 'beast'), the land equivalent of the Leviathan sea monster, is 'the size of a thousand mountains and drinks so much water each day that a special river flows out of Paradise to quench its thirst. It roars once a year in the month of Tammuz to frighten the wild animals of the world and keep them in control.'[22] Its flesh, too, will be eaten at the Messianic banquet. Both creatures are mentioned at length in the Book of Job:

> Look at the Behemoth, which I made just as I made you;
>   it eats grass like an ox.
> Its strength is in its loins, and its power in the muscles
>   of its belly.
> It makes its tail stiff like a cedar; the sinews of its thighs
>   are knit together.
> Its bones are tubes of bronze, its limbs like bars of iron.
> It is the first of the great acts of God.[23]

Along with the Leviathan and the Behemoth, there was another strange and mythical creature that played a part in the religious life of the Jews: the miraculous worm, the shamir. In Jewish legend, the worm was thought to have been created at twilight on the sixth day of Creation, just before the onset of Sabbath, for the sole purpose of helping to build the Temple. The shamir was as big as a grain of barley, and it had been brought from Paradise by a bird and kept hidden.[24]

Role in Birth and Origins of Humans

In Judaism, as seen in both creation accounts in Genesis, animals do not have a role in giving birth or in assisting in the creation of humans, which is a feature in some religions. In the second creation account animals are created as helpers or partners for the male human:

> 'It is not good that the man should be alone; I will make him a helper as his partner.' So out of the ground the Lord God formed every animal of the field and every bird of the air, and brought them to the man to see what he would call them; and whatever the man called every living creature, that was its name. (Genesis 2:18–19)

Here we note the acknowledgement of a bond between the human and the non-human; by 'naming' an animal, there is transference of power, as well as an acknowledgement of a relationship. While the notion of companionship is important in this cross-species relationship, it is interesting that the word 'helper' is used. The use of this word conjures up an image of working together, an idea that will be more closely examined in the next section.

On first reading, a Midrash would appear to suit a First People's creation account, rather than the creation accounts found in Judaism:

> Adam was created last of all creatures because the Holy One, blessed be He, asked all creatures to contribute their portion to Adam's body: the lion his might, the deer his speed, the eagle his agility, the fox his cleverness, etc. All these traits were given to Adam thus, the verse states: 'let us make man in our image . . .' (Genesis 1:26), indicating that the essential traits of all species are included in humankind.[25]

The intimacy of naming, of having companionship, is cut short due to the words of an animal, the serpent. Here we have gone from the positive, from acknowledging the gift and help of 'the other', from spending time considering the correct name for each being, to blaming one of the animals for a human act of disobedience, which led to eviction from Paradise. It is worth noting that the eviction involved humans only; we could say that the animals remain[ed] in the Garden.

In the apocryphal Book of Jubilees, its version of Genesis notes that after the eviction, the language that all creatures, human and non-human, could understand ceased (the language was probably Hebrew; in Jubilees 12 Hebrew is mentioned as being 'the tongue of creation'):

> And God made for them garments of skin and he dressed them and sent them from the garden of Eden . . . On that day the mouth of all the beasts and cattle and birds and whatever walked or moved was stopped from speaking because all of them used to speak with one another with one speech and one language. And he sent from the garden of Eden all of the flesh which was in the garden of Eden and all of the flesh was scattered, each according to its kind and each according to its family, into the place which was created for them.[26]

They were silenced after the Fall; was it because Adam and Eve had listened to the voice of the serpent? Perhaps that is part of the Fall: humans have lost the ability to communicate with other species.

After the eviction from the garden, Cain and Abel are born. There is a legend that Cain was not Adam's son, but was sired by the serpent Samael, who had cast lustful eyes at Eve.[27] Only after the Fall was the serpent cursed by God and made to crawl on its belly; before that, it is implied that the snake or serpent had legs and was like other animals. In one rabbinic tradition the snake 'was like a man, in appearance, standing upright on two legs'.[28]

Dominion

There is no real discussion in Judaism as to whether the opening chapters of Genesis are an allowance to exploit the created world.[29]

The account in Genesis 2:15, where Adam is placed in the Garden to care for it, suggests that we are to do the same.

Rabbi Samson Raphael Hirsch (1808–1888), one of the founders of Orthodoxy, spoke of what he saw as the Torah's universal vision for all creation:

> you have been given to the Earth, to treat it with respectful consideration, as God's Earth, and everything on it as God's creation, as your fellow creature, to be respected, loved, and helped to attain its purpose according to God's Will . . . to this end, your heartstrings vibrate sympathetically with every cry of distress sounding anywhere in creation, and with every glad sound uttered by a joyful creature.[30]

Brethren or Beasts of Burden?

In the second chapter of Genesis we see all creatures peacefully existing on vegetation alone for the first ten generations of humankind. Fish and fowl received the first explicit divine blessing, given on the fifth day of Creation (Genesis 1:22). The other animals were created on the sixth day, together with Adam and Eve, and they received a separate affirmation of divine favour (Genesis 1:25). 'The dignity of animals is borne out by a number of sources. The Talmud states that God conferred with the souls of all animals prior to Creation, and they readily agreed to be created as such, even choosing their own physical forms.'[31] They were worthy of God's consideration.

Prayer and Praise: Animal Songs of the Universe

In Judaism, animals, as mentioned earlier, are acknowledged as having the capacity to pray and also the ability to praise, and petition, their Creator. In Joel 1:20 there is the assurance that animals can speak to God; there is communication between the Creator and the created. In this passage, their anguish is expressed in a lament: 'Even the wild animals cry to you because the watercourses are dried up.' In Psalms 104:21, the lions petition God to provide for them: 'The young lions roar for their prey, seeking their food from God.'

Praise is the theme of the Sabbath and Festival prayer *Nishmat kol chai* ('The souls of all living things shall praise Your Name').[32] In this last verse of Psalm 150, which can also be translated as 'Let everything that breathes praise the Lord,' *soul* and *breath* being the same word, animals praise God for the gift of life. Following the *Nishmat* prayer we read, 'For such is the duty of all creatures (*hayetzurim*) in thy presence ... to thank, praise, laud, glorify, extol, honour, bless, exalt, and adore.' Here the important word is *hayetzurim*: 'creatures'. If the word *adam* had been used it would only refer to humans,[33] but here there is a wider meaning that includes all creatures, human and non-human.

The important notion of the bond of all creatures is detected in the Rosh Hashanah and Yom Kippur Amidah in the prayer book, after the introductory blessings: 'Now therefore, O Lord our God, impose Thine awe upon all Thy works, and Thy dread upon all that Thou hast created, that all may fear Thee and all creatures prostrate themselves before Thee, that they may all form a single bond to do Thy will with a perfect heart.'[34]

As mentioned earlier, Jewish prayers and liturgy contain a collection of songs of praise known as the *Perek Shirah*, in which the creatures declare that they are carrying out their assigned tasks; they are obedient to the will of God, which leads to praise. Some say that each creature sings its own song, but humans are unable to hear them. Others suggest that the singing is done by angels. A third opinion is that the creatures and elements of nature do not 'sing' as we know singing, it is not audible; instead, the 'song' is implicit in the nature of the creature and what that creature or part of creation (such as the ocean) can teach humans.

Although humans are not given a song to sing in this book, *Perek Shirah* does serve the human as well:

> Rabbi Paysach J. Krohn (*Reflections of the Maggid*) tells about a young family that was beset by scorpions. No other apartment in their complex was so smitten, and they were at their wit's end. The husband told Rabbi Chaim Pinchas Scheinberg of their plight. The elderly sage said that the song of the scorpion is ... 'God is good to all and His mercy is upon all of His handiwork' (Psalms 145:9). Had the couple failed to show mercy to anyone? The husband told him about an annoying guest that he and his wife had 'deserted'. Rabbi Scheinberg

told him to bring the man back to their home. They did – and the scorpions disappeared.³⁵

In *Perek Shirah* the animals and the rest of creation are dependent upon humans for their complete purpose. In the 'Song of the Rooster', for example, the rooster is given seven calls. These calls serve to link the earthly song with the heavenly song. Each hour, from midnight through the seventh hour, has its own message. The rooster symbolizes the call to 'awake' to the mission of the hour. Consider the final three calls of the rooster:

> At the Fifth Call he says:
> 'How long will you recline, O sluggard?
> When will you arise from your sleep?' (Proverbs 6:9)

The Fifth Call: It is two hours before dawn, and the rooster awakens everyone to arise and prepare for the time of prayer. Sluggard, how long will you sleep, as if the time of Divine Service will never come?

> At the Sixth Call he says:
> 'Do not love slumber, lest you become impoverished,
> open your eyes, [then] you will be sated with food.'
> (Proverbs 20:13)

The Sixth Call: It is an hour before dawn, time to go to the synagogue. Only God gives sustenance: prayer is not a luxury, it is your best way of assuring that you and your loved ones will not suffer hunger and poverty.

The Seventh Call: It is dawn. Prepare for the day and look around. Often we are surrounded by a culture amok and by people who live to negate the Torah. Dawn begins the time of activity and accomplishment – and man can have no greater accomplishment in life than to defeat those who oppose God's will.³⁶

The climax of *Perek Shirah* is the song of the dog: 'Come! Let us prostrate ourselves and bow, let us kneel before God, our Maker' (Psalms 95:6). This is quite unusual, for dogs are given a mixed press in Judaism. There are a number of derogatory and hostile references to dogs in Scripture: 'The dogs have a mighty appetite; they never have enough' (Isaiah 56:11); 'Each evening they come back, howling like dogs and prowling about the city' (Psalms 59:6); and 'Like a dog that returns to its vomit is a fool who reverts to his folly' (Proverbs 26:11). In rabbinical literature a distinction is made between wild dogs and domesticated dogs. Jews were allowed to break the Sabbath if they needed to kill a rabid dog, for rabies was a constant and real fear. Watchdogs were praised and Jews were advised: 'Dwell not in a town where no barking of dogs is heard.'[37] Dogs were praised for their silence during the night of preparation for the Exodus from Egypt: 'But not a dog shall growl at any of the Israelites – not at people, not at animals – so that you may know that the Lord makes a distinction between Egypt and Israel' (Exodus 11:7). According to the Mishnah, because of the dogs' silence when the Jewish slaves were fleeing Egypt, God commanded that any meat that was forbidden to the Jews should be given to their dogs as a reward. There is a story of a Talmudic sage who fasted and prayed in order that dogs should be allowed to sing God's praises. An angel appeared to him and told him his fasting was unnecessary, for dogs were specially favoured by God since they did not bark when the Israelites left Egypt.[38] In the Apocrypha, in the Book of Tobit, the dog is given an important role, as companion to the angel Gabriel.

Not only do animals pray, they are conscious of the majesty of the Holy. When the Torah was revealed, all creation was said to have been conscious of this awe-inspiring moment:

> When God gave the Law, no bird sang or flew, no ox bellowed. The angels did not fly. The Seraphim ceased saying: 'Holy, holy.' The sea was calm. No creature spoke. The world was silent and still, and the divine voice said: 'I am the Lord thy God' . . . at Sinai God made the whole world silent so that all the creatures would know that there is no god beside him.[39]

The Flood: A Rift in Relations

After the creation stories, the next narrative that speaks of humanity's responsibility to creation is that of the Flood. Flood stories are prevalent in many cultures' myths and religions. In Judaism (and in Christianity), the Flood/Deluge story reveals the consequences of the Flood, one being an alteration, or rift, in the relationship between the human and the non-human.

Jacques Tissot, *The Animals Enter the Ark*, c. 1896–1902, gouache on board.

In the Talmud, there is an account of the gathering of the animals, and how Noah was to choose the ones that would be saved:

> The Lord spoke to Noah, saying:
> 'Go thou with all thy household into the ark, and, behold, I will gather to thee all the beasts and fowls, and they will surround the ark.
> 'Then place thyself in the doorway of the ark, and the beasts and fowls will place themselves opposite to thee. Those that lie

down before thee let thy sons lead into the ark, and those that remain standing thou shalt abandon.'

As the Lord had spoken so happened it. The animals assembled in a great multitude opposite the ark. Those which lay down were led into the ark, and the others were abandoned.[40]

In this tale it appears that the animals who paid homage – those who would 'lie down', bow down, pray – were the ones allowed on board and thereby saved.

Classical rabbinic interpretation of the *Noach parsha* (story of Noah) contains some interesting stories and interpretations. Rabbi Achava bar Zeira taught that when Noah entered the Ark, he brought precious stones and jewels with him to keep track of day and night. When the jewels shone dimly he knew that it was daytime and when they shone brightly Noah knew that it was night-time. The Gemara noted that it was important that Noah could make this distinction, because there were some animals who needed to feed during the day, and others who would only eat at night. Even the placement of the animals and humans consumed rabbis' thoughts. A Tanna read 'with lower, second and third storeys shall you make it' (Genesis 6:16), to

Jan Brueghel the Elder, *Paradise Landscape with the Animals Entering Noah's Ark*, 1596, oil on copper.

'Noah in the Ark and the Dove Resting on it', illustration from the North French Hebrew Miscellany, c. 1278–98.

mean that the bottom storey was for the dung, the middle for the animals and the top level for Noah's family.⁴¹

The rabbis also viewed Genesis 6:19 and Genesis 8:16 as linked together, the former prohibiting cohabitation while on the Ark, and the latter allowing cohabitation to resume. The rabbis taught that three inhabitants broke the rules – the dog, the raven and Ham (one of Noah's sons) – and they were all punished: 'The dog was doomed to be tied, the raven expectorates [his seed into his mate's mouth] and Ham was smitten in his skin.'⁴²

Noah provides an example of the proper treatment of animals: 'he gave chopped straw to the camel, barley to the ass, vine tendrils to the elephant, and grass to the ostrich. So for twelve months he did not sleep by day or night, because all the time he was busy feeding the animals.'⁴³

In Genesis 8 there is a triumphant retort from the raven:

'Of all the birds that thou hast here thou sendest none but me!' 'What need then has the world of thee?' Noah rejoined, 'for food? for a sacrifice?' And the Holy One said to Noah: 'Take it back, because the world will need it in the future.' 'When?' Noah asked. 'A righteous man [Elijah] will arise and dry up the world, and I will cause him to have need of them [the ravens], as it is written, "And the ravens (orbim) brought him bread and flesh etc".' [1 Kings 17:6]⁴⁴

Not all the stories concerning the raven were favourable. When Noah went to send out the raven to check on the water level, the raven objected. The raven was classed as 'unclean' and therefore there was only a single pair of them in the ark: 'Why not send a clean animal?' the raven protested. 'There are seven each of them. If I die the whole raven species will disappear.'[45] But Noah insisted. The raven was angry and rebelled, and did not return; he found some carrion and remained on dry land, feasting and gorging himself.[46]

According to rabbinical literature, there were other mythical creatures during the Flood, including the re'em, a mythical creature of enormous size and ferocity. The Ark was not big enough to accommodate it, so it had to be towed behind.[47]

The Flood narrative was a seismic catastrophe in the domain of human-animal relations; even Noah had been changed, albeit physically, for according to Rav Huna, when Noah was leaving the Ark, a lion set on him and maimed him, so that he was not fit to offer sacrifices and his son Shem sacrificed in his stead.[48]

There were three monumental changes after the Flood: the introduction of animal sacrifice; permission granted to consume meat in one's diet; and, quite disturbingly, animals now feared humans. The

Simon de Myle, *Noah's Ark on Mount Ararat*, c. 1570, oil on panel.

The animals leaving the Ark, in a Byzantine mosaic of *c.* 1150 in the chapel of the Palazzo dei Normanni, Palermo.

peaceful paradisiacal relationship between human and animal had been changed forever.

After the Flood, burnt offerings, which consisted of one of every clean bird and one of every clean animal, were offered on an altar. This portion of the Flood story is generally overlooked in picture books of Noah's Ark: how would one explain to a child that the brave dove, who brought back the olive sprig to the ark, was later sacrificed?

Genesis 1:29 declares that humans were initially vegetarian, or meant to be vegetarian. Only after the Flood was meat consumption permitted (Genesis 9:3) and this was understood as a concession to human weakness and to a supposed scarcity of vegetable matter. Only after animals became permissible as a food source were dietary laws and prohibitions instituted. No vegetable is forbidden, only certain animals:[49]

> The fear and dread of you shall rest on every animal of the earth, and on every bird of the air, on everything that creeps on the ground, and on all the fish of the sea, into your hands they are delivered. Every moving thing that lives shall be food for you; and just as I gave you the green plants, I give you everything (Genesis 9:2–3).

According to the writer Elie Wiesel, the aftermath of the Flood meant a return to human mastery over animals:

> As a result of Adam's sin, animals and beasts had begun to rebel. Man was no longer their sovereign . . . He recaptured it only with the advent of Noah: birds and beasts 'calmed down' thanks to him whose name means 'calm'. Because of who he was, or what he was, they once again accepted man as their superior and master.[50]

I have not found this view expressed as openly elsewhere, but I would suggest that such a view is assumed by many. It refers to the notion of dominion and how that term is interpreted. There may not be the level of discussion concerning dominion in Judaism as there is in Christian circles, but there is the assumed hierarchical system where human beings are above the animals, having been created in the image of God.

Stained glass in the church of St-Aignan de Chartres, France. After the dove has proved that the Flood is receding (Genesis 8:8–12) Noah builds an altar and offers burnt offerings of every clean beast and very clean fowl (8:20); in return the covenant is made, with the rainbow as its symbol (8:21).

After this a covenant was established with Noah and his descendants, 'and with every living creature that is with you, the birds, the domestic animals, and every animal of the earth . . . This is the sign of the covenant that I make between me and you and every living creature' (Genesis 9:9 and 12). Animals were included in this covenant, reassuring all that never again would there be a flood of such proportions. The inclusion of animals alongside human beings as parties in the covenant is significant.

In Genesis 9, the Noahide Laws (Seven Laws of Noah) are set out, one being a prohibition against eating flesh cut from a living animal (Genesis 9:4). It was customary among pagan tribes to drink the blood and cut the limbs from living animals, the idea being that they thereby took in the strength of the creature. This may also have been instituted in response to wild Bacchanalian feasts, when revellers would tear limbs from living creatures.[51] Joseph was said to have brought bad reports of his brothers to his father (Genesis 37:2). According to one source, he accused them of transgressing the prohibition of eating the flesh of a living animal.[52] The Noahide Laws and the later Mosaic laws were designed to protect animals from these cruelties. These laws also prevented certain diseases by prohibiting the consumption of blood.[53]

Donkeys, Lambs, Spiders and Others: What they Reveal – and Conceal

Sometimes a particular animal was set apart, imbued with divine-given properties. In the story of the *akedah*, the near sacrifice of Isaac by Abraham, the ram that was substituted for Isaac was thought to be a very special one. In rabbinical literature: 'Its skin provided a mantle for Elijah, its gut the strings of David's harp, and its two horns the two trumpets: one to be sounded later at the great revelation of God at Mount Sinai, and the other to be blown at the end of time to announce the coming of the Messiah.'[54] It was thought that the site of the altar that Abraham had constructed was the same place that Abel and Noah had used for their animal sacrifices, and that in the future it was to be the site for the building of the Temple.[55]

In the Bible kindness toward animals is noted as a good character trait. When Abraham's servant was sent to find a wife for Isaac, Rebekah, his future wife, was found to have the qualities of kindness for humans and animals, because she gave water to the camels.[56]

'Jacob journeyed to Succoth [booths], and built himself a house, and made booths for his cattle; therefore the place is called Succoth' (Genesis 33:17). One commentary on this verse suggests that Jacob may have been the first person to build animal shelters, out of compassion for them.[57] Moses was chosen to lead the people because of the compassion he showed his herds:

> When Moses was feeding the sheep of his father-in-law in the wilderness, a young kid ran away. Moses pursued it until he reached a ravine where it found a well to drink from. When Moses reached it, he said, 'I did not know that you ran away because you were thirsty. Now you must be weary.' He carried the kid back. Then God said, 'Because you have shown pity in leading back one of a flock belonging to a man, you shall lead my flock, Israel.'[58]

Later Moses constructed a bronze serpent at God's command. In the wilderness there were venomous snakes. If someone was bitten, they were restored to health by looking at the bronze serpent. It is interesting to note that Hezekiah destroyed it when the people began to make offerings to it, transferring their worship from God to the snake. It seems a strange ritual to have allowed, for the pull of animal worship was a real and powerful presence in the region.

Another ritual that seems at odds is that of commanding an animal sacrifice in honour of the donkey. Donkeys had carried the Israelites and their possessions from slavery in Egypt. Because of their service, God ordered that every donkey be consecrated with the sacrifice of a lamb:

> When the Lord has brought you into the land of the Canaanites, as he swore to you and your ancestors, and has given it to you, you shall set apart to the Lord all that first opens the womb. All the firstborn of your livestock that are males shall be the Lord's. But every firstborn donkey you shall redeem with a sheep. (Exodus 13:11–13)

In Leviticus the ass (or donkey) is classed as 'unclean', yet the ass is never regarded in this way, because of its unstinting service. In the story of Balaam's donkey, the donkey can see the angel with a sword in his hand.[59] The donkey turns away from the angel, going from the road into a field. Balaam beats his donkey. Again, the donkey sees the angel so it veers and scrapes Balaam's foot against the wall near the vineyards. A third time the angel appears and the donkey lays down in the road, unable to proceed any further. Balaam strikes his animal for the third time. This time, the donkey opens its mouth and speaks to Balaam, protesting its innocence. In Judaism, the donkey is usually a symbol of stupidity and insensitivity; here the roles are reversed. The donkey asks: 'What have I done to you, that you have struck me these three times?' Balaam says to the donkey, 'Because you have made a fool of me! I wish I had a sword in my hand! I would kill you right now!' But the donkey says to Balaam, 'Am I not your donkey, which you have ridden all your life to this day? Have I been in the habit of treating you this way?' And he says, 'No.' Then, and only then, does Balaam see the angel. The lack of surprise on Balaam's part may give the impression that there were other conversations of this type, talks between humans and animals. The conversation between Eve and the serpent could be considered as another example of this.

The angel reprimands Balaam for his treatment of the donkey: 'Why have you struck your donkey these three times? I have come out as an adversary, because your way is perverse before me. The donkey saw me, and turned away from me these three times. If it had not turned away from me, surely just now I would have killed you and let it live.'

By speaking, Balaam's donkey saved his master's life. This narrative could be one of the earliest condemnations of cruelty to animals in the ancient world.

Certain stories are told about biblical characters being instructed by animals about the nature of God, or about ethical behaviour. One such tale concerns David, the future king of Israel. While David was resting after a hard day's work, he was disturbed by a large wasp attacking a spider. David cried out in protest, wanting to know why such 'useless' creatures were created.[60] The answer came:

> O David! Why dost thou despise the little creatures which I have made for the welfare of the world. An occasion will surely arise when thou wilt have great need of their wonderful help. Then indeed will thou know why they have been created by Me . . . Despise naught in the world. I love all things that are

Mosaic from a synagogue in Gaza, said to show animals listening to King David play the lyre, *c.* 500 CE (this might in fact depict animals listening to Orpheus play his harp).

the work of My hand. I hate none of the things which I have made. I spare all things because they are Mine . . . All My creatures praise Me.[61]

The years go by and David marries King Saul's daughter. Due to Saul's envy, David has to flee. While hiding in a cave from Saul's men, God, hearing his prayer for help, has a spider weave its web across the entrance. The men, thinking no one could be in there because of the intact web, move on. David then thanks God, and the spider.[62]

Solomon was thought to be able to converse with all living creatures. This idea came about due to this verse: 'He would speak of trees . . . he would speak of animals and birds, and reptiles, and fish' (1 Kings 4:33). The 'of' came to be interpreted as 'to' or 'with' them. In the Talmud, after Solomon asks for wisdom: 'He wandered into the fields, and he heard the voices of the animals; the ass brayed, the lion roared, the dog barked, the rooster crowed, and behold he understood what they said, one to the other.'[63] This has led to a number of legends about Solomon having animals carry out his requests, or judging a trial for them.

God's compassion for animals can also be seen in the story of Jonah, where God is concerned about the fate of Nineveh: 'And should I not be concerned about Nineveh, that great city, in which there are more than a hundred and twenty thousand persons . . . and also many animals?' (Jonah 4:11).

There is punishment for those who do not show compassion for other creatures; in the Talmud, Judah the Prince (Yehuda HaNasi) is remembered as having suffered for several years because of his negligence in this regard.[64]

> Rabbi Judah the Prince was sitting studying the Torah in front of the synagogue in Sepphoris when a calf passed before him on its way to slaughter. It began to cry out as though saying: 'Save me.' He replied: 'What can I do for you? It is for this that you were fashioned.' As punishment he suffered toothache for thirteen years. One day a creeping thing ran past his daughter who tried to kill it. He said: 'My daughter, let it alone, for it is written: "His mercies are over all his works" [Psalms 145:9].' Immediately he was restored to health.[65]

A Lesson from a Cow: for Jew and Gentile

In the story 'The Cow who Observed the Sabbath: The Medieval Legend of Rabbi Johanan ben Torta', found in Pesikta Rabbati 14,[66] the cow not only observes and keeps the Sabbath, but, through her practice, brings about the conversion of a Gentile to Judaism. A Jew had sold his cow to a Gentile:

> On the Sabbath he brought her out again to plough for him, but she lay down under the yoke.[67] Though he kept beating the cow, she would not budge from her place. Seeing this, he went to the Israelite who had sold him the cow, and said: 'Come, take your cow. Something is ailing her, though I beat her again and again, she will not budge from her place.'
>
> The Israelite understood that what the gentile was talking about had something to do with the Sabbath, the cow having become accustomed to rest on the Sabbath. So he said to the gentile: 'Come along, and I will get her up.' When he came to the cow, he spoke to her, [spoke right] into her ear: 'Cow, cow, you know that when you were in my hands, you ploughed six days in the week but were allowed to rest on the Sabbath. But my sins[68] having brought it about that you are in the hands of a gentile, I beg you to stand and plough.' At once she stood up and ploughed.

The gentile was fearful, thinking that the Jew had used magic in order to get the cow to plough. The Jew calmed him down; then the gentile, awe-struck, replied:

> 'If a cow, which has no speech and no understanding could acknowledge her Creator, shall not I, whose Maker made me in His own image and put understanding into me – shall I not go and acknowledge my Creator?' At once he went and became a convert and studied and acquired Torah. They used to call him Johanan ben Torta.[69] And to this day our Rabbis quote law in his name.[70]

Tza'ar ba'alei chayim: Kindness and Respect for All

One is not to inflict suffering on an animal or to pass by when one could ease its burden. If one finds cattle broken down under a load, one is legally bound to unload them, even if their owner is absent. In Scripture we find verses that imply that animals, as part of God's creation, are to be accorded both respect and protection. In Exodus and Deuteronomy there are instructions concerning the care of animals, to rescue those that have strayed, even if they belong to your enemy (Exodus 23:4–5). 'You shall not see your neighbour's donkey or ox fallen on the road and ignore it; you shall help to lift it up' (Deuteronomy 22:4). In an earlier verse, it is stated that you shall not withhold help. If you do not know who the owner is, then you must take the animal to your own house, and return it to its rightful owner when you learn who that is (Deuteronomy 22:1–3).

When using animals for work purposes, it is forbidden to hamper their instinct: 'You shall not muzzle an ox while it is treading out the grain' (Deuteronomy 25:4). When ploughing, you must yoke animals of similar sizes, otherwise it is cruel, for such a practice inflicts unnecessary pain on the animal: 'You shall not plough with an ox and a donkey yoked together' (Deuteronomy 22:10).

There is a positive command prohibiting the removal of eggs from a nest until the mother bird has flown away. This may not seem positive, but this was meant to lessen the emotional pain of the mother bird.[71] Some commentaries state that this practice also ensures the continuation of the species.

Even the ways of slaughter consist of rules to prohibit unnecessary suffering: 'When an ox or a sheep or a goat is born, it shall remain seven days with its mother . . . But you shall not slaughter, from the herd or the flock, an animal with its young on the same day' (Leviticus 22:26–8). This was to prevent the parent from witnessing the death of its young, or vice versa. Why add to its turmoil with additional (that is, emotional) suffering? The prohibition on separating the first-born of oxen and sheep (which were to be given to the Lord in sacrifice), from their mothers until the eighth day is also mentioned in Exodus 22:30. The twelfth-century philosopher Moshe ben Maimon (known as Maimonides) commented on these verses:

> The pain of animals under such circumstances is very great. There is no difference in this case between the pain of humans and the pain of other living beings, since the love and tenderness of the mother for her young is not produced by reasoning but by feeling and this faculty exists not only in humans but in most living things.[72]

The Ten Commandments include domestic animals in the Sabbath rest: 'But the seventh day is a Sabbath to the Lord your God; you shall not do any work – you, your son or your daughter, your male or female slaves, your livestock' (Exodus 20:10). This is probably one of the earliest written records of animal welfare in history.

In rabbinic law there is a concept known as *tza'ar ba'alei chayim* (the suffering/sorrow of living creatures). This teaching, or ethic, counsels for the protection of all God's creatures from undue pain or harm. It is acknowledged as a great mitzvah (deed). One instance of halakhic concern for animal welfare is a ruling that has been attributed to the third-century Babylonian Rav, that one should feed one's cattle before breaking bread oneself.[73] This continues: 'No man may take an animal, a beast or a bird, unless he provides them with food,'[74] 'No man may eat before feeding his animals,'[75] and 'It is a good sign for a man when his animals eat and are satisfied.'[76] 'Rabbi Elazar HaKapar taught: "It is forbidden for a person to buy an animal or bird unless he can feed it properly."'[77]

Tza'ar ba'alei chayim has a wider connotation: it meant the prohibition of gladiatorial fights in the Roman arenas[78] and, these days, other blood sports, such as fox hunting, bull fighting and cock and dog fighting. Prominent Polish rabbis and Jewish communal leaders wore fur-trimmed hats, popular among the Polish nobility from the thirteenth century onwards. Many Hasidim still wear the traditional *shtreimel*, made from tails of the sable or marten. Rabbi Hayim David HaLevi (1924–1998), Sephardic Chief Rabbi of Tel Aviv, spoke out against the cruelty of the fur industry, saying that it constitutes actual *tza'ar ba'alei*.[79] Today the laws of *tza'ar ba'alei chayim* would prohibit wearing the skins of baby seals clubbed to death and from eating veal from calves that have been kept in cages from birth until they are slaughtered. The Jewish teaching *tza'ar ba'alei chayim* needs to be considered in light of the modern practice of kashrut (Jewish dietary laws). It could be argued that products from animals that have endured intensive factory farming methods infringe the spirit, if not the letter, of kashrut.

Exceptions to the Rule: Cruelty Darkens the Page

Having stressed the Jewish concept of *tza'ar ba'alei chayim*, there are, however, three instances of cruelty in the Torah. The first is the *eglah arufah*, the calf used in a ritual when a murder victim is found and the murderer is unknown:

> The elders of the town nearest the body shall take a heifer that has never been worked ... the elders of that town shall bring the heifer down to a wadi with running water, which is neither ploughed nor sown, and shall break the heifer's neck there in the wadi. Then the priests, the sons of Levi, shall come forward ... and by their decision all cases of dispute and assault shall be settled. All the elders of that town nearest the body shall wash their hands over the heifer whose neck was broken in the wadi, and they shall declare: 'Our hands did not shed this blood, nor were we witnesses to it'. (Deuteronomy 21:3–7)

The second is the scapegoat of the Yom Kippur service, where a goat is taken to the top of a cliff and pushed off; and the third the Temple offerings. How can the Torah contain these commandments that involve brutality? Rabbi Natan Slifkin says that they are brutal to drive home the point; the calf's cruel death is to stress to the elders of the town that they were negligent in their leadership, the goat's grizzly death and the large number of animal sacrifices are to warn us to stay holy. Slifkin writes: 'cruelty to animals is clearly permitted for human benefit, and spiritual human benefits are just as important as material benefits. The benefits of atonement gained from the scapegoat are every bit as real as the benefits gained from eating an animal.'[80]

In Scripture, there are three instances in which animals are brought to trial before a court of 23 judges and, if found guilty, are executed. The transgressions seem to correspond to the cardinal sins of idolatry, murder and sexual immorality:

> Wandering onto Mt Sinai (parallels the sin of idolatry; showing disregard for the Creator).[81]
> The ox that kills a man (parallels the sin of murder).[82]
> The animal that is used for bestial purposes (parallels the sin of sexual immorality).[83]

Unwarranted killing of animals is rated as bloodshed that is only a little less severe than human bloodshed. The laws of putting an animal on trial are just as serious as putting a human being on trial. If there is any doubt as to whether the animal is liable for the offence, it is not killed. While this sounds positive, it is difficult to ascertain whether animals possess innate rights in Judaism, as there are conflicting statements in various sources.

Concession is Made: Meat May be Added to One's Diet

In Scripture, it was after the Flood that animal sacrifices were instituted and meat was permitted in one's diet. Animal sacrifice was thought to have been introduced in order to wean people from the ancient pagan practice of human sacrifice and of shamanism.

In Judaism, blood is viewed as containing the animal's life force, hence the prohibition concerning its consumption: 'For the life of every creature – its blood is its life; therefore I have said to the people of Israel: You shall not eat the blood of any creature, for the life of every creature is its blood: whoever eats it shall be cut off' (Leviticus 17:14). *Nephesh*, or life force, can also be translated as 'soul', to read: 'for the soul of every creature is its blood'.

'And anyone of the people of Israel, or of the aliens who reside among them, who hunts down an animal or bird that may be eaten shall pour out its blood and cover it with earth' (Leviticus 17:13). Rabbi Chaim ben Attar (1696–1743) wrote that an animal's blood represents its soul. It should therefore receive a burial, just as a dead human being is buried, out of respect.[84] According to Pick, 'even today when an animal is slaughtered, some of its blood is buried in the ground and a prayer is said over it in order to remind the slaughterer that he has taken a life.'[85] Hunting is prohibited in Judaism for a number of reasons:

> It is destructive and wasteful.
> It causes distress to animals.
> It actively produces non-kosher carcasses (since the prey, even if it was a kosher animal, will not have been slaughtered lawfully, and is therefore 'not kosher').
> It leads to trading with non-kosher communities.
> It wastes time that should be spent studying and/or carrying out charitable works.
> It is contrary to Jewish ethics.

Unlike surrounding religions and culture, where the hunt was spoken of in terms of victory and heroes, in Judaism, its villains, such as Esau and Nimrod, were associated with hunting, with Esau being viewed as a violent person.

Killing an animal for no legitimate human need was and is seen as wrong. Hunting for sport was not seen by the halakhic authorities as a human need; therefore it was wrong. Rabbi Saul Levi Morteira (c. 1596–1660) felt that hunting was not only cruel in its killing methods, but also because of the emotional trauma it caused the animal while being chased.[86] Another rabbi went further by saying that anyone who causes unnecessary suffering to animals by hunting them will not receive divine mercy. He added that Jews have a legacy of compassion, so there is an obligation not to act in such a manner.[87]

According to Slifkin, being cruel to a robotic animal or hunting animals on a computer game may still contravene the spirit of the prohibition of causing suffering to animals, as it may compromise one's sensitivity.[88]

Originally Jews lived mostly on vegetables. They ate meat only at festivals, when animals were slaughtered at the Temple, their fat burned on the altar, their blood spilled on its corners and a portion set aside for the priests. The eating of meat was thus part of the sacrificial service and only clean animals, those worthy of being offered to God, were consumed. Eating meat (observing the dietary laws) and worshipping

God were still closely linked. There was to be no compromise with the idolatry of the surrounding pagan society: 'Pagan worship . . . demanded as a sacrificial act the seething of a kid in its mother's milk. Blood was drunk to absorb divine qualities and used for idolatrous purposes. Judaism, therefore, absolutely forbade both.'[89]

There were severe penalties for killing an animal outside the gates of the Temple:

> If anyone of the house of Israel slaughters an ox or a lamb or a goat in the camp, or slaughters it outside the camp, and does not bring it to the entrance of the tent of meeting, to present it as an offering to the Lord before the tabernacle of the Lord, he shall be held guilty of bloodshed; he has shed blood, and he shall be cut off from the people. (Leviticus 17:3–4)

These verses refer to an animal that has already been consecrated for use in the Temple. Such an animal could only be slaughtered in the Temple. If the animal had been slaughtered elsewhere, that animal could not be used and so the animal's death would have been in vain; this waste of life was prohibited.

Animal sacrifice, a major form of worship, was a system overseen by the priests and sometimes questioned by the prophets, who warned that sacrifice without the right ethical behaviour did not count. In the days of the Temple, a man who brought an animal to be sacrificed would place his hands on the head of his offering, prior to its slaughter, to express that the sacrifice was his property and now the animal took his place before God.

Rituals surrounding animal sacrifice were instituted not because the animal itself was sacred, but in order to give God the best of the flock. The words surrounding the sacrificial rituals made it plain that regular sacrifices were made to appease God, and the priests and Levites could take some of the choicest meat for themselves. Later, after the Temple had been destroyed, the slaughter of animals was permitted elsewhere. The eating of meat was no longer confined to set times. The Jewish people were now 'priests'. Food rituals and dietary laws were transferred to the individual household. Even after its destruction there is still a connection to the Temple, since prayers are said at set times when the sacrifices were offered: morning (*shakharit*) and afternoon (*minkha*).

Rules of Meat Consumption

When the subject of Judaism and its relationship with animals is discussed, perhaps the most common association is that of the dietary laws derived from divine commandments found in the Bible and in the Talmud. Kashrut refers to the laws of kosher food. *Kasher* (or kosher, as it has come into English via its Ashkenazi pronunciation) means 'suitable' – what is legal and proper. In Judaism no distinction is made between religious and secular areas of life, for religion permeates all aspects of life. Eating, and what one eats, is as much a part of religious practice as prayer. In a sense, for Jews to observe these food laws is a way of bringing everything into the realm of the holy. The simple act of eating, or of food preparation, has now been transformed into a spiritual practice. Food laws go back to the very beginning; the first command that God gave referred to food: 'of the Tree of Knowledge of Good and Evil, thou shalt not eat of it' (Genesis 2:17).

The observance of kashrut acts as a separating factor between Jew and Gentile. Kashrut helps define who is a Jew. Three to four times a day it is a reminder of what it means to be Jewish. It is also a reminder that food is not created or provided by human beings, but by God. Food is not to be taken for granted and must always be acknowledged in prayer and with blessings.

Animals are divided into three groups: land, sea and air or winged (insects, with the exception of four species of grasshoppers, are impure). Animals must be specifically slaughtered as food; one cannot eat anything that has died itself – 'You shall not eat anything that dies of itself' (Deuteronomy 14:21) – so there can be no roadkill or animals wounded by predators.

> You shall not eat any abhorrent thing. These are the animals you may eat: the ox, the sheep, the goat, the deer, the gazelle, the roebuck, the wild goat, the ibex, the antelope, and the mountain sheep. Any animal that divides the hoof and has the hoof cleft in two, and chews the cud, among the animals, you may eat. Yet of those that chew the cud or have the hoof cleft you shall not eat these: the camel, the hare, and the rock badger, because they chew the cud but do not divide the hoof; they are unclean for you. And the pig, because it divides the hoof but does not chew the cud, is unclean for you. You shall not

eat their meat, and you shall not touch their carcasses. Of all that live in water you shall eat these: whatever has fins and scales you may eat. And whatever does not have fins and scales you shall not eat; it is unclean for you. You may eat any clean birds. But these are the ones that you shall not eat: the eagle, the vulture, the osprey, the buzzard, the kite, of any kind; every raven of any kind; the ostrich, the nighthawk, the sea gull, the hawk, of any kind; the little owl and the great owl, the water hen and the desert owl, the carrion vulture and the cormorant, the stork, the heron, of any kind; the hoopoe and the bat. And all winged insects are unclean for you; they shall not be eaten. You may eat any clean winged creatures. You shall not eat anything that dies of itself. (Deuteronomy 14:3–21)

Maimonides points out that all of the animals that are considered 'clean' and therefore able to be eaten are herbivores; the forbidden animals are carnivores, which rely upon killing and devouring their prey. The Talmud notes that one of the signs of a forbidden bird is that it has a talon to kill. Maimonides wonders whether we really are what we eat; perhaps food affects us in ways other than the purely physical.[90] If we do not eat the meat of carnivores, then maybe we are keeping ourselves compassionate.[91] The rabbis wrote: 'The bull flees from the lion, the sheep from the wolf, the goat from the tiger. Said the Holy One, blessed be He, "You shall not bring before Me such as pursue, but only such as are pursued".'[92]

To be kosher, or fit, animals have to chew their cud and have a split hoof. These animals include goats, deer, sheep and cattle. Animals that do not chew their cud, or do not have a split hoof, are deemed *treif* (or *trayf*), not kosher, therefore unacceptable. *Treif* is from the Hebrew word *terayfa* ('torn') and refers to animals torn by wild beasts and therefore not slaughtered correctly. Its meaning was extended by rabbinic tradition to include any animal afflicted with a potentially fatal wound or physical defect, even if it had not been 'torn' or ripped apart by a wild beast. The term *treif* has been applied to anything deemed unfit to be eaten (horse, donkeys, camels, pigs). Pigs have split hooves, but they do not chew their cud. The pig seems to be worse than the other animals deemed *treif*. The Midrash explains that the pig is deceptive, for it puts out its foot (you think it is kosher): on the outside it is kosher, but on the inside (not chewing its cud) it is *treif*.

The Mishneh Torah is the most renowned work of the medieval philosopher Moses Maimonides (1125–1204), and the text long served as the authoritative code of Jewish law. This *Mishneh Torah* was painted in Italy by the Master of the Barbo Missal, *c.* 1457. It is the only surviving example of this master's work for a non-Christian patron.

The prohibition on eating the flesh of pigs has been used as a means of oppression or torture of Jews throughout history. In the time of the Maccabees, the Greek-Syrian king Antiochus introduced the sacrifice of pigs to replace the Jewish Temple rites. Jews were commanded to eat pork in front of the gathered people, which would prove to the Greeks that the Jews had forsaken their faith. The Jews, however, chose martyrdom instead. In the Middles Ages the Jewish people were once again forced to eat pork in public, to amuse the crowd, and as a form of humiliation.[93]

Raising pigs is prohibited even for purposes separate from eating them (other non-kosher animals can be raised for other uses, such as keeping alpacas for their wool).[94] Why were pigs despised? Is it due to the likelihood of pork spoiling in the heat, and leading to diseases, such as trichinosis? The late F. E. Zeuner, a palaeontologist and leading expert on domestication, rejected this view. Zeuner felt that it had more to do with a dispute between nomads and settled farmers. Pigs were unable to be driven and were part of the settled farmer's livelihood. Nomads, who felt superior, came to despise not only the farmer, but also the farmer's stock (in this case, pigs).[95]

Another reason for the avoidance and disdain for pigs in Judaism is because of the role pigs played in Canaanite chthonic (underground) worship.[96] Pigs were used in worship by the Hittites. This was also a practice among the Greeks, who worshipped several gods of the underworld, including Demeter and Dionysus. Chthonic cults, with their reverence of pigs, penetrated Israel as late as the sixth century BCE, leading to the wrath of both prophets and priests.[97] This led to tirades from prophets and ritual taboos (dietary laws) instituted by the priests. Some scholars suggest that the prohibition against eating pork came about as a desire to be different from neighbouring tribes.

Certain parts of animals are also non-kosher, such as the sciatic nerve in the hindquarter, which is difficult to remove. It is present in the choicest cuts (filet mignon, rump and sirloin steaks, leg of lamb) so these items are not eaten by observant Jews. Its prohibition is based on the story of Jacob wrestling with God on the banks of the river Jabbok: 'The sun rose upon him as he passed Peniel, limping because of his hip. Therefore to this day the Israelites do not eat the thigh muscle that is on the hip socket, because he struck Jacob on the hip socket at the thigh muscle' (Genesis 32:30–32).

Another prohibition is suet, the hard fat formed below the diaphragm. Forbidden fats seem to be the ones that were specified for sacrifice: 'All its fat shall be offered: the broad tail, the fat that covers the entrails, the two kidneys with the fat that is on them at the loins, and the appendage of the liver, which shall be removed with the kidneys' (Leviticus 7:3–5). Three times in the Torah we read: 'You shall not boil a kid in the milk of its mother.' This suggested to Maimonides that in those times it was a common rite of idolatry. This led to a complete separation of flesh and dairy in the Hebrew diet.[98]

For fish to be deemed kosher, it must have both fins and scales: anchovies are fine, but shellfish, shrimp, lobsters, eels and oysters are not. Some fish have scales that are questionable, like swordfish and sturgeon, so they are usually classed as *treif*. Most domestic birds are kosher (turkeys, chickens, pigeons, ducks, geese) but wild birds and birds of prey are *treif*. Eggs have to be inspected as well; if there are blood spots, the egg has to be discarded.[99]

The Torah does not say why some creatures are kosher and others are not. The food laws fall into what is known as *hukim/chukkim* (where there may not be a reason given). About 150 of the Torah's 613 laws deal with sacrifices. Jews believe that dietary laws were handed down by God to Moses, or written down by humans owing to divine inspiration, or that they are a relic of a primitive past to do with sacrificial ritual.[100]

Some scholars suggest that in biblical times the dietary laws were only observed by the priesthood. The ordinary Jews observed them only when they went to the Temple, and they were viewed as a connection to the sacrifice. After the Temple was destroyed in 70 CE, the direct pathway to God now gone, new rituals and observances were instituted by the rabbis to replace the Temple's absence: 'The family dinner table was made into the primary replacement for the sacrificial altar. The rabbis called the family table the Mikdash mu'at, the "little Temple".'[101] The table rituals replaced the Temple rituals; now people could reside at the 'little Temple'. The ordinary Jew became the new priest; the laws of kashrut became their priestly rites. Along with washing hands and saying blessings over the food, the table becomes a sanctified place.

The prayer books of Reform, Orthodox and Conservative Judaism consider the history of sacrifice in different ways. Reform Judaism doesn't refer to it in its prayer book, seeing sacrifice as a primitive stage in Judaism. The prayer book used by the Conservatives speaks of sacrifice in the past tense; sacrifice is to be remembered, but the practice does not need to be reinstated. For the Orthodox, however, their prayer book hopes that the Temple will be rebuilt and sacrifices offered there again: 'While traditional Jewish theology commits Orthodox Jews to pray for the reinstitution of sacrifices, many are ambivalent about the prospect of again publicly slaughtering and sacrificing animals.'[102]

The differences extend to the upholding of the dietary laws. The Reform movement declared the dietary laws to be no longer in force, as these laws prevented them from socializing with non-Jews, and they felt this was undesirable. The Conservative movement compromised, saying they should observe the laws of kashrut, but allow for social mixing.

It is worth noting that kashrut laws can be taken to extremes. Some Hasidic families do not permit non-kosher animals in any form:

> My friend Reuven from Minneapolis doesn't allow his kids to have – as toys – any stuffed animals that aren't kosher. Toy cows and sheep and chickens are okay, but no horse, elephants, or lions are permitted. Miss Piggy cannot cross his threshold. 'We're looking for good role models,' Reuven told me.[103]

Some authorities say that this applies only to images created for idolatrous purposes, others that this prohibition is for three-dimensional images only, and others that it applies to images/pictures as well:

the late Lubavitcher Rebbe, Rabbi Menachem Mendel Schneerson (1902–1994), objected even to pictures of non-kosher animals, singling out a certain famous American cartoon mouse, and bemoaning how such illustrations were even to be found in Jewish publications. He requested that his followers not have pictures of non-kosher animals in their homes.[104]

Surely there is a discrepancy here, as viewing a non-kosher animal as harmful or dangerous contravenes the concept that all have been blessed and pronounced 'good'. Non-kosher animals are used as symbols for several of the Jewish tribes: the wolf for the tribe of Benjamin, the lion for the tribe of Judah, the donkey for the tribe of Issachar and the snake for the tribe of Dan. The throne of Solomon had statues of a lion and an eagle. In many synagogues, lions are featured on the embroidered curtains covering the ark of the Torah and on the covers of the Torah scrolls.

In the 1970s Rabbi Zalman Schachter-Shalomi set up a new standard, 'eco-kosher', which looked at whether chemicals had been added to food and questioned whether animals had received humane treatment while they were living. One such example would be whether free-range chickens were preferable to caged kosher ones deprived of sunlight, room and so on. Perhaps it would be better to be vegetarian, as this would mean no harm at all for other creatures. This former Lubavitch Hasid had broken away from a very narrow point of view and questioned what it meant to respect creation. His life reflected his ethics, even down to his name: his family name 'Schachter' means 'slaughterer', so he added 'Shalomi' from the word 'peace' to indicate the dramatic change.[105]

The Jewish method of slaughter (Hebrew: *shechita* or *shehitah*) is designed to minimize animal suffering. It requires a perfectly sharpened blade, free of nicks or any unevenness. The blade is passed swiftly over the wind and food pipes in a single motion so that the blood can drain out completely. The shechita method renders an animal unconscious in a matter of seconds. The animal must not be stunned before slaughtering, for this would prevent the free flow of blood, and the absorption of the blood into the meat makes the food prohibited. In Jewish law this method is seen as a humane death. If slaughter cannot be carried out this way, then a Jew is unable to eat the meat as it is not deemed to be kosher. The *shochet* (slaughterer) also cuts away the forbidden fat and removes the hip socket and sciatic nerve. When questions arise, the shochet consults a rabbi, who makes the final decision.

The shochet is not a tradesman but a professional. His appointment depends on possession of a rabbinical certificate. He must be learned in the duties of a normal butcher, as well as the regulations of shechita, and be able to recognize specific animal diseases. The shochet utters a special benediction before killing, reminding him of his responsibility towards God and God's creatures. He has to be a pious, observant Jew: 'Only those who understand the holiness of life are permitted to prepare an animal for human consumption.'[106] The shochet must slaughter correctly, otherwise there may be divine retribution: 'There is a kabbalistic tradition that the souls of animals protest before the Divine Throne against Jews and non-Jews alike for having slaughtered them improperly, unnecessarily, or in a cruel manner.'[107]

To Eat Meat . . . or Not to Eat Meat

Kashrut can encourage some to become vegetarian. It is thought that in the Messianic Age, no animal or human will be killed, and all will be vegetarian. Many Jews view vegetarianism as the ideal, for it appears to be the way of living in the 'end days':

> The wolf shall live with the lamb,[108]
> the leopard shall lie down with the kid,
> the calf and the lion and the fatling together,
> and a little child shall lead them.
> The cow and the bear shall graze,
> their young shall lie down together;
> and the lion shall eat straw like the ox.
> The nursing child shall play over the hole of the asp,
> and the weaned child shall put its hand on the adder's den.
> They will not hurt or destroy on all my holy mountain:
> for the earth will be full of the knowledge of the Lord
> as the waters cover the sea. (Isaiah 11:6–9)

During the Messianic Age, all animals will become ritually pure (kosher) and spiritually perfected, regaining their status prior to the sin of Adam.[109] They will also possess great wisdom and intellect. Sometimes this has already happened; there have been several cases cited in the Talmud where animals have refused to violate Torah laws,[110] although these laws apply to humans only. Some scholars also hold the view that during the Messianic Age the sacrificial offerings in the Holy Temple will consist of vegetation only.[111]

There is no single Torah view on vegetarianism. In Genesis 1 it appears that Adam and Eve ate a vegetarian diet. The Torah does not advocate this, but many Jewish philosophers and thinkers have pointed this way. Joseph Albo (1380–1435), a Spanish Jewish philosopher, wrote that Adam and Eve did not eat meat as they were forbidden to do so because of the cruelty involved in killing animals.[112]

Rashi (1040–1105), perhaps the most famous Torah commentator, taught that: 'God did not permit Adam and his wife to kill a creature and to eat its flesh. Only green herbs should they all eat together.'[113] Other major commentators, including Ibn Ezra (1092–1167), Maimonides and Nahmanides (1194–1270), have agreed that a vegetarian diet is the ideal. Umberto Cassuto (Moshe David Cassuto, 1883–1951) 'taught that Torah permits people to use animals for the services they can provide, but does not permit them to be used for food'.[114]

In Scripture, the subject of eating meat was not confined to conditions immediately following the Flood. During the time in the wilderness, the people cried out for meat, complaining about the manna that had been given to them (Numbers 11:4–6). God supplied quail and the people gathered them:

> But while the meat was still between their teeth, before it was consumed, the anger of the Lord was kindled against the people, and the Lord struck the people with a very great plague. So that place was called Kibroth-hattaavah [Graves of craving] because there they buried the people who had the craving. (Numbers 11:33–4)

This story has been interpreted by some to suggest that God tried to lead the people back to a vegetarian diet, by supplying them with manna; when they ate meat, they became ill. Perhaps this story was a warning, for the deaths were blamed on their cravings, or their lust, for meat. There are examples of biblical heroes and heroines, including Queen Esther, Daniel and his comrades, and the Maccabees, adopting a vegetarian diet in order to survive under hostile conditions.

Vegetarian society is viewed as the highest ideal. Eating meat is a concession, therefore one should minimize its consumption. Vegetarianism is viewed as a way of compassion, rather than as purely a diet. Its practice is seen as enhancing one's compassion for all of God's creatures. If this was God's intention, why does Judaism allow for the slaughtering and eating of animals? Some rabbis thought that after the Flood, meat was allowed because of the inability of the earth to produce enough fruits, vegetables and grains. The Polish rabbi Isaak Hebenstreit went on to add that once the taste for meat was acquired, it was hard to go back to a vegetarian diet.[115] Hebenstreit taught that the prohibition against consuming the blood of an animal was in place to remind humans that eating meat was a *concession* to human taste; it was not the ideal human diet.[116] Nahmanides (also known as Rabbi Mosses ben Nahman, and more commonly by his Hewbrew acronym, Ramban) explained that it is inappropriate for humans to eat animals, since animals are intelligent creatures and wish to live: 'animals have a certain quality in their souls . . . and they flee from pain and death.'[117]

The Release of Souls: Meat-eating and the Question of Transmigration

The distinction between vegetarian and non-vegetarian diets in Judaism becomes less clear when the mystical strand of Kabbalah is considered. In Kabbalah there is a school of thought that states that there is transmigration (reincarnation) and that eating meat releases the soul and therefore is of benefit to the animal. Souls, and the type of souls possessed by humans and non-humans, is also a subject for discussion. For the purposes of this chapter, the two are considered together.

According to Slifkin, in Judaism there are different categories of the soul; different types of souls can coexist in the same body. The form of soul that humans share with animals is called the *nefesh*, which is a lower form.[118] This is the soul responsible for intelligence and senses. Humans alone also possess a type of soul called a *neshamah*. This is a spiritual soul, as opposed to a physical or 'animal' soul (*nefesh*). Does this mean that non-humans are not immortal? According to Slifkin, this is the case: when an animal dies, its existence ceases; only humans live on in a spiritual realm.[119] Having argued this point, Slifkin, in a footnote, mentions a Midrash that seems to contradict these findings, speaking of resurrection for animals:

When God renews His world, He himself takes charge of the work of renewal. He arranges all the regulations of the last ones, those of the future world ... the order of each and every generation, of every being, of every animal, and of every bird ... I have caused all human beings and all creatures to die in this world, and I shall restore their spirit and soul to them and revive them in the World to Come.[120]

The classical texts of Judaism reflect a marked ambivalence towards meat-eating, but within the Kabbalah eating meat is a spiritual exercise, because it is a means of freeing the 'holy sparks' trapped within animals. Rabbi Isaac Luria taught that sparks of holiness are lodged in all things, including plants and animals.[121] Each person is to liberate the sacred that lies within everything. Consuming meat is therefore not just for one's physical well-being, it is also one's responsibility to God and towards all of creation. According to the Kabbalists, 'we human beings may elevate the holy sparks that have fallen to the lower levels of creation.'[122]

It is also important to recite the appropriate blessings before and after eating, to help the elevation of the holy sparks contained within the food. Rabbi Nachman Goldstein (1823–1898) included in his *tzava'ah*, or 'spiritual will', an apology to all souls on all levels of creation for having possibly failed to elevate them during his sojourn in this world,[123] while Rabbi Yaakov Yosef ben Yehuda of Ostrog (1738–1791) would apologize after every meal to the holy sparks in the leftover food for his inability to redeem them.[124]

One rabbi suggested that animals were given a choice in this matter, and chose to be a source of food for humans in order to elevate their souls to the level of human beings:

In the beginning of creation, God asked each animal if it agreed to be slaughtered, and the animal replied: 'It is good.' What was the reason for this? The animal does not have a higher soul with which to grasp the deeds and might of God. Therefore, in the beginning of creation God assembled all the animals before Him and said to them: 'Do you wish to be slaughtered and eaten by man, if by doing so you will ascend from the level of an ignorant beast to the level of a human being, who knows and recognizes God, May He be blessed?' The animals answered,

'We accept – and His mercy will be upon us.' For when man eats part of an animal, the animal becomes part of man. Thus, the rite of slaughter is an act of mercy, for it enables the animal to transcend its former level and to enter the human level. The subsequent death of the human is actually life for [the soul of] the animal, for now it ascends to the height of the angels . . . contemplate the mystery of animal slaughter, and you will realize that it is an act of God's mercy and compassion for all His creatures.[125]

Another argument, which differs from the fairly positive idea that animals wanted to be like humans in their understanding of God, is that animal souls are those of humans who have sinned deeply: 'The main purpose of *shechitah* is to elevate souls that have been reincarnated in the form of animals or birds. These souls were reincarnated in these lower forms because of the severity of their transgressions.'[126]

Whatever we may feel after reading about reincarnation as being a reason or a justification for eating meat, it certainly adds another layer to our understanding of how animals are viewed in the mystical tradition of Judaism. Through this lens, animals function as a means of liberating the holy sparks and therefore are seen to play a special role in the restoration of the world.

Fasts and Festivals

Enjoying meat on Sabbaths and festivals is supported by the Talmud and by legal codes: 'The sages considered this to be such an integral part of these sacred occasions that they permitted animal slaughter on the Festivals in order to provide for the needs of the day.'[127] It is scripturally prohibited, however, to slaughter an animal or even to kill an insect on the Sabbath unless it presents a threat to human life.[128] The Sabbath is a day when all of creation rests, people, animals and the environment, as set out in the Ten Commandments.

Passover

Until the destruction of the Temple in Jerusalem, the major ritual of Passover was to bring a lamb to the Temple to offer as a sacrifice in commemoration of the sacrifice made by every Hebrew family on their last night in Egypt. Part of the lamb was set aside as a sacrifice and the rest given back to the family to consume. The roasted shankbone placed on the Seder plate on Passover commemorates the Paschal lamb – the lamb sacrificed at the first Passover on the eve of the Exodus.[129]

In the Talmud another reason is given for the sacrifice of the lamb. This passage speaks openly of competing religious practices and of the temptations posed for the Jewish people:

> Moses said to the Israelites in the name of the Lord: 'Draw out and take for yourselves a lamb . . .'.
>
> Draw yourselves away from the idols which ye are worshipping with the Egyptians, the calves and lambs of stone and metal, and with one of the same animals through which ye sin, prepare to fulfil the commandments of your God.
>
> The planet sign of the month Nisan is a lamb; therefore, that the Egyptians might not think that through the powers of the lamb they had thrown off the yoke of slavery, God commanded His people to take a lamb and eat it.
>
> They were commanded to roast it whole and to break no bone of it, so that the Egyptians might know that it was indeed a lamb which they had consumed.[130]

During Passover no leaven is eaten, or even kept in the house, as a reminder of the haste in which they had to flee from Egypt. These days, this prohibition extends to feeding one's pets:

> A person is not only prohibited from eating *chametz* (leavened bread) on Passover, but also from owning it or deriving any benefit from it. Thus, one may not own pet food that contains *chametz* or feed one's pet with it during Passover. One may not even allow one's pet to eat *chametz* that is given to it by a non-Jew. However, a person is permitted to sell his pet to a non-Jew for the duration of Passover. The animals should be housed in the home of the non-Jew.[131]

There are a number of vegetarian alternatives to the eating of lamb at Passover, as well as liturgical resources to use as one celebrates the festival. Roberta Kalechofsky, a Jewish academic and animal rights activist, has compiled the *Haggadah for the Liberated Lamb*, 'a vegetarian haggadah that celebrates compassion for all creatures'.[132] Olives, grapes and grains of unfermented barley, which symbolize the commandments of compassion for the oppressed, are substituted in place of the shankbone on the Seder table. Within the Passover liturgy:

> This night is different because on this night we eat our ancient meal of herbs, seeds, and fruits of the earth, as we ate it in Eden ... We, the family of Israel sit down to our ancient meal, where there is no sign of blood, no memory of wounds. This is the meal of redemption from the wounds of the earth. This is the meal of healing. This is the table God set for us in Eden ... This is the table we shall all be together at in the holy mountain of the prophets, with the lion and the lamb.[133]

Yom Kippur

On the eve of Yom Kippur, Kapparot ('expiation of sin') is observed by Ashkenazi Jews.[134] After verses from Psalm 107 and Job 33 have been recited, a person takes a live fowl (the men swing roosters, the women hens – white is the preferred color) by the feet with his or her left hand, and the right hand is placed on its head. The fowl is swung overhead three times, saying, 'This is my atonement, this is my ransom, this is my substitute.'[135] Then the following words are spoken: 'The fowl will go to death, and I will enter upon a good, long life and peace.'[136] The fowl is immediately slaughtered and either the fowl or its equivalent value in money is given to the poor. The liver, kidneys and innards of the chicken are put outside for the birds to eat, in order to show compassion for God's creatures. In this act, the person's sins have been transferred to the fowl, thus increasing the prospect of his or her name being written in the Book of Life. Hasidic scholars are quick to point out that this is not a sacrifice, as no animal sacrifice has been permitted in Judaism since the destruction of the Temple; rather, this is a symbolic act of atonement.

Kapparot has its origins in the Temple custom of having a scapegoat receive the people's sins. The high priest would take the goat and place his hands on the head of the goat while confessing the sins of the people. Then the goat was taken a distance and pushed off a cliff, falling to its death. Afterwards, a red flag was waved to notify those near the Temple that their sins had been erased.[137]

Nowadays, the use of a live fowl, for the most part, has been replaced by the giving of money or by performing the ritual with money tied up in a handkerchief. For centuries great rabbinical scholars opposed Kapparot, saying that there are no grounds for this kind of 'vicarious' sacrifice,[138] and in Reform and Conservative congregations it has, for the most part, been abandoned. Sephardic Jews (of Spanish and Portuguese origin) regard it as a pagan practice and so do not observe this custom.

On Yom Kippur it is forbidden to wear leather shoes. Cloth ones are worn instead, for leather is seen as a luxury and much too fancy for the solemn day. Perhaps animal products are also to be avoided on the day when meat is not eaten. Philip Pick suggests another reason: 'The reason for this is not humility but to avoid hypocrisy. It is not devout to pray for compassion when one has shown no compassion in daily life.'[139]

> Rabbi Israel Salanter, a famous nineteenth-century Orthodox Rabbi, failed to appear one Yom Kippur eve to chant the sacred *Kol Nidrei* prayer. His congregation became concerned, for it was inconceivable that their saintly rabbi would be late or absent on this very holy day. They sent out a search party to look for him. After much time, their rabbi was found in the barn of a Christian neighbor. On his way to the synagogue, Rabbi Salanter had come upon one of his neighbor's calves, lost and tangled in the brush. Seeing that the animal was in distress, he freed it and led it through many fields and over many hills. This act of mercy represented the rabbi's prayers on that Yom Yippur evening.[140]

Rosh Hashanah: the New Year

On Rosh Hashanah, also known as Yom Teruah (the Day of the Sounding of the Shofar), the shofar, a ram's horn, is blown. The horn of a sheep, goat or an antelope may be used, but a ram's horn is favoured because it is a reminder that a ram was caught in the thicket, and Isaac was spared from being sacrificed, which led to the survival of the Jewish people. The only horn not allowed is that of a cow, in case it reminds one of the worship of the Golden Calf by the Israelites in the wilderness.[141]

On the first day of the new year, the ritual of Tashlikh (or Tashlich, 'wilt cast') takes place. People scatter bread, which symbolizes their sins, upon the waters and pray for God's forgiveness. According to one ancient tradition, running water is chosen because there will be fish in the river. Their eyes never close, 'reminding us of the ever watchful eyes of God, who is always looking down on his creatures on earth – in mercy'.[142]

Animals in the Synagogue: in Art and Language

Animals may not have a big presence in synagogue art but animals are seen within the building.[143] The Lion of Judah is often embroidered on the curtain of the Ark and engraved on the breastplate covering the mantle of the Sefer Torah (a handwritten scroll of the Torah). Apart from the lions, it may be hard to find pictures of animals, yet they are there in great number, for they are embedded within the Hebrew letters themselves. The Hebrew alphabet begins with aleph, א, originally the picture of the head of an ox. Gimel, ג, the third letter of the Hebrew alphabet, developed from the picture of a camel, and it is one of the words that Hebrew gave to the English language. Lamed, ל, is a surprising character; it represents the ox-goad, a pole used to prod cattle to move in a certain direction. Its choice shows that it was a common implement of early Jewish existence, a time when Jews were shepherds and peasants.[144] The fourteenth letter, nun, נ, means 'fish': 'fish intruded Jewish history and literature in strange and diverse ways. The name of Joshua's father was Nun – the Fish. The temple in which the Philistines displayed blinded Samson and gloated over his agony was dedicated to Dagon – the pagan fish god.'[145]

The letter pe (mouth), פ, plays its part in Jewish legend. During God's work of creation, on the Sabbath eve, God produced ten additional works that were to appear in the world at the right moment. One of these works was the mouth of Balaam's donkey. After pe comes tsade, צ, the fishing hook. Its existence tells of the plentiful fish in the region. Jews did not fish for sport, only for the food they required.

Animal names and certain characteristics became associated with the Jewish people. In Genesis 49, Jacob, on his deathbed, blesses his sons and compares five of them to animals in the field: Judah to a lion, Issachar to a strong donkey, Dan to a snake, Naphtali to a deer and Benjamin to a hungry wolf. These are not links to totemism, they are metaphors, telling something about their character. Through them we detect nobility, physical strength, swiftness and an ability to fight till the end. Thousands of years later, when Jews were seeking appropriate family or surnames, some took Genesis 49 as their guide: 'Benjamin called his family Wolf or Sief, its Hebrew translation; Naphtali chose Hirsch, the German stag, as his name; and Judah selected Loeb, Leibel, Liebvitch or Lew – all meaning lion.'[146] This continued, with the story of Jonah leading some to become a Mr Fisch or Fischl.[147] Sometimes pictures of these animals are carved on headstones in Jewish cemeteries.

In a passage from the Midrash, similar in content to a page of a Christian bestiary, we find the following:

> As the dove is whole (*tamah*), so Israel is whole-hearted [in its devotion to God]. As the dove is distinguished, so Israel is distinguished through circumcision and *tzitzis* (knotted strings on their four-cornered garments). As the dove is chaste, so Israel is chaste. As the dove stretches out her neck for slaughter, so does Israel; as the verse states, 'For Your sake, we are slaughtered all the day' (Psalms 44:23). As the dove atones for sin, so Israel atones for the nations of the world. As the dove is faithful to her mate from the first moment they meet, so Israel remains faithful to God. As the dove is saved by her wings, so Israel is saved by the commandments. As the dove never abandons its cote, even upon the loss of its young, so Israel continues to observe the pilgrim festivals each year, even after the destruction of the Holy Temple. As the dove produces a new brood each month, so does Israel produce new Torah insights and new good deeds each month. As the dove flies far away [in search of food] but always returns to her cote, so Israel shall return to her land.[148]

Here we note how a bird can demonstrate certain key spiritual characteristics of a people. Similar to the way a Christian bestiary reflects something of the nature of God, Christ or the church, here the dove, a symbol of peace and innocence from the time of Noah, in its habits, reinforces what is expected from the Israelites.

Finally it is important to note that Jews have been involved in, and are still active in, animal welfare and animal rights. Lewis Gompertz (1783–1865), for example, helped found the Society for the Prevention of Cruelty to Animals, although he left the SPCA on religious grounds. Lewis Gompertz was an interesting personality who was a practising vegan 120 years before the term was coined, wrote several books about animal welfare and refused to ride in horse-drawn carriages.

Parted: The Afterlife – Soul Bearers and Sharers in Another Existence

You save humans and animals alike, O Lord (Psalms 36:6)

Animals were present at the beginning of human existence and have also played a role in rites to honour the end of earthly human life. In Genesis there is the account of the first death, the murder of Abel by his brother Cain. How did they dispose of the body? They had no reference point. In a story found in the Pirke de-Rabbi Eliezer (Chapters of Rabbi Eliezer),[149] this problem is solved:

> for they did not know what to do with Abel since they had no experience of burial. Then a raven appeared who had been bereaved of one of his companions. He took the dead bird, and dug a hole in the ground and buried it. Adam saw this and said: 'I shall do the same as the raven.' He took Abel's corpse, dug a hole in the ground and buried it.[150]

In Dan Pagis's poem 'Autobiography', in which he retells the story of Cain and Abel, he makes reference to this Midrash:

> I died with the first blow and was buried
> in the stony field.
> The raven showed my parents
> what to do with me.[151]

In the Aggadah, the book of Jonah is linked to the end of time:

The fish that swallowed Jonah warns him that it is about to be eaten by Leviathan, the great monster of the deep. 'Take me to him', says Jonah. Jonah confronts Leviathan and tells him that in the days to come he, Jonah, will catch him and drag him out of the sea and feed his flesh to the righteous in paradise. Leviathan takes fright and swims away. The fish in gratitude for Jonah's intercession spews him out on to the dry land.[152]

The banquet for the righteous in heaven will be denied to those who hunt: 'Whoever hunts wild animals with dogs, as do the non-Jews in these regions, will not witness the celebration of the Leviathan [in the World to Come].'[153]

There is also punishment meted out to humans who are cruel to their own animals: 'A person who willfully intimidates his fellow-men or needlessly hurts his animals will receive the same punishment [at the hand of Heaven].'[154]

Some of the rabbis of the early medieval era claimed that animals received recompense in the next world for the suffering they underwent in this world. Rav Sherira Gaon stated that in the afterlife God compensates animals for the pain that they endure in this world: 'We are of the opinion that all living creatures, the slaughtering and killing of which God has permitted, have a reward which they may expect.'[155] This view has been disputed. Nahmanides (Rambam) wrote that this opinion originated with the school of Islamic thought known as the Mu`tazila.[156]

There is a belief is some circles that the souls of the righteous (the *tzadikim*) are reincarnated as doves:

> In the courtyard of Chassidic master Rabbi Nosson Dovid of Shidlovitz (d. 1865) hundreds of doves nested. Whenever the Rebbe leaned his head out of an open window, they would all flock to him in a great tumult of activity – and he would do with them whatever he would do.
>
> It once happened on Rosh Hashanah (the Jewish New Year), as the Rebbe ascended the raised platform prior to the sounding of the Shofar (ram's horn), that a dove flew into the synagogue through an opened window, and perched on the reader's table. The Rebbe gazed intently at the bird, and then asked that a bowl of water be placed in front of it. However, due to the

incline of the reader's table, it was impossible to do so. Therefore, the Rebbe removed his *shtreimel* (fur-trimmed hat), and placed the bowl upon it at the proper angle, so that the dove could drink.

At last, the time came for the Rebbe of Shidlovitz to leave this world. However, as soon as his holy soul ascended from his body, an amazing thing happened: all the doves immediately flew away from the courtyard and disappeared forever. Who can fathom the secrets of the *tzaddikim*?[157]

Transmigration

Earlier in this chapter, when discussing the concept of kashrut, I mentioned the belief in transmigration or reincarnation, which is found primarily in the mystical strand of Judaism. Not once does the Talmud or the Midrash mention reincarnation, yet today this theory is accepted by many authorities. The Baal Shem Tov (Rabbi Yisroel Ben Eliezer, 1698–1760), founder of the Hasidic movement, reinforced this belief. Reincarnation as animals and other non-human forms receives greater attention with the emergence of the Safed school of Kabbalah in the 1500s.[158] The Safed Kabbalists teach that there are many reasons why a human may be reincarnated as an animal. Some are related to sexual transgression, or to murder, damaging speech, causing other Jews to eat non-kosher food, omitting the blessing either before or after eating, stealing and gluttony.[159] 'He who behaves like an animal in this life [by pursuing physical desires] will be forced to labor as an animal in the next world.'[160]

It appears that a soul that has been reincarnated in an animal suffers because it is aware of its previous condition:

> The Kabbalists state that when a person is reincarnated as another human being, he does not remember his former life; however, when a person is reincarnated as an animal, beast, or bird, he does remember his former life. Therefore, the soul grieves and agonizes over how it has fallen from the heights of heaven, from the human form to an animal form.[161]

There is hope for the righteous and the wise: 'Sometimes even *tzaddikim* who dwell in the Garden of Eden must be reincarnated for some small matter that they did not fulfill. However, they are reborn as fish that need not endure the pain of *shechitah*.'¹⁶² In the following tale, we note the reincarnation of a pious man in a different form:

> Once Rabbi Mordcheleh of Nadvorna and his disciples were discussing some scholarly matter in the study hall, when suddenly the holy rabbi heard through the window the sound of music. Reb Mordcheleh looked out the window to see a troupe of gypsies leading a dancing bear by a leash. In those days, it was customary for gypsy entertainers to travel from town to town.
>
> No sooner did the *tzaddik* spy the bear, than he rushed out, telling the Chassidim he must purchase it, no matter the cost. He then entered into negotiations with the leader of the gypsies to buy his bear. The gypsy, a shrewd bargainer, smelled a good deal. 'I can't possibly sell the bear which is the source of my livelihood.' The price went up. Yet the Nadvorner was insistent on buying the bear. As his own funds were limited, he now turned to the Hasidim to contribute to the purchase of the bear. The Chassidim hadn't a clue why their beloved master should need a dancing bear, but a true Chassidim doesn't question the ways of the *tzaddik*. Finally, the fee, an exorbitant sum, was paid to the gypsy.
>
> The Rebbe then led the bear by its chain back to his *beis midrash* (study hall). Reb Mordcheleh stood with the bear in the middle of the hall, looked the bear straight in the eyes, and spoke these words: '*Schoen, genug getanzt!*' 'Danced enough already!' Immediately, the bear dropped dead on the floor of the *beis midrash*. The Chassidim stared in amazement. Reb Mordcheleh was renowned as a miracle worker, but this was too much!
>
> Before they had time to recover from their shock, Reb Mordcheleh commanded his faithful followers to perform a *taharah*, a ritual purification, on the dead bear. The Chassidim somehow managed to drag the hulk to the ritual bath next door for immersion in the cleansing waters. When they finished the *taharah,* Reb Mordcheleh demanded the bear be given a proper funeral, culminating in burial next to the ritual bath. From beginning to end, the Chassidim had not the slightest

clue what was going on in their beloved Rebbe's mind, but they knew the thoughts of the righteous are loftier than those of average men.

Sometime, maybe days, maybe weeks later, Reb Mordcheleh revealed to them what it was all about. There once lived a very pious Jew who observed all six hundred and thirteen commandments, with the exception of one: It seems he was a great scholar and deemed it beneath his dignity to dance at weddings in order to gladden the hearts of bride and groom. When he died, his soul was summoned before the heavenly court for judgment. It was decreed that since he failed to keep this supremely important commandment, his punishment would be to reincarnate as a performing bear and dance his whole life in town after town.

'I recognized him as soon as I saw him. When I pronounced those words "Danced enough already!" that was the *tikkun* of that poor soul. Having served its sentence and expiated its sin, the soul was thence liberated from within the body of the bear.'[163]

The story contains a mixed message of compassion: compassion for the former (human) soul, rather than for the bear's cruel plight.

Conclusion

In conclusion, animals, as subjects and in the role of functionaries, as objects, have been acknowledged from the very beginnings of Judaism. From Creation, through the sacred acts of naming, blessing and saving a remnant in the Flood, to the intricacies of animal sacrifice and the complexity of dietary laws, animals have always been included in Jewish religious debate, though sometimes with no agreement reached among the different schools of thought. The central tenet is that animals are to be accorded respect because they have been created by God, but, from a hierarchical religious position, they are viewed as lesser beings than humans. Even with such a divergent history, animals have never been worshipped in their own right, though there have been a few close calls. In Judaism there is a wide spectrum of opinion, an agreement to disagree, so the way animals are viewed within Judaism does, of course, differ. From calls to embrace a vegetarian lifestyle to a belief that eating meat liberates the animal's soul, there is a wide range of opinions. All would consent that God's creation is good; for in Genesis God pronounced 'it was good,' yet some would say, especially in relation to what is deemed to be kosher, that some animals are more 'good' than others.

Judaism, while not a religion based on ahimsa (non-violence), does follow an equivalent code of ethics, centred in the goodness of God's creation. This influences the method of slaughter, prohibits blood sports, advocates respect for what one eats, wears and uses (one may not waste, or use to excess), and reminds one of this through the blessings recited before each meal. The non-negotiable component is that animals are to be respected because they are part of God's creation. How one interprets 'respect' is another matter.

FIVE
Animals in Christianity

The earth is the Lord's and the fullness thereof,
Oh God, enlarge within us the sense of fellowship
with all living things, our brothers the animals . . .
　　　　　　Attributed to St Basil[1]

A model of being and knowing that begins with touch . . . will insist
on being bonded to skin, fur and feathers, to the smells and sounds
of the earth, to the intricate and detailed differences in people and
other life-forms . . . as the incarnation insists, God is found in the
depth and detail of life and the earth, not apart from or in spite of it.
　　　　　　Sallie McFague[2]

CHRISTIANITY GREW OUT OF the various religious traditions found in the Mediterranean world two thousand years ago. Judaism, mystery religions, pagan traditions and the state religion of the Roman Empire each played their part. Each of these religions had included and excluded animals, thus influencing the inclusion and exclusion of animals in Christianity. During and after the scientific revolution and the Enlightenment, Christianity, for the most part, severed ties with the rest of nature, seeing humanity at the top of the hierarchy, the sole subjects of the Divine, animals being objects purely for utilitarian use.

In considering how Christianity regards animals, it is important to note that viewpoints are fluid; there has been much change through the centuries. Even today there are some Christians, including theologians and clergy, who are making the near invisible, visible. Questions about the environment are being asked, with animals being included as a topic in some of these discussions. Christianity, though, to its

Roman tombstone from Chester. The dead woman is shown enjoying a banquet in the afterlife; two birds are perched above on garlands of leaves. In the upper corners can be seen two carvings of Triton (half man, half fish) blowing on a sea shell trumpet.

detriment, has emphasized all too often that humans have intrinsic value whereas the rest of creation has instrumental value for humans and/or for God.

Before Humanity: Dreams and Visions

'But what is my God?' I put my question to the earth. It answered, 'I am not God', and all things on earth declared the same. I asked the sea and the chasms of the deep and the living things that creep in them, but they answered, 'We are not your

Fragment of a mosaic pavement, featuring a peacock. Late Roman or Byzantine, Syria (5th–6th century CE), probably from a church. The peacock was a pagan symbol of springtime and renewal. This symbolism was used in Christianity for the eternal triumph of Christ.

> God. Seek what is above us.' I spoke to the winds that blow, and the whole air and all that lives in it replied . . . 'I am not God.' . . . I said, 'Since you are not my God, tell me about him. Tell me something of my God.' Clear and loud they answered, 'God is he who made us.' I asked these questions simply by gazing at these things, and their beauty was all the answer they gave.[3]

Christianity holds fast to the belief that God created everything; animals were not present before Creation, or co-creators, as in some religions.[4] The search always involves story: narratives from Scripture, from extra-canonical sources (material that is not part of the accepted biblical canon), and legend. Although legends do not carry the same weight as Scripture, many of them add insight and a glimpse into the importance of faith, and of the mystery of the Divine. This quirky example touches on the mystery of the Eucharist for all creation, as well as the notion that other creatures may possess the ability to worship God, their Creator:

> Cesaire de Hesterbach reported in the early thirteenth century that a peasant once placed the Eucharist in a hive, hoping it would inspire the bees to produce more honey. Later he found that the bees had made a little chapel of wax. It contained an altar on which lay a tiny chalice with the Host.[5]

Together: Animals as Brethren

Scripture

In Scripture animals are present at the birth of Jesus. Within the canon, their role is at times small, but in extra-canonical texts their presence is greater, especially at the Nativity and during the early years of Jesus.

In the New Testament there is considerable material concerning animals. In the New Testament the term 'lost sheep' embraces concern for animals as a basis for understanding God's care for humanity, as Jesus is known as 'the Good Shepherd'. The hymn of praise in Colossians 1:15–17 includes all of creation under Christ: 'He is the image of the invisible God, the firstborn of all creation; for in him all things in heaven and on earth were created, things visible and invisible . . . all things have been created through him and for him . . . and in him all things hold together.'

The first New Testament story we associate with animals is the narrative of the Nativity. In the account of Jesus' birth in Luke 2:7, 'And she gave birth to her firstborn son and wrapped him in bands of cloth, and laid him in a manger, because there was no place for them in the inn,' we note that the infant Jesus was born in a place that had first sheltered and nurtured animals. The animals in the stable were the first witnesses, apart from Mary and Joseph. The animals seem to recognize the revelation of the incarnation. The next verse introduces the first 'outside' witnesses, the shepherds. Some viewed them as outcasts,

Nativity scene from a French *Book of Hours, c.* 1500.

Workshop of Benedetto Buglioni, *Nativity*, c. 1520, glazed terracotta.

because of the nature of their work, which made it difficult for them to observe all the requirements and commandments necessary in order to lead a holy life. Shepherds, tending the sheep, protecting them from danger, were there ready to respond. So it was that the humans chosen to be the first to know the good news of Christ's coming, were men who cared for animals. The author J. Regina Hyland argues that Jesus' birth, surrounded by living animals and by shepherds, heralds a new era:

> The work of the shepherds who attended Jesus at his birth was the antithesis of those whose work centred around the holocaust of animals on the altars at Jerusalem . . . Just as the beginning of Judaism was marked by the rejection of human sacrifice, so the beginning of Christianity was marked by the rejection of animal sacrifice. It was a fulfillment of the call for reform that had been given by the prophets hundreds of years earlier.[6]

Mary Lewis, *The Joyful Mysteries, III: Birth of Jesus*, 1989, at the National Sanctuary of Our Sorrowful Mother ('The Grotto') in Portland, Oregon.

With Jesus' birth, peace with wild animals, as foretold by the prophets, becomes evident.[7] The creation narrative's message about the relationship between humans and animals becomes reality in Jesus' presence: 'The "community of the sixth day" is restored.'[8] In the post-biblical period, the ox and the ass were introduced into the birth narrative from the Gospel of Pseudo-Matthew. This was no mistake. These animals recognized what humans were incapable of doing, they understood who Jesus was. The theologian Lukas Vischer points out that these animals, and the lack of understanding on the part of humans, is a reference to Isaiah 1:3: 'The ox knows its owner, and the donkey its master's crib; but . . . my people do not understand.'[9] If animals were the first non-human witnesses at the birth of Jesus, and had an understanding of the nature of the event, then surely they are to be included in the 'good news'.

Jesus continually revealed a God of compassion whose concern extended to all creatures. In the New Testament the beautiful words of comfort, 'Come to me all that are heavy laden, and I will give you

Jacquelin de Montluçon, *Adoration of the Child*, c. 1490s, oil.

rest. For my yoke is easy' (Matthew 11:28–30), take up the imagery of the ox working the land. And there is also the Old Testament injunction against yoking an animal to another of a different size, because it was seen as a form of cruelty: 'You shall not plow with an ox and a donkey yoked together' (Deuteronomy 22:10).

Jesus speaks of relieving the suffering of domestic animals.[10] Not all Jews would have agreed with Jesus' account of what was permissible for other creatures to do on the Sabbath. The Essenes, inhabitants of the Dead Sea community at Qumran, whose interpretation of the Sabbath laws was extremely strict, forbade any such cases of mercy: 'No man shall assist a beast to give birth on the Sabbath day. And if it should fall into a cistern or pit, he shall not lift it out on the Sabbath' (Damascus Document, CD XI:12–14).[11] The accounts in the Gospels are remarkable in that the examples are of animals whose lives are not in danger; the motivation is compassion, to relieve suffering; action is not needed in order to save a life. Jesus places himself within the Jewish ethical and legal tradition, which held that God requires humans to treat all creation with compassion and respect.

Jesus invites his listeners to consider the natural world, God's creation, and to draw religious lessons from it. In Luke 12:24, when Jesus asks his listeners to consider the raven,[12] Jesus is saying that within the context of the dietary laws, the raven would be considered unclean, but God takes care to provide for even the unclean birds. Jesus highlights God's cares for all living creatures, even for the common sparrow: 'Are not two sparrows sold for a penny? Yet not one of them will fall to the ground apart from your Father' (Matthew 10:29). Sparrows were the cheapest birds for sale in the market. Jesus uses the example of the unimportant sparrow to demonstrate God's concern for the unimportant. In Matthew's version (which differs slightly from that in Luke 12:6–7), the sparrow's fall to the ground is not because it has died, but because it has been pulled to the ground, caught in a hunter's net.[13] Jesus draws on traditional Jewish teaching: 'In his hand is the life of every living thing' (Job 12:10); 'You save humans and animals alike, O Lord' (Psalms 36:6). God is not only concerned about the species, but with each individual within the species. Even that which seems of little worth in human eyes is of value in the sight of God.

In Matthew 23:37 Jesus likens his desire to protect and care for his people to that of a mother hen wishing to protect her chicks: 'Jerusalem, Jerusalem, the city that kills the prophets and stones those

Mary Lewis, *Agnus Dei*, 1989, at The Grotto, Portland, Oregon.

who are sent to it! How often have I desired to gather your children together as a hen gathers her brood under her wings, and you were not willing!'

Jesus referred to himself as 'the Good Shepherd' and frequently likened the relationship between the shepherd and his sheep to that of his own calling. Jesus linked his view of himself as 'the Good Shepherd' to the tradition of Isaiah, who wrote of God in this way:

> He will feed his flock like a shepherd;
> he will gather the lambs in his arms,
> and carry them in his bosom,
> and gently lead the mother sheep. (Isaiah 40:11)

Jesus reminded people that the ideal relationship with animals was one in which humans cared for the non-human.

In biblical times lambs were frequently sacrificed. Their gentleness made them ideal victims. They were slaughtered as atonement for sin, as thanksgiving offerings and as redemptors for more valuable animals. The non-violent nature of the lamb being led to the slaughter was also a basis for the designation of Jesus as 'the Lamb of God'. Jesus went to his death 'like a sheep . . . led to the slaughter' (Acts 8:32). After his death, Jesus, 'the Good Shepherd', was known as 'the Lamb of God'.

The episode of the Gerasene swine (Matthew 8:28–34; Mark 5:1–20; Luke 8:26–30) has been interpreted to mean that Jesus didn't care about animal life. In the accounts in Mark and Luke, Jesus permits the demons to enter the pigs, in response to their begging him to let them. In Matthew, Jesus commands them to do what they have begged to be allowed to do. Their destruction of the pigs manifests the inherent tendency of the demonic to destroy whatever it possesses. In this story Jesus permits a lesser evil. The principle that human beings are of more value than other animals operates here to the detriment of the latter.

The account of Jesus in the wilderness, 'He was in the wilderness forty days, tempted by Satan; and he was with the wild beasts; and the angels waited on him' (Mark 1:13), underscores Jesus' mission. Jesus, as the Son of God, is embarking on his mission to inaugurate the Kingdom of God. Here the desert, the non-human sphere, is a world outside human control.

Edward Hicks, *The Peaceable Kingdom*, c. 1834, oil on canvas.

In Jewish literature, there was the expectation that wild animals would be scared of humans. It was thought that they would become domestic animals and thereby serve humans. Such ideas are absent from Mark 1:13: 'Jesus does not terrorize or dominate the wild animals, he does not domesticate or even make pets of them. He is simply "with them".'[14] He lets them be themselves in peace, leaving them in their wildness. This image of Jesus in Mark's gospel gives hope for humans living peacefully with all living creatures, a possibility given by God in the creation accounts and then again in messianic times. The kingdom of God is only partially realized now, but that hope is there for the eschatological future.[15]

Jewish eschatological expectation included the hope that the righting of all wrongs in the Messianic Age would bring peace between wild animals and humans. The outcomes of messianic peace (a type of peace that is both relational and hopeful in its essence) are described in detail in Isaiah 11 (see p. 167). Peace among all animals is implied, as well as a restoration of paradise ('my holy mountain'). It was thought that the original paradise, in which humans and wild animals lived in peace and harmony, would be restored in the Messianic Age. Jesus establishes messianic peace with the wild animals. Over the course of twenty-five years the Quaker preacher-artist Edward Hicks (1780–1849) painted nearly one hundred versions of *The Peaceable Kingdom*. In the early period of his work Hicks concentrated on the figure of the messianic child, but the latter paintings emphasized harmonious relationships among the most unlikely of creatures.[16]

In the late Middle Ages and early Renaissance period there was a shift in the visual imagery of Jesus' crucifixion. A major source of this change was the incorporation into the Passion narrative of Psalm 22, in which bulls, lions and dogs enter the lament and are thus interpreted as torturers of Jesus:[17]

> Many bulls encircle me,
> strong bulls of Bashan surround me;
> they open wide their mouths at me,
> like a ravening and roaring lion . . .
> For dogs are all around me;
> a company of evildoers encircles me. (Psalm 22:12–13, 16)

Christ's coming calls into question the practice of expiatory sacrifice. Christ is the sacrificial animal, the Lamb who takes away the sins of the world. There is no need for animal sacrifice; indeed, it no longer has any meaning: 'we have been sanctified through the offering of the body of Jesus Christ once for all' (Hebrews 10:10). Jesus celebrates Passover with his disciples and becomes the Lamb of God, the sacrificial animal that was brought to the slaughter. This idea is developed into the Lamb of God ruling the world: 'To the one seated on the throne and to the Lamb be blessing and honour and glory and might forever and ever!' (Revelation 5:13). The Lamb's blood has ransomed the world, and brought about reconciliation.

In the New Testament animals are not classed as unclean or clean: 'there is nothing outside a person that by going in can defile, but the things that come out are what defile' (Mark 7:15). Animals have now been liberated from taboos. Dietary laws had been seen as imparting holiness, enabling the Israelites to maintain covenantal relations with God. The New Testament rejects ritual holiness and declares all foods clean; there is no food that renders a person unclean.

Jesus' attitude to animals, however, belongs wholly within the Old Testament and Jewish tradition. In this tradition it was permitted to kill certain animals for sacrifice to God in the temple and for food. After Jesus had healed lepers, he advised them to go to the Temple and offer the appropriate sacrifice. What he did oppose was the abuse of the ritual and the corruption of the priesthood. It is highly likely that Jesus participated in sacrificial worship: his attendance at the regular annual festivals in Jerusalem would have involved this.[18] If the Last Supper was a Passover meal, then Jesus would have eaten the Passover lamb, which would have been sacrificed in the Temple that afternoon.

The early Church saw Jesus' death as the only acceptable sacrifice and the end of all sacrifices. The author of the epistle to the Hebrews states that animal sacrifices were ineffective (Hebrews 10:1–18).[19] Eventually most early Christians came to believe that the sacrificial system had been made redundant by the sacrificial death of Christ. Gentile converts to Christianity were free from all the ritual requirements of Mosaic law.

Hyland offers a more radical view concerning Jesus' reaction to animal sacrifice. According to Hyland, the 'cleansing of the Temple' sets in motion the arrest, trial and death of Jesus, because in trying to end the slaughter of animals, he was attacking the economic foundation of Jerusalem: 'it was the slaughter of animals, in the name of God, that led to the only aggressive confrontation reported in his ministry ... He freed those animals who were about to be slaughtered and disrupted the entire procedure that surrounded the sacrificial rites.'[20] Hyland suggests that Jesus' attack on the Temple was premeditated, that it was not an impulsive act:[21] 'Then he entered Jerusalem and went to the temple; and when he had looked around at everything, as it was already late, he went out to Bethany with the twelve' (Mark 11:11). Hyland states that Jesus planned this to be a public spectacle, with many present, but by the time Jesus and his disciples had passed the crowds on their entry to Jerusalem, most had returned home from the Temple. When Jesus was going, he looked and saw everything, which included the animals, jammed into the Temple enclosure. The next day was the 10th of Nisan, the day that the male head of the household chose the animal to be killed for Passover. According to sources, the killing began at 3 p.m. and ended at sundown, with about 18,000 animals slaughtered.[22]

Isaiah and other Latter Prophets had called for an end to sacrificial religion. Now Jesus, who began his ministry claiming to be the fulfilment of Isaiah's prophecy (Luke 4:16–20) took action against that system. Jesus had been preaching against the religious establishment; now he was trying to overthrow the sacrificial system, which was its foundation.[23]

Apocryphal Texts

The extra-canonical stories of the apostles and martyrs were part of the religious world for earlier generations of Christians. This apocryphal literature is unfamiliar to many Christians today;[24] but the material says much about animals and our relationship with them.

The apocryphal acts were composed in the second and third centuries CE. The lives of Andrew, John, Peter, Thomas and Paul form the majority of the apocryphal acts. These popular stories helped raise the spirits of new Christians. The apocryphal texts came to be regarded as heretical by some early Christian leaders, but that did not diminish their popularity.

Some of the stories tell of martyrs and the animals used in the arenas throughout the Roman Empire. In these accounts wild animals refuse to harm Christians while harming those who confront Christianity. There are other stories that tell of people forming close bonds with animals and those same animals protecting them from cruelty. Apart from life and a right to a cruelty-free existence, have animals been recipients of other gifts or blessings from God? Consider this story from the Acts of Paul (the Coptic Papyrus):

> I [Paul] went out, accompanied by the widow Lemma and her daughter Ammia. I was walking in the night, meaning to go to Jericho in Phoenicia . . . There came a great and terrible lion out of the valley . . . But we were praying, so that through the prayer Lemma and Ammia did not come upon the beast. But when I had finished praying, the beast had cast himself at my feet. I was filled with the Spirit and looked upon him, and said to him, 'Lion, what do you want?' But he said, 'I wish to be baptized'. I glorified God, who had given speech to the beast and salvation to his servants. Now there was a great river in that place; I went down into it and he followed me . . . I myself

was in fear and wonderment, in that I was on the point of leading the lion like an ox and baptizing him in the water. But I stood on the bank . . . and cried out, saying, 'You who dwell in the heights . . . who with Daniel shut the mouths of the lions, who sent to me our Lord Jesus Christ, grant that we escape the beast, and accomplish the plan which you have appointed.' When I had prayed thus, I took the lion by his mane and in the name of Jesus Christ immersed him three times. But when he came up out of the water he shook his mane and said to me, 'Grace be with you!' And I said to him, 'And likewise with you.'[25]

Paul is later forced into the arena to face the lions. One of them is the lion that he had baptized earlier. Like Paul, the lion too had been captured.[26] The entertainment is disrupted by a severe hailstorm. Although many of the spectators are killed, Paul and the lion manage to escape.[27]

Although these works were not included in the canon, their popularity cannot be disputed. Hippolytus, in his *Commentary on Daniel* (written around 204 CE), accepts that the story of Paul and the lion is true: 'For if we believe that when Paul was condemned to death, a lion, let loose upon him, fell down and licked his feet, how shall we not believe the things that happened in the case of Daniel?'[28] These texts, entering the popular imagination and becoming influential in the development of early Christianity, flowed through art and hagiography.[29]

The Gospel of Pseudo-Matthew is a comparatively late text, perhaps from the eighth century, and it represents an effort to bring together the legends that had become popular among ordinary Christians. The text became an important channel through which the legends of the nativity became widely known, and it had a great impact on the art and literature of the medieval West. In the Gospel of Pseudo-Matthew, Jesus is viewed as the new Adam, adored at birth by the animals. This is where the 'ox and ass' are mentioned as being in the stable:

On the third day after the birth of our Lord Jesus Christ holy Mary went out from the cave, and went into a stable and put her child in a manger, and an ox and an ass worshipped him. Then was fulfilled that which was said through the prophet Isaiah: 'The ox knows his owner and the ass his master's crib.'

> Thus the beasts, ox and ass, with him between them, unceasingly worshipped him. Then was fulfilled that which was said through the prophet Habakkuk: 'Between two beasts are you known.' And Joseph remained in the same place with Mary for three days.[30]

The Holy Family later flees to Egypt to escape Herod's fury. This episode in the life of Jesus has fostered stories concerning animals, again, from apocryphal sources:

> Likewise lions and leopards worshipped him and accompanied them into the desert. Wherever Joseph and holy Mary went, they went before them, showing (them) the way and lowering their heads (in worship); they showed their servitude by wagging their tails and honoured him with great reverence. But when Mary saw the lions and leopards and all kinds of wild beasts surrounding them, she was at first gripped by violent fear. But the child Jesus looked at her face with a happy countenance, and said: 'Do not fear, mother; for they do not come to harm you, but they hasten to obey you and me.' With these words he removed all fear from her heart. And the lions went along with them, and with the oxen and asses and the beasts of burden which carried what they needed, and they harmed no one, although they remained (with them). Rather they were docile among the sheep and rams which they had brought with them from Judaea and had with them. They walked among wolves without fear, and neither was harmed by the other. Then was fulfilled that which was said through the prophet: 'The wolves pasture with the lambs: lions and oxen eat straw together.' And the lions guided on their journey the two oxen and the wagon in which they carried what they needed.[31]

In the Infancy Gospel of Thomas, an extra-canonical text written in the second century CE, we find stories about Jesus from birth until the age of twelve. One of the tales is a resurrection story, with fish as its subject:

> And when Jesus was three years old, and when he saw boys playing, he began to play with them. And he took a dry fish

and put it in a basin, and ordered it to breathe, and it began to breathe. And he said again to the fish, 'Reject the salt which you have, and go into the water', and so it came to pass.[32]

In another account from the Infancy Gospel of Thomas, Jesus is caught moulding birds from clay and is scolded by Joseph for doing this 'work' on the Sabbath. Jesus claps his hands, which brings the clay to life and the birds then fly away.[33] In both stories, Jesus brings new life to animals. Perhaps the story of the birds moulded from clay brings to mind the creation account and God's ability to breathe life into His creation.

Another story in the Infancy Gospel of Thomas is about a boy who was 'tormented by Satan . . . [and] used to bite all who came near him'. When the boy's mother brought him to the young Jesus, he 'wished to bite the Lord Jesus, but was not able'. Then the boy, probably in frustration, tried to hit Jesus: 'Satan went forth out of that boy . . . in the shape of a dog.'[34] The text goes on to state that this boy was named Judas, and he later became one of Jesus' disciples, the one who would betray him.[35]

These incidents, while not accepted as part of the canon of Scripture, serve the purpose of filling in some gaps, particularly the early years of Jesus. We know that legends contain a kernel of truth, as do these apocryphal stories. They deal with Jesus' compassion and insight. Cruelty towards animals was not the way of creation. In the following narrative the disciples are portrayed as lacking understanding: Jesus even pronounces 'woe' to them because they cannot hear the animal's agony. The donkey cries out to God, and God hears. Not only does God hear, but kindness to an animal is viewed as a means of grace:

> It happened that the Lord left the city and walked with his disciples over the mountains. And they came to a mountain, and the road which led up it was steep. There they found a man with a pack-mule. But the animal had fallen, because the man had loaded it too heavily, and now he beat it, so that it was bleeding. And Jesus came to him and said, 'Man, why do you beat your animal? Do you not see that it is too weak for its burden, and do you not know that it suffers pains?' But the man answered and said, 'What is that to you? I may beat it as much as I please, since it is my property, and I bought it for a

good sum of money. Ask those who are with you, for they know me and know about this.' And some of the disciples said, 'Yes, Lord, it is as he says. We have seen how he bought it.' But the Lord said, 'Do you then not see how it bleeds, and do you not hear how it groans and cries out?' But they answered and said, 'No, Lord, that it groans and cries out, we do not hear.' But Jesus was sad and exclaimed, 'Woe to you, that you do not hear how it complains to the Creator in heaven and cries out for mercy. But threefold woes to him about whom it cries out and complains in its pain.' And he came up and touched the animal. And it stood up and its wounds were healed. But Jesus said to the man, 'Now carry on and from now on do not beat it any more, so that you too may find mercy.'[36]

Nothing is known of this story, preserved in Coptic, so it is impossible to know whether it is from an early Gospel tradition. What is important though, is its warning to carry out the commandment, found in Exodus 23:4 and Deuteronomy 22:4, to rescue an animal that has fallen under its load.[37]

St Peter, too, encountered a talking animal, this time a dog:

Peter, seeing a great dog tied . . . with a massive chain, went up to him and let him loose. And when the dog was let loose he acquired a human voice and said to Peter, 'What do you bid me do, you servant of the ineffable living God?' And Peter said 'Go in and tell Simon in the presence of his company, "Peter says to you, Come out in public; for on your account I have come to Rome, you wicked man and troubler of simple souls."' And immediately the dog . . . rushed into the middle of Simon's companions and . . . called out with a loud voice, 'I tell you Simon, Peter the servant of Christ is standing at the door, and says to you, "Come out in public."' . . . But Simon said to the dog, 'Tell Peter that I am not in the house.' And the dog answered him in the presence of Marcellus, 'You most wicked and shameless man, you enemy of all that live and believe in Christ Jesus, here is a dumb animal sent to you and taking a human voice to convict you and prove you a cheat and a deceiver.' . . . Having said these words, the dog . . . came to Peter . . . and reported his dealings . . . So the dog said,

'Messenger and apostle of the true God, Peter, you shall have a great contest with Simon, the enemy of Christ and with his servants; and you shall convert many to the faith that were deceived by him.' ... And when the dog had said this, he fell down at the apostle Peter's feet and gave up his spirit.[38]

In this account, an animal can be given the role of prophet, ready to proclaim God's message to humans.[39]

The Gospel of the Holy Twelve, a controversial text first serialized in the *Lindsey and Lincolnshire Star* between 1898 and 1901, is largely dismissed by scholars. Rev. Gideon Jasper Richard Ouseley (1834–1906), a former clergyman, originally claimed that he had discovered the Original Gospel from which the present four Gospels were derived, preserved in a Buddhist monastery in Tibet, where it had been hidden by members of the Essene community to keep it safe from the hands of corrupters. This claim was later revised, stating that the text had been communicated by departed mystics in dreams and visions.

The description of the animals at Jesus' birth sets the tone:

And there were in the same cave an ox and a horse and an ass and a sheep, and beneath the manger was a cat with her little ones; and there were doves also, overhead; and each had its mate after its kind, the male with the female.

Thus it came to pass that He was born in the midst of the animals which, through redemption of man from ignorance and selfishness, He came to redeem from their sufferings by the manifestation of the sons and the daughters of God.[40]

The Gospel of the Holy Twelve presents vegetarian versions of traditional teachings and events described in the canonical New Testament. In this work all references to eating meat have been changed. There are now Twelve Commandments, instead of ten, the third one forbidding the eating of flesh.[41] The Gospel was probably created in support of animal welfare and vegetarianism. The work remains unrecognized by biblical scholars and has also been dismissed by modern theologians and historians of the animal rights movement. Though fictitious, the text is an interesting read, with many examples of Jesus' compassion towards animals, domestic and wild:

> And on a certain day, as he was passing by a mountain side nigh unto the desert, there met him a lion, and many men were pursuing him with stones and javelins to slay him.
>
> But Jesus rebuked them saying, Why hunt ye these creatures of God, which are more noble than you? By the cruelties of many generations, those were made the enemies of man which should have been his friends.
>
> If the power of God is shown in them, so also are shown his long suffering and compassion. Cease ye to persecute this creature, who desireth not to harm you; see ye not how he fleeth from you, and is terrified by your violence?
>
> And the lion came and lay at the feet of Jesus, and showed love to him; and the people were astonished and said, Lo this man loveth all creatures, and hath power to command even these beasts from the desert, and they obey him.[42]

Neglect of animals has repercussions: in the account of the visit of the wise men in *The Gospel of the Holy Twelve*, they lose sight of the star because they have neglected their animals. Once their camels and asses have been watered and rested, the star reappears to them: 'And when they saw it they rejoiced with exceeding great joy. And they praised God who had shewn his mercy unto them, even as they shewed mercy unto their thirsty beasts.'[43]

Another apocryphal work, though one that can be traced back to sources in the fourth century CE, is the Gospel of the Ebionites. Like the Jewish sect at Qumran,[44] the Ebionites were hostile to the practices undertaken at the Temple in Jerusalem, particularly the practice of animal sacrifice. In their writings they attempt to show that Jesus abolished this ritual: 'he came and declared, as their gospel . . . reports, "I am come to do away with sacrifices, and if you cease not from sacrificing, the wrath of God will not cease from you."'[45] The Ebionites were vegetarian and in their gospel they remove the reference to John the Baptist's diet of locusts (Matthew 3:4); their gospel also records Jesus' refusal to eat the Passover Lamb: '[The Ebionites] . . . let the disciples say [to Jesus], "Where will we prepare the Passover for you?" And him to answer, "Do I desire at this Passover to eat flesh with you?"'[46] Ebionites were not vegetarian because of compassion for animals, but because of gnostic dualism, where matter is seen as evil.[47] They abstained from eating meat since they believed flesh was defiled because it was the product of sexual intercourse, the same rationale behind the absence of meat consumption in gnostic Manichaeism.[48]

Some scholars have tried to prove that John the Baptist ate carob pods, rather than locusts. This was a widespread interpretation during the nineteenth century, but is unsupported by linguistic evidence. In the Gospel of the Ebionites it states that John the Baptist ate cake, not locusts. The change was made to legitimize their vegetarian beliefs.

The version of Josephus' *Jewish War* known as the *Slavonic Josephus* states that John the Baptist was a vegetarian: 'Every beast he abhorred [for food] . . . and fruits of the trees served for [his] needs.'[49] Lexical analysis has concluded that the vegetarian texts were interpolations, added perhaps as late as the eleventh century. These textual additions suggest, however, that there were vegetarian sects at work in the early centuries of the Church, and that individuals felt so strongly about their beliefs that they were prepared to alter manuscripts to make them conform to their beliefs.

Was John the Baptist an Essene?[50] This is questionable; John's father, Zachariah, as a follower of orthodox Judaism would hardly have encouraged his son to follow a heterodox Jewish sect, and John's open missionary world would not have been welcomed by the closed Qumran community.

There is also a question concerning whether Essenes were strict vegetarians. The Damascus Document states that fish and locusts could be eaten, if they were prepared according to the rule (CD XII:11–15). Animal bones and potsherds have been found at Qumran, which suggests that meat may have been consumed on festive occasions.[51]

In Manichaean dualism, divine Light was trapped in the earth when attacked by Darkness.[52] The Light was able to escape through the soil and through plants when cooked and digested, but if animals ate the plants, they defiled the divine Light because of their acts of procreation. Augustine challenged the Manichaean beliefs that part of God exists in plant matter and that meat is inherently evil and defiles the soul of its consumer. During this time, vegetarianism was discussed because of dualism, Gnosticism and spirituality, not because of moral issues. Meat-eating was a spiritual issue, not an ethical one.[53]

According to an Ebionite *Acts of the Apostles* quoted by the chronicler Hegesippus (d. *c.* 180 CE) (a source that itself is only known from a mention by Eusebius), James, the brother of Jesus, was thought to have been a vegetarian. St Peter, too, is described as vegetarian in the

Recognition of Clement, which originated in Syria in the mid-third century and was preserved by the Ebionites.

There have been several attempts to construct a vegetarian Jesus.[54] There have been claims that Jesus was an Essene, but the present academic consensus is that Jesus was not, as he rejected ritual purity laws and ate with sinners and tax collectors, all actions that Essenes would not have engaged in because of the risk of defilement.

While I'm not suggesting that Jesus was a vegetarian, it is interesting to note that today some Christians are vegetarian or vegan.[55] There are others who, though not vegetarian, find the references to sacrifice, particularly to blood, off-putting, even offensive, especially in relation to Communion. What does it mean to refer to Christ as the 'Lamb of God'? Does the phrase 'washed in the blood of the Lamb' bring to mind images of slaughter and violence? Is a new vocabulary needed in order to change this language of sacrifice?

Traditional Christian theology suggests that the Fall caused a rift, splitting apart all creation, as described in St Paul's letter to the Romans: 'For the creation was subjected to futility . . . creation itself will be set free from its bondage to decay and will obtain the freedom of the glory of the children of God' (Romans 8:20–21). Paul saw that creation was in bondage, like childbirth, but that there would be transformation. St John the Divine's vision of a new heaven and a new earth speaks of harmony and justice for all creation (Revelation 21).

Sometimes particular animals or birds are used to illustrate spiritual lessons, in this case, the gift of generosity (and the curse when it is withheld).[56] This folk tale is unusual in that its main character is Christ:

> In those days when our Lord and St Peter wandered upon earth, they came once to an old wife's house, who sat baking. Her name was Gertrude, and she had a red mutch on her head. They had walked a long way, and were both hungry, and our Lord begged hard for a bannock to stay their hunger. Yes, they should have it. So she took a tiny little piece of dough and rolled it out, but as she rolled it, it grew and grew till it covered the whole griddle.
>
> Nay, that was too big; they couldn't have that. So she took a tinier bit still; but when that was rolled out it covered the whole griddle just the same, and that bannock was too big, she said; they couldn't have that either.

The third time she took a still tinier bit – so tiny you could scarce see it; but it was the same story over again – the bannock was too big.

'Well,' said Gertrude, 'I can't give you anything; you must just go without, for all these bannocks are too big.'

Then our Lord waxed wrath, and said, 'Since you love me so little as to grudge me a morsel of food, you shall have this punishment – you shall become a bird, and seek your food between bark and bole, and never get a drop to drink save when it rains.'

He had scarce said the last word before she was turned into a great black woodpecker, or Gertrude's bird, and flew from her kneading-trough right up the chimney; and till this very day you may see her flying about, with her red mutch on her head, and her body all black, because of the soot in the chimney; and so she hacks and taps away at the trees for her food, and whistles when rain is coming, for she is ever athirst, and then she looks for a drop to cool her tongue.[57]

Saints

Oh, God, enlarge with us the sense of fellowship with all living things, our brothers the animals to whom Thou gavest the earth in common with us. We remember with shame that in the past we have exercised the high dominion of man with ruthless cruelty so that the voice of the earth, which should have gone up to thee in song, has been a groan of travail.[58]

What is a charitable heart? . . . It is a heart which is burning with love for the whole creation, for men, for the birds, for the beasts . . . for all creatures. He who has such a heart cannot see or call to mind a creature without his eyes being filled with tears by reason of the immense compassion which seizes his heart; a heart which is softened and can no longer bear to see or learn from others of any suffering, even the smallest pain being inflicted upon a creature. That is why such a man never ceases to pray for the animals . . . moved by the infinite purity which reigns in the hearts of those who are becoming united with God. (St Isaac the Syrian, d. *c.* 700 CE)

Bronze sculpture by Michael Florin Dente, 1993, of St Francis, in the garden of The Grotto sanctuary, Portland, Oregon.

In both the Eastern and Western branches of Christianity, legends of saints demonstrate Jesus' peace in the world. One aspect of Jesus' reign is the ability to live peacefully with all of creation. Certain saints are associated with animals, because animals were their companions; illustrations of St Jerome, for example, usually include a lion at his feet. Many of the saints lived as hermits in the forests and deserts, and attracted animals to them. The sixth-century Irish saint Ciarán (Kieran) of Saighir had a community of animals around him, including a boar, a fox, a badger, a wolf and a deer, and viewed them as pupils or disciples. Another Ciarán, this time Ciarán of Clonmacnoise, was assisted by a deer whose antlers served as a lectern at services. In the twelfth century St Godric had wild animals as his companions. In the third century Paul the Hermit withdrew to live in a cave for ninety years. St Anthony went to visit him and, according to legend, Anthony was greeted by a wolf, who led him to Paul's cave. After they met, another creature appeared, a crow carrying a loaf of bread. Paul told St Anthony that for the past sixty years a bird had brought him bread each day, During his sojourn in the wilderness, all of Paul the Hermit's companions were animals. When Anthony returned and found that Paul had died, two lions appeared and dug his grave.[59]

St Francis of Assisi, who was declared the patron saint of ecology in 1979, is the saint most popularly associated with animals. For Francis, all creation was part of the same family under God. All creatures were his brothers and sisters; if Jesus could become our brother, then surely we should view all of creation in the same way. In the 'Canticle of the Creatures', attributed to St Francis, all of creation praises God:

> Be praised then, my Lord God,
> In and through all your creatures,
> Especially among them.[60]

In *The Little Flowers of St Francis*, the piety of the birds is addressed. After St Francis had preached to them, stressing that they needed to praise God, their creator, 'all of the birds began to open their beaks, to stretch their necks, to spread out their wings, to reverently bow their heads to earth, and to show in gesture and in song that the words of the holy father gave them great joy'.[61] He blessed them and made the sign of the cross over them before they flew away.

> Then all the birds as one soared to heaven with sweet songs and, according to the sign of the cross that St Francis had made, flew in four different directions – toward the east, the west, the south and the north – each group continued to sing marvelously. Their flight signified that as St Francis, standard-bearer of the cross of Christ, had preached to them and had made the sign of the cross over them, they were now to set off singing throughout the four parts of the world.[62]

This example of birds committing their lives to God shifts the anthropocentric paradigm significantly. St Francis was neither the first nor the last to recognize that birds and animals can be a congregation; they not only hear the word, they respond to it.

Francis saw all of creation as loved by its Creator God. This was new in the teaching of the Church (with the exception of Celtic

Christianity) and was considered dangerous by some, for it smacked of paganism. The Church had had to contend with older nature religions, where different parts of nature were considered to be spirits or gods and were worshipped. The Church had tried to destroy these ideas because of its belief in the one God who had created all of nature, yet was not part of nature. As a result of this, it seemed as if the Church did not value nature, but Francis challenged this. Francis did not fear nature: instead, he praised it and saw nature as praising God. God gave birth to all, and loved all. For Francis, the coming of Jesus Christ to live among us was not just an event of importance for human beings, it was significant for all creation. His vision of a family type of relationship with all creatures was largely forgotten after he died, until it resurfaced in the 1960s, with the spirit of the Second Vatican Council. Francis's original vision of a familial relationship with all of creation was rediscovered and celebrated, and is still popular today, with many churches conducting services where animals are blessed on the feast day of St Francis (4 October). The Nativity tableau is also attributed to St Francis, who introduced live animals into the scene and perhaps had more to do with the association of animals in the stable at Jesus' birth than any other source, including Scripture.

It is interesting to note this quite forward-thinking, perhaps even unorthodox, view of G. K. Chesterton, in relation to St Francis:

> I cannot think how everybody, including myself, can have overlooked the fact that the whole tale of Saint Francis is of Totemistic origin. It is unquestionably a tale that simply swarms with totems. The Franciscan woods are as full of them as any Red Indian fable. Francis is made to call himself an ass, because in the original mythos Francis was merely the name given to the real four-footed donkey, afterward vaguely evolved into a half-human god or hero. And that, no doubt, is why I used to feel that the Brother Wolf and Sister Bird of Saint Francis were somehow like the Brer Fox and Sis Cow of Uncle Remus. Some say there is an innocent stage of infancy in which we do really believe that a cow talked or a fox made a tar baby. Anyhow there is an innocent period of intellectual growth in which we do sometimes really believe that Saint Patrick was a Sun-Myth or Saint Francis a Totem. But for the most of us both those phases of paradise are past.[63]

Later, commenting on Francis's death, Chesterton wrote:

> A man might fancy that the birds must have known when it happened; and made some motion in the evening sky. As they had once, according to the tale, scattered to the four winds of heaven in the pattern of a cross at his signal of dispersion, they might now have written in such dotted lines a more awful augury across the sky. Hidden in the woods perhaps were little cowering creatures never again to be so much noticed and understood; and it has been said that animals are sometimes conscious of things to which man, their spiritual superior, is for the moment blind.[64]

Francis believed in the virtue of humility. He tried to set up a democracy of all God's creatures. With him the ant is not simply an example for the lazy, but is now known as Brother Ant, praising the Creator in his own unique way.

> Later commentators have said that Francis preached to the birds as a rebuke to men who would not listen. The records do not read so: he urged the little birds to praise God, and in spiritual ecstasy they flapped their wings and chirped rejoicing. Legends of saints, especially the Irish saints, have long told of their dealings with animals but always, I believe, to show their human dominance over creatures. With Francis it is different ... What Sir Steven Runciman calls 'the Franciscan doctrine of the animal soul' was quickly stamped out.[65]

St Anthony (c. 251–356 CE), who is known by various names, including St Anthony the Great and St Anthony of Egypt, lived as a hermit in the desert with animals as his only companions. There is a legend that tells of how St Anthony and his companion pig brought fire to the world. St Anthony, who had earlier lived as a swineherd, travelled to the door of Hell accompanied by his pig, for all fire was in Hell and the people were suffering from the cold. St Anthony was not allowed to enter Hell, because the devils recognized him, but they allowed his pig inside, hoping he would end up as their meal. When the pig was let inside, he runs amok. In disgust, the devils asked St Anthony to come in to catch his pig. St Anthony calmed the pig with his staff and sat down to warm himself by the fire. A young devil tripped over the staff and angrily threw it into the fire. The pig started to misbehave and St Anthony told the young devil that the only way he could calm the pig was by using his staff. So the staff was given back to St Anthony, and he and the pig were evicted from Hell. What the devil didn't realize was that the saint had been able to capture fire through the staff, which was soft and dry in its centre, so flames from the fire remained hidden in the wood. St Anthony then spread fire throughout the land, before returning to the desert with the pig.[66] Perhaps, in this story, we can detect a similarity to First Peoples' narratives, where an animal is acknowledged and honoured because of the gift or blessing it has brought to humans. Such gifts could include knowledge concerning crop cultivation, how to divine water or, as in this tale, bringing the gift of fire to people.

Other saints highlight the bond between themselves and certain animals. One of the commonest is that of the dog. Many of these stories place the animal in the role of messenger or rescuer. In paintings, St Roch (1350–1380) is often depicted with a dog. He was working to help victims of the bubonic plague, when he himself became infected and his body became covered with sores. Roch went off into the woods to die, but a dog found him, licked his sores and later brought him some bread to eat. Roch was soon cured.

Carved wooden dog in the Grote Kerk, Haarlem, Netherlands.

Icon of St Christopher with a dog's head, *c.* 1561, in the Dormition Cathedral in Sviyazhsk, Republic of Tatarstan.

St John Bosco (1815–1888) was the founder of the Salesian Order, which was formed to care for homeless boys. In 1852, while Bosco was having problems reforming the boys, a mysterious dog came to the aid of the Italian priest. The dog, large, grey and friendly, was given the name Grigio. He appeared when he was needed, saving Bosco from attacks, escorting him to safety, even preventing him from entering a dangerous area:

> By now, John realized that something heavenly was going on. And as if to confirm it, the dog appeared one day as John was on his way to visit a farmer. When they arrived, John brought the dog inside. Grigio lay down quietly in a corner while the family ate. But when they had assembled leftovers for Grigio's dinner, they could not find him. No doors or windows had been open, yet he had vanished.[67]

Grigio accompanied Don Bosco for more than thirty years: 'To this day, if a Salesian priest is in danger, a large grey dog sometimes appears, just at the right time.'[68]

St Christopher's association with dogs is of a more personal nature. Most Eastern imagery depicts Christopher as a cynocephalic, having a dog's head. Icons of St Christopher with a dog's head date back to the reign of Justinian I (527–65), and this depiction continues throughout Eastern Orthodox history.[69] He is mentioned as dog-headed in the apocryphal Gnostic text, the *Acts of St Bartholomew*, and an eighteenth-century Greek Orthodox hymn recognizes him as 'St Christopher, dog-headed, valiant in faith, fervent in prayer'.[70] In one legend, St Christopher is said to have descended from a race of cynopheli, who were usually fierce and ate human flesh. He had no language other than a bark. He prayed to God, and God answered his prayers by giving him human speech.[71] Another legend states that Christopher was incredibly handsome and prayed to God for a head of a dog so that women would leave him alone.

One dog was given the highest honour, being named a saint. Guinefort was a greyhound who lived on the estate of Villars, near Lyons in France. One day Guinefort, a trusted dog, was left alone with an infant. When the father returned, he saw Guinefort next to the crib, with blood around his mouth. Assuming the dog had killed the baby, he immediately killed Guinefort by shooting an arrow through his heart and threw his body into a well. Approaching the crib, the father saw that the child had not been harmed, but instead there was a dead snake that the dog had killed. Guinefort's grave became a site of pilgrimage that appealed to parents with sick or deformed children. As they made their way to the well to pray for their children to be healed, 'Monks in a nearby monastery looked on in consternation as peasant women prayed to the dog, hung swaddling clothes in nearby bushes, and practiced what seemed to be pagan rituals.'[72] Sick children were brought to the well until the nineteenth century and reports of miraculous healings at Guinefort's shrine influenced generations of believers in southern France: 'Saint Guinefort, a martyr, received the popular designation of "saint", a title usually reserved for human animals. Apparently a dog cannot be an official saint, though he can be an official heretic.'[73] Various versions of this tale have been found in India, as early as the sixth century BCE, in a Greek legend and in a medieval Hebrew text. An almost identical tale about a greyhound called Gelert can be found in Welsh folklore.

St Martin de Porres (1579–1639) was the illegitimate son of a Spanish knight and a freed slave woman from Panama. His concern for better treatment of others extended to animals, for whom he felt a deep fondness and compassion. He created what was probably the first animal shelter for stray dogs and cats. He cared for mice, rats and reptiles, feeding them, as he believed that it was probably hunger that drove them to enter homes and kitchens.

Animals can also lead to conversion, as was the case in the legends of St Eustace and St Hubert. A Roman general named Placidus was out hunting when an image of Jesus on the cross appeared lodged between the antlers of a stag he was chasing. The stag told him that his charitable works were pleasing to Christ. His wife was also told in a vision that her family should become Christian. They did so, and Placidus changed his name to Eustace. Eustace refused to honour the Roman gods and was brought to the arena to face wild lions, but they became tame and left Eustace alone. Eustace and his family were then roasted alive inside a large bronze statue of a bull. The irony of this story is that Eustace was named the patron saint of hunters.

There are many other stories of saints and their relationship with animals, from St Pachomius, who was so beloved of animals that crocodiles would ferry him across the Nile river to wherever he wanted to go,[74] to St Jerome, who lived with many animals. One day a lion wandered into the courtyard of the monastery where St Jerome lived. Noticing that the lion was limping, Jerome removed a thorn from its paw. The lion remained with Jerome and was said to have been inconsolable when he died. This relationship inspired a well-known, though anonymous, poem:

> St Jerome in his study kept a great big cat,
> It's always in his pictures, with its feet upon the mat.
> Did he give it milk to drink, in a little dish?
> When it came to Fridays, did he give it fish?
> If I lost my little cat, I'd be sad without it;
> I should ask St Jeremy what to do about it;
> I should ask St Jeremy, just because of that,
> For he's the only saint I know who kept a pussy cat.[75]

There is even a patron saint for vegetarians: the Italian hermit St Nicholas of Tolentino (1245–1305). This affiliation is due to a miracle

Misericords in the Grote Kerk, Haarlem, Netherlands, *c.* early 16th century.

known in two different versions. In the first, Nicholas was given chicken to eat; he made the sign of the cross and it turned into roasted vegetables. According to the second, Nicholas was served partridge; he made the sign of the cross and the partridge was restored to life, then flew out the window. It is not known, however, if St Nicholas refrained from eating meat, or had a deep affinity for other creatures.

Other saintly figures have been reported as having a great love of animals. Perhaps this is partly due to living an ascetic lifestyle, coupled with infrequent encounters with humans, so animals have provided friendship or at least a relationship of some kind. Sometimes such a relationship is due to close observation, leading to a heightened awareness of kinship with the 'other'. One of the Desert Fathers, named Abba Didymus, lived on raw vegetables because he didn't want to hurt any living being. He believed that every living creature was created by God and therefore worthy of respect and humane treatment. Every night he would put out dishes of water and food for the hostile creatures of the desert. Many tracks to his home were seen in the desert. When asked why he put out the food and water he explained that he found great delight in creating his own version of a peaceable kingdom in the desert.

According to Laura Hobgood-Oster, Guinefort was not the only animal counted among the saints in Christianity:

They served as the locus for revelation, as exemplars of piety, as martyrs and servants, and, in their relationships with others, they have often been the source of agape – the love of the divine. Thus the sacred history, though often obscured, suggests that animals may indeed be counted among the holy ones in the Christian tradition.[76]

Two narratives concerning saints and their relationship with animals and birds are notably unusual. The first is the *Félire na Naomh Nerennach*, the *Martyrology of Donegal*, a calendar of the saints of Ireland, which includes the legend of Mochaoi, abbot of Nendrum (n'Aondruim) in Uladh. He is sitting with several companions near a forest, cutting wattles in order to build a church, when hears the song of a bright bird, singing on the blackthorn nearby, more beautiful than any birdsong he has ever heard before. He stops his work and asks the bird who is bringing him so much pleasure. The bird tells him that he is an angel, and proceeds to sing. Mochaoi is in a trance for three hundred years, listening to the angelic birdsong. When he awakes from the trance, he notices that time has passed, for there is a stone church standing front of him. Mochaoi erects a shrine in the wood:

> and surpassingly white angels often alighted there, or sang hymns to it from the branches of the forest trees, or leaned with their feet on tiptoe, their eyes on the horizon, their ear on the ground, their wings flapping, their bodies trembling, waiting to send tidings of prayer and repentance with a beat of their wings to the King of the Everlasting.[77]

The second narrative, which is more well known, is that of St Brendan, the legendary medieval Irish abbot, monk, seafarer, poet and prophet, who sailed among several islands with his followers for seven years in search of the promised land, the *Terra Repromissionis*. In his travels he met a whale, named Jasconius, who would allow the monks to celebrate Mass upon its back each Easter, and an island with many birds, who spoke so that they could be understood by St Brendan. The *Navigatio Sancti Brendani* (Voyage of St Brendan) was composed no later than the third quarter of the eighth century,[78] and contains many elements of myth and folklore. The work is very much allegory: everything ordinary is actually extraordinary. The mystical, spiritual realm is at the forefront, while earthly reality recedes into the background. The journey time is holy or liturgical time. Stops on the four islands coincide with religious holy days (Lent, Easter, Whit Sunday and Christmas). The closest I can describe it is as being akin to First Peoples' beliefs in the intersection of the spiritual and the material worlds, of them being 'one' (or the Celtic idea of the 'thin veil' between heaven and earth).[79]

The following passage demonstrates St Brendan's sense of humour, seen in how he conceals what he knows and in his description of the whale. It is interesting to note that the whale has been named, presumably by God. They came to an island that was 'stony and without grass. There were a few pieces of drift wood on it, but no sand on its shore . . . the man of God remained sitting inside in the boat. For he knew the kind of island it was, but he did not want to tell them, lest they be terrified.' They sang Mass in the morning. The brothers then carried some raw meat from the boat back to the island and placed a pot over a fire. 'When, however, they were plying the fire with wood and the pot began to boil, the island began to be in motion like a wave.' They scrambled onto the boat and set sail, while Brendan reassured them:

> My sons, do not be afraid. God revealed to me during the night in a vision the secret of this affair. Where we were was not an island, but a fish – the foremost of all that swim in the ocean. He is always trying to bring his tail to meet his head, but he cannot because of his length. His name is Jasconius.[80]

They came to another island that was covered with birds:

> When the hour of vespers had come all the birds in the tree chanted, as it were with one voice, beating their wings on their sides: 'A hymn is due to thee, O God, in Zion, and a vow shall be paid to you in Jerusalem.'
>
> They kept repeating this versicle for about the space of an hour. To the man of God and his companions the chant and the sound of their wings seemed in its sweetness like a rhythmical song. Then Saint Brendan said to his brothers: 'Repair your bodies, for today our souls are filled with divine food.'[81]

Dragon-shaped silver-gilt ewer, German, c. 1120.

Then the Divine Service is recited and the birds respond with praise; this continues through the saying of vespers, matins, terce, sext and nones: 'In this way, day and night, the birds gave praise to the Lord.'[82]

St Brendan meets Paul the Hermit, who tells the story of how he survived after he climbed onto a rocky island:

> About three o'clock in the afternoon, an otter brought me a meal from the sea, that is, one fish in his mouth. He also brought a small bundle of firewood to make a fire, carrying it between his front paws while walking on his two hind legs. When he had put the fish and kindling in front of me he returned where he came from. I took iron, struck flint, made a fire from the kindling and made a meal for myself on the fish. Thus it was for thirty years – always every third day the same servant brought the same food, that is one fish, to do for three days. I ate a third of the fish every day.[83]

Monasteries were often situated in the countryside, surrounded by the natural world. St Benedict (c. 480–550) formed a community that tried to live in harmony with nature. The Rule of Benedict was to help shape and form one's attitude towards nature. The Rule consisted of Praise (singing the Psalms, celebrating God's gift of nature), Humility, Stewardship (caring for what belongs to another), Manual

Labour (giving an appreciation of and respect for nature) and Community (living as equals). This way of life fostered a view of creation as good and helped diminish a need to dominate it. One saw nature as part of God's glory, and therefore treated nature with respect.

From the late Middle Ages there was a greater emphasis on the individual's role in the world. Animals were no longer prominent in the picture of the Christian world. Their differing roles as messenger, companion, moral instructor and embodiment of God's love were relegated to the edges. After the turn of the sixteenth century, little is heard of saints and communities of animals. This view of kinship with other species had almost entirely disappeared by the Renaissance and the beginnings of the modern era, as scientific developments distanced humans from other animals.[84]

> The saints are exceedingly loving and gentle to mankind, and even to brute beasts ... Surely we ought to show them [animals] great kindness and gentleness for many reasons, but, above all, because they are of the same origin as ourselves. (St John Chrysostom, 345–407 CE)

Animals as Beasts of Burden: The 'Gifts' of Science and Theology

As in Judaism, Christianity places humans at the centre of things. For the most part this has meant a belief in subduing and having dominion (in the sense of 'domination') over nature. This belief has been shaken at various times, for example, in response to the theories of Copernicus (that the earth is not the centre of the universe) and Charles Darwin (that humans are not separate from the rest of creation but have in fact evolved from it, and are part of it). Christianity has a long tradition of viewing nature from a utilitarian stance, seeing all of creation for its benefit, having been given it by God. For more than five hundred years Western Christianity has been part of European colonization, and alongside European economic expansion, the Church has bolstered the destruction of land and creatures by saying that, as humans, we have dominion over all the earth, including its creatures.

Domination, or dominion, was reinforced by the concept of the Great Chain of Being, which was derived from Plato and Aristotle.

This structure was a religious hierarchy of all life and matter, believed to have been decreed by God. God is at the top of the chain, viewed as external to creation. In descending order, there are angels, demons, stars and so on, and then humans, wild animals, domestic animals, plants and earth. Humans straddle the world of the spiritual, but they also belong to the physical world. Animals are placed below humans as they are thought to have limited intelligence and to lack spiritual and moral attributes. Wild animals are above domesticated because they defy training. Domesticated animals are divided into 'useful' (horses, dogs), and 'docile' (sheep). The avian are next, with the eagle at the top. Birds are connected to the air and are thought to be superior to creatures linked to the element of water. After fish and sea creatures, insects and arachnids put in an appearance, divided into 'useful' (spiders, bees), 'pretty' (ladybirds) and 'unpleasant' (flies). At the bottom of the animal section are snakes, placed last as punishment for the serpent's action in the Garden of Eden. This set hierarchy of species came into question during the eighteenth century, owing to the radical views of thinkers such as Jean-Baptiste Lamarck and, later, Darwin. Christian theologians tended to prefer the static, less radical view, which continued to hold sway over many Christian thinkers until, by the twentieth century, scientific progress caused the idea of the Great Chain of Being to be abandoned.

A sense of needing to subdue the earth, sometimes in order to hold back that which was feared, was not the belief of all. Some early Christian writers referred to the world as a living being, as holy. This was certainly the view in Celtic Christianity, where the earth was seen as a mother. The inhabitants, human and non-human, were blessed. When carrying out their daily chores the Celts recited prayers for their animals, which often included their cattle:

> Be blessing, O God, my little cow,
> And be blessing, O God, my intent;
> O God, my partnership blessing thou,
> And my hands that to milking are sent.
>
> Be blessing, O God, each teat of four,
> Be blessing, O God, each finger's pull;
> Be blessing thou each drop that doth pour
> Until, O God, my pitcher be full![85]

Prayers for protecting animals from harm often called on the saints to aid them:

> The peace of Columba be yours in the grazing,
> The peace of Brigit be yours in the grazing,
> The peace of Mary be yours in the grazing,
> And may you return home safe-guarded.[86]

Prayers were also recited for sick animals; this was not seen as something strange or unusual, but as part of the cycle and rhythm of life. All were under the care of their Creator God:

> Come now, O Columba,
> And heal my dear white cow.
> Come now, O Columba,
> For she is water-sick . . .
>
> Columba came up to the knoll,
> And laid hands on the cow,
> And healed it in the name of God,
> Lord of eternity.[87]

The Celtic way of living within nature, and seeing God as caring for creation, did not become the norm. Part of the reason for this was due to the incarnation; Jesus had become human and was grounded in history, rather than in nature. This had been the case in Judaism as well: 'Israel learned its faith through history, and it was in history rather than in nature that Israel and also Christianity expected to find God at work.'[88] History was viewed as salvation-history; Jesus was incarnation, within history. Seeing God's acts in nature was less common, and at times it was discouraged, in case admiring nature could be seen as delving into pantheism or local pagan worship. Christians (and Jews) worshipped a God who had created nature, but did not dwell in nature.

Greeks (and Romans) at the time of the early Church tended to be polytheistic, believing there were gods who influenced all natural phenomena. History did not play a major role in the way they viewed the divine. They placed more importance on the rhythm of nature, experienced through the movement of the stars and the repetition of the seasons. They saw the divine working through these patterns and events in nature. Christians, and the early Church, lived in both cultures, Christian and pagan. Christianity did not revert to paganism, because the world was God's creation, and it relied on God for its continuing sustenance and survival.

Gradually, in the West, the gap widened between humanity and nature, as humans began to see themselves as superior to the rest of nature. Theologians, such as St Augustine, believed that humans were superior in intelligence and reason, and were like their Creator. In *The City of God*, he wrote that animals are subordinate to our needs, 'not having been endowed with reason as we are . . . hence it is by a just arrangement of the Creator that their life and death is subordinated to our needs.'[89] He was not alone in this belief. Origen (d. *c.* 254 CE) wrote: 'But that He should have provided food even for the most savage animals is not a matter of surprise, for these very animals . . . have been created for the purpose of the rational creature.'[90]

One of the lesser known Christian thinkers from the fourth century was Arnobius of Sicca, a convert from Africa. In his treatise *Adversus nationes* (Against the Pagans/Heathens) he discusses the idea of sacrifice. He has the ox argue the following:

> Did not the same nature both beget and form me from the same beginnings? Is it not one breath of life which sways both them and me? . . . They love their young, and come together to beget children; and do not I both take care to procure offspring, and delight in it when it has been begotten? But they have reason, and utter articulate sounds; and how do they know whether I do what I do for my own reasons, and whether that sound which I give forth is my kind of words, and is understood by us alone?[91]

However, at the end of the argument it is clear that Arnobius' intention is to discredit pagan practices, rather than address the topic of the place of animals in creation's hierarchy.

The Church was drawing apart from the natural world and views such as those of St Augustine, that there is no place for nature in the Kingdom of God,[92] caused this gap to widen still further. This gulf was helped along by the Latin phrase *imago Dei* (image of God), which was seen as only applicable to human beings, consisting in some part of human reason. A distinction was made between the thinking, conscious observer and the non-thinking, non-conscious nature.[93]

For more than a millennium, most Christian views of animals were derived from non-scientific sources, particularly from the philosophical views of Aristotle, and St Thomas Aquinas. According to Aristotle, only humans possess rationality, but both humans and animals have the capacity for feeling. These ideas were adapted into the scholastic tradition by Aquinas. Earlier, the Stoic view that humans have no responsibility to animals was introduced into Christian thought by St Augustine. Both Aristotle and Aquinas thought that animals did not possess mind or reason; from this premise came the conclusion that humans bore no responsibility for other animals. Aquinas held the view that animals were for human use:

> hereby is refuted the error of those who said it is sinful for a man to kill brute animals, for by the divine providence they are intended for man's use according to the order of nature. Hence it is not wrong for man to make use of them, either by killing them or in any other way whatever.[94]

These ideas were carried over into the twentieth century, with the prominent Protestant theologian Karl Barth stating that animals are a secondary responsibility for humans. While animals and plants do not 'belong' to humans, 'they are provided for his use'.[95] Because God reveals himself to humans, Barth concludes that human life therefore has higher value than that of animals.[96] These views meant that Christians placed animals low on the list of human concerns. During the Enlightenment Voltaire and Rousseau spoke of adopting compassionate views towards animals. Immanuel Kant, on the other hand, declared that animals exist for human needs. In the same year as Kant's lectures (1780), Jeremy Bentham was posing the question: Can animals suffer?

In the West, the growth of scientific knowledge led to a separation from religious knowledge, as people began to view nature as consisting of 'things'. The universe had been reduced to objects that obeyed a series of laws, such as the laws of gravity, growth and respiration. This development increased knowledge, yet it came at the expense of the spiritual. God had been reduced to the role of the 'giant watchmaker' who had set the world in operation according to unchanging rules, and was no longer involved with His creation. Creation was studied in 'parts' rather than as a whole; therefore relationships between all things were ignored. Scientific study and research became a separate discipline cut off from Christianity and its practical components of ethics and morals. Later Western theology was studied in towns and cities, rather than in rural communities, which led to a geographical separation from nature.

There was a general unease, even in the Middle Ages, that people could be dehumanized by having a close relationship with an animal; people feared they would become 'animals' themselves or 'debased'. Sometimes a close relationship between a woman and an animal, particularly a cat, would lead to accusations of witchcraft, with the animals seen as 'familiars', or demons in animal form. People were worried that these women worshipped animals and took their instructions from them. In the Middle Ages, the role of animals was ambiguous, because of their association with paganism. One writer suggests that the Middle Ages, with the continuing influence of paganism and the rise of Christianity, remained a time when animals, and stories about animals, were included within the Christian tradition.[97] Edmund Leach points out the connection between 'God' and 'dog' in English. Not only is there a linguistic inversion, but there is an actual inversion as well. In the seventeenth-century witchcraft trials in England, 'it was commonly asserted that the Devil appeared in the form of a Dog – that is, God backwards'.[98]

The cat became identified with the Devil and came to symbolize the heretic, because of its secretive nature. Alain de Lille, in the late twelfth century, defamed the cat, and his ideas that heretics conducted secret rites with cats became popular. He also asserted that the Cathars were named after the cat, 'because they kiss the hind parts of a cat in whose form . . . Lucifer appears to them'.[99] Similar accusations appear elsewhere, including a report that 'a black cat descended a rope into nighttime gatherings of heretics and offered itself for adoration – kisses on its feet, anus, and private parts.'[100] The Dominican preacher Stephen of Bourbon reported a similar story, this one concerning the foundation of the first Dominican house in southern France. Dominic had been preaching in the town of Fanjeaux, in the heart of Cathar country, when nine women approached and asked him for a sign to help them discern whether they should follow the Cathars. Dominic prayed and told the women to stand still and wait, for the Lord would show them whom they had been serving. A large mean cat with a long tongue then appeared and the beast released horrid smells. The cat, a sign of the Devil, frightened the women into orthodoxy and several of them became the first sisters at Prouille, Dominic's first religious house.[101] The ritual of cat-kissing can be seen in some Bible illustrations produced in the early thirteenth century. Examples of the *Bible moralisée*, a visual and literary commentary on the Bible, have illustrations of heretics and Jews kissing cats under the tail.[102] A pact with the Devil was sealed with a cat's paw print on the body of an accused witch. The ceremonial killing of cats continued for hundreds of years: 'Cats were burned alive on Ash Wednesday in Metz and other Continental cities during the Middle Ages to produce the ash for the Mass.'[103]

Christopher Smart's poem 'Jubilate Agno' challenges the common ideas concerning the cat and its demonic nature. The 74-line section concerning his cat, Jeoffry, presents the cat as embodying the divine, rather than the diabolic:

> For I will consider my Cat Jeoffry.
> For he is the servant of the Living God duly and daily
>   serving him.
> For at the first glance of the glory of God in the East he
>   worships in his way . . .
> For having consider'd God and himself he will consider
>   his neighbour.
> For if he meets another cat he will kiss her in kindness.
> For when he takes his prey he plays with it to give it a chance.
> For one mouse in seven escapes by his dallying.
> For when his day's work is done his business more
>   properly begins.
> For he keeps the Lord's watch in the night against
>   the adversary.
> For he counteracts the powers of darkness by his electrical skin
>   and glaring eyes.
> For he counteracts the Devil, who is death, by brisking
>   about the life . . .
> For he purrs in thankfulness, when God tells him he's
>   a good Cat.
> For he is an instrument for the children to learn
>   benevolence upon.
> For every house is incomplete without him and a blessing
>   is lacking in the spirit.

> For the Lord commanded Moses concerning the cats
>   at the departure of the
> Children of Israel from Egypt.
> For every family had one cat at least in the bag . . .
> For he knows that God is his Saviour . . .
> For I perceived God's light about him both wax and fire.
> For the Electrical fire is the spiritual substance, which God
>   sends from heaven to
> Sustain the bodies both of man and beast.
> For God has blessed him in the variety of his movements.[104]

Some artists included dogs in their artwork depicting the Last Supper; dogs tend to be present where there is food, but dogs can also symbolize those who are deemed unworthy to receive the Eucharist. A canine in the scene can represent both a physical and symbolic reminder of Scripture: 'Do not give what is holy to dogs' (Matthew 7:6). The *Didache*, an early Christian pedagogical text, echoes this sentiment, referring to the Eucharist and baptism: 'Let no one eat or drink of your Eucharist save those who have been baptized in the name of the Lord, since the Lord has said, "Do not give what is holy to the dogs".'[105] This text probably uses dogs as a metaphor for the unbaptized, or for those deemed unworthy. Though a metaphor, this association remains with the readers or listeners. Thomas Aquinas, in his liturgy for the Feast of Corpus Christi, includes these Latin lines: '*Ecce, panis, angelorum . . . non mittendus canibus*' (Behold, the bread of Angels . . . denied to dogs).[106] In the Bible, dogs are considered unworthy for admittance to heaven: 'Outside are the dogs and sorcerers and fornicators and murderers and idolaters, and everyone who loves and practices falsehood' (Revelation 22:14).

In the early 1600s a new natural history was on the rise, owing to the work of John Ray, an English biologist and ornithologist. Ray became the central figure in England's scientific revolution. This was a break away from an Aristotelian view and from uncertainty. Ray had a new vision of the natural world. He overturned the idea of people living as sinners under the watchful eye of an angry and jealous God; instead, Ray offered an alternative – a cheerful and benign God.[107] This God was responsible for all of the natural world and its beauty, and all that God had created fitted together within its environment in an intricate manner. Ray called this 'physico-theology' (later known as natural theology), a process that today is known as adaptation.[108] Physico-theology is the belief that God was responsible for the fit between an individual and the environment. Ray's life's work is laid out in his book *The Wisdom of God*, first published in 1691, which was as significant as Darwin's would be one hundred and fifty years later.[109]

Ray studied plants, then moved on to birds. His focus was on how birds fitted together in God's scheme. He came up with a definition of what constituted a species, a way of naming and arranging them that would inspire Linnaeus sixty years later to bring to the fore his classification, which we still use today.[110]

The essence of physico-theology was that God had created a perfect world, and creation was there to be decoded and interpreted. Sometimes, in creation itself, God had provided clues, such as the presence of yellow flowers on certain plants possessing the necessary properties to treat jaundice. These clues were known as the 'doctrine of signatures'.[111]

The impetus for Ray's theory arose out of a belief that René Descartes' view of animals as soulless automata that do not feel pain was wrong. Ray believed that Descartes' view was medieval in outlook and, if carried through, could lead to an elimination of certain species. Physico-theology proved extremely popular and influenced the English clergyman-naturalist tradition, epitomized by Gilbert White.[112] In the early 1700s physico-theology was embraced in Europe, particularly in the Netherlands and Germany. Physico-theology also influenced William Paley's *Natural Theology* (1802) – indeed, he plagiarized Ray's work.[113] In the end, physico-theology failed; its flaw was its inability to account for the balance of nature.

The great change in the scientific and philosophical worlds of Europe between the fifteenth and seventeenth centuries coincided with the religious turmoil of the Protestant Reformation, which began in 1517. The two great reformers that emerged from this theological watershed, Luther and Calvin, had their own observations concerning the animal world. Scott Ickert, writing about Luther's lectures on Genesis, notes that Luther viewed animals as subject to Adam's fall; just as humans lose paradise, so do animals.[114] After the Flood, human dominion changes, as animals 'are made subject to man for the purpose of serving him even to the extent of dying'; for Adam, 'it would have been an abomination to kill a little bird for food,' but Luther contends 'because the Word is added, we realize that it is an extraordinary blessing that in this way God has provided the kitchen with all kinds of meat.'[115] For Calvin, the primary purpose of animals was to guide the human to God. He saw them as 'messengers and witnesses'. Peter Huff observes that for Calvin 'the most effective form of insult was comparison with the animal world.'[116] On the other hand, in the Genevan theocracy established by Calvin,[117] citizens were to take care of their animals and were even allowed to miss attending church for that purpose.[118]

The Protestant emphasis on personal salvation meant that they generally saw themselves only in relation to God, and not as part of creation. The Puritan tradition tended to view the material world as savage and dangerous, and therefore needing to be conquered and tamed. Protestant individualism, with personal salvation, meant that the gift of creation seen in nature was overlooked. 'To a large extent, the Reformation marked the demise of animals as saints disappeared, as people removed iconography from the sanctuary, and as a new focus centered on the spoken Word (preaching) as the only true source of revelation. All of this dominated the Protestant religious worldview.'[119]

Not all Protestants viewed nature as being created for their use and abuse. The seventeenth-century metaphysical poets, such as John Donne (1572–1631), saw nature as evidence of God's glory and challenged some of the assumptions of the day:

> Why are we by all creatures waited on?
> Why do the prodigal elements supply
> Life and food to me, being more pure than I,
> Simple, and further from corruption?
> Why brook'st thou, ignorant horse, subjection?
> Why does thou bull, and boar so sillily
> Dissemble weakness, and by one man's stroke die,
> Whose whole kind, you might swallow and feed upon?
> Weaker I am, woe is me, and worse than you,
> You have not sinned, nor need be timorous.
> But wonder at a greater wonder, for to us
> Created nature doth these things subdue,
> But their Creator, whom sin, nor nature tied,
> For us, his creatures, and his foes, hath died.[120]

At the same time, many English Puritans were happy to follow the new way of thinking. In *An Antidote against Atheism* (1653), Henry More, one of the Cambridge Platonists, wrote that cattle showed God's goodness because by being alive, they kept their meat fresh and pure until humans decided it was time to eat it![121]

The Quakers, who were among the more free-thinking Protestants, saw a place for creation in the purpose of God. One of their founders, George Fox (1624–1691), had this to say:

> What wages doth the Lord desire of you for his earth that he giveth to you teachers, and great men, and to all the sons of men, and all creatures, but that you give him the praises, and the thanks, and the glory; and not that you should spend the creatures upon your lusts, but to do good with them; you that have much, to them that have little; and so to honour God with your substance; for nothing brought you into the world, nor nothing shall you take out of the world, but leave all creatures behind you as you found them.[122]

Quakers also took a lead in the campaigns against several blood sports, including bear-baiting and cockfights, although these were not banned until the passing of the Cruelty to Animals Act 1835.

Anna Sewell, the author of *Black Beauty*, was a Quaker and wrote her story to alert the general reader to the plight of the London working horse. Its popularity succeeded in getting the cruel conditions changed. Sewell wrote: 'There is no religion without love, and people may talk as much as they like about their religion, but if it does not teach them to be good and kind to other animals as well as humans, it is all a sham.'[123]

Do Animals Have Souls?

The soul, the breath of life (*nephesh*), is that which makes humans and animals animated. The popular notion of the soul in Christian theology restricts it to the immaterial aspect of humans that enables them to have communion with God and to experience salvation. This comes from Greek philosophy, where only the rational soul is immortal and only humans possess it. According to this interpretation, the non-human world lies outside the realm of God's salvific intent and outside the realm of moral obligation. The scientific revolution, with Descartes' move to view animals as machines, advanced humans to just below the divine. Humans were above the rest of creation, for humans alone were thought to possess intelligence, a soul and the ability to use words. Descartes argued that animals have mechanical souls, unlike the incorporeal souls of humans.[124] Humans' immortal, rational souls were seen as a sign of their superiority.

John Wesley, a vegetarian, thought that animals had souls. In his journal he recorded a visit to the Tower of London's menagerie on 31 December 1764 accompanied by a friend, a flautist. Wesley thought that by watching animals' reaction to music (in this case, several lions and a tiger) one could ascertain whether they possessed souls. One of the lions and the tiger reacted to the music in a playful manner.

Wesley could find no explanation for the animals' reactions, aside from the possibility that they had some kind of divine soul moving them to react as they did: 'Can we account for this by any principle of mechanism? Can we account for it at all?'[125] Wesley addressed this topic in his sermon 'The General Deliverance', published in 1781:

> What then is the barrier between men and brutes? The line which they cannot pass? It was not reason. Set aside that ambiguous term: exchange it for the plain word, understanding; and who can deny that brutes have this? We may as well deny that they have sight or hearing.[126]

It was a sign of this divinity, not merely reason or 'understanding', that Wesley was looking for in the animals' responses to music. Animals were recipients of eternal life:

> They will be restored, not only to that measure of understanding which they had in paradise, but to a degree of it as much higher than that . . . And whatever affections they had in the garden of God, will be restored with vast increase; being exalted and refined in a manner which we ourselves are not now able to comprehend . . . No rage shall be found in any creature, no fierceness, no cruelty, or thirst for blood.
>
> As there will be nothing within, so there will be nothing without, to give them any uneasiness: no heat or cold, no storm or tempest, but one perennial spring. In the new earth, as well

as the new heavens, there will be nothing to give pain, but everything that the wisdom and goodness of God can create to give happiness. As a recompense for what they once suffered, while under the 'bondage of corruption', when God has 'renewed the face of the earth', and their corruptible body has put on incorruption, they shall enjoy happiness suited to their state, without alloy, without interruption, and without end.[127]

Yet Wesley does not perceive animals to be on the same footing as human beings:

But though I doubt not that the Father of All has a tender regard for even his lowest creatures, and that, in consequence of this, he will make them large amends for all they suffer while under their present bondage; yet I dare not affirm that he has an equal regard for them and for the children of men ... God regards his meanest creatures much; but he regards man much more.[128]

It is important to note that while some Protestants maintained their interpretation of Genesis to mean that divine permission had been given to exploit or subdue the world, others saw any use of animals beyond the necessities of life (food, clothing) as a form of blasphemy, for all God's creatures had been entrusted to humans for safe keeping. In 1824 Rev. Arthur Broome, an Anglican clergyman, was a key figure in setting up the Society for the Prevention of Cruelty to Animals and he based its formation on Christian principles. Some of the abolitionists, including William Wilberforce, added their voice and support to animal welfare issues.

In more modern times, Christian writers have emphasized our kinship with animals, calling for Christians to honour all subjects in God's creation.[129] One theologian who helped pave the way was Albert Schweitzer (1875–1965), who adapted the Jain ethic of ahimsa (non-violence), as 'Reverence for Life', for a Christian audience. In 1952 Schweitzer was awarded the Nobel Peace Prize for the practical implementation of this ethic. He thought that Western civilization was decaying because it had abandoned reverence for life as its ethical foundation. While he acknowledged that Jainism was the first to expand ethics from concern for humans to concern for all living beings,

Schweitzer's philosophy of 'Reverence for Life' was deeply embedded in Christian theology:

> A man is truly ethical only when he obeys the compulsion to help all life which he is able to assist, and shrinks from injuring anything that lives . . . He is not afraid of being laughed at as sentimental. It is the fate of every truth to be a subject for laughter until it is generally recognized . . . The time is coming, however, when people will be astonished that mankind needed so long a time to learn to regard thoughtless injury to life as incompatible with ethics.[130]

Schweitzer's plea for an end to cruelty is used in much modern-day animal activist literature:

> While so much ill-treatment of animals goes on, while the moans of thirsty animals in railway trucks sound unheard, while so much brutality prevails in our slaughter-houses, while animals have to suffer in our kitchens painful death from unskilled hands, while animals have to endure intolerable treatment from heartless men, or are left to the cruel play of children, we all share the guilt.[131]

As a boy, Schweitzer composed a prayer that he recited every night: 'Dear God, protect and bless all living beings. Keep them from evil and let them sleep in peace.' He later wrote: 'From childhood, I felt a compassion for animals. Even before I started school, I found it impossible to understand why, in my evening prayers, I should pray only for human beings.'[132]

Unlike in Judaism, in mainstream Christianity there are no dietary restrictions, but there have been Christians who believed that God ordained a vegetarian diet for humans. Refraining from eating meat was crucial to William Cowherd (1763–1816), who founded the Bible Christian Church in Salford, west of Manchester, in 1809. His tiny chapel, nicknamed the Beefsteak Chapel, was England's first vegetarian church and was the British birthplace of the meat-free diet. Cowherd is credited with being the main figure advocating the theory of vegetarianism at the time. One of the philosophical forerunners of the Vegetarian Society (founded in 1847), he encouraged his followers, known as 'Cowherdites', to abstain from eating meat. Cowherd taught his congregation that it was a sin to eat meat, because God inhabited every animal: 'If God had meant us to eat meat, then it would have come to us in edible form as is the ripened fruit.'[133] He also wrote vegetarian hymns for his congregation:

> 'Eaters of flesh!' could you decry,
> Our food and sacred laws,
> Did you behold the lambkin die,
> And feel yourself the cause?[134]

Forty-one members of the Bible Christian Church later emigrated across the Atlantic, setting up a branch in Philadelphia and spreading their ideas.

Most Seventh Day Adventists follow a vegetarian diet. This is not due to a sense of compassion for animals, but because of what they interpret to be the original and ideal diet found in Genesis 1:29. Seventh Day Adventists state that the Bible does not condemn the eating of clean animals, but God's original diet, the diet for humans, did not include meat. In this diet, flesh foods are not included because it is thought that God did not envision the taking of any animal's life and because a balanced vegetarian diet is viewed as the best for health.

Sadly it was God's incarnation as a human, and not as an animal, combined with scientific ideas developed during the Enlightenment, alongside Protestantism's focus on the individual, that relegated animals to be viewed as mere objects, rather than subjects. This greatly contrasted with the medieval tradition exemplified by the German mystic Meister Eckhart (c. 1260–c. 1328):

> Apprehend God in all things,
> For God is in all things.
> Every single creature is full of God,
> And is a book about God.
> Every creature is a word of God.
> If I spent enough time with the tiniest creature –
> Even a caterpillar –
> I would never have to prepare a sermon
> So full of God
> Is every creature.[135]

Animals feature in ecclesiastical writings, mainly in the form of bestiaries. The bestiary designates a corpus of animal lore that derives from the *Physiologus*, which was compiled in Greek during the second century CE and then translated into Armenian, Syrian and other languages; a Latin translation was certainly in circulation by the early sixth century. The *Physiologus* was an attempt to redefine the natural world within a Christian framework. Material was gathered from a range of sources, including Aristotle, Pliny and Lucan. By the thirteenth century its original 39 chapters had expanded fourfold to include new species. Bestiaries tended to be a mixture of zoology and Christian moralizing, combining both fact and a great deal of fantasy, but during their day they were viewed as the natural history texts of the time. Bestiaries are an insight into the medieval world. These works, which examine animals, birds and reptiles, as well as mythical or magical beasts, were not written in order to describe the natural world, or indeed to critique it, but to draw on the natural world as instruction on the religious and moral aspects of human lives. The writers knew that their Creator had a purpose for everything: the natural world was there to remind humans of their sinful nature and to lead them back to the way of redemption.[136] Each creature, if read correctly, could be a sign to the path of salvation. The bestiaries had three aspects: a description (of natural lore), a moral meaning and the mystical significance of each creature, as reflected in Holy Scripture.[137] One example is that of the pigeon: its twin offspring were seen to represent the love of God, and the love of one's neighbour.[138]

Although there were magical beasts in the bestiaries, the majority were species that could be encountered in daily life, so that their messages, such as the bees displaying the virtues of humility and industry, might be easily understood:

> The dove is a simple bird, free of gall, which looks lovingly at its mate. In the same way, preachers are free from rage and bitterness, because although they may be angry, it cannot be called rage when they are angry with good reason. The dove sighs rather than sings; and so the preachers not caring for love-songs, sigh for their own sins and those of others. The dove does not mangle things with its beak: again, this applies to the preachers, who do not falsify the Holy Scriptures as the heretics do. The dove chooses its grain, plucking out the best, just as

preachers choose the best sentences from the Scriptures. It brings up the chicks of other birds: the preachers nourish the children of this world who are estranged from God by their sins, and bring them again to Christ. The bird sits near running water so that if it sees a hawk it can dive in and escape. In the same way the preachers have the Holy Scriptures close at hand, so that, seeing the devil attacking them with temptations, they can immerse themselves in the actions prescribed by Scripture and thus escape. The dove uses its wings to defend itself: and the preachers strengthen their defences with the words of the fathers. It nests in holes in the rock, just as preachers take refuge in their belief in the wounds of Christ, of which it is said: 'The rock moreover was Jesus.' They make a nest and a defence there for themselves and others. The dove can also recover from blindness: the preachers of the Holy Church, if some gift of the Holy Spirit has been lost through a person's sin, recover it just as David recovered the gift of prophecy which he had lost. It flies in flocks, just as the preachers who believe in the faith gather in flocks and follow good works. For such good works as we do are steps towards God.[139]

Animals were also used in other forms of literature, usually in negative portrayals. By the late twelfth century animals were included in a number of types of anti-heretical literature. Europe at that time was consumed by the beginnings of popular heresy and the use of animals in literature became a means by which authors preached and wrote against it. Animals and their behaviour became a way to symbolize dissident Christians and their conduct. A number of commentaries on Scripture linked certain creatures with heretics, including wolves, foxes, cats, dogs, leopards, jackals and moths.[140] Hildegard of Bingen (1098–1179) selected an animal to represent each of the five eras in her visionary *Book of Divine Works*. The fifth era, represented by the grey wolf, would herald persecution against Christians by the wolf-like Antichrist, who would follow the heretics who helped pave the way in the fourth era, which was represented by the black pig.[141]

Henry of Albano (also Henry de Marcy, d. 1188) who was abbot of the Cistercian abbey at Clairvaux from 1176 to 1179, used foxes, wolves, moles and moths to symbolize the heretic and the heretic's nature and intentions. The moth is seen to have destructive tendencies,

Early 13th-century French gilt-copper Eucharistic dove.

gnawing away at orthodoxy. Moths appear in a number of places in the Bible to represent various sins, including greed and lust.[142] This identification of moths with heresy did not originate with Henry of Albano, but can be found in Christian exegetic writings as early as the fourth century. Moths destroy clothing, in the same way that heretics destroy the Word of God.[143] Once certain animals became identified with evil and therefore viewed as diabolical, it wasn't long before they, particularly cats, were persecuted alongside heretics.

Churches are filled with illustrations or images of animals. Sax comments that 'Most religious institutions have made an uneasy accommodation with zoolatry. Our churches are filled with sacred images of animals.'[144] Many Christian symbols are of animals. Three of the Evangelists are represented by animals: St Matthew (lion), St Luke (ox), and St John (eagle). The Holy Spirit, one of the persons of the Trinity, is represented by a dove. Sax reminds us that 'The Father, Son and Holy Spirit correspond respectively to natural force, human being and animal – three aspects of nearly every pagan deity.'[145]

Early theologians found the four Evangelists corresponded with or were associated with the four living creatures surrounding God's throne in Ezekiel 1:4–11, 10:1 and 10:14–15.[146] John the Divine's

The four beasts for the Four Evangelists, on the portal of the Church of St Trophime, Arles.

vision of heaven in Revelation 4:6–8 includes all creation around the throne of God:

> Around the throne, and on each side of the throne, are four living creatures, full of eyes in front and behind: the first living creature like a lion, the second living creature like an ox, the third living creature with a face like a human face, and the fourth living creature like a flying eagle. And the four living creatures, each of them with six wings, are full of eyes all around and inside. Day and night without ceasing they sing, 'Holy, holy, holy, the Lord God the Almighty; who was and is and is to come.'

The Latter Prophets had foretold a time when animals and humans would exist in harmony and peace. In Revelation the vision includes both humans and animals partaking in the afterlife, which scholars were quick to dispute. Around one hundred years after John's vision, the first official refusal came from Irenaeus, bishop of Lyons from about 177 CE, who stated that these animals were not symbols of animal creation; rather, they were human beings in disguise: the

Evangelists, Matthew, Mark, Luke and John.[147] Despite scholars continuing to deny that the presence of animals in heaven is portrayed in Revelation, some think otherwise. Four kinds of God's creatures are represented in heaven: 'the heads of animate creation; the lion of wild beasts, the ox of tame beasts, the eagle of birds, the man of all (mankind)'.[148]

When the four Evangelists are painted with the bodies of human beings and the heads of animals, references to Egyptian mythology can be made. St John, as eagle, is like archaic pictures of Toth, the Egyptian god of learning, who is often shown with the head of an ibis. Both Toth and St John are often depicted holding writing implements in their hands.[149]

Parted: The Afterlife – Soul Bearers and Sharers in Another Existence

And for these also, O Lord, the humble beasts, who bear with us the heat and burden of the day, we beg you to extend your great kindness of heart, for you promised to save both humans and beasts, and great is your loving kindness.[150]

Do animals have an afterlife? Martin Luther was once asked by a child whether her dog would be allowed into heaven. Luther gently patted the dog's head and replied: 'Be thou comforted, little dog, Thou too in the Resurrection shall have a little golden tail.' Was this a theological view or just a pastoral utterance? I have already mentioned John Wesley's view. Joseph Victor Widmann (1842–1911) addressed the redemption of animals in his verse play *Der Heilige und die Tiere* (The Holy One and the Animals, 1905). Jesus asks the angels: 'Tell me, does my Father's vast habitation, arrayed with shining mansions, not contain a single peaceful retreat where the least of all animals can take refuge after earthly sufferings?'[151] The angels have no answer, for 'the last things are hidden from us too.' When Jesus departs from the suffering animals, he says:

> I too could not find the power to solve so immense a problem. So live and die as best you can. Now I must follow other paths. At least I was permitted to learn from you. You good,

unassuming creatures have taught me one thing: how to be true to oneself and to bleed even though innocent.[152]

C. S. Lewis thought that there was animal resurrection, but only for tame animals:

> The error we must avoid is that of considering them in themselves. Man is to be understood only in his relation to God. The beasts are to be understood only in their relation to man and, through man, to God . . . Now it will be seen that, in so far as the tame animal has a real self or personality, it owes this almost entirely to its master. If a good sheepdog seems 'almost human' that is because a good shepherd has made it so . . . you must not think of a beast by itself, and call that a personality and then inquire whether God will raise and bless that. You must take the whole context in which the beast acquires its selfhood – namely 'The-goodman-and-the-goodwife-ruling-their-children-and-their-beasts-in-the-good-homestead.' That whole context may be regarded as a 'body' in the Pauline (or a closely sub-Pauline) sense; and how much of that 'body' may be raised along with the goodman and the goodwife, who can predict? . . . And in this way it seems to me possible that certain animals may have an immortality, not in themselves, but in the immortality of their masters . . . My picture of the good sheepdog in the good homestead does not, of course, cover wild animals nor (a matter even more urgent) ill-treated domestic animals.[153]

Evelyn Underhill, in a letter to Lewis, challenges him on this matter:

> Is the cow which we have turned into a milk machine or the hen we have turned into an egg machine really nearer the mind of God than its wild ancestors? This seems like saying that the black slave is the only natural negro. You surely can't mean that, or think that the robin red breast in a cage doesn't put heaven in a rage . . . And if we ever get a sideway glimpse of the animal-in-itself, the animal existing for God's glory & pleasure & lit by His light (& what a lovely experience that is!), we don't owe it to the Pekinese, the Persian cat or the canary, but

to some wild free creature living in completeness of adjustment to Nature, a life that is utterly independent of man . . . Of course I agree that animals too are involved in the Fall & await redemption and transfiguration . . . And man is no doubt offered the chance of being the mediator of that redemption. But not by taming, surely? Rather by loving and reverencing the creatures enough to leave them free . . . I feel your concept of God would be improved by just a touch of wildness.[154]

While some Christians argue that animals possess souls and will, as a result, obtain eternal life, others disagree.

A similar split occurs over the significance of the Blessing of the Animals services held on 4 October, the feast day of St Francis of Assisi, or on the nearest Sunday; the secular world has also adopted this date as World Animal Day. Services that used to be held in Catholic churches belonging to the Franciscan order are now conducted in many Protestant churches in the West, as well as adapted for use within inter-faith gatherings. In some communities a different date is set aside: 17 January, the feast day of St Anthony.

The Blessing of the Animals dates back to an ancient Roman celebration of a pre-spring fertility festival to honour the goddesses Ceres and Terra, during which a pregnant animal was sacrificed and garlanded oxen were paraded by the crowds. Traces of this Roman festival lingered on into the eighth century, when the work animals were given a symbolic 'day off', while their owners sought the Church's divine protection for their work animals (so they could perform the work needed, rather than out of any fondness or love).

Conclusion

The way Christianity has viewed, and still views, animals is mixed. There is a negative tradition, due in large part to Descartes, in which theologians state that animals have no rational souls, mind or sentience, and are thereby reduced to mere instruments or commodities, slaves for the sole use of humans. On the other hand, there are positives as well: animals will be beneficiaries of the Messianic Age; animals are acknowledged as part of the environment; they have been blessed, within the Celtic tradition and today in special church services. Stories, especially in the non-canonical texts, tell of Jesus' compassion for animals. Due to the incarnation, God becoming human, the notion of human superiority has dominated Christian theology, but surely the incarnation can be seen as an act that embraces and includes all of creation: God's redemptive act is not for humans alone. Perhaps one of the major problems is the way that good and evil has been portrayed, at least in the past. Certain animals, or parts thereof, have long been associated with the demonic:

> While the Christian tradition represents God and the angels anthropomorphically, except for their wings, it gives the devils, identified with old animal deities, bestial features. Satan is traditionally shown with a tail, horns, and pointed ears. Often, he will have the teeth of a large carnivore, tusks of a boar, and perhaps a cloven hoof. The demon Beelzebub is known as the 'Lord of the Flies' and is often pictured as an enormous insect. Representations of the Christian Hell traditionally reverse accustomed roles and hierarchies, as animals are shown herding, cooking, and eating human beings.[155]

Within the Christian tradition animals have never been worshipped. Partly out of fear of being linked with pagan practices, this reservation has at times kept animals at a distance and diminished the goodness of all God's creation:

> For many Christians, a first step will be to dwell in the presence of animals already in their midst. It will begin, not with theology, but with touch: flesh-upon-flesh, as enlivened by the Spirit. For a religion that celebrates enfleshment, supremely realized in incarnation, salvation by touch is an appropriate beginning.[156]

In *The Three Languages*, a fairy tale collected by the Brothers Grimm, the son of a count is sent away to learn wisdom. He returns having learned the languages of the dog, the frog and the birds, much to the disgust of his father. He is sent into exile and uses his newly acquired knowledge to find treasure. One day he sets off to Rome with his wife, a lord's daughter:

On their way thither, they passed a swamp, where the frogs sat croaking. The young Count listened, and when he heard what they said, he became quite thoughtful and sad, but he did not tell his wife the reason. At last they arrived at Rome, and found the Pope was just dead, and there was a great contention among the Cardinals as to who should be his successor. They at length resolved that he on whom some miraculous sign should be shown should be elected. Just as they had thus resolved, at the same moment the young Count stepped into the church, and suddenly two snow-white doves flew down, one on each of his shoulders, and remained perched there. The clergy recognised in this circumstance the sign they required, and asked him on the spot whether he would be Pope. The young Count was undecided, and knew not whether he were worthy; but the Doves whispered to him that he might take the honour, so he consented. Then he was anointed and consecrated; and so was fulfilled what the Frogs had prophesied – and which had so disturbed him, – that he should become the Pope. Upon his election he had to sing a mass, of which he knew nothing; but the two Doves sitting upon his shoulder told him all that he required.[157]

David Guss suggests that the young count was chosen as the new pope to fulfil the role of being a 'bridge' between the human-dominated world and the animal realm.[158] Surely the Christian is called to 'bridge' the two worlds, recognizing that both have been created by a loving God, and both mirror particular qualities or attributes of their Creator.

SIX
Animals in Islam

There is not a creature on the earth but God provides its sustenance. He knows its dwelling and its resting place. All is recorded in a glorious book.

(Qur'an 11:6)

He laid the earth for His creatures, with all its fruits and blossom-bearing palm, chaff-covered grain and scented herbs.

(Qur'an 55:10)

All the beasts that roam the earth and all the birds that soar on high are but communities like your own.

(Qur'an 6:38)

Brethren or Beasts of Burden?

ISLAM IS A MONOTHEISTIC RELIGION, as are Judaism and Christianity. Muslims believe that Islam is not a new religion, but a continuation of all the previous monotheistic religions that came before it.[1] There is a tripartite relationship between Judaism, Christianity and Islam.

Islam does not believe in a pantheon of gods and its creation story does not involve animals assisting in helping birth humans, or showing or giving them keys to civilization, such as the gift of fire, because all has been created by Allah. While acknowledging the absence of pivotal roles for animals in creation, there is still much in Islam that concerns animals, including the respect to be shown to all of Allah's creation. Each creature is made for itself and in order to praise its Creator. There is no unified Islamic view of non-human animals, and Islam does not make a distinction between politics and religion; therefore attitudes and behaviour in one area affect other areas also.

Islam ('submission') as an ideal is understood by believers as the state God wills for His creation (*khalq*).[2] Animals are mentioned in Islam in varying degrees. When dealing with non-human animals, three sources are called upon for guidance and direction: the Qur'an (revealed scripture), the Hadith (reports about the words and deeds of the Prophet Muhammad) and the sharia (*shari'a*, Islamic law), which consists of a comprehensive code of life set out in the legal texts of the Classical period (eighth to tenth centuries CE).

The Qur'an

Islamic tradition is rich indeed with references to animals and for the need to respect all of God's/Allah's creation. In the Qur'an animals and insects are mentioned and accorded dignity. Unlike in the majority of Islamic literature and within popular culture, where animals are seen as provision for humans, in the Qur'an animals are viewed as having value of their own.

In the Qur'an everything that God has created submits to His will. Everything has been created as God wished it to be; therefore everything in creation works properly and creation is sacred. Muhammad said: 'The whole of this earth is a mosque; that is, a place of worship.' Everything that God has created praises God, for everything has been created like a faithful Muslim: 'All that is in the heavens and the earth gives glory to God, the Sovereign Lord, the Holy One, the Almighty, the Wise One' (Qur'an 62:1).

The Islamic religion is governed by the Qur'an, so it is important to establish what the Qur'an states about non-human animals. Opening the Qur'an, and looking at its table of contents, one notes that of the 114 suras (chapters), six are named after animals: The Cow (sura 2), The Cattle (sura 6), The Bee (sura 16), The Ant (sura 28), The Spider (sura 29) and The Elephant (sura 105). Apart from these names, other non-human animals are mentioned as well, including camels, mosquitoes, horses, mules, donkeys, sheep, monkeys, dogs, pigs and worms. First and foremost, the Qur'an states that all animals were created by God:

> He raised the heavens without visible pillars, and set firm mountains on the earth lest it shake with you. He dispersed upon it all manner of beasts. (Qur'an 31:9–10)

> Among His signs is the creation of the heavens and the earth and the living things He has dispersed over them. If He will, He can gather them all together. (Qur'an 42:29)

> [He] who has created all living things in pairs and made for you the ships and beasts on which you ride, so that, as you mount upon their backs, you may recall the goodness of your Lord. (Qur'an 43:11)

Unlike in Genesis, all species (including humans) have been created by water: 'God created every beast from water. Some creep upon their bellies, others walk on two legs, and others yet on four. God creates what He pleases. God has power over all things' (Qur'an 24:44–5).

All animals are viewed as belonging to a community: 'All the beasts that roam the earth and all the birds that soar on high are but communities like your own' (Qur'an 6:38). These communities operate in their own right. They are not in a hierarchy, comparable with human values. Even those considered to be dangerous, or insignificant, are to be treated as communities. It is about recognizing their *intrinsic* value, not about their usefulness:

> Abū Hurayrah reported the Prophet as telling of an incident that happened to another prophet in the past. This prophet was stung by an ant and, in anger, he ordered the whole of the ant's nest to be burned. At this God reprimanded this prophet in these words: 'because one ant stung you, you have burned a whole community which glorified Me.'[3]

The Qur'an and that particular Hadith remind us that ants are as much a community as the human community, loved and created by God. Every creature on earth has a share in the earth's natural resources, and is to be respected as belonging to God and to its particular and unique community. The Iranian-American philosopher Seyyed Hossein Nasr, referring to the Qur'anic verses that state that 'all creation praises

Jonah and the Whale, mentioned in the Qur'an 37:139. From the *Compendium of Chronicles* (*Jāmi 'al-tawārīkh*) by Rashid al-Din Hamadani, c. 1400.

God,'[4] notes that 'In destroying a species, we are in reality silencing a whole class of God's worshippers.'[5]

In the Qur'an, language and rationality are ascribed to some species: 'It is noteworthy that in the brief utterances made by the two non-human animals that speak in the Qur'an, the hoopoe and ant, these animals emerge as rational and wise beings.'[6] Animals have an awareness of their Creator, and pay homage to their Creator by adoration and worship: 'Do you not see how God is praised by those in the heavens and those on earth? The very birds praise Him as they wing their way. He notes the prayers and praises of all His creatures; God has knowledge of all their actions' (Qur'an 24:41).

In the Qur'an animals are noted as having the ability to pray, yet to pray involves qualities greater than instinct; to pray gives credence to something or someone mightier than oneself, usually accompanied by a sense of awe. In the Qur'an it is acknowledged that it is hard for many humans to understand that this ability exists in other animals: 'The seven heavens, the earth, and all who dwell in them give glory to Him. All creatures celebrate His praises. You cannot understand their praises' (Qur'an 17:44).

God also communicates with His creation: 'Your Lord inspired the bee, saying: "Make your homes in the mountains, in the trees, and in the hives which men shall build for you"' (Qur'an 16:68). The

Qur'an uses the same Arabic word *wahy* for God's revelation to his prophets, and here, in the case of the bee.[7] Animals are thought to understand their Creator's messages.

One of the pivotal points in Islam is that all non-human animals are viewed as believers, or 'Muslim': 'none yet approaches the inclusiveness of the Islamic tradition which states that unlike humans, *all* non-human animals are believers.'[8] Animals, as believers, are therefore spiritual in nature; they glorify, praise and worship God: 'To God bow all creatures of the heavens and the earth, and the angels too. They are not disdainful; they fear their Lord on high and do as they are bidden' (Qur'an 16:49). Sarra Tlili categorizes their acts of devotion in this way: 'The Qur'an . . . ascribes to non-human animals in particular several types of devotional acts, including prayer (*salat*), glorification of (*tasbh*) and prostration (*sujud*) to God.'[9]

Having stated an affirming and quite radical view of the spiritual nature of non-human animals, it is important to note that the Islamic view of the world is a hierarchical one, in which the human community occupies a higher rank, a special and privileged status, above those of all other animal communities: 'Do you not see how God has subdued for you all that is in the earth?' (Qur'an 22:65). Islam describes humans as the *khalifah*, which means that the human is the vice-regent of God/Allah on earth, and has the duty and responsibility of looking after the earth. The term the Qur'an applies to humans is defined by contemporary Muslims as 'vice-regent' (Qur'an 2:30 and 6:165),[10] which implies caretaker, or steward, rather than exploiter. But this vice-regency is not unconditional. If humans fail to conform, they are reduced to the lowest of the low, to certain categories of animals, which is interesting after earlier observations: 'Those whom God has cursed and with whom He has been angry, transforming them into apes and swine' (Qur'an 5:60); and 'they are like cattle, nay, even less cognizant of what is right' (Qur'an 7:179).[11]

According to Masri, superiority of the human is only because of their special spiritual volition, called in the Qur'an, *taqwa*. But this does not mean that humans cannot learn from animals. Imam Ali, cousin and son-in-law of the Prophet Muhammad, said: 'Be like a bee; anything it eats is clean, anything it drops is sweet and any branch it sits upon does not break.'[12] We might view the Islamic stance as anthropocentric, though Muslims would prefer to see their worldview as theocentric, placing God in the centre, with all creation surrounding him.

Finally, the Qur'an invites us to remember that the earth was not created for humans, but for every living being. All are interconnected as signs to worship their Creator: 'Here is God's she-camel: a sign for you' (Qur'an 7:73).

Hadiths

Hadiths (or Ahadith, plural of Hadith) are reports about the words and deeds of the Prophet Muhammad and are universally accepted by Muslims as interpretations of the Qur'an. There are six major compilations of the Hadith and above the Hadith compilers are the scholar jurists who created four schools of law. In Sunni Islam, the Hadiths are known by the name of the scholar-jurist who originated them: Al-Shafi'i, Abu Hanifa, Ahmad ibn Hanbal and Malik ibn Anas. Shi'ite Hadith collections differ from those used by Sunnis, because Shi'ite Hadiths also contain reports of Muhammad's successors, the Twelve Imams, which makes their collection of Hadiths more extensive and more diverse, because many Imams lived and travelled outside Arabia. Sufis (who can be Sunni or Shi'ite) also defer to the authority of their spiritual guides (sheikhs, or Pirs).

There are some differences, one being that in Shi'ite Hadith accounts, Muhammad and the Imams are portrayed as being able to converse with animals.[13] Occasionally there are accounts in the Sunni Hadiths as well, but these are rare. In Shi'ite Hadiths, Muhammad is often reported as talking with camels, birds and other species, listening to their complaints and responding with compassion:

> One day the Holy Prophet (Peace be Upon Him) was sitting somewhere when a camel came up and kneeled down beside him, and began to lament, complaining to the Holy Prophet (Peace be Upon Him) in its own language. The Holy Prophet (Peace be Upon Him) asked, 'Who is the owner of this camel?' He was told that such-and-such was the camel's owner. The Holy Prophet (Peace be Upon Him) said, 'Bring him to me.' So the camel's owner came to the Holy Prophet (Peace be Upon Him). His Excellency told him, 'Your camel said, "I've been working at their service, but now they want to kill me."'
>
> The camel's owner explained, 'O Messenger of God, we have the knife ready and wish to sacrifice him.' The Holy

Prophet (Peace be Upon Him) replied, 'For my sake, spare him and don't sacrifice him.' The camel's owner immediately offered him to the Holy Prophet (Peace be Upon Him), who set the camel free. The camel then went round to the homes of the Ansar [literally the 'helpers' of Medina], who fed him his fill, saying, 'This must be the camel which the Messenger of God (Peace be Upon Him) set free.' And in this way the camel was looked after and cared for.[14]

In another Hadith, the fourth Shi'ite Iman, Zayn al-'Abidin (658–713) shows compassion to a hungry deer:

The Archangel Gabriel meeting a shepherd, from a 16th-century manuscript of the *Siyer-i Nebi* (Life of the Prophet, c. 1388) by al-Darir.

One day His Excellency Imam Sajjad (Zayn al-'Abidin), Peace be Upon Him, had gone to a garden accompanied by some friends. The food arrived and His Excellency ordered it to be spread out. No sooner had the group begun to eat, than a deer came up alongside Imam Sajjad, Peace be Upon Him, and began conversing with the Imam. The group asked His Excellency what the deer had spoken to him about. His Excellency replied that the deer had complained to him of hunger, saying it was three days since he had eaten.

Then, Imam Sajjad, Peace be Upon Him, told the group, 'Don't do anything to this deer; because I would like to invite him to eat with us.' The group all gave their word not to bother or molest the deer, and to allow it to eat freely until it was full.

Imam Sajjad, Peace be Upon Him, motioned to the deer and invited it to eat. The animal then came and began eating. At this time one man from the group got up and grabbed the deer around the waist; because of this, the deer took fright and ran away from the group. Imam Sajjad, Peace be Upon Him, turned to the group and said, 'Didn't you promise me you were going to leave this deer alone?' The man who had put his arm around the deer and was the cause of its fleeing swore that he hadn't meant any harm and didn't intend to frighten the deer.

His Excellency Imam Sajjad, Peace be Upon Him, then spoke to the deer and invited it once again to come and eat, and promised the deer that there was nothing to be afraid of and that nobody from the group would bother it. So the deer returned once again and began eating until it had had its fill. Once it was full, the deer spoke to Imam Sajjad, Peace be Upon Him, in its own language, and then left the group.

The group asked His Excellency Imam Sajjad, Peace be Upon Him, what the deer had said to him. His Excellency Imam Sajjad, Peace be Upon Him, replied, 'This deer has prayed for your well-being.'[15]

In another Hadith, a pregnant lioness asks Imam Musa al-Kazim to pray for an easy delivery for her. The Imam does so, and in return the lioness prays for the Imam, and for 'his children, his partisans (shi'ites) and his friends'.[16]

Richard Foltz makes the observation that the Shi'ite accounts are quite striking, in that Muhammad and/or the community converse with animals (humans are able to communicate in animal languages), animals pray and their prayers are respected. In Shi'ite Hadiths animals pray for humans and can incite God's wrath against humans who are not compassionate. In one Hadith, attributed to the eighth Imam, Ali al-Ridha (also spelled Ali Reza), he warned his followers to respect the lark and not to eat it, because 'this species of bird prays repeatedly to God to curse the enemies of the Prophet's family.'[17]

There are many legends about Muslim saints and other holy men being able to converse with animals. This is also mentioned in the Qur'an: 'Solomon succeeded David. He said: "Know, you people, we have been taught the tongue of birds"' (Quran 27:16). The Turkish Sufi master Bediüzzaman Said Nursi (1877–1960) was known to be a great animal lover. He claimed to understand animal languages:

> One day I looked at the cats; all they were doing was eating, playing, and sleeping. I wondered, how is it these little monsters which perform no duties are known as blessed? Later, I lay down to sleep for the night. I looked; one of the cats had come. It lay against my pillow and put its mouth against my ear, and murmuring: 'O Most Compassionate One! O Most Compassionate One!' in the most clear manner, as though refuting in the name of the species the objection and insult which had occurred to me, throwing it in my face. Then this occurred to me:
>
> I wonder if this recitation is particular to this cat, or is it general among cats? And is it only an unfair objector like me who hears it, or if anyone listens carefully, can they hear it? The next morning I listened to the other cats; it was not so clear, but to varying degrees they were repeating the same invocation. At first, 'O Most Compassionate!' was discernible following their purring. Then gradually their purrings and meowings became the same 'O Most Merciful!' It became an unarticulated, eloquent and sorrowful recitation. They would close their mouths and utter a fine 'O Most Compassionate!' I related the story to the brothers who visited me, and they listened carefully as well, and said that they heard it to an extent.[18]

Many Hadiths deal with Muhammad's teachings or reactions to non-human animals, such as in the following example:

> A man was walking on a road when he became very thirsty. He found a well and went into it and drank and came out. There was a dog panting and eating earth out of thirst. The man said, 'This dog has become as thirsty as I was.' He went down into the well and filled his shoe and then held it to his mouth until he climbed out and gave the dog water to drink. Allah thanked him for it and forgave him [for his sins].
>
> They said, 'Messenger of Allah, do we have a reward for taking care of beasts?' He said, 'There is a reward for [compassion shown to] everyone with a moist liver [this is, for every living thing].'[19]

Muhammad went to some lengths to instruct his followers on proper care of and respect for animals. Animals in service, for example, should only be used when necessary, and only for the purpose for which they are meant:

> The Prophet once saw a man sitting on the back of his camel in a market place, addressing people. He said to him: 'do not use the backs of your beasts as pulpits, for God has made them subject to you so that they may take you to places you could not otherwise reach without fatigue of body.'[20]

Muhammad is said to have praised the rooster, for its crowing signals the time for morning prayer, and elsewhere the crowing itself is seen as prayer.[21]

Sharia: Animals in Islamic Law

On the basis of God's guidance in the Qur'an, Muslim legal scholars have defined the ultimate objective of sharia as the universal common good of all created beings, both in this life and in the afterlife. Working for the good of all creation is the only way that one can truly serve Allah/God.

Islamic law consists of a comprehensive code of life set out in the legal texts of the classical period (eighth to tenth centuries). As in other religions, many animal welfare issues did not exist when the religion was forming, so there were no specific laws passed to deal with them, but in Islam there are general principles or guidelines. The two overriding principles are that people should not be overburdened by restrictions, and that anything not specifically forbidden is lawful. It is assumed that animals are going to be eaten and used for other purposes, so laws address the type of animal that may be consumed, the proper methods of slaughter and the responsibilities humans have to them. The ethical question regarding whether humans have the right to eat and/or use animals does not arise in the sharia.[22]

The actual practices and attitudes of Muslims have always been shaped by Islamic sources in combination with non-universal sources, such as Islamic cultural ones. Arabs in pre-Islamic times practised animal cults, various meat taboos and possibly totemism. Some tribes took on animal names, such as the Assad ('lion') and the Quraysh ('shark'), which was the tribe of the Prophet Muhammad.[23] Certain animals were believed to carry blessings (camels, horse, bees and others), while others were associated with evil (cats and dogs). Genies (*djinn* or jinn) were thought at times to take on animal forms.[24] These examples from Islamic culture have influenced and continue to influence how animals are viewed in Islam.

Within these sources and popular traditions, non-human animals appear to be regarded in terms of the value they pose for humans, or for the lessons that humans can derive from them. During the Abbasid caliphate, a great jurist was asked why flies were created. He replied: 'In my humble opinion the purpose is to show those in power their own helplessness.'[25]

According to the overall spirit and teaching of Islam, pain and suffering inflicted on innocent creatures is not justifiable. In pre-Islamic times, some cruel polytheistic and pagan practices were undertaken against animals. All such practices were condemned and stopped by Islamic influence.[26] Disfiguration of an animal was forbidden: 'The Prophet said: "Do not clip the forelock of a horse, for a decency is attached to its forelock; nor its mane, for it protects it; nor its tail, for it is its fly trap."'[27]

This Hadith is concerned with disfigurement and unnecessary pain because of branding on a sensitive part of the body: 'Jābir told that God's Messenger forbade striking the face or branding on the face of animals.' The same Sahabah, or companion of the Prophet, reported that when an ass that had been branded on the face passed by him, he exclaimed, 'God curse the one who branded it.'[28]

Another practice that was condemned was that of cutting off camels' humps and the fat tails of sheep. Muhammad had observed these practices when he moved from Mecca to Medina. One of the reasons for this barbaric practice was that this was performed on live animals, so that the animal could be used later. To prevent this practice, Muhammad declared: 'whatever is cut off an animal while it is still alive, is carrion and is unlawful (*haram*) to eat.'[29]

To make sure no injury was inflicted on a live animal, other prohibitions were brought in to ensure that the animal had died first. It was forbidden to break an animal's neck, skin the animal or slice off any of its limbs until the body was completely cold, to ensure that the animal was dead. There seems to be an equality of treatment between humans and animals, as noted in this Hadith: 'A good deed done to a beast is as good as doing good to a human being; while an act of cruelty to a beast is as bad as an act of cruelty to a human being.'[30]

One Hadith tells of Muhammad being reprimanded by God for neglecting his horse: 'The Prophet was seen wiping the face of his horse with his gown. When asked why he was doing that, he replied: "Last night I had a reprimand from Allah regarding my horse for having neglected him."'[31] If people did not provide for animals, they risked divine retribution. In the Qur'anic story of the tribe of Thamud, the tribe, supposedly the descendants of Noah, demanded that the prophet Sālih show them a sign to prove that he was a prophet of God. At the time, there was a food shortage, so livestock were being neglected. Sālih singled out a she-camel, as a symbol, and asked the people of the tribe to give her a fair share of food and water. The people agreed, but later they killed the camel. The tribe was annihilated as divine retribution.[32] This incident is mentioned in the Qur'an in different contexts.[33]

Emotional care of animals was also important. Once Muhammad reprimanded his wife for treating a camel offhandedly, telling her to treat the camel more gently. There are other instances of emotional trauma:

> We were on a journey with the Apostle of God and he left us for a while. During his absence, we saw a bird called *hummarah* with its two young and took the young ones. The mother-bird

was circling above us in the air, beating its wings in grief, when the Prophet came back and said: 'who has hurt the *feelings* of this bird by taking its young? Return them to her.'[34]

According to the teachings of the Qur'an, a man cannot milk an animal at a time that is wrong for it, or in a way that would damage the young, for the milk belongs to the young. Before a Muslim goes to milk his cows, he must cut his nails so that he does not hurt the cow when he milks her. Protection of an animal includes the emotional: one is forbidden to curse an animal.

When travelling, animals' needs are to be considered. Muhammad would say: 'When you journey through a verdant land [go slow to] let your camels graze. When you pass through an arid area, quicken your pace [lest hunger should enfeeble the animals]. Do not pitch your tents for the night on the beaten tracks, for they are the pathways of nocturnal creatures.'[35]

A Caravan of pilgrims in Ramleh, from a 13th-century manuscript of the *Maqamat al-Hariri* of al-Hariri of Basra (Muhammad al-Hariri, 1054–1122).

The saying of daily prayers is one of the five most important obligations of the Muslim religion.[36] In the following Hadith, one of Muhammad's Sahabah says that Muhammad and his travellers would even delay reciting prayers until they had given food to their animals: 'When we stopped at a halt, we did not say our prayers until we had taken the burden off our camels' backs and attended to their needs.'[37]

God has placed upon humans certain obligations towards other living creatures; there is both divine reward and divine punishment for the way animals have been treated: 'The Prophet told his Companions of a woman who would be sent to Hell for having locked up a cat; not feeding it, nor even releasing it so that it could feed itself.'[38] According to Shu'ab al-Imam: 'All creatures are like a family (*ayal*) of God: and He loves the most those who are the most beneficent to His family.'[39] A Hadith from the *Mishkat al-Masabih* states that: 'There is no Muslim who plants a tree or sows a field, and a human, bird or animal eats from it, but it shall be reckoned as charity from him.'[40]

Dietary Rules

How does respect for animals translate into dietary rules and dietary norms? Meat is allowed in the Muslim diet. The majority of Muslims consume meat; indeed it is mentioned in the Qur'an as one of God's gifts to humans, and as one of the delights of heaven:

> He created the beasts which give you warmth and food and other benefits. How pleasant they look when you bring them home to rest and when you lead them out to pasture! They carry your burdens to far-off lands, which you could not otherwise reach except with painful toil. Compassionate is your Lord, and merciful. He has given you horses, mules, and donkeys, which you may ride or put on show; and He has created other things beyond your knowledge. (Qur'an 16:5–8)

> In cattle too you have a worthy lesson. We give you to drink of that which is in their bellies, between the bowels and the blood streams: pure milk, pleasant for those who drink it. (Qur'an 16:66)

> It is God who has provided you with beasts, that you may ride on some and eat the flesh of others. You put them to many uses; they take you where you wish to go, carrying you by land as ships carry you by sea. (Qur'an 40:79–80)

> They shall recline on jewelled couches . . . with fruits of their own choice and flesh of fowls that they relish. (Qur'an 56:21)

Scriptures of both Judaism and Islam allow the consumption of meat, but the moral philosophy underlying this covenant between God and themselves is not the same. In Genesis 1:29–30 a vegetarian diet is set out as the ideal; in Islam, eating meat is considered a neutral choice. The Qur'an does stipulate that one should eat in moderation: 'Eat and drink, but avoid excess. He does not love the intemperate' (Qur'an 7:31).

There are different laws for the rearing and breeding of animals, and care of them before and after slaughter. These requirements must be carried out in order for the flesh to be regarded as lawful and pure (*halal* and *tayyib* – 'clean, good, wholesome'). In both Islam and Judaism, God's name is invoked before slaughter, and both religions prescribe a method of slaughter that allows blood to drain out. In terms of ritual observance when carrying out sacrificial slaughter, the only conditions are the invocation of the name of God, and the use of a sharp knife. This is the same for normal slaughter for food. Slaughter is to be performed as painlessly as possible, and emotional as well as physical aspects are to be considered. Physical and emotional care includes allowing animals to have access to food and water before slaughter, and to prevent them having to await death. 'The Holy Prophet said to a man who was sharpening his knife in the presence of the animal: "Do you intend inflicting death on the animal twice – once by sharpening the knife within its sight, and once by cutting its throat?"'[41]

Ritual slaughter, or *dhabihah*, is said to follow the principle of compassion for the animal being slaughtered. In one Hadith:

> Shaddid ibn Aws said: Two are the things which I remember Allah's Messenger (may peace be upon him) having said: 'Verily Allah has enjoined goodness to everything; so when you kill, kill in a good way and when you slaughter, slaughter in a good way. So every one of you should sharpen his knife, and let the slaughtered animal die comfortably.'[42]

Although ritual sacrifice is not proscribed as a duty in the Qur'an, the following Hadith is sometimes quoted, with that connotation attached to it:

> He who can afford (sacrifice) but he does not offer it, he should not come near our places of worship. On the day of sacrifice no one does a deed more pleasing to Allah than the shedding of blood of a sacrificed animal who will come on the Day of Resurrection with its horns, its hair, its hoofs, and will make the scales of its action heavy, and verily its blood reaches acceptance of Allah before it falls upon the ground; therefore be joyful for sacrificing animals.[43]

In Islam, laws in all schools regarding animals as food classify animals in terms of whether eating them is *halal* (permissible), *haram* (forbidden) or *makruh* (discouraged). All schools place the majority of animals in the halal category. The underlying principle appears to be that animals are to be killed in order to be eaten (and only what is needed to satisfy one's hunger) or if necessary to protect oneself from danger. Animals that can be eaten include cud-chewing animals (ruminants) such as cattle, sheep, goats, camels, buffaloes and wild ruminants, fish and most birds.

Certain foods are prohibited: these include pigs, amphibians, all carnivores, animals that are zoologically similar to humans (such as monkeys and apes), most reptiles, and animals that feed on carrion (scavengers). The killing of some animals is forbidden by certain Hadiths: Muslims are never to kill hoopoes, magpies, frogs, ants or bees. Muhammad forbade the killing of frogs because it was thought that their croaking was their way of praising Allah. Magpies were not to be killed, as it was believed that they were the first to perform the fast.[44] Muslims are forbidden to kill while in a state of ritual purity (on pilgrimage, or in prayer).[45]

> Forbidden to you is that which dies of itself; blood; flesh of swine; that on which any name other than that of Allah has been invoked; the strangled animals; that beaten to death; that killed by a fall; that gorged to death with the horn; that [parts of] which wild beasts have eaten – except those which you [are able to] slaughter; that which is sacrificed on stones set up [as

idols]; and that on which you draw lots by arrows. This day I have perfected your religion for you . . . However, if one is compelled by hunger – not inclining wilfully to sin – then surely Allah is Forgiving, Merciful (Qur'an 5:3).[46]

A careful analysis of this verse shows that the prohibited food falls into four categories: carrion, blood, pork and animals killed for idolatrous purposes. These prohibitions are based on two considerations: physical welfare and metaphysical welfare. Pork, blood or the flesh of animals that are dead for any reason before being cleansed of blood are seen as being physically unhealthy, or unhygienic to consume. Animals sacrificed to idols are considered dangerous to spiritual health. There is a reference in this passage from the Qur'an to stone altars on which sacrifices used to be offered to deities and idols by pagans. 'Draw lots by arrows' refers to the pagan practice of portioning out the sacrificial meat by shooting arrows at them.[47] This verse was revealed to Muhammad several months before he died, and is his final word on the Qur'anic dietary laws.[48]

Two exceptions to these prohibitions are included in the Qur'an. When on pilgrimage, for example, 'It is lawful for you to eat the flesh of all beasts other than that which is hereby announced to you. Game is forbidden while you are on pilgrimage' (Qur'an 5:1). Special mention is made of food deemed 'unclean' and food offered to idols: 'I find nothing in what has been revealed to me that forbids people to eat of any food except carrion, running blood and the flesh of swine – for these are unclean – and any flesh that has been profanely consecrated to gods other than God' (Qur'an 6:145). And all restrictions are lifted in circumstances of genuine need and distress: 'But whoever is driven by necessity, intending neither to sin nor to transgress, will find that God is forgiving and merciful' (Qur'an 16:115).[49]

It is interesting to note that it is permitted to eat all injured animals, provided they are alive enough to be bled: 'You are forbidden the flesh of strangled animals and of those beaten or gored to death; of those killed by a fall or mangled by beasts of prey (unless you make it clean by giving the death-stroke yourselves)' (Qur'an 5:3). This Qur'anic ruling is quite different from the Jewish objection to any injury or blemish to an animal before slaughter. It is based on the Islamic view of the utility value of all food, yet food obtained by any illegal or unethical means, such as subjecting animals to cruelties in their breeding, transport, slaughter or general welfare, cannot be regarded as *tayyib*, 'good, pure, wholesome', both in the physical and the moral sense. *Tayyib* is not limited to physical cleanliness; there is a moral dimension, too, that states that food is not *tayyib* if it has been obtained by illegal, unethical or cruel means.

In Islam, blood is only a symbol of life because it supplies nutrients to the body; it does not possess sacred significance. It is only important in that it keeps the body alive. Islam's prohibition of blood is due to reasons of hygiene, not to mysterious or sacred qualities.[50]

In order for meat to be termed halal, two laws have to be followed: the first deals with the method of slaughter and the cleaning of the carcass (*dhabihah* and *tadhkiyah* respectively), the second concerns the invocation of God's name at the time of slaughter. Two phrases are uttered: the Basmala (or Bismillah), '*bismillah ir-Rahman ir-Rahim*', meaning 'in the name of God, the Most Gracious, the Most Merciful'; and the Takbir, '*Allahu akbar*', meaning 'God is [the] Greatest'. No other prayer or supplication is required for halal slaughter: '*bismillah Allahu akbar*' is the only utterance needed.[51]

This invocation is much more than mere ritual: it reminds the slaughterer of the sanctity of all life, of the fact that he has to ask God's permission in order to take this life, and that the slaughter is to be performed in a spirit of thankfulness and humility. It appears that Islamic law places greater emphasis on the invocation of the Takbir than on the method of slaughter (*dhabihah*): 'He (Allah) has forbidden you . . . the flesh of that animal over which any name other than that of Allah has been invoked' (Qur'an 2:173).

Unlike Judaism, Islam allows Muslims to obtain their food by hunting: 'All wholesome things are lawful for you, as well as that which you have taught the birds and beasts of prey to catch, training them as God has taught you. Eat of what they catch for you, pronouncing upon it the name of God' (Qur'an 5:4). The flesh of game hunted for food is lawful (halal) if the Takbir has been pronounced before shooting, or before setting the dogs or birds of prey after the animal, even though the animal dies before the hunter has had a chance to kill it. One can only hunt for basic necessities of life. There are numerous Hadiths forbidding the hunting of animals for uses other than for food. It appears from the Hadiths that wild animals should be left alone, except if they threaten or endanger a human. If they are killed this should be done in the correct manner, mentioning the name of the Creator.

There are Hadiths forbidding blood sports and the use of animals as targets, for example: 'Ibn 'Umar happened to pass by a party of men who had tied up a hen and were shooting arrows at it. When they saw Ibn 'Umar coming, they scampered off. Ibn 'Umar angrily remarked: "Who has done this? Verily! Allah's Messenger has invoked a curse upon one who does this kind of thing."'[52] Muhammad's words prohibiting blood sports were repeated many times, which shows that he took the matter seriously. It was also forbidden (*haram*) to consume the body of an animal that had been used as a target for shooting, or who had died in a fight.

Animals needed to be killed for their furs and skins, because these were necessities for survival, but these skins and furs were obtained from domestic animals, which had either been killed to provide food or had died a natural death. Wild animals were not to be killed just for their skins, for it was seen as a waste to leave their bodies to rot: 'The Holy Prophet Muhammad prohibited the use of skins of wild animals.'[53]

Animal Sacrifice

Islam is a continuation of all the previous monotheistic religions, so Islam's links with animal sacrifice should be considered in the light of this religious background. Abraham's sacrifice is the basic source of the Islamic concept of sacrifice. According to Muslims, this story serves as a prohibition of human sacrifices. At the annual 'Festival of the Sacrifice', Eid al-Adah, animals are sacrificed for distribution among the poor. Muhammad was once asked by his Companions why animal sacrifice was still allowed in Islam; he replied: 'This is a commemorative tradition (Sunnah) of your patriarch Abraham.'[54]

The tradition of animal sacrifice in Islam is based on several verses in the Qur'an, including the following:

> Exhort all people to make the pilgrimage . . . they will come to avail themselves of many a benefit, and to pronounce on the appointed days the name of God over the cattle which He has given them for food. Eat of their flesh, and feed the poor and the unfortunate. (Qur'an 22:28)

> Pronounce over them the name of God as you draw them up in line and slaughter them; and when they have fallen to the

ground eat of their flesh and feed the uncomplaining beggar and the demanding suppliant. Thus have We subjected them to your service, so that you may give thanks. (Qur'an 22:36)

Their flesh and blood does not reach God; it is your piety that reaches Him. Thus has He subjected them to your service, so that you may give glory to God for guiding you. (Qur'an 22:37)

According to Masri: 'Muslims generally believe that the above verses lay down a canonical law to offer animal sacrifices during the festival of pilgrimage and that replacement of animals with any other kind of offering would be wrong.'[55]

There are three occasions when sacrifice is permitted: towards the end of Hajj or pilgrimage (this sacrifice is primarily for the poor); on the birth of a child; and when one is offered as an act of generosity in pure and simple charity (*sadaqah*). It is important to note that animal sacrifice is not an end in itself: it is a means to serve the less fortunate. All the verses mention that the meat is to be given to the poor. In some cases, the one offering the sacrifice is allowed to keep a portion of the meat; in other instances all of the animal is to be given to the needy. Sacrifice is to be an act of benevolence (*ihsan*). If any of the sacrifice goes to waste, that is viewed as a sinful act and a violation of sharia, for it would appear as being ungrateful to God, and a misuse of God's creation.

The original purpose of offering gifts at the sacred house (Kaaba, at Mecca) was to care for the ancient Makkans, who were the descendants of Abraham, and in response to Abraham's prayer in the Qur'an: 'Lord, I have settled some of my offspring in a barren valley near Your Sacred House, so that they may observe true worship, Lord. Put in people's hearts kindness towards them, and provide them with the earth's fruits, so that they may give thanks' (Qur'an 14:37). Food would have been appreciated, as the area was arid desert. The Qur'an does mention animal sacrifice to expiate certain offences committed during the Hajj, but it also mentions alternative offerings and acts of devotion, such as fasting.

There are two kinds of wildlife preserves in Islamic Law; the first is *hima*, a protected area or sanctuary, the second is the *harīm*, green areas around the sacred cities of Mecca and Medina where hunting is outlawed. According to the Hadiths, Muhammad declared Mecca 'sacred by virtue of the sanctity conferred on it by God until the day of resurrection. Its thorn trees shall not be cut down, its game shall not be disturbed.'[56] Medina was a sanctuary whose 'trees shall not be cut down and its game shall not be hunted'.[57] The precincts of Mecca are declared an animal and bird sanctuary during the period of pilgrimage. Various reasons have been suggested for this prohibition of hunting. One reason is that there is enough meat for all to eat during this time, so extra meat would be wasted, which would be a violation of Islamic law.

We have already noted the prohibition on hunting while on pilgrimage: 'kill no game while on pilgrimage. He that kills game by design shall present, as an offering to the Ka'bah, an animal equivalent to the one he killed' (Qur'an 5:95). 'But you are forbidden the game of the land while you are on pilgrimage' (Qur'an 5:96). Perhaps the reason is more to do with God than with the protection of the animals for their own sake. The penalty to be paid for transgressing this law against hunting was to pay the equivalent in one's own domestic livestock.[58] Atonement by substituting one animal for another cannot be seen as an act for the animals themselves, rather it is about God's creation. This ruling is not about preserving and protecting wildlife in its own right (the individual), but about God's creation (the collective).

Animal Rights

In Islam, animals are to be treated with respect, and without cruelty. Insects may be killed for food if they are edible, but it is forbidden to kill them for no just reason. Even if pests are killed, there is a greater reward for killing them with the first blow than with the second.[59]

It is a distinctive characteristic of Islamic law that all animals have legal rights. The Muslim legal scholar 'Izz al-Din ibn 'Abd al-Salam (c. 1181–1262), in his *Qawa'id al-ahkam fi masalih al-anam* (Rules for Judgement in the Cases of Living Beings), wrote the following about Islam's obligation to animals, based on stories and sayings of the Prophet:

> *The rights of livestock and animals upon man:*
> These are that he spend on them the provision that their kinds require, even if they have aged or sickened such that no benefit comes from them; that he not burden them beyond what they can bear; that he not put them together with anything by which they would be injured, whether of their own kind or other species, whether by breaking their bones or butting or wounding; that he slaughter them with kindness; that when he slaughters them he neither flay their skins nor break their bones until their bodies have become cold and their lives have passed away; that he not slaughter their young within their sight but that he isolate them; that he make comfortable their resting places and watering places; that he put their males and females together during their mating seasons; that he not discard those which he takes as game; and neither shoot them with anything that breaks their bones nor bring about their destruction by any means that renders their meat unlawful to eat.[60]

The legal category of water rights extends to animals through the law of 'the right of thirst' (*haqq al-shurb*). This law has its basis in the Qur'anic verse: 'This is God's own she-camel. Let her drink' (Qur'an 91:13).[61]

It needs to be said, however, that although the rights of non-human animals are guaranteed in the legal tradition of Islam, their interests are subordinate to those of humans. Ibn 'Abd al-Salam writes: 'The unbeliever who prohibits the slaughtering of an animal [for no reason but] to achieve the interest of the animal is incorrect because in so doing he gives preference to a lower, *khasis*, animal over a higher, *nafis*, animal.'[62]

The Syrian poet Al-Ma'arri (973–1057), who became a vegan late in life, was accused by a leading theologian of the time of 'trying to be more compassionate than God'.[63] An early Sufi, Zaynab, was persecuted for her refusal to eat meat.[64]

Early Islamic philosophy (*falsafa*, a loanword from the Greek *philosophia*) of the eighth and ninth centuries was heavily influenced by Hellenistic tradition, following the Aristotelian view of the Great Chain of Being, with each stage being more developed than the previous one. This hierarchy corresponds to that found in the Qur'an.[65]

The Case of the Animals versus Man before the King of the Jinn is a fascinating work written in the late tenth century by a group of anonymous authors known as the Brethren of Purity (Ikhwan al-Safa), a group of radical Muslim philosophers from the Iraqi city of Basra. This is their best-known work and has been described as 'the most extensive critique of mainstream human attitudes towards animals in the entire vast corpus of Muslim literature'.[66] Within the work there is underlying tension between Islam and the influence of Neoplatonism. This is evident in the arguments concerning hierarchy of species; Neoplatonism draws on the Great Chain of Being, where there is a set order, a hierarchy of all creatures. The tension here is with Islam's monotheism, where God creates at will and has full control over his creation.

The text begins by narrating how humans were once small in number, whereas the wild beasts were many. Gradually the human population grew and enslaved the animals. But some of the animals escaped to a lush island. A group of travellers were shipwrecked on the island, which was governed by a righteous king, a Muslim jinni. The animals and birds had lived in harmony until the arrival of the human travellers, who, upon seeing the island and its bounty, which included the island's animal inhabitants, wished to have it for themselves. The story consists of representatives from the animal kingdom bringing a case against the human race, whom they accuse of abusing their superior position. They state that before humans were created they had lived in peace and harmony:

> We were fully occupied in caring for our broods and rearing our young with all the good food and water God had allotted us, secure and unmolested in our own lands. Night and day we praised and sanctified God, and God alone.
>
> Ages passed and God created Adam, father of mankind, and made him his vice-regent on earth. His offspring reproduced, and his seed multiplied. They spread over the earth – land and sea, mountain and plain. Men encroached on our ancestral lands. They captured sheep, cows, horses, mules, and asses from among us and enslaved them, subjecting them to the exhausting toil and drudgery of hauling, being ridden, plowing, drawing water, and turning mills. They forced us to these things under duress, with beatings, bludgeonings, and every kind of torture and chastisement our whole lives long. Some of us fled to deserts, wastelands, or mountaintops, but the Adamites pressed

after us, hunting us with every kind of wile and device. Whoever fell into their hands was yoked, haltered, and fettered. They slaughtered and flayed him, ripped open his belly, cut off his limbs and broke his bones, tore out his eyes; plucked his feathers or sheared off his hair or fleece, and put him onto the fire to be cooked, or on the spit to be roasted, or subjected him to even more dire tortures, whose full extent is beyond description. Despite these cruelties, these sons of Adam are not through with us but must claim that this is their inviolable right, that they are our masters and we are their slaves, deeming any of us who escape a fugitive, rebel, shirker of duty – all with no proof or explanation beyond sheer force.[67]

The animals refute the humans' claim to a rightfully deserved superior status founded on species membership. This cut to the core of prevalent anthropocentric views of the time. As the trial proceeds, the humans present arguments about their uniqueness; the animals provide their own examples. In the next stage of the trial, humans highlight the negative characteristics of particular animals, with the maligned species speaking up in their own defence. The parrot, upon hearing the humans' claim of possessing superior linguistic skills, argues:

You mentioned that you have poets, orators, theologians, and such. But if you could follow the discourse of the birds . . ., the anthems of the swarming creatures, the hymns of the crawling creatures, the hosannas of the beasts, the meditative murmur of the cricket, entreaty of the frog, admonitions of the bulbul, homilies of the larks, the sand grouse's lauds and the cranes celebration, the cock's call to worship, the poetry doves utter in their cooing and the soothsaying ravens in their croaking, what the swallows describe and the hoopoe reports . . . you would know, O human race, you would realize that among these throngs are orators and eloquent speakers, theologians, preachers, admonishers, and diviners, just as there are among the sons of Adam.[68]

The parrot continues his argument, drawing on quotes from the Qur'an:

There's ample argument and proof of what I say in God's words in the Qur'an: 'There is not a thing that does not praise and exalt Him, but you understand not their praises.' God calls you dim and benighted when he says *you understand not*. He connects us with insight, good sense, and awareness when He says 'Each knows His worship and praise.'[69]

The bee is quick to point out that non-human animals constantly worship God and possess rationality, for they are able to manage and order their own affairs and interests. Thus, the assumption that humans are the only articulate species is a misconception, due to humans' inability to decipher the languages of the animals.

The humans point out their perfect form and the irregularities of the animals' bodies: the big ears of the small rabbit, the tiny eyes of the massive elephant. The animals respond, stating that humans have missed the beauty and wisdom inherent in the animals, created by a wise Creator who alone knew the purpose and reason for the forms given to them.[70] The animals have been able to argue that beauty is relative to function; each species has been created with this in mind, echoing the Qur'an 20:52: 'Our Lord . . . is He that gave all creatures their distinctive form and then rightly guided them.'

The humans move on to the issue of property, explaining that as masters of the animals, they water them, shelter them, protect them. The animals respond by questioning the compassion of humans: where is the compassion seen when the animals are brutally beaten, when they have to carry heavy loads, when kids and lambs are separated from their mothers? They argue that these actions are in direct contradiction of the Qur'anic injunction to 'show compassion and indulgence'.[71]

The humans, concerned that they may lose the case, wonder whether they should bribe the judges. They are concerned that they cannot do without animals. They resolve to accept the judgement to improve the conditions of the animals that they have enslaved, to 'lighten their load, and show more kindness and compassion toward them, for they are flesh and blood like us, and they feel and suffer. We have no superiority to them in the eyes of God for which He was rewarding us when He made them subject to us,' admitting that the subjugation of animals to humans was not due to human superiority in the eyes of God, but instead a signal of God's grace towards humans.[72]

Another striking argument is that concerning spirituality: one human states that humans are superior, because humans have been ennobled with prophecy, divine laws and prayer. The nightingale points out that these measures are needed for humans who forget God's goodness, or dispute God's lordship. Animals, on the other hand, 'are free of all these things, for we acknowledge our Lord, believe in Him, submit to Him and proclaim His unity without doubt or hesitation'.[73]

The animals elect a representative from each group to present their case to the King of the Jinn.[74] Here, even the Prophet Muhammad's ruling about killing poisonous snakes is challenged. The snake, representing the category of 'crawling things', makes the case that poisonous snakes have been created in order to keep down the numbers of predators, as well as to provide poison, which can be utilized for medicinal purposes.[75]

The writers recognize that every species has an assigned place and each knows its proper place, with the exception of humans. It has sometimes been claimed that this work foreshadowed Darwinism,[76] yet the Brethren were operating out of a creationist model, not an evolutionary one. The animals occupy special roles, solely because they are created by God and this is God's purpose for them. For the Ikhwan, human beings are not viewed as being part of the animal world, which is at odds with the majority of medieval Arabic works. They treat humans as a separate class with its own subdivisions, whereas the animals are seen as one unit, or group.

In the book, the animals are seen as subjects in their own right until the final pages, when the King of the Jinn decides in favour of the humans, basing his judgement on the notion that only humans can obtain eternal life. The ruling seems to be in conflict with the writings of the Qur'an, especially 6:38: 'Before their Lord they shall be gathered all.'[77] What is more disturbing is that the animals agree with the verdict: 'They, surprisingly, readily admit that they have no share in the blessings of the hereafter, but this is not pure loss, because lack of resurrection also shields them from the torture of hell.'[78]

The pleading of the case comes to an end. The King of the Jinn delivers his judgement: 'All the animals were to be subject to the commands and prohibitions of the humans and were to be subservient to the humans and accept their direction contentedly and return in peace and security under God's protection.'[79] Perhaps the purpose of the text is fulfilled when the humans realize their responsibility towards God's creatures.

If the goal of the work had been to assert the uniqueness of the human, then why are the arguments of the animals so convincing? Foltz suggests one reason: 'is the reader's frustration meant to be turned against God, for having established the hierarchy of creation on the basis of such unfair and arbitrary principles?'[80]

Within this work, the Ikhwan draw on animals as seen in the Qur'an. The work views animals as 'signs'; signs point to God: 'Do they never reflect on the camels, and how they were created?' (Qur'an 88:17). The diversity of creation is an awe-inspiring aspect of God's creation. The king is amazed; the Jinni philosopher comments thus:

> Your majesty is amazed at them, and I am amazed at the wisdom of the Creator who formed and fashioned them, raised and reared them, who gave them being and preserves and provides for them still, who knows their every lair and refuge. All this, writ plain in His Book, with nothing left out or forgotten, but each detail clear and precise.[81]

This is echoed in the Qur'an 11:6: 'There is not a creature on the earth but God provides its sustenance. He knows its dwelling and its resting place. All is recorded in a glorious book.'

The Ikhwan give voice to the animal characters in a way that is more in line with the Qur'an than with fables. This story is not allegorical, with animals taking on human functions; it is, like the verses in which they are addressed in the Qur'an, taking account of their own concerns as well as highlighting several human failings, including insensitivity and lack of piety. Indeed, the Qur'an is cited more than two hundred times, being the main source drawn on (supplemented at times from the Hadith).[82]

At the close, it is important to note that the Ikhwan needed to adhere to their principle of hierarchy, so the outcome had to be consistent with their Neoplatonistic philosophy. The Brethren of Purity were never accepted by the mainstream of Islamic thought, because they were seen as too radical. Only the heterodox Isma'ili Shi'ite sect adopted their writings as authoritative.[83]

Other Works Featuring Animals

Muslim scientists composed many important works on zoology. Al-Jahiz (Abu 'Uthman 'Amr ibn Bahr al-Kinani al-Basri (776–c. 869) is one of the most famous figures in Arabic literature. His incomplete seven-volume *Kitab al-Hayawan* (Book of Animals) is a comprehensive zoological catalogue, yet its priority is to demonstrate the magnificence of God through a study of his creation. Al-Jahiz's classification of animals is derived mainly from the Qur'an. He divides animals into three broad categories: 'walking animals', which include humans, noncarnivorous quadrupeds (*bahima, baha'im*) and those that are carnivorous (*siba'*); 'flying things' (*tayr*), which include insects and birds; and 'crawling things' (*hasharat*), which include non-flying insects, snakes and so on. According to Al-Jahiz, all animals are miraculous signs from God, and able to help humans in their spiritual life:

> the animal that one thinks the least useful of all may turn out to be, perhaps, the most useful, if not in terms of the life below then to that of the life to come . . . Therefore, if you notice that an animal is uninterested in providing any service to humans, inapt and unwilling to render any aid or assistance, or even very much a pest . . . know that their usefulness resides in the fact that they constitute a test, a difficulty, which God Almighty – may He be exalted and glorified – has prepared precisely to test the endurance and patience of humans . . . The reflective man will perceive the purpose to which is served the creation of the scorpion, and what value the Divine Work has placed in that of the snake. May he not despise, therefore, the mosquito, the butterfly, nor ants and flies. Pause to reflect . . . you will surely be filled with praise for the Almighty for having created flying insects, crawling things, and animals with fangs and venom; just as you will praise Him for having created the nourishments of the earth, the waters, and the air.[84]

Al-Jahiz also notes examples of animals being better equipped at performing certain tasks than humans, yet he accepts the Qur'anic interpretation that humans are above animals in the cosmic hierarchy, owing to their capacity for reason.

Buraq, on whose back Muhammad ascended to heaven,
from a 17th-century Indian album painting.

Al-Damiri's (Kamal al-Din Muhammad ibn Musa al-Damiri, 1344–1405) most famous work was *Hayat al-Hayawan* (The Lives of Animals). In this work there are references to mythical creatures, including to the Buraq, a horse-like creature who, according to Muslim folklore, served as Muhammad's mount on his miraculous night journey to heaven.[85] This text remained a standard reference book up to modern times.

At the beginning of the tenth century, when the Persian language superseded Arabic as the language used for Muslim literature throughout the Islamic East, new animals, including the mythical bird, the simorgh (simurgh), were introduced to a wider audience.[86] In *Tutinama* (Tales of a Parrot), compiled in the fourteenth century by Ziya al-Din Nakhshabi, a Persian speaker of Central Asian origin, we hear of a parrot who can recite the Qur'an. In reply to the merchant's disbelief, the parrot says:

> Though I may be a handful of feathers, because of the extent of my knowledge, I triumph over all. Theologians are amazed at my eloquence, and men of great wisdom are astonished at my ability in debating. I am not a messenger of God though I am wearing green [the colour of the Prophet]. I am not a *houri* [heavenly maiden] with a cloak over my shoulder. I am

Buraq ascending to heaven with Muhammad, from the 12th-century *Khamsa* (Five Poems) of Nizami Ganjavi, *c.* 1540.

not a zealot, but I can travel as a devout servant of God. I am religious, but I have wings. I am not a king, but I am worthy of a high position. I am not a scribe, but I am eloquent. Praise be to God, I am an excellent speaker.[87]

In another story in the *Tutinama*, Moses saves a pigeon from an eagle. Moses offers his own flesh in exchange for the life of the pigeon. The birds reveal their true identities: they are the angels Michael and Gabriel and they have come to test his generosity.[88]

On the ninth night, the parrot tells a tale about King Solomon, who according to the Qur'an could converse with animals – a common thread through the Abrahamic faiths. King Solomon was wondering whether he should drink the elixir of life, so he consulted all the animals for their opinions. The porcupine did not come, so King Solomon sent the horse to request the porcupine's presence. The porcupine still did not come. King Solomon sent the dog, and the porcupine then showed up. This perplexed the king: why did the porcupine refuse the noble horse, but come for the lowly dog? The porcupine answered:

O King Solomon, a man like you looks at appearances. It is a pity that your judgment rests on external traits. We thank God that our decisions are supported by inner qualities. What do you see besides the visible beauty of the horse? You should consider his inner callousness for there is no hope of finding loyalty in him. He always wants to throw his master off his back and thinks of tricks to escape from his stable. On the other hand when a piece of bread or a fragment of bone is given to a dog by anyone, even if he sees him a thousand times a day, he will wag his tail and show affection for him. It must be because of this quality in him that he is mentioned in the story of the Companions of the Cave [Qur'an 18:22] . . . A soiled appearance may conceal a gentle heart but a sordid heart cannot be seen from the outside.[89]

Sufism: A Mystical Interpretation of 'Communities'

It is important to consider the mystical dimension of Islam, which is Sufism. Its central doctrine is that of Divine Unity. A Sufi is a lover of Truth, of the perfection of the Absolute. Does Islamic mysticism view animals differently from other Islamic schools? In Islamic mysticism animals are sometimes used to emphasize exemplary faith in their Creator. One of the most well-known Sufi poets is Rumi (Jalal ad-Din Muhammad Rumi, 1207–1273), the founder of the Sufi Mevlevi Order (the 'Whirling Dervishes'). Rumi's poems speak of the spiritual aspects of Sufism, while remaining true to Islamic orthodoxy. Rumi's genius is recorded in two great bodies of literature: the *Divan-e Shams-e Tabrizi* (The Works of Sams Tabrizi) and the six volumes of the *Masnavi* (*Mathnawi al-ma'nawi*, sometimes referred to as the Persian Qur'an). Images of animals are used frequently in Rumi's stories and poems to reflect spiritual truths. These stories and parables include 'The Grocer and the Parrot', 'The Lion and the Beasts', 'Camels on the Roof' and 'The Gazelle in the Donkey Stable', as well as perhaps Rumi's most famous story, 'The Elephant in the Dark House'. In Rumi's *Masnavi* we read the following, in which he highlights the exemplary faith of animals:

> The dove on the tree is uttering thanks to
> God, though her food is not yet ready.
> The nightingale is singing glory to God,
> Saying, 'I rely on Thee for my daily
> Bread, O Thou who answerest prayer.
> You may take every animal from the gnat
> To the elephant: they have all become
> God's dependents.'[90]

'The Elephant in the Dark House' appears in the third book of the *Masnavi*. An elephant was being kept in a dark house. Many went to see the creature, but it was so dark they had to feel it to determine what it was. To the one feeling its trunk, it was a water pipe; to the one touching its ear, it was thought to be a fan; to another fondling its leg it was a pillar; and to another touching its back it was believed to be a throne. Rumi's story illustrates the impossibility of completely knowing the Divine, or comprehending all of Divine Truth.

In the fourth book of the *Masnavi*, the tale 'Camels on the Roof' encapsulates the elusiveness of the search for God. A man hears footsteps on his roof. He encounters a magical man who says that he searches for camels on his roof, in the same way that the man seeks God on His throne. 'Is this so much more extraordinary?' Rumi continues with his explanation: 'he made his point of the madness of man, that a camel that flies is no more crazy than he who seeks God on the throne of delight.'[91]

In the fifth book of the *Masnavi*, the story 'The Gazelle in the Donkey Stable' illustrates the fine, refined nature of Muhammad, and the beauty of Islam. A captured gazelle is placed in a stable with cows and donkeys. He is not used to their ways, to their crudeness; he is from another region, another home:

> And how is the Prophet in relation to this tale? He is a lion in the shape of a cow; behold him from a distance but do not investigate too closely; for the lion will rip the cow to pieces, expelling the bovine nature from your head and uprooting the animal nature from your head. If you are a cow you will become a lion when near him, but if you prefer to remain a cow do not seek the lion.[92]

On occasions, Rumi writes of animals that excel humans in some qualities, particularly that of devotion:

> Wolf and bear and lion know what love is:
> He that is blind to love is inferior to a dog!
> If the dog had not a vein of love,
> How should the dog of the Cave have sought to win the
> Heart of the Seven Sleepers?[93]
> You have not smelt the heart in your own kind:
> How should you smell the heart in wolf and sheep?[94]

Yet in Rumi's mystical quest, the soul continues to follow Aristotle's Great Chain of Being, from a vegetable state, to animal to human, before becoming lost in its Creator:

> I died to the inorganic state and became endowed with growth
> and [then] I died to [vegetable] growth and attained the animal

... I died from animality and became Adam [man], why then should I fear?[95]

Even in the literature that praises non-human qualities, the value seems to be mainly instructive. Humans are above animals in nature, as seen in their place in the cosmic hierarchy. In Sufi literature, animals tend to be used as symbols of human character and behaviour. In Sufism, the 'animal self' (*nafs*) is of a negative nature, referring to the baser instincts that the mystic is to overcome. This 'animal self' is sometimes referred to as a dog.[96] Use of this animal imagery, is, for the most part, unflattering.

A more positive image is that of the bird. An anonymous sixteenth-century Sufi poet wrote in Hindi about birds:

Oh that I could be a bird and fly,
I would rush to the Beloved!

Many have regarded birds as ensouled beings that have a special relationship with God. They fly to heaven, and have easier access to the Divine. They are symbols of the soul. This is not unique to Islam: a bird as symbol of the soul can be found in many cultures and religions, but 'no other tradition of mysticism has developed as elaborate a symbolism and imagery related to soul-birds as Sufism.'[97] Each bird has its own distinctive manner of prayer: 'The very birds praise Him as they wing their way. He notes the prayers and praises of all His creatures' (Qur'an 24:41).

Solomon was believed to have been taught the language of the birds: 'Solomon succeeded David. He said: "Know, you people, we have been taught the tongue of birds and endowed with all good things"' (Qur'an 27:16).[98]

The example of Solomon inspired the Persian poet Sanai (1080– c. 1131) to compose a long poem entitled *Tasbih at-tuyur* (The Rosary of the Birds), in which Sanai interprets individual birdsong, looking at the way particular species praise God. When the stork utters 'lak, lak' it is praising God by saying (in Arabic): '*al-mulk lak al-amr-lak*' ('Kingdom belongs to You; Command belongs to You').[99] The pigeon's 'ku ku' is interpreted as a way of searching for God; for in Persian it means 'Where is He? Where is He?'[100] For Muslim mystics on the Indian subcontinent, the cries of the papiha bird's 'piu piu' represent its call (in Hindi): 'The Beloved, the Beloved'.[101]

Birds and their songs were interpreted in other ways concerning the soul and its search for the Beloved. At times the birds represented various stages of spiritual development and different spiritual experiences. The nightingale fascinated the Sufi poets, for the song seemed to be that of a yearning lover. This led to the famous pairing of the nightingale and the rose. In mysticism, the bird is singing of its yearning for the Beloved (God). The nightingale sings to the rose, hoping to win its love:

> in innumerable poems in Persian, Turkish, Urdu, and other related languages, the nightingale represents the longing soul-bird who is forever bound to the rose, the symbol of divine beauty. In as far as the nightingale never tires of singing of its love for the rose and patiently endures thorn pricks, it embodies the soul longing for eternal beauty . . . For many poets, the unrequited longing of the nightingale is the highest state the soul can reach.[102]

Another bird that captured the imagination of the Sufi poets was the falcon. The falcon soars into the heavens, free, returning to the outstretched hand of its master when summoned. *Baz* is the Persian word for falcon and part of the phrase 'to come back' (*baz ayad*). Rumi viewed the falcon as the noble soul that returns to God (the falconer) when it hears the call of His drum: 'O serene soul! Return to your Lord, joyful and pleasing in His sight' (Qur'an 89:27). After the falcon returns to the King, Rumi proclaims:

> The falcon rubs its wings on the King's hand
> Without tongue he says 'I have sinned'.[103]

One of the most famous poems is *The Conference of the Birds*, an epic of nearly five thousand couplets by Attar of Nishapur (Farid al-Din 'Attar, *c.* 1142–*c.* 1220). It describes how the birds of the world gather, as they have decided they need a king. The hoopoe says that they already have one, known as the simorgh (a mythical bird from Iranian/Persian mythology),[104] but they must set out to find him. They have to travel to Mount Qaf, going through seven valleys, each valley representing a different stage on the spiritual path. Attar interprets the actions of each bird as an indication of the development of its soul. Many make excuses in order to avoid making the journey. In the case

Detail of an illustration from a 15th-century manuscript of Farid al-Din 'Attar's
The Conference of the Birds (1177).

of the nightingale, her love for the rose prevents her from journeying to the simorgh. Attar points out that the nightingale represents one attached to the superficial and transitory world.[105] When excuses are given, the duck says the following:

> Now none of you can argue with the fact
> That both in this world and the next I am
> The purest bird that ever flew or swam;
> I spread my prayer-mat out, and all the time
> I clean myself of every bit of grime
> As God commands. There's no doubt in my mind
> That purity like mine is hard to find.[106]

The hoopoe questions the duck, explaining that physical purity does not mean a pure and spiritual life. The duck's lifetime of rituals can mean a life empty of spiritual meaning. The hoopoe is frequently identified as one who guides the lover to the Beloved. The hoopoe gives advice, points out their limitations and encourages them to persevere. The hoopoe possesses wisdom and spiritual knowledge, perhaps because of his association with Solomon:

> I come as Solomon's close friend and claim
> The matchless wisdom of that mighty name.[107]

It is not only birds whose true nature is discussed:

> Behold the spider, her delicate dawn web
> With tears glistening on its geometrical lines
> A symmetry for the eye charmed by the ebb
> And flow of appearance. Then a fly finds
> Itself trapped and, struggling, dies beside her.
> Food for the patient creature. Suddenly a broom
> Sweeps all away, fly, web and spinning spider –
> So this contingent world is native to doom.
> Thus you may possess a thousand things
> But be wary that they don't possess you.[108]

This passage is a commentary on Qur'an 29:41: 'Those who serve other masters besides God may be compared to the spider which builds a cobweb for itself. Surely the spider's is the frailest of all dwellings, if they but knew it. God knows whatever they invoke besides Him; He is the Mighty, the Wise One.'

Near the end of the quest, only thirty birds remain. The conjunction of Persian words for 'thirty' (*si*) and for 'birds' (*morgh*) indicate that they have already discovered what they have been searching for: *simorgh*.[109] The king they are seeking is God.

Other Sufi literature draws on compassion shown towards animals and sees these acts as devotion to God. Abu Bakr Shibli (861–946) was visited in a dream by a deceased friend, who told him that, despite his devotion to prayer and fasting, the only reason he was enjoying the afterlife was because he once took in a cat from the cold.[110]

Another Sufi tale concerns the eighth-century female mystic Rabi'a of Basra:

> Rabi'a had gone up on a mountain. Wild goats and gazelles gathered around, gazing upon her. Suddenly Hasan Basri [another well-known early Muslim mystic] appeared. All the animals shied away. When Hasan saw that, he was perplexed and said, 'Rabi'a, why do they shy away from me when they were so intimate with you?'
>
> Rabi'a said, 'What did you eat today?'
>
> 'Soup.'
>
> 'You ate their lard. How would they not shy away from you?'[111]

Like ascetics in other religious traditions, Muslim ascetics would often withdraw from society and spend their lives among nature. This would sometimes lead to a greater appreciation of nature and of the animals living within it. A number became vegetarian. Most of the stories concerning Sufi vegetarians originate in South Asia, so perhaps they were influenced by Hindus or Buddhists, although some stories were also found in North Africa and the Ottoman world.[112] Although it may suggest a bond with their animal brethren, this practice had more to do with spiritual discipline than with a concern for animals.

Earlier I mentioned the Turkish Sufi master Bediüzzaman Said Nursi, an exceptional animal lover who was believed to understand the language of animals. He was particularly vocal about the less lovely, including flies (on which he wrote a treatise):

flies are charged with duties of cleaning away poisonous substances and microbes which breed disease and are invisible to the human eye. They do not transmit microbes; on the contrary, through sucking up and imbibing harmful microbes they destroy them and cause them to be transformed into a different state; they prevent the spread of many contagious diseases. A sign that they are both health workers and cleansing officials and chemists and that they exhibit extensive wisdom is the fact that they are extremely numerous. For valuable and beneficial things are multiplied.[113]

Nursi included mosquitoes and fleas in his praise; he believed that the universe was 'clean' because of these unloved animal species keeping it that way: 'Mosquitoes and fleas fall upon the turbid blood flowing in the veins polluted by harmful substances, indeed they are charged with consuming the polluted blood, so in hot weather when there is blood surplus to the body's needs, why should they not be natural cuppers?'[114]

Nursi used to share his food with a variety of animals, including ants, mice and pigeons. It is recorded that he once reprimanded a student for killing a lizard, asking him, 'Did you create it?'[115]

Nursi believed that animals had eternal souls. His writings and teachings embraced nature as a form of divine revelation and boldly stated that Creation is the original form of revelation, whereas the Qur'an is only commentary. If we follow Nursi's argument, then we could see that when animal species and their habitats are destroyed it is 'like burning the pages of the divine text by which God makes it possible for us to know Him'.[116]

In conclusion, Sufism does tend to display a greater sensitivity towards animals than the legal tradition, with an acceptance of the Qur'anic interpretation of animals as 'communities' able to worship God alongside human beings.

The Problem of Dogs

Islamic attitudes towards dogs are mixed, yet for the most part they are negative. This seems to be in sharp contrast to the rather positive consideration given to animals in both the Qur'an and in the Hadiths.

There has been, and continues to be, a basic hostility towards dogs among Semitic peoples that pre-dates Islam. In the Qur'an there is a verse in which dogs are used to describe our baser instincts: 'Had it been Our will, We would have exalted him through Our signs: but he clung to this earthly life and succumbed to his desires. He was like the dog which pants if you chase it away, but pants still if you leave it alone' (Qur'an 7:176).

One suggestion is that hostility towards dogs may have arisen after the Muslim conquest of Zoroastrian Persia in the seventh century CE,[117] since it is a common practice to do the opposite of one's rivals.[118] This may have been a contributing factor, but not the whole picture, for it seems that Muhammad was not a dog lover and there are Hadiths that record him as saying that angels will not enter a home where there is a dog.[119] Keeping a dog appears to reduce the merit of a Muslim's good deeds. Black dogs are sometimes viewed as demons in canine form. Muhammad said that a dog walking past a Muslim man saying his prayers would cause those prayers to be without value.[120]

A famous Hadith mentions a woman who, due to her actions in saving a dog from thirst, is forgiven her sins and granted eternal life in paradise.[121] While this seems to be an encouraging Hadith, the point of the story is that this woman's compassion extends even to dogs.

Although dogs had been part of the Arab world before Islam, guarding and shepherding, and accompanying hunting trips,[122] in most schools of Islamic law dogs are listed as being ritually unclean (*najis*).[123] The shunning of pigs comes from their classification in the Qur'an as being unclean, whereas for dogs this classification comes from the Hadiths.[124] One of the outcomes of classifying dogs as unclean is that a Muslim man may not pray after being touched by a dog.[125]

There is, however, one positive reference to dogs in the Qur'an. 'The Companion of the Caves', probably derived from the narrative of the 'Seven Sleepers of Ephesus', tells the tale of seven devout young men who hide from their persecutors in a cave. Their dog guards the entrance.[126] Positive references to dogs in Islamic texts usually refer to qualities that are lacking in humans, such as loyalty and faithfulness. 'Ali ibn Abi Talib, the nephew and son-in-law of Muhammad and the most important figure in Shi'a Islam, said this about dogs:

> Happy is the one who leads the life of a dog! For the dog has ten characteristics which everyone should possess. First, the

dog has no status among creatures; second, the dog is a pauper having no worldly goods; third, the entire earth is his resting place; fourth, the dog goes hungry most of the time; fifth, the dog will not leave his master's door even after receiving a hundred lashes; sixth, he protects his master and his friend, and when someone approaches he will attack the foe and let the friend pass; seventh, he guards his master by night, never sleeping; eighth, he performs most of his duties silently; ninth, he is content with whatever his master gives him; and tenth, when he dies, he leaves no inheritance.[127]

Dogs in Sufi Literature

In Sufi literature, there are many references to dogs, usually in terms of the 'dog' symbolizing one's baser (*nafs*) instincts, which the mystic needs to overcome through spiritual discipline and practices:

> You have fallen low because of this miserable dog of a *nafs* (lower self); you have become drowned in pollution. That dog of hell which you have heard about sleeps within you, and you are blissfully unaware. Whatever you feed this fire-eating dog of hell, it devours with relish. You may be sure that tomorrow this dog of a *nafs* will raise its head up out of hell as your enemy. This *nafs* is your enemy, worse than a dog; how long will you nourish this dog, O ignorant one![128]

There are a number of references, usually unfavourable, to dogs in *The Conference of the Birds*:

> Vanity, resentment, envy and anger shall be cemented
> Into your inner state: you shall be like a demented
> Dog with lolling tongue, infected with indolence of sin.[129]

> you must burn
> For goodness and the real, eschew the dogs of desire.[130]

> We are built not to last but yet our canine lust
> Bears a dogged determination that puts us to shame.[131]

Such references, though literary devices, draw on the common Muslim perception of dogs as low in status, and classed as unclean. Some of the stories talk about cruelty to dogs as though it was common and accepted as normal behaviour. In one story, a Sufi novice hits and cripples a stray dog. When his guide chastises him for such a cruel action, he responds that 'it was not my fault, but the dog's. Since he had made my clothes ritually impure, I hit him with my staff with good reason.'[132]

Many Sufi mystics kept company with dogs, learning from the 'lowest of the low'. The dogs were only a means to an end, a way for the greater exaltation of a saintly figure.[133] They were not loved in their own right, as subjects, but merely as objects, as illustrated in this story about Rumi, who requests some fine food from his disciples and then disappears. Later he is discovered giving the food to a dog and her newborn puppies. This has been interpreted in terms of Rumi's compassion; Rumi's compassion extends *even* to dogs (the lowest of the low). Another point is that God spoke to Rumi directly, asking him to look after the dog.[134]

In another story, kindness to a dog is rewarded by God:

> There was once a man walking along a road who became very thirsty. He found a well and so went down into it and drank from it. When he came out he saw a dog which was panting and eating earth because if its thirst, and he said to himself, 'This dog is as thirsty as I was.' So he went down into the well again, filled up his shoe with water, and, holding it in his mouth, came up again and gave it to the dog to drink. Allah thanked him for this and forgave him.[135]

The great Sufi saint Bayazid Bistami (804–874/877) tells of how the lower and higher come together in spiritual transformation. He meets a dog on the road:

> 'You are outwardly impure and I inwardly. Come let us put the two together so that the combination will bring purity to both of us.' The dog then said, 'You are not worthy of my companionship, for I am rejected by mankind while you are accepted. Stones are thrown at me while you are greeted as the "Monarch of the Gnostics". I never leave so much as a bone

for tomorrow but you have a whole crock of wheat stored up.' Bayazid replied, 'If I am not a worthy companion to a dog, how can I accompany the Eternal? Glory be to God Who cultivates the finest of creation through the basest thereof!'[136]

Another example of a spiritual comparison between a human and a dog is from *The Conference of the Birds*:

> A dog brushed up against a sheikh, who made
> No move to draw his skirts in or evade
> The filthy stray – a puzzled passer-by
> Who'd noticed his behaviour asked him why.
> He said; 'The dog is filthy, as you see,
> But what is outside him is inside me –
> What's clear on him is hidden in my heart;
> Why should such close companions stay apart?'[137]

Another positive reference is from Hafiz, which sets out the idea that everything, including dogs, can be a way to God:

> Where is the door to God?
> In the sound of a barking dog.[138]

Modern-day Opinions about Dogs

There is still some uncertainty about the texts concerning the status of dogs and whether dogs are ritually impure. Abou El Fadl, a Muslim legalist, has examined classical legal sources to see if the anti-dog stance holds up. He has concluded that the Hadiths used to justify hatred towards dogs are highly questionable, and has found Hadiths that suggest that dogs were commonly accepted during Muhammad's time, and that dogs were allowed inside mosques.[139]

Parted: The Afterlife – Soul Bearers and Sharers in Another Existence

If non-human animals are classed as 'Muslim', does this mean that they will partake of the afterlife? While most mainstream Muslims would say that non-human animals do not have an afterlife, one Hadith states that:

> On the Day of Arising, all of creation will be gathered together: the cattle, the riding-beasts, the birds, and every other thing, and it shall be God's justice [Exalted is He!] that He takes the hornless sheep's case against the horned-one. Then he shall say, 'Be dust!' which is the time at which the unbeliever says, 'Would that I were dust!'[140]

While this may appear quite harsh, the reasoning behind it isn't. The logic is that non-human animals will be extinguished on the Day of Judgement, which will be a kinder fate than being consumed by hellfire (a fate for non-Muslim humans).

In the Qur'an animals are seen as possessing that all-important element in any discussion concerning animals and religion: a 'soul'. Before we become too excited, note that mainstream Islam believes animal souls differ from human souls, they are not 'eternal'.[141] Muslim philosophers and Sufis follow the ancient Greeks in making a distinction between the 'animal soul' and the 'rational soul', the latter being found only in the human.[142] The animal soul is located in the heart, is material and is therefore subject to eventual destruction. The rational soul is immaterial and eternal and, in the mind of Muslim mystics, its aim is to be reunited with God. Non-human animals, lacking a rational soul, cannot aspire to eternal life.

Yet according to some of the Mu'tazilites, good animals, like good humans, will enjoy eternal life in heaven while bad animals will join bad humans in hell.[143] One theologian, Abu Ishaq an-Nazzam (c. 775–c. 845), even believed that all animals would go to heaven, a view that displeased some. The theologian al-Baghdadi responded: 'He is very welcome to a heaven which contains pigs, dogs and snakes.'[144]

The question of whether animals will participate in an afterlife has been discussed by a number of Qur'an commentators. Muhammad ibn Jarir al-Tabari (839–923) states that non-human species:

> have knowledge in the way you (human beings) have knowledge, manage their lives in the way you do, and their good and bad deeds are preserved in the Mother of the Book (the same way

yours are). Then, God will cause them to die, will resurrect them, and will compensate them for their deeds and misdeeds on the Judgement Day.[145]

The term 'mustered' in the Qur'anic verse 'No creature is there crawling on the earth, no bird flying with its wings, but they are like nations to you. We have neglected nothing in the Book; then to their Lord they shall be mustered' (Qur'an 6:38)[146] is interpreted by Al-Mawardi (972–1058) to mean that animals:

> will be resurrected in order that God compensate them for any suffering or injustice that is inflicted on them in this life. After that, He will turn some of them into dust, whereas others will be admitted into heaven whereby believers can enjoy their company.[147]

These interpretations show that the theme of resurrection of animals has been considered. It is significant that their deeds are recorded in the Heavenly Book and they are held accountable for their acts. Although opinions among Muslim scholars differ, a number, drawing on the Qur'an and the Hadiths, seem to agree that animals will be resurrected: 'We will provide them with a fine abode in this life: yet better still is the reward of the life to come, if they but knew it' (Qur'an 16:42).

Muhammad ibn Zakariya al-Razi (d. 925 or 932), often known by his Latinized name as Rhazes, states in *Al Syrat al-Falsafiah* (The Philosophical Way) that slaughtering an animal allows liberation of its soul and thus gives the soul the opportunity to transmigrate into a superior body, bringing it closer to salvation.[148] Transmigration, however, was not a popular view and was generally seen as heretical.

What happens to animals in the afterlife? In *Resalat al-ghufran* (The Treatise of Forgiveness) the poet Al-Ma'arri expresses the belief that there are animals in heaven; some are already there for humans (for heavenly hunting parties), and others because they have earned eternal life through their sufferings on earth.[149] In several verses of the Qur'an, eating meat in the afterlife is mentioned, indeed, listed as one of the pleasures of paradise: 'such meats as they desire' (Qur'an 52:22) and 'flesh of fowls that they relish' (Qur'an 56:21). This does beg the question concerning the benefits of an afterlife for non-human animals. Are animals purely for utilitarian use, objects for human use, rather than seen as individuals? What does this mean for the concept of 'communities'? Are some communities of more value than others?

Conclusion

Muhammad was reported as saying: 'All creatures are like a family ['*iyal*] of God: and He loves them most who are the most beneficent to His family.'[150] In Islam, the idea that all species are Muslim, or believers, is a noble one; all praise their Creator, and form communities that are able to praise, as well as receive, divine revelation. Yet there is the rather glaring discrepancy concerning how dogs are viewed; surely they too are a community of Muslims, created by God?

The Qur'an, Hadiths and Islamic law may not list modern problems relating to animals, but the letter of the law, or the essence of Islam, is that life is respected. Although there are no set laws in the Qur'an and the Hadiths prohibiting such practices as vivisection, the texts and guidelines one can see in Islam indicate that all life is sacrosanct and has the right of protection. There is a system of divine rewards and divine punishment for offenders. Muhammad declared that: 'There is no man who kills [even] a sparrow or anything smaller, without its deserving it, but God will question him about it.'[151] 'He who takes pity [even] on a sparrow and spares its life, Allah will be merciful on him on the Day of Judgement.'[152]

There are differences of opinion concerning diet. On the one hand we read that all is given to enjoy and that there will be meat to feast on in the afterlife; while at the other end of the spectrum, others advocate vegetarianism:

> All your life you have been drinking the blood and eating the flesh of animals without realizing what you have been doing. You love flesh and enjoy murder. If you had any conscience or any sense of justice, if you were born as a true human being, you would think about this. God is looking at me and you. Tomorrow his truth and his justice will inquire into this.[153]

Perhaps, in the final analysis, the best phrase to describe mainstream Islamic views about animals is 'compassionate anthropocentrism'.[154] In Islam humans are accorded higher status than other animals, yet that belief should prompt a corresponding level of responsibility towards the protection of other communities, for all are believers.

SEVEN
Animals in Hinduism

In the beginning, there was only the Great Self in the form of a Person . . . it desired a mate . . . He united with her; and from that human beings were born.

  She thought: 'How can he unite with me, after producing me from himself? Well, let me hide.' She became a cow, he a bull, and united with her. From that cattle were born. She became a mare, he a stallion; she a she-ass, he a he-ass; and united with her. From that one-hoofed beasts were born. She became a she-goat, he a he-goat; she became a ewe, he a ram; and he united with her. From that goats and sheep were born. In this way he projected all things existing in pairs, down to the ants.

  Then he realized: 'I, indeed, am this creation; for I have poured it forth from myself.' In that way he became this creation. And verily, he who knows this becomes in this creation a creator.
Brihadaranyaka Upanishad[1]

I am the seed of all existence. There is no being moving or still, that exists without me.
Krishna in the *Bhagavad Gita* 10.39

The sage sees the One in all beings . . .
In a Brahmana endued with wisdom and humility,
in a cow, in an elephant, as also in a dog . . .
the wise see the same.
Bhagavad Gita[2]

Hinduism: Ancient History, Animal Sacrifice and the Presence of Unicorns

ANIMALS OCCUPY AN IMPORTANT PLACE in Hindu myths and legends. In the Hindu pantheon they provide the vehicles of many gods and goddesses, as divinities and as incarnations or aspects of Vishnu or Shiva. Animals also embellish and beautify Hindu decorative art and temple architecture, sometimes being installed inside as objects of veneration.

The religious tradition known as Hinduism is the result of five thousand years of development, yet the name dates only from about 1200 CE, as a result of the invading Muslims wishing to distinguish their faith from that of the people of India.[3] 'Hindu' is the Persian word for 'Indian': both 'India' and 'Hindu' derive from *Sindhu*, the traditional name of the Indus river. In ancient inscriptions and documents 'Hindu' refers to the people of 'Hind', the Indian subcontinent. Only after the late eighteenth century did the term come to be used to refer to the dominant religion of the Indian people.

It seems appropriate that the name of the religion is derived from the land, for the adherents of Hinduism have been close to the land, its plants and its animals. Another name sometimes given to Hinduism is Sanatana Dharma, which roughly translates as 'the eternal essence of life' or 'eternal natural law'.[4] This essence is not limited to humans, but extends to include and unite all beings – humans, animals and plants – in the world that they dwell in and ultimately with the source of their existence, the Godhead. This unity means that for Hindus there is little that divides the living out of their daily life from their religion.

Hinduism has no founder and no prophet; it has no ecclesiastical or institutional structure and no set creed. No single holy book is universally acknowledged as being of primary importance. Early Hinduism is not marked by great personalities, but by the composition of orally transmitted sacred texts expressing concepts of what we now call Hinduism. The emphasis is on a way of living rather than on a set body of thought or beliefs. However, ascetics, monks, swamis, sadhus and gurus are considered essential to the preservation and passing on of Hindu traditions. Hindu sacred scriptures include the Vedas and Agamas, Upanishads, *Bhagavad Gita*, the epics, such as the *Mahabharata* and *Ramayana*, the Puranas, law books and many other philosophical and sectarian texts.

Hinduism is a religion, a culture and a way of life. The boundaries between the sacred and the secular do not exist in the way they do in the West.

Hinduism is the world's oldest living religion, a rich collection of hundreds of spiritual and philosophical traditions followed throughout Asia for more than five thousand years. Followers of Hinduism believe that the Divine (Brahman), the infinite reality of Truth, is beyond the comprehension of undisciplined minds, and is understood and worshipped by individuals in various ways. This is reflected in the diversity of practice and paths in Hinduism, as well as an acknowledgement that no one path can claim exclusivity over the ways of knowing the Truth.

Bhakti (the devotion to a particular god) demands acts of worship. Apart from ritual acts and ceremonies, there are the hymns of praise to be sung and statues to be venerated and adored. It is not 'idol-worship' as such, but rather the idol becomes the focus through which God (who cannot be represented in any image) is worshipped. Although there are gods who are paid homage, they are not the ultimate reality. They direct one to the ultimate reality of oneness. Hindu destination is One and these gods are the vehicles to take a Hindu to that destination. All these deities are manifestations of that One.

There are two main branches of Hinduism: Vaishnavism, which focuses on Vishnu and his avatars, and Shaivism, which follows Shiva. Most Hindus believe in one, all-pervasive supreme Divine, though the Divine may manifest and be worshipped in different forms, both male and female, by different names and in different ways. As such, Hinduism's complex understanding of the Divine cannot be adequately categorized as either monotheistic or polytheistic, but Hinduism is understood as being monotheistic.[5] 'Although the Hindus accept the existence of three hundred and thirty three million deities or *Sahasranama*, they all exhibit oneness.'[6]

All Hindus believe in Brahman, the supreme being: 'I am the soul that abides in the heart of all beings' (*Bhagavad Gita*).

The vast majority of Hinduism's leading *sampradayas* (traditions) regard the ethical treatment of animals as fundamental to the core Hindu belief that the Divine exists in all living beings, both human and non-human: the whole world is one family (*Vasudhaiva Kutumbakam*). Animals and plants are equally embodied with the existence of the Divine and are fully deserving of respect and human compassion, known as ahimsa (non-violence). Some Hindus believe that we should respect all living creatures and maintain a vegetarian lifestyle; there are others who uphold animal sacrifice and eat meat. From this we can see that Hinduism is an umbrella term covering a wide range of customs and beliefs.

Hinduism is closely intertwined with tradition and the customs and culture of the land of India, including its social system and its history. Each district has its own language and customs, as well as particular religious ideas and practices. The vast majority live in small villages and their lives are influenced by agrarian principles. Hinduism has been portrayed in the last two centuries as being a more or less unified religion, but it is important to note that there are hundreds of internal divisions created by caste, community, language and geography. At times it may be more helpful to speak of many Hindu traditions or, at other times, of one tradition.

Hinduism cannot date its origin, yet it is generally believed that its beginnings lie in the ancient indigenous culture of India and the Indo-European people who appeared in India four thousand years ago. Excavations at the Indus Valley archaeological sites show that animals played an important role in the religious and economic lives of the Indus people. They domesticated cows, buffaloes, sheep and bulls, and probably worshipped animals along with the mother goddess.[7] Archaeological evidence of cities dated as early as 3000 BCE points to the presence of a civilization in the Indus Valley characterized by orderly cities and extensive use of terracotta seals. Excavations undertaken since 1922 in the Punjab and the Indus Valley, at sites such as Mohenjo-daro, Lothal and Harappa (whose inhabitants have become known as Harappans), have revealed structures including temple citadels. The people of this civilization were literate, but their script remains undeciphered.

The seals of the Indus Valley civilization depict a variety of scenes. Several show adorned bulls or meditative figures surrounded by animals. The finds have unearthed figures of a male god, with horns and three faces (seemingly the original of the *Trimurti*, later expressed by the three deities Brahma, Vishnu and Shiva). The figure is in the position of a yogi in a state of contemplation, surrounded by animals, which may suggest that he is the original form of the great god Shiva, known as 'Lord of the Beasts'.[8] Were the animals worshipped as sacred? Or was it an indication of shamanic initiation?[9] If this were the case, it could indicate that these animals were protected from harm and may have benefited from the practice of ahimsa (non-violence). Putting these unanswered questions aside, these seals suggest that some form of religious practice involving meditation and veneration of animals flourished in the Indus Valley cities.

On other seals there are figures of mythical or fantastic creatures, several of which might be identified as unicorns. The animal, a well-fed looking bovine, has a small head, a long neck and a single horn. It is shown in a standing pose, with its neck adorned or decorated. It is thought that the unicorn was viewed as sacred, 'as it bears the ceremonial regalia in its representation, sometimes a trough or an incense burner is placed on it'.[10]

The Harappan culture was followed by the 'Age of the Vedas', the sacred compositions of the Indo-European peoples who invaded India from Central Asia in the middle of the second millennium BCE, bringing their languages and traditions and influencing the older religions. They referred to themselves as 'Aryans' or 'Noble Ones'.[11] Their language developed within India into what we know as Sanskrit. Their earliest compositions were collectively known as Vedas (Sanskrit for 'knowledge'). The Vedas, which include laws, rituals and philosophy, are the sacred books of the Hindus and contain the collected wisdom of the Vedic culture, which has come to be known as Hinduism.

Whereas the older Indus Valley religion seems to have included yoga and rites of renunciation and purification, the Aryans appear to have been more world-affirming. Originally nomads, they made their sacrifices to gods representing the forces of nature, with animal sacrifice a feature of their rites. Pre-Aryan worshippers seem to have used meeting places beside rivers, whereas the Aryans gathered around sacred fires to perform their ceremonies.[12]

There have been no archaeological finds from the early period of Aryan settlement, but the Vedic texts – which were written down about 800 BCE, although they reflect a much older oral tradition – are a means to understand something of the original Aryan faith. A dominant feature of religious life in the Vedic period was ritual sacrifice. Most rituals involved fire and were conducted by priests, who also supervised the making of altars and the recitation of hymns. Vedic religion perceived a delicate connection between ritual and *rta* (truth/justice/rightness). According to Vedic hymns,[13] the world itself may have come into being through an act of cosmic sacrifice.[14]

> The ancient sages saw the Universe as an eternal ritual of sacrifice. It is the self-sacrifice of the Absolute which gives birth to the relative and the very nature of life is one of transformation of energies. Every aspect of creation, divine or human, reflects this transformation . . . We cannot live without taking part in this cosmic ritual, both as instrument and as victims, and it is through this conscious participation in the sacrificial ritual that cosmic order is maintained.[15]

The early Hindu community performed intricate rituals that culminated in the sacrifice of live animals, which included cows, sheep, oxen, buffaloes and horses. One such ritual, the horse sacrifice (Asvamedha), entailed releasing a horse for one year, following it as it wandered throughout India, and then killing and dismembering it. This ritual eventually became internalized and symbolic, the process visualized but no longer enacted.[16]

Horses are not indigenous to India. They were either imported from outside by the Indus Valley people or they accompanied the Vedic people. In Vedic mythology, horses originated from Uchchaihshravas, a mythical white winged horse that emerged from the waters during the churning of the oceans by gods and demons, and was taken by Indra, the leader of the gods. Indra cut its wings and gave it to humans for their use.[17]

Vedic people valued cattle as wealth and preferred to receive them as gifts. The scriptures emphasize the virtue of donating cows to members of the priestly order, the Brahmins. Cows became sacred and could not be killed because of economic and religious reasons. Killing cows became a social taboo and a capital offence.

The Rigveda (Verses of Knowledge) are the oldest Vedic texts; some of the religious songs may have been composed when the Vedic peoples were still in Central Asia. In later times they were considered to be a revelation from Brahman. The texts emphasize the priority of the Brahmins, who are described in a poem about creation as the mouth of the World Soul, linking them with the importance of sacrifice and incantations: 'The priests alone could bring the people into touch with the cosmic powers and guarantee the continuation of life.'[18] By about 600 BCE the ascendancy of the priestly class was commonly accepted in northern India, with the priestly ritual of sacrifice set out in priestly manuals. Changes were on the way, however, for

Hinduism was to be influenced by the movements of Jainism and Buddhism.

The sacrifice-based world view of the early Vedic age gave way to philosophical inquiry and discussion in later texts known as the Aranyakas and Upanishads. These were composed around the early sixth century BCE, a time of great spiritual power when both Siddhartha Gautama (the Buddha) and Mahavira, the founder of Jainism, were challenging the notion that the Vedas were divine revelation. They relied on their own spiritual experiences to proclaim a path to liberation that was for all, not just for the higher castes of society. Both emphasized the concept of non-violence (ahimsa), a virtue that has been significant in Hinduism.

Hinduism developed as a religion of synthesis of Aryan and non-Aryan ideas, evolving to become highly tolerant and receptive in nature. When Buddhism rose as a challenge to Hinduism, it sanctified Buddha as the ninth incarnation of Vishnu. Similarly, the Jainist concept of ahimsa was readily accepted and incorporated into Hinduism.

Yet there was tension between the *himsa*, violence of the sacrificial requirements of the Vedic age, and the ahimsa, non-violence associated with the Atman, or soul-based sensitivities of the post-Vedic age. These Atmans were perceived to be equal, irrespective of the material form (animal or human). This was enforced later by the notion of reincarnation, which held that all souls in animal form will eventually incarnate in human form, and all human forms could become animal in future births, depending upon the nature of their activities.

Much of the philosophical development had parallels with the earlier schools of Buddhist thought, but there was one fundamental difference: Buddhism rejected the notion of a continuing self and saw everything as subject to flux, but all Hindu thought presupposed the permanence of the self or soul (Atman).[19]

Texts

The Vedic period is the earliest era in South Asia for which we have written literary records. The prominent religious expression at the time was animal sacrifice, offered to the gods through the medium of fire.

The four Vedic collections (Rigveda, Samaveda, Yajurveda and Atharvaveda) are the oldest Indian sacred texts and were first collected about 800 BCE, although some are centuries older in origin. Each contains hymns and ritual treatises. The Aranyakas ('compositions for the forest') and Upanishads ('sitting near' [the teacher]) are philosophical works composed about 600 BCE. Many Hindu traditions consider the Vedas to be revealed and not authored by human beings. They are said to be eternal in nature and revealed in every cycle of time. For centuries it was considered taboo to write them down, so they were transmitted orally by seers to their disciples.

The oldest and most revered Vedic text, the Rigveda, has many references to people eating meat. Indra, a prominent god of the early Vedic period, boasts of being offered more than fifteen oxen: 'They have cooked for me fifteen bulls, and twenty, so that I may eat the fat as well. Both sides of my belly are full.'[20] Horses, oxen, barren cows and rams were offered to Agni, the god of fire.[21] Most of the references to meat-eating and animal slaughter in the Vedic period are within the context of sacrifice, the most famous being that of the Asvamedha, the horse sacrifice.

There were signs of unease about such slaughter. As early as the Rigveda, sensitivity is shown towards the slaughtered beasts; one hymn notes that mantras are chanted so that animals will not feel pain and will go to heaven when sacrificed: 'You do not really die through this, nor are you harmed. You go to the gods on paths pleasant to go on.'[22]

The requirements necessary for offering a cow at a funeral procession are listed in the *Taittiriiya Aranyaka*, but further on in the text it advises one to release the cow, rather than kill her.[23]

This tension, or ambivalence, can be seen in a later text, the *Satapatha Brahmana*, where it states that eating the flesh of the bull and cow is prohibited. The text outlines that the gods decree that these animals support everything in the world, so to consume them would be similar to eating everything and, as punishment, one would be reborn as a sinful being. Yet the text goes on to acknowledge that Yajnavalkya, a renowned sage, eats the flesh of cows and oxen.[24]

In the Yajurveda, the third of the four Vedas, it is stated that: 'You must not use your God-given body for killing God's creatures, whether they are human, animal or whatever' (12.32.90).

Near the close of the Vedic age, in the *smriti* genre of law books, there is a growing sense of discomfort surrounding the sacrificial cult and more references to the benefits of abstinence from the eating of meat. Yet even in these texts we note conflict. In the *Yajnavalkya Smrti*, it states that one can eat meat if one's life is in danger, when making offerings to the ancestors, when it has been sprinkled with water and the appropriate mantras recited or when the meat has been offered to the gods.[25] Yet the verses following this state 'that one slaying beasts outside of the ritual context dwells in hell for as many days as there are hairs on the body of the beast', and the one who does not eat meat will obtain all desires and become like a sage.[26]

Brahman: The One Essence

In the Vedas, the ultimate absolute is Brahman, defying every attempt at definition. Brahman is neutral and impersonal, the origin, the cause and basis of all existence. Brahman is unknowable but the only way he can be considered is in terms of a personal deity, so it was natural that Hindus saw the functions of divinity in a multiplicity of forms, not purely in human terms, for the gods are also manifestations of nature or cosmic forces. The divine names may be countless, but they are all understood as expressions of Brahman: there are limitless forms, but only one essence.

The Upanishads are a distillation of Vedic teaching and are primarily concerned with the Absolute from which all existence has come. They are about liberation from the cycle of life and death and introduce the notion of immortality as reality. This has become the ultimate quest of the Hindu tradition: to achieve the immortality of the soul and happiness in this life.

Within the Upanishads, there are many references to animals, which, together with nature, are used as symbols and metaphor to highlight something of Brahman:

> Brahma is the first-born among the gods.
> He is the creator of everything,
> who, remaining hidden,
> sustains all he has made.[27]

> Just as a spider spins forth its thread
> and draws it in again,
> The whole creation is woven from Brahman
> and unto it returns.

> Just as plants are rooted in the earth,
> All beings are supported by Brahman.
> Just as hair grows from a person's head,
> So does everything arise from Brahman.[28]
>
> From Him are born the many deities,
> From Him are born the angelic beings,
> and man,
> and the beasts and birds.[29]
>
> Two birds,
> inseparable companions,
> perch on the same tree.
> One eats the fruit,
> the other looks on.
>
> The first bird is our individual self,
> feeding on the pleasures and pains of this world;
> The other is the universal Self,
> silently witnessing all.[30]

Nearly all of the Upanishadic teachings can be found in seed form within the Brihadaranyaka Upanishad (The Great Forest Teaching), which is both the oldest of the Upanishads, dating from about 800 BCE, and the longest, containing more than 400 verses:

> When the bees collect the nectar from many different plants, blending them all into one honey, the individual nectars no longer think, 'I come from this plant', 'I come from that plant'. In the same way, my son, all creatures when they contact Being lose all awareness of their individual natures. But when they return from Being they regain their individuality. Whether tiger, or lion, or wolf, or boar, or worm, or fly, or gnat, or even mosquito, they become themselves again.[31]

Prana comes from the root *an* ('to breathe'), which signifies not only human breath but the breath of the Universe, the life force.[32] Prana is the energy behind both mind and matter:

And Indra continued:
'I am Prana, the life breath,
and the consciousness in all beings.
Glorify me, for I am life and I am immortality.'[33]

Brahman, Thou art One,
though formless,
Through Thine own power,
and for Thine own unfathomable purpose,
Thou givest rise to the many forms.
Thou createst the whole Universe from Thyself,
and, at the end of time,
drawest it back within Thyself . . .

Thou art Prajapati, the Lord of all creation . . .
Thou art the deep blue butterfly,
Thou art the parrot, green with red eyes.[34]

The Vedic tradition ended with the Upanishads and the emergence of the notion of the identity of the individual self (*atman*) with the absolute (Brahman). The next step was to postulate that there is only one reality; this is called monism and is the basis of Vedantic philosophy.

Classical Hinduism emerged during the period from 300 BCE to 300 CE. Although Buddhism and Jainism reached their widest growth within India at this time, it was also the period when Vedantic 'orthodoxy' was developing.[35] Sutras were written, highlighting the teaching of the Vedas and the Upanishads. This was a time when *bhakti* (devotion to one of the gods) entered religion, so that what was already happening at the grassroots level was now given approval. There was a wider synthesis of Aryan and non-Aryan elements in the tradition. This was also the time of the epics, using legends and stories of the past to tackle the issues of good versus evil, cosmos and chaos in human affairs.

The Vedic corpus was followed by a body of work called *smriti* or 'remembered' literature. This consists of Puranas (ancient stories), epics and codes of law and ethics. The two *smriti* epics, the *Ramayana* (Story of Rama) and the *Mahabharata* (Great Epic of India, or Great Sons of Bharata) are the best-known works of the Hindu tradition, and form the heart of Hindu sacred literature.

Ravana fighting the monkey Hanuman, in a Kalighat print of c. 1850.

The *Mahabharata* is considered the world's longest poem (approximately one hundred thousand verses). It is the story of a great struggle between the descendants of a king. In both the *Ramayana* and the *Mahabharata* history is viewed as being in two cycles: at the beginning there is order and righteousness, but then, through four ages, standards deteriorate and the gods decide to destroy the world and start again. The epics indicate a need to discover meaning and purpose, even during the period of disorder.

The *Ramayana* is placed within the second age, when order, though under attack, is still largely intact. Animals play an important role in the epic battle. Jatayu, a mythical bird, loses his fight against Ravana when Ravana is carrying away Sita after kidnapping her. An army of bears, monkeys and other animals accompany Rama to Lanka to rescue Sita, his wife. They build a bridge across the ocean to the island country of Ravana. They destroy the army of

Ravana and help Rama rescue Sita. The story of the *Ramayana* is a reminder of the Hindu belief that in the universal scheme of things God does not distinguish between humans and animals; all living beings have an equal status but play different roles. Hanuman, the monkey god, is the symbol of loyal service and ingenuity, for he assists in the rescue of Sita by establishing the monkey bridge. Hanuman is believed to appear wherever the *Ramayana* is being read. Because of this association, monkeys are treated as sacred in India.

The squirrel is also considered sacred in India because of its association with Lord Rama. There is a legend that explains the stripes on the backs of most squirrels:

> During the construction of the Adi Sethu (bridge) at Rameswaram by Lord Rama and the vanara sena, a little squirrel also contributed in its own way. It rolled in the beach sand and then ran to the end of the Sethu to shake off the sand from its back (chanting Lord Rama's name all along). Lord Rama, pleased by the creature's dedication, caressed the squirrel's back and ever since, the Indian squirrel carried white stripes on its back, which are believed to be the mark of Lord Rama's fingers.[36]

In popular Hinduism the Rama story is not only heard in childhood, but continues at the heart of many everyday activities. Rama is invoked at the start of every undertaking and thanked on its successful completion. Rama's name is said in order to console the sick and the aged, and is chanted by assembled mourners as bodies of the dead are taken away to be cremated.

The *Mahabharata* emphasizes the important goals of human life and our interconnection with one another. One myth associates the writing of it with Ganesha, the elephant-headed deity who has only one tusk: 'He was traditionally the first scribe of the great Hindu epic, the *Mahabharata*. He was said to have been so keen to write it down that he tore off one of his tusks to use as a pen.'[37]

The *Mahabharata* is set in the third age and tells the story of the war that ushers in the fourth age, the era of final disintegration. The high point of the epic is the section entitled *Bhagavad Gita* (Song of the Lord), which is one of the most important and revered sacred

A carved stone relief of Ganesha in the Andhra Vishnu temple in Srikakulam, Andhra Pradesh, India.

scriptures of Hinduism. In the story, Arjuna, hesitating about entering into battle, is engaged in dialogue with his charioteer, who is none other than Krishna, the eighth incarnation of Vishnu. Through devotion to Krishna (in whom the impersonal Brahman becomes a personal, loving god), Arjuna can be freed from his doubts and attachments.

The *Bhagavad Gita* contains a number of passages that deal with animals and compassion towards them, including:

> I look upon all creatures equally; none are less dear to me and none more dear. (9.29)

> He alone sees truly who sees the Lord the same in every creature ... seeing the same Lord everywhere, he does not harm himself or others. (13.27–8)

> non-violence ... and mercy to all life forms are the goals of godly persons who are endowed with My nature. (16.1)

The *Bhagavata Purana* states: 'Avoiding harm ... and working towards the happiness of all living creatures is the duty of everyone' (11:17–21). Further passages may be found elsewhere in the *Mahabharata*:

> He who desires to augment his own flesh by eating the flesh of other creatures lives in misery in whatever species he may take his birth. (115.47)

> The purchaser of flesh performs violence by his wealth; he who eats flesh does so by enjoying its taste; the killer does violence by actually tying and killing the animal. Thus, there are three forms of killing. He who brings flesh or sends for it, he who cuts off the limbs of an animal, and he who purchases, sells, or cooks flesh and eats it – all these are to be considered meat-eaters. (115.40)

> Abstention from cruelty is the highest Religion. Abstention from cruelty is the greatest self-restraint. Abstention from cruelty is the highest gift. Abstention from cruelty is the highest penance. Abstention from cruelty is the highest sacrifice. Abstention from cruelty is the highest power. Abstention from cruelty is the greatest friend. Abstention from cruelty is the greatest happiness. (116.38–9)

The most important of a further cycle of stories about Krishna is the *Bhagavata Purana*. The fact that Krishna is commonly portrayed as a cowherd is significant, for it brings Krishna worship into the context of the ancient cult of the mother-goddess.[38] The cow is the living symbol of Mother Earth and of the bounty she bestows upon humankind. Feeding the cow is in itself an act of worship. The majority of Hindus are vegetarian; the reverence shown towards the cow is also a symbol of reverence for all animals.

The *Manusmriti* (Laws of Manu), from the Epic Period (600 BCE–200 CE), the second stage of Indian religious development, is attributed to ancient seers, the most important of whom was Manu. It is one of eighteen *smritis* ('what is remembered') of the *Dharmasastra*, or 'laws of righteous conduct'. The *Dharmasastra* constitutes a body of precepts related to three goals (*trivarga*) that a Hindu is to seek: *dharma* (righteousness), *artha* (material well-being) and *kama* (pleasure). The successful pursuit of the *trivarga* is believed necessary for achieving *moksha*, final liberation from the cycle of birth, death and rebirth. These texts are highly revered by orthodox devotees of Brahmanism, for they offer an account of the conduct of life and its proper social organization. The date of the *Manusmriti* is uncertain, but is probably between 200 BCE and 100 CE.

In its treatment of foods, the *Manusmriti* emphasizes not hurting living things as well as the importance of refraining from remote actions that cause suffering to sentient creatures. Concern for the good of all beings is identified as a prerequisite to heavenly bliss. The *Manusmriti* had been described as 'the earliest explicit vegetarian writing from India'.[39] Spiritual liberation is linked to desiring the good of all beings and vowing non-injury to all creatures. Not only is the eating of meat forbidden, but the person who permits the slaughter or cooks the meat is also condemned: 'Thus the entire social and economic structure of meat eating is condemned as spiritually impure.'[40]

> He who injures innoxious beings from a wish to give himself pleasure, never finds happiness, neither living nor dead. (5.45)

> He who does not seek to cause the sufferings of bonds and death to living creatures, but desires the good of all beings, obtains endless bliss. (5.46–7)

> Meat can never be obtained without injury to living creatures, and injury to sentient beings is detrimental to the attainment of heavenly bliss; let him therefore shun the use of meat. (5.48–9)

> He who permits the slaughter of an animal, he who cuts it up, he who kills it, he who buys or sells meat, he who cooks it, he who serves it up, and he who eats it, must all be considered as the slayers of the animal. (5.51–2)[41]

The *Puranas* 'of ancient times' are a group of important Hindu (or Jain and Buddhist) religious texts, notably consisting of narratives of the history of the universe from creation to destruction, genealogies of kings, heroes, sages and demigods, and descriptions of Hindu cosmology, philosophy and geography. In the *Padma Purana*, one of the major eighteen *Puranas*, it is stated that: 'Of all the gifts only one is supreme. It is the freedom from fear for all of the creatures of this universe. There is no other gift greater than this.'

A Puranic story tells of King Usinara, who was a generous king. One day a dove, being pursued by a hawk, flew to him for help. The king gave it protection, but the hawk protested at being deprived of its food. The King offered his own flesh as a substitute, but it didn't matter how much he cut from his body, the weight of the dove was always heavier. Only when Usinara offered himself in entirety did the scales balance. Indra and Agni had taken on avian form in order to test the king.[42]

The Universe as a Forest: All Beings are Here

The Hindu idea of the world as a forest led to an understanding that the different aspects of the Ultimate Reality could be found in the various forms that are in the forest (trees, plants and animals). All of life is encompassed and interconnected in the forest. In the *Bhagavad Gita* Krishna compares the world to a single banyan tree with many branches in which all species of humans, demigods and animals live.[43]

In Hinduism the forest was set aside for the practice of religion. Sages lived in ashrams or hermitages; from their forest setting, surrounded by natural beauty and wildlife, arose the Vedic teachings of the Upanishads, including the Brihadaranyaka (The Great Forest Teaching). The spiritual tradition of yogis incorporated a quasi-shamanic communion with animals. They learned detachment, humility and compassion. The presence of the sages guaranteed the protection of the animals, for none were to be harmed where the sages lived. Even kings who violated the sanctity of the area by hunting faced punishment.[44] *Mahavana* is the concept of the great ancestral forest where all species of life find shelter.[45] This helps explain the presence of cows in cities, for the cities are but an extension of the world forest. The world village must include aspects of the forest, including animals. The forest is part of Hindu identity, part of Hindu spirituality. Ethics are involved, for one must be kind to the forest, including its inhabitants, animal and human. One cannot separate the two: Vedic culture taught that the earth and the cow are to be loved and cared for as mothers;[46] if we are kind to nature, then we are kind to others.[47] Hindus may say '*Om shanti, shanti, shanti*' ('peace, peace, peace') before every prayer. The first shanti means peace with nature, or ecological peace.

Animals: Divine Companions, Vehicles and Avatars

Most Hindus view divinities as manifestations of a single godhead. The Upanishads refer to this supreme being as Brahman, who is beyond all human comprehension, but the Puranas claim that this divine entity assumes a form and a name to make itself accessible to humankind. Hindus worship the supreme being in temples in the form of an image or form. Most Hindus think of a sacred image as an actual incarnation of the supreme being.[48]

With the passage of time, animals acquired a new dimension in the life and consciousness of religious people. Most deities became associated with one or more animals, or with birds. Gods and goddesses all have their own iconographic characteristics and their association with animals has a special significance. In the Hindu pantheon each god and goddess is aligned with an animal as a vehicle or *vahana*. Symbolically their vehicles represent the animals' energies or qualities, which need to be strengthened or sublimated in human beings' lower nature with the help of the divinities who can transform them. Ganesha, the Remover of Obstacles, for example, is associated with wisdom, while Hanuman, the monkey, is sometimes linked to the fickleness of the human mind, which tends to jump from one thing to the next. Worshipped as the perfect devotee of the Divine, Hanuman also represents the ability to gain complete control over an ever-racing mind. Ganesha's elephant head and mouse companion represent his power to overcome hindrances, as an elephant can crush enormous obstacles, and a mouse can gnaw through small ones.[49] The knowledge of vehicles is therefore very useful in knowing which divinity can help in transforming inner energies.

Animals are not only viewed as vehicles, they are acknowledged as assistants or companions to the gods and goddesses. Spiritually this hints that an animal is also part of the divine spirit and therefore not inferior in spirit. This companionship demonstrates divine love and equality to animals. The animals that are associated with particular gods and goddesses are considered to have been gifted with power as representatives of the gods they accompany. They are also accorded protection. It may be no coincidence that animals most susceptible to human attacks, such as the elephant, lion, tiger, mouse and snake, are placed as assistants and vehicles to the gods and goddesses under their protection.

Some of the principal gods and goddesses and their corresponding vehicles and animal assistants include:

Divinity	Vehicle/*Vahana*
Ganesha	Mouse
Brahma	Swan
Vishnu	Garuda or eagle
Shiva	Nandi or bull
Indra	Elephant (Airavata)
Agni	Ram
Vayu	Thousands of horses, antelopes, lions
Varuna	Swans or crocodile (Makara)
The Sun	Chariot driven by seven horses
Skanda Kumara	Peacock
Saraswathi	Peacock or swan
Lakshmi	Owl
Parvathi or Durga or Chandi	Lion
Maheswari	Bull
Vaisnavi	Eagle
Kaumari	Peacock
Brahmi	Swan
Aindri	Elephant
Kama	Parrot, cuckoo or swan
Soma	Two- or three-wheeled chariot drawn by ten horses
Mangala	Ram
Buddha	Chariot drawn by eight horses

Brihaspathi	Golden chariot drawn by eight horses
Sukra	Eight horses
Sani	Vulture, crow, buffalo or an iron chariot drawn by eight horses
Rahu	Black lion
Ketu	Vulture
Kubera	Shoulders of a man, a carriage drawn by men or an elephant or ram
Yama	Male buffalo
Nritti	Donkey, lion or man
Ishana	Bull
Ganga	Crocodile

In Hinduism planets are also deified and are thought to influence evil or good efforts. Planets are worshipped by both Hindus and Buddhists. Six of the nine planets have animal vehicles: Aditya (a chariot with seven horses), Chandra (a swan), Mangala (a goat). Brihaspati (a frog), Sani (a tortoise) and Ketu (a snake).

Hindus revere many divinities in animal form. Lord Vishnu incarnated upon earth first as a fish, then as a tortoise, next as a boar. In another incarnation he appeared as half lion, half man. He is worshipped in all these forms. Hanuman, the monkey god who assisted Lord Rama in the battle of Ramayana, is another, as well as elephant-headed Ganesha, son of Lord Shiva.

The main gods of the Vedic period include Agni, Indra and Varuna. Agni, the god of fire and sacrifice, is the one who unites earth, heaven and the atmosphere in between. He is seen as the life force within nature and is depicted as a handsome man riding a blue ram. The Rigveda hails him as the one who 'restores life to all beings'.[50] Indra, king of gods, is the guardian deity of the world. He is the god most frequently invoked in the Veda, as the sky god and god of war. He took the elephant Airavata as his vehicle when he changed his character from the war god to the god of rain. With his thunderbolt he was able to suppress Vrita, an evil dragon who sought to stem the flow of the waters. Killing Vrita brought rain to the earth, as well as Varuna, the upholder of cosmic order, with the power to punish or reward. Varuna, also known as the god of waters, is seated on Makara (a mythical crocodile), holding a cord noose and an umbrella in the form of a cobra. Indra is sometimes accompanied by a dog named Sarama, which is sometimes identified with Usha, the dawn.[51]

Life involves creation, preservation and destruction. Therefore Hinduism has three major deities: Brahma the creator, Vishnu the preserver and Shiva the destroyer. This is the Hindu triad, or trinity. Early writings express this idea of a divine trinity (*trimurti*). In time, Brahma became marginal and the functions of creation, preservation and destruction were often combined in one deity, usually Vishnu or Shiva, depending on the individual devotee. In Hinduism a god can assume the form of other deities, even with opposite qualities, so Vishnu may be a destroyer and Shiva the creator.

Vishnu

Vishnu, the great preserver, is sometimes depicted reclining or asleep on the ocean (symbolizing chaos) in the form of a thousand-hooded primeval serpent, Adishesha. Lord Vishnu, who rises from the primeval waters (*ksiramudra*) at the beginning of Creation, rests on the endless coils, the thousand hoods providing him with a canopy. The serpent represents time and the thousand hoods divisions of time.[52]

Vishnu, also a symbol of the sun, may appear mounted upon his vehicle, the heavenly eagle Garuda. Garuda can be depicted in different forms, from half-man/half-bird, to having a human body and face, the wings of a bird, or just a beak. One legend about Garuda concerns his ambition. Garuda was devoted to Vishnu, but ambitious, and wanted to be greater than Vishnu. Vishnu understood this and said that he would grant him one request. Garuda took this opportunity to ask that he be given a seat higher than Vishnu. Vishnu smiled and made a seat for Garuda on the roof of his chariot and told him to sit there. He also made his flag fly higher than Vishnu's head, which pleased Garuda. Vishnu is also known and worshipped as Garuradhvaja ('God with Garuda on Flag'). This story brings to the fore that animals are more than assistants: they are also friends. The fish and conch shell are also associated with Vishnu.

Vishnu's Avatars

Vishnu draws close to humankind through his ten avatars (from Sanskrit *avatara*, 'descent').[53] Vishnu exists outside the material realm as the creator and he exists within every being as the Supersoul. It is thought that Vishnu incarnates in all species of life. It is believed that over the ages Vishnu has descended to earth several times in animal and human form to overthrow evil and establish dharma, or righteousness, so restoring balance. By the fifth century CE, ten incarnations, through which Vishnu had saved and recreated the universe after the Great Flood, had come to be considered the most important. His first, as a fish, saved Manu (the progenitor of the human race), his family and many animals from a flood. The progression of the incarnations from fish to full human is understood by some Hindus today as anticipating evolutionary theory,[54] with Vishnu progressing from fairly simple life forms (such as the fish) to more developed forms, such as the boar, and finally to human form. This sounds plausible, but the more prevalent explanation is that Vishnu takes the form most suited to the crisis at hand. It is important to emphasize that the idea that a deity should incarnate as an animal shows that animals have an important role to play. They are living expressions of the spirit and presence of God. The stories that accompany each of the avatars have had a profound influence on Hindu culture.

Matsya, the Fish

The first incarnation was that of Matsya, 'Fish', who appeared at the time of the Great Flood to warn humankind. The fish incarnation is suggested in a number of different stories. One version is about Manu, who was saved from a deluge by a long-horned fish. One day Manu was washing in the river, when he found a tiny fish, Matsya, who begged Manu to protect it. Manu took the fish home, where it grew bigger and bigger until Matsya asked to be taken to the sea to be released. Before the fish swam away, it warned Manu that there would be a huge flood and advised him to build a boat. He did as the fish advised, taking on board all kinds of creatures and seeds of plants. Then it began to rain and the waters threatened to destroy the boat. Then Matsya, now a gigantic fish, appeared and towed the boat safely through the waters. After the waters subsided, the fish confessed to Manu that he was Vishnu.[55] Another version replaces Manu with a king named Satyavrata, who had been performing a sacred ceremony beside a river, when he scooped up the little fish. During the flood, the giant serpent Vasuki was used to tie the boat to Matsya, and the boat was towed across the waters of devastation for many years. During the long voyage, Vishnu-Matsya instructed the king and his companions in the spiritual knowledge of the Vedas.[56]

Another legend tells of a time when there was a partial dissolution of the universe in which the earth and the other worlds were submerged in the depths of the ocean. Vishnu advised King Satyavrata to take seeds of plants, the *rishis* (sages) and Brahma to a safe place on a boat, which also contained the four Vedas. While being rescued, Brahma fell asleep and the horse-headed demon, Hayagriva, stole the Vedas. Seeing this, the gods asked Vishnu to rescue the Vedas. Vishnu then took on the form of a gigantic fish, killed Hayagriva and rescued the Vedas. Another account of the fish incarnation of Vishnu is given in the *Agni Purana*.[57]

In artwork depicting the first avatar, the image of the fish may be either in its theriomorphic form (in the form of an animal) or in its therianthropic form.[58] (A therianthropic form contains qualities of both animal and human, and can also imply that humans can metamorphose into animals by means of shape-shifting.)

Kurma, the Tortoise

The second incarnation was that of Kurma the tortoise, who rescued treasures from the flood. This incarnation has been described in the *Bhagvata Purana*. It is said that the forces of evil were once again gaining the upper hand. Amrita, the ambrosia that is the nectar of the ocean, as well as the nectar of immortality, had been lost, so Vishnu churned the ocean. He manifested himself in the form of a tortoise. The mountain, Mandara, was placed on his back. The churning rope was Ananta, the snake lord. The gods held one end of Ananta, while the other end was held by the demons. The *ratnas* (jewels) that came out of the churning waters were of great significance. They included the divine cow, Surabhi (or Kamadhenu), offering milk to human beings, as well as several other treasures, including the conch shell, which Vishnu took for himself; the white elephant, Airavata, which became Indra's vehicle; and the amrita itself. Vishnu gave the amrita to the gods and they once again became immortal.[59]

The *Bhagvata Purana* says that the churning of the ocean was possible only when Vishnu went to the bottom in the form of a tortoise to support the load of the mountain. This creative myth is symbolized in art by a picture of a half-man, half-tortoise form.

Varaha, the Boar

The third incarnation of Vishnu is as Varaha, the boar who raised the earth from the flood. There are several versions of this story. The first is that the boar took pity on the earth; in the *Mahabharata* it is said that the population of the earth and all the grain increased to such an extent that the earth began to sink due to its weight. Vishnu took the form of a boar and lifted the earth up from the depths of the nether world into which it had sunk.

Another version narrates that the earth had lost its balance on account of the demon Hiranyaksha, who wore many golden ornaments which he had obtained by mining the earth. He had dug so deep that the earth had lost its balance and fallen from space into the depths, coming to rest in the primeval waters, which lie at the very bottom of the universe. Vishnu saw the earth's distress and took on the form of a gigantic boar, Varaha, and entered the universe to rescue the earth from the deep. As Varaha was picking up the earth on his tusks, Hiranyaksha challenged Varaha to a fight. Varaha was victorious and restored the earth to its rightful place in space.[60]

Vishnu as Varaha (the Boar) in an illustration from an unknown manuscript of *c.* 1800.

The image of this incarnation varies, but the most common is that of a figure with the face of a boar and the body of a man.

Narasimha, the Man-lion

Vishnu's fourth incarnation was as Narasimha (Sanskrit for 'man-lion', Narasimha is often depicted as having a human torso, a lion's face and claws). The demon Hiranyakashipu, the brother of Hiranyaksha, swore vengeance when he saw his brother had been killed. He had a son, Prahlada, who became a devotee of Vishnu. Unable to turn his son into a demon, Hiranyakashipu set about trying to kill him. Finally, after being told by Prahlada that Vishnu is everywhere, Hiranyakashipu rushed at a nearby pillar of the palace and struck it. The pillar opened up and from it emerged a terrifying form, with the head of a lion and the body of a man. This was Narasimha, the man-lion incarnation of Vishnu, who had come to protect his devotee, Prahlada; Narasimha then killed the demon.

Rama, the King

The story of the seventh incarnation,[61] Rama, involves a number of different animals. The full story of Rama and Sita, as told in the *Ramayana*, mentions a number of animals who played key roles: Hanuman and the army of monkeys, a vulture named Jatayu, who gave his life trying to save Sita from being captured, and Jambavan the bear, who helped in the battle. The role these animals played has helped give them – monkeys in particular – special status in Hindu culture.

Balarama, the Cowherd

The eighth incarnation is that of Balarama the cowherd, who lived in the forest with his brother Krishna and their friends, alongside the cows, monkeys, peacocks and deer. He is always shown carrying a plough and is associated with the earth and rivers. Some also place Krishna as the eighth avatar, or at number nine, while other traditions think of Krishna as the supreme deity, the 'full' descent (not an avatar). The significance of Krishna, the most popular manifestation of Vishnu, is that in him the being of Vishnu is held to be totally present.

Krishna is one of the most popular Hindu gods, celebrated in folk songs and narratives (such as the *Bhagavad Gita*) and in many paintings. He is depicted as a cowherd who dances with peacocks and lives in simplicity in the forest. Devotees of Krishna care about the environment because Krishna loves nature.

> When Krishna played His flute to call the cows, the river stopped flowing, her waters stunned with ecstasy. Instead of swimming or flying, the cranes, swans, ducks and other birds closed their eyes and entered a trance. The cows and deer stopped chewing, their ears raised. They became motionless like painted animals.[62]

Krishna defeated the venomous serpent Kaliya, who had entered the Yamuna river. Krishna fought the serpent for more than two hours, climbing on his many heads and dancing. The serpent begged for mercy and left the Yamuna river, which was restored to its natural state. On another occasion Krishna swallowed a forest fire to protect the forest. It is also said that he spoke to the birds in their own languages.[63]

Krishna rejected ritualistic worship in favour of an earth-based practice of religion that recognized the sacred in the environment. One was to live in harmony with nature, to show love for all creatures and never to harm a living being.

Buddha, the Teacher

The ninth incarnation is that of Buddha, the teacher. Many of the recorded teachings of Buddha, such as the Four Noble Truths and the Eightfold Path, are readily accepted and endorsed by Hindus. Buddha stopped the ritual slaughter of animals, which was undertaken in the name of Vedic sacrifice, and taught compassion for all living beings. Buddha is also remembered for his teaching of ahimsa: non-violence.

Kalki, the Slayer

The tenth avatar will be Vishnu's future incarnation. At the end of the present dark age, a Brahman named Kalki will be born. He will be a hero and will ride a white horse. Kalki will bring about the final destruction of the evil world and then a new Creation will begin. Some authors believe that Vishnu will be with Kalki as a white horse: 'All glories to you, O Lord of the universe, who will take the form of Kalki. Like a comet you will appear riding a white horse and carrying a terrible sword,'[64] 'but there is no ancient indication of a horse-headed Vishnu.'[65]

The avatars are also useful in personal devotional contexts, for the divine One is believed capable of infinite manifestations or 'descents' (avatars), as Krishna, or Rama, or in animal form, such as elephant, fish, serpent, boar or monkey.

Shiva

Shiva, the destroyer, is also credited with being the one who recreates new life. Shiva is identified with fertility and procreation (in most of the temples dedicated to Shiva there is a statue of a bull, the symbol of virility). Shiva is the source of birth, of good and evil. He is also known as Pashupati, Lord of the Animals (*pashu*, 'beast'; *pati*, 'lord'). Pashupati is the presiding deity of Nepal. Pashupatinath Temple, near Kathmandu, is the holiest temple in Nepal and inside it there is a huge gold-plated image of a bull in a kneeling position.

Shiva is accompanied by this great bull, named Nandi. Nandi is usually depicted in a joyful mood, in a sitting or standing position. In some paintings Shiva is shown seated on Nandi, his vehicle. In all Shiva temples, Nandi faces the figure of Shiva, symbolizing the soul of the human yearning for Paramatma, the Supreme Soul. Nandi is the son of Surabhi, the divine cow who arose from the churning of the ocean. Nandi is not only Shiva's vehicle, but is also guardian of all four-legged creatures and stands guard at the four corners of the earth. Nandi's loyalty and devotion to Shiva is mentioned in all *Purana* stories. As well as his vehicle and companion Nandi, animal emblems of Shiva include tiger skin and snakes. Many Shiva temples give shelter to snakes.

In Nepal, Shiva, known as Nasa Deva, is offered rice beer and animal sacrifices.[66] This is a clear example of the paradoxical aspects of the deities, for in Nepal Shiva is also known as Bhairav (the dreadful aspect). This manifestation of Shiva, considered a Tantric god of Hinduism, is a wrathful aspect of Shiva and said to be satisfied only by blood sacrifice. Cocks are sacrificed by the Tantrics in the premises

An 11th–12th-century stone statue of Nandi, the sacred bull, from Tamil Nadu, India.

of Pashupatinath, but due to objections raised by Hindu Shaivites (devotees of Shiva), the number of sacrifices has decreased.[67]

One of the most popular associations with Shiva is through his son, Ganesha, the single-tusked elephant-headed deity. Ganesha, one of the most worshipped deities in Hinduism, is depicted riding a mouse and is venerated before one embarks on any journey, task or project. There are several myths surrounding Ganesha's acquisition of an elephant's head, the best-known of which highlights the ramifications of outbursts of anger: that asking questions before taking action can have tragic results. While Shiva was away from home, his wife Parvati became bored and lonely. She decided to make herself a baby and created Ganesha, either from the rubbings of her own body, from dew and dust or from clay. She later ordered the child to stand guard outside the entrance to her rooms, while she took a bath. When Shiva returned home and tried to see his wife, Ganesha, not realizing who he was, barred his entrance. In his anger Shiva chopped off Ganesha's head. Parvati was distraught and demanded that her son be brought back to life. The first head Shiva could find was that of an elephant.[68]

Another version is that Vishnu went in search of another head for Ganesha and returned with that of the elephant Airavata, the great white elephant ridden by Indra, the king of the gods.[69] According to another myth, Parvati invited the god Shani (or Sani), embodied in the planet Saturn, to visit her son. However, she had forgotten how dangerous the god could be and when he looked at Ganesha, the child's head burst into flames. Brahma told Parvati to repair her child with whatever she could find, which turned out to be the head of the elephant Airavata.[70]

Ganesha has many roles in Hinduism, as the Hindu god of wisdom and literature (credited as the first scribe of the *Mahabharata*), and the patron of business (business people hold ceremonies in his honour). Ganesha is also known as Ganapati or Vinayaka, and is the first deity to be worshipped during any ritual, as he is considered the remover of obstacles. Ganesha's appearance is a visual spiritual lesson. His huge body represents the cosmos or the universe and his trunk the Pranava or Om, the symbol of Brahman.[71] The snake around his waist represents cosmic energy, the noose is to remind us that worldly attachments are nooses and the hook on his hand is to prod humans on to the path of righteousness. The rosary beads are for the pursuit of prayer. The *modak* (sweet dumpling) in his hand is to remind us of the sweetness of one's inner self. The awkward form of Ganesha is to teach us that the outward form has no connection with inner beauty or spiritual perfection.[72] Ganesha on his vehicle, the mouse, symbolizes the equal importance of the biggest and the smallest of creatures to the Great God. The mouse was originally a demon who was transformed by Ganesha.

The other son of Shiva, Kartikeya (also known as Kumara, Skanda and Subramaniyan), rides the peacock, reminding us not to let pride or egotism get the better of us.

Other gods and goddesses connected with animals include the Goddess, sometimes called Devi, usually seen as a manifestation of Parvati. She is a beneficent deity, often called Amba and widely venerated as Shri or Lakshmi, mother of all creation. As Kali, she is dark and dishevelled. As a warrior goddess riding a tiger or lion she is Durga, one of the most popular goddesses in India. In one story she manifests herself with the energies of all other deities in order to combat a buffalo-demon, Mahishasura. After nine nights of struggle, she emerges victorious; this event is commemorated in the autumn festival of Navaratri ('Nine Nights'). In Nepal it is called the Dashain or the Durga Puja festival and is celebrated with the sacrifice of hundreds of goats and buffaloes to commemorate the event. As the goddess of strength, Devi Durga is accompanied by the king of the forest, the great lion. The Goddess may have been worshipped by the pre-Hindu Harappan civilization.

In the *Bhagavata Purana* (10.21.10–14) all of nature is portrayed as responding to Lord Krishna, the divine incarnation, and the call of his flute: the deer worship, the birds are dumbstruck, cows hold Krishna reverently in their minds. But these birds, we learn later, are not birds but ancient sages, incarnated to enjoy the Divine play on earth.[73] Even Hanuman, the beloved monkey god, is more deity than monkey. Animals are accorded respect, coming from Brahma, and because of their association with certain gods, especially with Vishnu, but animal sacrifice is still practised in Hinduism, particularly in worship of Durga and Shiva. Are animals valued for their uniqueness, or for the help they accord a god or goddess?

Liberation and Moksha

> Gods take animal form, human beings have had past animal lives, animals have had past human lives.[74]

One concept embraced by all Hindus is that of transmigration and reincarnation. *Samsara* is the cycle of birth–death–rebirth. The concept of karma is linked to samsara, for each action has either negative or positive consequences, or 'karma', which flow into the next existence and influence its character and dictate the form of one's rebirth. Hindus hope for enlightenment, which will mean a release or liberation (moksha) from this cycle of birth and rebirth. All life, from the smallest plant to the largest animal, goes through the process of reincarnation, with the soul or Atman continuing its journey, carrying forward unfulfilled karmic outcomes from previous lives and assuming new physical forms until it attains moksha or spiritual perfection. These life forms are not seen as equal in their material or physical form, but spiritually they are of the same importance because the material/physical form encloses or covers the spiritual.

Karma, a belief first documented around the seventh century BCE, means 'action'. In the context of the Rigveda, karma means ritual action: through one's actions in the sacrificial process, certain benefits can be assured. These texts from the Vedas do not place as great an emphasis on ethics as do the later Hindu texts, which list non-violence as pre-eminent. After the Upanishads, karma came to mean the concept of reward and punishment attached to various acts. Human beings gain merit (*punya*) or demerit (*papa*) from every action they perform.[75] The balance of *punya* and *papa* acquired in one lifetime determines the nature and quality of one's next existence.[76] Karmic consequences may span several lifetimes; there are serious karmic repercussions for taking an innocent life or for causing unnecessary suffering to another life form.

According to various schools of Hindu spirituality, there is no distinction between human beings and other life forms. All life forms, including plants and animals, are manifestations of God as limited beings (*jivas*) and possess souls. Even microorganisms are *jivas*, having souls of their own.[77] The Isa Upanishad states that everything, from a blade of grass to the whole cosmos, is the home of God.[78] The whole of creation is therefore sacred: any differences between creatures are in terms of their physical bodies and the number of *tattvas* (principles), *gunas* (qualities) and *mahabhutas* (elements) associated with them.[79]

The concept that all beings have souls may suggest compassion, but this does not entail any developed moral life in animals, or any real communion between animal and human. According to Nelson, the Atman (soul) in its transcendence is aloof, inactive and non-communicative; there is no Atman-to-Atman (soul-to-soul) communication.[80] In Hindu thinking communication takes place at the level of the mind, not at the level of Atman.[81] Hinduism credits animals with possessing Atman, yet they are dominated by *tamas* (darkness due to ignorance).

According to Hinduism, animals are not inferior creatures, but manifestations of God on the lower scale of evolution, containing a spark of the divine and capable of becoming human and achieving salvation. Human life is precious *only* because it comes after many lives of existence as lower life forms.

There are stories about certain people being reborn as animals. The temple of the fifteenth-century female mystic Karni Mata, who was regarded as an incarnation of the goddess Durga, is known as the 'Temple of Rats' because the many rats that live there are believed to be deceased members of the clan of Karni Mata. Due to a boon given to the saint, the rats, her relatives, never descend to the kingdom of the god of death, Yama, but wait in the bodies of rats until their next human birth, protected from harm.[82] The rats are fed by the offerings left for them by devotees. It is thought that if the devotees eat any leftover offering that has been nibbled by the sacred rats, this will bring the human good fortune.

Another story concerns Lakshmi, a cow, who was one of the most faithful devotees of Bhagavan Ramana Maharshi, waiting on the saint every day. At the time of her death, the saint placed his hand on her head and heart in a gesture of blessing.[83] A statue of Lakshmi was placed on the cow's tomb, which was in a prominent location, and there was an engraved epitaph, composed by the saint, declaring that the cow had attained moksha.[84] There was much speculation about this, prompting this remark:

> Although Lakshmi now wore the form of a cow, she must have attached herself to Sri Bhagavan and won his Grace by love and surrender in a previous birth. It seemed hard to explain in any other way the great solicitude and tenderness that Sri Bhagavan always showed in his dealings with her.[85]

It was decided that Lakshmi must be the reincarnation of Keeraipatti, an elderly woman who had been devoted to Ramana Maharshi, before her death.

In another example of animal liberation, the noble Jatayu, the vulture king of the *Ramayana*, sacrificed his own life attempting to save Sita, the wife of Rama. The bird's funeral rites were performed by the divine incarnation, Rama, and he thereby obtained moksha.[86]

In the *Bhagavata Purana* (8.2–4) there is a story dealing with animal spirituality. It tells of the liberation of an elephant that has been caught in the jaws of a crocodile. The elephant, Gajendra, focuses his mind and repeats a Sanskrit hymn in praise of Lord Vishnu. Then Vishnu appears, riding his heavenly vehicle, Garuda. The elephant struggles to utter 'Hail to Thee, O Narayana [Vishnu], Preceptor of the Universe!' (*Bhagavata Purana* 8.3.32). Vishnu dismounts, pulls Gajendra and the crocodile out of the lake, opens the crocodile's jaws and frees the elephant.[87] It turns out that the crocodile, a heavenly being, was a celestial musician incarnated as a crocodile as the result of a curse. Now freed from the curse, he returns to his heavenly abode. Gajendra is then delivered from his elephant body and granted moksha by Vishnu. In a previous life the elephant had been Indradyumna, a noble king turned ascetic, who had been devoted to Vishnu. It was in this former life that he had learned the long Sanskrit hymn that he recites. In that life, too, Indradyumna had made the mistake of upsetting a Brahmin sage, who cursed him thus: 'May this impious, malevolent, and feeble-minded fellow, who has insulted a Brahmin just now, sink into blinding ignorance. Since he is stupid like an elephant, let him be born as one.'[88]

In the *Chaitanya Charitamruta*, a biography of the sixteenth-century Bengali saint Caitanya (Chaitanya Mahaprabhu), a story is told of a dog who follows a group of disciples on a journey to meet their master, Lord Caitanya. One of the disciples, Sivānanda Sena, looks after the dog, feeding it and obtaining passage for it on the boat they use to cross a river. The dog disappears, but when the followers arrive at Jagannath Temple, at Puri, they are surprised to see the dog at the feet of Caitanya, chanting 'Krishna! Krishna!'[89] Later they learn that the dog's love for God had been awakened by contact with Caitanya, and that the dog had been granted moksha; it had been liberated from its canine body into Krishna's heavenly paradise.[90]

Commenting on this episode, A. C. Bhaktivedanta Swami Prabhupada (1896–1977) makes the point that the attachment and care of the dog by Sivananda Sena was a great boon to it and that the dog's salvation was made possible by *sadhu-sanga*, the spiritually uplifting effect of association with a holy person. 'This result is possible,' he remarks, 'even for a dog'.[91]

> The great emperor Yudhishthira, at the end of his reign, sets off on a final trek north, toward the Himalaya. He is accompanied by his four brothers, the Pandavas as they are known, and their common wife, Draupadi. A small pariah dog attaches himself to the retinue as well. Slowly, every member of this royal troupe dies along the way. The four brothers and his wife all succumb. Yudhishthira and the dog continue on their way alone. Eventually, they reach the end of their journey. At the gates of heaven, Indra, the King of the Gods, comes to greet the emperor in a golden chariot. He invites him to climb into the chariot and accompany him in regal and godly splendour into heaven. Yudhishthira replies: 'This dog, O Lord of the

Past and the Present, has been a constant and faithful companion to me. He should go with me. My heart is full of compassion for him.'

The King of the Gods says to him: 'Immortality equal to mine, O King, prosperity extending over all the earth, renown and all the joys of heaven have you won today. Leave the dog. There is nothing cruel in this.'

Yudhishthira says: 'O god of a thousand eyes, O you of righteous behaviour, I have always behaved righteously, it is hard now to perpetrate an act that is unrighteous. I do not wish for wealth for whose sake I must abandon one that is devoted to me.'

Indra says: 'There is no place in Heaven for persons with dogs. Besides, the deities called the Krodhavas take away all the merits of such persons. Think about this, O King of the righteous. Abandon the dog. It is not cruelty.'

Yudhishthira tells the King of the Gods: 'I will in no circumstances abandon this dog now to achieve happiness for myself.'

The king of the Gods tries to convince him one last time: 'If you give up this dog, you will acquire the world of heaven. You have already given up your brothers and wife. You have obtained heaven through your very own deeds. You have already abandoned everything. How can you be so confused as not to give up a mere dog?'

Yudhishthira still refuses, saying he abandoned his wife and brothers because they were already dead, but he will not abandon this living dog.

At that point, the dog reveals himself to the none other than the God of Righteousness himself [Dharma]. (*Mahabharata* 17.2–3)[92]

Stories of animals attaining moksha are quite challenging. They speak of the unexpected, for orthodox teachers say that only humans have this privilege. The despised species may become the profound; the divine is to be waited upon by all life forms, the sacred can manifest itself through all life forms. These stories are perhaps more to do with humans than with animals. In the story of Lakshmi the cow, the devotees could not understand their master's devotion to her, until they had decided that she had been human in her previous life. Would Gajendra the elephant have remembered the hymn if he had not been a royal ascetic in his previous life? Sivananda Sena's dog had been blessed because of his contact with devotees whose spirituality was transferred to the dog.

Karma and Dharma: Hindu Ethics and Sacrifice

In the *Bhagavad Gita* Krishna says: 'I am the Self seated in the heart of all creatures. I am the beginning, the middle and the very end of all beings. All beings have, therefore, to be treated alike.'

In classical Hinduism, actions (karma) and duty (dharma) were the dominant concepts. Karma, as the accumulation of good and bad acts, would influence a person's destiny. Early in the Veda there had been the notion of an overriding moral law: *Rta* (order, truth). Humanity had to recognize a divine imperative, and prayer and sacrifice were necessary to maintain a right relationship between the divine and the human. In modern times, more weight is placed on universal values such as truthfulness, kindness and love, as well as the need to alleviate suffering.

The classical Hindu view of the world is hierarchical and anthropocentric. Superiority of the human is not based on the possession of the soul (we have already seen that the same Atman is in all beings). The difference is that of morality, for only humans have the capacity to receive the appropriate revelation in the form of the Veda, and only humans have what proceeds from the Veda, which is dharma (correct ritual behaviour and morality). Although we have noted exceptions to this rule, the majority of Hindus would say that only human beings have access to moksha (spiritual liberation).

All Hindu teachers agree that one's journey through samsara is determined by one's karma, the moral consequences of one's actions. The circumstances of one's birth, whether in human or animal form, is attributed to one's karma. In Manu 12.40, 'people of darkness [*tamas*] always become animals.'[93] Rebirth as an animal, is, for humans, a frightening prospect: 'Violent men become carnivorous (beasts); people who eat impure things become worms; thieves (become animals that) devour one another... Women, too, who steal in this way incur guilt; they become the wives of these very same creatures' (Manu 12.59.69).[94]

The Chandogya Upanishad (6.10.7–8) promises rebirth as a dog or pig to those whose conduct has been evil. Those who neglect Vedic values 'take birth as these small creatures – gadflies, mosquitoes, and other insects – which are reborn again and again . . . They spend their time in mere birth and death, having opportunity for neither ritual nor enjoyment' (5.108).[95]

Is there equality or a type of caste system in transmigration? In the *Bhagavad Gita* (5.18) Brahmins and cows are seen as being alike as the highest beings, both pure and holy, whereas the dog and the outcaste are marginalized; both are oppressed. Dogs are viewed as unclean and therefore impure, the outcastes of the animal world: 'the dog [is] to the cow in the world of beasts what the outcaste is to the Brahmin in the world of men.'[96]

In orthodox tradition, dogs are seen as indiscriminate in their eating habits and their sexual behaviour. Designated as 'vomit-eaters', they prowl in cremation grounds and eat carrion. The commentator Vyasa wrote about the *yogin* in this way: 'If I, the very person who had once given up perverse thoughts [of violence], were to revert to them, I would be behaving like a dog . . . One who reverts to what has once been renounced is like a dog licking up its own vomit.'[97] Dog behaviour can resemble that attributed to outcastes.[98] It is thought that if dogs (and outcastes) glance at the food of Brahmins, they pollute it.

Yet there are also positive references:

> The dog is associated with Indra, Yama and Siva. Indra had a dog called Sarama, whose progeny became the watchdogs of Yamaloka, the nether world of Lord Yama . . . The dog is also associated with Lord Siva who is known as svapathi, or the lord of the dogs. Bhairava, a fierce form of Siva, has a dog as an attendant. Khanoba, an aspect of Siva, who is worshipped in Maharashtra, had a dog as his vehicle. Lord Dattatreya who is the personification of the Brahma, Vishnu and Siva is always accompanied by four dogs who symbolize the four Vedas.[99]

In some instances, ancient Hindu ritual and scripture call for sacrifice. For a marginal number of Hindus, this translates into the practice of animal sacrifice. The vast majority of Hindus do not participate in, or condone, animal sacrifice. Most Hindus carry out their sacrifice to the Divine using foods such as fruit, grains and clarified butter, and through fasting. Because Hinduism is a term that includes many different, though related, religious ideas, there is no clear single Hindu view on the right way to treat animals.

There are certain passages that deal with ethical treatment of animals (usually concerning abstaining from injury or violence) and also some that view animals as teachers:

> By not killing any living being, one becomes fit for salvation. (Manu samhita 6.60)

> Deer, camel, donkey, monkey, rats, creeping animals, birds and flies – one should consider them like one's own children, and not differentiate between one's children and these creatures. (*Bhagavata Purana* 7.14.9)

> He should not satiate his hunger and thirst without first giving water and grain to his animals. (*Vishnu Dharma Sutra* 63.18)

> The ascetic should live the life of a bee, accepting little alms from several homes, so that he does not burden any particular home too much, and take only that much which fulfils his hunger. A clever man takes the essence from multiple sources and scriptures, just as the bee extracts nectar from several flowers. (*Bhagavata Purana* 11.8.9–10)

> The ascetic calls these animals as his teachers. (*Bhagavata Purana* 11.9.24)

Other questions can be raised, as well as a number of contradictions to ponder: are these actions undertaken in order to gain a better result in the next life, in the next rebirth? Is ethical care of animals undertaken because one recognizes the sacredness in all, or as a means to a better end? It is understood that karma cannot be earned, yet many of the writings seem to suggest the opposite. There is discrepancy in the concept of the sacredness of all, as shown in some of the material concerning how dogs are sometimes viewed and their alignment or association with outcastes. There is also fear surrounding the notion of being reborn in animal form.

Animal Sacrifice

> Meat can never be obtained without injury to living creatures, and injury to sentient beings is detrimental to the attainment of heavenly bliss; let him therefore shun the use of meat. (Manu Smriti 5.48, Vishnu Dharma Sutra 51.71)

During the Vedic period, animal sacrifice was frequent and preceded almost any endeavour for which the outcome was uncertain. Obligations of the Vedic sacrificial cult still held sway for many years, though the practice of animal sacrifice was in decline by the time of the major Hindu law books (200 BCE–200 CE). This was due to an unease regarding sacrificial violence and concern about future consequences for those involved in the sacrifices.[100] There was also pressure from Buddhist and Jain advocates of ahimsa, but animal sacrifice was permitted in general households. Manu 5.39 states that animals were created for sacrifice and that 'killing in sacrifice is not killing.'[101]

This conflict is seen in the most authoritative legal text in Hinduism, the *Manusmriti*. He is very specific when it comes to the sacrificial aspect of meat-eating: one should not eat meat without a sacred purpose, and eating meat is only allowed in a sacrificial setting. It is interesting to note that, according to Manu, birds and animals slaughtered in sacrifice attain a higher existence in their next life, as does the Brahmin priest who performs the ritual.[102]

Manu follows the injunction and customs of his Vedic forefathers, yet he departs from them on the issue of meat consumption outside the ritual context. If an animal is slaughtered unlawfully, the man 'will be slain as many times as there are hairs on the body of the animal.'[103]

Perhaps from these examples (several among many) we see that Manu is obliged to defer to the sanctity of Vedic injunctions, and therefore allows animal sacrifices to be performed and meat to be eaten in ritualistic contexts.[104] However, the number of his sayings about not eating meat for the purpose of satisfying the palate suggests that if it were not for scripture he would not tolerate animal sacrifice. Manu even undermines the ritual practices by suggesting that an offering made of butter and flour be substituted instead.

In the *Brahmana Satya*, it is stated that someone who has engaged in violent sacrifices will lose any merit that has been gained.[105] This text states that in the *satya yuga* – the golden age – there was no sacrifice;

animal sacrifice was only introduced during the second of the four ages, when people began to resort to violence. This implies that animal sacrifice developed during a less compassionate age. The Vedic prescriptions promoting animal sacrifice are thereby assigned to a less enlightened era.

In many *Puranas* there is evidence for conflicting beliefs within the sacrificial cult. The *Kurma Purana* requires that Brahmins are to be fed rice and meat during the rites to departed ancestors; any higher caste person who does not eat the flesh at such sacrifices will become like an animal for 21 births.[106] The same text, however, also states that Brahma created the institution of sacrifice *without* the slaughter of animals.[107]

The tension in these post-Vedic texts is probably due to later editing, when arguments against meat-eating and animal sacrifice were added at a time when sacrifice was fading in appeal, yet older sections of the texts, which acknowledged such practices, were preserved. Part of the reason was the idea of the later Vedic period that humans and animals had the same Atman, or life force. Animals began to be seen more as subjects rather than as objects for consumption. Many innovative thinkers of this period moved away from the Vedic sacrificial rites and Vedic texts, and became Jains or Buddhists. They preached ahimsa without having to struggle within the orthodox Brahmana group.

In the *Skandha Purana* it was said that the sages were dismayed to see the violence of animal sacrifice. When King Vasu, who had sacrificed a great number of animals, was asked by the sages whether animals or herbs were to be offered as sacrifice, he was reported as falling from heaven to earth for saying that it was to be animals.[108] The *Skandha Purana* also gives a reason for the introduction of animal sacrifice, stating that it was a concession to an emergency that had arisen when there was famine. It was therefore a concession to humanity, but was never intended to be the norm.

The text that distances itself the most from animal sacrifice is the *Bhagavata Purana*, which states that a person who truly understands dharma does not eat meat at sacred rites; a refusal to cause harm is seen as the highest dharma. The Bhagavata tells the story of Pracinabarhis, who had killed many animals, through both hunting and animal sacrifice. He received a vision of these animals waiting for his death so they could carry out violence against him by cutting him with their horns.[109]

Over time the ahimsa ethic triumphed over the ancient sacrificial cult and animal sacrifice was no longer allowed, especially by the *bhakti* (devotional) traditions. The *Purana* attributes awareness of human intent and animal fear to animals confronted by sacrificial death: 'Seeing someone about to sacrifice with material offerings, beings are filled with dread, fearing "This self-indulgent [human], having no compassion, will slay me."'[110] From the tenth century Hindu legal writings prohibited animal sacrifice and by the thirteenth century animal effigies were suggested as worthy substitutions. Even though the numbers declined, the practice of animal sacrifice continued in the temples of the goddesses Kali and Durga, in tantric rites and in regional village traditions.

In some remote areas of India animal sacrifice continues today. Though formal animal sacrifices of the early Vedic period gradually lost their importance, due to the reformatory movements of the Upanishadic sages, Jainism and Buddhism:

> a new type of animal sacrifice got into the fabric of Hinduism during later ages as aboriginal cultures got integrated into the Hindu fold. The Deity was invariably an aspect of Durga or Kali and the rituals were very simple. Buffaloes, goats, sheep and cockerels were the usual sacrificial victims. It was believed that these victims would go to heaven.[111]

Blood is used to consecrate the image of the god or goddess being worshipped and a portion of the animal is presented to the god or goddess. It is thought that it is an honour for an animal to be selected for sacrifice. Before sacrifice, the person performing the sacrifice consults the animal, requiring it to 'nod' its assent before the sacrifice can take place. If there is no response, then water is sprinkled on its head to make it nod. If this does not elicit a nod, then the sacrifice is delayed and other methods used to make the animal nod.

The rise of Tantricism in the post-Mauryan period and the integration of folk religions into Hinduism contributed to the rise in animal sacrifice.[112] Practices of Hindu animal sacrifice are mostly associated with Shaktism.[113] In current folk Hinduism they are strongly rooted in local tribal traditions. Animal sacrifice is now mainly confined to the southern state of Tamil Nadu (performed in front of local or clan deities), the eastern states of India and Nepal. It is also conducted by some Hindus on the Indonesian island of Bali. Adherents of the Shakta sect of Hinduism hold this to be a central tenet of their belief. The ritual slaughter forms part of a festival to honour a Hindu god. In Nepal, for example, the goddess Gadhimai is honoured every five years with the slaughter of 250,000 animals. In Bali sacrifice is common at the Shakta shrines of the goddess Kali. While most Indian Hindus oppose animal sacrifice and eating meat, based on the prevailing Hindu principle of ahimsa, only a few Balinese Hindus seem to share this view. They believe that animal sacrifice leads to the attainment of a human birth for the animal. Every home makes an animal sacrifice to Kali every fifteen days. At the Ekadasa Rudra festival, which is held once every one hundred years, more than two hundred kinds of animals are sacrificed.

Jhatka bali is the prescribed method for Hindu ritual slaughter. The *jhatka* method requires the instant killing of the animal in a single decapitating blow with an axe or sword, for it is seen as a bad omen if the animal makes a noise.

Ritual animal sacrifice also includes the practice of Tabuh Rah, a religious cockfight that is an exercise in spiritual appeasement in Balinese Hinduism. The spilling of blood is thought necessary in order to appease evil spirits. Ritual fights usually take place outside the temple proper, and follow a complex ancient ritual set out in the sacred lontar manuscripts.

Ahimsa and Meat Consumption

The concept of ahimsa (non-injury or non-violence) emerges from a world view based on notions of karma that link violent activity to future painful retribution. The doctrine of ahimsa is not exclusively a Hindu concept, but is upheld in both Jainism and Buddhism.

The Mahabharata states many times that 'ahimsa is the highest duty (dharma)' (for example, 1.11.12 and 3.198.69) and the Hindu law books state that non-injury is the duty of all human beings.[114] The *Manusmriti*, which have played a great role in shaping Hindu society, list ahimsa among the rules to be performed by all castes. In the Hindu tradition, ascetics, as part of their call to renunciation, promise to give safety to all living beings: the renouncer 'should inspect the ground constantly as he walks, by night or by day' (*Manusmriti*, or *The Laws of Manu*, 6:68).[115]

In the *Mahabharata*, the Hindu epic about war between two sets of cousins, there is extensive discussion concerning non-violence. The wise grand-uncle Bhisma explains that ahimsa involves two elements: doing no physical harm and seeing all beings as similar to oneself: 'The meat of other animals is like the flesh of one's son. The foolish person, stupefied by folly, who eats meat, is regarded as the vilest of human beings' (13.114.11).[116] The Golden Rule that everyone should observe is that 'Persons endowed with intelligence and purified selves should always behave toward other beings after the manner of that behaviour which they like others to observe towards themselves' (13.115.22).[117] '*Ahimsa* is the dharma. It is the highest purification. It is also the highest truth from which all dharma proceeds' (13.125.25).[118] In these and similar passages ahimsa is cited as the best of all actions, giving birth to righteousness (dharma) and serving as the best path for purification.

In the classical Yoga system, part of the renouncer school of the Hindu tradition, ahimsa is mentioned as the basis of and the reason for all ethical practices and is to be strictly adhered to by aspiring yogis. Ascetics seek to rid themselves of violent thoughts. Those who succeed are thought to be able to pacify dangerous animals and to cause species that are mutual enemies to live together in harmony.

The *Bhagavad Gita* echoes the Golden Rule: 'When one sees the pleasure and pain in all beings as the same in comparison with self . . . one is considered the highest *yogin*' (6.32).[119] Elsewhere it is stated that the ideal sages are those who 'delight in the welfare of all beings' (5.25).[120] Those who are not ascetics do not have to observe the ethic of ahimsa as rigidly as the renouncers.

A Hindu sage from the twentieth century, Bhagavan (Blessed One) Ramana Maharshi, was known for his extraordinary affection for animals, as well as his ability to communicate with them. He knew their habits, likes and dislikes, and their individual personalities. Many species shared his ashram with his human devotees, including dogs, cats, squirrels, peacocks, monkeys, cows, snakes and scorpions. He called them by name and did not discriminate between his human and his animal devotees: 'We do not know what souls may be tenanting these bodies . . . and for finishing what portion of their unfinished karma they may seek our company.'[121] It is said that he understood the language of the monkeys that lived in the area, and that they would seek him out in order to settle their disputes.[122]

As stated in the *Bhagavad Gita*, the person of knowledge 'sees no difference between a learned Brahmin, a cow, an elephant, a dog, or an outcaste'.[123] In the language of the Vedas, the Brahman is inseparable from its individual manifestations. To violate another creature is to violate Brahman itself.

Christopher Key Chapple, a theologian of the religions of India, tells a story about a development worker from the United States being called in to investigate food shortages in India. One of the main reasons for the shortage was the vast number of rats devouring the grain. The American's suggestion of using poison horrified his Indian co-workers, for it would violate ahimsa. A solution was found by placing the grain storage facilities on stilts, thereby decreasing the number of rats without injuring them.[124]

Chapple narrates another story that encompasses the ethic of ahimsa from a practical angle:

> A woman from India told me a story that occurred during her childhood in West Bengal. An important local temple had become overrun with ants. The offerings to the enshrined deity were being consumed, not by the god or the resident priests, but by swarms of industrious insects. To kill them was unthinkable, but their presence grew increasingly intolerable. Finally, one enterprising temple-goer proposed a solution that at first seemed preposterous but, due to lack of alternatives, was given a try. Next to the existing temple a new shrine was erected, to and for the ants. Rather than being composed of stone, this religious centre was comprised solely of sugar cane, and included offerings of refined sugar. Soon, the human temple was free of pestilence and, judging by the numbers of devotees, the ant temple soon outstripped its human counterpart in popularity.[125]

But can one say that Hinduism embraces ahimsa? Animal sacrifice, inseparable from the all-important Vedic ritual tradition, is still practised in some places, so ahimsa cannot be stated to be an all-embracing ethic observed by all Hindus.

Meat Consumption

Eating meat was not forbidden in ancient India. The Vedic people ate cooked meats of certain animals, and meat was cooked and consumed at the end of particular sacrificial ceremonies, such as the horse sacrifice. Oxen and bulls were sacrificed to the gods and their meat was eaten, but the slaughter of milk-producing cows was increasingly prohibited, and in the middle of the first millennium CE, killing a cow was made a capital offence. Even when meat-eating was permitted, however, the ancient Vedic scriptures encouraged vegetarianism. One scripture states: 'There is no sin in eating meat . . . but abstention brings great rewards' (*The Laws of Manu*, 5.56).

The *Apastamba Sutras* forbid meats of certain animals, such as one-hoofed animals, camels, certain birds, fish, deer, village pigs and cattle, but hedgehogs, rhinoceros and hares are allowed.[126] Later, in the spiritually fertile period that produced Buddhism and Jainism, most Hindus stopped eating meat. This would have been for practical as well as spiritual reasons: it was expensive to slaughter an animal for religious rituals, or for a guest, and the cow produced important products, such as milk, butter and dung for fuel. This era, and the incorporation of Jain traditions, may have had a direct influence on Hindu texts and teachings as they developed, for ahimsa became an important religious value. Jainism exercised a great influence in changing the food habits of the people of the subcontinent, for many ancient rulers of India were Jains.

In regard to meat-eating, the *Manusmriti* contain several recommendations, including that only meat obtained through ritual sacrifice may be eaten and that one should eat no meat:[127] 'Live on flowers, roots, and fruits alone, which are ripened by the time and fallen spontaneously (6.21). He who for a hundred years annually sacrifices a horse sacrifice and he who does not eat meat [at all]: for both of these the fruit of their meritorious deeds is the same.'[128] All those involved in the killing of animals, from the slaughterer, the butcher and the cook to those who consume the meat, are seen as murderers and are liable for punishment.[129]

The *Mahabharata* contains some of the strongest statements against the slaughter of animals and the consumption of meat. Although there are references to eating meat and to sacrificial rites, the *Mahabharata* contains stories glorifying non-violence against animals. There is a story about a sage who was impaled by thieves on a large pike. When the sage asked Dharma, the god of righteousness, what his offence had been to warrant this negative karmic reaction, he was told that he had once pricked an insect with a blade of grass and was now suffering the karmic consequences.[130] Another sage, Cyavana, while meditating underwater, was caught in a net along with many fish. Seeing the great slaughter of fish, the sage declared that he had lived with the fish for so long that he would not abandon them: he would either die with them or be sold alongside them.[131]

Strong protests against eating meat can be found in the *Mahabharata*, where three chapters are devoted to the evils of meat consumption. Bhisma, grandsire of the Kuru dynasty, explains that compassion is the highest religious principle. Eating meat is compared to eating the flesh of one's own son. Bhisma says that consumers of meat will not gain the joys of heaven; in fact, 'the righteous gained entrance into heaven in previous ages by giving up their own bodies to protect the lives of other creatures.'[132] Bhisma also allows sacrifices to be performed with seeds rather than with animals, so providing a way of fulfilling the Vedic sacrificial requirements without having to slaughter animals.

According to Bhisma, becoming a vegetarian is the highest form of religion and will mean one will gain the confidence of other creatures. Those who eat meat will suffer torment in various future births by the same animals one has eaten, and this suffering will be in the same form as that which was inflicted on animals in this life. The one who does not eat meat will see heaven in the next life and will never see hell. In contrast, one who shortens the lifespan of other creatures will see their own lifespan shortened and will be tormented in hell.[133]

The *Bhagavata Purana* graphically portrays what happens to those who kill or harm animals:

> a man cooking animals and birds is merciless and goes to *kumbhipaka* hell where he in turn is fried in boiling oil; unlawful animal killers are made the target of the arrows of the servants of Yama, the lord of death; those killing animals in sham sacrifices are themselves cut to pieces in *visasana* hell; those harming insects and other lesser creatures go to the *andhakupa* hell where, deprived of sleep and unable to rest anywhere, they are tortured by those very creatures.[134]

By the ninth century vegetarianism was becoming the norm for Brahmins and followers of the devotional sects, although the ruling castes, the Kshatriyas, continued to observe the hunting of game and eating meat.[135] Nowadays vegetarianism is common practice among many followers of Hinduism, and Hindus make up the largest percentage of vegetarians in the world. It is an ethical and practical way of observing ahimsa. Some branches of Hinduism consider vegetarianism a core virtue. Most Hindu temples do not allow meat products on their premises.

Before concluding this analysis of animals in Hinduism, it is worth considering in more depth the role and status of the cow. Two other creatures will also be explored: the snake and the elephant. While they are of lesser importance, both play pivotal roles in Hinduism.

The Sacred Cow

In Hinduism the cow is revered as a source of food and a symbol of life. It may never be killed, although there are examples that contradict this. Most Hindus do not worship the cow, and cows do not always lead charmed lives in India, but the cow is still viewed as sacred.

Cows have been considered sacred from the early Rigvedic period and were associated with the sacred in the ancient hymns of the Vedas. The Vedas prohibit the killing of cows for either religious or secular purposes. During the Gupta rule, cow slaughter became a capital offence and remained so for a long time under successive generations of Hindu rulers.

Kamadhenu-Surabhi, considered to be a sacred cow, emerged from the churning of the cosmic ocean, in order to acquire ambrosia, the elixir of life. Lord Krishna spent most of his childhood in the midst of cowherds and became one himself. His flute had a soothing effect on the cows, causing them to produce more milk. Krishna is also known as the cow-protector, 'Gopala'. Goloka, or the land of the cows, is another name for Vaikuntha, the world of Vishnu. The pastoral element in the Krishna stories from the tenth century onwards further reinforced the sanctity of the cow.

There are fewer representations of cows in Hindu art than of other animals, because the cow is not associated with any deity, either in the form of a vehicle or as an attribute, except as the companion of Krishna.

Sacred cows by a temple on the ghats of Maheshwar on the shore of the Narmada River, central India.

The sacred cow is known by several names; in Puranic myth she is Kamadhenu, 'yielder of the milk of all desire' or the 'cow of plenty'.[136] The name Surabhi (which is also used to refer to an ordinary cow) means The Fragrant One, perhaps alluding to the particular scent of cows; it can also mean 'charming' or 'pleasing'. It is said that Surabhi was created by Prajapati from his breath. Cows are regarded as the daughters of the heavenly Surabhi, as well as the embodiment of Lakshmi, the goddess of wealth. The residence of Surabhi is Goloka, which is mentioned in the epics and the *Puranas*, and is depicted as a paradise of great splendour and happiness. It can only be attained by the most pious, and it is assumed that donors and worshippers of cows will attain this heaven.[137]

In the *Satapatha Brahmana* the cow is praised with these words: 'the shower of wealth, the body (from which it flows) is the sky, the udder the cloud, the teat is lightning and the shower (of *ghee*) is the rain-shower from the sky.'[138]

When someone in a Hindu family dies, there is a tradition of giving a cow as a gift to a Brahmin. A cow donated to the Brahmins is thought to carry the departing soul across the river Vaitarani, which separates the world of the living from the world of the dead. In a Vaitarani ritual, this belief is enacted when the worshipper clutches the tail of a cow.[139] The cow is held in such high regard by the

Brahmins that it is thought to be the animal that is most inhabited by souls prior to their incarnation as Brahmins.[140] Killing a cow is considered equal to killing a Brahmin. A researcher in the holy city of Varanasi, where Brahmins perform cow worship (*go-puja*), was told: 'We believe that 330 million Hindu gods live in every atom of the cow's body' and 'We believe in going to heaven by the aid of the cow.'[141]

Every part of a cow's body is thought to be occupied by a divinity; so everything the cow produces is considered sacred, including its dung and urine, which are used in certain rites and rituals. The five products (*pancagavya*) of the cow – milk, curds, ghee, urine and dung – are used in *puja* (worship) as well as in rites of penance.[142] Cow dung is sometimes used in the materials for *tilak*, the ritual mark on the forehead. Elderly cows are also looked after; there are records of shelter and care being given to unproductive cattle as early as the fourth century BCE, and homes (*goshalas*) established for ageing cattle by the sixteenth century CE.[143] *Goshalas* continue to be a prominent feature of Hindu religious establishments.

Gandhi considered care of the cow paramount in Hinduism; this practical application of the principle of ahimsa had universal scope, for it was to include all other creatures:

> The central fact of Hinduism is cow protection. It is to me one of the most wonderful phenomena in human evolution. It takes the human beyond his species. The cow to me means the entire sub-human world. Man through the cow is enjoined to realize his identity with all that lives. Why the cow was selected for apotheosis is obvious to me. The cow was in India the best companion. She was the giver of plenty. Not only did she give milk, but she also made agriculture possible. The cow is a poem of pity. One reads pity in the gentle animal. She is the mother to millions of Indian mankind. Protection of the cow means protection of the whole dumb creation of God. The appeal of the lower order is all the more forcible because it is speechless. Cow protection is the gift of Hinduism to the world.[144]

Serpent Deities

The worship of snakes is a very ancient tradition in India. The Vedic people did not worship snakes, but many native people across the subcontinent did. According to Hindu mythology, the serpent deities are semi-divine beings descended from the sage Kashyapa and his wife Kadru, and they live in the subterranean world of Nagaloka.[145] They guard gems, minerals and precious stones. Known for their wisdom, skill and magical powers, they are depicted in Hindu iconography with a lower snake body covered by bejewelled garments and a human head adorned with three to seven cobra hoods.[146] The snake deities are charming personalities who can bewitch human beings with their grace and beauty. There is eternal enmity between them and their cousin Garuda, the celestial bird and vehicle of Vishnu.

In certain parts of southern India the serpent deities are associated with fertility and tree worship: 'Women, desiring offspring, worship snake stones having the images of a snake goddess carrying two offspring in her arms. The stones are installed under either a pipal or a neem tree after keeping them submerged under water for six months and worshipped with flowers and vermilion.'[147]

Prominent serpent deities include Ananta, Kaliya and Vasuki. Ananta is the king of the serpent world. Kaliya was a five-headed serpent who was subdued by Lord Krishna after a prolonged fight. Vasuki was a giant serpent who helped gods and demons in the churning of the oceans for the nectar of immortality.

The serpent deities constitute an important aspect of Hinduism even today. Devout men and women in the rural areas of North and South India worship them with milk, incense and flowers, seeking their help and grace. In some parts of India, killing a snake is a bad omen and brings bad karma. People avoid killing cobras because of the belief that they can recognize their attackers and take revenge. If a snake or a cobra is accidentally killed, it is customary to perform certain rites before cremating or burying it to avoid retribution from the serpent deities.

Serpents are still involved in worship: on the eve of Nag Panchami, snakes are worshipped throughout India and are not killed on this day. Snakes are closely associated with Lord Shiva. In a temple of Lord Shiva in Marleshwar, in Maharashtra, there are hundreds of snakes on the road to the temple.

The Elephant

According to legend, the first elephant was produced from the cosmic golden egg, or *Hiranyagarbha*. Brahma took two halves of the broken shell in his hands and breathed life into them.[148] Out of one half came Airavata and seven other male elephants, while from the second half came eight female elephants. The eight male elephants became the *vahana*, or vehicle, of the *Ashta-Dikpalas*, the Guardians of the Eight Directions. They support the universe at four quarters and at four points. Airavata is associated with water, the rainbow (Indra's weapon) and lightning. Depictions of elephants have been in various Hindu temples from the eighth century.[149] In some temples, especially in Nepal and Tibet, elephant statues are set up to serve as door guardians. They assume the attitude of devotion to the deities, whose places of worship they guard.

There is another legend about the origin of the first elephant, Airavata, and his consort Abhramu. The *Vishnu Purana* and the *Matsya Purana* say that after the gods worked for more than a thousand years, strange personifications and symbols came out of the milk of the universe, first the goddess Kamala and then Airavata, the milky white elephant. Airavata had a huge body with two pairs of white tusks. Indra, the chief of the gods, appropriated him as his mount. Since then the elephant has been associated with might.[150] Airavata also guards the entrance to the heavens. He is regarded as an ancient serpent king, reborn at the time of the churning of the ocean. Abhramu, Airavata's consort, produces monsoon clouds that bring down rain to the crops.[151]

White elephants are accorded special significance: they suggest the origin of their ancestors from the milk of the universe and are thought to have the power to produce clouds. Elephants are regarded as sacred beings as they bestow upon the people the boons of earthly happiness, abundance of crops and cattle, prosperity, offspring, long life and health. A popular legend surrounding Shiva and Parvati is that they took the form of elephants and lived in the mountains, enjoying being animals. They were called Matanga and Matangi. During this intense period of love their first son, Ganesha, was born.[152]

Conclusion

Although there is an underlying and all-abiding essence of 'oneness' in Hinduism, with all life imbued with the same *atman* from Brahman, the ethic of ahimsa is not as developed as in Buddhism and Jainism. Although Hinduism does not require a vegetarian diet, many Hindus avoid eating meat, since they believe that this minimizes the harming of other life forms. There is also still some concern as to how ahimsa can be aligned with a religion that allows animal sacrifice to continue.

It is interesting to note that the stories pertaining to animals are mainly associated with gods, such as Vishnu's avatars; there are few, except for those about Bhagavan Ramana Maharshi, that deal with the human. Does this mean that animals are more mythical than real? Does this change the way we perceive them? Or the way we care for them? Could the 'unicorn' seal from the Indus valley thousands of years ago have contributed to this mythical view of animals?

The concepts of karma and samsara tend to imply passiveness: our ways are set; this is our path (and the path of others, human and animal) in this life. This view does not hold with activism, particularly in the domain of animal welfare. One could also interpret transmigration as a way of according human beings a higher status than non-human animals: only humans can attain liberation.

While animals are vehicles and/or companions for deities, and are linked with all other life forms in the path of reincarnation, in many instances they are still viewed as commodities or as a means to an end, as in ritual sacrifice. The application of ahimsa is inconsistent, as has been shown. In Hinduism animals embody the roles of midwives, messengers and beasts of burden.

EIGHT
Animals in Jainism

In the Jain *Kritanga Sutra* the teaching goes beyond people: 'Treat all creatures in the world as you want to be treated.'
Stephanie Dowrick, *Seeking the Sacred*[1]

In Jainism, the spiritual well-being of a human being is tied to the physical well-being of all forms of life.
Kristi Wiley, 'Five-sensed Animals in Jainism'[2]

There is no quality of soul more subtle than non-violence and no virtue of spirit greater than reverence for life.
Vardhamana Mahavira

If you kill someone, it is yourself you kill. If you overpower someone, it is yourself you overpower. If you torment someone, it is yourself you torment. If you harm someone, it is yourself you harm.
Vardhamana Mahavira

Together: *Parasparopagraho Jivanam* (Interdependence of Life)[3]

IN THE JAIN RELIGION and within its practice, the guiding principle is a conviction in the phrase *Parasparopagraho jivanam*, translated as 'All life is bound together by mutual support and interdependence.' Jains are well known for their commitment to a vegetarian diet, their concern for the environment and their involvement in human and animal welfare.

Overview of Jainism

Jainism is one of the most ancient of India's indigenous traditions and the oldest of the surviving non-Vedic schools.[4] Jainism is a minority religion, with less than 1 per cent of the Indian population being Jain, yet it has had a major influence in developing a system of philosophy and ethics that has influenced other religions, with concepts such as karma, ahimsa, moksha[5] and reincarnation propagated and developed by Jain teachers. Jainism has no single founder, yet its strong ethical ideals, especially its emphasis on ahimsa (non-violence) have been much admired through the centuries. Jains do not worship animal gods, yet animals, and their relationship with humans, pervade all of Jain teaching. The heart of Jainism is non-violence to all beings, making it a religion of compassion, for it considers the welfare of all living beings, not just humans. The practice and protest of Jainism helped end Vedic animal sacrifice and influenced both Buddhist and Hindu religions. The cosmology, logic and ethics of Jain beliefs have remained unaltered for more than two and a half thousand years.

In the sixth century BCE there was a backlash against the traditional priesthood in the ancient world that led to the appearance of seven new world religions within fifty years of each other, one being Jainism.[6] Up to this point, Indian life had been dominated by the Brahmin priesthood. North India was experiencing social and political upheaval. During this time, teachers who were seen as heterodox came to be associated with Buddhism, Jainism and the Ajivika sect.[7] These teachers may have been influenced by the Sramanas, who differed from the Brahmins because they followed ascetic practices and rejected the authority of the Vedas, the institution of the caste system and animal sacrifice. Sramanas were part of what became known as the Renouncer (ascetic) tradition. Jainism started spreading in South India from the third century BCE. Several different traditions developed, but all unanimously accept and believe in the core Jain philosophies, including the major vows of non-violence, truthfulness, non-stealing, celibacy and non-possession.

Mahavira is often credited with founding Jainism, but the religion existed long before. India's great Vedic traditions were coalescing into Hinduism, and Mahavira was born only a few years before his contemporary, Gautama Buddha. Jainism has influenced Hindu rituals and the concept of non-violence was incorporated into Hinduism.

(Many Hindus and Jains regard Hinduism to have been derived from Jainism.) The concepts of karma, nirvana and ahimsa are present in Hinduism and Buddhism, meaning that both track their roots to early Jainism. The main difference between Jain and Buddhist practice is the extent to which Mahavira imposed his dictates of total abstinence.

In Jainism there is no creator or personal god: it is atheistic. Jains therefore do not hold a deity responsible for creation or for the ongoing governance of the universe; instead, the universe changes over time as governed by the laws of nature. Rather than a deity, Jains believe that *tirthankaras* ('ford builders' or 'crossing makers') assist people. *Tirthankaras* are Jain saints or guides who have achieved enlightenment by conquering their emotions and desires. By leading others to enlightenment, they achieve their status and bring an end to samsara, the cycle of reincarnation. The *tirthankaras*' spiritual guidance helps souls cross the 'river of human suffering'. *Tirthankaras* are rare: Jains believe that only 24 beings in the past eight million years have achieved moksha and ascended to the supreme throne at the top of the universe.[8]

Jains believe that time rotates in an infinite cycle, descending and ascending. According to Jain cosmology, there was no beginning to the universe; nor will there be an end. The cyclic nature of the universe is a constant motif in Jainism:

> The Jain cosmos exists in a set of layers or states: Siddha is the supreme condition, resting 'at the top of the universe' where the souls who achieve moksa reside; the upper world is made up of thirty heavens all occupied by celestial beings; the middle world consists of our world and universe; the nether region is comprised of seven hells of various miseries and punishments; the Nigoda is where the lowest forms of life reside; and the void beyond is merely infinite space without soul, time or matter.[9]

Depending on their actions, animals may be reborn in one of eight heavens or seven hells. If animals perform auspicious deeds, they may be reborn in heaven.[10]

In each half of the cycle, 24 *tirthankaras* establish the fourfold order (*sangha*), consisting of monks, nuns, laymen and laywomen. The first *tirthankara* in the descending cycle was Risabhdeva, who is believed to have lived thousands of centuries ago. The twenty-third was

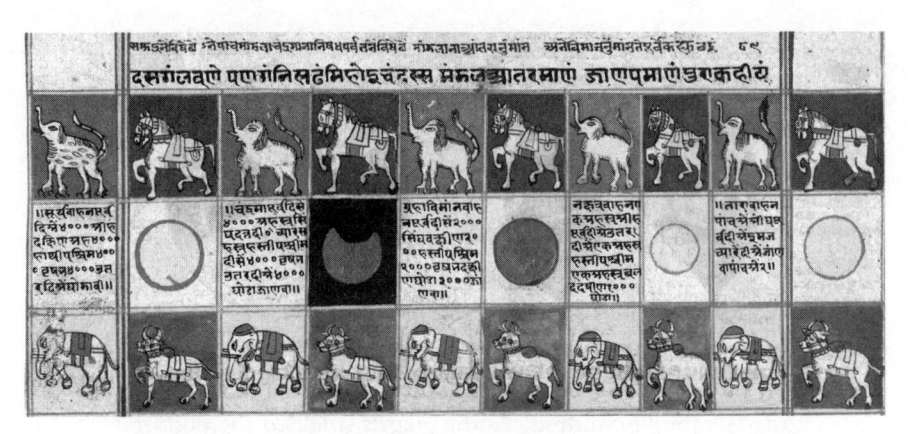

Animal *vahanas* of celestial bodies, from an 18th-century manuscript of a Jain cosmological tract, the *Sangrahani Sutra*.

Parsvanatha (870–770 BCE); the twenty-fourth, and last, was Vardhamana Mahavira (599–527 BCE).

Mahavira and his Connection with Animals

Vardhamana Mahavira ('Great Hero') was, like Buddha, a prince of the warrior caste (Kshatriyas). He reacted against what he saw as the amorality of the Brahmin priesthood and stressed the need to perform good deeds and lead an ethical life. Mahavira's ethical way included vegetarianism, a result of forbidding harm to any form of life. He gave to India the word ahimsa (non-violence). Mahavira was a rationalist; he rejected revelation and based his religion on experience and logic.

Jains are followers of the Jina ('conqueror' or 'victor'), a title given to Vardhamana Mahavira to indicate that he had overcome his passions and his self. Those that have achieved this are called *tirthankaras*, for they have attained omniscience by shedding destructive karma and teaching the spiritual path of perfection to all humans.

It is common for legends to surround birth narratives of pivotal religious leaders. Mahavira's mother had several dreams about animals before his birth: one about an elephant, another featuring a bull and a third concerning a lion. The dream about the lion was the most significant, for it is said that Mahavira was born as a lion. Two Jain monks, impressed by the lion's intelligence, instructed him to be kind and to stop killing animals for food. The lion, moved by their sermon about ahimsa, stopped hunting and, as a result, starved to death. He was reborn in heaven and later became Mahavira.[11] In these stories the animals appear to be able to make moral choices, deciding whether to do good or evil. Their actions result in consequences that can be immediate or in the future, as in rebirth.

Perhaps the most significant encounter with an animal that shaped Mahavira's life took place when he was only five years old:

> He and his childhood friends were playing on the palace grounds when an elephant of the guard suddenly became spooked. Crushing everything in its path, the elephant careered towards the trembling children. As the guards shielded the children and prepared to kill the beast, Vardhamana stood his ground. The charging elephant lowered its head, aiming its lethal tusks at the boy, but Vardhamana deftly grabbed its trunk, planted his foot on the animal's knee and hurled himself onto its neck. He patted the elephant's cheek, whispered in its ear and brought it under control, saving both the noble animal and the children. When he rode the pacified elephant into the palace, the entire court turned out to marvel. Vardhamana was hailed as a 'great hero', and so the name Mahavira came to be.[12]

At the age of thirty Mahavira was recognized by two great sages as an evolved soul and was released from his royal duties in order to continue his spiritual journey. For the next twelve years he wandered and lived as an ascetic. It is said that he harmed no animals, was not afraid of wild animals or snakes and respected all souls. During his twelve years of asceticism, Mahavira took on some of the qualities of animals and birds. According to the *Kalpa Sutra*: 'His senses were well protected like those of a tortoise; he was single and alone like the horn of a rhinoceros; he was free like a bird; he was always waking like the fabulous bird Bharunda; valorous like an elephant, strong like a bull, difficult to attack like a lion.'[13]

Owing to these qualities, Mahavira went on to become a great religious leader. In his thirteenth year of abstinence, he at last achieved divine knowledge while sitting beneath an ashoka tree in deep meditation.[14] Mahavira became a Jina at the age of 42. As a great reformer, he addressed the problems of the day, including the killing or harming of life for religious rituals or for pleasure of the senses. Mahavira then fulfilled his destiny by becoming the twenty-fourth and final Jain *tirthankara*. Mahavira's renunciation is described in the *Acaranga Sutra*, the oldest text of the Jain canon. Sakra, the leader and king of the gods, praises him and clothes him in beautiful robes, one of which is decorated with designs of flamingos. He then creates a giant palanquin 'adorned with pictures of wolves, bulls, horses, men, dolphins, birds, monkeys, elephants, antelopes, *sarabhas* (fantastic animals with eight legs), yaks, tigers, lions'.[15] Even at his renunciation, Mahavira is surrounded by animals, is linked with animals and perhaps is seen as living in harmony with all creatures.

A 6th–7th-century statue of the Jain goddess Ambika, the protector goddess of Neminatha, the 22nd *tirthankara*, with her lioness.

Mahavira had reframed Jainism as a world religion, and for the next 23 years he spread the Jain philosophy to mainstream Indian life. Mahavira's contribution during his earthly life was enormous; by the time of his death he had more than 400,000 followers, who vowed to live ethically, committed to non-violence.[16]

In Jainism, most of the 24 *tirthankaras* are associated with a particular animal, as listed here:

1 Rsabha (bull)
2 Ajita (elephant)
3 Sambhava (horse)
4 Abhinanda (ape)
5 Sumati (partridge)
9 Suvidhi/Puspadanta (crocodile)
11 Sreyamsa (rhinoceros)
12 Vasupujya (water buffalo)
13 Vimala (boar)
14 Ananta (hawk or bear)
16 Santi (deer)
17 Kunthu (goat)
18 Ara (fish)
20 Munisuvrata (tortoise)
23 Parsvanatha (snake)
24 Mahavira (lion)[17]

In Jain iconography the specific *tirthankara* is usually identified by the use of his particular symbol.

Animals also play an important role in a story about Parsvanatha, the twenty-third *tirthankara*. Two cobras, Dharanendra and Padmavati, saved the life of Parsvanatha, but they were soon killed by non-Jains. Due to their life-saving deed, they were reborn in the heavenly abode of the *yaksha*s (deities).[18]

Animals in the Jaina Universe

The Jain universe contains animals in many forms and species. In the Jain cosmology there is the upper world, containing the heavens and the celestial beings who live there. Humans, animals, plants, astral bodies and lower kinds of heavenly beings occupy the earthly realm or 'middle world'; and the infernal beings live in the lower world, in one of the seven hells. Ultimate liberation is possible only from the earthly realm.

The 24 *tirthankaras* (or Jinas) share their knowledge of salvation with others by preaching in a specially constructed circular assembly hall. Encircling the Jina on the first level are the Jain monks, nuns, laymen and laywomen. On the second ring is a congregation of the five-sensed rational animals; they, too have come to listen to the Jina:

> It is believed that the sounds uttered by the Jina are in a form that each living being is able to understand, in his or her own language. This truly constitutes a communion of subjects, humans and animals together experiencing the sight of the Jina and sharing in his sacred knowledge.[19]

In the assembly hall it is possible for humans and animals to attain insight into the true nature of reality. Although other life forms are not represented in the assembly hall, they are part of a larger community of beings that live in the universe. All undergo desire and suffering, yet not all species are able to reach liberation, 'because less developed life-forms do not have the capacity for reasoning, they lack the ability to attain true spiritual insight (*samyak-darshana*), the first step toward salvation (*moksa*).'[20]

In Jainism there are 8,400,000 different species of life that are part of the cycle of birth, life, death and rebirth (samsara).[21] Every living thing has a *jiva*, a life force, and when the body dies the *jiva* finds another body to inhabit. The soul incarnates in various life forms during its journey over time. Human, sub-human (animals, which include birds, insects and other forms of living creatures), super-humans (heavenly beings) and hellish beings are the four forms of soul incarnations. A living being's thoughts and actions give rise to the accumulation of karma, which determines its future in the form of rewards or punishment. If the animal has lived a virtuous life, then it may return in a higher life form; if it has been savage, then it will return in a lower life form, or perhaps as a microorganism.[22] There is extensive classification of various living organisms, including microorganisms that form the earth, air and water. This helps foster a sense of respect for all life forms. The life forms fall into two main categories:

Immobile single senses: clay, trees, roots

Mobile and multi-sensed: these are classified by their senses:

> Two-sensed: touch and taste (shells, worms, leeches, snails, oysters, microbes)
> Three-sensed: touch, taste, smell (lice, ants, moths)
> Four-sensed: touch, taste, smell, sight (scorpions, crickets, spiders, fleas, butterflies, flies, bees)
> Five-sensed: touch, taste, smell, sight, hearing (humans, birds, reptiles, mammals)
> Infernal (in one of the hells)

The state of the soul is due to the karma accumulated over the years as a result of transmigration and rebirth. Unlike the Hindu and Buddhist views of karma as a law of nature, Jains believe that karma consists of fine particles of matter and this can be controlled through personal effort and discipline. Careless, selfish acts lead to heavy karma, which weighs one down, whereas karma resulting from good deeds helps to lighten the soul.[23] The quantity, size, type and density of karmic particles determine the severity of karmic bondage and the form that the soul will assume in forthcoming births. Jains believe that every soul's original state is pure but becomes contaminated by these karmic particles; the ultimate spiritual goal is the liberation of the soul from all these particles.

To achieve salvation (moksha) the soul must be free from matter; then it will float to the top of the universe to dwell in a blissful state. Souls like that of Mahavira rise higher, to the eternal rest of nirvana. While souls are the same in all forms, the most important state to achieve is that of a human being, as this is the only state in which a living being can be freed totally from karmic bondage.[24]

The Heartbeat of Jainism: Ahimsa

Owing to the infinite number of souls in the universe, and the length of the cycle of rebirth, it is rare that a soul obtains human birth. This means that the opportunity to follow the path to salvation is very important. The way of salvation is acquired by the Three Jewels

A depiction of *himsa* (violence), including cruelty to animals, from a 17th-century manuscript of the Jain *Sangrahani Sutra*.

(*triratna*): Right Knowledge, Right Faith and Right Conduct (*mahavratas*). To break the karmic cycle, Mahavira taught that a soul must embrace the Three Jewels. The first two are worthless without the last, right conduct, the most important and all-embracing of which is non-violence, known as ahimsa. Ahimsa, a Sanskrit term that literally translates as 'avoidance of violence', is an attitude to life that refuses to enjoy any pleasure at the cost of another's pain. Mahavira put the concept of ahimsa at the very core of the Jain religion. One could say that ahimsa is the essence of Jainism, its very heart.

Ahimsa is a commandment against killing or harming any living being. It is non-violence of thought, action, deed and speech.[25] Violence, whether intentional or accidental, is thought to incur negative karma, so it is crucial to avoid it. All other vows stem from this fundamental one. Mahavira organized much of the ethical and metaphysical aspects of Jainism around the concept of ahimsa. It was this vow that brought the Jain saints into conflict with the Vedic practice of animal sacrifices. Acarya Somadeva, for example, offered a warning to royalty, who often paid for these elaborate sacrifices:

> A king who constantly desires longevity, strength, and health must not cause injury to living creatures himself, nor allow it to take place when planned by others. One may give away the Meru mountain of gold as well as the entire earth. The result will not be equal to that of saving the life of a single sentient being.[26]

Animals and Ahimsa in Jain Religious Texts and Practice

Mahavira's belief in the sanctity of all life led to the abolition of animal sacrifice, as well as to an increase in the importance of a vegetarian diet. His teachings were gathered together in the *Agam Sutras*, which were passed on orally until they were written down about one thousand years after his death. These teachings restructured Jainism around non-violence and placed a new emphasis on the sanctity and equality of all life.

The Acaranga Sutra is a canonical sacred text of Jainism based on Mahavira's teachings and dating from the fourth or fifth century BCE. It is the first of the eleven *angas*[27] that form part of the *agamas* (religious texts).[28] The Acaranga discusses the conduct of a Jain monk, in particular the actions that monks must take to avoid harming other living beings, including the microscopic life forms that the ancient Jains believed pervaded the universe. In antiquity the Acaranga was the first text studied by the Jain monks. The first part of the Acaranga says this about the treatment of animals:

> Some slay animals for sacrificial purposes, some slay animals for the sake of their skin, some kill them for the sake of their flesh, some kill them for the sake of their blood; others for the sake of their heart, their bile, the feathers of their tail, their big or small horns, their teeth, their tusks, their nails, their sinews, their bones; with a purpose and without a purpose. Some kill animals because they have been wounded by them, or are wounded, or will be wounded. He who injures these animals does not comprehend and renounce the sinful acts; he who does not injure these, comprehends and renounces the sinful acts. Knowing them, a wise man should not act sinfully toward animals, nor cause others to act so, nor allow others to act so.[29]

This sutra states that the teachings of all the *tirthankaras* agree: 'Do not kill any living beings, or overpower them, or enslave them, or harass them, or drive them away.'

> The Arhats and Bhagavats of the past, present, and future, all say thus, speak thus, declare thus, explain thus: all breathing, existing, living, sentient creatures should not be slain, nor treated

with violence, nor abused, nor tormented, nor driven away.
   Propagate the religion which is a blessing to all creatures in the world.

The Sutrakritanga, the second *angas* of the main *agamas* of the Jain canon, contains instructions for the conduct of monks: 'All breathing, existing, living, sentient creatures should not be slain nor treated with violence, nor abused, nor tormented, nor driven away. This is the pure unchangeable law.' 'All beings hate pain; therefore one should not kill them. This is the quintessence of wisdom: not to kill anything.'

The text of the *Purushartha-Siddhyupaya*, written by Amrtachandra, a mystic scholar who was said to have lived around the tenth century CE, is themed around ahimsa and deals with non-violence in all its aspects. It states, for example: 'Flesh cannot be procured without causing destruction of life; one who uses flesh, therefore, commits *hisma* (injury) unavoidably.'

In the *Yoga Shastra* of Hemachandra, Mahavira is quoted as saying the first truth of Jainism is that: 'Non-injury to all living beings is the only religion.' Mahavira elaborated by stating that all creatures should be treated in the same manner as that in which we treat each other. He continued, listing actions that are prohibited, and then underlined the virtue of non-violent behaviour, for non-injury is at the core of wisdom:

> This is the quintessence of wisdom; not to kill anything. All breathing, existing, living sentient creatures should not be slain, nor treated with violence, nor abused, nor tormented, nor driven away. This is the pure unchangeable Law. Therefore, cease to injure living things.

What does this mean in practice for animals? Non-violence means to take seriously the welfare of all kinds of animals, both visible and invisible. It involves minimizing intentional as well as unintentional harm to another living creatures (*jiva*), human and non-human. Jains believe that every living being has a soul; therefore every soul is worthy of respect because it has the potential to become a *siddha* ('highest soul'). Jains believe that life (soul) is sacred regardless of faith, caste, race or species. Because all living beings possess a soul, great care is needed when carrying out one's actions. Life is seen as equal, from the largest animal to microscopic organisms, from the largest mammals to the smallest bacteria. Every soul is potentially divine, with innate qualities of infinite knowledge, perception, power and bliss (masked by its karmas). One should therefore regard every living being as one would regard oneself, being kind to all. Every soul is born as a heavenly being, a human, a sub-human or a hellish being, according to its karma. Every soul has the potential to achieve divine consciousness through its own efforts. From this it is clear that Jains believe in the concept of spiritual advancement for animals, but there are limitations, as will be explained later.

Before Mahavira, who took it to a more radical and comprehensive extreme, ahimsa was an essential part of the 'Fourfold Restraints' dictated by Parsvanatha, the twenty-third *tirthankara*. Parsvanatha once saved a snake from being burned by a mendicant in a sacrificial fire. This incident showed that he would not allow violence for a religious purpose. Mahavira was even more radical; he made every effort to extend the notion of ahimsa to all life, from plants to animals, microorganisms to humans. He was concerned about cultivating crops and ploughing, because of the harm done to creatures in the earth, and advocated strict vegetarianism. There is kinship because of the process of reincarnation. Since each soul has 'transmigrated' as an animal, plant or microorganism innumerable times, a karmic kinship is created between all life forms. Essential to Jainism is *Parasparopagraho Jivanam*, an aphorism that declares that 'all life is interrelated and it is the duty of all souls to assist each other.'[30]

> Because of the Jaina view of the interchangeability of life forms and because of their unique cosmological view that sees all live forms possessing five senses as hierarchically equal, Jainism establishes a truly unprecedented philosophical foundation for compassionate behavior toward animals.[31]

In Jainism there is the assumption that every human being has experienced numerous animal births in prior incarnations. This means that we are all interrelated; we are kin: 'One of the great acts of wrongdoing that will cause rebirth as an animal is undue harm to an animal or human, both of which are to be seen as akin to oneself.'[32] Animals in Jainism, in contrast to how they are perceived in Western philosophy and Western religion, are not viewed as created for human use and for human exploitation. However, (here is the sting) the reason for respecting animals is *not* for the sake of the animal – but for the sake of karma, of lightening one's own karmic burden. Surely the animal is then viewed as a functionary, rather than appreciated for its own integral worth as a different species.

Ambivalence towards animals continues, from positive stories about some animals reaching heavenly birth, to stories that narrate their shortcomings. The Tattvartha Sutra states that 'Deceitfulness leads to birth in animal realms,' which suggests that 'animals are born as animals because of their karmic impulses.'[33]

Jainism sees animals as former or potential human beings paying for past sins, but these sins can be overcome. Human birth is considered to be the highest birth, because, as stated earlier, the earthly realm is the only one through which final liberation (*kevala*) might be entered:

> It is said that animals who have attained proper insight can observe restraint with respect to killing, and so forth. Thus, they are able to follow a mode of conduct equivalent to that of a human who has formally accepted the vows of restraint . . . that a Jain lay person may have formally taken to refrain from harmful actions . . . from telling lies . . . from stealing . . . from inappropriate sexual activity . . . and from possessiveness . . . Like lay people, animals may undertake a fast ending in death.[34]

This notion of animal laity in Jainism is mentioned in the Aupapaatika Sutra and in other texts, indicating that instinctive animals possessing five senses, such as elephants, frogs, snakes and lions, can behave like human lay Jains because they possess the following: the instinct for the desirable and avoidance of the undesirable; a discriminating capacity for good and evil; a capacity to remember their past lives; the capacity to fast, perform penance and self-control, and change their behaviour; the capacity to hear religious sermons and receive instructions; and the capacity to acquire sensory, scriptural and clairvoyant knowledge:

> It is claimed that the holy assembly of Mahariva consisted of living beings of all forms, and his sermons were in a language, which miraculously could be understood by all . . . animals are

often more reliable friends than human beings . . . many are vegetarian and do not harm others . . . If we think about their behaviour, they live a life similar to that of the human laity.[35]

There are accounts of five-sensed rational animals attaining meritorious births as a result of behaving in a similar manner to that of the lay people who have made lay vows. There is, however, a difference: animals are unable to take the more formal vows and they do not have the capacity to destroy karma, which binds one in a cycle of rebirth. This means that only human beings are able to reach the bliss of salvation and end their suffering in the cycle of rebirth. Human life is therefore deemed the *highest* form of life, for only as a human can the highest spiritual undertaking be accomplished:

> Although attaining *moksa* in some future life is possible for five-sensed rational animals, as it is for all living beings, if they are reborn as humans, a human birth is still considered superior to birth as a five-sensed animal because greater spiritual progress can be made, especially for those who choose to take the mendicant vow.[36]

The Jain tradition attributes a thinking faculty (*manas*) to animals; this special ability has given rise to numerous stories in which animals make reasoned choices, particularly in regard to non-violent behaviour, that subsequently advance them from animal to human or godly status. One story tells of a frog being trampled by an elephant while en route to hear a lecture by Mahavira; he is said to have been reborn in heaven. A wonderful story about compassion for other living beings demonstrates the Jain belief that animals can exhibit remarkable powers of both intellect and will:

> Long ago, there was a forest fire, and all the animals of the forest fled and gathered around a lake, including a herd of elephants, deer, rabbits, squirrels, etc. For hours the animals crowded together in their small refuge, cowering from the fire. The leader of the elephant herd got an itch, and raised a leg to scratch himself. A tiny rabbit quickly occupied the space vacated by the elephant's foot. The elephant, out of an overwhelming desire not to hurt the rabbit, stood on three legs for more than

three days until the fire died down and the rabbit scampered off. By then, his leg was numb and he toppled over. Still retaining a pure mind and heart, the elephant died. As a reward for his compassion he overcame the need for embodiment as an animal and was born as a prince by the name of Megha and eventually became a disciple of Mahāvira, taking the vows of a monk in hopes of transcending all forms of existence.[37]

This story is noteworthy for its confidence in animal abilities, illustrating the Jain conviction that animals can hold a very high place in the greater order of things. If we carefully reread the story, however, we may be struck by its ending, because the elephant did not incarnate as another animal, but as a human being, a form viewed as spiritual progression: 'Jains believe that animals can behave like the human laity, progress spiritually and improve their future rebirth, and the Jain scriptures claim that there are more animals following the life of the Jain laity in the universe, than humans.'[38] Although animals may progress spiritually, especially in matters of incarnation, this still implies a hierarchy of species and a preference to remain within human form in order to achieve liberation.

Jain Influence in History

Jainism has played a significant role in history, from protesting against animal sacrifice, which led to the cessation of many Vedic rituals, to changing the behaviour of influential persons by their practice of ahimsa. One of the most influential non-Jain rulers in India to have been persuaded to adopt ahimsa as a government policy was Akbar, the Mughal emperor who ruled between 1556 and 1605. He extended Muslim control throughout most of India. Akbar had invited the Jain monk Hiravijaya Suri to visit him in order to learn the basic principles of Jainism. The monk arrived with 67 monks and stayed for two years. Hiravijaya asked that Akbar use his influence to spread the teaching of non-violence throughout the empire.[39] Jains were influential in having the Moghul emperor issue a decree to free caged birds. Due to Hiravijaya's influence and instruction, animal slaughter was prohibited during Jain festival days (such as the Jain festival of Paryushana) in regions where Jains lived. Akbar gave up eating meat for the most part and he gave up hunting: 'According to the *Akbar Nama*, he passed laws requiring the protection of mice, oxen, leopards, hares, fish, serpents, horse, sheep, monkeys, roosters, dogs, and hogs, either banning or limiting their slaughter.'[40]

Mahavira's teachings form the basis of Eastern non-violent thought and action. Gandhi's mother was descended from Jains, and ahimsa formed the central component of Gandhi's strategy of *satyagraha*,[41] the non-violent civil disobedience movement that led to India's independence from Great Britain. The Jain notion that life forms are sacred and merit preservation has exerted direct influence on Indian and Asian cultures. The concepts of karma, moksha, reincarnation and ahimsa either originated with or evolved through Jain teachings.[42]

Jain literature has many examples of animal rescue. It is said that Neminatha, the twenty-second *tirthankara*, staged a non-violent demonstration by sacrificing his nuptial pleasure in order to save the helpless animals that were kept in cages for the occasion of his marriage.[43]

Living a Life Dominated by the Vow of Ahimsa

In Jainism, in order to uphold the vows of ahimsa, two paths of practice were developed: one for the Jain monks, who adhere to greater vows, and another for the Jain lay community, who follow a less rigorous discipline. The biggest part ahimsa plays in the lives of Jains is in their daily diet. All Jains are strict vegetarians, living on one-sensed beings (vegetables) and milk products. Alcohol, honey and certain kinds of figs are also prohibited, because they are said to harbour many forms of life, especially *nigodas* (microorganisms).[44] It is claimed that 'flesh-eaters have no kindness, drunkards never speak the truth, and people who take honey . . . feel no pity.'[45] Jains avoid root vegetables, as cutting the root from a plant kills it, unlike the other parts of the plant (seeds, fruit, leaves). According to Jain texts, root vegetables contain infinite *nigodas*. Jains refuse anything for any purpose in which animals have been slaughtered, including medicine. Jains are strictly forbidden to use any leather products as these are derived from killing animals. When fasting, Jains drink only boiled water; all living microorganisms have died and there are no new ones, so this decreases the amount of

Gouache painting of two monks, the one on the right a Jain, 19th century.

himsa (violence) the fasting person does. Water is filtered to remove small insects that may be present. Jains tend to eat during daylight hours to avoid ingesting insects. They don't use cloth where its production has hurt animals or humans.

Apart from diet, occupations are an important consideration for Jains when observing the ethic of ahimsa. Jains avoid employment in jobs that cause harm, such as those involving furnaces or fire; occupations in which trees are cut down; those involving fermentation; those trading in meat products, honey or eggs; trading in silk or leather; or selling pesticides. Even farming is to be shunned, because farming involves digging and ploughing, which can harm creatures. Other occupations that involve animals are also avoided, including work in circuses and zoos.

Everyday activities are carried out in such a manner as to avoid accidental violence. Jain monks carry whisks or brushes, which they use to brush chairs before sitting on them, for to squash a microbe would constitute violence to a living being, resulting in unwanted karma. Muslin cloth covers the mouth to stop the person from inhaling insects. Jain monks walk barefoot and sweep temples with utmost care so as to avoid accidentally crushing crawling insects. Jains also avoid extensive travel, to prevent harming creatures during the journey. If a creature is seen on a path or road, it is removed. During the Jain festival of Paryushana, which takes place in late August or early September, normal activities are kept to a minimum to reduce the harm to worms and insects that thrive during this season.

Fasting is an important part of Jain religious life for lay people and monastics. Even this ascetic practice, which is seen as one way to purge various forms of negative karma, encompasses the principle of ahimsa: 'By not eating, one renounces harm to the *jivas* present in the food that normally would be consumed, thereby expelling previous karma and preventing the accrual of new karma.'[46]

Ahimsa is practised even when preparing for one's own death. The ideal way for a Jain to die is to fast to death, for in this way no harm will be done to any living being on the way to rebirth.[47]

One positive outcome of the Jain principle of ahimsa has been the establishment of animal hospitals (*pinjrapole*) and cow shelters (*goshala*). Many of the *pinjrapoles* include rooms for birds and insects. The rooms for insects consist of the sweepings that people bring from their homes, for this dust will include insects. The dust is kept in the room for fifteen years, sometimes with grain for nutrition, until it is assumed that the life of the insects has ended. According to a 1955 study, there were more than 3,000 animal homes in India at that time.[48]

In these Jain shelters, some of the animals should have been euthanised, but two reasons are given for not ending life. The first is that the person who carried out the euthanasia would incur negative karma. This would bind to their life force (*jiva*) and impede the progress of their spiritual liberation (*kevala*). The second reason is that it would not be in the animal's best interests, as each life earns its status on its past actions. Here the view is that the animal deserved its suffering. If this suffering is cut short by euthanasia, this would mean that the killed animal would have to endure another painful life to finish the atonement process.[49] This does not mean that suffering is not relieved: if it can be then it is, but only up to the point of dulling the animal's pain.[50]

Jains do not tend to have pets, for this would involve feeding them meat, as most dogs and cats are carnivores. Having to feed them meat would be in direct conflict with Jain teachings and would also incur negative karma.

In Jainism there is a very moving ritual of repentance (*pratikramana*), in which one asks forgiveness from all living things; this must be performed at least once a year:

I want to make *pratikramana* for injury on the path of my movement, in coming and in going, in treading on living things, in treading on seeds, in treading on green plants, in treading on dew, on beetles, on mould, on moist earth, and on cobwebs; whatever living organisms with one or two or three or four or five senses have been injured by me or knocked over or crushed or squashed or touched or mangled or hurt or affrightened or removed from one place to another or deprived of life – may all that evil have been done in vain . . . I ask pardon of all living creatures, may all of them pardon me, may I have friendship with all beings and enmity with none.[51]

Influence Today and Conclusion

Jains are among the wealthiest and best-educated citizens in India today. Although they make up less than 0.5 per cent of the Indian population (10–12 million people), they contribute nearly 25 per cent of Indian taxation.[52] Their vegetarian diet has and continues to have an impact, but there are ethical issues concerning animal welfare and conservation that have not been addressed because these are modern problems, hence they have not been discussed in Jain classical texts, a common problem that faces all religions.

> To kill any living being amounts to killing oneself.
> Compassion to others is compassion to one's own self.
> Therefore one should avoid violence like poison and thorn [that cause pain]. (*Bhagavati Aradhana*)

In conclusion, I would suggest that in Jainism the relationship with animals is marked by ambivalence. On the one hand, the principle of ahimsa upholds the sacredness of all life, yet to respect life, preventing harm to others, appears to have more to do with lightening one's own human karmic bondage than recognizing another species as kin. The above quotation illustrates this observation; one may read it and be overwhelmed by its universal message of peace for all species, but, on another level, it may be interpreted as anthropocentric. A vegetarian diet is followed, water is boiled, certain occupations are avoided . . . all well and good, but the question remains whether the avoidance of negative karma is using animals for human spiritual wellbeing. The words by Kristi Wiley that open this chapter bring this matter to the fore: 'In Jainism, the spiritual well-being of a human being is tied to the physical well-being of all forms of life.'[53] In Jainism, are animals mere functionaries?

When a Jain looks at an animal does he or she see a former human, or a potential human, paying for his or her mistakes, rather than marvelling at that animal's uniqueness? Within Jainism there seems to be a movement away from forming a relationship with other species, except for the maintenance of the animal hospitals and cow shelters. Instead there is an avoidance of contact, in case injury or harm is done. This avoidance decreases the possibility of bonding with an animal, where ahimsa, or reverence, could arise from love, rather than as a remedy to aid one's own (that is, one's human) spiritual progress. Jainism is not a religion that believes in a Creator; yet I wonder if this partially explains the perceived absence of reverence? Also, I admit, I find it hard to reconcile ahimsa with the Jain practice of allowing an animal to continue to suffer by refusing euthanasia. Perhaps my Western mindset detects a rift between theory and practice. Is the Jain guiding principle of *Parasparopagraho Jivanam*, the interdependence of life, in reality one-sided, a means of human spiritual advancement rather than a general concern and respect for other life forms?

NINE

Animals in Buddhism

May all beings be happy and have the cause of happiness. May they be free of suffering and the cause of suffering.
Buddhist prayer[1]

As a mother even with her own life protects her only child, so should one cultivate immeasurable loving-kindness towards all living beings.
Metta Sutta

The Cycle of Rebirth: A Shared Cosmic Status

'Buddha' is a Sanskrit word that embodies two meanings: ultimate truth or absolute truth; and one awakened or enlightened to the true nature of existence.[2]

Buddhism was part of a religious revival that swept through India for two hundred years from the beginning of the seventh century BCE. It arose from the Shramana, or 'Renouncer', movement led by ascetics who sought spiritual fulfilment through meditation, discipline and the renunciation of worldly goods and worldly pleasures.[3] Out of this movement arose Buddhism, Jainism and Hinduism, the three Indian religions based on ahimsa.[4] Buddhism, like Jainism, originated as a religious movement easily distinguishable from Hinduism due to its lack of allegiance to Vedic texts and its disdain for animal sacrifice. Buddhism, too, does not believe in a creator God, believing instead that the cycle of life has been present for all time, which has no beginning. Unlike Jainism, however, it does not assent to an abiding life force (*jiva*). Buddhism does not believe in a lasting self. Another difference is that Buddhism developed several distinct schools of thought and practice and reached far beyond its native India, spreading to China, Japan, Southeast Asia and Indonesia.

Buddhism, like Hinduism and Jainism, is a way of achieving liberation. Trapped by our negative emotions in an illusory world of suffering (samsara), there is no escape except to awaken to the higher level of consciousness known as nirvana (enlightenment). Until we achieve enlightenment, we will be reborn again and again. Buddhism emphasizes the continuous flow of life through the realm of rebirth. Suffering arises from desire and craving, conditioned by the karmic effects of both animal and human.

Siddhartha Gautama, later known as the Buddha ('the Enlightened One'), was born about 560 BCE in Lumbini, a village near the modern-day border between Nepal and India. His father was the Rajah of Kapilavastu, and so Siddhartha was brought up as a prince. According to the *Buddhacharita* (Acts of the Buddha), an account of the Buddha's life by the poet Ashvaghosha (second century CE), an animal was part of the legend of his conception. Before the future Buddha was conceived, his mother, Queen Maya, dreamt that a white elephant,[5] holding a white lotus flower in its trunk, circled her three times and then entered her womb from her right side. When Queen Maya awoke, she knew that the dream was important, because the elephant is a symbol of greatness in India. According to Buddhist tradition, the Buddha-to-be was residing as a bodhisattva in one of the heavens,[6] and decided to take the shape of a white elephant to be reborn on earth for the last time.

As a young boy, Siddhartha showed concern for animals: when he saw a peasant ploughing, for example, he was concerned not only for the man and the ox, but also for the suffering of the animals and insects in the soil who were killed or maimed by the man's labour.[7] It was also an animal that gave the boy Siddhartha his first experience of pain and started him on his journey to achieve enlightenment. A swan had been shot by his cousin, Devadatta, but Siddhartha picked it up, calmed it down and then managed to remove the arrow. He wondered why the bird should have fallen, so he pricked his skin with the arrow and felt pain for the first time. 'When his cousin claimed the bird as his by right of conquest, the prince said that it was his, for he had saved its life.'[8]

When Siddhartha was 29 he felt compelled to leave his luxurious life and live as a homeless holy man in the mountains with hermits

Statues outside one of the modern temples in Lumbini, Nepal, the birthplace of Siddhartha Gautama.

and sages. He sought release from samsara, the eternal cycle of birth, death and rebirth. After seven years of spiritual exercises and meditation, he reached enlightenment and began to teach. The site for his first preaching engagement was among animals in the deer park at Sarnath, near Varanasi.

One story tells of Siddhartha seeing a flock of sheep being driven towards the city of Rajagaha to be sacrificed, noticing that among them was an injured lamb. Siddhartha, feeling compassion, picked up the poor creature and followed the shepherds into the city and prevented the sacrifice from taking place. He also asked King Bimbisara to stop animal sacrifices, saying:

> All beings tremble before danger, all fear death.
> When a man considers this, he does not kill or cause to kill.
> All beings fear before danger, life is dear to all.
> When a man considers this, he does not kill or cause to kill
> (Dhammapada 129–32).[9]

Moved by Siddhartha's words, the king became a follower of the Buddha.

By this act in saving the lamb, Siddhartha was demonstrating his opposition to animal sacrifice, seeing it as a cruel and inappropriate practice. The Buddha compared the kind of religious ceremony he approved of with those common in his time: 'In this sacrifice, Brahmin, no bulls were slain, no goats or sheep, no cocks or pigs, nor were various living beings subjected to slaughter.'[10]

There are two main schools of Buddhism: Theravada ('Southern school') and Mahayana ('Northern school').[11] These two groups formed as a result of the schism of the Sanga. By the time of the second Buddhist council (Vesali, 383 BCE) two opposing groups stood out: the strict and conservative Theravadins and the more liberal Mahasanghikas. Theravada ('teaching of the ancients') keep to the original teaching as found in the earliest Buddhist writings. The group had acquired the nickname Hinayana (Smaller Vehicle), which they found insulting, for it originated in a scripture of their rival group, in which the world is seen as a burning house from which the inhabitants have to escape in a cart pulled by an animal but the cart is small, so only the few true believers can fit in.[12] This strict lifestyle did not suit the masses, so the Mahasanghikas formed the Mahayana (Great Vehicle) from about the first century BCE, with a greater emphasis on the laity's capacity for enlightenment, since salvation was intended for all, not just for monks. It stresses loving kindness and compassion. The Mahayana also makes reference to other Buddhist texts.

Theravadin Buddhism emphasized the transitory nature of all beings, with nirvana as the goal of existence. The Mahayana tradition emphasized the Buddha-nature or Buddha-essence found in all sentient beings. All sentient beings are believed to possess the innate potential of Buddhahood.

This underlying tension between the 'conservative' (Theravada) and the 'liberal' (Mahayana) groups will later help to explain the reason for two different versions of the Buddha's attitude towards eating meat found in monks' begging bowls: in the Mahayana Sutras no meat is permitted), but in the Pali Canon meat is permitted provided the animal was not killed specifically for the monks.[13]

Both schools trace their origin to the Buddha. His teachings were transmitted orally for four hundred years before being written down, in what became known as the Pali Canon. This is the only scripture accepted by Theravadins. Mahayanists accept the Theravadic Pali Canon as scripture, but they place a greater emphasis on a separate body of scriptures originally written in Sanskrit. Many of these texts have survived only in Chinese or Tibetan translations.

Manjushri seated on a lion, 11th-century Chinese sculpture. Manjushri is the oldest and most significant bodhisattva in Mahayana literature, and he is one of the Four Great Bodhisattvas of Chinese Buddhism. He is often depicted riding or seated on a lion, representing the use of wisdom to tame the mind, which is compared to riding or subduing a ferocious lion.

Both sets of scripture are divided into three categories, known as the Tripitaka, the 'three baskets': the Vinaya Pitaka (rules of monastic discipline), the Sutta Pitaka (discourses of the Buddha) and the Abhidhamma Pitaka (treatises on philosophy and psychology).[14]

In the Mahayana school of Buddhist thought, a combination of infinite compassion and wisdom equals *bodhichitta*, enlightened mind. Those who have perfected it are called bodhisattvas (enlightened beings). They are so moved by compassion that they forego the bliss of nirvana and are voluntarily reborn in samsara for countless lifetimes

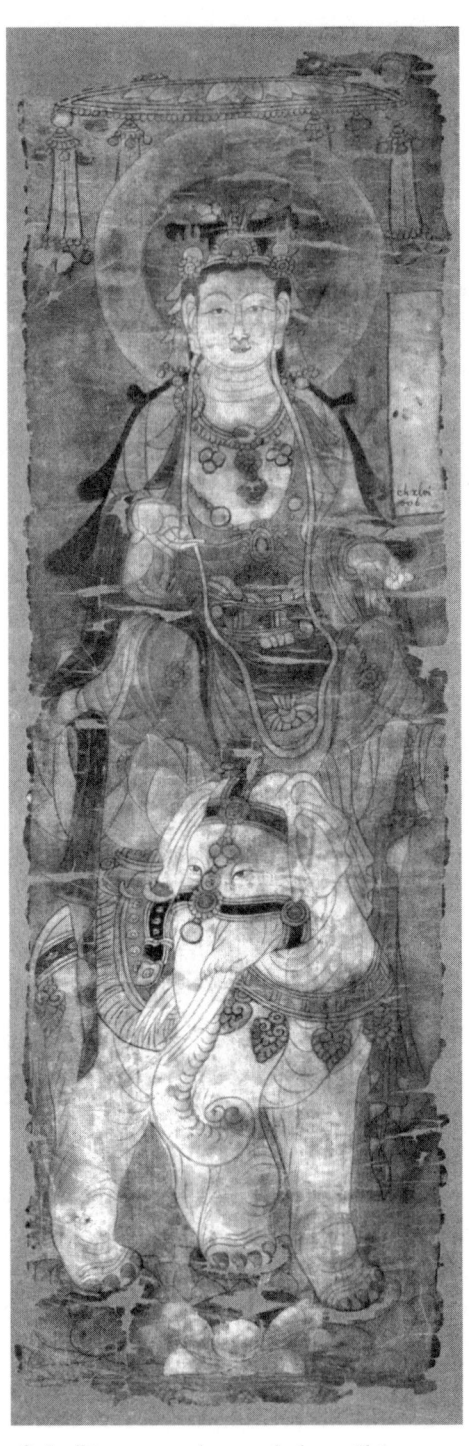

Painting of a bodhisattva seated on an elephant, China, *c.* 750–850 CE.

to alleviate the suffering of those trapped in the cycle of birth and death. Five hundred years after the Buddha, the Indian philosopher Nagarjuna expressed what it means to be a bodhisattva: 'The essential nature of all bodhisattvas is a great compassionate heart, and all living beings are the object of its compassion.'[15]

> The bodhisattva should adopt the same attitude toward all beings, his mind should be even toward all beings, he should not handle others with an uneven mind, but with a mind which is friendly, well-disposed, helpful, free from aversions, avoiding harm and hurt; he should handle others as if they were his mother, father, son, or daughter. As a savior of all beings should a bodhisattva behave toward all beings. So should he train himself if he wants to know full enlightenment.[16]

Later, other paths or types of Buddhism evolved, including Vajrayana Buddhism, Lamaism and Zen Buddhism. Vajrayana Buddhism derived its name from the *vajra*, the thunderbolt of the god Indra. It came to mean a bright substance as indestructible as diamond, so is often known as 'the diamond vehicle'.[17] This version of Buddhism spread to Nepal, Tibet, China and Japan, and has become overlaid with occult, magical and mystical elements. Easing the suffering of living beings is also part of Vajrayana Buddhism. Avalokiteshvara (Tibetan: Chenrezig) is the bodhisattva of compassion, and a very popular meditational deity (*yidam*) in Vajrayana Buddhism:

> Many ages ago, Avalokiteshvara was so moved by compassion for the suffering of living beings that he made a vow not to rest until he had relieved the suffering of them all, sealing the vow with the wish that if his resolve should fail, his body might shatter into a thousand pieces. After eons of tireless effort, Avalokiteshvara paused to look around and see how much progress he had made. Seeing that beings beyond number were still mired in suffering, he grew discouraged and gave up his efforts. Immediately, his body shattered into a thousand pieces. Taking pity on him, Amitabha, the Buddha of Boundless Light, collected the pieces and put Avalokiteshvara back together, but with one difference: The reassembled bodhisattva had a thousand arms, one for each

Guanyin seated on a lion, Chinese hanging scroll, 16th century.

of the pieces into which his body had broken, the better to be able to help living beings.[18]

In Chinese and Japanese Buddhism Avalokiteshvara is in female form and known as Guanyin (Japanese: Kanzeon, Kannon). And answers prayers for help and eases the suffering of sentient beings.[19]

Phelps makes an astute observation concerning action versus theory and counsels against selective compassionate acts: 'The existence of an important Vajrayana *yidam* who is specifically devoted to alleviating the suffering of sentient beings while they remain in samsara is proof that Vajrayana compassion should be active in the world and not confined to meditational practices or to helping certain living beings attain enlightenment.'[20]

In Buddhism, compassion creates the foundation for a balanced view of the world. It is only by exercising loving compassion towards all that a human being can perfect him- or herself and become a sustainer of life. Buddhism teaches the unity of all life and considers kindness and compassion to be the highest virtues. Animals are therefore an integral component of Buddhism's moral universe.

In Buddhist culture, nature was considered sacred. Significant occasions for the Buddha took place in nature: he was born in a garden, he preached his first sermon in a deer park and he spent time in the forest with wild animals. In Buddhist stories animals and plants could talk and respond to human beings. This unity, enveloped by boundless compassion, was seen as the basis of Buddhist life.

Ajahn Pongsak, a Buddhist monk in Thailand, pointed out an even closer connection between Buddhism and nature, for dharma, the Buddhist word for truth and teachings, is also the word for 'nature', because they are the same: 'Nature is the manifestation of truth and of the teachings. When we destroy nature we destroy the truth and the teachings. When we protect nature, we protect the truth and the teachings.'[21]

Cleanliness, both in the person and in the environment, is highly commended. Several rules prohibit monks from polluting green grass and water with saliva, urine and faeces.[22] Rules about keeping grass clean were prompted not only by ethical and aesthetic considerations, but also because grass is the main food source for many animals.

A tradition in Ladakh, a region adjoining Tibet, considers the activity of sowing, and has a ritual to honour the earth and its inhabitants:

> Next the spirits of the earth and water, the lu (or nagas) and sadak must be pacified; the worms of the soil, the fish of the streams, the soul of the land. Any interference with the soil, digging earth, or breaking stones, is liable to upset or anger them. Before sowing, a feast is prepared in their honour. For an entire day, a group of monks recites prayers . . . In a cluster of trees at the edge of the village, where a small mound of clay bricks has been built for the spirits, milk is offered. As the sun sets, other offerings are thrown into the streams.[23]

Concern for the welfare of the natural world has been an important element throughout the history of Buddhism. There is recognition of dependence upon and interconnectedness with the environment, with an overriding respect for nature.

Respect for nature is evident in this exchange between the Buddha and his disciple Maudgalyayana (also Maha Moggallana) when the monks' custom of receiving their daily food as charity from local people was undermined by famine:

> The venerable Maha Moggallana went to the Blessed One. He said: 'Lord, alms food is hard to get in Veranja now. There is a famine and food tickets have been issued. It is not easy to survive even by strenuous gleaning. Lord, this earth's under-surface is rich and as sweet as pure honey. It would be good if I turned the earth over. Then the bhikkhus (monks) will be able to eat the humus that water plants live on.'
>
> 'But Moggallana, what will become of the creatures that depend on the earth's surface?'
>
> 'Lord, I shall make one hand as broad as the Great Earth and get the creatures that depend on the earth's surface to go on to it. I shall turn the earth over with the other hand.'
>
> 'Enough, Moggallana, do not suggest turning the earth over. Creatures will be confounded.'[24]

Perhaps one of the key factors in Buddhism's respect for nature is the way Buddhists perceive the world. Buddhism tends to divide the world into sentient beings and the non-sentient environment. Western thought tends to divide the world into 'humans' and 'nature'. Buddhism places humans and animals together, whereas Western thought places animals with nature, separate from humans.[25] The Buddhist concept of the unity of all existence, the idea that all are one, can have radical implications for the natural world.

Two of the most important qualities to be incorporated into Buddhism are those of loving kindness (the desire for others to be happy) and compassion (alleviating suffering, ahimsa). In one of the earliest texts of Buddhism there is a description about how to cultivate the quality of loving kindness, a quality that extends to all living beings:

[Then let him think:] 'In joy and safety
Let every creature's heart rejoice,
Whatever breathing beings there are,
No matter whether timid or bold,
With none excepted, long or big
Or middle-sized or short or thin
Or thick or those seen or unseen
Or whether dwelling far or near;
That are or that yet seek to be.
Let every creature's heart rejoice.

Let none betray another's trust
Or offer any slight at all,
Or even let them wish in wrath
Or in revenge each other's ill.'

Thus as a mother with her life
Will guard her son, her only child,
Let him extend without bounds
His heart to every living being.
And so with love for all the world
Let him extend without bounds
His heart, above, below, around,
Unchecked, with no ill will or hate.
Whether he stands, or sits, or walks,
Or lies down (while yet not asleep),
Let him such mindfulness pursue.
This is Holy Abiding here, they say.[26]

Buddha is understood to be an embodiment of Great Compassion (*Maha Karuna*) and Great Wisdom (*Maha Prajna*). There is a Buddhist saying that compassion and wisdom are like the two wings of a bird; you need both in order to fly.[27] Without both, a person cannot reach nirvana.

Ethics and Karma

In Buddhism animals are viewed as having the capacity to suffer as well as being able to experience joy, just as humans are. The Buddha's statement in the Dhammapada, 'See yourself in others,' is the Buddhist litmus test for ethical claims. Buddhist ethics are not a legal set of rules that one adheres to; rather, they emphasize intent. They are guidelines for putting loving kindness, compassion and non-violence into daily living. Precepts are not commandments (for there is no deity in Buddhism to issue them); they are voluntary commitments. They are more like instructions or suggestions about how to live a non-violent life.

Buddhism, as a religion that follows ahimsa, has this concept at its forefront. If a being can suffer, it needs our compassion. The only quality that matters for compassion is sentience.[28] The idea of non-violence is based on a perception of sameness among human beings, and between humans and the natural world. It is not *life* that confers moral standing (the right to be treated with compassion), but *sentience*. Ethical conduct (*sila*) arises out of the concept of universal love and compassion for all beings, on which the Buddha's teachings are based.

The Five Precepts (Pancasila) form the minimum code of ethics that every lay Buddhist is expected to follow. The Five Precepts (ethical guidelines) are all expressions of ahimsa: Do not kill (non-injury to life); Do not steal; Do not lie; Do not commit sexual misconduct; Do not use intoxicants. The first four prohibit actions that harm living beings directly, the fifth attacks our judgement and self-control, which may cause us to commit harmful acts and cause suffering to others, as well as to ourselves. They are expressed in negative terms, yet their message is positive, because all of them preserve or save life.

The First Precept, 'Do not kill', takes precedence over the others. Unlike the equivalent biblical commandment, the First Precept has always been held to apply to animals as well as to humans. In Buddhist scripture, the word *prana* (Sanskrit) or *pana* (Pali) means 'living beings' or 'sentient beings', not 'human beings', and translates as 'anything that breathes'.[29] All schools of Buddhism agree on this.

Buddha's basic instructions for life, known as the 'Noble Eightfold Path', are concerned with morality, spiritual discipline and insight. This is also known as the 'Middle Way', since it avoids the extremes of asceticism and sensuality.

The fifth step of the Eightfold Path is 'right livelihood', meaning that one must earn a living consistent with the Five Precepts. A Buddhist may take up an occupation that does not cause harm or injustice to others, but trades that cause harm, such as dealing in arms or living beings, are to be avoided. Nowadays that list would include work in circuses, bullfights, zoos – any occupation that supports the killing of animals or inflicts suffering upon them (physical and emotional or mental) is prohibited to Buddhists. Buddhists are also encouraged to dissuade people from engaging in these livelihoods, because Buddhists believe that when one eats meat, one is the reason that the butcher has taken on such a livelihood – and thus one is also culpable.

Buddhist nuns and monks follow a stricter code than the laity. They must abstain from practices that would even unintentionally harm living creatures. The Buddha made a rule against travelling in the rainy season because of possible injury to worms and insects that come to the surface in wet weather. Monks and nuns are forbidden to drink unstrained water. Monks are not to dig the ground:

> Once a monk, who was a potter before he was ordained, built himself a clay hut and set it on fire to give it a fine finish. The Buddha strongly objected to this as so many living creatures would have been burnt in the process. The hut was taken down on the Buddha's instructions to prevent it from setting a bad example for later generations.[30]

In Buddhism there is no hierarchy of sentient beings: all are equal and all are equally capable, over many lifetimes, of gaining enlightenment or achieving nirvana. Buddhists believe that humans will experience many births, as mammals, insects, fish and so on, as well as human births. Humans, as fellow travellers on the path, should neither harm non-human animals nor impede their progress. Ideally followers of Buddhism should treat all creatures without discrimination regardless of species or intellect. Because of this equality, all are entitled to protection and compassion, as the Buddha taught:

> All beings tremble before danger, all fear death. When a man considers this, he does not kill or cause to kill. All beings fear before danger, life is dear to all. When a man considers this, he does not kill or cause to kill. He who for the sake of happiness hurts others who also want happiness, shall not hereafter find happiness. He who for the sake of happiness does not hurt others who also want happiness, shall hereafter find happiness.[31]

The Buddha warned his disciples to remember the traditional Indian doctrine of karma. Karma literally means 'actions'. The law of karma states that all our thoughts, words and deeds shape our experiences in the future. What we are experiencing now is the outcome of what we have thought, done or said in the past. In Buddhism, to escape the cycle of rebirth one must learn the truths of suffering, which leads the seeker to embrace compassion for all life.

Buddhism does not use the term 'soul', for this does not equate with the Buddhist doctrine of 'no self'. Theravadin teachers do not name the essence or form that journeys through samsara and is able to attain nirvana, but Mahayana teachers speak of it as 'Buddha nature' or 'true nature of mind', 'the clear light of awareness'. Both schools agree that the Buddha nature of every living being without exception is identical. Lama Kelsang Gyaltsen said: 'There is no difference between the Buddha nature of His Holiness the Dalai Lama and the Buddha nature of the most unfortunate homeless dog on the street.'[32]

The hierarchy of samsara is a hierarchy of suffering; it is not a hierarchy of beings. According to Buddhist thought, animals inhabit a realm where suffering is worse for them than for humans. This animal realm is called *Tiryagyoni* (Sanskrit) or *Tiracchanayoni* (Pali). In Buddhism there are six realms in the cycle of rebirth into which sentient beings may be incarnated or born. The other five are *Deva* (the realm of the gods), *Asura* (the realm of the demigods), *Manusa* (the human realm), *Preta* (hungry ghost realm) and *Naraka* (a hell realm).[33] Some types of Buddhism see these as literal places of existence, others as symbolic states of mind.

The animal realm is deemed 'lower' because there is usually more suffering there than in the human realm. Suffering can be caused by non-human activities, such as being attacked and eaten by other animals, living in constant fear, no security of habitation or enduring extremes of weather. Suffering can also be caused by humans: animals are slaughtered for meat or for their skins, used for work or for experimentation, or confined to zoos or circuses for entertainment. Buddhists believe that animals endure this suffering, lacking the intellectual ability to understand what is happening to them; they act out of instinct and, unable to recite mantras or meditate, they are unable to attain enlightenment in this realm.[34] Buddhist teaching refers to 'precious human birth', meaning 'spiritually advantageous', for humans are fortunate in that they can engage in spiritual practices that can help them make progress towards achieving nirvana. Humans are not better than animals; humans just happen to be more fortunate in their present circumstances.

Animals are not inherently inferior to human beings or less entitled to human respect and compassion. Indeed, the more a being needs our compassion, the greater is our obligation to offer it. For a hell being or a hungry ghost to be reborn in the animal realm would be good fortune and the result of positive karma.

Arguments have been made that assert that animals are in the position they are in because of previous actions, and to intervene would be to disturb their karma. This idea of 'non-interference' can stop one alleviating suffering. To participate in cruelty to another living being under the guise of helping them work out their karma, and their need to do this by suffering, is not Buddhist teaching.

The Buddhist notion that all sentient beings are identical in Buddha nature, and therefore there is no hierarchy of beings, is quite different from Western thought, yet Buddhism considers birth as a human being extremely desirable and birth as an animal as a misfortune. Perhaps there is a hierarchy after all, or at least an inconsistency in this view of the ability and/or opportunity to achieve nirvana. Is this changed by the belief that the Buddha took birth many times as an animal (for example, as a monkey, fish, dog and deer), and therefore was thought to know what it was like to be an animal?

There are two other reasons why Buddhism instructs us to make all living beings the equal objects of our compassion: before one can obtain nirvana, compassion must encompass all who suffer; and reincarnation and transmigration are to be understood literally.[35]

Some Western Buddhists interpret the teaching that human beings can be reborn as animals metaphorically, with certain animals representing different kinds of circumstances. For example, being reborn as a pig meant that you would be reborn in dirty conditions: 'This was a speciesist misunderstanding of the dharma based on old Western habits of thought. Many in this first generation of Western Buddhists simply could not bring themselves to accept that there is no fundamental difference between human and nonhuman animals.'[36]

Although all sentient beings are thought to possess Buddha nature, some Buddhists have a low opinion of the intelligence of non-human species: 'In the animal realm stupidity and ignorance lead to blind instinctive behavior and to the preying of one species upon another.'[37]

Animals possess the faculty of thought, though their ability to develop useful insights into the true nature of things is perceived as being limited. This is thought to be partially due to their inability to cultivate and then act from a calm mental state.[38] This is one reason for their exclusion from admittance to the monastic order (*sangha*), for they cannot easily act upon the teachings of a Buddha since 'recitation of the monastic rules in an animal's presence is an offence (Vinaya Pitaka 1.135) and monks are prohibited from imitating their behavior.'[39] Buddha condemned a monk who decided that he would graze like a cow (Vinaya Pitaka 2.134), while an ascetic who copied the manners of a dog was castigated (Majjhima Nikaya 1.387–9).[40]

The term *tiracchanakatha*, which means 'low conversation', is literally 'animal talk'.[41] Animal behaviour, with its breaking of human taboos, such as cannibalism and incest, is thought to demonstrate that animals lack insight into what constitutes the true nature of reality. In terms of incest, goats, sheep, chickens, pigs, dogs and jackals are mentioned (Digha Nikāya 3.72), and it is not unusual to see animals put alongside human murderers, hermaphrodites, thieves and Buddha-killers (Vinaya Pitaka 1.320).[42]

In the Tibetan Buddhist tradition, the animal realm mentality is characterized by dullness, or stupidity, but this attitude is not one of contempt; rather it is compassionate concern for the less fortunate. They are seen as less fortunate because they are less powerful and at the mercy of nature. In Buddhism, including Tibetan Buddhism, it is Buddha nature, *not* intelligence, that is the guide to one's worth.

A popular Buddhist technique for generating compassion is to view all sentient beings as relatives. Buddhists believe that all beings are interconnected, part of one single family:

> It is believed that if you were able to retrace your previous incarnations you would realize that every creature was related to you in some way. Beings currently living in the animal realm may have been your mothers, fathers, brothers, sisters, children, spouses or your friends. An animal that you care for or conversely mistreat may well have been a departed relative either fairly recently or at some time during the infinite number of lives you have lived. Put simply: every creature who has lived, is, was or will be related to you in this or a former incarnation. Therefore, for this reason it is important to make a commitment

to abide by the first precept and not to harm, kill or eat the flesh of any sentient being as to do so would be tantamount to harming, killing and eating your own child or mother or sibling or any other relation or indeed any human being.[43]

Tibetan Buddhists often refer to all living beings as 'mother beings', to indicate that we are to regard them as highly as we do our own human mother, because at some time they have been our mother. A Tibetan tale illustrates this point:

> There was a lama, who, because of his high level of realization, was able to see the past lives of the beings whom he encountered. Returning to his monastery ... he stopped at the home of a farmer for lunch. Back at the monastery the next day, he described the scene to his abbot. 'The wife was cooking a fish, the husband and the eldest son were butchering a yak, and the daughter was swatting flies. In past lives, the fish had been the wife's sister, the yak had been the husband's father, and one of the flies had been their child. So the wife was frying her sister, the husband was slitting his father's throat and the son his grandfather's, while the daughter was squishing her baby brother. I couldn't stand it. I excused myself and went on my way. It was better to travel hungry than eat with those barbarians.[44]

This idea of kinship, or interconnectedness, has been used to highlight the opposition to the practice of animal sacrifice:

> It is said that offering to the wisdom deities the flesh and blood of a slaughtered animal is like offering to a mother her murdered child. If you invite a mother for a meal and then set before her the flesh of her own child, how would she feel? It is with the same love as a mother for her only child that the Buddhas and Bodhisattvas look on all beings of the three worlds.[45]

The Buddhist notion of loving kindness (*metta*) embodies this notion of relatedness: 'Just as a mother would protect with her life her own son ... so one should cultivate an unbounded mind towards all beings, and loving kindness towards all the world' (Sutta Nipata 149–50).[46]

The eighth-century Buddhist poet Shantideva wrote:

> In the same way as the hands and so forth
> Are regarded as limbs of the body,
> Likewise, why are living things
> Not regarded as limbs of life?
>
> I should dispel the misery of others
> Because it is suffering, just like my own,
> And I should benefit others
> Because they are living things, just like myself.
>
> When I work in this way for the sake of others
> I should not let conceit or feelings of amazement arise.
> It is just like feeding myself –
> I hope for nothing in return.[47]

'According to the *Macchuddana Jataka*, in a previous life, the Buddha-to-be threw his leftover food into a river to feed the fish, and by the power of that merit he was saved from an impending disaster.'[48] Thus kindness to animals is a source of merit, which human beings need to improve their lot in the cycle of rebirths and to approach the final goal of nirvana. In the end, the purpose of morality in Buddhism is to create the conditions for the realization of spiritual fulfilment, which is nirvana. In Mahayana Buddhism the reflection on morality is extended to consider how everything we use in our daily life is derived from other living beings. The Korean Zen Master Ya Un told his monks:

> From the time of ploughing and sowing until the food reaches your mouth and the clothes your body, not only do men and oxen suffer great pains in producing them, but countless insects are also killed and injured. It is improper to benefit in this way from the hardships of others. Even more, how can you endure the thought that others have died in order that you can live ... A very heavy debt is incurred through wearing fine clothes and eating fine food.[49]

The Theravada Vinaya states that butchers, fletchers, hunters, fowlers and animal tamers are all destined to suffer a horrible death. A later text, the *Sutra of the Remembrance of the Good Law*, states that in one of the eight levels of hell there is a region called the hell of repetition, where those who have killed birds and deer without any regret are forced to eat dung alive with flesh-eating worms as punishment for their actions.[50]

Is the Buddhist notion of loving kindness, and the implementation of ahimsa, similar to the Jain notion of receiving merit for these loving acts? Is the ethical dimension of Buddhism self-serving?

Confucianists saw humans as being vastly superior to other species. The notion of reincarnation ran counter to the most basic of Chinese beliefs. Nonetheless, a Buddhist-inspired respect for animals is found in a variety of contexts in Chinese and Japanese culture. There are a number of Chinese Buddhist stories that narrate dreadful punishments for persons who eat meat. In one, a peasant named Chih-tsung, who lived during the Song dynasty, fell into a coma for a long period of time. When he finally regained consciousness, he told of being bound and taken away by one hundred men to a Buddhist shrine. Then a monk spoke to him:

> 'You are fond of hunting and fishing and ought now to receive retribution.' He then took Chih-tsung, peeled off his skin, and pared away his flesh the way one would go about dressing down an animal. Next he was placed deep down under water, and then pulled out by a hook in the mouth, to be split in two and chopped up into a fine hash, boiled in a cauldron, and roasted over a brazier. Reduced to a pulp, he was made whole again and the process repeated with great pain and suffering. After a third time the monk stopped and asked whether or not he would like to live. Chih-tsung then bowed his head to the ground and pleaded for his life . . .
>
> Seeing several ants, the priest pointed to them and said, 'Even though these are very insignificant beings, still they must not be killed. How much the less those that are larger!' . . .
>
> Chih-tsung then returned to life and after several days was able to get up. Thereafter he ceased his hunting and fishing.[51]

In the *Yu-Li* (Precious Records), a volume of Chinese Taoist scripture, there are warnings regarding the fate of those who take the lives of animals:

Those who kill the ox (which ploughs the field) or the dog (who guards the house), or animal life in general, their souls shall be placed before the mirror of reflection. After suffering the torments of the . . . hells a red-haired, black-faced demon shall cut such from the head to the buttocks. The suffering is intense. After healing, they shall be cast for ten years into a great hell, then in the scalding water hell for fifteen years. They shall appear before the judge, who shall condemn them to receive 1,500 calamities in the boundless hell. At the expiration of this ordeal they shall be sent to the wheel of life and be born again as beasts.[52]

Although these stories and others emerge from the folk tradition, the concept of punishment for those who have injured or killed animals first appears in China in the early fifth century CE, at a time when Buddhism was becoming integrated into Chinese culture. The difference is that little is said about enlightenment.

Hue Shen Hua Chi, a collection of illustrated Chinese poems by both Buddhist monks and laypeople, was compiled in 1928. In the poem 'Flesh of our Flesh' the lowly pig is seen to be similar to a human:

> The swine are also sentient beings.
> Their bodies possess the same elements as ours.
> Seeing their grievance and helplessness
> Rouses the all-mighty heart of sympathy.
> An appeal to the world of man –
> For the sake of protecting life,
> Do not kill.
> And, when you do not eat flesh,
> You have already done a job for the love of humanity.[53]

Another poem grapples with feelings of revulsion at what the world deems acceptable:

> How can they be called delicious dishes?
> They are merely rotten, stinking, unnatural and what not;
> Tears well up in one's eyes,
> Sick is one's heart,
> When the scene is viewed.
> The wise feels ashamed and downcast.[54]

These poems, and others in the work, communicate a commitment to the ethic of non-violence and indicate how widespread it was in some parts of China.

There is an argument that activism is a waste of time for it only treats the symptoms. The end of suffering can only be found in nirvana; therefore Buddhists should spend more time in meditation so that they can achieve enlightenment and thereby be able to help others reach nirvana. Yet one should not use nirvana or the goal of enlightenment as a way to shield oneself from suffering, or cut oneself off by meditation and study. Those disciplines are a means of cultivating compassion and empathy, because compassion becomes tangible when it is lived out in the world. Buddhist action on behalf of animals is a non-violent expression of *Maha Karuna*, the Great Compassion.[55]

As distinct from Descartes and Aristotle, and the Great Chain of Being, as well as from Thomas Aquinas, who thought that only humans have souls and therefore ethical duties only extend to humans, this notion of a qualitative difference between humans and animals, which dominates Western thinking, does not govern Buddhism. In Buddhism loving kindness is extended to all, regardless of intelligence, use of language, self-awareness and so on. In the spirit of Jeremy Bentham's question of 1789, the key question is 'Can they suffer?'[56]

Sacred Texts

In Buddhism the term *sutra* refers primarily to canonical scriptures, many of which are regarded as records of the oral teachings of the Buddha. Within the scriptures there are many references to animals and the call to extend loving kindness to them.

The Dhammapada is a versified Buddhist scripture spoken by the Buddha on various occasions. It records Buddha as saying: 'If a person does not harm any living being . . . and does not kill or cause others to kill – that person is a true spiritual practitioner.'

The *Avatamsaka Sutra* (Flower Adornment Sutra) is a Mahayana Buddhist sutra that explores the teachings of the Buddha. It describes an assembly in the palace of Indra, where the Buddha teaches that all beings have the Buddha nature:

I should be a hostel for all sentient beings, to let them escape from all painful things. I should be a protector for all sentient beings, to let them all be liberated from all afflictions. I should be a refuge for all sentient beings, to free them from all fears ... I should accept all sufferings for the sake of sentient beings, and enable them to escape from the abyss of immeasurable woes of birth and death. I should accept all suffering for the sake of all sentient beings in all worlds, in all states of misery, forever and ever, and still always cultivate foundations of goodness for the sake of all beings. Why? I would rather take all this suffering on myself than to allow sentient beings to fall into hell. I should be a hostage to those perilous places – hells, animal realms, the nether world – as a ransom to rescue all sentient beings in states of woe and enable them to gain liberation.[57]

There is an abundance of mythical, actual and magical animals in Buddhist narrative art and literature. Lions, deer, elephants, yaks, horses, serpents, dragons and hybrids (animal–human) were often adopted

A statue of a lion guards a large prayer wheel outside the Buddhist stupa Boudhanath in Nepal.

from earlier pre-Buddhist motifs and transformed by the Buddhist tradition. India was an agrarian society in the early Buddhist period, which is another reason for the inclusion of animals in Buddhist works.

One of the most important Buddhist sacred narratives imbued with animals is a collection of ancient stories known as the *Jataka*. This body of Pali Buddhist scriptures describes the 550 previous lives, or bodhisattvas, of the Buddha, before his birth as Siddhartha Gautama. Sometimes the stories are called the Buddha birth stories. In his previous 550 lives, the Buddha existed in a variety of forms, both non-human and human. It is believed that Buddha himself used the stories to help his followers understand his teachings. These didactic tales draw on his past lives as a rabbit, a swan, a fish, a quail, an ape, a woodpecker, an elephant and a deer.

Sculptured scenes from the *Jatakas*, found upon the carved railings around the relic shrines of Sanchi, Amaravati and Bharhut, indicate that the 'birth stories' were widely known in the third century BCE and were considered part of the sacred history of Buddhism.[58] Compilations of these stories were made by Buddhist monks, especially during the reign of Ashoka, known as the Monk Emperor, who sent out Buddhists to instruct others using the *Jataka* stories as part of their teaching method. These stories, or legends, were continually introduced into the religious discourse of the Buddhist teachers to illustrate or explain some element or doctrine of their faith. These tales spread throughout Sri Lanka, Tibet, Burma, China, Mongolia and Japan.[59] They even became incorporated into the tales of Aesop's fables and Chaucer's *Canterbury Tales*.[60]

The tales of the Buddha's previous incarnations deal primarily with the human condition, pointing out human faults and failings, stressing the qualities of compassion, love, understanding and loyalty, but using animal form in order to do this (similar to Aesop's fables). Although the tales deal with the human, there are some examples where the non-human condition is considered and compassion extended, for example, in pointing out the cruel practice of hunting, the duty of kindness to animals or highlighting the beauty of nature. It is worth noting that when the tales deal with animals, there is little or no evil in them, but when the stories deal with human beings, there is much cruelty.[61]

In the tale 'The Alert Antelope' the peace-loving manner of the antelope is contrasted with that of a cruel hunter. The hunter tries to outsmart the antelope, but the cleverness of the antelope means that she outwits the hunter. Furious, he yells:

> 'Begone with you! You have escaped me today, but another day my spear will find its mark!' . . .
>
> The antelope turned one last time with some words of advice, 'Hunter, you might want to reconsider your way of life. Anyone who uses such trickery to slay the gentle creatures of the forest will eventually reap very harsh rewards. Think again about your actions here today.'[62]

In another *Jataka* tale, the Buddha, in a prior incarnation as a deer, offers his own life in place of a pregnant doe heading off to be slaughtered. The deer's generosity moves the king to an overwhelming outpouring of compassion. He guarantees protection for all deer in the park and then extends his care to include all animals in his kingdom.[63]

Animals are often subjects and active agents in the transmission of Buddhist ideas. They can be transformative players in key Buddhist narratives. In some Buddhist literature, animals are portrayed as sacrificing their lives for the sake of human beings. In the *Sasa Jataka*, a rabbit offers his body to a Brahmin for food, jumping into the fire that the rabbit had piled up. The Brahmin turns out to be the god Indra in disguise, and Indra rewards the rabbit by placing the figure of the rabbit in the moon.[64] In other cases, humans are seen as giving up their lives so that animals may live. There are several accounts of a Buddhist throwing himself in front of a hungry tigress so that she may feed her cubs.[65] It was believed that even wild animals could be tamed through the example of loving kindness.

One *Jataka* tale includes within its narrative several key Buddhist teachings, including karma, rebirth and compassion, as well as the Buddhist indictment of animal sacrifice:

> Once upon a time, a goat was led to a temple and was about to be sacrificed by the presiding Brahman. Suddenly, the goat let out a laugh and then uttered a moaning cry. The Brahman, startled by his odd behaviour, asked the goat what was happening. The goat responded as follows: 'Sir, I have just remembered the history of what has led up to this event. The reason I have laughed is that I realized that in the last of 500

births I have suffered as a goat; in my next life I will return again as a human. The reason I have cried is out of compassion for you. You see, 500 births ago, I was a Brahman, leading a goat to the sacrifice. After killing the goat, I was condemned to 500 births as a goat. If you kill me, you will suffer the same fate.' The Brahman, visibly shaken, immediately freed the goat, who trotted away. A few minutes later, lightning struck the goat and he was freed to again become human. The Brahman likewise was spared, due to the goat's compassionate intervention.[66]

Animals are deemed receptive to hearing and learning the teachings of the Buddha. In one story the Buddha was approached by a wild buffalo who had been causing problems in a small village. He preached to him about 'impermanence, lack of substance, and peaceful *nirvana*. He also reminded him of his past births . . . Overcome with remorse, the buffalo died and was reborn in the Devaloka,'[67] the realm of the gods. In another story the Buddha pacified a greedy cobra and chastised him for his behaviour, warning him that his action would cause rebirth in hell. The snake 'died thinking of the Buddha and was reborn in one of the heavens'.[68]

The natural environment was also respected as the ideal place for cultivating spiritual insights. In such settings it is not surprising to find nature metaphors used to make spiritual insights understandable, such as in the following example:

> A fish swims in the ocean, and no matter how far it swims there is no end to the water. A bird flies in the sky, and no matter how far it flies there is no end to the air. However, the fish and the bird have never left their elements. When their activity is large their field is large. When their need is small their field is small. Thus, each of them totally covers its full range, and each of them totally experiences its realm. If the bird leaves the air it will die at once. If the fish leaves the water it will die at once.
>
> Know that water is life and air is life. The bird is life and the fish is life. Life must be the bird and life must be the fish.[69]

In East Asia, Buddhists often preferred to express themselves in poems, especially in the form of haiku, rather than in philosophical utterances:

Clouds of mosquitos –
It would be bare
Without them.⁷⁰

Ashoka's Vision: Buddha Dharma in Practice

I have enforced the law against killing certain animals and many others, but the greatest progress of righteousness among men comes from exhortation in favor of noninjury to life and abstention from killing living beings.⁷¹

From Magadha, where three centuries earlier the Buddha had lived and taught, Emperor Ashoka of the Maurya dynasty (r. 269–232 BCE) ruled a powerful empire. Magadha was also a stronghold of Jainism, for it had been the home of Mahavira, and Ashoka had been a Jain prior to his conversion to Buddhism at a time of military crisis. After a triumphant battle Ashoka was overwhelmed by the destruction and, deciding to devote the remainder of his reign to providing compassionate rule, he became a lay follower. He instituted what became known as the 'reign of dharma', or Buddhadharma, and he tried to establish righteousness throughout the country, extending this to animals as well as to humans. Ashoka's aim was to create something unique in the world, a compassionate state dedicated to relieving the suffering of all who lived there. Stone billboards erected across his empire list (or perhaps boast of) his charitable achievements: 'On men and animals, birds and fish, I have conferred many boons, even to saving their lives; and I have done many other good deeds.'⁷² These stone billboards are known as 'pillar edicts' and 'rock edicts'.⁷³ One of the most striking things about these Edicts of Ashoka is their inclusion of animals under Ashoka's protection.

Among Ashoka's many imperial edicts, were teachings that spoke of generosity, compassion and the need to refrain from killing animals. He established some of the first animal rights laws. In his edicts he expressed his concern about the number of animals killed in order to provide him with a meal and his intention to stop this practice. Ashoka urged people to become vegetarian and, in a more radical edict, he forbade animal sacrifice: 'Here (in my domain) no living beings are to be slaughtered or offered in sacrifice'.[74] He stopped royal hunting parties and made it illegal to kill many species: 'Twenty-six years after my coronation various animals were declared to be protected.'[75]

Animals were included as beneficiaries of his programmes for obtaining medicinal plants, planting trees and digging wells: 'Along roads I have had banyan trees planted so that they can give shade to animals and men . . . And in various places, I have had watering places made for the use of animals and men.'[76] 'Everywhere has [Ashoka] made provision for two types of medical treatment: medical treatment for humans and medical treatment for animals'.[77]

In his fifth pillar edict Ashoka decreed protection from slaughter for young animals and mothers still feeding their young, he prohibits forests from being burned, in order to protect the creatures living in them, and bans a number of hunting practices harmful to animals. Ashoka decreed that certain days were 'non-killing days', and on these days fish could not be caught, nor any other animals killed. He also established hospitals for humans and animals alike.[78] By taking these actions and making these decrees Ashoka was carrying out the advice to the Chakravartin king given in the *Cakkavatti Sihanada Sutta*, that a good king should extent his protection not only to different classes of people equally, but also to beasts and birds.[79] In summary, 'pity . . . should be felt for all creatures.'[80]

Not everyone in Ashoka's empire agreed with his efforts; in some cases he was forced to compromise, limiting some of his reforms to certain times during the month or to specific holidays. Ashoka also had to withdraw his initial ban on the slaughter of all animals. Some of this resistance may have come from within the palace:

> Formerly, in the [royal] kitchen . . . hundreds of thousands of animals were killed every day to make curry. But now with the writing of the Dhamma edict only three creatures, two peacocks and a deer are killed, and the deer not always. And in time, not even these three creatures will be killed.[81]

Ashoka hoped that his public campaign would convince his people to follow a non-violent way of life, but in this he failed. By the end of his reign there was only a partial concession to animal welfare, yet these inscriptions reveal compassion from a temporal ruler on behalf of his subjects, human and animal. Part of this failure was due to Ashoka's heirs, as after his death they undid his reforms. It is worth noting, however, that Ashoka's reforms influenced others in the Buddhist world, for he had sent missionaries to other kingdoms to spread the Buddhist message of compassion and non-violence to all beings. Due to Ashoka's patronage, Buddhism spread through the Indian subcontinent and his influence was strong in China.[82]

'One who Takes Flesh Kills the Seed of Great Compassion':[83] The Meat Controversy

In Buddhism the First Precept, 'Do not kill,' applies to treatment of both animals and human beings. Meat consumption can be seen as a direct violation of the First Precept. Eating meat is thought to block the growth of compassion and create negative karma, which causes rebirth in realms of great suffering from which it is hard to gain release. Consuming meat also violates the Buddhist principles of ahimsa and compassion, as is stated in the Dhammapada:

> To avoid terror to living beings, let the disciple refrain from eating meat . . . the food of the wise is that which is consumed by the Sadhus (holy men); it does not consist of meat . . . There may be some foolish people in the future that will say that I permitted meat-eating and partook of meat myself, but . . . meat-eating I have not permitted to anyone, I do not permit . . . I will not permit meat-eating in any form, in any manner or in any place; it is unconditionally prohibited for all.

The Mahayana sutras portray the Buddha condemning the eating of meat. The *Surangama Sutra*, which is part of the *Mahayana Sutra*,[84] vividly depicts the punishment that awaits eaters of meat. They become earthbound *raksasas*, blood-eating and flesh-devouring demons who remain trapped in the continual cycle of birth and death.[85] There will be no liberation, no *Bodhi* enlightenment for those who eat the flesh of living beings:

> if living beings in the six worlds of existence cease to kill they will not be subject to the continual round of births and deaths

> ... You should know that those who eat meat, though their minds may open and realize a semblance of *Samādhi* [contemplation], are but great *rāksasas* who, after this life, will sink back into the bitter ocean of *samsara* and cannot be my disciples. They will kill and devour one another ceaselessly; how then can they escape from the three worlds of existence?[86]

Also in the *Surangama Sutra* the Buddha emphasizes that meat-eating cannot coexist with the Great Compassion. The prohibition is against all animal products, inciting the monks to follow what nowadays we would define as a vegan lifestyle:

> How then can those who practice great compassion feed on the flesh and blood of living beings? If *bhiksus* [monks] do not wear garments made of Chinese silk, boots of local leather and furs, and refrain from consuming milk, cream and butter, they will really be liberated from the worldly; after paying their former debts, they will not transmigrate in the three realms of existence ... If a man can control his body and mind and thereby refrains from eating animal flesh and wearing animal products, I say he will really be liberated. This teaching of mine is that of the Buddha.[87]

The *Lankavatara Sutra* belongs to the sacred writings of the *Yogacara* tradition, a branch of Mahayana Buddhism that believes consciousness is inherent in all and the potential for enlightenment is therefore possible for all beings. The *Lankavatara Sutra* contains perhaps the strongest advocacy of vegetarianism in the Buddhist tradition, and helped shape strict adherence to this practice in the Chinese monastic tradition. It was composed before 433 CE, although the chapter on meat-eating is modified in a translation from 513 CE.[88] The entire eighth chapter is devoted to the issue of meat-eating, with the Buddha instructing a disciple about the dangers of eating meat, giving 24 reasons why he should abstain from meat consumption. These reasons include:

> To those who eat meat there are detrimental effects, to those who do not, merits [no. 4].

For profit sentient beings are destroyed, for flesh money is paid out, they are both evil-doers and the deed matures in the hells called *Raurava* (screaming) [no. 9].

The meat-eater is ill-smelling, contemptuous, and born deprived of intelligence; he will be born again and again among the families of the *Candāla*, the *Pukkasa* and the *Domba* [various classes of outcastes] [no. 14].[89]

Three stories are also told to illustrate the dangers of eating meat. The first one concerns a king whose fondness for meat led him to eat human flesh. This led to his alienation from society and he was forced to renounce his throne. The second story is about the god Indra, who assumed the form of a hawk because in a previous existence he had eaten meat. The final story, concerning a king who sired children with a lioness, is particularly strange. The children ate meat and gave birth to flesh-eating demons, who ate human flesh. This cautionary tale addresses what will befall them during transmigration: they will be pursued by flesh-eating animals, such as lions and tigers. It will be difficult for them to obtain a human womb for the higher stage of transmigration, so it will be highly unlikely that they will ever attain nirvana.[90]

Nowhere in the sutras is meat perceived as something enjoyable, or as food permitted for Buddha's followers: 'But in the present sutra all meat-eating in any form, in any manner, and in any place, is unconditionally and once for all, prohibited for all . . . meat-eating I have not permitted to anyone, I do not permit, I will not permit.'[91]

The *Dasabhumika Sutra*, another important Mahayana text, states that a Buddhist 'must not hate any being and cannot kill a living creature even in thought.'[92]

In the *Bodhisattva Bhumi,* in a discussion concerning the principle of giving (*dana*), the Buddhist is not allowed to give anything that 'may be used to inflict injury on other living beings', no 'poisons, weapons, intoxicating liquors, and nets for the capture of animals'. A Buddhist must 'not bestow upon others a piece of land on which the animals may be hunted or killed'.[93]

In the sixteenth minor precept in the *Fan-wang jing* (*Brahmajala Sutra*), a text popular in China, it states that: 'One should be willing to forsake one's entire body, one's flesh, hands, and feet as an offering to starving tigers, wolves, lions, and hungry ghosts.'[94]

The *Mahayana Mahaparinirvana Sutra* reports that Kasyapa, one of the Buddha's most senior followers, proposed a total abstention from meat. The Buddha replied: 'Well said, well said! . . . From now on, I do not permit my sravaka disciples to take flesh.'[95]

The Pali Canon reports that the Buddha gave a different answer, and this is part of the controversy concerning whether Buddhists are permitted to consume meat. The scriptural defence of meat-eating in the Pali Canon states that Buddhist monks are not permitted to eat meat unless they know that the animals were not killed for them. In the *Jivaka Sutta* there is a story about the Buddha's personal physician, who tells the Buddha of a rumour he has heard stating that the Buddha is eating meat from animals that people have slaughtered, so that they can serve him meat. The Buddha denies this, saying: 'Jivaka, I say that there are three instances in which meat should not be eaten, when it is seen, heard, or suspected [that the living being has been slaughtered for oneself]. I say that meat should not be eaten in those three instances.'[96]

This saying was for the begging Buddhist monks who were given leftover food. This exception would not apply if the monks had been invited to a meal, for the animal would have been butchered especially for the occasion, and served with the expectation of gaining merit, or positive karma, by virtue of it being an offering to the Buddha and his disciples. The *Jivaka Sutta* explains, however, that such an action would have the opposite effect:

> If anyone slaughters a living being for the Tathagata [the Buddha] or his disciples, he lays up much demerit [negative karma] in five instances. When he says: 'Go and fetch that living being,' this is the first instance in which he lays up much demerit. When that living being experiences pain and grief on being led along with a neck-halter, this is the second instance in which he lays up much demerit. When he says: 'Go and slaughter that living being,' this is the third instance in which he lays up much demerit. When that living being experiences pain and grief on being slaughtered, this is the fourth instance in which he lays up much demerit. When he provides the Tathagata or his disciples with food that is not permissible, this is the fifth instance in which he lays up much demerit. Anyone

who slaughters a living being for the Tathagata or his disciples lays up much demerit in these five instances.[97]

The question of meat-eating is controversial and there is much confusion. Many Buddhists eat meat and monks, priests and teachers sometimes defend meat-eating as consistent with Buddhist teachings. Some Buddhist meat-eaters use the argument of karmic connection: when an animal is killed a karmic connection is established. The animal will benefit from a favourable birth and will eventually attain enlightenment; therefore, we are helping the animal when we kill and eat it.[98] This rationale has no scriptural basis.[99]

Vegetarianism is mandated by the First Precept in Buddhism. To take life is a form of cannibalism, because in Buddhism there is:

> not a single being that has not been our mother, our father, husband, wife, sister, brother, son or daughter in its ascent and descent of the ladder of cause and effect through countless rebirths – not one being whose kinship with us even while in the animal state has not continued. How then can one who approaches all living beings as though they were himself eat the flesh of something that is of the same nature as himself and not be guilty of cannibalism of a sort?[100]

The highest proportion of Buddhist meat-eaters is found in Tibetan Buddhism, originally from necessity, due to the climate and the soil. Tibetan Buddhism doesn't require strict vegetarianism, but it does condemn the killing of animals for food. Tibetan Buddhism has a stronger tradition of compassionate animal protection and vegetarianism than many people realize. Jigme Lingpa (1729–1798) was a practitioner of Tibetan Buddhism who felt compassion for animals. His biographer tells of 'his sorrow . . . when he witnessed the butchering of animals by humans. He often bought and set free animals about to be slaughtered.'[101] When he learned of an extensive massacre of bees for honey taking place on a mountain, he purchased that mountain and 'sealed it until the end of the eon'.[102] Shabkar Tsogdruk Rangdrol (1781–1851), one of the most beloved teachers in Tibet, was a vegetarian for most of his life. In his autobiography he mentions the circumstances that led to this:

I saw many sheep and goats that had been slaughtered. Feeling unbearable compassion for all animals in the world who are killed for food, I went back before the Jowo Rinpoche, prostrated myself, and made this vow: 'From today on, I give up the negative act that is eating the flesh of beings, each one of whom has been my mother.'[103]

Shabkar frequently took part in animal liberation and insisted that all slaughter of animals be stopped. On a trip to Nepal he convinced many professional hunters that their way of life was contrary to the teachings of Buddha, which led to meat merchants complaining that he was ruining their livelihood.[104]

Patrul Rinpoche, one of the most-respected Tibetan teachers of the nineteenth century, wrote these profound words:

In Buddhism, once we have taken refuge in the dharma we have to give up harming others. To have an animal killed everywhere we go, and to enjoy its flesh and blood, is surely against the precepts of taking refuge, is it not? More particularly, in the Bodhisattva tradition of the Great Vehicle [Mahayana Buddhism], we are supposed to be the refuge and protector of all infinite beings [all living beings without exception]. The beings with unfortunate karma that we are supposed to be protecting are instead being killed without the slightest compassion, and their boiled flesh and blood are being presented to us, and we – their protectors, the Bodhisattvas – then gobble it all up gleefully, smacking our lips. What could be worse than that?[105]

The fourteenth Dalai Lama is believed by the faithful to be a reincarnation of the Bodhisattva Avalokiteshvara. He is thought to embody Avalokiteshvara's essence: compassion. He gave up eating meat after witnessing a chicken being killed for his lunch: 'I thought of how much suffering the poor creature was enduring. The realization filled me with remorse and I decided it was time to become a vegetarian.'[106] Although he is no longer a strict vegetarian,[107] the Dalai Lama continues to believe that a meatless diet is one of the practical ways that Buddhism helps all sentient beings. He believes that our basic nature as human beings is to be vegetarian, and humans are to make every effort not to harm other living beings. He remains an advocate for animal rights:

One day I went to visit a small lake to offer food to the fish that we had previously freed there. On my way back someone said, 'By the way, did you see the poultry farm?' All of a sudden I had a vision of chickens carrying banners on which it was written, 'The Dalai Lama not only saves fish, but even feeds them. What does he do for us poor chickens?' I felt terribly sad and sorry for the chickens. We no longer raise poultry in our settlements.[108]

Buddhism encountered opposition in China, for it was seen as a challenge to the threatened Confucian world view and thereby came to be associated with the downfall of dynasties and the destruction of family values, mainly because of its emphasis on renunciation. The non-violent ethic threatened the Confucian viewpoint, which was that a heavenly decree controls the fate of kingdoms and of all nature, and there is little humans can do about it. The doctrine of karma came into direct conflict with this Chinese cosmological view that heaven and earth are the parents of all things, that fate is predestined and not changed or brought about by good or bad karma. By the time of the Song dynasty (960–1279 CE) Buddhist dietary practices introduced from India, including vegetarianism, gained ascendancy over Taoist practices.[109] In the Mahayana tradition, which spread from northern India to East Asia, vegetarianism became a requirement, particularly for Chinese monks, causing a clash with indigenous Confucian culture, but securing a place within Chinese folk tradition.

Another reason for opposition to a vegetarian diet in China was because of the pre-Buddhist practice of animal sacrifice. The killing of animals was a standard element of many ritual occasions, from imperial commemorations to weddings and birthdays. Animal sacrifice was considered essential for the sustenance of departed ancestors, as well as for placating evil spirits.[110] Buddhist monks had to provide alternative means of ensuring the well-being of ancestors and dealing with evil spirits. One solution was to provide a vegetarian feast, to which monks would be invited and merit accrued through this offering.[111] Many tracts dealing with this topic were written by monks for the laity.

One of the best known of these tracts is *Verses on Resolving Doubts and Replacing Blood Sacrifice with Vegetarian Feasts and Fasts*, written by the monk Ciyun Zunshi (964–1032). Zunshi compiled a number of Buddhist ritual tracts as a means of converting the local population from animal sacrifice to Buddhist observances. He stressed that virtuous deeds done in the past are the reason for present happiness, not animal sacrifice.[112] One dilemma he anticipated is that of a new convert, concerned about the negative karma acquired by the previous practice of slaughtering animals. Zunshi counselled each household to create a shrine with a copy of the *Sutra of Golden Light*, and to make offerings to it, dedicating the merit of doing this to the animals slain.[113]

Another important work, *Tract Against Taking Life* by Zhu Hong (1535–1615), a Chinese monk of the Ming dynasty, was composed five centuries after Zunshi's treatise. This tract is very different, since Zhu Hong does not cite Buddhist texts against blood sacrifice; rather, he considers individual occasions when an animal is usually sacrificed, such as weddings and birthdays, and provides an argument stating why such a sacrifice is both unnatural and inappropriate. He combines passionate argument with dramatic stories, to create tension and horror:[114]

> Point One: Birthday celebrations are not suitable occasions for taking life . . . How could one be so callous as to forget a mother's pain and take the life of living souls? . . . The fact that the whole world engages in this without realizing it's wrong can surely be considered something so painful that one weeps endlessly with grief.[115]

> Point Two: It is not right to kill living creatures in order to celebrate the birth of a son . . . They do not stop to think that every bird and beast also loves its son. How could one rest comfortably with the idea of celebrating the birth of one's own child by causing the death of another's? . . . There was a hunter who one night became exceedingly drunk. When he spied his young son he mistook him for a roebuck. He sharpened his knife and prepared to kill him. His wife pleaded tearfully with him, but he would not listen. Finally he slit open the boy's abdomen and took out his intestines [as though to dress his carcass]. When he was finished he went peacefully to sleep. At the break of day he awoke and called for his son to go to the market to sell the roebuck meat for him. His wife, weeping, said, 'The creature you killed last night was your own son.' The father flung his body [to the floor] and his five viscera

burst into pieces [at the grief]. Alas! Humans and animals, different though they be, are united in heart by the love for their children. How could one condone killing?[116]

Point Four: In marriage celebrations it is not appropriate to take life ... marriage is the beginning of reproduction of human life. To practice taking life at the beginning of life is simply contrary to principle ... Whenever a person gets married, it is required by custom to offer prayers that the husband and wife will grow old together. But if we wish [human couples] to grow old together, does this mean that animals wish that they should die first?[117]

Point Five: It is not appropriate to take life in order to entertain guests ... People gorge themselves from cup and tray to the music of reed pipe and song, as butchered animals scream on the chopping block ... When you know that the creatures on your tray come, struggling and squealing, from the chopping block, then you are making their extreme anguish your greatest delight.[118]

Point Seven: It is not appropriate to take life in order to make one's living ... To make one's living by taking life is something that in principle is condemned by the gods ... There is no more certain means than this when it comes to planting the seeds for [rebirth in] the hells and evil retribution in lives to come. How could you face such pain and not seek a different livelihood? ... I have personally seen butchers of sheep who, on their deathbed, have made bleating sounds from their mouths, or the heads of eel-sellers writhe and gasp like eels as they near their end ... I tell you people that, if [you] have no other means to make a living, it is far better to beg for your meals. To live by killing is no match for bearing your hunger and dying of starvation.[119]

Near the close of the tract, Zhu Hong urges the reader to pass the text on to others, explaining that it will save the lives of millions of creatures and gain the reader merit: 'your unpublicized good deeds will be vast, and the rewards you reap will be inexhaustible ... the buddhas will be filled with joy, and the myriad gods and spirits will extend their protection to you.'[120]

As well as meat-eating, there were other forms of animal abuse condemned by the Buddha. In the *Mahayana Mahaparinirvana Sutra*, out of sixteen deeds listed as evil, thirteen concern the ill-treatment of animals.[121] Using animals for transportation or for labour seems to have been permissible, providing the animals were not overworked or mistreated.

Buddha taught that it was wrong to gain happiness at the expense of another being. A basic teaching common to all schools of Buddhism is that one may not build happiness on the sufferings of others, as is stated in the Dhammapada 1.31: 'He who for the sake of happiness hurts others who also want happiness, shall not hereafter find happiness.' This principle, along with those of compassion and ahimsa, has governed the Buddhist practice of animal protection or animal liberation ('ransoming of sentient beings'). Animal protection has a long history in Buddhist Asia. In the *Jataka* there is a story of Prince Vessantara who, on his return to his kingdom, releases all animals from servitude as a thank-offering.[122] In another story, Sakka, the chief of the gods, commands his charioteers, even though they are fleeing from enemies, to drive in such a way that birds' nests are not pulled down from the trees, for 'it is better to give up one's own life than make a bird nestless.'[123] In another tale, a devout boy is told that his mother can be cured if she eats the flesh of a hare. He catches one, but then releases it, sorry for his action. His mother is cured because of her son's rejection of violence.[124]

Animal liberation practices are taught in all of the major traditions of Buddhism and are considered extremely virtuous. This practice of 'releasing life' (*fangsheng yi*) is one of the main activities of lay Chinese Buddhism. Birds, turtles and fish are the most popular animals to release, because they require no further assistance once released into the air or water. Spiritual release is encouraged to accompany the physical release. In the *Sutra of Golden Light* it is written that the previous buddha Ratnasikhin had made known that any being living in the ten directions who heard his name would ascend to rebirth in the Heaven of the Thirty-three.[125] 'A young man named Jalavahana [Shakyamuni Buddha in a previous life] came upon ten thousand dying fish. After filling their dry pond with water, he recited ten epithets of Ratnabhava, causing the fish to be reborn in heaven.'[126]

Ceremonies to accompany the liberation of the animals were devised by prominent Buddhist monks. At the stage of preparing for the service: 'The congregation should look upon the [bound] creatures with the eye of loving kindness, pondering their [plight] and arousing a profound empathy for their being mired deeply [in the cycle of samsara].'¹²⁷ The officiating monk then calls on the deities:

> Today there are various creatures of the air, water and land who have been captured by others and are about to enter death's door. We . . . intent on carrying out our *bodhisattva* practice, arouse a heart of loving-kindness and compassion and [prepare] to be the cause that will grant them long life. Through this act of releasing life we redeem for them their bodies and lives, releasing them to wander in ease and freedom.¹²⁸

The monk asks that the Three Jewels purify the animals, so that they will be able to understand what is to be said.¹²⁹ He then recites the epithets of Ratnabhava so that the animals will be reborn in their next life in the Heaven of the Thirty-three, and so that they will eventually achieve enlightenment. A lecture follows, then a confession on behalf of the animals and, finally, a prayer for rebirth.¹³⁰

One of the most startling components of the liturgy is the wording that accompanies the 'Administering of the Three Refuges'. Animals are assumed to be capable of professing refuge in the Buddha, in the dharma and in the *sangha*:¹³¹

> These sentient creatures that stand before us now, of species different from our own, [hereby] profess that they have taken refuge in the Buddha, have taken refuge in the dharma, have taken refuge in the *sangha*. [Repeat three times.] From this day forward, they will proclaim the Buddha as their master.¹³²

Liberation of condemned animals includes rescuing one or more animals doomed to an early death (either as food or as bait), performing a ceremony to strengthen one's compassion and then releasing the animals into a secure and safe environment.¹³³ Such a practice decreases suffering, increases compassion and increases positive karma. This positive karma can be invoked on behalf of someone else. In 2002, when the Dalai Lama was ill in hospital, Lama Zopa Rinpoche asked

Buddhists to conduct animal liberation practices dedicated to the long life of His Holiness. More than one million animals were liberated as a result of this request.[134]

Animal protection or liberation, first declared by Ashoka, spread with Buddhism to China and Japan, where it became a means of earning merit. The twentieth precept of the *Fanwang jing* (*Brahmajala Sutra*) declares: 'if one is a son of Buddha, one must, with a merciful heart, intentionally practice the work of liberating living beings.'[135]

This text and others influenced Chinese and Japanese leaders to declare the institution of *hojo-e* or 'meetings for liberating living beings'.[136] In the sixth century the monk Chi-i reportedly convinced more than one thousand fishermen to give up their livelihood. He also purchased three hundred miles of land as a protected area where animals could be released. In 759 CE the Chinese Emperor Suh Tsung established 81 ponds where fish could be released.[137]

Zhu Hong proposed a practical path to enlightenment based on a combination of Zen Buddhism and Pure Land Buddhism.[138] Rewards await those who set animals free, because releasing animals accords with the mind of heaven and the teaching of Buddha:

> Of the persons who set creatures free, some receive honor and prestige, some receive added years of life, some are spared from disasters, some recover from mental illnesses, some achieve rebirth in heaven, and some attain enlightenment in the Way. There is clear evidence that as one releases life, he assuredly receives a reward.[139]

In Japan reforms were carried out by Emperor Tenmu (Tenmu-tennō), who in 675 CE restricted the use of certain hunting devices, as well as the eating of cows, horses, dogs and monkeys. In the following year he ordered that various provinces 'let loose living things'.[140] The release of living things continues to be practised in East Asia, primarily as a ceremonial event, and is now practised by Buddhists in the West.

With the transmission of Buddhism from China to Japan, the ahimsa doctrine underwent yet another cultural transformation. As in China, stories were told to encourage the protection of animals and of those releasing animals. The Japanese Shinto tradition was supportive of the Buddhist views of the sanctity of animal life, unlike the resistance of Confucianists in China.[141]

Stories similar to the ones told in China were circulated in Japan to emphasize the importance of practising non-violence towards all creatures. In one tale a monk advises some people to buy four large sea turtles and then set them free. Later the monk is thrown overboard by thieving sailors. The four turtles that he had helped rescue come to save him, after nodding to him three times.[142] In another story a cruel man is punished:

> In Yamato province there was a man whose name and native place are not identified. He was not benevolent and liked to kill living beings. He caught a rabbit and set it free in the fields after skinning it alive. Before long he contracted a fatal illness; his whole body was covered with scabs that broke out in extremely painful sores. He was never cured and died groaning loudly.
>
> Ah! How soon wicked deeds incur a penalty in this life! We should be considerate and benevolent. Above all, we should show mercy.[143]

The Presence of Animals in Indian and Tibetan Vajrayana Traditions

As has already been mentioned, Buddhism can take on different forms depending on the particular country and its accompanying folk and cultural traditions. Buddhism has always found room for the reverence of local deities and spirits. Ideas about animals in the Indian Buddhist and Tibetan Vajrayana traditions are quite complex. Animals are prominent in creation stories of the Tibetan people. Divine animals appear in the Tibetan Buddhist tradition in their role as creators of a whole culture. In a Tibetan text, the bodhisattva of compassion, Avalokiteshvara, is incarnated as a monkey who is seduced by a rock demoness; their offspring are the first Tibetans. 'A passage in this text explicitly attributes the compassionate qualities (that are also deeply embedded in the Tibetan character) to this paternal monkey.'[144]

Elephants are important in Buddhism: cosmologically, eight (or sixteen) elephants support the physical universe.[145] Elephants also carry kings; therefore, the Buddha is depicted on an elephant, reminding the follower of his royal pedigree. Parileyya was a wild elephant who

Lumbini, Nepal, animal relief on a *dorje* (Tibetan for the *vajra*, the thunderbolt symbol). Around the pedestal are animals of the Tibetan calendar.

waited on the Buddha when he spent time in the forest away from the monks.[146] Another elephant, the angry Nalagiri, was tamed by the Buddha through the power of loving kindness.[147]

The elephant is also one of the possessions of the Chakravartin ('the turners of the wheel'). On the wheel of samsara, the cycle of rebirth, there are several animal images, with the perimeter ringed with twelve preconditions that create rebirth.[148] Three animals represent human values: the cock (desire), the snake (hatred) and the pig (delusion). These three 'poisons', as they were known in early Indian tradition, are the propelling forces of the cycle of existence.[149] Karmic retribution determines where on the wheel each person will be reborn. Deer were present at the Buddha's first sermon; this event is commemorated in Indian and Tibetan monasteries by deer depicted on the wheel of the dharma (replacing the wheel of samsara).[150]

Nagas (snakes) have often been at the centre of Buddhist traditions and their transmission. They are considered both dangerous and beneficial. They dwell underground or in rivers and are thought to control fertility. They can destroy because of their power over rain and are thought to be agents of diseases, such as leprosy and epilepsy. Shrines and temples have been built in their honour. *Nagas* have been Buddha's adversaries, as well as the guardians of Buddha and his teaching (it is

Buddha sheltered by the head of a naga *at a Buddhist temple complex in Chiang Mai, Thailand.*

believed that *nagas* guard the treasures of the Buddhist tradition). The Buddha himself is said to have been protected by a *naga*. The nature of *nagas* is not always predictable; they need to be appeased, hence the use of snake charmers in Indian courts.

Belief in the power of *nagas* (from local beliefs) led monastics as well as Buddha himself to incorporate the *nagas* into the Buddhist framework. In one story about the *nagas* Apalala and Gopala, these *nagas* are described as disgruntled monastics from previous lives set on damaging the Buddhist teachings. The Buddha subdued them with his presence in the form of a reflection in a pond they inhabit.[151]

Nagas will provide stability, wealth and well-being, as long as they are respected. For example, a *naga* appears early on in the life of the historical Buddha, Siddartha, in the role of the *naga* king Mucalinda. This serpent shelters the future Buddha from the rain, coiling himself around Siddartha seven times as he meditated prior to his full enlightenment. One interpretation of the Mucalinda story is that the Buddha received royal authorization from the *nagas*, reinforcing the Buddha's connection with divine kinship to guide all people from then on.[152] The Buddha's appreciation for the *naga* is visible; the marks on the head of the monocled cobra are said to have been made by the Buddha's fingers after he had blessed it.[153]

The Buddhist concern for order and legitimacy is reflected in the construction of shrines to *nagas*. At the Ajanta Caves in Maharashtra, India, a site of thirty rock-cut Buddhist cave monuments, cave 16 is an example of the Buddhist tradition's accommodation of the *nagas*. According to the dedicatory inscription, the Buddha took over the abode of a *naga* who originally resided in the cave, but he relocated the *naga* to a place further inside.[154]

In the Tibetan tradition, the *naga* is known as *klu*. The universe is thought to consist of three worlds: the gods or the celestial world, the human world and the *naga* world.[155] As in the Indian tradition, Tibetan temples for the *klu* are erected in order to appease and honour them. In Lhasa there is a temple situated on an island near the Potala Palace. The lake was formed after the building of the palace and the temple built to appease the *klu*, who had been disturbed by the building of the palace. The site became a place of personal retreat for the Dalai Lamas. Even today, patients from the hospital in Lhasa are sent there to undergo a purification ritual and to request prayers dedicated to the *klu*.[156]

Animals not only protect and preserve the Buddhist teachings, but act as vehicles of transmission of the doctrine. Both Indian and Tibetan Buddhist literature includes an elaborate pantheon with deities mounted on animals.[157] In the Tibetan case, the mounts of guardian figures show animals whose actual and mythical qualities are closely linked with the powers of the deities on top of them.

Examples of the Tibetan tradition of therianthropic deities include Hayagriva ('the Horse-headed one'; Tibetan: Rta mgrin), and the four female figures known as *Phra men ma* (animal-headed sorceresses) that point to the importance of animals in Tibetan Buddhist ritual.[158] The horse-headed figure is prominent in narratives in Asia as a god of horses, expeller of demons, or messenger of prayer (as depicted on prayer flags). The Buddha Ratnasambhava is often depicted as sitting on a yellow throne supported by four horses.[159]

The *Phra men ma* have the bodies of beautiful women and the faces of animals (a raven, pig, dog and owl). The origin of these figures is complex and may be a mixture of different traditions from India, Tibet and areas of Central Asia. These animal-headed figures are associated with the directions, the doors of monasteries or mandalas and certain independent powers.[160]

In the Tibetan religious tradition, both before and after the introduction of Buddhism, there is the concept of animals being the seat of life power or principle. The life force (*bla*) in the body is connected with external objects and attached to an individual, community, animal, tree or mountain.[161] This life force can take the form of a tiger, lion, elephant or bear for those with royal connections, and for others will be a horse, mule, sheep, ox or yak.[162] Because of this belief, these animals are often protected from harm.

In summary, animals represent complex roles in Indian and Tibetan Buddhist narrative traditions: as attributes of deities, as modes of transportation, as protectors of sacred teachings and as divine beings.[163] Animals are therefore key in Indian and Tibetan Buddhist traditions, aiding the spread of the Buddhist tradition.

Conclusion

> Today, more than ever before, life must be characterized by a sense of Universal Responsibility, not only nation to nation and human to human, but also human to other forms of life.[164]

> And, no matter whether they belong to the higher groups such as human beings or to the lower groups such as animals, all beings primarily seek peace, comfort, and security. Life is dear to a mute creature as it is to man. Even the lowliest insect strives for protection against dangers that threaten its life. Just as each one of us want happiness and fear pain, just as each other one of us want to live and not to die, so do all other creatures.[165]

In summary, Buddhism has developed an extensive tradition of emphasizing and fostering a positive link between the human realm and that of animals. Due to rebirth, humans can regard non-humans as relatives. Although Buddhism considers human birth superior, in that only humans can achieve nirvana, various texts remind people that they once were animals and can again take animal form if they behave incorrectly. Several stories tell of animals who perform virtuous acts and thus ensure for themselves either heavenly or human birth. The

The Death of Buddha Attended by Animals, in a 14th-century Japanese hanging scroll, ink, colour and gold on silk.

principles of loving kindness, compassion and ahimsa are emphasized. Although there are different forms of Buddhism, all assent to the above principles, lived out by observing the Precepts and following the Noble Eightfold Path. Because there are no commandments per se, people are to live out their Buddhist lives in the knowledge of 'the Way', which includes seeing non-human companions as fellow beings. Yet, it is with some hesitation that I point out that in Buddhism, loving acts can accrue merit. Sometimes this practice of loving kindness, and its use as a meditative exercise, is to benefit the human's spiritual enhancement rather than for the alleviation of the suffering of animals. Negative karma will be cancelled out and the human's journey towards nirvana will be hastened. Are Buddhist practice and ideals similar to Jainism in that both embrace positive outcomes for humans as well as for sentient beings? While applauding compassion for sentient creatures, what about the non-sentient?

I wish to draw attention to two contemporary animal concerns that are not addressed in Buddhism. The first, raised by Harris, is about conservation. He notes that Buddhism is not an ecological religion because, from the Buddhist perspective, 'some of the major ecological issues of our day, such as the extinction of species, are really pseudo problems that can be straightforwardly resolved through . . . rebirth in a variety of different destinies . . . within *samsara*.'[166] The second, taking up the principle of happiness, as well as that of alleviating suffering, is raised by Phelps. Conservation issues may not figure highly in Buddhism, but, Phelps argues, vivisection – which is mostly ignored as an ethical dilemma by many religions – is contrary to Buddhist teachings. The suffering the animals experience is suffering that in some way contributes to humanity's happiness or well-being. It is contrary to the Buddhist teachings concerning the unity of all life. Sacrifice of animals to the gods was thought to bring blessings to humans; Phelps stresses that 'Vivisection is the modern equivalent of religious animal sacrifice, both being attempts to purchase our own well-being with the lives of animals.'[167]

The Animals and the Hermit

Long ago a holy man wishing to develop a deeper understanding of life came to live as a hermit in a remote area of the Himalayan foothills. One summer a parching drought went on month after month. As all the streams had dried up in the sweltering sun, the hermit dug a well to provide himself with water.

The animals of the area began suffering deeply from the lack of water and many were on the verge of perishing. The hermit felt a deep compassion for the animals and decided to help them. He cut down a large dead tree and hollowed out the centre to make a large drinking trough. It was very difficult work in the extreme heat of the drought but, knowing the animals would not survive much longer, he persisted. When he had finished the trough, he began filling it with buckets from his well. Once again, it was strenuous work, but he accomplished it.

The animals of the forest could smell the water they so desperately craved and slowly began to come to the trough to drink. First the birds, rabbits and squirrels came. The deer and wild boar arrived to drink. And finally even the great tiger came in the spirit of peace and drank from the hermit's trough.

The hermit had to work almost continuously to keep the trough full of water for the steady stream of thirsty animals. His labour was so time-consuming that he neglected to forage for the roots and fruits that made up his diet. The animals could see that he was growing weak and they decided to return his kindness. They knew the places deep in the woods where edible roots, berries and even some fruits still remained, and they went out and gathered some for the hermit. When they returned with the food the hermit was deeply moved by this display of their gratitude. During the drought the hermit kept filling the trough for the animals and the animals kept bringing him food. When the drought finally ended and the rains came, the streams filled once again. The hermit no longer needed to fill the trough and he could now gather his own food. But his close relationship to the animals did not end. The animals often came and rested by his hut or perched in nearby trees, happy to be with the friend who had saved their lives.[168]

TEN

Animals in Religion in China and Japan

China

ANCIENT CHINA WAS A WORLD rich in animals, for it was a land of lush forests, rich grasslands, fertile mountains and wetlands. In ancient China local fauna varied across the regions as did the perceptions of animals and their role in religious belief and practice. The Han historian Sima Qian noted that people in the southern states seemed to be preoccupied with beliefs in demons and carried out divination by means of chicken bones (as opposed to the more widespread use of turtles, known as plastromancy).[1] Wooden figurines with horns and long tongues have been found in graves from the Eastern Zhou period (771–221 BCE) in the southern state of Chu.[2] In early Chinese (pre-Buddhist) religion, animals were both mediums or agents and objects. The Chinese did not see the demarcation of the human and animal realms as permanent; they were part of the larger natural world.

Chinese religion is unique in that it developed in isolation, without the influence of other great religions. Confucianism and Taoism, two of the three faiths of China (the other is Buddhism), developed their distinct forms before they had significant contact with other religions and with the rest of the world. In many aspects of Chinese culture and religion the line between historical fact and mythology is blurred. When discussing Chinese religions, mythology plays a very important role, especially in terms of the presence of animals, real and imaginary. Chinese deities did not systematically manifest themselves as animals and the Chinese pantheon did not include many gods and spirits that were identified with certain animals.

Creation of the World

Chinese religion lacks a formal doctrine of creation; instead, we encounter cosmogonies that are mainly the product of scholarly compilers, written as parables in order to illustrate philosophical theories. Creation for the Chinese is an act of reducing chaos to order: it is not about explaining the creation of humans and animals. Mythology provides different stories to help explain the origins of the universe.[3] The most extensive creation account involves a giant, Pangu ('antiquity'), said to be the child of Yin and Yang, the vital forces of the universe.[4] According to a text of the third century CE, when neither Earth nor Heaven existed, Chaos was like a hen's egg. From this egg Pangu was born. He slept and grew inside the egg for 18,000 years until, eventually, he woke up and stretched. The egg separated, with the heavy part becoming the earth (*yin*) and the light part the sky (*yang*). He fell asleep again, and eventually died. The giant's corpse gave rise to all the elements.[5] Details of Pangu's changes vary from text to text. One has fleas on his body becoming the human race; another account has him being dissatisfied with the animals 'because here was no reasoning being who could develop and utilise other living creatures, these being incapable of any action on their own account,'[6] so he moulded man and woman from clay.

There were also important symbolic animals appointed to the four cardinal directions, which grew from the dead Pangu and were ultimately derived from the principles of *yin* and *yang*:

> The Green Dragon of the east and of spring: the bringer of regenerating rain. It embodied the *yang* principle, positive and male.
>
> The Red Bird of the south, the phoenix or feng-huang: fire and summer. It symbolized drought and embodied the *yin* principle, negative and female. The phoenix represented the Empress, while the dragon stood for the Emperor. The phoenix was a symbol of happiness and of heaven's favour. The phoenix was also believed to mark buried treasure.
>
> The White Tiger of the east: king of the beasts, autumn. In the autumn it descended from the mountains in the west. Though known to the Chinese, it was often treated as a fabulous beast.
>
> Dark Warrior, the tortoise and snake, associated with the north and winter, and with water.[7]

Chaos (Hundun) was not only thought to have taken the form of an egg; sometimes Chaos was conceived of as a bird, sometimes an owl. These nocturnal creatures represented the dark, negative *yin* elements of the universe, which had to be destroyed to bring order into the world. Another version has Hundun as a mythical bird, either yellow or red. It has six feet, four wings and no face. It can dance and sing despite the absence of a mouth and lives on the Mountain of the Sky.[8]

The Dragon and Other Important Creatures

The dragon is one of the four heavenly creatures of Chinese mythology, along with the tortoise, the male phoenix and a female *qilin*.

During the Shang dynasty (c. 1600–c. 1050 BCE) there were many representations of imaginary creatures, such as dragons, but few portrayals of real animals. In the West, the dragon represents evil, as depicted in the New Testament (Revelation) and in tales about St George, the dragon slayer. In contrast, in China the dragon, known as the 'long beneficent spirit of the moist', is chiefly a benign figure associated with storms and clouds, rain and fertility, rivers and imperial power.[9] The dragon of Chinese mythology that appeared to the legendary ruler Fu Xi out of the Luo River resembled a crocodile with its teeth and short legs. The Chinese dragon was a mythical creature with the 'horns of a deer, head of a camel, abdomen of a cockle, scales of a carp, claws of an eagle, feet of a tiger, and ears of an ox'.[10] The dragon as a supernatural creature embodied the forces of nature. Taoist dragons were benevolent spirits associated with happiness and prosperity, but when Buddhism became popular their character was modified by the Indian concept of the *naga*, or snake god, a more terrifying creature.[11]

Dragon processions were held in spring to welcome the return of the dragons, who had spent the winter underground. Their arrival was announced by thunder and the beginnings of the spring rains. Sometimes dragons were depicted carrying a flaming ball or pearl, which symbolized thunder. As the dragons emerged from the mud beneath the waters in the spring, they became rain and fertility symbols.

There were five types of dragons: heavenly, which guarded the mansions of the gods; spiritual, which controlled winds and rains and only accidentally caused flooding; earthly, which cleared rivers and deepened seas; those of hidden treasure; and Imperial dragons, which

Painting of the Kangxi Emperor, c. 1700, with a painted dragon, symbol of imperial power, behind him.

were marked by five claws, whereas the other types had four.¹² Four claws signified the status of a prince, while court officials were only allowed to embroider dragons with three claws on their robes.¹³

Imperial dragons represented the 'Sun of Heaven', the emperor of China: 'The legendary emperor Yu, founder of the Xia dynasty, had originally appeared in the form of a winged dragon who emerged from his father's body when it was slashed open. Each succeeding emperor was said to be the reincarnation of Yu.'¹⁴ After a flood, Yu ('the Great', c. 2200–2100 BCE), in the form of a winged dragon, was given permission to take the earth, and he formed mountains from it and with his tail he cut ditches to channel the flood waters.

The Han dynasty (206 BCE–220 CE) had the five-clawed dragon as its emblem. The dragon symbol was used on clothing, the throne and on ceremonial and household items. Dragons were sometimes depicted on doors as door guardians, usually beneficent, but not always. The dragon's male power (*yang*) was offset by the phoenix, the symbol of the Empress (*yin*).

According to the Taoists, dragons were symbolic of the Way (*tao* means 'way' or 'path'), the central truth of their philosophy, which revealed itself momentarily, only to vanish in mystery. On the one hand the dragon is believed to be life-giving (due to its ability to bring rain), yet it is also to be feared for the destruction it could bring. At festivals, such as the lunar Chinese New Year, the dragon dance continues to be one of the highlights.

Four thousand years ago, together with the dragon, there were other mythical creatures. They included the *taotie* or *t'ao-t'ieh*, an ogre with open jaws and feline characteristics. It is said that it resembled a tiger and served as a guardian to protect graves from evil spirits, and perhaps even to suggest that the ground was a divine force, from which we all come and to which we shall all eventually return.[15] The *taotie* was a common motif on the Chinese vessels used for ritual offerings (*ding*).

The carp is associated with the mythological dragons. It is thought that once a year all carp attempt to leap the Longmen Falls, or Dragon Gate, on the Yellow River at the border between Shaanxi and Shanxi provinces. Those who succeed are transformed into dragons and rise up into the sky.[16]

Another popular creature, real rather than mythical, was the tortoise, which was extremely important in divination rituals. The tortoise was seen as divine because of its physical longevity and for the designs on its shell. In Eastern Han apocryphal literature, the tortoise was viewed as a divine medium through which writing was revealed to humankind. According to legend, 'Fu Xi based the composition of the trigrams on the patterns he observed on the back of a tortoise emerging from the river Luo. These designs allegedly inspired the composition of the famous Book of Changes.'[17] The tortoise was also a symbol of stability, often portrayed holding up the foundations of the earth. It is interesting to note that the tortoise was accorded this special status, because the tortoise was not native to China and had to be imported from southern regions to serve this exalted purpose.[18]

Tigers were worshipped in different regions; the Ba, who lived in the eastern part of present-day Sichuan, worshipped the white tiger with the sacrifice of human victims. Legend stated that the Ba were descendants of a king whose soul had transformed into a white tiger after he had died.¹⁹ Tigers were associated with death.

Gaoyao, the judge of Shun, the last of the Five Emperors and predecessor of Yu, had as his emblem a *qilin*, an auspicious creature:

> Its body was that of a deer, with the tail of an ox, horse's hooves and a single, fleshy horn. The hair on its back was varicoloured, that on its belly was yellow. When it walked it did not crush the grass and it consumed no living creature. It spared the innocent but struck the guilty with its single horn.²⁰

When the judgements of a prince achieved ideal justice, a *qilin* was born in his court. The appearance of miraculous beasts at the imperial court was proof of the favour of heaven and of the emperor's supreme virtue, for it was only when the cosmic order had achieved a perfect balance that there was a sufficient amount of cosmic force to allow the production of such wonders.²¹

Animals in Pre-Buddhist China

Chinese mythology remains scattered and interspersed in later texts. Archaeological discoveries have disclosed a past of war and violence, when warriors were buried with their horses and chariots. Mythological records speak of an age of legendary gods and heroes, especially the Three Sovereigns (*San Huang*; sage-like figures) and the Five Emperors (*Wu Di:* Yellow Emperor, Zuanxu, Yao, Shun and Yu). The Three Sovereigns have sometimes been identified with such figures as Fu Xi ('Animal Tamer') and Shennong ('Divine Farmer'), bearing names that speak about their merits.²² The ox-headed divine farmer Shennong taught humans the acts of agriculture.

Were the ancient sages and the five emperors human or divine? Scholars who consider the ancient sages to be deities do not always agree about what it means to be a deity. Some see them as supreme beings, as personal gods. Others regard them as ancestral spirits, or god-ancestors, lower on the rung of the divine. This is closer to what we would consider to be totemism. Oracle and bronze inscriptions have been discovered bearing pictographs derived from animal symbols and associated with totemic clans.²³ The sage Shun is associated with the phoenix and has been regarded as the ancestor of the Bird Tribe,

Earthenware tomb figure of a horse, China, c. 700–800 CE.

while the flood-controller Yu (with dragon connections) has been called the ancestor of the Reptile Tribe.[24] In any case, the primordial sages were ancestral figures in a country where people considered themselves as children of a divine or semi-divine order.

One of the significant factors about a figurine of a mother goddess excavated in Liaoning province, northeast of Beijing, and dated to about 4400 to 2500 BCE, is that it was found with representations of animals: jade dragons, tortoises, birds and cicadas.[25] The powerful dead were accompanied in the grave by pieces of jade ritually placed on the body. Cicadas were viewed as a symbol of immortality and resurrection, since they emerge fully formed after seven years underground. A jade sculpture of the cicada was placed on the tongue of a corpse before burial as an emblem of resurrection.[26]

In mythology, another female deity figure is Nu-wa ('woman'), sometimes alleged to be the consort of Fu Xi, the culture hero. She is supposed to have a human head and a serpent's body. A text of the second century BCE, the *Huainanzi*, contains a description of an early cosmic disaster, whereby the pillar attaching earth to heaven was broken. Nu-wa repaired the universe, using coloured pebbles to mend the sky, cutting turtle legs to establish the four compass points and killing the black dragon responsible for causing a great flood.[27]

A hierarchy of gods and spirits was worshipped in Chinese antiquity. Above all the spirits and deities stood a supreme deity called Di (or Ti, 'Lord') or Shangdi ('Lord-on-high'), who reigned over a host of nature deities. Besides this supreme deity, there were the nature deities, the high ancestors and the ancestral spirits of the common people. Under the category of 'high ancestors', there were three dynasties – Xia, Shang and Zhou' – founded by members of different clans.

The emergence of the Shang dynasty is intimately connected with a bird: according to the *Shijing* (Classic of Poetry or Book of Odes), *Tian* (Heaven) gave orders to the blackbird (*xuan niao*), which descended and gave birth to Shang.[28] Another version of the origins of the Shang dynasty has as its principal high ancestor a mythical hero whose mother became pregnant after devouring a dark bird's egg.[29]

Like many ancient peoples, the ancient Chinese had a three-tiered world view of heaven existing above, the dead below and the living in between, on earth. The royal ancestors were often believed to be on high, in the presence of the divine, and were still able to have power over the living, either to bless or to curse. The ancestors also expected their descendants to provide sacrificial 'blood' offerings for their nurture and enjoyment.[30]

Little is known about the religion of the great Shang dynasty, but its followers lived in a world thought of as inhabited by spirits with power that could influence their success or failure. It was thought necessary to appease or gain favour with the spirits by offering sacrifices.

The use of animals as mediums of communication with the divine can be traced back to China's oldest-known form of writing, the inscriptions on Shang oracle bones. The diviner would pose the question to the spirit and record its answer either on the carapace of a turtle or on the shoulder blade of an ox.[31] The turtle was associated with spirit powers, for its shell was said to resemble the Shang vision of the cosmos with the undershell being flat and roughly shaped like the earth, and the domed and rounded upper shell resembling heaven; the turtle thereby resembled the universe in miniature. These oracle bone inscriptions offer evidence of ancestral cult, divination, animal sacrifice, priesthood and shamanism.[32] The bones were prepared after the animal victims had been offered in sacrificial ritual. The assumption was that the dead animals would have special power and be able to contact others in the spiritual world.[33] The ritual took place under the direct supervision of the emperor and his court. Questions were addressed to the ancestral spirits, fire was applied, cracks appeared on the bones and these were then interpreted. Oracle bone inscriptions often refer to dreams, which may carry warnings from the spiritual world. Sometimes the spirits demanded sacrificial offerings, which were brought to altars, sanctified and killed in order to avert evil or to invite benefits.[34]

In early China ritual sacrifice constituted the single most important act of organized religion and was at the heart of social and political life. The types of animals suitable, as well as the occasions on which they were killed, are documented as far back as the divination records of the late Shang. Oracle bone inscriptions, which record ancestral offerings, also note the type of animal sacrificed, which include domestic sheep, cattle and dogs, as well as animals found in Shang mortuary rituals:[35] 'We do not use black sheep, there will be no rain. It should be white sheep that are used for it, then there will be heavy rain'.[36] Texts dating from the Warring States, Qin and Han periods state that there was sacrificial worship of horse, dragon, chicken and cat and tiger spirits; the last two were worshipped because of their skill in catching mice and killing wild pigs.[37]

The Chinese word for sacrifice (*ji*) is represented by a compound Chinese character that combines the symbols for 'hand', 'meat' and 'altar'.[38] Originally the practice simply involved providing food for dead ancestors. During the Shang period, burnt offerings were also made to other heavenly spirits. Later state sacrifices came into being, with more elaborate rituals. The usual victims were cattle, goats and pigs, with young bulls set aside for the most important sacrifices. The animals were to be the best available. After the animal was killed, the fat was burned to make smoke, inviting the spirits to descend, and the internal organs prepared and cooked. In the royal ancestral temples, there were special halls and yards for the different kinds of animal sacrifice, with many different sizes of bronze vessels to hold the raw and cooked offerings.[39] These vessels (*ding*) often had a two-eyed motif of a *taotie*. Later they were more complex, with highly defined faces and various animal features, such as snouts, fangs and horns.[40]

The cult of Heaven involved annual sacrifices offered by the emperor to heaven and earth. Its ritual developed very early, existing already at the time of Confucius (551–479 BCE). Attendance was strictly limited, with the privilege of carrying out the sacred duty being reserved for the Son of Heaven – the emperor. The annual sacrifice took place within the temple compound at the winter solstice.[41] The emperor prepared himself for this priestly function with a three-day fast and vigil, in which his princes and officials also took part. The animal victim, a bullock, was to be of one colour and perfectly healthy, without blemish.

Spirits were invoked to protect domestic animals and safeguard their fertility. There were a number of spirits related to domestic animals, including horse spirits, reflecting their importance in transport and military affairs. By Han times spirits known as the 'horse traveller', 'horse ancestor', 'first herdsman', 'first equestrian' and 'horse walk demon' received sacrificial offerings.[42] A horse fertility spirit known as the 'horse begetter' was worshipped by the elite in the late third century BCE. This spirit was called upon to 'make [the foal's] noses able to savor fragrances, their ears sharp and sight clear . . . to make their stomachs become sacks for all kinds of grasses, and their four feet fit for walking'.[43]

With the replacement of the Shang dynasty by the Zhou there began a shift from Di to Tian, Heaven, as the central figure in worship.[44] The concept of the Mandate of Heaven became more complex. The first emperor of the Qin dynasty, Qin Shi Huang (260–210 BCE), later reverted to Shang practice and chariot burials, with the horses interred separately, have been excavated on the west side of the emperor's necropolis near Xi'an.

Information about the sacrificial use of animals is found on Zhou bronze vessel inscriptions and texts. They mention the use of animal sacrifices in honour of ancestral kings, as gifts at visits and before and after military campaigns. A well-known inscription on an early Western Zhou ritual wine container known as the Ling *fangyi* records how the son of the Duke of Zhou followed his administrative duties with animal sacrifices at temples dedicated to the deceased kings Wu and Kang:

> After he had completed the commands, (on) *jiashen* (day 210) Duke Ming used sacrificial animals at Jing *gong*; (on) *yiyou* (day 22) (he) used sacrificial animals at Kang *gong*. Completely having used sacrificial animals at Wang, Duke Ming returned

from Wang. Duke Ming awarded Captain Kang fragrant wine, metal, and a small ox saying, 'Use (them in) ritual entreaty.'[45]

The preparation and ritual cooking of animals is included in several early sacrificial liturgies preserved in China's oldest compilation of poetry, the *Shijing*:

> Of a tawny bull we make offering;
> It is accepted, it is approved,
> Many blessings are sent down.
> The Duke of Zhou is a mighty ancestor;
> Surely he will bless you.
> In autumn we offer the first-fruits;
> In summer we bind the thwart
> Upon white bull and upon tawny.
> In many a sacrificial vessel roast pork,
> mince, and soup.[46]

As well as oxen, which were the most important animal sacrifice, other animals included horses, pigs, sheep and dogs.

The animals set apart for sacrifice were looked after by various specialized officers. There were 'animal fatteners' responsible for tethering the sacrificial victims in their stables and feeding them, and also for announcing when the victims were ready to be sacrificed. Different standards were set for particular sacrifices. According to one ritual code an ox destined for sacrifice to the high god Di had to be kept in a cleansed stable and fattened for three months; in an account from the Han period[47] bulls that were to be sacrificed to Heaven were fed over a five-year period until they reached a weight of 3,000 *jin* (approximately 700 kg).[48]

The victim and the day of the sacrifice were determined by divination. Failure to obtain a favourable answer could lead to the cancellation of the sacrifice.[49] If an animal set aside for sacrifice was ill, wounded or physically imperfect, it was thought that this would provoke an unfavourable response from the spirits. To avoid this, the animals were carefully inspected. As animals set aside for sacrifice, they were accorded special status. A ruler was to alight from his chariot if he passed a ritually cleansed sacrificial ox. Sacrificial animals were not to be sold at the market together with common animals. Meats destined for sacrifice could not be consumed as food on secular occasions. Such sacrificial demands could, however, create economic problems in communities that had to supply animals for religious ceremonies.[50] One account from the mid-first century CE tells of a community that had been hard pressed by local shamans; they had been informed that if they ate ox meat destined to appease local spirits, they would make a mooing noise and then die. This incident prompted the Han court to send a new governor to the region in order to stop the excessive activities of the local shamans.[51]

As well as special procedures for the breeding, inspection and ritual cleansing of the animals prior to their sacrifice, special appellations were given and through the use of sacrificial names the animal's status was transformed from secular to sacred. These ritual words were to endow the victim with special qualities or powers. Oxen were referred to as 'creatures with a large foot', pigs as 'stiff bristles', sheep as 'soft hair', a cockerel as 'red shriek', a dog as 'broth offering', a pheasant as 'wide toes' and a hare as 'the clairvoyant'[52] – oxen would grow large feet because they were well fed; the distance between the pheasant's toes was seen as an indication that it had been well nourished; and the eyes of a hare were believed to be wide open when it was in peak health.[53] These names were called out as part of the ritual, acknowledging ritual power and as a mark of respect for the animals about to be killed.

In addition to being used in ancestral sacrifice, in sacrifices to various spirits and deities, and in rituals to consecrate buildings and roads, animals were also used to seal covenants. In these covenants, oaths were made, an animal was slaughtered and the people smeared their lips with its blood and buried the inscribed covenant tablets together with the victim in a pit.[54] The animals included sheep, oxen, pigs, dogs, chickens and cockerels. Covenant fields have been excavated at Houma (Shanxi province, early fifth century BCE) and Wenxian (Henan province, 497 BCE).[55]

Dogs were thought to act as spirit mediums in pre-Buddhist China, for they lived in both the human and the animal worlds. Dogs were seen as guardians for the passage into different territory; this is confirmed by the use of dog sacrifices to the road. During these sacrifices dogs were crushed by chariots or dismembered before people set out on a journey (the ritual was known as 'the driving over' sacrifice).[56] Sometimes the dog's blood was smeared on the wheels of the chariot as part of the ritual. Dogs were also sacrificed to gates and paths, places close to human residences.

The pivotal role of animal sacrifice in pre-Buddhist China is reflected in the practice of Chinese philosophers using sacrifice in support of their own arguments. The *Zhuangzi* (*c.* fourth century BCE) suggests that simplicity is a good way to preserve one's life:

> The invocator of the ancestors wearing a ceremonial hat and robe was nearing the sacrificial animal corral and said to the pigs: 'Why are you afraid of dying? I will fatten you with grain for three months (before the sacrifice), then I will fast for ten days and purify myself for three days. Next I will spread out white woolly grass on the ground and place your shoulders and rumps on the carved sacrificial stands. You'll go along with that, won't you?'[57]

Thus physical perfection leads to an unhappy end. In another example, the *Zhuangzi* uses the image of the sacrificial ox as a reason to refuse the gifts of a ruler, for to serve in office is similar to being offered up in sacrifice, with no way back to the ordinary, simple life.

The ancient Chinese engaged in cultic worship of several animal spirits related to agriculture and military affairs. Evidence of this can be traced back to the late Shang period. Oracle bone inscriptions indicate that the Shang performed divinations involving silkworms. During the Han dynasty, sheep and pigs were sacrificed to a silkworm spirit prior to the ceremonial feeding of the imperial silkworms in the spring season.[58]

The cultivation of silk is still very important in China. Its mythological beginnings are linked to an incident that involved cruelty to an animal:

> In ancient times a man had to leave on business for a long time. His young daughter missed him very much, and one day, as she was grooming her stallion, she declared that she'd marry anyone who brought her father home to her. Suddenly the horse bolted and disappeared into the distance.
>
> The next day, in a distant town, her father was much surprised to see her stallion. He climbed onto his back and galloped home, thinking something was wrong. When he arrived, he

was relieved to find that all was well. The daughter said that her horse must have known how much she missed him. The man was grateful, and for several days he gave the stallion extra helpings. The horse, however, hardly touched his food and became very excited every time the girl came near him. After several days, the girl remembered her promise and told her father. Furious that a horse would even dare to think of marrying his daughter, he killed the stallion and laid its hide out to dry.

Later, as the girl and her friends were taunting the skin as though it were alive, it suddenly wrapped itself around her and flew off into the distance. Her father and neighbours eventually found it, on the top of a tree. Inside it, the girl had become a caterpillar-like creature, now named Can Nu (Lady Silkworm). As she waved her horse-like head from side to side, a fine white thread emerged from her mouth. This thread was strong, and could be spun and woven into beautiful garments.[59]

This heavenly weaver-girl was the granddaughter of heaven.[60]

Weaving silk was of such importance as one of the basic arts of Chinese civilization that it was thought that the skills and knowledge needed had been taught by the serpent-bodied Fu Xi, the first of the mythical Three Sovereigns. Fu Xi was also credited with having taught the people how to fish and how to domesticate animals.[61]

Animals played a significant role in the religious world of pre-Buddhist China. Literature may not have debated their fate, or considered their relationships with humans, or even set out a simple ethical justification for the use of animals, but they were present in the household and in the institutionalized state cults.[62] Animal spirits related to agriculture were recipients of sacrificial worship: the spirit world was called on regarding animals' well-being and fertility, for they were believed to be intermediaries between the world of gods and the human world. Animals were sacrificed to ancestors, deities, spirits and demons in many places, in temples and shrines, and on altars and sacrificial mounds throughout China. When the new Taoist religious movement called for an end to animal sacrifice, it brought into question one of the most commonly practised religious rituals, which had been part of the Chinese landscape for centuries.[63]

Taoism and Confucianism

Yin and *yang*, the cardinal principles of the universe, were thought from late Zhou times to constitute the Tao, or Way, the principle of the universe, and were the basis of court ritual.[64] Tao meant the proper way of living, acting and governing. The term 'Taoism' has been attributed to Sima Tan in *Shiji* (Historical Records, *c.* 100 BCE) and has been widely used to refer to the teachings of its principal texts: the *Tao Te Ching* or *Laozi* (probably compiled *c.* 200 BCE), attributed to the sage Laozi, and the *Zhuangzi*, attributed to Zhuang Zhou (*c.* fourth century BCE).[65] Laozi was Taoism's legendary founder. It is both a philosophy and a religion, and it has interacted with popular Chinese religion during its diverse history. During the first millennium CE it developed an elaborate pantheon of gods and goddesses.

Taoism was also a quest for freedom from the political and social constraints of a Confucian state, as well as a profound search for immortality. For some it was the search for oneness with the Tao itself, for the Tao was the sum total of all that is and of all that will change. In the Taoist religion there is a realization that life is beautiful, but that some transformations are frightening.

There is a dimension in the *Zhuangzi* that goes beyond nature mysticism; it seems to echo more ancient customs, including shamanism:

> There is a Holy Man living on the distant Ku-she Mountain, with skin like ice or snow . . . He does not eat the five grains, but sucks the wind, drinks the dew, mounts the clouds and mist, rides a flying dragon, and wanders beyond the four seas. By concentrating his spirit, he can protect creatures from sickness and plague and make the harvest plentiful.[66]

Another important source was the *Chu Ci* (Songs of Chu or Songs of the South), a collection of early poems by court officials of Han and pre-Han times; many of the poems are shamanistic in nature. It is rich in animal images, mentioning at least 88 animal species, many of which are imaginary, with 'wasps as big as gourds, and ants as big as elephants'.[67] Animals appear in many contexts in these writings, valued for providing food, clothing, medicine, as a means of transport and as an item of sacrifice to gods and ancestors. There is little in the texts that protests against these sacrificial practices.

Animals had varying degrees of spiritual or numinous power. The most numinous were the imaginary (the dragons and phoenixes), but some ordinary animals, such as tortoises, snakes and cranes, were seen as possessing numinous attributes. Cranes in particular were associated with mystical experiences: Taoists kept tame cranes until they became too rare to be available.[68]

It is significant that the early Chinese texts devote little attention to animal powers, except for attributing power to imaginary creatures such as dragons, which is in marked contrast to shamanistic societies of north and central Asia. Taoist writers found animals useful as a source of metaphors and subjects for teaching, but they were more than pure examples. In one famous story, Zhuang Zhou used to flutter about as a butterfly at night. On waking, he would continue to feel the motion of wings in his shoulders, unsure whether he was a man or a butterfly. Laozi explained: 'Formerly you were a white butterfly which ... should have been immortalized, but one day you stole some peaches and flowers ... The guardian of the garden slew you, and that is how you came to be reincarnated.'[69] It is interesting to note that in many cultures the butterfly is a symbol of the soul. There is a striking similarity to this dream in a story about deer in a later Taoist text, the *Liezi* (compiled *c.* 300 CE, though attributed to Lie Yukou, *fl. c.* 400 BCE), which resembles the shamanistic concept of deer found among the Mongols of northern China.[70]

The foundational Taoists are silent on the matter of ethics in regard to animals, apart from a general charter to leave them in as natural a state as possible. 'Taoists seem not to have conceived of a world in which animals were not used for food, clothing, traction, and medicine. They saw eating animals as a natural thing, and therefore appropriate for humans. Tigers, and even mosquitoes, eat humans; why should not humans eat other animals?'[71] Sacrifice was and still is important in Taoist ritual. Today their ceremonies involve sacrifice and consumption of chickens, pigs and sometimes other animals.[72] Taoism therefore differs from Buddhism in its views on animal sacrifice.

Shamanism was a form of religious and curing activity widespread in Asia and involved shamans who sent their souls to other realms in order to search out the cause and cure of personal ills and misfortunes. The Han Chinese world was surrounded by shamanistic societies:

The English word 'shaman' is borrowed from the Tungus languages. Many Tungus groups live in China. It would be inconceivable that China would not be influenced by shamanism. Indeed, the Chinese word *wu*, which now covers a range of spirit mediums, once clearly applied to shamans very similar in their practices to the Tungus and Mongol ones. *Wu* and Daoist adepts could both send their souls to the heavens and to the lands of the immortals, as is clearly seen in the *Songs of the South* and in many later Daoist writings. Daoist adepts live in a universe of meditation and inner travel, similar to the shamanic one.[73]

Shamanic practices used animal masks and animal hides. During the Han an annual festival called the 'Great Exorcism' took place at the beginning of the new year, during which the spirit medium covered his face with an animal mask and donned a bearskin hood. His role was to drive away evil spirits from the palace.[74]

Taoism believes that transformation is an important aspect of animal life; an essential part of nature. Everything changes; one can only resign oneself to the natural flow of things. A clear link with shamanic animal lore is this notion of transformation. Statements in Taoist texts about transformation of all things may have roots in shamanistic traditions.

There are differences, however, for the shamanistic bond with animals is not very visible in the Taoist texts: 'Animals are not the sources of spiritual power, nor are they companions or guides in supernatural travel, as they are in shamanism. The nearest we come are the dragons and cranes used as mounts for travel to empyrean realms.'[75] Shamans ride spirit horses, and sometimes birds, but the connection is not close. The importance of the animal that reaches incredible heights, which is prevalent in Central Asia, seems absent from Taoism, except in regards to general Chinese beliefs about sacrifice and the significance of certain creatures, such as the dragon and the turtle. Even the tiger, so prominent in folk cults, gets no special mention in Taoist texts; nor does the fox.[76]

The early Taoist sources also seem to lack the strong moral component so prominent in shamanistic lore about hunting, such as not taking too many animals and reverence for the animal. The early Taoists were keen to move one away from moral rules towards a meditative state in which one can naturally make the correct decisions. Later

Taoist religious communities adopted a number of moral codes relating to animals, but these came from Confucian and Buddhist teachings rather than from shamanism.

Having said this, Taoist texts do possess an underlying moral view of animals, in that animals have their own natures, their own Tao, and humans should not interfere with that unless it is necessary to do so. Destructive uses violate the animals' Tao. Animals are to be admired, for they live their own lives without worrying about rites and ceremonies, duties and responsibilities, so Taoists are to learn from them.

Taoist texts, including the *Liexian Zhuan* (a collection of biographies of Taoist personalities, compiled during the Han period), are sparse in their mention of animals. When animals appear, they are usually ordinary, everyday creatures such as birds, chickens, fish and butterflies.[77] Some interact with the animal associated with immortality: the dragon. A red bird is said to have appeared to Tao Angong, a blacksmith, telling him that he would be spirited away by a red dragon.[78] In a story about Mashi Huang, a horse doctor in the time of the Yellow Emperor, an ill dragon comes to rely on the doctor's curative skills: 'Afterwards, whenever the dragon was ailing, it issued from its watery lair and presented itself for treatment. One morning the dragon took Huang on its back and bore him away.'[79] Despite these examples, animals are not a key feature in the *Liexian Zhuan*, apart from being vehicles for humans to ride to cross the boundary between heaven and earth.

Other creatures are found within the mythical texts. On the east of the great mountain Tai Shan was a creature called *Fei*, which resembled a white-headed, one-eyed bull with a serpent tail. According to the classic *Shan Hai Jing*, if it waded in a river, it dried up; as it grazed the grass died; it brought pestilence to the realm.[80] Mount Tai (Tai Shan), in Shandong province, was a very sacred site. Taoists believed the mountain was an abode of the immortals. The white tiger leads the immortal beings: 'If you climb Mount Tai, you may see the immortal beings . . . They yoke the scaly dragons to their carriages, they mount the floating clouds . . . The white tiger leads them . . . they ascend straight to heaven.'[81]

Supernatural creatures, hybrid animals with elephant ears, wings and cloven hooves, were supposed to guard the entrances to the mythical mountain Kunlun. On Kunlun there lived Xi Wangmu, Queen

Mother of the West (associated with the elixir of immortality), a formidable figure who had tiger's teeth and a leopard's tail.[82] In the late Han period she was closely associated with Taoism: 'When Laozi died, he departed towards the west on the back of a buffalo bound for her paradise.'[83] She travelled on the back of a crane or phoenix. For Taoists she is the primal breath of Tao Yin (Taoist breathing exercises) and is served by three-legged birds who bring her food.

In summary, the Taoists did not see a sharp barrier between people and animals, between humanity and nature. They viewed them as mutually dependent. This implies a respect for the inner nature of things and for the place of all things in the cosmic flow. Mythical creatures were associated with the deities, perhaps more so than real animals.

The Confucian Perspective

Confucianism emerged in the sixth century BCE, but it was not until the Han dynasty (206 BCE–220 CE) that it was adopted as the philosophy of the state. Confucianism is the moral and political teaching of Kong Qiu (Kong Fuzi, 'Master Kong', 551–479 BCE), known in the West as Confucius, the Latinized form of his name, and it was developed during a period of violence and upheaval in China. It emphasized that human fulfilment was best achieved in a highly structured and ordered society. Classical Confucian tradition emphasized a specific set of moral relations. Animals may be absent from the list, but one animal that has been associated with these relations is the bat. In China the word 'bat' also means 'joy'. Bats seemed to demonstrate the Confucian virtue of filial piety, for bats would live together in a single cave. They were believed to live for centuries. Shouxing, the god of long life, is often depicted with two bats.[84]

In its religious teachings Confucianism does not restrict the scope of moral relations to human beings. Tian (Heaven) is the source of ultimate religious authority and *tianli* (the Principle of Heaven) permeates all living things, animals as well as humans.[85] The natural order is a moral order. To act reasonably and sensitively towards other forms of life is expressive of the relation between the moral nature of humans and that of heaven.[86] Moral responsibilities towards human beings are deemed to be more important than the moral relations to living things that are not human.

In this example of whether a sheep was required for sacrifice, we see how important it is to keep order: 'Zigong wanted to do away with the presentation of a sacrificial sheep at the Announcement of each New Moon. The Master said, "Si! [or Ci, Zigong's personal name]. You grudge sheep, but I grudge ritual."'[87] The matter here is maintenance of traditional sacrificial codes of state religion, rather than feelings for the sheep. An announcement is made to the ancestors at the start of each new month, accompanied by a sacrifice that includes a sheep. Zigong, one of Confucius's disciples, felt that the sacrifice of the sheep was unnecessary. Confucius's response shows that he felt it was more important for the ritual to take place than for the sheep to be spared. For Confucius, his primary task was to restore the moral order that prevailed in China during the reigns of the founding fathers of the Zhou dynasty, and this included rituals and ceremonies.

In the Confucian world, everything has a fixed place. In this 'address' Han Yu reads crocodiles their rights.[88] They had been eating animals and humans who had strayed too near the water's edge, and by doing so, had acted against Confucian principles. The crocodiles could either accept the order of the world, or, if they did not, then divine justice would be carried out.

> On the 24th day of the 4th month of the year 819, Han Yu, Governor of Chao-zhou (Canton), instructed his officer Qin Ji to take one sheep and one pig and hurl them into the deep waters of the river Wu as an offering of food for the crocodiles. When the crocodiles had gathered, Han Yu addressed them in the following manner:
>
> '... The governor, under the command of the Son of Heaven, has been entrusted with the protection of this land and of its people. But you, bubble-eyed crocodiles, you are not satisfied with the river depths, but must take every opportunity to seize and devour people and their livestock, bears and boars, stags and deer, to extend your bellies and to multiply your line. You are thus in discord with the governor, and seemingly rival his authority ... To the south of this province lies the great sea. In it there are places for creatures as great as the whale or shark, insignificant as the shrimp or crab. All there have a home in which to live and eat. If you left this morning, crocodiles, you would be there tonight ... Those who defy the deputies of the

Son of Heaven, who do not listen to their words or refuse to accept them ... will be put to death.'

That night, a violent storm struck the province. When it subsided, some days later, it was discovered that the crocodiles were gone. They were not seen again for a hundred years, when the Empire was again in ruin.[89]

Confucianism seeks to perfect human beings within the world, whereas Taoism prefers to turn away from society to the contemplation of nature. The great heyday of cross fertilization of religions in China came in the Ming dynasty (1369–1644).

The Shan Hai Jing

The *Shan Hai Jing* (Classic of Mountains and Seas), is a classical text that provides a fabled geographical and cultural/mythical account of pre-Qin China. It existed before the fourth century BCE and had reached its final form by the early Han period (*c.* 200 BCE). It consists of eighteen scrolls or sections. Authorship is attributed to Emperor Yu, mythical founder of the Xia dynasty (seventeenth to fifteenth centuries BCE), but there is no single author. It was seen as a type of bestiary and was assumed to be accurate. There are two sections: the first consists of Taoist writings relevant for Taoist shamans (possibly compiled in the fourth to third centuries BCE) and the second section contains mythical tales about animals and people (late third century or second century BCE).

The *Shan Hai Jing* tells how a horned monster, Gong Gong, having failed in an attempt to overthrow one of the Five Emperors, impaled Mount Buzhou, the northwest pillar of the universe, causing a great flood and tearing a hole in the sky. There was no sky or sun; instead, there was a flaming dragon with a human face. When its eyes were open, it was daytime; when they were closed, it was night. When Gong Gong exhaled it was winter; when he inhaled it was summer. When he stopped breathing, there was no rain or wind; when he did breathe, the wind blew. The monster neither ate nor drank.[90]

After Gong Gong's attack, the nearby Islands of the Immortals floated freely, which meant there were collisions. The Ruler of Heaven sent Yuqiang, god of the ocean wind, to fix them. He employed giant tortoises in teams of three to take it in turns (each period of duty was 60,000 years) to hold the islands in place.⁹¹

Yuqiang has a bird's body and a human face; green serpents hang from his ears and red serpents are under his feet. As a spirit linked to the sea, he has the form of a great whale with human hands and feet and rides upon a pair of dragons. The whale (*gun*) can turn into a giant bird (*peng*) whose wings, when it rises from the water, make huge waves. As it flies south for six months, the spread of its wings darkens the sky; it comes to rest in the southern sea.⁹²

In addition to Yuqiang, there was a Count of the Wind, Feng Bo, also known as Fei Lian. He is described as having 'a body like a stag, a head like a sparrow, a serpent's tail, horns and the markings of a panther'.⁹³

The Heavenly and Earthly Empires

For the Chinese, the divine world reflects much of the earthly bureaucracy, but on a heavenly scale. The principal aide of Yu Huang, the sky god, was Dong-yo Da-di, Supreme Ruler of the Eastern Peak, birthplace of *yang*. Dong-yo Da-di was head of a ministry of no fewer than 75 departments.⁹⁴ Here were fixed the times of birth and death, and the way of every living creature, human and animal. Human and animal life formed a continuum because of the Buddhist belief in transmigration, adopted in its entirety by the Taoists. In this system, rebirth as an animal was seen as a typical punishment for an erring human, whereas transmigration in human form was a suitable reward for a good animal.⁹⁵

The high role attributed to the sky deity in ancient China was paralleled by a cult of the god of the soil, Cheng-huang (also known as Chenghuangshen), who was thought to control the ravages of wild beasts or beasts that could destroy the harvest.⁹⁶ Dong-yo Da-di and Cheng-huang were both concerned with human and animal destinies and how those existences were lived out in the earthly realm.

Peasant Myths

Sometimes the role of animals in Chinese religion is best seen in the tales of ordinary people. In a Chinese folk tale explaining how humans were provided with plough oxen, we learn that the ox came from heaven. In the past, people struggled for food and could only eat on every third or fourth day. The Emperor of Heaven was disturbed about this and sent down the Ox star to tell humans to work hard and then they would be able to eat every third day. But the ox was too hasty and told them that they could eat three times a day. Since he had made a mistake, the ox was sent back to earth to help with the ploughing.

In a Buddhist version of this story, Dayuan Dizang Pusa, the bodhisattva Ksitigarbha, had compassion for the people. He suggested to the Jade Emperor (Yu Huang) that the heavenly ox be sent down to earth to help. The Jade Emperor did not agree, saying that the people would care for the ox only while it was able to pull the plough. Once it became feeble they would kill it and eat its flesh and use its hide. Dizang didn't agree and pledged that if such a thing were to happen he would suffer the punishment of being banished to Hell. Events unfolded as the Emperor predicted, with Dizang being banished to Hell.[97]

In another story about agriculture, a dog is given credit for the introduction of rice as a crop. After floods had been brought under control by Yu, the people discovered that their crops had been destroyed, so they took up hunting. One day a dog came out of a waterlogged field with bunches of a long yellow plant, full of seeds, on its tail. The people planted these seeds, the grain grew and it became known as rice. They were very thankful to the dog for its gift, so whenever they ate rice they would always offer some food to the dog before eating and at the first meal after the rice harvest food was always shared with the dog.[98]

Another crop origin story, this time about the lobok radish, is a morality tale with its origins in the practice of eating meat. It is not certain whether this tale cautions against the eating of meat, or whether it has more to do with being punished because of greed. Mu-lien's mother killed many animals to eat. He reproached his mother, but she kept eating them. One day she fell ill. As she lay dying, she knew that she was being punished because she had killed so many living creatures. She died and descended to hell. By his merit Mu-lien became a Buddha and was able to enter hell and rescue his mother. They escaped and lay down in a field, exhausted. His mother, starving, saw a radish in the field and pulled it up and ate it. Mu-lien, knowing this would offend the deity of heaven and lead to his mother's return to hell, cut off one of his fingers and pushed it in the hole to replace the gap left from the stolen radish. It grew into a red-cored radish, known as the lobu radish (in mythology, Mu-lien's personal name is *Lo Bu*).[99] It is a story that involves sacrifice, with the implication that Mu-lien's hardships could have been avoided if his mother had not eaten so many animals.[100]

There were animal demons in Chinese folk culture (one of the most common, the fox, will be examined later). Demons were thought to be prevalent if the animals were old and if they had a long association with humans. Statues of horses outside the ancient tombs of high officials were believed to travel at night and take on human form.[101] The souls of people eaten by tigers became slaves to the tigers and hunted other humans on their behalf. By doing this they hoped to gain their release, for having died violently they were *guei*, demon spirits, and removed from the cycle of reincarnation and rebirth until they could find another soul to take their place. Door knockers were sometimes in the form of a tiger to repel demons over which the domestic gods had no power. The tiger's protection was particularly required on the fifth day of the fifth month, which was seen as a day of great risk. Drawings of tigers were placed on doors and windows, and the character for 'tiger' written on the foreheads of young children.[102]

'Monkey' from *Journey to the West*, Japanese print, *c.* 1820s.

One key non-mythical animal is the monkey. How the monkey became part of the Chinese pantheon is told in the *Da Tang Xiyu Ji* (Great Tang Records on the Western Regions), an account of a journey to the western paradise in order to obtain Buddhist scriptures for the Emperor of China. The story is of Xuanzang (also Tang Sanzang, Tang Seng), who travelled to India as a pilgrim to bring back texts of Buddha's teachings. Xuanzang was accompanied by the Monkey King, Sun Wukong, who was prone to evil deeds; an ogre or monster known as Sha Wujing, or 'Sandy'; and Zhu Bajie, also known as Zhu Wuneng. Xuanzang gave Zhu Wuneng the nickname 'Bajie', which means 'eight restraints' or 'eight commandments', to remind him of his Buddhist diet. The name Zhu Wuneng was given to him by Bodhisattva Guanyin and means 'pig who rises to power'; he is also known as 'Pigsy' or 'Pig'.[103]

Monkey became skilful at magic and learned much from a Taoist immortal who taught him to change his shape at will and how to fly. After many fiascos, he was brought before the Jade Emperor, because he had upset the gods and goddesses. He was condemned to death, but because he had eaten the pills of immortality, the sentence could not be carried out. In despair, the Jade Emperor sent for the Buddha and, after a flying trial, the Buddha created a magic mountain and enclosed Monkey within it. He was released in order to accompany Xuanzang on his pilgrimage to fetch the Buddha's teachings. Monkey swore to faithfully obey his new master and to protect him, which he did. On their return Monkey was declared the God of Victorious Strife and Pig was given the role of Chief Divine Altar Cleanser. The horse that had carried Xuanzang and the scriptures was turned into a four-clawed dragon and named chief of the celestial dragons who guard the mansions of the gods.[104]

Animals in the Afterlife

Some of the most common animal figures in Chinese art fall into the category of beasts whose presence demonstrated the favour of heaven. Lions, a creature not native to China, were treated as fantastic animals, often used to guard tombs. They were lined up in pairs along the Spirit Road to the south of the tomb. Another common creature was the peacock, a symbol of beauty and dignity, also found as decoration on some tombs.

A lion ornaments the road to the Ming Xiaoling Mausoleum (the tomb of the founder of the Ming dynasty, the Hongwu Emperor), built in the late 14th-century outside Nanking.

During the Han period, bronze figures of battle chariots, complete with 'celestial horses' of the type brought from Fergana about 100 BCE, were buried in tombs. Han burial sites of the ruling elite at Shizhaishan, Yunnan, have revealed a rich animal repertory and evidence of a bird-snake theme, similar to the Indian *garuda-naga* motif. Leopards are found in various contexts in Han funerary rites, for they guard the ramp that leads from the earthly level to the entrance to heaven.[105] Gilt leopards decorate the late second-century BCE tomb of Princess Dou Wan at Mancheng, Hebei. Some burial chambers had masks of the four creatures of the Chinese constellations, known as the Four Guardians of the Four Compass Directions: the Black Turtle (North), the Vermilion Bird (South), the Azure Dragon (East) and the White Tiger (West).

Unlike in Hinduism and Buddhism, in Chinese religions, few alliances between animals and gods are recorded. One notable exception was the legend surrounding the goddess Xi Wangmu (Queen Mother of the West). From Han times onwards, when she became associated with the quest for immortality, she appears in art 'surrounded by an array of animal acolytes, including a three-legged crow, a nine-tailed fox, a dancing toad, and a hare pounding the elixir of immortality'.[106]

The Fox Cult

There are some malevolent creatures in Chinese mythology. As they aged, some of these animals developed the power to transform themselves into human form. The animal best known for this ability is the fox.

The emperor Yu was said to have observed a white fox as an auspicious omen when seeking a bride, but mostly the fox was seen as evil. Because it would sleep during the day and roam at night, it was thought to receive an excess of the dark, inferior female half of the *yin-yang*. Foxes were thought to have the power to make fire, either by banging their tails on the ground or by emitting a fireball from their mouths.[107] They would often inhabit ancient tombs and therefore came to be associated with the spirits of the dead. But the fox itself, seen to possess a power to foresee the future and thus its own death, was also the epitome of a seemly death: 'The fox died correctly with his head on the mound' is a phrase used to describe a proper death.[108] According to Xiaofei Kang:

> My mother recalls that the backyard of her childhood home in a suburb of Beijing during the 1940s contained a small shrine. It was dedicated to a '*xianjia*,' the respectful term for fox spirits in the local language . . . it was common, if unspoken knowledge in the family that maintaining the shrine would ensure good fortune and well-being. When my uncle, my mother's only brother, fell seriously ill and had a high fever at age fourteen, my grandmother made offerings at the fox shrine and prayed. That night, my mother told me, my grandmother dreamed of a gray-haired, white-bearded man who descended to my uncle's bedside and wiped his face once with his long sleeves. Next morning the fever subsided, and the boy soon recovered. The family believed that the white-bearded man was a fox spirit.[109]

The fox cult is a tradition that has been deeply entrenched in the local life of north China for centuries, for stories are found from the Ming (1368–1644), Qing (1644–1911) and Republican (1911–49) periods. The fox cult was branded 'feudal superstition' and banned during both the Republican and the Communist eras. The fox cult was a phenomenon particular to the north, even though it expanded to many other parts of China during the late nineteenth and early twentieth centuries. Worship of the fox was a personal, familial, local and regional practice.[110]

Fox shrines were usually established in insignificant and private places, such as backyards and doorways, and were simple in design, such as a wooden box. These shrines were easy to erect and quick to tear down. If they were worshipped in public places, foxes were usually shielded in temples dedicated to prominent gods or goddesses. Worship of the fox did not mean people lost their commitment to other religious cults and traditions. *Xian*, *xianjia* and *huxian* were names used to address fox spirits. *Xian* means 'immortal', 'perfected' or 'transcendent', and *huxian* means 'fox immortal'.

The fox, as omen, was one of the animals used as a symbol of premonition in ancient Chinese texts. The *Shan Hai Jing* mentions several legendary creatures, including the man-eating nine-tailed fox.[111] In a Han esoteric text, however, the nine-tailed fox is not a man-eating beast, but an auspicious omen that is said to have appeared when King Tang of the Shang dynasty ascended the throne and when the 'Eastern Barbarians' submitted themselves to the rule of King Wen.[112] A white nine-tailed fox appeared to the legendary emperor, Yu the Great, when he turned thirty years old, as a divine indication of his forthcoming marriage.

The use of omens for political ends persisted during the Six Dynasties. Guo Pu (276–324 CE), a scholar and diviner, wrote this famous eulogy about the nine-tailed fox:

> An extraordinary beast on the Green Hill,
> The fox of nine tails.
> It manifests itself when the Way prevails,
> And it appears with a book in its mouth:
> It sends an auspicious omen to the Zhou [dynasty]
> To promulgate a mystical talisman.[113]

The fox was thought to be able to bewitch people. Fox spirits were also blamed for causing illnesses, as recorded in two Han medicinal prescriptions unearthed in Mawangdui.[114] The fox also assumed the roles of shaman and celestial being at the same time. Foxes were thought to carry skulls before going to haunt; by wearing the skull they would metamorphose into human form. Age played a significant role in gaining the power of metamorphosis. The alchemist Ge Hong (283–343 CE) pointed out that 'Foxes and wolves live to eight hundred, and at five hundred they assume human shape.'[115]

The Fox and Xi Wangmu, Queen Mother of the West

The image of the nine-tailed fox, one of Xi Wangmu's animal attendants, is found on archaeological artefacts: 'The early depiction of the Queen Mother in the *Shanhaijing*, with her special headdress, panther's tail, tiger's fangs, and skill in whistling, is closely tied to shamanistic practices.'[116] She was believed to grant immortality, but also to destroy life. She is featured on funerary art, as the Han people believed that, accompanied by the fox as a helping spirit, she was able to transcend the three worlds and could escort the dead to heaven.

Guo Pu's eulogy quoted above, in which a nine-tailed fox appears holding a mystic book in its mouth to illuminate the Way of the sage kings, reflects the possibility that the fox might well be Xi Wangmu's divine messenger. Tang writings also reveal a connection between the fox and higher divinities: 'Among the arts of the Way, there is a specific doctrine of the celestial fox. [The doctrine] says that the celestial fox has nine tails and a golden color. It serves in the Palace of the Sun and Moon and has its own *fu* (talisman) . . . It can transcend *yin* and *yang*.'[117] The concept of the 'celestial fox', over a thousand years old and able to ascend to heaven, is now blended with the legendary nine-tailed fox. The doctrine it had mastered, plus the heavenly sign of the *fu*, all used by the Taoists, distinguish the celestial fox from demonic spirits. Tang tales describe the activities of foxes in the inner court as well as among elite and rural families, suggesting that fox worship involved a broad segment of Tang society.

North China has remained the heartland of fox cult practices till the present day. Sources from the late nineteenth and twentieth centuries also mention that the fox was commonly worshipped as one of a group of five sacred animals, named the Five Great Xian (*wudaxian*), Five Great Households (*wudamen*) or Five Great Families (*wudajia*).[118] In some places the cult comprised four animal spirits instead of five: usually the fox, weasel, hedgehog and snake. While the fox and the weasel always remained the first two members of the cult, others in the group of sacred animals varied in different regions, and might include the tiger, turtle, hare or wolf.[119]

The Fox and the Cult of Bixia Yuanjun (Mother Taishan)

Bixia Yuanjun's cult first emerged during the Song dynasty (960–1279) and became one of the most celebrated in north China after the mid-Ming (c. 1500). She was adopted into the Taoist pantheon. Her cult and that of the fox spirit both prospered in roughly the same area (north China and later Manchuria) and around the same period, from the mid-Ming dynasty to the early twentieth century:

> During Ming-Qing times, in the Taishan Palace and many local temples, the goddess was pictured with small bound feet wearing embroidered slippers as her special trademark. The same motif also appears in many Ming-Qing accounts of foxes. The main offerings to fox shrines in Shandong consisted of tiny women's shoes, based on the belief that foxes had bound feet when they transformed themselves into women. Daji, the infamous fox concubine of the Zhou King of the Shang dynasty in Ming-Qing popular literature, was believed to be the inventor of foot binding.[120]

People thought that the fox spirit and Bixia Yuanjun had similar functions. In folk stories she was sometimes a fox spirit.

In the early twentieth century rural people worshipped *huxian* chiefly in two forms: as *Jiaxian* (family *xian*) and *Tanxian* (altar *xian*). The *Jiaxian* were worshipped in private homes; they had the potential to haunt, but once properly propitiated, they protected the family's financial situation, guaranteed bountiful harvests and protected the family in other ways too. The *Tanxian* exercised their power through spirit mediums and were approached by people in times of need. They cured illness, warded off evil beings and foretold the future.[121] These two forms of *xian* worship dominated fox cult practices throughout north China and Manchuria during late imperial and modern times.[122] Ordinary people tended to associate daily struggles with the capricious character of fox spirits, whom they pacified through mediums in order to gain peace and harmony in their family and social life. Fox spirits are also found at side altars in major Buddhist and Taoist temples.

During the late nineteenth and early twentieth centuries images of fox deities were commercially printed and widely distributed in northern China and Manchuria. Some popular prints depict foxes as

Qing mandarins wearing official uniforms; others show the fox as an old man with grey hair and a beard.

The fox cult thrived on the practices of worshipping, exorcising, narrating and recording fox spirits at local, regional and national levels. Fox spirits are both respected and detested, and in Chinese culture they embody tensions between official order and unofficial practices, and among different social groups.

———

ANIMALS HAVE A PRESENCE within Chinese religion and philosophy, for they are part of the Chinese pantheon and the established order. This is reflected in the way they are portrayed. From sacrificial victims to fox cults, animals conform to the *yin* and *yang* principles, to the orderly view of the Confucian mindset and to the Taoist 'Way'. Mythical creatures are granted a larger canvas. There is a sense of the 'unreal' in this relationship with animals; even the 'real' animals – the tortoise, fox and monkey – are viewed more in terms of their divine nature. Their status is linked to heavenly duties: holding up the earth, being used to appease ancestral spirits or, by merit of their shell, for the purposes of divination, rather than for their earthly presence. It would take the influence of Buddhism to raise the status of animals and to enlarge the brushstrokes of the real (while still keeping the mythical), particularly in regards to the principle of ahimsa.

Japan

Ainu Culture

The Ainu are the indigenous people of Japan, subjugated by the Japanese in 812 CE and forced to retreat to the northern islands of Hokkaido and Sakhalin. They are probably remnants of a proto-Nordic people that once spread over western Asia. Their language is unrelated to any other.[123]

Ainu religion is classed as animistic, but it has dualistic features as well. A supreme god dwells in the highest heaven and many lesser deities, including an evil one who created death and disease, dwell in the lower regions. Ancestor worship, conquering evil spirits and belief in an afterlife are the major features of Ainu religion.[124]

The Ainu creation myth shares similarities with other creation myths: there is water, slush that needs to dry out to form land, and a pivotal animal, in this case, a bird, the little wagtail. Unlike in some myths, where the birds use their wings to dry the land, here the wagtail also treads the mud to mould the earth:

> In the beginning the world was slush, for the waters and the mud were all stirred in together. All was silence; there was no sound. It was cold. There were no birds in the air. There was no living thing.
>
> At last the Creator made a little wagtail and sent him down from his far place in the sky. 'Produce the earth,' he said.
>
> The bird flew down over the black waters and the dismal swamp. He did not know what to do. He did not know how to begin.
>
> He fluttered the water with his wings and splashed it here and there. He ran up and down in the slush with his feet and tried to trample it into firmness. He beat on it with his tail, beating it down. After a long time of this treading and tail-wagging a few dry places began to appear in the big ocean which now surround them – the islands of the Ainu. The Ainu word for earth is *moshiri*, floating land, and the wagtail is reverenced.[125]

In another myth the Ainu, who were thought to have a great deal of body hair, are said to have descended from the polar bear or from a Bear god.[126] As will be described in more depth, a bear sacrifice, in which the sacrificed bear is sent 'home' to the ancestors, is still practised by the Ainu. Many Ainu myths are contained in several heroic narratives, which are often sung by female shamans.

Animals as Gods in Disguise

The Ainu believe that everything surrounding humans and nature embodies a spirit. These spirits are called *kamui* and can bring blessings. *Kamui* are thought of as gods or deities who embody plants, animals, fire, water and everything that comes into a human's life. *Kamui* are closely associated with everything the Ainu do, including hunting, fishing, farming and gathering. The *kamui* 'live in anthropomorphic form in their own separate god-worlds, invisible to human eyes, but who pay frequent visits to the humans in disguise'.[127] The Ainu perform rituals and ceremonies to thank the gods for the abundance in their lives.

In the story 'The Ainu and the Fox', the fox argues that the salmon were created neither by the fox nor by the Ainu, but by the gods, for all creatures to use as food. All the animals are to yield to one another and only take what they need. The collector of this tale, Shigeru Kayano (1926–2006), a leading Ainu figure of the twentieth century, wrote in the notes to this narrative:

> This story reminds me of a time, about seventy years ago, when I helped my father set out the salmon nets. After we had caught about ten salmon, my father made diagonal cuts with his knife in each side of one of these fish and laid it on the gravel river bank, explaining that this was the 'crow's portion'. My father, Aleainu, knew that the crows could not tear at the tough salmon skin with their beaks. I did not realize then, as I do now, that this is a custom observed by the hunting peoples.[128]

The Ainu believe that the world is a common territory shared by different orders of beings; animals are accorded high ranking and are of great importance, for they are viewed as being gods in disguise.

In the Ainu world, humans and deities are fairly equal, with the humans having a slight advantage. There is dependency on both sides; the gods fear the humans, and depend on them and are subject to their power: 'A god can enhance his social prestige in his own community when he is worshipped and given presents by the humans. In fact, the wealth of the gods consists of the presents they receive from humans.'[129] In return, the humans are guarded and protected from evil deities.

No matter where the gods may be living, they always follow the human (*Ainu*) pattern. When home in their god-world, they have human form, build homes, wear clothes, love their families and pray to their gods.[130] They treasure the gifts of wine and *inau* (whittled sticks of wood with wood shavings attached to them). When the deities come to visit humans it is usually in order to conduct business and for this, they put on their best costumes:

the god of the mountain (*kimun kamui*), the ruler of the mountain game, comes wearing a bear costume. The god of the sea (*repun kamui*), who rules the food animals in the ocean, comes in the guise of a grampus, or killer whale. Another important deity, the guardian spirit of the land (*kotan-kor-kamui*), assumes the form of an owl. Pestilence deities come in the form of flocks of little birds.[131]

The underlying concept of 'gift' lies at the heart of Ainu hunting ritual. A human hunter does not choose to kill; it is the deity, masquerading as an animal, who chooses the hunter and blesses him by leaving his animal costume for him as a present. These presents left behind by the deities enable the humans to survive. When a god's costume (*hayokpe*, an Ainu word for 'armour', 'disguise' or 'costume') is broken, his spirit is released. By killing the animal, the human has released the spirit of the god trapped inside the disguise and this enables him to return to his own world.[132]

Ritual is important, for the very existence of the Ainu community depends on correct religious observance by hunters and fishermen: 'Ainu fishermen gave *inau* symbolically to the salmon by beating each fish over the head with a special decorated club called *i-sapa-kik-ni* ("head-beating club"). The deer were also given presents of curled wood shavings (*inau-kike*), which had the same potency as the *inau*.'[133] The mythic songs emphasize that if the Ainu neglect to perform rituals, the spirits of the gods will go home in tears and will complain to their species rulers, the 'masters' of the game or of the fish, which will lead to famine.

In order to survive, humans developed ways of communicating with other species (the *kamui*), one of the most common ways being through prayer. When they were hunting, the Ainu men would address prayers to gods who appeared to them in the costumes of birds or animals. The following prayer would be spoken by an Ainu hunter to game animals, probably deer, after they had been shot: 'Let your spirits return atop the summit of our native country. May you abide there as newborn gods. Take these *inau*, these lovely *inau*, and may you enhance with them your glory as deities!'[134]

Another means of communication was through shamanism and dreams as well as through poetry or narratives.[135] In the 'god epics' the speakers were thought to be the deities who borrowed the lips of the epic reciter in the same way that a god would use the lips of a female shaman.[136]

The Ainu practised an elaborate bear cult into the 1920s; in fact they are the only people to have retained a fully fledged bear cult into the twentieth century. They would capture a bear cub, look after it for months and then sacrifice it in an elaborate ceremony. During its stay, the housewife would be given the task of caring for the bear cub and feeding him; the cub was seen as an adopted god-child.

The masculine bear is the earthly representation of the mountain god, Chira-Mante-Kamui, the bear form being his disguise when visiting earth.[137] The Ainu gods wish to be on good terms because of the offerings humans make that reach the kingdom of the gods. The flesh and skin of the deity's disguise is the god's offering to humans. The sacrifice frees the god to return to his kingdom where the deities enjoy the fruits of the ritual.

One of the most important Ainu ceremonies is the Iomante, a festival of the dead that honours and sends animal spirits to the world of the gods. People from many villages gather together to participate in this ceremony. It is also known as 'the Bear Festival', Kumamatsuri, and is held in midwinter. A sacrifice takes place when the bear reaches two or three years of age. After the bear is killed, the bear's head is laid in state and offerings of food and wine are made to him. After the god's spirit has been released from the *hayokpe*, it remains with the humans for several days as an honoured guest. The Ainu dance, eat and sing in his honour and he is said to delight in this, watching as he lies in the place of honour at the head of the fireplace. The festivities last for three days and three nights.

When the feast is over, the god is sent home. This is called *iomante*, which means 'sending-off': the ritual dismissal has come to be applied to the bear festival itself. The god returns home with many gifts from the humans. When he returns, he will have a feast with his relatives and friends. As he speaks of the wonders of the humans, he will encourage the other gods to visit, thus ensuring the continued survival of the humans. The ritual is not about making peace with the bear's spirit; rather it is about the Ainu relationship with a god.

In the mythic epics, bear cubs speak of their human masters as 'my human father and my human mother'. One of the most interesting mythic epics with bear cubs as speakers is one that Kubodera Itsuhiko recorded in writing in 1932 from the female reciter Hiraga Etenoa of Shin-Piraka village in Hokkaido. It is entitled 'Song of a Bear Cub':

This went on
until finally
they said it was time
For me to be sent home.
After that
my father
went about with
the young men
and let me play[138]
for a while until
finally
it was time
for me to be given dismissal.
I was worshipped
magnificently
with trade wine,
trade liquor,
and also
with Ainu wine,
as well as
bundles of dumplings
and bundles of *inau* . . .
After that,
carrying
Bundles of wine
and bundles of *inau*,
I came home
to the place of
my divine father
and my divine mother.
Before I arrived there,
the floor at the head of the fireplace
of our house
was filled
with much wine
as well as dumplings
and fine food . . .
and my divine father
sent out messages [of invitation] to all

> the gods living nearby
> and the gods living far away.
> The invited gods
> were shown in
> with much ceremony . . .
> Then I turned back
> and cast my glance at
> my human mother
> and my human father.
> I looked and saw that
> they had no children between them.
> I felt so exceedingly
> sorry for them
> that I blessed them
> with a boy and a girl.
> I showed this
> to my human father
> in a dream.
> Since then
> my human father
> worships me
> as his dearest god,
> his most honored god . . .
> These things
> a bear-cub deity
> recounted concerning himself.[139]

The complex interrelations between humans and deities in Ainu culture were intended to increase the prosperity of both humans and the gods.

The Island of the Dragonfly

The very essence of Japan is connected to an insect, the dragonfly, loved by the Japanese for thousands of years. One of the old names for Japan is *Akitsushima*, which means 'The Island of the Dragonfly' and is written with the character that represents the dragonfly.[140]

The earliest of Japanese writings reveal a world where humans and animals existed side by side. Many creatures shared the mythological cosmos with both deities and humans, as described in the *Kojiki*

Hanging scroll showing dragonflies and butterflies, Japan, Edo period (1603–1868).

(Record of Ancient Matters, *c.* 712) and the *Nihon Shoki* or *Nihongi* (Chronicles of Japan, 720).[141] These records tell of the importance of beasts, fowl, fish and insects to the ancient Japanese.

Religion in Japan is a rich tapestry of diverse traditions with a history of nearly 2,000 years. From the Asian continent it received the religions of Buddhism and Confucianism. It was in reaction to these imported religions that Shinto, Japan's native religion, became better organized and defined. Buddhist missionaries in Japan drew parallels between the two faiths and proclaimed the identities of the deities to be the same. This peaceful coexistence made it easy for the two religions to prosper alongside each other. One deity, Fukurokuju,[142] who was perhaps originally a Taoist sage, was the god of long life. His traditional companions were animals associated with longevity: the crane, the stag and the tortoise. Daikoku was regarded as the god of wealth and a patron of farmers. He is often depicted sitting on bales of rice, which sometimes have rats eating them. He remains untroubled by the rats' theft, because he is wealthy. Another is Ebisu, the patron of labourers, also regarded as one of the ancestors of the Ainu, the first people of Japan. In some areas of Japan he is called on by fishermen; he holds a fishing rod in one hand and a sea bream (a symbol of good luck) in the other.[143] Benzaiten, or Benten, the only female of the seven deities, is said to have married a dragon in order to subdue him. She is sometimes depicted riding a dragon or sea serpent.

Kangiten is a Japanese form of the Indian elephant-headed god Ganesha, who was adopted by certain Buddhist sects. The Hindu icon travelled to China, where he was incorporated into Buddhism, and from there was taken to Japan in the ninth century, where his cult was incorporated into Shingon Buddhism and a number of esoteric sects. Kangiten, the god of bliss,[144] is also known as the Dual-bodied Kangiten or the Embracing Kangiten, for the god may be represented as an elephant-headed male and female human couple in an embrace. The explicit sexual connotations meant that the statue was kept hidden from public eye, according to Confucian ethics. Less frequently Kangiten is depicted as a single male with two, four, six, eight or twelve arms; when shown with four arms he holds a radish and a *modak*, an Indian sweet dumpling. Kangiten is seen as a protector of temples and is worshipped by gamblers, actors and geishas. He both creates obstacles and overcomes them. The god's power is believed to help people gain enlightenment.

Kangiten (centre), a Japanese form of Ganesha, at a temple in Miyajima, Japan.

A sense of being in harmony with nature underpins Japanese religions and Japanese culture, but the presence of animals is not as noticeable as in some other religions. There are, however, demons, called *oni*, which can take on animal form or certain animal features. *Oni* are said to be giant horned demons, brought to Japan from China with the arrival of Buddhism; Buddhist priests perform annual rites to expel them. The *oni* of hell are said to have the heads of oxen or horses; they hunt down sinners and transport them in their chariots of fire to the underworld.[145]

Shinto has its roots in prehistoric Japan. Little is known about Japanese religion before the emergence of a unified state in the Yamato period (*c.* 300–710 CE), but it was broadly animist, believing that supernatural power resided in natural objects, such as mountains, trees and animals.[146] In animist societies these spirits or souls must be propitiated to maintain prosperity and social harmony. Shinto, 'The Way of the Gods', has no fixed doctrine and no official sacred texts; it centres on worship of *kami*, divinities believed to inhabit every phenomenon in nature.[147]

Shinto shrines house the god or *kami*. The ancient shrine at Kashima, for example, has a fenced enclosure surrounding a large stone that is thought to hold down a giant catfish, believed to be responsible for earthquakes.[148] An ancient tradition of dedicating horses to Shinto shrines was later modified to presenting pictures of

horses on wooden plaques to the shrines. Sesson Shukei (*c.* 1504–
c. 1590) was a Zen monk and the last of the great ink painters of
the Muromachi period. His designs of horses, prepared originally
for a Shinto shrine, are some of the earliest designs ever printed in
woodblock-book format.[149]

Although there is no overt moral ethic that states how one should
act towards animals in Shinto (with the exception of Buddhist tenets),
there is a well-known story that encompasses the call for compassion
and highlights certain benefits that follow as a result of caring for
another species. Okuninushi was the god of medicine and magic. He
had eighty brothers, all of whom wished to marry the beautiful Princess
Yakami:

> While the brothers were on their way to visit the princess, a
> flayed hare stopped them and asked them for help. The brothers
> told the hare to wash in the sea and then dry itself in the wind.
> The hare suffered excruciating pain and distress. The creature
> then met Okuninushi who, feeling sorry for it, told it to bathe
> in fresh water and then roll around in the pollen of kama grass.
> The hare did as Okuninushi advised and immediately felt better.
> In gratitude, the hare, who was really a god, told Okuninushi
> that the beautiful princess Yakami would be his.[150]

While one of the story's themes may be that of exercising caution,
because gods can take on various forms, its poignant message is about
having compassion for another, regardless of its species.

There are always exceptions of course, and these can be due to
historical events. White dogs, for example, were extremely unpopular
in Japan for about a dozen years after the Second World War.[151] One
reason for this is that white is a colour associated with death and is
worn at Shinto funerals: 'The funny thing was, lots of old snow country
legends portrayed white dogs as magical spirits or spiritual rescuers.
And in ink drawings and paintings done by Zen monks centuries ago,
a white dog was often a representation of Buddha, an expression of
pure goodness and compassion.'[152]

The introduction of Buddhism gave new impetus to the Japanese
respect for all living creatures. In stories of former lives of the Buddha
(the *Jataka* tales), the Buddha was born, and performed meritorious
acts, in the forms of animals.[153] Elephant images came to Japan from

An Edo period (1603–1868) ceramic fire box in the form of a *tanuki*.

China with Buddhism in the sixth century. When the elephant appears in Japanese art, it is usually as a Buddhist symbol. The importance of all living creatures in Japanese art became especially notable during the Heian period (794–1185).[154] Artistic motifs of living beings were used as decoration on objects made for use as offerings to Shinto and Buddhist deities.

In the writings of Lafcadio Hearn (1850–1904), an American who lived in Japan, we find a rich set of names and associations with animals, which helped to instil a sense of reverence: 'The Japanese warbler was imagined to be calling out "hok-ke'-kyō", the title of the holy Lotus Sutra . . . even the hammer-head shark was referred to as a priest of the Nembutsa chant because its T-shaped head resembled the mallet used by the pious to strike a gong during prayers.'[155]

The traditional Japanese short form of poetry, haiku, embodies an understanding and respect for all living beings, traditionally incorporating natural themes.[156] Haiku sometimes incorporates animals with symbolic meanings, especially the crane and the tortoise (both symbols of longevity). Issa (1763–1828) wrote poems of great compassion for all living creatures and became one of the three most loved poets in the haiku tradition. Issa was especially sensitive to insects, which are usually ignored or scorned in the literature of the West:

Sculpture of *kitsune* at the Fushimi Inari-taisha shrine near Kyoto, Japan.

Where there are people
there are flies, and also
there are Buddhas.¹⁵⁷

Mosquito larvae,
dancing a Buddhist chant
in the water by the grave.¹⁵⁸

Animals and humans are seen as fellow members of the same world and they are viewed with empathy. Haiku masters established personal relationships with the natural world and their ability to link the animal with the divine is further expressed in the following examples by

Takamasa (*c.* late seventeenth to early eighteenth centuries), Issa and Kansetsu (eighteenth century), respectively:

Running across the altar
and stealing a chrysanthemum –
the temple rat.[159]

From the nostril
of the Great Buddha comes
a swallow.[160]

Could they be hymns?
frogs are chanting
in the temple as well.[161]

In Japan the cicada is associated with death, and particularly with Obon (or Bon), the festival of the dead. One reason for this is that the small red marks on their heads are said to represent the names of the deceased.[162] A *netsuke*, or miniature sculpture, in the form of a cicada may have been worn on the day of the festival to guarantee a long life.

Sculptures of *kitsune* at the Fushimi Inari-taisha shrine near Kyoto, Japan.

Utagawa Hiroshige, *New Year's Eve Foxfires at the Changing Tree*, c. 1857, woodblock print. Foxes gather at the old *enoki* (hackberry) tree on New Year's Eve to prepare to pay homage to Inari at the Ōji Inari shrine.

Japanese religions share common elements with China, including the hare, symbolizing longevity and believed to live on the moon, and the carp. In China and Japan the carp symbolizes abundance or success through perseverance. A Children's Day festival (previously known as Boys' Day) is held in Japan on 5 May and kimonos, kites and streamers (one for each male child) are all decorated with designs of carp, which are believed to transform into dragons.

Another common theme is that of fox worship, found in China, Japan, Korea and other cultures. Foxes and humans have lived together in Japan since ancient times, closely associated with Inari Okami, a Shinto *kami* or spirit messenger and rice deity. Inari is venerated not only as the deity who ensures an abundant rice harvest, but also as the patron of general prosperity. Inari's messenger is the fox, a pair of which usually flank his image at every Inari shrine. The Japanese word for fox is *kitsune* and this name was originally given to a messenger of Inari, but the line is now blurred and Inari may be depicted as a fox. While priests insist that the fox is the spirit messenger of Inari, Japanese worshippers in both Buddhist and Shinto traditions generally worship the fox as Inari himself. Fox statues stand at entrances to Shinto shrines and Buddhist temples, and beside roads, tombs, rice paddies, hills and farmhouses. According to Kang, 'The Buddhist form of the deity features a female bodhisattva astride a white fox.'[163] Chinese influence may have shaped the development of Inari worship. There are some similarities with Chinese fox worship, including connections with shamans and affiliation with a female goddess, but there are differences too. There are many Inari shrines all over Japan, whereas fox worship in China remains largely regional, a phenomenon of the north. In China it is almost impossible to find images of foxes in Chinese fox shrines and temples, whereas Inari foxes in Japan are generally given physical expression, placed in public spaces and in religious settings.[164] Chinese fox spirits never entered Buddhist or Taoist

Tsukioka Yoshitoshi, *The Fox-woman Kuzunoha Leaving Her Child*, c. 1889–92, woodblock print.

pantheons, whereas Japanese Inari foxes are incorporated in Buddhist, Shinto and folk customs.

In Japan it is common to think of the fox as an intelligent being with magical abilities that increase with age and wisdom. Sometimes the fox is thought to assume human form (as in China). The more tails the *kitsune* has – as many as nine – the older, wiser and more powerful it is. Because of the fox's potential power, some people make offerings to them. There are shrines dedicated to *kitsune* where offerings are left. The fox spirits are said to be partial to fried, sliced tofu (*aburaage*) and when *aburaage* is added to *udon* or *soba* noodle soups, the dishes are named after the fox spirits: *kitsune udon* and *kitsune soba*.

Depictions of *kitsune* often include round or onion-shaped white balls known as *hoshi no tama* (star ball). These are magical jewels or pearls that emit a glow. When the *kitsune* is not in human form, the fox keeps the ball in its mouth or carries it on its tail. The pearl holds some of its magical power. Another tradition states that the pearl represents the *kitsune*'s soul and the fox will die if separated from it for long. *Kitsune* stories are thought either to have originated from foreign sources (China, Korea or India) or to be a Japanese indigenous tradition from the fifth century BCE.

Butterflies are also special in Japan, serving as symbols of conjugal love and of death. One story tells of an old man named Takahama, who was dying. His nephew, at his bedside, noticed a white butterfly near his uncle's bed. He shooed it away, then followed it through the house and outside until it reached a gravestone, when it promptly disappeared. The man read the name on the gravestone: Akiko. He returned to find that his uncle had died while he was out of the room. He told his mother what had happened, and she was not surprised: 'Akiko was a young girl that Takahama had planned to marry, but she died of consumption at the age of eighteen. For the rest of his life, Takahama had remained faithful to her memory and visited her grave every day.' The nephew then realized that the soul of Akiko had come in the form of a butterfly to accompany the spirit of his uncle to the next world.[165]

In a Japanese folk tale from Chiba prefecture, *tanuki*, or racoon dogs, became associated with Shojo-ji temple in Kisarazu and its new priest. The Shinto temple, in the midst of the Tanuki Woods, was quite isolated. The new priest, who was very fond of music, was lonely. One night, when the moon was full, he heard voices and strange sounds in the temple grounds. Investigating the noise, he discovered the noise to be that of a group of one hundred *tanuki*, dancing and singing in the moonlight. Some were beating their paws on their pot-bellies like drums; others were playing flutes made from leaves and reeds, or were dancing or singing. Their song was a plea to the priest:

Shojo-ji priest . . . dum diddle dee dum.
Please be our friend . . . bom diddle dee bom.

The priest noted what fine musicians and dancers the *tanuki* were. Then he remembered he had heard people saying that the *tanuki* waited in the woods until a man they really liked came to live in Shojo-ji, and then they would come and sing and dance their approval. The priest joined in, drumming on the floor and door, while the *tanuki* drummed on their bellies. A competition ensued to see who would be the strongest. This continued until dawn, then they retired to rest. This continued over the next few nights, but on each night there were fewer *tanuki*. On the fourth night the priest decided that the contest would have to end; he realized that he was beaten and that they were stronger. He dressed in his best purple robe and waited for his friends to arrive, but that night no *tanuki* came. The next day, he found a large *tanuki* lying on his back, asleep, under the main hall of the temple. It was the *tanuki* who had led the drumming. The priest noticed that the poor *tanuki*'s tummy was a raw, pink patch, for its beautiful fur had been worn away through drumming so hard. The priest took the *tanuki* into the temple and cared for him, giving him the best food and wine. After seven days the *tanuki* thanked the kind priest and trotted back into the woods, carrying a bottle of rice wine under his arm.

From then on, on the night of every full moon, the priest and the *tanuki* held a concert in the garden. The priest provided wine and food for all in the hour before dawn, so that there were no sore throats or tummies or aching legs. No one became too tired to join in the festivities. The *tanuki* changed their song to 'Shojo-ji Priest . . . Is our friend.'

Even today, people of the area say that in the garden of the old Shojo-ji in Kisarazu *tanuki* still dance and sing, accompanied in their singing by an old priest. When morning comes the *tanuki* disappear into the Tanuki Woods, the old priest following them, carrying a bottle of wine under his arm.[166] The Japanese raccoon dog, sometimes translated as 'badger', is a common creature in Japanese folklore in the form of *tanuki*. The *tanuki* tends to be a mischievous animal, possessing shape-shifting abilities. Perhaps the *tanuki* in this folk tale are former Shinto priests, visiting in order to encourage new priests while demonstrating harmony in nature?

In the Shadows

For the Ainu, animals are gods and are pivotal in all aspects of daily life, but elsewhere in Japanese religions animals do not have a strong presence. That does not mean, however, that they are absent. Rather than being seen as separate entities, they are incorporated into nature as a whole and valued in a more passive sense. They undergird the Shinto belief in the harmony of nature, as well as the Buddhist tenet of ahimsa, reverence for life. They are present as *kitsune*, messengers of the rice god, or as the rice god himself. They may be seen in the form of a two-headed Ganesha couple, or as badgers entertaining a Shinto priest. Perhaps they are more like the haiku in which they are nearly always present; they may not merit many words in religious texts, but they are always part of the landscape.

Conclusion

Henry Beston's well-known observation is not always quoted complete with its opening sentence, which links animals to the sacred:

> We need another and wiser and perhaps a more mystical concept of animals ... In a world older and more complete than ours, they move finished and complete, gifted with extensions of the senses we have lost or never attained, living by voices we shall never hear. They are not brethren; they are not underlings; they are other nations, caught with ourselves in the net of life and time, fellow prisoners of the splendor and travail of the earth.[1]

While acknowledging the power of these words, I disagree with Beston's statement that animals are 'not brethren'. Animals are our brethren, our kin. When Adam names the animals, he (and we) sees them as companions, created from the same material as ourselves, earth (*adaman* means earth). Rather than interpreting this ritual of naming to mean that humans have power over animals, which is a common reading of this text, this myth 'grounds' us in relationship. When God brings the animals to Adam, it is a question of recognition.[2] Naming the animals is about identity, not power; we are of the same source: 'Surely we ought to show them [animals] great kindness and gentleness for many reasons, but, above all, because they are of the same origin as ourselves' (St John Chrysostom, 345–407 CE).

If religion is relational, which I suggest it is, then we want the best for each other, regardless of species. The guiding principle, for it is the essence of the Divine, should be love. Love must inform ethics, doctrine and commandments. Only love can move us from our human-centred, narrow frame of reference. Only love can shatter the exclusive fence

At the waterhole, Namibia.

of human superiority that divides. Only love can transform our hearts and our worship.

On a recent trip to Africa, I spent many hours sitting at waterholes.[3] Animals gathered at the water, to partake of that which is essential to life. Some of the animals were bold, others fearful, but, ultimately, all came to drink; all were refreshed by the same source. Sitting in the hide, compass on my lap, I was awash in a sense of the sacred, here at the waterhole. The waterhole was a holy space, the compass pointing due north, to the sacred. In front of me, and in the shadows, in the spaces where I could not see them but I knew they were there . . . were, in the Lakota term, *Mitakuye Oyasin* (All My Relations/All are Related). I was involved in worship, for, in the words of Simone Weil, 'absolutely unmixed attention is prayer.'[4] Were not my non-human brethren also involved in a form of prayer? Were they not totally focused on the ritual, partaking in and of the sacramental and the real, the life-giving water? Animals had raised my sacramental consciousness. McDaniel writes that each animal is 'a holy icon, a stained glass window, through which holy light shines'.[5] As I watched huge, lumbering elephants, I was reminded of Ganesha; elegant giraffes brought to mind the ancient Bushman legend of Tutwa, the Giraffe.[6] Zebras, their stripes as individual as our fingerprints, displayed the wonders of the Creator's imagination and design. A lone jackal, scurrying through the scrub, was a long way from the Egyptian underworld. A colourful hornbill perched on a bush, to the side of the water, close to the jackal; how appropriate, having an escort of souls near Anubis, guardian of the dead. Warthogs, deemed 'unclean' were here, joining in as the clowns of the waterhole community, tails like radars, rod-stiff, pointing to heaven. All were welcome at this sanctuary.

And what of the water, which gives life and is full of life, visible and invisible? The waters in Genesis, with God's spirit often portrayed in the form of a dove, hovering above; the churning of the ocean in Hinduism, with the serpent as the churn stick; Buddha resting on the coils of a cobra; the rivers full of the salmon people; Muskrat diving into the deep to retrieve the mud needed to create the world . . . holy, holy, holy . . . animals are here, even if religious traditions do not fully acknowledge them.

Throughout this book we have encountered animals assisting in Creation, as prophets (bearers of messages from God or the Divine), or dismissed as mere machines, 'soulless automata', or beasts of burden. What hurt do we inflict when we ignore messages from the Divine? What are the consequences when we humans act as machines, without feelings? To conclude with a story that addresses these sins:

> The Nass River people of the Northwest coast tell of a time when the people caught more salmon than they could use – so many that excess fish were thrown away, carelessly. There was a canyon near the head of a fast-moving river where the people could always find food, salmon, berries, and skins. The villagers who lived near there were wealthy traders. They were respected on account of their wealth.
>
> Over time, this wealth made the younger people lazy, thoughtless, and cruel. They would kill small animals and leave the meat to rot for the crows. The Officers called the young people to a meeting. Some young people came, but others did not. The Officers told the young people that the Chief of the Sky would show his anger at their thoughtlessness. The young people listened, went out, and did as they pleased.
>
> One young man experimented with the salmon. He found that if a fish were slit down the back, it could still swim. He put burning pitch in the slit salmon and placed it back into

the water. The salmon frantically swam in circles, lighting up the river. The men of the Wolf Clan thought this amusing.

The Wolf Clan caught fish for this purpose alone. They lit up the river with burning salmon at night. The pain of this cruel amusement was felt in the sky. Thunder rolled out across the land as the Wolf Clan netted the salmon. The fish cried out in their pain, and the cruelty of this slow death was echoed to the Great Above.

The Officers called the Wolf Clan to a meeting, but the men only laughed. They didn't go to the meeting, for they were eager to light up the river. They lit the hot pitch that lay in the slits of the struggling salmon. They pushed the fish into the river and sat back to watch. The sky grew dark. Thunder shook the land. The earth rattled. Rocks fell down from the canyon into the river, crushing the suffering salmon and bringing them a quick, painless death.

The Wolf Clan laughed. 'It is the ghosts waking up,' someone said. 'They want to see the river light up with the floating fish.' The Wolf Clan men returned the next night to repeat their cruelty. The night sky rolled out in anger, and the sound of drums reverberated across it. The Wolf Clan men became afraid.

The sound grew louder and louder and louder and *louder*. The noise became deafening as the mountain broke open. Black pitch from every salmon that was ignited poured forth and surrounded the people.

They tried to escape, but burning, red-hot pitch blocked the rivers. Fire poured down through the forest, fell from the sky, and enveloped the people. A few got away or we would not know of this story.

It is said that the young men of the Wolf Clan carried the burning, red-hot pitch on their backs and turned into burning salmon that suffer in the bottom of the Nass River. They lie frozen in the black pitch of the mountain forever.[7]

The whole earth is a living icon of the face of God. (John of Damascus)

References

Introduction

1. Walt Whitman, 'Song of Myself', *The Complete Poems* (Harmondsworth, 1975), p. 94.
2. Jay McDaniel, 'Practicing the Presence of God: A Christian Approach to Animals', in *A Communion of Subjects: Animals in Religion, Science and Ethics*, ed. Paul Waldau and Kimberley Patton (New York, 2006), p. 142.
3. The oldest-known cave art is located in Cueva de El Castillo, the 'Cave of the Castle', in Cantabria, Spain. It is 40,800 years old. Chauvet's cave art covers two distinct periods, the Aurignacian (30,000–32,000 BP), and the Gravettian (28,000–23,000 BP). These dates are based on radiocarbon dating. At Lascaux, in southwest France, some of the best-known Upper Palaeolithic cave art can be found. Over 2,000 figures have been found, with more than 900 of them identifiable as animals. These paintings are 17,000 years old.
4. Kimberley Patton, 'Caught with Ourselves in the Net of Life and Time', in *A Communion of Subjects*, ed. Waldau and Patton, p. 29.
5. The oldest shrine, in Switzerland, is thought to be that of a bear.
6. Alistair Moffat, *The Wildwood*, in Graeme Gibson, *The Bedside Book of Beasts: A Wildlife Miscellany* (London, 2009), p. 316.
7. Susan Chernak McElroy, *Animals as Teachers and Healers* (London, 1996), p. 15.
8. Susan Chernak McElroy, *Heart in the Wild* (New York, 2002), p. xix.
9. A term we need to exercise with caution when using, for no one can really 'own' another living creature. I prefer the terms 'animal companion' and 'guardian'. Figures from 2011 for rates of pet ownership: New Zealand: 68 per cent of households had a pet; Australia: 63 per cent; United States: 62 per cent (in 2013 statistics from the American Pet Products Manufacturers Association, the United States had increased pet ownership from 62 per cent to 63 per cent); and Britain: 48 per cent. 'Pet Ownership in Australia – 2013', at www.animalmedicinesaustralia.org.au.
10. 'The Lord opened the mouth of the donkey, and it said to Balaam, "What have I done to you, that you have struck me these three times?"' (Numbers 22:28).
11. It is interesting to note that there are only two instances of an animal speaking (and being understood by humans) in the Bible: Balaam's donkey and the serpent in Genesis.
12. Gary Kowalski, *The Souls of Animals* (Walpole, NH, 1990), p. 140.

ONE: Animals in Tribal and First Peoples' Religions

1 Chief Letakots-Lesa of the Pawnee Tribe, to Natalie Curtis, *c.* 1904, in Natalie Curtis, *The Indians' Book: An Offering by the American Indians of Indian Lore, Musical and Narrative, to Form a Record of the Songs and Legends of Their Race* (New York, 1907), p. 96; cited in Joseph Campbell, *Historical Atlas of World Mythology*, vol. I: *The Way of the Animal Powers* (London, 1984), p. 8.
2 Hubert Howe Bancroft, 'The Native Races', *Myths and Legends*, vol. III (San Francisco, CA, 1883), p. 305, cited in Richard Erdoes and Alfonso Ortiz, *American Indian Myths and Legends* (New York, 1984), p. xiii.
3 N. Scott Momaday, 'Foreword', in Michael J. Caduto and Joseph Bruchac, *The Native Stories from Keepers of the Earth* (Saskatoon, SK, 1991).
4 Irving Hexham, *Concise Dictionary of Religion* (Downers Grove, IL, 1993), p. 187.
5 Warren Pohatu, *Māori Animal Myths* (Auckland, 2001), p. 22.
6 'First Peoples' refers to indigenous peoples (the first people to live in a region). First Nation is a term used for Aboriginal peoples in Canada (who are neither Inuit nor Metis). A more recent trend is for First Peoples/Nations to refer to themselves by their tribal or national identity, for example, 'I am Haida.' Tribal identity is usually based upon cultural regions, geography and linguistics. Within this work I usually use the term 'First Peoples', which encompasses tribal/indigenous peoples of Africa, the Americas, the Arctic, Asia and Oceania. Occasionally I use the term 'Native American'. I acknowledge that the terms used will be inadequate, and will date in time. This does not set out to be an exhaustive account, and the subject matter cannot be contained within the limits of one chapter. This chapter, given its scope, is more of an overview. If readers want to learn more, then the footnotes and Bibliography will guide them to additional information. The majority of this chapter will address the First Peoples/Nations of North America, but references will be made to other First Peoples/Nations.
7 Boria Sax, *The Serpent and the Swan: The Animal Bride in Folklore and Literature* (Blacksburg, VA, 1998), p. 220.
8 Evan T. Pritchard, *Native American Stories of the Sacred* (Woodstock, VT, 2005), p. xviii.
9 Ella E. Clark, *Indian Legends of the Pacific Northwest* (1953) (Los Angeles, CA, 2003), p. 8.
10 Ibid.
11 Northwest tribes include the Salish, the Chinook, the Tlingit and the Haida.
12 The Plains tribes include Blackfoot, North Cheyenne, Pawnee and Lakota (Sioux).
13 Southwest/Pueblo tribes include the West Apache, Hopi, Navajo and Apache.
14 Southeast and Woodlands tribes include the Cherokee, Shawnee, Iroquois and Huron.
15 Roy Willis, ed., *World Mythology: The Illustrated Guide* (London, 1993), p. 221.

16 William Bright, cited in David M. Guss, ed., *The Language of Birds: Tales, Texts and Poems of Interspecies Communication* (San Francisco, CA, 1985), p. 5. Perhaps it would be more appropriate to define animals as 'First Peoples', rather than using this term for human beings, because in the majority of the myths or tales animals precede humans.
17 Richard and Judy Dockrey Young, 'Introduction', in Teresa Pijoan (collected and retold), *White Wolf Woman and Other Native American Transformation Myths* (Little Rock, AK, 1992), p. 14.
18 Tezcatlipoca could see through darkness, like his alter ego the jaguar. He was the supreme god of the Mesoamerican pantheon. His feet had been cut off by the primeval earth monster and had been replaced by a mirror in the shape of a curled-up rabbit.
19 The Chavin culture worshipped a jaguar god (the culture disappeared around 33 BCE). The Maya sun god, Kinich Ahau (Ahau Kin), journeyed between sunset and sunrise in the underworld as the Jaguar God. Gods were often portrayed wearing jaguar pelts as sacred dress. For the Aztec, elite warriors were known as the 'Jaguar Knights', who played a role in the rituals that preceded human sacrifice. In southern Mexico many still believe that the jaguar is in charge of rain, and will only send rain in exchange for blood. Nowadays this takes the form of young men dressing in jaguar costumes and having fist-fights; Nicholas J. Saunders, *Animal Spirits* (London, 1995), p. 72. Sinaa, the feline ancestor of the Brazilian Yudja (Juruna) tribe, is the offspring of a huge jaguar and a female human.
20 The roots of his name indicate a symbolic combination of the gentle quetzal bird and a water serpent. He represented the force of life. In one myth he took the form of a black ant in order to steal maize from the red ants for humanity.
21 The Toltecs also worshipped the sky god Mixcoatl, the Cloud Serpent (also the god of hunting), the father of the more important Quetzalcoatl. Mixcoatl's wife was Coatlicue ('Snake Skirt' or 'Goddess of the Serpent Petticoat'). In Aztec myth she was also a creator earth goddess, the fertile force from which everything was created. In some accounts the South American continent was thought to have been formed from her body and upper jaw, after her lower jaw was torn off during a fight in which she took the form of a crocodile. Several of her names allude to animals: Itzpapalotl (Flint Butterfly) and Tlaltecuhtli (Earth-Toad-Knife); Kenneth McLeish, *Myth: Myths and Legends of the World Explored* (London, 1996), p. 125.

She may have been a shape-changer; the most common depiction of her is as a woman wearing a skirt or petticoat of writhing snakes, and a necklace of the skulls, hands and hearts of her sacrificial victims. She had clawed hands and feet and fed on corpses.
22 Jo Forty, *Mythology: A Visual Encyclopedia* (London, 2004), p. 398.
23 Erdoes and Ortiz, *American Indian Myths and Legends*, p. 389.
24 Guss, ed., *The Language of Birds*, p. ix.
25 Sax, *The Serpent and the Swan*, p. 27.
26 Ibid.

27 Exogamous refers to a custom or act of a person marrying outside their tribe, clan or other social unit, often as required by law.
28 Kimberley Patton, 'Caught with Ourselves in the Net of Life and Time: Traditional Views of Animals in Religion', in *A Communion of Subjects: Animals in Religion, Science and Ethics*, ed. Paul Waldau and Kimberley Patton (New York, 2006), p. 28.
29 Tom Lowenstein and Piers Vitebsky, *Native American Myth and Mankind: Mother Earth, Father Sky* (London, 1997), p. 103.
30 Ibid.
31 Willis, *World Mythology*, p. 279.
32 For example, the Blue Tongue Lizard, known as Lungkata, stole a fat emu from two Bell Bird brothers, and buried it at the site of what is known as Uluru (Ayer's Rock), ibid., p. 286.
33 Ibid., p. 279.
34 A. W. Reed, *Aboriginal Legends: Animal Tales* (Sydney, 1978), p. 9.
35 Ibid.
36 Jan Knappert, *African Mythology* (London, 1990), p. 245.
37 Ibid., p. 246.
38 Gary Wyatt, *Mythic Beings: Spirit Art of the Northwest Coast* (Seattle, WA, 1999), p. 11.
39 Claude Lévi-Strauss, *Savage Mind*, trans. George Weidenfeld et al. (Chicago, IL, 1962), p. 37; cited in Sax, *The Serpent and the Swan*, p. 31.
40 Masson, Jeffrey, *The Pig who Sang to the Moon* (London, 2005), p. 242.
41 Ibid., p. 52.
42 Ibid.
43 Ibid., p. 243.
44 Bronislaw Malinowski, cited in Erdoes and Ortiz, *American Indian Myths and Legends*, p. xv.
45 Nick Greaves, with Rod Clement, *When Hippo was Hairy, and Other Tales from Africa* (Cape Town, 2000), p. 14.
46 David Leeming, *The Oxford Illustrated Companion to World Mythology* (New York, 2008), p. 7.
47 McLeish, *Myth: Myths and Legends of the World Explored*, p. 246. Speed is an appropriate attribute, for Heitsi-Eibib is also the patron of hunters.
48 Leeming, *The Oxford Illustrated Companion to World Mythology*, p. 7.
49 Ibid. Khonvum is thought to still visit the earth, most often in the form of a chameleon.
50 Forty, *Mythology: A Visual Encyclopedia*, p. 448.
51 Willis, *World Mythology*, p. 222.
52 Pritchard, *Native American Stories of the Sacred*, p. 36.
53 Other animals had cosmic meaning: the eagle symbolized the sun, the jaguar the night. Both the owl and the dog were associated with death, whereas the sea-snail and the butterflies were aligned with rebirth; Veronica Ions, *The World's Mythology in Colour* (London, 1974), p. 248.
54 Wyatt, *Mythic Beings: Spirit Art of the Northwest Coast*, p. 12.
55 Robyn Maxwell, *Life, Death and Magic: 2,000 Years of Southeast Asian Ancestral Art* (Canberra, 2010), p. 51.

References

56 Kofi Opoku, 'Animals in African Mythology', in *A Communion of Subjects*, ed. Waldau and Patton, p. 354.
57 Ibid.
58 Pritchard, *Native American Stories of the Sacred*, p. xxii.
59 In a myth about the creation of the Klamath people (from the region of Northern California), Kemush created the world and 'sent Mushmush, the white-tailed deer, Wan, the red fox, and Ketch-katch, the little gray fox, to run through the forest he had created. Up in the mountains he placed Luk, the grizzly bear. High on the mountains, on the rocks and snow fields, he placed Koil, the mountain sheep. On Mount Shasta he placed Gray Wolf.' Clark, *Indian Legends of the Pacific Northwest*, p. 13. These animals are gently placed into their natural habitat, where they belong. Peace reigns. This myth is similar to the creation myth of Judaism (Genesis 1).
60 There is a scarcity of early accounts dealing with Mesoamerican mythologies, which makes *Popol Vuh* such a precious find.
61 Darwin did not state that humans evolved from apes; his evolutionary theories suggest that humans and other hominoids all evolved from a common ancestor. If we picture evolution as a tree, there was a time when the branch that leads to humans and the branch that leads to apes converged.
62 From Dennis Tedlock, trans., *Popol Vuh: The Definitive Edition of the Mayan Book of the Dawn of Life and the Glories of Gods and Kings* (New York, 1996), cited on www.criscenzo.com, accessed 30 June 2015.
63 Ibid.
64 Ibid.
65 Ibid.
66 Or present before the concept of time.
67 The principal tricksters in African mythology are Anansi and the hare. Owing to the slave trade, tales of these tricksters travelled to the Americas and to the Caribbean, the hare becoming better known as Brer Rabbit. Anansi was introduced to a wider audience through Neil Gaiman's novel *Anansi Boys* (2005). Anansi claimed the Spider Stories as his own from the sky god. This came at a price; he had to capture a python, hornet, leopard and a nature spirit, which he did by tricking each creature into trapping itself. Anansi, in common with other tricksters, brought harmful things as well: through a mistake he spread disease among the tribes.
68 Leeming, *The Oxford Illustrated Companion to World Mythology*, p. 15.
69 Ibid., p. 16.
70 Only the Southwest lacks the episode of a diving creature fashioning the earth from mud.
71 Pritchard, *Native American Stories of the Sacred*, p. 9.
72 Ibid., pp. 6, 10. Pritchard points out that the Mordvin people of Estonia and Russia have stories similar to certain Native American stories. In their Earth Diver story God sits on a rock in the middle of the primeval sea. The devil comes out of the sea in the form of a goose and the goose is ordered to dive for earth at the bottom of the sea. On his third attempt he succeeds, but hides some of the earth in his mouth. Ibid., p. 6.

73 Willis, *World Mythology*, p. 222. In a myth from the Onondaga people, from the Northeast Woodlands, little Muskrat places the dirt on Great Turtle's back (it is thought that the marks from Muskrat can still be seen on Turtle's shell) and then Turtle and the bit of earth grow larger until they become the whole world. Sky Woman is brought to rest on the earth and she brings seeds, which fall on the bare soil; life on earth then begins. Caduto and Bruchac, *The Native Stories from Keepers of the Earth*, p. 9.
74 Pijoan, *White Wolf Woman and Other Native American Transformation Myths*, p. 110.
75 Opoku, 'Animals in African Mythology', p. 353.
76 The Sea Mother is known by a number of names: Nuliajuk, Takanakapsaluk and Sedna ('The Great Food Dish').
77 Tony Allan, Charles Phillips and Michael Kerrigan, *Arctic Myth and Mankind: Spirits of the Snow* (London, 1999), pp. 58–9. In another version of the myth, Sedna is forced by her father to marry a dog. The dog dies, she runs away and her father comes after her in a boat. She clings to the boat during a storm; a large bird appears, and the father tries to throw his daughter to the bird. As she clings to the boat, her father cuts off her fingers. The smaller seals are from her fingertips, the bearded seals from the middle joints and the walruses from the last joints. Willis, *World Mythology*, p. 217. Other versions have seals, ground seals, walruses and, from her thumb, whales.
78 Helen Caswell, 'Sedna, the Sea Goddess', in *Eskimo Folk Tales: Shadows from the Singing House* (Tokyo, 1968), p. 32. It is also believed that humanity's sins accumulate as filth in her hair; hence the need to comb them out. When her hair gets dirty her anger causes epidemics or storms, or makes her withhold the seals and other animals on which the people depend.
79 Alistair Campbell, *Maori Legends* (Paraparaumu, 1969), p. 18.
80 Ibid., p. 19.
81 The Yao live on the shores of Lake Nyasa in northern Mozambique.
82 Maria Leach, *The Beginning* (New York, 1956), pp. 143–4; retold from material in Duff Macdonald, *Africana: The Heart of Heathen Africa*, vol. I (London, 1882), pp. 295ff. Cited in Barbara C. Sproul, *Primal Myths: Creating the World* (London, 1980), pp. 36–7.
83 A hunter was stalking game. Suddenly he saw a group of buxom women bathing in the river. As he was slowly coming closer he came across a row of buffalo hides neatly laid out on the bank. He chose the finest and the softest and took it away, wanting to keep it for his bedcloth. Great was his surprise when the nude women emerged from the river and started walking in his direction. As an experienced hunter, he managed to remain invisible behind the bushes while the women approached. They picked up the buffalo hides and proceeded to put them on, whereupon they became buffalo cows. Except one, a lovely big girl who searched frantically for her skin, but in vain. The buffaloes finally walked away and the hunter came out of his hiding place. When the girl saw him she wanted to run away but he quickly caught up with her, talking soothingly to her. He persuaded her to marry him and took her home. They had a son, but

References

when they went to visit his grandparents in the buffalo-bush, the hunter asked his parents-in-law to change him into a buffalo too, for he no longer wanted to live in the wicked world of people. Knappert, *African Mythology*, p. 42.

84 Michael J. Rosen, *The Dog who Walked with God* (London, 2000), author's notes, inside back cover, n.p. In 1906 Pliny Earle Goddard, an anthropologist, recorded the words of one of the last of the Kato; these words form the majority of Rosen's narrative.
85 Ibid.
86 Ibid.
87 Pritchard, *Native American Stories of the Sacred*, p. iv.
88 Evelyn Dahl Reed, *Coyote Tales from the Indian Pueblos* (Sante Fe, NM, 1988), p. 6.
89 Thomas George, 'The Great Reformation', in *Coyote Tales of the Northwest* (Edmonton, 2010), pp. 25–9.
90 George, 'Coyote Moves the Heavens', ibid., pp. 77–92.
91 George, 'The End', ibid., p. 206.
92 George, 'The Visitors', ibid., p. 199.
93 This is similar to one of the variants of the Sedna myth.
94 Caswell's book pre-dates the use of the term 'Inuit', so 'Eskimo' is used.
95 Caswell, 'The First White Men', *Eskimo Folk Tales*, p. 25.
96 Ibid.
97 Allan, Phillips and Kerrigan, *Arctic Myth and Mankind: Spirits of the Snow*, p. 79.
98 Willis, *World Mythology*, p. 217.
99 George, 'To the Moon', *Coyote Tales of the Northwest*, p. 106.
100 Willis, *World Mythology*, p. 276. The Khoisan peoples of southwest Africa attribute the invention of words to the praying mantis.
101 Ibid., p. 263. In some versions of this myth, when the men were carrying fire back to their village, some of the birds picked up the sparks to prevent a forest fire. Several of the birds were burned as they did so, which is why some species have flame-coloured beaks, legs and feet.
102 Ibid., p. 261.
103 Allan et al., *Arctic Myth and Mankind*, p. 34.
104 Willis, *World Mythology*, p. 218.
105 Ibid., p. 290.
106 The Dayaks are the indigenous non-Muslim population of the interior of southern and western Borneo.
107 Willis, *World Mythology*, p. 302.
108 Ibid.
109 Forty, *Mythology: A Visual Encyclopedia*, p. 448.
110 Ibid.
111 Pijoan, 'First People', in *White Wolf Woman and Other Native American Transformation Myths*, p. 122.
112 Pohatu, *Māori Animal Myths*, p. 4.
113 Ibid.
114 Lowenstein and Vitebsky, *Native American Myth and Mankind*, p. 54.
115 Caswell, 'The Flood', *Eskimo Folk Tales*, pp. 93–5.

116 Clark, *Indian Legends of the Pacific Northwest*, pp. 32–3.
117 Caduto and Bruchac, *The Native Stories from Keepers of the Earth*, p. 103. Kokopilau, the insect person, led the Hopi into the new land. As he played his flute, the land grew warm. On his back he carried seeds of useful plants, and so corn and beans and squash and flowers began to grow as they travelled. The insect person thus assisted the Hopi with produce and the beginnings of agriculture.
118 Therianthropy: metamorphosis of humans into animals, from the Greek *therion* (wild beast) and *anthropos* (human being); sometimes this was via shape-shifting. In some Native American tribes this presents itself as a tutelary spirit. The youth kills the animal of which he dreams during his initiation fast. The claws, skin and/or feathers of the animal or bird are placed in a bag and they become his 'medicine'.
119 Pijoan, *White Wolf Woman and Other Native American Transformation Myths*, p. 19.
120 Knud Rasmussen's notes of an Inuit, cited in Waldau and Patton, eds, *A Communion of Subjects*, p. 34.
121 Howard Norman, 'Introduction to the Wishing Bone Cycle', *The Wishing Bone Cycle: Narrative Poems from the Swampy Cree Indians* (Paris, 1982); cited in Guss, ed., *The Language of Birds*, pp. 19–20.
122 Ibid.
123 Knappert, *African Mythology*, p. 124.
124 Clark, *Indian Legends of the Pacific Northwest*, p. 81.
125 'Changer' is the name used by Clark; most other accounts of Coyote use 'Trickster'. 'Trickster' in its broadest definition includes both 'trickster' and 'culture hero/creator', so when I use that label I mean it in its more inclusive sense, rather than limiting it to a purely negative connotation.
126 Ibid., p. 82.
127 Ibid.
128 The belief in *nagualism* varies from region to region; some limit a *nagual* to powerful leaders, while others believe that every individual has his/her own animal guardian spirit. Many modern Mesoamerican Indians believe that the first animal to pass over ashes spread before a newborn will become that child's *nagual*; www.britannica.com.
129 Ions, *The World's Mythology in Colour*, p. 248.
130 Lowenstein and Vitebsky, *Native American Myth and Mankind*, p. 69.
131 Clark, *Indian Legends of the Pacific Northwest*, pp. 203–4.
132 Willis, *World Mythology*, p. 305.
133 Maxwell, *Life, Death and Magic*, p. 217.
134 Ibid.
135 Pohatu, *Māori Animal Myths*, p.6.
136 Allan et al., *Arctic Myth and Mankind*, p. 53.
137 Caswell, Prologue to 'Sedna, the Sea Goddess', in *Eskimo Folk Tales*, p. 12.
138 Vivianne Crowley and Christopher Crowley, *Spirit of the Earth: Ancient Belief Systems in the Modern World* (London, 2004), p. 124.
139 Knud Rasmussen, *Intellectual Culture of the Iglulik Eskimo*, cited in Graeme Gibson, *The Bedside Book of Beasts: A Wildlife Miscellany* (London, 2009), p. 174. Gibson continues with this observation: 'If Bergson is right

when he says that "the past collects in the fibre of the body" then this kind of fear lives deep within urban man as well.'
140 Knud Rasmussen, cited in Peter Knudtson and David Suzuki, *Wisdom of the Elders* (Toronto, 1992), p. 86.
141 Allan et al., *Arctic Myth and Mankind*, p. 53.
142 The Yupik (or Yupiit) of Alaska and Siberia do not consider themselves Inuit, and ethnographers agree they are a distinct people. They prefer the terminology Yupik, Yupiit or Eskimo ('eaters of raw flesh'). The Yupik languages are linguistically distinct from the Inuit languages.
143 Allan et al., *Arctic Myth and Mankind*, p. 110.
144 Ibid.
145 Ibid. A similar myth from northwest Alaska tells of the soul of a Tikigaq man named Aquppak who lived among the whales for a whole winter; this experience brought him great power, which he used to seek revenge on those who had murdered his sister. In the following spring, when Aquppak's soul swims with the whales to the region of Yikigaq, he sees his relatives in one of the boats and offers himself to their harpoon. They did not know the whale contained his soul, but when they brought the whale back to shore and cut it up, Aqippak's soul was released and entered his human body again. Ibid., p. 77.
146 Told by Naukatjik, Inuit, trans. Knud Rasmussen, cited in Gibson, *The Bedside Book of Beasts*, pp. 106–8.
147 Willis, *World Mythology*, p. 259.
148 Ibid.
149 Ibid.
150 Not all tribes existed on meat. The Osage tribe formerly inhabited western Missouri and southeast Kansas and now live mainly in north-central Oklahoma. The Osage followed a typical Plains area culture, with one great difference: there was tribal division between the Wazhazhe (meat-eaters) and the Tsi shu (vegetarians). This was also mentioned in the writings of Lewis and Clark. Rita Laws states that the Choctaw of Mississippi and Oklahoma ate mainly vegetables and lived in houses constructed not of skins, but of wood, mud bark and cane. Laws mentions a Cherokee legend in which humans, plants and animals lived in harmony. The needs of all were met without having to kill. When humans became aggressive and ate some of the animals, the animals invented diseases. The plants, however, remained friendly and offered themselves to humans as food and as medicine, in order to combat the new illnesses. Rita Laws, 'Native Americans and Vegetarianism', *Vegetarian Journal* (September 1994), p. 2, available at www.ivu.org, accessed 1 July 2015.
151 Allan et al., *Arctic Myth and Mankind*, p. 45.
152 Gerardo Reichel-Dolmatoff, *Amazonian Cosmos: The Sexual and Religious Symbolism of the Tukano Indians* (Chicago, IL, 1971), pp. 80–86, 218–25, 274–5; Reichel-Dolmatoff, *The Shaman and the Jaguar: A Study of Narcotic Drugs among the Indians of Colombia* (Philadelphia, PA, 1975), p. 92, cited in Knudtson and Suzuki, *Wisdom of the Elders*, p. 96.
153 Ibid., p. 97.
154 Reichel-Dolmatoff, cited in Knudtson and Suzuki, *Wisdom of the Elders*, p. 98.

155 Knappert, *African Mythology*, p. 112.
156 Opoku, 'Animals in African Mythology', in *A Communion of Subjects*, ed. Waldau and Patton, p. 356.
157 Ibid., p. 357.
158 Ibid.
159 Saunders, *Animal Spirits*, p. 55.
160 Back when the world was young, humans and the animals could speak with each other. At first they lived in peace, but after a while, when humans discovered the bow and arrow, they began killing animals when they did not need them for food or clothing. The animals met together to decide what to do. Finally, Awi Usdi, Little Deer, who was their leader, said that humans had to respect the animals, and that he would go and tell them: 'Whenever they wish to kill a deer, they must prepare in a ceremonial way. They must ask me for permission to kill one of us. Then, after they kill a deer, they must show respect to its spirit and ask for pardon. If the hunters do not do this, then I shall track them down. With my magic I will make their limbs crippled. Then they will no longer be able to walk or shoot a bow and arrow.' That evening Awi Usdi whispered into the ears of the hunters. In the days that followed, most did as they were told, only hunting when an animal was needed for food and clothing, asking permission before killing, and afterwards showing respect. Some of the hunters, though, paid no attention and continued to kill animals for no reason. Aswi Usdi visited them and crippled them with arthritis. Before long, all of the hunters began to treat animals with respect and to follow Little Deer's teachings. Even though animals and humans no longer speak to each other as in the old days, the people must still show respect and give thanks to the animals they hunt. Caduto and Bruchac, *The Native Stories from Keepers of the Earth*, p. 117.
161 Pijoan, *White Wolf Woman and Other Native American Transformation Myths*, p. 52.
162 Pijoan, 'Greedy Brothers', ibid., p. 49.
163 Ibid., p. 50.
164 Ibid.
165 Ernest Thompson Seton (compiler), *The Gospel of the Redman* (Bloomington, IN, 2005), pp. 90–91.
166 Bruce Trigger, *Handbook of North American Indians*, cited in Gibson, *The Bedside Book of Beasts*, p. 51.
167 Allan et al., *Arctic Myth and Mankind*, p. 63.
168 Lowenstein and Vitebsky, *Native American Myth and Mankind*, p. 123.
169 Ibid.
170 Ibid., p. 95.
171 Ibid.
172 Ibid.
173 An Ainu story, translated by Arthur Waley (1889–1966), cited in Gibson, *The Bedside Book of Beasts*, pp. 75–6.
174 Lowenstein and Vitebsky, *Native American Myth and Mankind*, p. 62.
175 Ibid.
176 Pijoan, 'Bears', in *White Wolf Woman and Other Native American*

Transformation Myths, p. 79.
177 Sax, *The Serpent and the Swan*, p. 219.
178 Arlene Hirschfelder and Pauline Molin, *Encyclopedia of Native American Religions* (New York, 2000), p. 265.
179 M. Leakey, *Africa's Vanishing Art: The Rock Paintings of Tanzania* (London, 1983), cited in n. 22 in Opoku, 'Animals in African Mythology', in *A Communion of Subjects*, ed. Waldau and Patton, p. 357.
180 Guss, ed., *The Language of Birds*, p. x.
181 Ibid., pp. x–xi.
182 Hirschfelder and Molin, *Encyclopedia of Native American Religions*, p. 267.
183 Wyatt, *Mythic Beings*, p. 14.
184 Guss, ed., *The Language of Birds*, p. xi.
185 Allan et al., *Arctic Myth and Mankind*, p. 78. Apparently the ravens would speak in a contrary way, saying the opposite of what they meant, often letting forth a string of abuse. It is said that the ravens have kept their contrary nature and are still prone to angry outbursts.
186 Guss, ed., *The Language of Birds*, p. xi.
187 Ibid.
188 Willis, *World Mythology*, p. 261.
189 Ibid.
190 The Pima are a people belonging to the Uto-Aztecan family, inhabiting the valleys of the Gila and Salt rivers in Arizona. They were closely allied with the Papago (Bean People). Pima believe that staying sickness was created along with the Pima, and affects no other peoples. Pima perceive that 38 or so dangerous objects (bear, deer, dog, lightning, mouse, owl, rattlesnake, wind, etc.) outside the body have a 'way'. A human must observe certain rites when encountering these objects, as specified by rites set down at the time of Creation. One gets a 'staying sickness' by transgressing in some way, not merely by encountering one of the 38 objects. After the transgression, the 'strength' of the dangerous object will enter the body to produce symptoms of disease. Hirschfelder and Molin, *Encyclopedia of Native American Religions*, p. 284.
191 Ibid., p. 267.
192 Allan et al., *Arctic Myth and Mankind*, p. 87.
193 Ibid., p. 95.
194 Ibid., p. 86.
195 Ibid., p. 89.
196 Ibid.
197 Lowenstein and Vitebsky, *Native American Myth and Mankind*, p. 110.
198 The five types of salmon are Chinook, sockeye, humpback, coho and dog salmon. Lowenstein and Vitebsky, *Native American Myth and Mankind*, p. 54. Although the salmon clans set out together, the dog salmon arrived later, for they were inclined to capsize canoes.
199 Ibid., p. 55.
200 Adapted from Joe Washington, Lummi Nation, former leader of First Salmon Ceremony, 1973, Burke Museum, Seattle.
201 Pritchard, *Native American Stories of the Sacred*, pp. 164–7. In another version, Coyote turns the two sisters into swallows and pronounces that

they will eat insects instead, saying: 'The fish is for the people that will inherit this land.' George, 'Saving the Salmon', in *Coyote Tales of the Northwest*, p. 163.
202 Pritchard, *Native American Stories of the Sacred*, p. 166.
203 Ibid.
204 Ibid.
205 Clark, *Indian Legends of the Pacific Northwest*, p. 98.
206 Stan Jones, Chair, Tulalip Tribes, Burke Museum, Seattle.
207 On an information board, Seattle Art Museum.
208 Teresa Sligar, Tulalip Tribes (on an information board, Burke Museum, Seattle). Another version concerning the care given to salmon because they are relatives comes from the Haida; in their myth a young nobleman was unfairly chastened in his village and he went to live with the Salmon People. Unwittingly his tribesmen caught a salmon with him inside it. He then grew life-size and taught the people about treating salmon with respect.
209 George, 'The Hungry Woman and the Great River Rock', in *Coyote Tales of the Northwest*, p. 175. Her husband is so upset that his tears form the small rivers and streams that run down from the mountains into the mighty Fraser River.
210 Wasco Museum information board.
211 Pijoan, 'Bears', in *White Wolf Woman and Other Native American Transformation Myths*, pp. 80–81.
212 Lewis Spence, *North American Indians: Myths and Legends* (New York, 1985), p. 311.
213 Pijoan, 'Bear Songs', in *White Wolf Woman and Other Native American Transformation Myths*, p. 91.
214 Ibid., pp. 92–3.
215 Black Elk (1863–1950), a medicine man (shaman) from the Lakota. After John G. Neihardt interviewed him, the holy man's life was revealed to outsiders. He shared his sacred teachings and old Lakota ways in order to save his vision for future generations. He witnessed the Ghost Dance of 1890 and the slaughter of Lakota at Wounded Knee in 1890. He gave detailed descriptions of Lakota ceremonies to Joseph Epres Brown in *The Sacred Pipe* (1947).
216 Pritchard, *Native American Stories of the Sacred*, pp. 69–71.
217 Lowenstein and Vitebsky, *Native American Myth and Mankind*, p. 129. In a different legend, the origin of the Sun Dance is much later than the other rites, introduced because the Sioux had become negligent in their respect for the sacred pipe. A man named Kablaya received a vision about a new form of prayer to help restore the faith of the people; this became what is now known as the Sun Dance; ibid., p. 129.
218 Pauline E. Johnson (Tekahionwake), *Legends of Vancouver* (Vancouver, 1913), p. 25.
219 Margret Carey, *Myths and Legends of Africa* (London, 1970), p. 8.
220 Ibid., p. 9.
221 Ibid.
222 Ions, *The World's Mythology in Colour*, p. 317. The Zulu have a similar

myth, with the chameleon being the one whose slowness brought death to humankind. For the Luyia, death came about through the chameleon, not due to slowness or because of miscommunication, but because of the chameleon's curse, for the chameleon had not received proper hospitality.

223 McLeish, *Myth: Myths and Legends of the World Explored*, p. 121. In another source, Chuku sends a dog, but the dog grows hungry and weary and never completes his mission, so a sheep is sent out, but becomes hungry, stops to eat and garbles the message, suggesting that people are to bury their people instead. Forty, *Mythology: A Visual Encyclopedia*, p. 438.

224 Forty, *Mythology: A Visual Encyclopedia*, p. 440. In a slightly different form of the myth, Kalumba, the creator deity of the Luba tribe of Zaire in central Africa, wished to protect humans from death and disease. He ordered Goat and Dog to guard the road down which Life and Death would journey; they are only to allow Life through, and they were instructed to turn back Death. But the animals split up because of a disagreement. Dog slept, so Death got through. The next day, when it was Goat's turn to guard the path, he prevented Life from passing. Owing to the animals' mismanagement, humans could not be saved from Death. Forty, *Mythology: A Visual Encyclopedia*, p. 442.

225 Willis, *World Mythology*, p. 224.

226 Lowenstein and Vitebsky, *Native American Myth and Mankind*, p. 43.

227 George, 'Coyote Rattles Some Bones', in *Coyote Tales of the Northwest*, p. 112.

228 Ibid., p. 113.

229 Ibid., p. 115. In the tale 'The Pine Gum Baby', reference is made to caring for the bones of the dead, for they have the power to resurrect: 'But please don't eat me here,' begged Rabbit. 'The rain would carry my bones away and scatter them so that I could never come to life again. Then you would have no more rabbit to eat.' From 'The Pine Gum Baby' (from Santa Clara), in Reed, *Coyote Tales from the Indian Pueblos*, p. 58.

230 Forty, *Mythology: A Visual Encyclopedia*, p. 458.

231 Willis, *World Mythology*, p. 282. These actions are thought to be the founding of the traditional Aboriginal rite of showing grief.

232 Ibid., p. 282.

233 Ibid.

234 Ibid.

235 Lowenstein and Vitebsky, *Native American Myth and Mankind*, p. 69.

236 Pijoan, *White Wolf Woman and Other Native American Transformation Myths*, p. 21. Snakes are often seen as holding power to the underworld. For some tribes, snakes are empowered with the ability to remove the spirit of the dead and take it to its next place.

237 The Toltec civilization (8th–12th centuries CE) pre-dated the Aztec. The Toltecs worshipped the sky god Mixcoatl, the Cloud Serpent, and his more important son Quetzalcoatl, the Green Feathered Serpent, who was a culture hero, war leader, priest, king and a god.

238 Willis, *World Mythology*, p. 243.

239 Jean Houston, *Mystical Dogs* (Makawao, HI, 2002), p. 152.

240 In other accounts he is portrayed as a trickster. One reference states that he

was a deformed dog, for his face pointed forwards, but his feet ran backwards. Rather than supporting Quetzalcoatl, he dragged Quetzalcoatl (aligned as the Sun) to the world of darkness each evening. His contradictory nature, symbolized by his shape, meant that he was unpredictable and would bring bad luck. McLeish, *Myth: Myths and Legends of the World Explored*, p. 668. Xolotl was also the god of deformed people, who were sacrificed to the sun at the time of eclipse. Forty, *Mythology: A Visual Encyclopedia*, p. 410.

241 'I was once asked by a Native Northern Mewuk if I had ever seen the broad belt of bony plates which surround the eyeball of the Great Horned Owl. On replying that I had, I was assured that these closely imbricating plates are the "fingernails all jammed tight together of the ghosts caught by the owl".' Traditional Miwok tale, in Merriman, *The Dawn of the World*, cited in Graeme Gibson, *The Bedside Book of Birds: An Avian Miscellany* (London, 2005), p. 170. See Margaret Craven's *I Heard the Owl Call My Name* (London, 1974).

242 Pohatu, *Māori Animal Myths*, p. 26.
243 Maxwell, *Life, Death and Magic*, p. 235.
244 Boria Sax, *The Mythical Zoo: An Encyclopedia of Animals in World Myth, Legend, and Literature* (Santa Barbara, CA, 2001), p. 21.
245 Ibid., p. 22.
246 George, 'Coyote and his Beautiful Daughter', *Coyote Tales of the Northwest*, pp. 182–3.
247 George, 'The End', ibid., pp. 215–16.
248 Although some evidence suggests certain tribes, such as one band of the Osage, were vegetarian, or mainly vegetarian, I do not have enough information to make definitive statements concerning this, and/or linking their vegetarian diet to particular Osage creation myths.
249 Lowenstein and Vitebsky, *Native American Myth and Mankind: Mother Earth, Father Sky*, p. 110.
250 Forty, *Mythology: A Visual Encyclopedia*, p. 460.

TWO: Animals in Ancient Egyptian Religion and Mythology

1 Predynastic and Protodynastic Periods (5500–3100 BCE):

Early Dynastic Period (3100–2686 BCE): Dynasties I–II
Old Kingdom (2686–2181 BCE): Dynasties III–VIII
First Intermediate Period (2181–2055 BCE): Dynasties IX–XI
Middle Kingdom (2055–1650 BCE): Dynasties XII–XIV
Second Intermediate Period (1650–1550 BCE): Dynasties XV–XVII
New Kingdom (1550–1069 BCE): Dynasties XVIII–XX
Third Intermediate Period (1069–747 BCE): Dynasties XXI–XXIV
Late Period (747–332 BCE): Dynasties XXV–XXX
Ptolemaic Period: (332–30 BCE)

From 30 BCE Egypt became part of the Roman Empire. By the mid-fourth century CE Egypt had adopted Christianity. I have used the listing

from Lucia Gahlin, *Egypt: Gods, Myths and Religion* (London, 2001), pp. 90–91, most of which follows the chronology in Ian Shaw and Paul Nicholson, *The British Museum Dictionary of Ancient Egypt* (London, 2008). Dates vary by several years in other references; these are approximate only. Dates may vary within this chapter, depending on the source consulted.
2 Richard Patrick, *All Colour Book of Egyptian Mythology* (London, 1972), p. 5.
3 Ibid., p. 66.
4 Gahlin, *Egypt: Gods, Myths and Religion*, p. 19. Some writers suggest that baboons (the god Thoth manifested himself as a baboon) were indigenous; others suggest they were an introduced species, brought back from travels. Some exotica, such as giraffes, though depicted in Egyptian artwork, were never represented as deities.
5 Angela McDonald, *Pocket Dictionary of Ancient Egyptian Animals* (London, 2004), p. 38.
6 Gahlin, *Egypt: Gods, Myths and Religion*, p. 210.
7 Ibid.
8 Ibid.
9 Ibid., p. 211.
10 McDonald, *Pocket Dictionary of Ancient Egyptian Animals*, p. 28.
11 Ibid., p. 32.
12 Ibid., p. 35.
13 Jaromir Malek, *The Cat in Ancient Egypt* (London, 1993), p. 75.
14 Ibid.
15 'It is commonly said that cats were "deified", but this misses the point.' Ibid., p. 76.
16 Ibid.
17 Ibid., p. 75. 'Camyses acquired a bad reputation for his disrespect towards Egyptian religion. According to Herodotus, he was responsible for mortally wounding the Apis-bull at Memphis, a crime so heinous that there was no punishment available for it.' Ibid.
18 Ibid., p. 76.
19 Roy Willis, ed., *World Mythology: The Illustrated Guide* (London, 1993), p. 37.
20 Ibid.
21 It was the goddess Maat's feather that was placed on the scales for the judgement ceremony, 'The Weighing of the Heart', to determine if the deceased would gain a place in the afterlife. The deceased's heart was weighed against the principle of *maat* (truth and justice); if the heart balanced against the feather, the deceased would be granted a place in the afterlife, but if it was heavy with the weight of wrongdoings the scales would sink and the heart eaten by the beast Ammit, 'Devourer' or 'Gobbler'. Ammit was a composite animal with the head of a crocodile, the front legs and body of a lion or leopard, and the back legs of a hippopotamus.
22 The Heliopolitan cosmogony is considered to be the most orthodox. The texts are thought to be dated from approximately 2350 BCE.

23 David Leeming, *The Oxford Illustrated Companion to World Mythology* (New York, 2008), p. 99.
24 Willis, *World Mythology*, p. 38.
25 In another myth, Amun is in goose form and the goose lays the cosmic egg, from which all life comes.
26 Willis, *World Mythology*, p. 38. The Greeks identified the Benu bird with the phoenix, which burned itself to death every 500 years and then rose from the ashes.
27 Gahlin, *Egypt: Gods, Myths and Religion*, p. 177.
28 Khepri is also spelled Khepera. The scarab is a type of dung beetle; its Latin binomial, *Scarabaeus sacer*, means 'sacred scarab beetle'.
29 Patrick, *All Colour Book of Egyptian Mythology*, p. 24.
30 Willis, *World Mythology*, p. 38.
31 Ibid., p. 39.
32 Leeming, *The Oxford Illustrated Companion to World Mythology*, p. 101.
33 McDonald, *Pocket Dictionary of Ancient Egyptian Animals*, p. 13.
34 Willis, *World Mythology*, p. 40. The Nine Gods of Heliopolis, or the Ennead, were Atum, Shu, Tefenet, Geb, Nut, Osiris, Isis, Seth and Nephthys.
35 It was thought that people from Libya were early conquerors of Egypt. Patrick, *All Colour Book of Egyptian Mythology*, p. 71.
36 Malek, *The Cat in Ancient Egypt*, p. 32.
37 Ibid., p. 83.
38 Willis, *World Mythology*, p. 47.
39 McDonald, *Pocket Dictionary of Ancient Egyptian Animals*, p. 16.
40 Leeming, *The Oxford Illustrated Companion to World Mythology*, p. 98.
41 Willis, *World Mythology*, p. 41.
42 Another expression of the high creator god was Khnum at Esna, south of Thebes. He too was depicted with the head of a ram.
43 McDonald, *Pocket Dictionary of Ancient Egyptian Animals*, p. 17.
44 Ibid., p. 12.
45 Boria Sax, *The Mythical Zoo: An Encyclopedia of Animals in World Myth, Legend, and Literature* (Santa Barbara, CA, 2001), p. 69. There are a number of variations in the spelling of Sobek.
46 Herodotus, *Histories*, II.148; trans A. D. Godley, 4 vols (New York, 1926); cited in Sax, *The Mythical Zoo*, p. 70.
47 Malek, *The Cat in Ancient Egypt*, p. 93.
48 Willis, *World Mythology*, p. 45.
49 McDonald, *Pocket Dictionary of Ancient Egyptian Animals*, p. 41.
50 Gahlin, *Egypt: Gods, Myths and Religion*, p. 44.
51 Malek, *The Cat in Ancient Egypt*, p. 96.
52 Willis, *World Mythology*, p. 50.
53 Malek, *The Cat in Ancient Egypt*, p. 73.
54 The city of Bubastis rose to prominence during the Twenty-second Dynasty. The name of one of the kings of this dynasty was Pamiu, 'The Tomcat' (773–767 BCE). Ibid., p. 95.
55 Ibid., p. 94.
56 In the mid-fifth century BCE Herodotus wrote that when a cat died, the

inhabitants of the house shaved their eyebrows as a sign of mourning.
57 Malek, *The Cat in Ancient Egypt*, p. 133.
58 Ibid.
59 Ibid., p. 96.
60 The white crown represented power over Upper Egypt, whereas the red crown represented power over Lower Egypt.
61 Malek, *The Cat in Ancient Egypt*, p. 95.
62 Ibid., p. 96.
63 Willis, *World Mythology*, p. 50.
64 Malek, *The Cat in Ancient Egypt*, p. 99.
65 Willis, *World Mythology*, p. 42.
66 McDonald, *Pocket Dictionary of Ancient Egyptian Animals*, p. 42.
67 Ibid., p. 44.
68 Ibid., p. 11.
69 Malek, *The Cat in Ancient Egypt*, p. 82.
70 Gahlin, *Egypt: Gods, Myths and Religion*, p. 162.
71 Ibid., p. 163.
72 Ibid., p. 159.
73 McDonald, *Pocket Dictionary of Ancient Egyptian Animals*, p. 29.
74 Patrick, *All Colour Book of Egyptian Mythology*, p. 70.
75 Ibid. During the New Kingdom Period, Min, a god of fertility, was sometimes depicted as a white bull.
76 Leeming, *The Oxford Illustrated Companion to World Mythology*, p. 102.
77 Patrick, *All Colour Book of Egyptian Mythology*, p. 67. During the time of the Ptolemies, the centre of the Apis cult was moved to Alexandria.
78 Also known as Shabti. From the Middle Kingdom (c. 2055 BCE), the ancient Egyptians were buried with small human statuettes known as *ushabti*. They were inscribed with Chapter 6 of the Book of the Dead, a spell to ensure that the *ushabti*, and not the deceased, did the hard work in the Afterlife. Gahlin, *Egypt: Gods, Myths and Religion*, p. 161.
79 McDonald, *Pocket Dictionary of Ancient Egyptian Animals*, p. 8.
80 Forty-eight boxes of mummified food were found in Tutankhamun's tomb.
81 McDonald, *Pocket Dictionary of Ancient Egyptian Animals*, p. 26.
82 'This is the earliest evidence for the apotropaic [protective] role of the cat.' Malek, *The Cat in Ancient Egypt*, p. 79.
83 Ibid., pp. 128–9.
84 Ibid., p. 133.
85 Ibid., p. 98.
86 This also meant that the cult of some, such as Isis and Serapis, spread to the ends of the Roman Empire. Patrick, *All Colour Book of Egyptian Mythology*, p. 9.

THREE: Animals in Celtic and Viking Myth and Ritual

1 Celtic myths and legends were recorded by monks in the seventh century.
2 Along with seers and bards.
3 Jo Forty, *Mythology: A Visual Encyclopedia* (London, 2004), p. 272.

4 For example, the Roman writer Pliny the Elder (23–79 CE) noted that the Celts sacrificed bulls and oxen.
5 Fergus Fleming, Shahrukh Husain, C. Scott Littleton and Linda A. Malcor, *Heroes of the Dawn: Celtic Myth* (London, 1996), p. 38.
6 Ibid, p. 42.
7 Forty, *Mythology: A Visual Encyclopedia*, p. 266. See chapter on Hinduism for another representation of an antlered male deity.
8 Nicholas J. Saunders, *Animal Spirits* (London, 1995), p. 87.
9 Roy Willis, ed., *World Mythology: The Illustrated Guide* (London, 1993), p. 179.
10 Ibid.
11 Saunders, *Animal Spirits*, p. 84.
12 Willis, *World Mythology*, p. 184.
13 A silver cauldron, 690 mm in diameter, found in 1891 in a peat bog at Gundestrup in Denmark. It was probably made by Celts in southeastern Europe about 250 BCE. On the panels are many scenes and divinities, including the Horned God, sitting among animals, and a bull hunt. Cauldrons were used to catch the blood of sacrifice victims and for cooking flesh. Fleming et al., *Heroes of the Dawn*, p. 22.
14 Ibid., p. 64.
15 Fleming et al., *Heroes of the Dawn*, p. 68.
16 Saunders, *Animal Spirits*, p. 82.
17 Willis, *World Mythology*, p. 186. Her cult was also adopted by Roman cavalry units; Forty, *Mythology: A Visual Encyclopedia*, p. 272.
18 Forty, *Mythology: A Visual Encyclopedia*, p. 272.
19 Bran's head was thought to have been buried under the 'White Mount' in London, possibly at the site of what is now the Tower. Fleming et al., *Heroes of the Dawn*, p. 83.
20 Ibid., p. 43.
21 Ibid., p. 29.
22 Ibid.
23 For example, after he has been wounded by his enemy Gronw, Lleu changes into an eagle that perches at the top of a tree possessing magical properties.
24 Veronica Ions, *The World's Mythology in Colour* (London, 1974), p. 163.
25 Willis, *World Mythology*, p. 194.
26 Ibid., p. 193.
27 Odin was also symbolized as a wolf or raven, creatures of the battlefield.
28 Ions, *The World's Mythology in Colour*, p. 162.
29 In one myth Thor is challenged by a giant to lift a grey cat off the floor. This was actually the World Serpent and the world was almost destroyed when he lifted one of the cat's paws off the floor. This could be another version of the myth of Thor pulling the World Serpent from the ocean. Willis, *World Mythology*, p. 199.
30 The Vanir was a group of deities, male and female, mainly associated with the earth and the water (as opposed to the Aesir, the gods of the sky). The Vanir brought peace and prosperity to the land. The cult of Freyr was popular in Sweden in the Viking age, and eventually spread to Norway and Iceland.

31 Willis, *World Mythology*, p. 200.
32 Ibid., p. 202.
33 Dragons may owe something to the form of serpent monsters in earlier myth and legend.
34 Willis, *World Mythology*, p. 205. In Celtic myth, Finn received his gift of prophecy after he placed his thumb in his mouth, having burned it on the cooked flesh of a magic salmon, the Salmon of Linn Feic.

FOUR: Animals in Judaism

1 Aubrey Rose, ed., *Judaism and Ecology* (London, 1992), p. xi.
2 Midrash: Bereshis Rabbah 10:7; David Sears, *The Vision of Eden: Animal Welfare and Vegetarianism in Jewish Law and Mysticism* (Spring Valley, NY, 2003), p. 199.
3 *Kav ha-Yashar*, chapter 83, cited in Rabbi Natan Slifkin, *Man and Beast: Our Relationships with Animals in Jewish Law and Thought* (New York, 2006), p. 51. Slifkin points out that this contrasts with the midrashic statement 'the best among snakes – crush its head' (Mechilta, Beshalach 1).
4 Maharal of Prague, *Nesivos Olam, Ahavas Re'a*, 1, cited in Sears, *The Vision of Eden*, pp. 207–8. The Maharal of Prague was Rabbi Judah Loew ben Bezalel (1512–1609).
5 From the Talmud, cited in Dan Cohn-Sherbok, *The Wisdom of Judaism* (Oxford, 2000), p. 22.
6 Sears, *The Vision of Eden*, p. 33.
7 Rabbi Tanchum Bar Chiyah said: 'A day of rain is greater than the day on which the Torah was given. For the giving of the Torah brought joy to the Israelites, whereas a day of rain brings joy to all nations and to the entire world, including the animals and beasts' (Midrash Shocher Tov on Tehillim 117). Sears, *The Vision of Eden*, p. 203.
8 Rabbi Ishmael, Rabbi Akiva, Rabbi Nechunya ben Hakanah and Rabbi Eliezer ben Hurkenos, Publishers' Preface to *Perek Shirah: The Song of the Universe* (New York, 2004).
9 Norman Solomon, 'Judaism and the Environment', in *Judaism and Ecology*, ed. Rose, p. 25. No one knows for sure who composed this 'song', but this ancient rabbinic work is mentioned in the Talmud and is much favoured by the Kabbalists.
10 Alan Unterman, *Dictionary of Jewish Lore and Legend* (London, 1997), p. 14.
11 Ibid., p. 134.
12 Rose, ed., *Judaism and Ecology*, pp. 2–3.
13 Talmud, Berakhot (Berachos) 58b, cited in Slifkin, *Man and Beast*, p. 21.
14 Cited in Slifkin, cited in *Man and Beast*, p. 24.
15 Meleches Shlomo to Mishnah Kilayim 8:6, cited in Slifkin, *Man and Beast*, p. 24.
16 Azariah 1:57–9: from *The Song of the Three Jews*, in the Apocrypha.
17 From the Midrash Rabba, Genesis, cited in Victor Malka (compiler), *The Wisdom of Judaism* (New York, 1996).

18 'The Holy One, blessed be He, sustains all creatures, from the horned *r'eimim* (gargantuan beasts) to the eggs of lice' (Talmud: Shabbos 107b); Sears, *The Vision of Eden*, p. 201.
19 From Genesis Rabbah 5:4, cited in David Goldstein, *Jewish Mythology* (London, 1988), p. 32.
20 Unterman, *Dictionary of Jewish Lore and Legend*, p. 119.
21 Rabbi Judah, speculating how God spends his twelve-hour day, mentions God playing with the Leviathan: 'in the next three hours he sits and feeds the whole world from the horned buffalo to the eggs of the louse; in the last three he sits and sports with Leviathan, as it says, "Leviathan whom you have made to sport with"' [Psalm 114:26] (Avodah Zarah 3b), Goldstein, *Jewish Mythology*, p. 33. In Jewish legend, Leviathan was the ruler of the kingdom below the sea. 'In the story "King Leviathan and the Charitable Boy" . . . a young man heard the commandment "Cast thy bread upon the waters . . .". Not understanding but wishing to do right, he went out every day and threw bread into the sea. A single fish noticed, waited every day for the boy, and ate the bread. The fish grew bigger than all the others in the sea. The smaller fish became afraid, and they complained to King Leviathan. When he learned what had happened, King Leviathan commanded the big fish to bring the young boy. When the boy came to the sea on the following day, the big fish swallowed him, carried him to King Leviathan, and vomited him out. The boy told King Leviathan that he had tried to follow the commandments of God. The Ruler of the Sea took the boy on as a pupil, taught him the Torah, and instructed him in every language of man and beast. The boy finally returned home to become a man of great scholarship and wealth.' Boria Sax, *The Mythological Zoo: An Encyclopedia of Animals in World Myth, Legend, and Literature* (Santa Barbara, CA, 2011), p. 264. This story is interesting in that it casts Leviathan in the role of the archetypal Jewish teacher, the rabbi, instructing the boy in the ways of Torah and teaching him the languages of the world, both human and animal, for that knowledge is true wisdom.
22 Unterman, *Dictionary of Jewish Lore and Legend*, p. 36.
23 Job 40:15–19; see also Job 40:20–24 and 41:1–34.
24 Unterman, *Dictionary of Jewish Lore and Legend*, p. 178.
25 Rabbi Eliyahu ben Shlomo, the Vilna Gaon, *Aderes Eliyahu*, Bereishis 1:26; cited in Sears, *The Vision of Eden*, p. 43.
26 J. R. Porter, *The Lost Bible: Forgotten Scriptures Revealed* (London, 2001), p. 27.
27 Goldstein, *Jewish Mythology*, p. 43.
28 Ibid., p. 40.
29 The concept of 'dominion' will be explored in more depth in Chapter Five.
30 Rabbi Samson Raphael Hirsch, from *The Nineteen Letters*, Letter Four, trans. Karin Partitzky, commentary by R. Joseph Elias (Feldheim, 1995); cited in Sears, *The Vision of Eden*, p. 214.
31 Chullin 60a, with Rashi, s.v. *li'tzivyonam*; cited in Sears, *The Vision of Eden*, p. 47.
32 Sears, *The Vision of Eden*, p. 48.

33 Shlomo Pesach Toperoff, *The Animal Kingdom in Jewish Thought* (Northvale, NJ, 1995), p. lii.
34 Ibid.
35 *Perek Shirah: The Song of the Universe*, p. 15.
36 Ibid., pp. 64–5.
37 Loyd Grossman, *The Dog's Tale: A History of Man's Best Friend* (London, 1993), p. 82.
38 Unterman, *Dictionary of Jewish Lore and Legend*, p. 154.
39 From Exodus Rabbah, cited in Cohn-Sherbok, *The Wisdom of Judaism*, p. 33.
40 Talmud, cited in Louis Ginzberg, *The Legends of the Jews* (Philadelphia, PA, 1988), vol. i, p. 157.
41 Genesis Rabbah 31:11.
42 From the Babylonian Talmud: Tractate Sanhedrin, 108b, available at www.come-and-hear.com (accessed 3 July 2015).
43 Cohn-Sherbok, *The Wisdom of Judaism*, p. 136.
44 Genesis Rabbah 33:5.
45 Goldstein, *Jewish Mythology*, p. 47.
46 From Sanhedrin 108a–b, cited in Goldstein, *Jewish Mythology*, p. 47.
47 From Genesis Rabbah 31, cited in Goldstein, *Jewish Mythology*, p. 45. 'On one occasion David mistook the sleeping re'em for a mountain, which he started to climb. The beast suddenly roused itself and David was lifted high in the air on its horns. He prayed to God promising that he would build a Temple as high as those very horns. God listened to his prayer and sent a lion of whom even the re'em was terrified. The huge monster bowed down to the lion, thus enabling David to dismount; and he was saved from the lion, too, because God sent a deer who drew the lion away in pursuit.' from *Midrash to Psalms* 22, 91, 92, cited in Goldstein, *Jewish Mythology*, p. 113.
48 Genesis Rabbah 30:6.
49 This will be discussed below in more depth in the section concerning dietary laws.
50 Elie Wiesel, *Sages and Dreamers* (New York, 1991), p. 25.
51 Toperoff, *The Animal Kingdom in Jewish Thought*, p. xxvi.
52 Goldstein, *Jewish Mythology*, p. 70.
53 The significance of the prohibition against the consumption of blood will be considered in more depth when the specific dietary laws are examined.
54 Goldstein, *Jewish Mythology*, pp. 57–8.
55 Ibid., p. 58.
56 'I will draw for your camels also, until they have finished drinking' (Genesis 24:19).
57 Rabbi Chaim ibn Attar, *Ohr HaChaim*, cited in Sears, *The Vision of Eden*, p. 36.
58 From Exodus Rabbah, cited in Cohn-Sherbok, *The Wisdom of Judaism*, p. 136. David was thought to possess similar qualities. God is thought to search for the righteous, by judging the manner in which they tend the flocks entrusted to their care: 'David, the son of Jesse, He tried in this manner. Before the lambs David set tender grass for food; to the old sheep

he gave soft herbs and tender grass, while to the young sheep, able to chew well, he gave the old grass; feeding each according to its wants and strength. Therefore the Lord said, "David, who is able to care for the wants of the flocks entrusted to him, will be able to rule properly over my flock, the people of Israel."' Talmud, cited in Ginzberg, *The Legends of the Jews*, vol. II, pp. 300–301.
59 Numbers 22:22–34.
60 Gerald Friedlander, *Jewish Fairy Tales* (Mineola, NY, 1997), p. 65.
61 Ibid.
62 A similar story is told about Robert the Bruce. Another time, David and his men came upon Saul and his men in a cave, fast asleep. David cut off a piece of Saul's robe to prove that he had spared his life. On the way out, David was wedged in by the legs of the giant Abner. David prayed to God for help: 'The Lord heard his cry. At that moment the Holy One, blessed be He, worked a miracle by sending there and then a wasp to sting Abner. The pain caused the giant in his sleep to pull up his legs sharply. Thus David was released . . . At once he praised God for His mercy in creating wasps. Never again did he have any doubt of God's wisdom in creating insects, which at first had seemed to him to be useless and even harmful. Never should we despise anything which seemed worthy to be created by the Holy One, blessed be He.' Ibid., p. 70. In the Talmud the wasp is a mosquito.
63 Talmud, cited in Ginzberg, *The Legends of the Jews*, vol. IV, p. 142.
64 Liat Collins, 'Noah's Sanctuaries', in *Judaism and Ecology*, ed. Rose, p. 110.
65 From Genesis Rabbah; cited in Cohn-Sherbok, *The Wisdom of Judaism*, p. 134.
66 *Torta* is Aramaic for 'cow'; the Pesikta Rabbati (sixth or seventh century) is a collection of aggadic midrash, addressing, for the most part, the Pentateuchal and Prophetic lessons. My version of the rabbinic tale comes from a handout received at the *Animals as Religious Subjects* conference, Chester, 2011, 'The Cow Who Observed the Sabbath: The Medieval Legend of Yohanan ben Torta'. The lecture was given by Dr Berel Dov Lerner.
67 The point was made by Dr Lerner that this was a religious cow; she observed the Sabbath and was preventing her new owner from committing the sin of working on the Sabbath. Lerner comments that this story has similarities with that of Balaam.
68 He coaxes her to sin on the Sabbath.
69 'Son of the cow'.
70 We learn from the cow, not from the lax owner.
71 'If you come on a bird's nest in any tree or on the ground, with fledglings or eggs, with the mother sitting on the fledglings or on the eggs, you shall not take the mother with the young. Let the mother go, taking only the young for yourself, in order that it may go well with you and you may live long' (Deuteronomy 22:6–7).
72 From *Guide for the Perplexed* 3:48; cited in Rose, ed., *Judaism and Ecology*, p. 63. This commandment has also been twisted and used in a cruel way against the Jews. During the time of Jerusalem's destruction, a woman

named Hannah and her seven sons were commanded to pay homage to the conqueror, which they refused to do. Six of the brothers were slain. Then the seventh, and youngest, was to be killed: 'She threw her arms around the lad, clasping him tightly to her bosom, and pressing her lips to his. "Take my life," she cried; "kill me first before my child." "Nay," he answered, scoffingly, "I cannot do it, for thy own laws forbid; 'Whether it be ox or sheep ye shall not kill it and its young in one day.'" *The Talmud (Selections from)*, p. 327.

73 Solomon, in Rose, ed., *Judaism and Ecology*, p. 29.
74 Yerushalmi, Yevamot 15:3, cited in Yosef Orr and Yossi Spanier, 'Traditional Jewish Attitudes towards Plant and Animal Conservation', in *Judaism and Ecology*, ed. Rose, p. 59.
75 *Berkhot* 40a 1; cited ibid. 'Rav Yehudah said in the name of Rav: It is forbidden for a person to eat before feeding his animal. [This is derived from the verse which first] states, "And I shall provide grass in your field for your cattle" (Deuteronomy 11:15), and then concludes, "And you shall eat and be satisfied" (Talmud: Berachos 40a); Sears, *The Vision of Eden*, p. 203.
76 Sifri, Eikev, 43; cited in Orr and Spanier, 'Traditional Jewish Attitudes', in *Judaism and Ecology*, ed. Rose, p. 59.
77 Jerusalem Talmud: Kesubos 4:8, cited in Sears, *The Vision of Eden*, p. 201.
78 The Talmud forbids gladiatorial shows and hunting. The author of *Chavas Da'as* (a classic work on Jewish law) deems that 'It is forbidden to watch a bullfight. Moreover, one who goes as a spectator and pays an entrance fee is deemed an accomplice to murder.' Avodah Zarah 18b; cited in Rose, ed., *Judaism and Ecology*, p. 64.
79 Sears, *The Vision of Eden*, p. 88.
80 Slifkin, *Man and Beast*, p. 150.
81 'Be careful not to go up the mountain or to touch the edge of it. Any who touch the mountain shall be put to death. No hand shall touch them, but they shall be stoned or shot with arrows; whether animal or human being, they shall not live' (Exodus 19:12–13).
82 'When an ox gores a man or a woman to death, the ox shall be stoned, and its flesh shall not be eaten' (Exodus 21:28). See also Exodus 21:29.
83 'Whoever lies with an animal shall be put to death' (Exodus 22:19). See also Leviticus 18:23. Slifkin, *Man and Beast*, p. 105.
84 Cited in Slifkin, *Man and Beast*, p. 145.
85 Philip L. Pick, 'The Sources of Vegetarian Inspiration', in *Judaism and Ecology*, ed. Rose, p. 78.
86 Slifkin, *Man and Beast*, p. 185.
87 Ibid.
88 Ibid., p. 130.
89 R. Brasch, *The Star of David: The Story of Judaism, its Teachings, Philosophy and Symbols* (Sydney, 1999), p. 258. 'I have separated you from the peoples. You shall therefore make a distinction between the clean animal and the unclean, and between the unclean bird and the clean; you shall not bring abomination on yourselves by animal or bird or by anything with which the ground teems, which I have set apart for you to hold

unclean. You shall be holy to me; for I the Lord am holy, and I have separated you from the other peoples to be mine' (Leviticus 20:24–6).
90 Rabbi Benjamin Blech, *The Complete Idiot's Guide to Understanding Judaism* (New York, 1999), p. 237.
91 Ibid.
92 Vayikrah Rabbah [Leviticus Rabbah] 27; cited in Rabbi Joseph Telushkin, *Jewish Literacy: The Most Important Things to Know about the Jewish Religion, its People and its History* (New York, 2001), p. 47.
93 This was also used as a form of torture or humiliation during the Holocaust.
94 Ramban writes: 'The principal reason why the Torah regards [the pig] as loathsome is due to its extreme dirtiness and its feeding on repulsive things. It is already known how particular the Torah is regarding seeing dirty things, even in the wilderness when there is an army encampment; all the more so in the city. If eating pig were to be permitted, the streets and houses would be dirtier than any cesspool, as one sees nowadays in the lands of France. The saying of the Sages is known: "The mouth of a pig is like excrement."' Talmud, Berachos 25a, from *Guide for the Perplexed* 3:48; cited in Slifkin, *Man and Beast*, p. 213.
95 Jeffrey Masson, *The Pig Who Sang to the Moon* (London, 2005), pp. 18 and 240.
96 Jonathan Klawans, 'Sacrifice in Ancient Israel: Pure Bodies, Domesticated Animals, and the Divine Shepherd', in *A Communion of Subjects: Animals in Religion, Science and Ethics*, ed. Paul Waldau and Kimberley Patton (New York, 2006), p. 67.
97 Jacob Milgrom, *Leviticus: A Continental Commentary* (Minneapolis, MN, 2004), p. 116. Milgrom suggests that some of the references in Isaiah 66 refer to chthonic deities, including this verse: 'Those who sanctify and purify themselves to go into the gardens, following the one in the center, eating the flesh of pigs, vermin, and rodents, shall come to an end together, says the Lord' (Isaiah 66:17).
98 This prohibition is mentioned three times in Scripture: Exodus 23:19, Exodus 34:26 and Deuteronomy 14:21.
99 Any food that is neither meat nor dairy (that is, neutral) is known as *pareve* (fruits and vegetables, nuts, eggs, tofu). These foods can be eaten with either meat or dairy. Fish can also be eaten with dairy.
100 Julia Neuberger, *On Being Jewish* (London, 1996), p. 195.
101 Stephen M. Wylen, *Settings of Silver: An Introduction to Judaism* (New York, 2000), p. 97.
102 Telushkin, *Jewish Literacy*, p. 48. After the Six Day War, some Orthodox Jews established the Ateret Kohanim Yeshiva in the Old City of Jerusalem: 'One of the school's primary curricular concerns is the laws of sacrifices, and preparing the *Kohanim* [priests] among its students to resume some day their functions at a rebuilt Temple in Jerusalem'; ibid.
103 Ari L. Goldman, *Being Jewish: The Spiritual and Cultural Practice of Judaism Today* (New York, 2000), p. 231.
104 Slifkin, *Man and Beast*, p. 36. The cartoon strip he objected to was the popular 'Mendel the Mouse' in *Olomeinu* magazine. It was replaced by the kosher 'Duvi the Duck'.

105 Goldman, *Being Jewish*, p. 232.
106 Blech, *The Complete Idiot's Guide to Understanding Judaism*, p. 240. For a very different perspective, see Isaac Bashevis Singer's short story 'The Slaughterer', in *The Collected Stories of Isaac Bashevis Singer* (New York, 1996), pp. 207–16.
107 From *Galya Raza*, cited in Sears, *The Vision of Eden*, p. 70 n. 29.
108 Woody Allen puts it like this: 'And the wolf and the lamb shall lie down together, but the lamb won't get any sleep.' Telushkin, *Jewish Literacy*, p. 84.
109 Sears, *The Vision of Eden*, p. 54.
110 See the story considered earlier, in which the cow refused to work on the Sabbath.
111 Rav Kook (1865–1935) expressed this view; *Olat Rayah*, 1:292, cited in Sears, *The Vision of Eden*, p. 161.
112 Norman Solomon, 'Judaism and the Environment' in *Judaism and Ecology*, ed. Rose, p. 29; Joseph Albo, *Sefer ha-Ikkarim*, 3:15.
113 Rashi on Genesis 1:29, cited in Rabbi Rami Shapiro, *Minyan: Ten Principles for Living a Life of Integrity* (New York, 1997), p. 144.
114 Cited ibid., p. 146.
115 Cited ibid., p. 147.
116 Cited ibid., p. 148.
117 Ramban, Commentary to Genesis 1:29, cited in Slifkin, *Man and Beast*, p. 163
118 Slifkin, *Man and Beast*, p. 70.
119 Ibid., p. 71.
120 *Osiyos d'Rabbi Akiva, os aleph*, cited in Slifkin, *Man and Beast*, p. 71.
121 Isaac Luria (1543–1572), mystic and founder of Lurianic Kabbalah, introduced new rituals into Judaism and new forms of mystical prayer. He said he was the reincarnation of the soul of Moses.
122 Sears, *The Vision of Eden*, p. 111: 'The centrality of humankind in the divine scheme is reflected by the symbolism of Ezekiel's vision of the *Merkavah* (Divine Chariot). Kabbalistically, the lowest level of the *Merkava* corresponds to the mineral realm and to vegetation; the angels (*Chayos*) in the vision correspond to the animal kingdom; and the Human Form (*Adam*) seated on the Supernal Throne corresponds to the perfection of all human souls. This indicates that humankind is the crown of creation, through which everything is spiritually elevated.' Ibid., n.24.
123 Ibid., p. 112.
124 Ibid.
125 Rabbi Yosef Gikatilla, *Sha'arei Orah*, Gate 6, cited in Sears, *The Vision of Eden*, p. 312.
126 *Likutei Halachos*, Shechitah 3:2, 4.3, cited in Sears, *The Vision of Eden*, p. 287.
127 Sears, *The Vision of Eden*, p. 173.
128 *Shulchan Aruch*, Orach Chaim, 316:9, cited in Sears, *The Vision of Eden*, pp. 173–4.
129 Seder is the ritual meal eaten at home on the first night of the festival of Passover (Hebrew: Pesach).

130 *The Talmud (Selections from)*, p. 332.
131 Slifkin, *Man and Beast*, p. 245.
132 Roberta Kalechofsky, *Haggadah for the Liberated Lamb* (Marblehead, MA, 2002). A Haggadah is a text read during Passover, containing prayers, Scripture, stories, discussion by rabbis and songs.
133 Ibid., p. 6.
134 Jews originally of German extraction. This rite is less common now, usually practised only within Orthodox communities.
135 Scott-Martin Kosofsky, *The Book of Customs: A Complete Handbook for the Jewish Year* (New York, 2004), p. 248. 'The tradition held further that the father of the family did this for himself and his household, a cock for each male and a hen for each female, and both a cock and a hen for a pregnant woman – the first for a boy, the second for a girl.' Ibid., p. 249.
136 Arthur Waskow, *Seasons of Our Joy: A Modern Guide to the Jewish Holidays* (Boston, MA, 1982), p. 34.
137 Kosofsky, *The Book of Customs*, p. 248. See Leviticus 16:7–10.
138 Kapparot is not mentioned in the Talmud.
139 Pick, 'The Sources of Vegetarian Inspiration', in *Judaism and Ecology*, ed. Rose, p. 79.
140 S. Y. Agnon, *Days of Awe* (New York, 1995); cited in Sears, *The Vision of Eden*, pp. 215–16.
141 Martin Gilbert, *Letters to Auntie Flori: The 5,000-year History of the Jewish People and their Faith* (London, 2002), p. 275. The story of the Akedah, the near sacrifice of Isaac at the hands of his father Abraham, appears in Genesis 22. The Golden Calf or idol was worshipped by the Israelites while Moses was on Mount Sinai receiving the Ten Commandments (Exodus 32).
142 Gilbert, *Letters to Auntie Flori*, p. 276. In this ritual the fish is a symbol for God's watchful presence, never sleeping, always alert.
143 There is little art in order to prevent creating a 'graven image', adhering to the strict monotheism of Judaism and obeying the Second Commandment: 'You shall not make for yourself an idol, whether in the form of anything that is in heaven above, or that is on the earth beneath, or that is in the water under the earth. You shall not bow down to them or worship them' (Exodus 20:4–5).
144 Brasch, *The Star of David*, p. 199.
145 Ibid., p. 204.
146 Ibid., p. 329.
147 Ibid., p. 330.
148 Midrash, Shir HaShirim, Rabbah 1:63, with Eitz Yosef, abridged, cited in Sears, *The Vision of Eden*, p. 201.
149 A midrashic work on Genesis, ascribed to Rabbi Eliezer ben Hyrcanus (first century CE) but probably written in Palestine in the eighth century.
150 Pirke de-Rabbi Eliezer 21, cited in Goldstein, *Jewish Mythology*, p. 8.
151 David C. Jacobson, *Modern Midrash: The Retelling of Traditional Jewish Narratives by Twentieth Century Hebrew Writers* (Albany, NY, 1987), p. 148 (Pagis's poem) and p. 204 n.: 'The image of the raven teaching Adam and Eve how to bury Abel is derived from the rabbinic legend which tells that

the fowl and the ritually clean animals buried Abel' (Bereshit Rabbah 22:18).
152 Pirke de-Rabbi Eliezer 10, cited in Goldstein, *Jewish Mythology*, p. 9.
153 Rabbi Isaac ben Moses (Yitzchak ben Moshe) of Vienna, *Or Zarua*, 83:17, cited in Sears, *The Vision of Eden*, p. 97.
154 Sefer Chassidim, 169, cited in Sears, *The Vision of Eden*, p. 97.
155 *Teshuvot HaGeonim*, no. 375, cited in Slifkin, *Man and Beast*, p. 114.
156 Slifkin, *Man and Beast*, p. 114.
157 *Alim L'Terufah-Chassidei Belz*, 5 Marcheshvan 5757/1996, citing *Tiferes Avos-Biala*), cited in Sears, *The Vision of Eden*, p. 220. 'R. Moshe of Ujhely, *Yismach Moshe, Noach*, s.v. *V'hinei HaGaon Baal Tevu'os Shor*, pp. 142b–143a, discusses the teaching of the Ari that the souls of *tzaddikim* sometimes reincarnate as doves or other birds of a kosher species, whereas the souls of the wicked sometimes reincarnate as birds of a non-kosher species. The Talmud states in Chullin 59a that the latter are typically predators. Galya Raza, p. 95, cites a somewhat different tradition that reincarnation as a dove or pigeon is designated for those who did not transgress the cardinal sins of idolatry, murder, or forbidden relations. Sefer HaKanah states: "One who sins with speech and action reincarnates with the wild animals of the field. One who sins with action but not with speech reincarnates with the birds of the sky. As for pigeons and doves, however, the souls of *tzaddikim* rest upon them, and [during the Temple period] they were called 'a gratifying fragrance'", see Sod HaShechitah Chayos U'Behamos, p. 282; Sears, *The Vision of Eden*, n.12, p. 220.
158 Sears, *The Vision of Eden*, p. 137. Sears states in a footnote that mention of reincarnation into non-human forms may be found in earlier documents, in the Torah commentary of R. Menachem Recanti (late thirteenth century) and in the *Sefer HaKanah, Sod V'Onesh Gilgul al HaArayos*.
159 Sears, *The Vision of Eden*, p. 138.
160 Sefer Chassidim, 169, cited in Sears, *The Vision of Eden*, p. 97.
161 Rabbi Eliezer Azkari, *Sefer Chareidim*, chap. 33, cited in Sears, *The Vision of Eden*, p. 281.
162 Rabbi Tzvi Elimelech Spira of Dinov, *Bnei Yissaschar, Chodesh Sivan, Ma'amar* 5:18, abridged, cited in Sears, *The Vision of Eden*, p. 285.
163 Rabbi Bezalel Naor, *Kabbalah and the Holocaust* (Spring Valley, NY, 2001), pp. 31–3, cited in Sears, *The Vision of Eden*, pp. 302–3.

FIVE: Animals in Christianity

1 Attributed to St Basil (d. 379 CE). For the complete history of this misattribution of part of 'For this World' (1910) by Walter Rauschenbusch, see Philip Johnson, 'St. Basil's "Animal Prayers" are a "Hoax"', parts One to Seven, https://animalsmattertogod.wordpress.com, 1–13 May 2012.
2 Sallie McFague, describing an ecological model of being for Christians; cited in Jenny Wightman, 'Preface', *The Earth Bible*, vol. III: *The Earth Story in Wisdom Traditions*, ed. Norman Habel and Shirley Wurst

(Sheffield, 2001), p. 16. In Wightman's footnote she lists the source's year and page number, but not a title; a search has shown, however, that it is not in the book of the year she lists.

3 St Augustine, *Confessions*, 10:6; trans. R. S. Coffin-Pine (Harmondsworth, 1961), p. 212.

4 This argument has been set out in Chapter Four of this volume, so I will not repeat myself here.

5 Boria Sax, *The Mythical Zoo: An Encyclopedia of Animals in World Myth, Legend, and Literature* (Santa Barbara, CA, 2001), p. 38.

6 J. R. Hyland, *God's Covenant with Animals: A Biblical Basis for the Humane Treatment of All Creatures* (New York, 2000), p. 45.

7 'You . . . shall not fear the wild animals of the earth . . . the wild animals shall be at peace with you' (Job 5:22–3).

8 Charles Birch and Lukas Vischer, *Living with the Animals: The Community of God's Creatures* (Geneva, 1997), p. 16. The 'community of the sixth day' is a reference to Genesis 1:26–31, when animals and humans are created. Young suggests that the sixth day consists of three components: the first consists of God creating humans in the divine image and giving them dominion over the earth; the second is God announcing a vegetarian diet for all; and the third is God pronouncing that all things are very good. Richard Alan Young, *Is God a Vegetarian? Christianity, Vegetarianism, and Animal Rights* (Chicago and La Salle, IL, 1999), p. 19.

9 Birch and Vischer, *Living with the Animals*, p. 16.

10 'He said to them, "Suppose one of you has only one sheep and it falls into a pit on the Sabbath; will you not lay hold of it and lift it out?"' (Matthew 12:11); 'Then he said to them, "If one of you has a child or an ox that has fallen into a well, will you not immediately pull it out on a Sabbath day?"' (Luke 14:5); 'You hypocrites! Does not each of you on the Sabbath untie his ox or his donkey from the manger, and lead it away to give it water?' (Luke 13:15).

11 Translation from G. Vermes, *The Dead Sea Scrolls in English*, 3rd edn (Harmondsworth, 1987), p. 95; cited in Richard Bauckham, 'Jesus and the Animals 1: What did he Teach?', in *Animals on the Agenda*, ed. Andrew Linzey and Dorothy Yamamoto (London, 1998), p. 37.

12 This is probably a reference to Psalm 147:9: 'He gives to the animals their food, and to the young ravens when they cry,' and to Job 38:41: 'Who provides for the raven its prey, when the young ones cry to God, and wander about for lack of food?'

13 There is a later rabbinic story that tells of Rabbi Simeon ben Yohai (mid-second century CE) who at the end of the second Jewish war had spent thirteen years hiding in a cave with his son: 'At the end of this period he emerged and sat at the entrance of the cave and saw a hunter engaged in catching birds. Now whenever R. Simeon heard a heavenly voice exclaim from heaven, "Mercy!" [i.e. a legal sentence of release], it escaped; if it exclaimed, "Death!" it was caught. "Even a bird is not caught without the assent of Providence", he remarked; "how much more then the life of a human being!" Thereupon he went forth and found that the trouble had subsided' (Genesis Rabbah 79.6), from H. Freeman, *Midrash Rabbah:*

Genesis, vol. II (London, 1939), p. 730; cited in Bauckham, 'Jesus and Animals: What did He Teach?', p. 43.
14 Richard Bauckham, 'Jesus and Animals 1', in *Animals on the Agenda*, ed. Andrew Linzey and Dorothy Yamamoto (London, 1998), p. 59.
15 Eschatology ('discourse about the last things') is the branch of theology concerned with the end of the world and all creation.
16 John F. A. Sawyer, *The Fifth Gospel: Isaiah in the History of Christianity* (Cambridge, 1996), p. 237.
17 Laura Hobgood-Oster, *Holy Dogs and Asses: Animals in the Christian Tradition* (Urbana and Chicago, IL, 2008), p. 105.
18 Luke 2:41–2, John 2:13, 7:1–10, 10:22–3.
19 'For it is impossible for the blood of bulls and goats to take away sins' (Hebrews 10:4).
20 Hyland, *God's Covenant with Animals*, p. 48.
21 Ibid., p. 49.
22 Ibid., p. 50.
23 Ibid., p. 51.
24 Apocrypha (Greek, 'hidden things'). Apocryphal writings were rejected because they did not teach orthodox doctrines and were usually of questionable authenticity.
25 J. R. Porter, *The Lost Bible: Forgotten Scriptures Revealed* (London, 2001), p. 189.
26 Wilhelm Schneemelcher, *New Testament Apocrypha*, vol. II: *Writings Relating to the Apostles, Apocalypses and Related Subjects* (Cambridge, 1992), pp. 372–3.
27 Porter, *The Lost Bible*, p. 188.
28 Cited in Hobgood-Oster, *Holy Dogs and Asses*, p. 56.
29 Lives and biographies of the saints.
30 Wilhelm Schneemelcher, ed., *New Testament Apocrypha*, vol. I: *Gospels and Other Writings* (London, 1963), p. 410.
31 Gospel of Pseudo-Matthew 19:1–2; Schneemelcher, ed., *New Testament Apocrypha*, vol. I, pp. 410–11.
32 Cited in Hobgood-Oster, *Holy Dogs and Asses*, p. 46.
33 Ibid., p. 47.
34 *Infancy Gospel of Thomas* [Latin text], p. 103, cited in Hobgood-Oster, *Holy Dogs and Asses*, p. 88.
35 Ibid.
36 Cited in Bauckham, 'Jesus and Animals 1', pp. 38–9. This is Bauckham's translation from the German translation of the Coptic in J. Boehmer, *Neutestamentliche Parallelen und Verwandte aus altchristlicher Literatur* (Stuttgart, 1903), pp. 26–7.
37 'When you come upon your enemy's ox or donkey going astray, you shall bring it back' (Exodus 23:4). 'You shall not see your neighbour's donkey or ox fallen on the road and ignore it; you shall help to lift it up' (Deuteronomy 22:4).
38 Acts of Peter 9 and 12, cited in Porter, *The Lost Bible*, p. 175.
39 In the Acts of Thomas there are a number of incidents concerning animals and animal welfare, including the following: 'While the apostle was still

standing in the highway and speaking with the crowd, an ass's colt came and stood before him, opened its mouth and said: "Twin brother of Christ, apostle of the Most High and fellow-initiate into the hidden word of Christ, who dost receive his secret sayings, fellow-worker of the Son of God, who being free didst become a slave and being sold didst lead many to freedom; thou kinsman of the great race which condemned the enemy and redeemed his own who hast become a cause of life for many in the land of the Indians – for thou didst come to the men who erred, and through thine appearance and thy divine words they are now turning to the God of truth who sent thee – mount and sit upon me and rest until thou enter the city." And in answer the apostle said: "O Jesus Christ (son) of the perfect compassion! O peace and quiet, who art now spoken of even among unreasoning beasts! . . . the good shepherd who didst give thyself for thine own sheep, and conquer the wolf and redeem thine own lambs and lead them into good pasture; we glorify and praise thee and thine invisible Father and thy Holy Spirit and the Mother of all creation" . . .

'But after the apostle had stood for a long time (as if in a trance), and had looked up to heaven, he said to the colt: "(Who are thou), and to whom dost thou belong? For astonishing are the things shown forth by thy mouth, and beyond expectation, such as are hidden from the many." And the colt in answer said: "I am of that race that served Balaam and thy Lord and teacher also sat upon one that belonged to me by race. And now am I sent to give thee rest as thou dost sit upon me, and (that these may receive faith) and that to me may be given that portion which I am now to obtain through the service which (I render to thee), and which if I serve thee (not) is taken from me." But the apostle said to it: "He who has bestowed on thee this gift (of speech) is able to cause it to be fulfilled to the end in thee and in those who belong to thee by race; for as to this mystery I am weak and feeble." And he would not sit upon it. But the colt prayed and entreated that he would bless it (by riding upon it). Then the apostle mounted and sat, and they followed with him, some going before and some following after. And they all ran, wishing to see the end and how he would dismiss the colt . . .

'But when he came near to the gates of the city, he dismounted from it, saying: "Go, and be thou kept safe where thou wert." But immediately the colt fell down on the ground at the apostle's feet and died. All those who were present were sorrowful, and said to the apostle: "Bring it to life and raise it up!" But he said in reply: "I could indeed raise it up through the name of Jesus Christ. But this is (not) expedient at all. For he who gave it speech that it might speak was able also to make it not die. But I do not raise it up, not because I am not able but because this is what is useful and helpful for it." And he instructed those who were present to dig a pit and bury its body; and they did as he commanded.' Acts of Thomas, Fourth Act: 'Concerning the Colt', 39–41; cited in Schneemelcher, ed., *New Testament Apocrypha*, vol. II, pp. 355–7.

40 Rev. G. J. Ouseley, *The Gospel of the Holy Twelve* (London, 1923), IV:5, p. 7.
41 Young, *Is God a Vegetarian?*, p. 5.
42 Ouseley, *The Gospel of the Holy Twelve*, VI:18–21, p. 14.

43 Ibid., v:10–11, p. 10.
44 The place where a Jewish sect known as the Essenes lived between 150 BCE and 68 CE, and near to where the Dead Sea Scrolls were discovered.
45 Porter, *The Gospel of the Ebionites*, in *The Lost Bible*, p. 143.
46 Ibid.
47 A religious and philosophical movement popular in the Graeco-Roman world. Gnostic groups claimed to possess secret knowledge (gnosis) about the nature of the universe and human existence.
48 Young, *Is God a Vegetarian?*, p. 97.
49 Josephus, *The Jewish War*, trans. H. St. J. Thackeray, Loeb Classical Library (London and Cambridge, MA, 1928), vol. III, pp. 645 and 648, cited in Young, *Is God a Vegetarian?*, p. 93.
50 An ascetic Jewish sect dwelling in the Dead Sea region about whom little is known, despite much speculation. They are generally believed to have lived in strictly organized communities and to have been associated with the Dead Sea Scrolls.
51 Young, *Is God a Vegetarian?*, p. 95.
52 A religion founded by Mani, a Persian prophet, that thrived between the third and seventh centuries CE. Its elaborate, dualistic cosmology was based on a supposed primordial conflict between light and dark, or between good (spiritual elements) and evil (material elements).
53 Young, *Is God a Vegetarian?*, p. 138.
54 German vegetarian Carl Anders Skriver (1903–1983), in his book *The Forgotten Beginnings of Creation and Christianity* (Denver, CO, 1990), argues that the true meaning of the word 'Nazorean', a title given to Jesus but suppressed, comes from the Hebrew word *metzer*, which means 'a greening sprout' ('vegetarian'); cited in Sawyer, *The Fifth Gospel*, p. 239.
55 Vegans abstain from the use of all animal products, including honey and leather. Veganism is a lifestyle, as well as a diet.
56 For more examples, see the section below on bestiaries.
57 Traditional Norwegian folktale, in Peter Christen Asbjørnsen and Jørgen Engebretsen Moe, *East o' the Sun and West o' the Moon*; cited in Graeme Gibson, ed., *The Bedside Book of Birds: An Avian Miscellany* (London, 2005), pp. 53–4.
58 Attributed to St Basil (d. 379 CE), cited in Matthew Scully, *Dominion* (New York, 2002), p. 13.
59 Hobgood-Oster, *Holy Dogs and Asses*, p. 63.
60 Fr Peter Hooper and Martin Palmer, 'St Francis and Ecology', in *Christianity and Ecology*, ed. Elizabeth Breuilly and Martin Palmer (London, 1992), p. 82.
61 *The Little Flowers of St Francis and other Franciscan Writings*, trans. Serge Hughes (New York, 1964), p. 78.
62 Ibid.
63 G. K. Chesterton, *Saint Francis of Assisi* (Peabody, MA, 2008), p. 111.
64 Ibid.
65 Lynn White Jr, 'The Historical Roots of our Ecological Crisis', *Science*, 155 (1967), pp. 1203–7; cited in David M. Guss, ed., *The Language of the*

Birds: Tales, Texts and Poems of Interspecies Communication (San Francisco, CA, 1985), pp. 354–5.
66 Boria Sax, 'How Saint Anthony Brought Fire to the World', www.h-net.org, accessed 10 July 2015.
67 Joan Wester Anderson, 'Saint John Bosco's Four-legged Angel', in *The Big Book of Angels*, ed. Wendy Schuman (Dingley, 2005), p. 337.
68 Ibid.
69 Hobgood-Oster, *Holy Dogs and Asses*, p. 101.
70 Mary Thurston, *The Lost History of the Canine Race: Our 15,000-year Love Affair with Dogs* (Kansas City, KS, 1996), p. 65; cited in Hobgood-Oster, *Holy Dogs and Asses*, p. 101.
71 Sax, *The Mythical Zoo*, p. 89.
72 Ibid., p. 92.
73 Hobgood-Oster, *Holy Dogs and Asses*, p. 104.
74 Sax, *The Mythical Zoo*, p. 70.
75 Arnold Silcock, ed., *Verse and Worse: A Private Collection* (London, 1958), p. 162. The poet obviously did not know that a cat frequented the cell of Julian of Norwich.
76 Hobgood-Oster, *Holy Dogs and Asses*, p. 79.
77 Fiona Macleod [William Sharp], 'Iona', in *The Works of Fiona Macleod*, vol. IV (London, 1912), p. 98.
78 Rosangela Barone, 'Introduction', in *The Voyage of Saint Brendan*, trans. John O'Meara (Dublin, 1994), p. 9.
79 Melita Cataldi and Piero De Gennaro, writing in the Introduction to a catalogue of paintings by Daniel De'Angeli exhibited in Rome in 1993, state that 'the border between the material and the immaterial is weak'; cited in Barone, 'Introduction', *The Voyage of Saint Brendan*, p. 14.
80 *The Voyage of Saint Brendan*, p. 36.
81 Ibid., p. 39.
82 Ibid., p. 40.
83 Ibid., p. 84.
84 One exception is the example of St Rose of Lima (1586–1617), a Peruvian mystic who would sing with birds and insects, even performing duets with them; Birch and Vischer, *Living with the Animals*, p. 27.
85 G.R.D. McLean, *Celtic Spiritual Verse: Poems of the Western Highlanders* (London, 1961), p. 222; cited in David Adams, *The Cry of the Deer* (London, 1987), p. 89.
86 'Columba's Herding', in *The Celtic Vision: Prayers and Blessings from the Outer Hebrides*, ed. Esther De Waal (London, 1988), p. 58.
87 'Columba and the White Cow', in *The Celtic Vision*, ed. De Waal, p. 38; 'stopping to heal an old woman's one cow, is typical of many anecdotes told about him,' ibid., p. 39. Columba had a close bond with his favourite packhorse. On the day before his death, the horse, sensing that Columba was soon to die, lowered its head onto his chest, with tears streaming from its eyes; Ruth Sanderson, *Saints: Lives and Illuminations* (Grand Rapids, MI, 2003).
88 Dr Ruth Page, 'The Influence of the Bible on Christian Belief about the Natural World', in *Christianity and Ecology*, ed. Breuilly and Palmer, p. 41.

89 St Augustine, *City of God* 1.20; ed. G. R. Evans (Harmondsworth, 1984), p. 32. In an earlier translation this appears as 'by the just appointment of the Creator subjected to us to kill or keep alive for our own uses', trans. Rev. Marcus Dods (Edinburgh, 1872), vol. 1, p. 31.
90 Origen, *Contra Celsum* 4:531, cited in Hobgood-Oster, *Holy Dogs and Asses*, p. 59.
91 Cited in Hobgood-Oster, *Holy Dogs and Asses*, p. 60.
92 Greek Orthodox Metropolitan John of Pergamon, 'Preserving God's Creation', in *Christianity and Ecology*, ed. Breuilly and Palmer, p. 51.
93 Ibid., p. 52. This view was later challenged by Darwinism, for Darwin pointed out that human beings were not the sole intelligent beings in creation and that consciousness could also be found in animals. The definition of the *imago Dei* as consisting of reason or intelligence had to be taken back to the drawing board – and is still there.
94 St Thomas Aquinas, *Summa contra gentiles* 3:112, cited in Gary Steiner, 'Descartes, Christianity and Contemporary Speciesism', in *A Communion of Subjects: Animals in Religion, Science and Ethics*, ed. Paul Waldau and Kimberley Patton (New York, 2006), p. 122.
95 Andrew Linzey and Tom Regan, eds, *Animals and Christianity: A Book of Readings* (London, 1989), p. 114.
96 Ibid.
97 Hobgood-Oster, *Holy Dogs and Asses*, p. 32.
98 Edmund Leach, 'Anthropological Aspects of Language: Animal Categories and Verbal Abuse', in *Reader in Comparative Religion: An Anthropological Approach*, ed. William Lessa and Evon Vogt (New York, 1958), p. 208; cited in Hobgood-Oster, *Holy Dogs and Asses*, p. 106.
99 Cited in Beverly Kienzle, 'The Bestiary of Heretics: Imaging Medieval Christian Heresy with Insects and Animals', in *A Communion of Subjects*, ed. Waldau and Patton, p. 109.
100 Walter Map, *De nugis curialium*; cited in Kienzle, 'The Bestiary of Heretics', p. 109. Map's work, a collection of gossip and trivia, was composed around 1185.
101 Etienne de Bourbon, *Anecdotes historiques: Légendes et apologues tirés du recueil inédit d'Etienne de Bourbon*, ed. A. Lecoy de la Marche (Paris, 1877), pp. 34–5; cited in Kienzle, 'The Bestiary of Heretics', p. 109.
102 Kienzle, 'The Bestiary of Heretics', p. 109. The earliest examples of this illustrated Bible commentary were probably produced by the Dominicans in Paris in the first half of the thirteenth century. In the commentary the wolf symbolizes Paul before his conversion, and the lamb Peter (John 21:15); Sawyer, *The Fifth Gospel*, p. 235.
103 Sax, *The Mythical Zoo*, p. 60.
104 Christopher Smart, *Jubilate Agno* (1759–63), Fragment B; published as *Rejoice in the Lamb: A Song from Bedlam*, ed. W. F. Stead (London, 1939).
105 *Didache* 9:5, cited in Hobgood-Oster, *Holy Dogs and Asses*, p. 87.
106 As noted in Hobgood-Oster, *Holy Dogs and Asses*, p. 97.
107 Tim Birkhead, *The Wisdom of Birds* (New York, 2008), p. 7.
108 Ibid.
109 Ibid.

110 Ibid., p. 49. Linnaeus was convinced that he alone had been chosen by God to decode God's natural system.
111 Ibid., p. 43.
112 Ibid., p. 47. Another famous clergyman-naturalist was Charles Kingsley, who was rector of Eversley, Hampshire, for 31 years and, among many other posts, Regius Professor of Modern History at Oxford. During his time as a canon of Chester Cathedral (1870–73) he founded the Chester Society for Natural Science, Literature and Art. 'Charles's love of nature was unique. Every natural object held a fascination for him. These included toads living in the garden, sand wasps in his dressing room, and a favourite slow worm in the church yard. It was not to be disturbed or killed. One Sunday, he briefly disappeared on the way to the pulpit; he had rescued a lame butterfly from the church floor in case it was trodden on' (from notes in a display case at the Grosvenor Museum, Chester, visited 2011).
113 Paley is best known for his parable of the watch, which he used to explain the universe. The parable states that the intricate design of the watch tells you that it had a designer; nature too has been designed and fits together in an intricate fashion, like a watch – God is the giant watchmaker. The problem here is that the watchmaker is seen as having set the world in operation, according to unchanging rules; God is no longer seen as being involved in the operation of the world, or of day-to-day affairs; God is now thought to be remote, uninvolved. This theory paved the way for the separation of science from ethics. Darwin was inspired by Paley's idea, but felt there was no need for God; instead, natural selection was the designer.
114 Scott Ickert, 'Luther and Animals: Subject to Adam's Fall?', in *Animals on the Agenda*, ed. Linzey and Yamamoto, pp. 90–99.
115 Ibid.
116 Peter Huff, 'Calvin and the Beasts: Animals in John Calvin's Theological Discourse', *Journal of the Evangelical Theology Society*, XLII/1 (1999), pp. 67–75.
117 Theocracy is government ruled by or subject to religious authority, with laws interpreted by ecclesiastical authorities.
118 Huff, 'Calvin and the Beasts'.
119 Hobgood-Oster, *Holy Dogs and Asses*, p. 131.
120 John Donne, 'Why are we by all creatures waited on?', 'Holy Sonnets', in *John Donne: The Major Works*, ed. John Carey (Oxford, 1990), p. 177.
121 Cited in Martin Palmer, 'The Protestant Tradition', in *Christianity and Ecology*, ed. Breuilly and Palmer, p. 89.
122 George Fox, *To All Sorts of People in Christendom* (c. 1673), cited in Palmer, 'The Protestant Tradition', p. 94.
123 Anna Sewell, *Black Beauty* (London, 1877), Chapter 13.
124 Corporeal souls are without material form, therefore spiritual or metaphysical in nature.
125 John Wesley, *The Works of the Rev. John Wesley, am*, vol. III (London, 1829), pp. 202–3; cited in Daniel Hahn, *The Tower Menagerie* (London, 2003), p. 3.
126 John Wesley, 'The General Deliverance', in *Sermons on Several Occasions*,

vol. II, intro. John Beecham (London, 1874), pp. 281–6; cited in Linzey and Regan, eds, *Animals and Christianity*, pp. 102–3.
127 Ibid.
128 Ibid.
129 The most significant Christian theologian writing on this subject in recent years is Andrew Linzey, but others have included Tom Regan, Stephen Webb and Jay McDaniel. Some concerned Christians are involved in the arena of animal welfare, which is a separate topic and can only be mentioned in passing. Having said that, 'The Bells of Heaven', a poem by Ralph Hodgson (1871–1962), is worth noting for its passion and anger; available at www.poemhunter.com, accessed 21 December 2015.
130 Albert Schweitzer, 'The Ethic of Reverence for Life', in *Civilization and Ethics* (London, 1967), pp. 214–22; cited in Linzey and Regan, eds, *Animals and Christianity*, pp. 118–19.
131 Schweitzer, in *Animals and Christianity*, ed. Linzey and Regan, p. 120. A slightly different translation reads as follows: 'When abuse of animals is widespread, when the bellowing of thirsty animals in cattle cars is heard and ignored, when cruelty still prevails in many slaughterhouses, when animals are clumsily and painfully butchered in our kitchens, when brutish people inflict unimaginable torments upon animals and when some animals are exposed to the cruel games of children, all of us share in the guilt'; cited in Jay B. McDaniel, *Of God and Pelicans: A Theology of Reverence for Life* (Louisville, KY, 1989), p. 58.
132 David Fitzpatrick Grippo, 'Albert Schweitzer: Be a Healing Presence in a Hurting World' (St Meinrad, IN, 2009), p. 2.
133 Karen Millington, 'Vegetarian Roots: The Extraordinary Tale of William Cowherd', BBC News, 17 December 2012, www.bbc.co.uk, accessed 12 July 2015.
134 William Cowherd and James Scholefield, *Select Hymns for the Use of Bible-Christians* (Manchester, 1841).
135 Matthew Fox, ed., *Meditations with Meister Eckhart* (Santa Fe, NM, 1982), p. 14.
136 Richard Barber, *Bestiary* (Woodbridge, 1993), p. 7.
137 Ibid.
138 Birkhead, *The Wisdom of Birds*, p. 22.
139 Barber, *Bestiary*, pp. 161–3.
140 Kienzle, 'The Bestiary of Heretics', in *A Communion of Subjects*, ed. Waldau and Patton, p. 106.
141 Ibid., p. 107.
142 Ibid., p. 111: Job 4:19, 13:28, Psalms 39:11, Isaiah 50:9, Matthew 6:19, James 5:2.
143 Ibid.
144 Boria Sax, *The Serpent and the Swan: The Animal Bride in Folklore and Literature* (Blacksburg, VA, 1998), p. 50.
145 Ibid.
146 'As I looked, a stormy wind came out of the north: a great cloud with brightness around it and fire flashing forth continually, and in the middle of the fire, something like gleaming amber. In the middle of it was

something like four living creatures. This was their appearance: they were of human form. Each had four faces, and each of them had four wings. Their legs were straight, and the soles of their feet were like the sole of a calf's foot; and they sparkled like burnished bronze. Under their wings on their four sides they had human hands. And the four had their faces and their wings thus: their wings touched one another, each of them moved straight ahead, without turning as they moved. As for the appearance of their faces: the four had the face of a human being, the face of a lion on the right side, the face of an ox on the left side, and the face of an eagle; such were their faces. Their wings were spread out above; each creature had two wings, each of which touched the wing of another, while two covered their bodies' (Ezekiel 1:4–11).

147 Hyland, *God's Covenant with Animals*, p. 59.
148 E. W. Bullinger, *A Critical Lexicon and Concordance to the English and Greek New Testament* (Grand Rapids, MI, 1975), p. 147; cited in Hyland, *God's Covenant with Animals*, p. 60.
149 Sax, *The Serpent and the Swan*, p. 52.
150 Attributed to St Basil (d. 379 CE), cited in Charles Birch, 'Respect for Animals', in *Living with the Animals*, ed. Birch and Vischer, p. 59. Adapted from a prayer devised in 1915 by Arthur Winnington-Ingram, Bishop of London; see Philip Johnson, 'St Basil "Animal Prayers"'.
151 Cited in Birch and Vischer, eds, *Living with the Animals*, p. 17. I have been unable to access the original *Schauspiel* (play) in rhyming couplets. German original text at www.archive.org, accessed 21 December 2015.
152 Ibid., p. 17.
153 C. S. Lewis, 'Animal Resurrection', in *The Problem of Pain* (London, 1967), pp. 125–8.
154 Evelyn Underhill to C. S. Lewis, 13 January 1941, *The Making of a Mystic: New and Selected Letters of Evelyn Underhill*, ed. Carol Poston (Urbana and Chicago, IL, 2010), pp. 341–2.
155 Sax, *The Serpent and the Swan*, p. 47.
156 Jay McDaniel, 'Practicing the Presence of God', in *A Communion of Subjects*, ed. Waldau and Patton, p. 144.
157 Jacob Grimm and Wilhelm Grimm, 'The Three Languages', in *The Complete Illustrated Works of the Brothers Grimm* (London, 1984), p. 144.
158 Guss, *The Language of the Birds*, p. 339.

six: Animals in Islam

1 Al-Hafiz Basheer Ahmad Masri, *Animal Welfare in Islam* (Markfield, 2007), p. 84.
2 Richard Foltz, '"This She-camel of God is a Sign to You": Dimensions of Animals in Islamic Tradition and Muslim Culture', in *A Communion of Subjects: Animals in Religion, Science, and Ethics*, ed. Paul Waldau and Kimberley Patton (New York, 2006), p. 149.
3 Footnote no. 7, *Bukhārī* and *Muslim*, cited in Al-Masri, *Animal Welfare in Islam*, p. 8. These are both collections of Hadiths; among the many collections produced in the eighth and ninth centuries, Sunni Muslims

accept the collections of *Bukhari* (d. 870) and *Muslim* (d. 875) as the best.
4   'All who dwell in the heavens and on the earth shall prostrate themselves before God' (Qur'an 13:15); 'All creatures celebrate His praises. Yet you cannot understand their praises' (17:44); 'Do you not see that those in the heavens and the earth . . . the beasts, and countless men – all do homage to God?' (22:18).
5   Seyyed Hossein Nasr, 'Islam, the Contemporary World, and the Environmental Crisis', in *Islam and Ecology: A Bestowed Trust*, ed. Richard C. Foltz, Frederick M. Denny and Azizan Baharuddin (Cambridge, MA, 2003), p. 96; cited in Richard C. Foltz, *Animals in Islamic Tradition and Muslim Cultures* (Oxford, 2006), p. 103.
6   Sarra Tlili, 'All Animals Are Equal, or Are They? The Ikhwān al-Safā's Animal Epistle and its Unhappy End', unpublished article, 2011, p. 30.
7   Masri, *Animal Welfare in Islam*, p. 21.
8   Foltz, *Animals in Islamic Tradition*, p. 5.
9   Tlili, 'All Animals Are Equal, or Are They?', p. 30.
10 In *The Koran*, trans. N. J. Dawood (London, 2006), the term is translated as 'Deputy' (2:30) and 'exalted some of you in rank above others' (6:165).
11 'They are like beasts – indeed, they are more misguided'; ibid.
12 *Maxims of 'Alī*, trans. Al-Halal (Lahore, 1963), p. 436. Ali ibn Talib was the son-in-law of Muhammad, and the fourth Caliph. Cited in Masri, *Animal Welfare in Islam*, p. 7.
13 Foltz, *Animals in Islamic Tradition*, p. 21.
14 Muhammad ibn Muhammad al-Nu'man al-Mufid, *Al-Ikhtisās* (Beirut, n.d.), pp. 295–6; cited in Foltz, *Animals in Islamic Tradition*, p. 23.
15 Said ibn Hibatullah al-Rawandi, *Al-kharā'ij wa'al-jarā'ih* (Qom, 1409 [1989]), p. 321; cited in Foltz, *Animals in Islamic Tradition*, pp. 23–4.
16 Ibid., pp. 249–50; cited in Foltz, *Animals in Islamic Tradition*, p. 24.
17 Foltz, *Animals in Islamic Tradition*, p. 25. The footnote attributes this to Al-Kulayni, *Al-Kāfī*, 3:225.
18 Bediuzzaman Said Nursi, *The Flashes Collection* (Istanbul, 1995), pp. 384–5; cited in Foltz, '"This She-camel of God is a Sign to You"', in *A Communion of Subjects*, ed. Waldau and Patton, p. 156. After a time spent in prison, Nursi became concerned about the killing of insects with insecticides and wrote a treatise on the importance of flies: *The Flashes Collection*, pp. 339–43. Muhammad had a fondness for cats: 'He told her once he had sailed to an eastern port where the people believed that the markings of a tabby cat were traces left by the fingerprints of the Prophet Mahommed;' Brenda Walker, *Poe's Cat* (Ringwood, Vic., 1999), p. 85. The source for this is: 'Islamic religion displays considerable tolerance towards them. The Prophet Muhammad is said to have cut off a sleeve of his cloak so that he would not disturb a cat which had fallen asleep on it, and the streaks on the fur of the Egyptian cat are described as the marks left where the Prophet's hand stroked it. There are records of medieval donations left to provide food for the homeless cats of Cairo, some of which still existed in the last century. The best-known of such charities is perhaps that of the Sultan Baibars (1260–1277) whose emblem was one of the big cats and

who left a garden near his mosque for the upkeep of destitute Cairo cats.' Jaromir Malek, *The Cat in Ancient Egypt* (London, 1993), p. 137.
19 The beginning of the saying sets out its long line of truthful witness: 'Yahya related to me from Malik from Sumayy, the *mawla* (client) of Abu Nakr from Abu Salih al-Samman from Abu Hurayra that the Messenger of Allah, may Allah bless him and grant him peace, said . . .'; Muwatta Malik, 49:10:23, cited in Foltz, *Animals in Islamic Tradition*, p. 19.
20 Narrated by Abū Hurayrah. '*Awn al-Ma'būd Sharh Abū Dāwūd*', 7:235; Hadith no. 2550; cited in Masri, *Animal Welfare in Islam*, p. 47.
21 Al-Kulayni, *Al-Kāfī*, 6.550, cited in Foltz, *Animals in Islamic Tradition*, p. 25.
22 Foltz, *Animals in Islamic Tradition*, p. 30.
23 Foltz, '"This She-camel of God is a Sign to You"', in *A Communion of Subjects*, ed. Waldau and Patton, p. 150.
24 Ibid. In Muslim mythology, *jinn* are spirits who can assume human or animal form. They are thought to influence humans by use of their supernatural powers.
25 Zia al-din Nakhshabi, *Tales of a Parrot: The Cleveland Museum of Art's Tūtī-nāma*, trans. Muhammad A. Simsar (Cleveland, OH, 1978), p. 109; cited in Foltz, *Animals in Islamic Tradition*, p. 4.
26 Masri, *Animal Welfare in Islam*, p. 34.
27 Narrated by Urbah ibn Farqad Abū Abdullāh al-Sulami, Hadith no. 2525; cited ibid., p. 36.
28 Narrated by Jābir ibn Abdullah. *Muslim*, vol. III, Hadith no. 2116; cited ibid., p. 34.
29 Narrated by Abū Wāqid al-Laythī. *Tirmidhī* Hadith no. 1480, chapter on *Al-At'imah*; cited ibid., p. 35.
30 *Mishkat al-Masabih*, cited in Fazlun Khalid and Joanne O'Brien, eds, *Islam and Ecology* (London, 1992), p. 18.
31 *al-Muwatta'* (Norwich, 1982), p. 205, cited in Masri, *Animal Welfare in Islam*, p. 36.
32 Masri, *Animal Welfare in Islam*, p. 25.
33 Qur'an 7:73, 11:64, 26:155, 54:27–31.
34 Narrated by 'Ad al-Rahmān ibn 'Abdullāh ibn Mas'ūd, *Muslim*; cited in Masri, *Animal Welfare in Islam*, p. 49.
35 Narrated by Abū Hurayrah. *Sahih Muslim- Kitāb al-Imān*, vol. III, chap. 807, Hadith no. 4724, pp. 1062, 1063, cited in Masri, *Animal Welfare in Islam*, p. 47.
36 A cycle of prayers is said five times daily at designated times: at sunset, between sunset and midnight, at dawn, at midday and in the afternoon, following the rite of ritual cleansing.
37 Narrated by Anas. '*Awn*, 7:223; Hadith no. 5234; cited in Masri, *Animal Welfare in Islam*, p. 48.
38 Narrated by 'Abdullāh ibn 'Umar Bukhārī, 4:337; recorded in *Riyād*, Hadith no. 1605, p. 271; cited in Masri, *Animal Welfare in Islam*, p. 46. This Hadith has been recorded by almost all the authentic books of Hadith.
39 Khalid and O'Brien, eds, *Islam and Ecology*, p. 18.

40 Cited in Othman Llewellyn, 'Desert Reclamation and Conservation in Islamic Law', ibid., p. 89.
41 *Al-Furū min al-Kāfī lil-Kulaynī*, 6:230; cited in Masri, *Animal Welfare in Islam*, p. 50.
42 *Sahih Muslim*, 21:4810, cited in Foltz, *Animals in Islamic Tradition*, p. 26.
43 *Sunān* of both Tirmidhi and Ibn Maja; cited in Abduljalil Sajid, 'Slaughter of Animals at Eidul Adha'; cited in Foltz, *Animals in Islamic Tradition*, p. 26.
44 Foltz, *Animals in Islamic Tradition*, p. 20.
45 Foltz, '"This She-camel of God is a Sign to You"', in *A Communion of Subjects*, ed. Waldau and Patton, p. 152.
46 Masri, *Animal Welfare in Islam*, p. 135. The quote is from the translation of the Qur'an used by Masri: by A. Yusuf Ali (Lahore, 1938).
47 Ibid. The translation by N. J. Dawood, *The Koran* (London, 2006) reads: 'You are forbidden to settle disputes by consulting the Arrows. That is a pernicious practice.'
48 Masri, *Animal Welfare in Islam*, p. 135.
49 Repeated in Qur'an 2:173.
50 Masri, *Animal Welfare in Islam*, p. 145.
51 Ibid., p. 146.
52 Narrated by Sa'īd ibn Jubayr. *Sahīh Muslim – Kitāh al-Sayd Wa'l-Dhabā'ih*, vol. III, chap. 827 (Lahore, 1976), Hadith no. 4813, p. 1079; cited in Masri, *Animal Welfare in Islam*, p. 37.
53 Narrated by Abū Mālik on the authority of his father. Abu Dawood and Imam at-Tirmidhi as recorded in *Garden of the Righteous – Riyād al-Sālihīn* of Imām Nawāwī, trans. M. Z. Khan (London, 1975), p. 160; cited in Masri, *Animal Welfare in Islam*, pp. 33 and 53 n.28.
54 *Ibn Kathīr*, vol. III, p. 221, cited in Masri, *Animal Welfare in Islam*, p. 113.
55 Ibid., p. 116.
56 Foltz, *Animals in Islamic Tradition*, p. 39.
57 Ibid.
58 Ibid.
59 This ruling is contained in the *Muwatta* of Iman Malik, cited in Yassim Dutton, 'Natural Resources in Islam', in Khalid and O'Brien, eds, *Islam and Ecology*, p. 63.
60 Cited in Llewellyn, 'Desert Reclamation and Conservation in Islamic Law', in Khalid and O'Brien, eds, *Islam and Ecology*, p. 91.
61 Foltz, '"This She-camel of God is a Sign to You"', in *A Communion of Subjects*, ed. Waldau and Patton, p. 153.
62 Ibid.
63 Ibid.
64 Ibid., p. 154.
65 Foltz, *Animals in Islamic Tradition*, p. 49.
66 Ibid., p. 50.
67 Ikhwān al-Safā, *The Case of the Animals versus Man before the King of the Jinn: A Tenth-century Ecological Fable of the Pure Brethren of Basra*, trans. Lenn Evan Goodman (Boston, MA, 1978), pp. 5–6; cited in Foltz, *Animals in Islamic Tradition*, pp. 50–51.

68 Ibid. pp. 279–80, cited in Tlili, 'All Animals Are Equal, or Are They?', p. 31.
69 Ibid.
70 Zayn Kassam, 'The Case of the Animals Versus Man: Toward an Ecology of Being', in *A Communion of Subjects*, ed. Waldau and Patton (New York, 2006), p. 164.
71 Ibid.; Qur'an 24:22.
72 Kassam, 'The Case of the Animals Versus Man', in *A Communion of Subjects*, ed. Waldau and Patton, p. 165.
73 Ibid., p. 166.
74 Foltz, *Animals in Islamic Tradition*, p. 51.
75 Ibid., p. 52.
76 Seyyed Hossein Nasr, *Science and Civilization in Islam* (Cambridge, MA, 1968), p. 71; cited in Foltz, *Animals in Islamic Tradition*, p. 159 n. 6.
77 The notion of an afterlife for non-human animals will be examined in the final section of this chapter.
78 Tlili, 'All Animals are Equal, or Are They?', p. 15.
79 Kassam, 'The Case of the Animals Versus Man', in *A Communion of Subjects*, ed. Waldau and Patton, p. 167.
80 Foltz, *Animals in Islamic Tradition*, p. 52.
81 Ikhwān al-Safā, *The Case of the Animals versus Man before the King of the Jinn*, trans. Lenn Evan Goodman, cited in Tlili, 'All Animals are Equal, or Are They?', p. 23.
82 Ibid., p. 27.
83 Foltz, *Animals in Islamic Tradition*, p. 53.
84 Abi Uthman Amr ibn Badr al-Jahiz, *Kitāb al-hayawān*, 7 vols (Cairo, 1357–64 AH [1938–45]), vol. III, pp. 300–301; cited in Foltz, *Animals in Islamic Tradition*, p. 57.
85 The Buraq (Al-Buraq) is a creature said to have transported Muhammad to heaven. It was white, half mule, half donkey, with wings. It would carry Muhammad on his 'Night Journey' (the Isra and Miraj), from Mecca to Jerusalem and back. Part of the Western Wall in Jerusalem is referred to as the Al-Buraq Wall, as it is said that Muhammad tied the Buraq to that wall during his Night Journey. Al-Buraq would also transport other prophets; the Buraq was said to have carried Abraham (Ibrahim) when he visited his wife Hagar and son Ishmael.
86 For more information, see ref. 104 below.
87 Zia al-din Nakhshabi, *Tales of a Parrot: The Cleveland Museum of Art's Tūtī-nāma*, trans. Muhammad A. Simsar (Cleveland, OH, 1978), cited in Foltz, *Animals in Islamic Tradition*, p. 74.
88 Ibid., p. 76.
89 Zia al-din Nakhshabi, *Tales of a Parrot*, p. 72, cited in Foltz, *Animals in Islamic Tradition*, p. 139.
90 Jalal ad-Din Rumi, *The Mathnawī of Jalalu'ddin Rumi*, trans. R. A. Nicholson, 5 vols (London, 1925–40), vol. I, pp. 2291–6; cited in Foltz, '"This She-camel of God is a Sign to You"', in *A Communion of Subjects*, ed. Waldau and Patton, pp. 153–4.
91 Philip Dunn, Manuela Dunn-Mascetti and R. A. Nicholson, *The*

Illustrated Rumi: A Treasury of Wisdom from the Poet of the Soul (New York, 2000), p. 115.
92 Ibid., p. 132.
93 This reference is to the story of the Seven Sleepers (Qur'an 18:17–21).
94 Rumi, *Mathnawī al-ma'anawī*, vol. v, pp. 2008–11, cited in Foltz, *Animals in Islamic Tradition*, pp. 79–80.
95 Ibid., vol. III, pp. 3901–2, cited in Foltz, '"This She-camel of God is a Sign to You"', in *A Communion of Subjects*, ed. Waldau and Patton, p. 154.
96 Foltz, *Animals in Islamic Tradition*, p. 77.
97 Ali Asani, '"Oh that I Could be a Bird and Fly, I would Rush to the Beloved": Birds in Islamic Mystical Poetry', in *A Communion of Subjects: Animals in Religion, Science and Ethics*, ed. Paul Waldau and Kimberley Patton (New York, 2006), p. 170.
98 Two verses later, Solomon listens to an ant.
99 Asani, '"Oh that I Could be a Bird and Fly"', p. 171.
100 Ibid.
101 Ibid.
102 Ibid.
103 Ibid., p. 172.
104 In classical and modern Persian literature, the simorgh, senmuru or simurgh is a metaphor for God in Sufi mysticism. In Iranian legend, the simorgh is so old that it has witnessed the destruction of the world three times over. In all that time, the simorgh has learned so much that it is thought to possess the knowledge of all ages. In Iranian art the simorgh is a winged creature in the shape of a bird, gigantic enough to carry off an elephant or a whale. Its wings are as large as clouds. It has the head of a dog and the claws of a lion.
105 Asani, '"Oh that I Could be a Bird and Fly"', p. 173.
106 Farid ud-Din Attar, *The Conference of the Birds* (London, 1984), p. 40.
107 Ibid., p. 33.
108 Farid ud-Din-Attar, *The Conference of the Birds*, new interpretations by Raficq Abdulla (London, 2002), p. 52.
109 Foltz, *Animals in Islamic Tradition*, p. 77.
110 Al-Damiri, *Hayāt al-bayawān*, cited in Foltz, *Animals in Islamic Tradition*, p. 80.
111 Farid al-din 'Attar, *Tazkirat al-Awliyā*, trans. Paul Losensky and Michael Sells, in Michael Sells, *Early Islamic Mysticism* (Mahwah, NJ, 1996), p. 160. A similar story is told by 'Abd al-Karim al-Qushayri (986–1074) of the early Sufi Ibrahim ibn Adham, who liked hunting. One day, while pursuing an antelope, he heard a voice asking him: 'O Ibrahim, is it for this that We have created you?' Immediately he got off his horse, gave his fine clothing to the shepherd in exchange for a simple wool tunic, and became a wandering dervish. Qushayri, cited in Emile Dermenghem, *La Culte des saints dans I'Islam Maghrebin* (Paris, 1954), p. 100.
112 K. A. Nizami, *The Life and Times of Shaikh Farid-ud-Din Ganj-i Shakar* (Aligarh, 1955), p. 36.
113 Quoted in Davud Ayduz, 'The Approach to the Environmental Question of the Qur'an and its Contemporary Commentary the *Risale-i Nur*',

Fourth International Symposium on Bediuzzaman Said Nursi, Istanbul, 20–22 September 1998; cited in Foltz, *Animals in Islamic Tradition*, pp. 95–6.
114 Ibid., p. 96.
115 Quoted in Ibrahim Ozdemir, 'Bediuzzaman Said Nursi's Approach to the Environment', Fourth International Symposium on Bediuzzaman Said Nursi, Istanbul, 20–22 September 1998; cited in Foltz, *Animals in Islamic Tradition*, p. 95.
116 Ibid., p. 96.
117 Loyd Grossman, *The Dog's Tale: A History of Man's Best Friend* (London, 1993), p. 77.
118 Dogs were held in high regard by Zoroastrians: 'whoever wounds a cattle-dog is to receive 800 blows with a horse goad, whoever wounds a young dog is to receive 500 blows;' ibid., p. 76. Zoroastrians would have a dog brought in to see if a person had died and to scare away the corpse demoness. The dog would then be given some food, so that it would lead the deceased across the Bridge of Separation to judgement. The dog, believed to be the leader of the soul, also accompanied the funeral procession.
119 Sahih Muslim, 4:174–5, cited in Foltz, *Animals in Islamic Tradition*, p. 129.
120 Sahih Muslim, 4:1038–9, cited in Foltz, *Animals in Islamic Tradition*, p. 130.
121 Ibid.
122 Salukis were the most popular breed, loved and cherished by later Middle Eastern princes.
123 Pariah dogs roamed the streets; rabid strays were feared.
124 Foltz, *Animals in Islamic Tradition*, p. 131.
125 Ibid., p. 130 n.12: 'The Hanafi school of law, more lenient than the others in many respects, does not have this restriction.'
126 In the Islamic version (Surah 18:9–26), a dog accompanies the youths into the cave and keeps watch at the entrance. Muhammad made the sleepers prophesy his coming, and he gave the dog the name Kratim (or Kratimir). Kratim sleeps with them and is endowed with the gift of prophesy. As a special favour, this dog is one of the ten animals admitted into paradise.
127 Hafiz Hussain ibn Karbala'i, *Rawzāt al-jinān wa jannāt al-janān* (Tehran, 1965), p. 414; cited in Foltz, *Animals in Islamic Tradition*, p. 133. In 1453 this appears to have been expanded and the work attributed to Abu Abdullah Muhammad Al-Jazuli Al-Simlali in *How to be Holy*: 'In order to eliminate feelings of self-importance, he who would become holy would do well to acquire the *Ten Praiseworthy Attributes of the Dog*: 1. He sleeps only a little at night; this is a sign of the God-lover. 2. He complains of neither heat nor cold; this is a sign of patient endurance. 3. When he dies, he leaves nothing behind to be disposed of; this is a sign of asceticism. 4. He is neither angry nor hateful; this is a quality of the faithful. 5. He is not sorrowful at the loss of a close relative, nor does he accept assistance; this is an attribute of the unshakeable. 6. If he is given something, he consumes it and is happy; this is a sign of the never-demanding. 7. He has

no place of refuge; this is the quality of holy wandering. 8. He sleeps in any place that he finds; this is a quality of the never-complaining. 9. He is incapable of hate, even if the owner beats or starves him; this is a quality of the knowers of wisdom. 10. He is always hungry; which is a sign of the virtuous.

128 Farid al-din 'Attar, *Musibat-nāma* (Tehran, 1977), p. 182; cited in Foltz, *Animals in Islamic Tradition*, p. 139.
129 Farid ud-Din Attar, *The Conference of the Birds*, new interpretations by Raficq Abdulla, p. 15.
130 Ibid., p. 46.
131 Ibid., p. 47.
132 Farid al-din 'Attar, *Elāhī-nāmeh* (Tehran, 1980), p. 46, cited in Foltz, *Animals in Islamic Tradition*, p. 140.
133 Ibid., p. 141.
134 Awhad al-din Kermani, *Manāqib* (Tehran, 1969), vol. I, p. 377, cited in Foltz, *Animals in Islamic Tradition*, p. 141.
135 Yassin Dutton, 'Natural Resources in Islam', in *Islam and Ecology*, ed. Khalid and O'Brien, p. 62.
136 Javad Nurbakhsh, *Dogs from a Sufi Point of View* (New York and London, 1989), p. 6; cited in Hilary Hart, *Pearlie of Great Price* (Ropley, Hants, 2007), p. 39.
137 Farid Ud-Din Attar, *The Conference of the Birds*, p. 151.
138 Hart, 'Introduction', in *Pearlie of Great Price*.
139 Khalid Abou El-Fadl, 'Dogs in Islam', in *Encyclopedia of Religion and Nature*, ed. Bron Taylor (New York, 2005), pp. 498–500; cited in Foltz, *Animals in Islamic Tradition*, p. 142. I have been informed by organizations that train and supply dogs to help the blind that it is difficult to persuade blind Muslims to use a seeing-eye dog. Education programmes have been set up in the Middle East to reverse this negative attitude towards dogs, in order to help the visually impaired.
140 Muhammad al-Ghazali, *The Remembrance of Death and the Afterlife*, trans. T. Winter (Cambridge, 1989), pp. 200–201; cited in Foltz, *Animals in Islamic Tradition*, p. 6.
141 Ibid.
142 Ibid.
143 Mu'tazilites were a radical school of Islamic theologians who became prominent in the early ninth century; Foltz, *Animals in Islamic Tradition*, p. 6.
144 Muhammad al-Ghazali, *The Remembrance of Death and the Afterlife*, p. 201.
145 Ibn Jarīr al-Tabarī, *Jāmi al-bayān an ta wīl al-Qur ān* (Beirut, 1999), vol. V, p. 186; cited in Tlili, 'All Animals Are Equal, or Are They?', p. 8.
146 Dawood translates the word as 'gathered' rather than 'mustered', *The Koran* (London, 2006).
147 Alī Muhammad b. Habīb Al-Māwardī, *al Nukat wa-al-uyūn* (Beirut, n.d.), 2:112–13; cited in Tlili, 'All Animals Are Equal, or Are They?', p. 8.
148 Foltz, *Animals in Islamic Tradition*, p. 48. This view is similar to the Kabbalistic concept (see Chapter Four).

149 Ibid., p. 68.
150 Narrated by Anas, *Mishkāt al-Masābīh*, trans. James D. Robson (Lahore, 1963), vol. III, p. 1392; cited in Masri, *Animal Welfare in Islam*, p. 7.
151 This quote is narrated in a number of Islamic texts, including the *Mishkāt al-Masābih*; cited in Masri, *Animal Welfare in Islam*, p. 28.
152 Narrated by Abū Umāmah, transmitted by Al-Tabarānī, cited in Masri, *Animal Welfare in Islam*, p. 29.
153 M. R. Bawa Muhaiyadeen, *Come to the Secret Garden: Sufi Tales of Wisdom* (Philadelphia, PA, 1985), p. 26, cited in Foltz, '"This She-camel of God is a Sign to You"', in *A Communion of Subjects*, ed. Waldau and Patton, p. 156.
154 Foltz, *Animals in Islamic Tradition*, p. 146, suggested this term: I cannot think of one that better embraces the sentiments, yet it still assumes the higher status of the human animal.

SEVEN: Animals in Hinduism

1 Brihadaranyaka Upanishad, 1.4.1–5, cited in Joseph Campbell, *The Way of the Animal Powers* (London, 1984), p. 13.
2 From *The Bhagavad Gita with Commentary by Sri Sankaracharya*, trans. Alladi Mahadeva Sastry (Madras, 1987), p. 171; cited in Allen Anderson and Linda Anderson, *Dogs and the Women who Love Them* (Novato, CA, 2010), p. 219.
3 Raymond Hammer, *The World's Religions* (London, 1994), p. 170.
4 Ranchor Prime, ed., *Hinduism and Ecology: Seeds of Truth* (London, 1992), p. x.
5 A belief in the existence of one god or in the oneness of God. Monotheism can be defined even further: there is exclusive monotheism (as seen in Judaism, Christianity and Islam), inclusive monotheism and pluriform monotheism, which, while recognizing many distinct gods, postulates some underlying unity. Hinduism fits into this last definition.
6 Trilok Chandra Majupuria, *Sacred Animals of Nepal and India* (Lashkar, 2000), p. 9.
7 Jayaram V, 'Treatment of Animals in Hinduism', www.hinduwebsite.com, accessed 17 July 2015.
8 Hammer, *The World's Religions*, p. 173.
9 Shaman: a practitioner taking on the powers of a particular animal. In some societies a clan or even an unrelated group of people will devote themselves to a particular animal. The chosen animal becomes sacred and members of that group will not kill it, though the animal might be used for food. See Christopher Key Chapple, *Nonviolence to Animals, Earth, and Self in Asian Traditions* (Delhi, 1993), p. 7.
10 Majupuria, *Sacred Animals of Nepal and India*, p. 75.
11 Vasudha Narayanan, in *World Religions: The Illustrated Guide*, ed. Michael Coogan (London, 2003), p. 131.
12 Hammer, *The World's Religions*, p. 174.
13 Composed before 1000 BCE.
14 Narayanan, in *World Religions: The Illustrated Guide*, p. 131.

15 *The Upanishads*, trans. Alistair Shearer and Peter Russell (London, 1978), p. 43.
16 Chapple, *Nonviolence to Animals, Earth, and Self in Asian Traditions*, p. 42.
17 Jayaram V, 'Treatment of Animals in Hinduism'.
18 Hammer, *The World's Religions*, p. 175.
19 Ibid., p. 183.
20 Rigveda 10.86.14, trans. and ed. Wendy O'Flaherty (London, 1981), p. 260.
21 Rigveda 1.162.12, in Edwin Bryant, 'Strategies of Vedic Subversion: The Emergence of Vegetarianism in Post-Vedic India', in *A Communion of Subjects: Animals in Religion, Science and Ethics*, ed. Paul Waldau and Kimberley Patton (New York, 2006), p. 195.
22 Rigveda 1.162.21, trans. O'Flaherty, p. 91.
23 Bryant, 'Strategies of Vedic Subversion', in *A Communion of Subjects*, ed. Waldau and Patton, p. 196.
24 Ibid.
25 Yajnavalkya Smriti 7.179, in Bryant, 'Strategies of Vedic Subversion', in *A Communion of Subjects*, ed. Waldau and Patton, p. 197.
26 Yajnavalkya Smriti 7.181.
27 *The Upanishads*, trans. Shearer and Russell, p. 24.
28 Ibid., p. 26.
29 Ibid., p. 31.
30 Selections from the Mundaka Upanishad, trans. Shearer and Russell, pp. 26–41.
31 Chandogya Upanishad 6, trans. Shearer and Russell, p. 65.
32 Similar to *chi* in Taoism, *ruah* in Judaism and *pneuma* in Greek philosophy.
33 Kaushitaki Upanishad 111, trans. Shearer and Russell, p. 80.
34 Shvetashvatara Upanishad 4, trans. Shearer and Russell, p. 95. This is similar to: 'This is the truth:/ as from a well-blazing fire, sparks/ by the thousand issue forth of like form,/ so from the Imperishable, my friend,/ beings manifold/ are produced, and thither also go.' Mundaka Upanishad, cited in Kerry S. Walters and Lisa Portmess, *Religious Vegetarianism* (Albany, NY, 2001), p. 37.
35 Hammer, *The World's Religions*, p. 180.
36 Vishal Rao, 'What are the Sacred Animals of Hinduism?', www.answers.com, accessed 17 July 2015.
37 Rachel Storm, *Mythology of India: Myths and Legends of India, Tibet and Sri Lanka* (London, 2000), p. 36.
38 Hammer, *The World's Religions*, p. 182.
39 Walters and Portmess, *Religious Vegetarianism*, p. 38.
40 Ibid.
41 From *Manusmriti*, cited in Walters and Portmess, *Religious Vegetarianism*, pp. 41–2. Verse numbers are not given and have been added from other sources.
42 Shakunthala Jagannathan, *Hinduism: An Introduction* (Mumbai, 1984), p. 25.
43 Banwari, the day-editor of *Jansata*, a Hindi daily newspaper published in

Delhi, in conversation with Ranchor Prime, cited in Prime, ed., *Hinduism and Ecology*, p. 10.
44 Ibid., p. 12.
45 Ibid., p. 10.
46 The goddess Bhumi (or Prithri) was given the earth. Hindus view the earth as their mother who gave them life and without whom they would die.
47 Prime, ed., *Hinduism and Ecology*, p. 22.
48 Narayanan, in *World Religions: The Illustrated Guide*, p. 134.
49 Ibid., p. 136.
50 Hammer, *The World's Religions*, p. 185.
51 Majupuria, *Sacred Animals of Nepal and India*, p. 20.
52 Other sources state that Vishnu, asleep in the ocean, rests on a bed formed from the coils of Ananta, the chief of snake gods.
53 It has been suggested that a more suitable word to explain incarnation is *pradurbhava*, or 'manifestation', rather than *avatara*, which means 'descending'.
54 Narayanan, in *World Religions: The Illustrated Guide*, p. 137.
55 According to Hindu mythology, Manu was the first man and the precursor of humankind, either the son of Brahma or the son of the sun god Surya. Storm, *Mythology of India*, p. 55. This legend is mentioned in the Satapatha Brahmana.
56 Prime, ed., *Hinduism and Ecology*, p. 38.
57 Majupuria, *Sacred Animals of Nepal and India*, p. 65.
58 Ibid.
59 Ibid., pp. 65–6.
60 Prime, ed., *Hinduism and Ecology*, p. 41. Another version concerns the demon Hiranyakashipu, who had received a boon from Brahma that he would be safe from gods, beasts and men. However, Brahma had forgotten to include the boar in the list of animals. Hiranyakashipu dragged the earth to his home and placed it under the waters. Vishnu took on the form of a boar named Emusa, killed the demon with his tusks and put the earth back into its rightful position. Majupuria, *Sacred Animals of Nepal and India*, p. 66.
61 The next two incarnations do not include animals: Vamana the dwarf and Parasurama the warrior.
62 Bhagavata Purana (also known as Srimad Bhagavatam) 10.35, cited in Prime, ed., *Hinduism and Ecology*, p. 53.
63 Ibid., p. 56.
64 Jayadeva, the *Gita Govinda*, an elaborate poem of devotion to Krishna, cited in Prime, ed., *Hinduism and Ecology*, p. 51.
65 Majupuria, *Sacred Animals of Nepal and India*, p. 73.
66 Ibid., p. 33.
67 Ibid., p. 34.
68 Storm, *Mythology of India*, p. 36. There are slight variants of the story; in a well-known one, Lord Shiva commands his soldiers to bring him the head of the first creature they encounter, to replace Ganesha's head; they see an elephant and bring back its head.
69 Ibid., p. 13; see also Sister Nivedita and Ananda K. Coomaraswamy, *Myths*

and Legends of the Hindus and Buddhists (Kolkata, 2006), p. 275.
70 Storm, *Mythology of India*, p. 36.
71 Jagannathan, *Hinduism: An Introduction*, p. 48.
72 Ibid.
73 Lance Nelson, 'Cows, Elephants, Dogs and other Lesser Embodiments of Ātman: Reflections on Hindu Attitudes toward Non-human Animals', in *A Communion of Subjects*, ed. Waldau and Patton, p. 189.
74 Walters and Portmess, *Religious Vegetarianism*, p. 37.
75 Narayanan, in *World Religions: The Illustrated Guide*, p. 156.
76 Underlying the hierarchical social or 'caste' system is the fundamental Hindu idea that people are born into an existence that is due to their past karma. One's social status in this life is therefore traditionally viewed as predetermined, and the individual must adhere to the particular ritual practices and dietary rules of his or her *jati* (birth group). The untouchables are those who undertake occupations considered 'unclean' and 'defiling' to the 'higher' castes. 'Such occupations included dealing with animal hides and corpses because dead skin and flesh are considered polluting (the use of the Tamil word *pariah* – "drummer" – to mean "outcaste" derives from the fact that drumskins were made of "unclean" animal hides)', Narayanan, in *World Religions: The Illustrated Guide*, p. 161.
77 Jayaram V, 'Treatment of Animals in Hinduism'.
78 Prime, ed., *Hinduism and Ecology*, p. 72.
79 Jayaram V, 'Treatment of Animals in Hinduism'.
80 Nelson, 'Cows, Elephants, Dogs and Other Lesser Embodiments of Ātman', in *A Communion of Subjects*, ed. Waldau and Patton, p. 189.
81 Ibid.
82 Nelson, 'Cows, Elephants, Dogs and Other Lesser Embodiments of Ātman', in *A Communion of Subjects*, ed. Waldau and Patton, p. 182.
83 Ibid., p. 187.
84 Ibid.
85 A. D. Mudaliar, *The Cow, Lakshmi* (Tiruvannamalai, 1996), p. 11, cited in Nelson, 'Cows, Elephants, Dogs and Other Lesser Embodiments of Ātman', in *A Communion of Subjects*, ed. Waldau and Patton, p. 187.
86 Ibid.
87 Ibid.
88 Bhagavata Purana 8.4.10; cited in Nelson, 'Cows, Elephants, Dogs and Other Lesser Embodiments of Ātman', in *A Communion of Subjects*, ed. Waldau and Patton, p. 188.
89 Ibid.
90 *Caitanya Caritamrta of Krsnadasa Kaviraja*, trans. Edward C. Dimock, ed. Tony Stewart (Cambridge, 1999).
91 A. C. Bhaktivedanta Swami Prabhupada, *Sri Caitanya-caritāmrta of Krsnadāsa Kavirāja Gosvāmi*, Part 3, vol. 1 (New York, 1975), pp. 13 and 17.
92 Jeffrey Moussaieff Masson, *Dogs Never Lie about Love* (London, 1998), pp. 187–8. The *Mahabharata* ends with this story about the faithfulness of the dog and the human. This is from Masson's own translation from the

original Sanskrit in *Critical Text of the Mahabharata*, vol. IV (Pune, 1933–66), 17.3.7ff. It is retold in Jean Houston's *Mystical Dogs* (Maui, 2002), with several changes. In Liz Rosenberg's poem, 'Elegy for a Beagle Mutt', in *The Fire Music* (Pittsburgh, PA, 1986), she writes 'and I stay here, reminded of the Buddhist saint who waited at the gates of heaven ten thousand years with his faithful dog, till both were permitted in.' Thanks to Jeffrey Moussaieff Masson's footnote about this poem.

93 Cited in Nelson, 'Cows, Elephants, Dogs and Other Lesser Embodiments of Ātman', in *A Communion of Subjects*, ed. Waldau and Patton, p. 185.
94 Ibid.
95 Ibid.
96 Wendy Doniger O'Flaherty, *The Origin of Evil in Hindu Mythology* (Berkeley, CA, 1976), p. 173.
97 *Yogabhāsya* of Vyāsa, 2.33, cited in Nelson, 'Cows, Elephants, Dogs and Other Lesser Embodiments of Ātman', in *A Communion of Subjects*, ed. Waldau and Patton, p. 182.
98 Ibid., p. 186.
99 Jayaram V, 'Treatment of Animals in Hinduism'.
100 There are a number of passages in the Brāhmanas that express fear that in the next world the sacrificer will be eaten by his victim. *Manu* 5.55 warns that one who eats meat in this life will, in the next, be eaten by the same animal. Nelson, 'Cows, Elephants, Dogs and Other Lesser Embodiments of Ātman', in *A Communion of Subjects*, ed. Waldau and Patton, p. 192 n. 21.
101 Ibid., p. 184.
102 *Manu* 5.42, cited in Bryant, 'Strategies of Vedic Subversion', in *A Communion of Subjects*, ed. Waldau and Patton, p. 197.
103 *Manu* 5.38, cited in Bryant, 'Strategies of Vedic Subversion', in *A Communion of Subjects*, ed. Waldau and Patton, p. 197.
104 Ibid., p. 198.
105 *Santiparva Parva* 272.
106 Kurma Purana 2.22.75.
107 Kurma Purana 1.29.42.
108 Skanda Purana 2.9.6.
109 Bhagavata Purana 4.25.7–8.
110 Bhagavata Purana 7.15.10, cited in Nelson, 'Cows, Elephants, Dogs and Other Lesser Embodiments of Ātman', in *A Communion of Subjects*, ed. Waldau and Patton, p. 184.
111 Swami Harshananda, in *A Concise Encyclopaedia of Hinduism*, 3 vols (Bangalore, 2008); cited in Rajiv Malik, 'The Reality of Animal Sacrifice', *Hinduism Today* (April–June 2012), pp. 62–3; available at www.hinduismtoday.com, accessed 20 July 2015.
112 Tantric Hinduism is a system of practices for purification of the body and mind. It is a name scholars give to a style of meditation and ritual that arose in India no later than the fifth century CE. The earliest documented use of the word 'tantra' is in the Rigveda (10.71.9). It combines beliefs in magic and esoteric philosophy and emphasizes mystic symbols, sacred chants and other esoteric devotional techniques. Based on ancient animist

religions, it sometimes uses shamans to dispel demons and appease the gods. Among Hindus, Tantricism is closely associated with Kali, the goddess Shakti (worshipping female energy) or Lord Shiva.
113 A branch of Hinduism that worships Shakti (or Devi), the female principle of the divine, in her many forms. Practitioners of Shaktism (also known as Shaktas) believe the goddess to be the personification of the universe's primordial energy and the source of the cosmos. In philosophy and practice, Shaktism greatly resembles Shaivism, as the god Shiva is commonly considered to be the consort of Shakti.
114 Nelson, 'Cows, Elephants, Dogs and Other Lesser Embodiments of Ātman', in *A Communion of Subjects*, ed. Waldau and Patton, p. 182.
115 Cited ibid. Renouncers are ascetics. This movement emerged as a reactionary and revolutionary process against Vedic ritualism. Disillusionment with the Vedic tradition by the 6th century BCE, later combined with the influence of Buddhism and Jainism, led to a rise in ascetic sects. Discipline and personal sacrifice were aids to inner purification.
116 Cited in Chapple, *Nonviolence to Animals, Earth, and Self in Asian Traditions*, p. 16. Chapple (pp. 79–80) also cites:

The one who, desiring the pleasure of the self,
abstains from killing helpless animals with a stick,
would attain happiness.

That person who indeed sees beings as like his own self
Who has cast aside his stick
and whose anger is conquered

. . . who sees all beings
with the being of oneself as that of all beings

. . . the person who sees all things as the self . . . (*Mahabharata* 13.114).

117 Ibid., p. 17.
118 Ibid.
119 Cited ibid., p. 181.
120 Ibid., p. 182.
121 Arthur Osborne, *Ramana Maharshi and the Path of Self-knowledge* (London, 1973), p. 110.
122 T.M.P. Mahadevan, *Ramana Maharshi: The Sage of Arunacala* (London, 1977), p. 55.
123 *Bhagavad Gita* 5.18, cited in Chapple, *Nonviolence to Animals, Earth, and Self in Asian Traditions*, p. 52.
124 Ibid.
125 Ibid., p. 53.
126 *Apastamba Sutras*, Prasna 1, Patala 5, Khanda 17. 'The *Gautama sutras* forbid meat of animals that had five toes, or double rows of teeth or excessive quantity of hair, but exempted the meat of hedgehog, hare,

porcupine, the iguana, the rhinoceros and the tortoise'; Jayaram V, 'Treatment of Animals in Hinduism'.

127 Chapple, *Nonviolence to Animals, Earth, and Self in Asian Traditions*, p. 16.
128 Ibid.
129 *Manusmriti* 5.51, cited in Prime, *Hinduism and Ecology: Seeds of Truth*, p. 102.
130 Bryant, 'Strategies of Vedic Subversion', in *A Communion of Subjects*, ed. Waldau and Patton, p. 198.
131 Ibid., p. 198 (*Asvamedha Parva* 50).
132 Ibid. (*Asvamedha Parva* 115, 116).
133 Ibid., p. 199 (*Asvamedha Parva* 115, 116).
134 Bhagavata Purana 5.26.13–25, summarized in Bryant, 'Strategies of Vedic Subversion', in *A Communion of Subjects*, ed. Waldau and Patton, p. 201.
135 Nelson, 'Cows, Elephants, Dogs and Other Lesser Embodiments of Ātman', in *A Communion of Subjects*, ed. Waldau and Patton, p. 184.
136 Ibid., p. 180.
137 Majupuria, *Sacred Animals of Nepal and India*, p. 82.
138 Ibid., p. 79.
139 Nelson, 'Cows, Elephants, Dogs and Other Lesser Embodiments of Ātman', in *A Communion of Subjects*, ed. Waldau and Patton, p. 180.
140 Madeleine Biardeau, 'Kāmadhenu: The Mythical Cow, Symbol of Prosperity', in *Asian Mythologies*, ed. Yves Bonnefoy (Chicago, IL, 1995), p. 99.
141 Deryck O. Lodrick, 'On Religion and Milk Bovines in an Urban Indian Setting', *Current Anthropology*, xx (March 1979), p. 242.
142 Ibid.
143 Ibid.
144 M. K. Gandhi, *Young India*, 6 October 1921, p. 318. A. C. Bhaktivedanta Swami Prabhupada, a twentieth-century teacher of Hinduism, considered cattle a symbol of all that is necessary for a healthy, flourishing society: 'The protection of the cow and the bull . . . the basis for a simple and prosperous life. In Hindu tradition the bull represents dharma, moral principles, and the cow represents the earth. If they are both happy, society will flourish.' Srila Prabhupada dedicated himself to teaching the Krishna tradition to the Western world. His alternative vision for society was the twin concept of protecting Brahmins (spiritual teachers) and protecting cows. Prime, ed., *Hinduism and Ecology: Seeds of Truth*, p. 102.
145 Jayaram V, 'Treatment of Animals in Hinduism'.
146 Ibid.
147 Ibid.
148 Majupuria, *Sacred Animals of Nepal and India*, p. 96.
149 Ibid., pp. 96–7.
150 Ibid., p. 99.
151 Ibid., p. 100.
152 Ibid., p. 98.

References

EIGHT: Animals in Jainism

1 Stephanie Dowrick, *Seeking the Sacred* (Crows Nest, NSW, 2010), p. 236.
2 Kristi Wiley, 'Five-sensed Animals in Jainism', in *A Communion of Subjects: Animals in Religion, Science, and Ethics*, ed. Paul Waldau and Kimberley Patton (New York, 2006), p. 253.
3 The categories I use in most of the chapters do not apply here, because Jain cosmology is quite different from that found in monotheistic religions. Jains do not believe that there was a beginning to the universe, or that there was a time when particular species were created. The headings 'Solo', 'Birthing' and 'Parted' have been discarded as they do not address the themes found within Jainism.
4 There are two philosophical streams of thought within Jainism: the Sramana-Jain movements; and the Brahmana/Vedic/Puranic schools (Vedanta, Vaishnava and others).
5 Moksha: the 'release' from the endless cycle of death and rebirth known as samsara. It is achieved by the annihilation of all karmas and the attainment of the 'purest self' known as *siddha*.
6 Robert Brow, 'Origins of Religion', in *The World's Religions*, ed. Pat Alexander (Oxford, 1994), p. 42. The other six religions were Zoroastrianism, Judaism, Buddhism, Confucianism, Vedanta Monism and Taoism.
7 Myrtle Langley, 'Respect for All Life: Jainism', in *The World's Religions*, ed. Alexander, p. 207.
8 Erin Ladd Sanders, *In the Name of Peace* (London, 2010), p. 12.
9 Ibid.
10 Christopher Chapple, 'Inherent Values without Nostalgia: Animals and the Jaina Tradition', in *A Communion of Subjects*, ed. Waldau and Patton, p. 242.
11 Ibid.
12 Sanders, *In the Name of Peace*, p. 5.
13 Hermann Jacobi, *Jaina Sūtras Translated from the Prakrit* (Oxford, 1884), p. 260, cited in Chapple, 'Inherent Values without Nostalgia', in *A Communion of Subjects*, ed. Waldau and Patton, p. 244.
14 Sanders, *In the Name of Peace*, p. 10.
15 Acaranga Sutra 11.15.21, cited in Christopher Key Chapple, *Nonviolence to Animals, Earth, and Self in Asian Traditions* (Delhi, 1993), p. 7.
16 Sanders, *In the Name of Peace*, p. 13.
17 Chapple, 'Inherent Values without Nostalgia', in *A Communion of Subjects*, ed. Waldau and Patton, p. 245. Perhaps due to difficulties of translation, there are some minor variations in lists of the *tirthankaras*: Rsabha may be a bull or ox, Abhinanda an ape or monkey, Sumati a partridge or goose or curlew, and Ananta may be given as falcon or porcupine.
18 Chapple, 'Inherent Values without Nostalgia', in *A Communion of Subjects*, ed. Waldau and Patton, p. 242.
19 Wiley, 'Five-sensed Animals in Jainism', in *A Communion of Subjects*, ed. Waldau and Patton, p. 250.
20 Ibid., p. 252.

21 Chapple, 'Inherent Values without Nostalgia', in *A Communion of Subjects*, ed. Waldau and Patton, p. 241.
22 Ibid., p. 241.
23 Langley, 'Respect for All Life: Jainism', in *The World's Religions*, ed. Alexander, p. 212.
24 Chapple, *Nonviolence to Animals, Earth, and Self in Asian Traditions*, p. 13.
25 'The sadhaka [one who practises spiritual discipline] speaks words that are measured and beneficial to all living beings.' *Kartikeyanupreksa* 334.
26 'The Idea of Ahimsa and Vegetarianism', www.jainworld.com, accessed 21 July 2015.
27 Some sources list twelve *angas*.
28 *Agamas* are canonical texts of Jainism based on Mahavira's teachings and are the most ancient works in Jain literature.
29 Jacobi, *Jaina Sūtras*, p. 12, cited in Chapple, 'Inherent Values without Nostalgia', in *A Communion of Subjects*, ed. Waldau and Patton, p. 244.
30 Sanders, *In the Name of Peace*, p. 14.
31 Chapple, 'Inherent Values without Nostalgia', in *A Communion of Subjects*, ed. Waldau and Patton, p. 242.
32 Chapple, *Nonviolence to Animals, Earth, and Self in Asian Traditions*, p. 42.
33 Tattvartha Sutra 6.27, cited in Chapple, 'Inherent Values without Nostalgia', *A Communion of Subjects*, ed. Waldau and Patton, p. 248.
34 Wiley, 'Five-Sensed Animals in Jainism', in *A Communion of Subjects*, ed. Waldau and Patton, p. 252.
35 Natubhai Shah, *Jainism: The World of the Conquerer*, vol. 1 (Brighton, 1998), pp. 153–4.
36 Wiley, 'Five-Sensed Animals in Jainism', in *A Communion of Subjects*, ed. Waldau and Patton, p. 253.
37 Chapple, *Nonviolence to Animals, Earth, and Self in Asian Traditions*, pp. 12–13.
38 Shah, *Jainism: the World of the Conquerer*, 1, pp. 153–4.
39 Chapple, *Nonviolence to Animals, Earth, and Self in Asian Traditions*, p. 18.
40 Ibid.
41 Sanders, *In the Name of Peace*, p. 17.
42 Ibid., p. 16.
43 'The Idea of Ahimsa and Vegetarianism', www.jainworld.com.
44 Chapple, *Nonviolence to Animals, Earth, and Self in Asian Traditions*, p. 10. *Nigoda*: a realm in which the lowest forms of life reside in endless numbers and without any hope of release by self-effort. Jain scriptures describe *nigodas* as having a very short life and are said to pervade each and every part of the universe, even in the tissues of plants and the flesh of animals.
45 'The Idea of Ahimsa and Vegetarianism', www.jainworld.com.
46 Chapple, *Nonviolence to Animals, Earth, and Self in Asian Traditions*, p. 99.
47 Chapple, 'Inherent Values without Nostalgia', in *A Communion of Subjects*, ed. Waldau and Patton, p. 245.
48 Deryck O. Lodrick, *Sacred Cows, Sacred Places: Origins and Survivals of Animal Homes in India* (Berkeley, CA, 1981), p. 13.
49 Chapple, 'Inherent Values without Nostalgia', in *A Communion of Subjects*, ed. Waldau and Patton, p. 247.

50 Ibid.
51 Pratikramana Sutra, cited in Wiley, 'Five-Sensed Animals in Jainism', in *A Communion of Subjects*, ed. Waldau and Patton, p. 254.
52 Sanders, *In the Name of Peace*, p. 16.
53 Wiley, 'Five-sensed Animals in Jainism', in *A Communion of Subjects*, ed. Waldau and Patton, p. 253.

NINE: Animals in Buddhism

1 Cited in Norm Phelps, *The Great Compassion: Buddhism and Animal Rights* (New York, 2004), p. 45. This prayer includes elements of Buddhist compassion and loving kindness. The longer version reads: 'May all beings be free from enmity; May all beings be free from injury; May all beings be free from suffering; May all beings be happy.'
2 Kerry S. Walters and Lisa Portmess, *Religious Vegetarianism* (Albany, NY, 2001), p. 86.
3 Phelps, *The Great Compassion*, p. 73.
4 For more information on ahimsa, see Chapters Seven and Eight.
5 In Buddhism, the elephant is held to be sacred because it is also said that the elephant offered flowers to Buddha, and carried the gem of wishes and his sacred alms-bowl.
6 Bodhisattva is a Sanskrit word meaning 'enlightened being'; one who is destined for enlightenment, or Buddhahood. In the Mahayana tradition, the bodhisattva postpones his goal of becoming a Buddha in order to relieve the suffering of sentient beings.
7 'Why Animals Matter: A Religious and Philosophical Perspective: Buddhism', www.think-differently-about-sheep.com, accessed 21 July 2015.
8 Ethel Beswick, *Jataka Tales: Birth Stories of Buddha* (New Delhi, 1999), p. 3.
9 Dhammapada 129–32, cited in Phelps, *The Great Compassion*, p. 47. The Dhammapada is a collection of the Buddha's sayings that forms part of the Pali Canon.
10 Kutadanta Sutta 5, 18. Maurice Walshe, trans., *Thus I Have Heard* (London, 1987), p. 138.
11 Theravada is prominent in Sri Lanka, Southeast Asia, Burma and Thailand. Mahayana is found in China, Nepal, Tibet, Korea, Japan and Vietnam. Martine Batchelor and Kerry Brown, eds, *Buddhism and Ecology* (London, 1992), p. 8.
12 Wulf Metz, 'The Enlightened One: Buddhism', in *The World's Religions*, ed. Pat Alexander (London, 1994), p. 235.
13 Which version is authentic? Both forms of scripture were not written down until at least 55 years after the Buddha's death, and both report traditions that date to the same period. We do not know, but, apart from the matter of meat found in alms-bowls, both sets of scripture agree that the Buddha forbade his disciples to eat meat. Phelps, *The Great Compassion*, pp. 77 and 80. The Buddha's cousin, Devadatta, pursued the more conservative path. His ruling on meat was that if monks found

scraps of meat in their alms-bowl, they could not eat it. Buddha, on the other hand, said that monks have to accept whatever they find in their alms-bowl, including meat scraps, provided the animal had not been killed in order to provide meat for them.
14 Phelps, *The Great Compassion*, p. xviii.
15 Nagarjuna and Sakya Pandita, *Elegant Sayings* (Emeryville, CA, 1977).
16 *Buddhism Perfection of Wisdom in Eight Thousand Lines* 321–2, the earliest of the Prajnaparamita Sutras, a genre of Mahayana Buddhist scriptures dealing with the subject of the Perfection of Wisdom. 'Why Animals Matter: A Religious and Philosophical Perspective: Buddhism', www.think-differently-about-sheep.com.
17 Metz, 'One Goal, Many Paths', in *The World's Religions*, ed. Alexander, p. 237.
18 Jonathan Landaw and Andy Weber, *Images of Enlightenment: Tibetan Art in Practice* (Ithaca, NY, 1993), pp. 58–9; cited in Phelps, *The Great Compassion*, p. 153.
19 Ibid., p. 154.
20 Ibid.
21 Ajahn Pongsak, cited in Kerry Brown, 'In the Water there were Fish and the Fields were Full of Rice', in *Buddhism and Ecology*, ed. Batchelor and Brown, p. 99.
22 Vinaya Pitaka 4.205–6, cited in Lily de Silva, 'The Hills Wherein My Soul Delights: Exploring the Stories and Teachings', in *Buddhism and Ecology*, ed. Batchelor and Brown, p. 25.
23 Helena Norberg-Hodge, 'May a Hundred Plants Grow from One Seed: The Ecological Tradition of Ladakh Meets the Future', in *Buddhism and Ecology*, ed. Batchelor and Brown, p. 43.
24 Vinaya Pitaka, Sutta-vighanga, para. 1, cited in Batchelor and Brown, eds, *Buddhism and Ecology*, p. 13.
25 Peter Harvey, *An Introduction to Buddhist Ethics* (Cambridge, 2000), p. 151.
26 Sutta Nipata 1.8, transmitted orally from the fifth century BCE until it was recorded in Sri Lanka in the first century CE; cited in Batchelor and Brown, eds, *Buddhism and Ecology*, pp. 4–5.
27 Phelps, *The Great Compassion*, p. 45.
28 Sentient beings are classed as those equipped with the physical make-up to support consciousness.
29 Phelps, *The Great Compassion*, p. 49.
30 Vinaya Pitaka 111.42, cited in de Silva, 'The Hills Wherein my Soul Delights', in *Buddhism and Ecology*, ed. Batchelor and Brown, p. 23.
31 Dhammapada 129–32, cited in Phelps, *The Great Compassion*, p. 47. This is another example of 'the Golden Rule', also proposed in the Jewish sage Hillel the Elder's admonition not to do to another what we would not want done to us, and Jesus' 'do unto others . . .'.
32 Phelps, *The Great Compassion*, p. 31.
33 Cited in 'Why Animals Matter: A Religious and Philosophical Perspective: Buddhism', www.think-differently-about-sheep.com.
34 Ibid.

35 Phelps, *The Great Compassion*, p. 32.
36 Ibid., p. 33.
37 Kalu Rinpoche, *The Dharma that Illuminates All Beings Impartially Like the Light of the Sun and the Moon* (Albany, NY, 1986), p. 25.
38 Ian Harris, '"A Vast Unsupervised Recycling Plant": Animals and the Buddhist Cosmos', in *A Communion of Subjects*, ed. Waldau and Patton, p. 208.
39 In the Vinaya Pitaka 1.87f there is a story about a *naga* (snake) who gains admission to the *sangha* by taking on the form of a youth. He reverts back to his snake form at night. When he is discovered to be a snake, he is expelled from the order by the Buddha: 'You *nagas* are not capable of spiritual growth in this doctrine and discipline. However . . . observe the fast on the fourteenth, fifteenth, and eighth day of the half month. Thus you will be released from being a *naga* and quickly attain human form.' Cited ibid., p. 214 n. 8.
40 Ibid., p. 208.
41 Ibid.
42 Ibid.
43 'Why Animals Matter: A Religious and Philosophical Perspective: Buddhism', www.think-differently-about-sheep.com.
44 Cited in Phelps, *The Great Compassion*, p. 34. Phelps had heard it from his teacher, Lama Kalsang Gyaltsen.
45 Patrul Rinpoche was a nineteenth-century Tibetan yogi born in eastern Tibet; 'Why Animals Matter: A Religious and Philosophical Perspective: Buddhism', www.think-differently-about-sheep.com.
46 Cited in Harris, '"A Vast Unsupervised Recycling Plant"', in *A Communion of Subjects*, ed. Waldau and Patton, p. 211.
47 Shantideva, *Bodhicaryavatara* 8.114. *A Guide to the Bodhisattva's Way of Life*, trans. Stephen Batchelor (Dharamsala, 1979), p. 118.
48 *Jataka* 11.423, cited in de Silva, 'The Hills Wherein my Soul Delights', in *Buddhism and Ecology*, ed. Batchelor and Brown, p. 24. The Buddhist concept of merit also encourages a gentle non-violent attitude towards living creatures. It is said that if someone throws dish-washing water into a pool where there are small creatures so that they can feed on the tiny particles of food washed away, that person accumulates spiritual merit even by such trivial generosity. Anguttara Nikaya 1.161, cited ibid.
49 Ya Un Sunim, 'On Self-admonition', unpublished translation by Martine Batchelor, cited in Batchelor and Brown, eds, *Buddhism and Ecology*, p. 8.
50 Harris, '"A Vast Unsupervised Recycling Plant"', in *A Communion of Subjects*, ed. Waldau and Patton, p. 209.
51 Donald E. Gjertson, *Ghosts, Gods, and Retribution: Nine Buddhist Miracle Tales from Six Dynasties and Early T'ang China* (Amherst, MA, 1978), pp. 14–15.
52 George W. Clarke, 'The Yü-Li or Precious Records', *Journal of the China Branch of the Royal Asiatic Society*, XXVIII (1898), p. 309.
53 Raghu Vira, *Chinese Poems and Pictures on Ahimsa* (Nagpur, 1934), p. 2.
54 Ibid., p. 70.
55 Phelps, *The Great Compassion*, p. 165.

56 Bentham's famous question: 'The question is not, Can they [animals] *reason*? Nor can they *talk*? but can they *suffer*?'
57 Cited in 'Why Animals Matter: A Religious and Philosophical Perspective: Buddhism', www.think-differently-about-sheep.com.
58 They were handed down orally, and it is not known when they were gathered together; Ellen. C. Babbitt, Introduction to *More Jataka Tales* (Varanasi, 2003).
59 Noor Inayat, Introduction to *Twenty Jataka Tales* (Varanasi, 2003).
60 Ibid.
61 Beswick, *Jataka Tales*, p. 2.
62 Mark W. McGinnis, *Buddhist Animal Wisdom Stories* (Boston, MA, 2004), p. 16.
63 Chapple, *Nonviolence to Animals, Earth, and Self in Asian Traditions*, p. 23.
64 'Animals', in *Encyclopedia of Buddhism*, ed. G. P. Malalasekara (Colombo, 1965), vol. I, pp. 667–72.
65 Chapple, *Nonviolence to Animals, Earth, and Self in Asian Traditions*, p. 24.
66 *Jataka* Tale 18, retold from H. T. Francis and E. J. Thomas, *Jataka Tales* (Cambridge, 1916), pp. 20–22.
67 Padmanabh S. Jaini, 'Indian Perspectives on the Spirituality of Animals', *Buddhist Philosophy and Culture: Essays in Honour of N. A. Jayawickrema*, ed. David. J. Kalupahana and W. G. Weeraratne (Colombo, 1987), pp. 172–3.
68 Ibid., p. 173.
69 Kazuaki Tanahashi, ed., *Moon in a Dewdrop: Writings of Zen Master Dogen* (Albany, NY, 1985), pp. 71–2.
70 Kobayashi Issa (1763–1828). Lucien Stryk and Takashi Ikemoto, eds and trans., *Zen Poetry: Let the Spring Breeze Enter* (Athens, OH, 1977), p. 60. Another version is 'Swarms of mosquitos –/ but without them / it's a little lonely'; Stephen Addiss, *A Haiku Menagerie* (New York, 1992), p. 82.
71 Pillar edict cited in Walters and Portmess, *Religious Vegetarianism*, p. 77.
72 Cited ibid., p. 76. 'To two-footed and four-footed beings, to birds and aquatic animals, I have given various things including the gift of life'; Ashoka, 'Pillar Edict 2', in Ven. S. Dhannika, *The Edicts of King Ashoka: An English Rendering* (Kandy, 1993); available at www.cs.colostate.edu, accessed 24 July 2015.
73 Ibid.
74 'Rock Edict 1', ibid.
75 'Pillar Edict 3', ibid. The list of 24 species includes parrots, geese, ducks, fish, turtles, pigeons, porcupines, squirrels, deer and donkeys. The translator notes that the identification of some of the animals is 'conjectural'; ibid. p. 175.
76 'Pillar Edict 7', ibid.
77 'Rock Edict 2', ibid.
78 'Why Animals Matter: A Religious and Philosophical Perspective: Buddhism', www.think-differently-about-sheep.com.
79 Ibid.
80 Cited in Walters and Portmess, *Religious Vegetarianism*, p. 75.
81 'Rock Edict 1', in Dhannika, *The Edicts of King Ashoka*.

82 Ibid. In China, a number of rulers in the seventh and eighth centuries followed Ashoka's example by restricting hunting and the consumption of flesh.
83 Mahayana Mahaparinirvana Sutra, cited in Phelps, *The Great Compassion*, p. 127.
84 Composed in India between the first century BCE and the sixth century CE.
85 Walters and Portmess, *Religious Vegetarianism*, p. 64. The suggested dates of composition vary between 350 and 400 CE, with the introductory chapter and the last two chapters being added at a later date. A number of translations of the text were made from Sanskrit into Chinese from the early fifth century CE.
86 *Surangama Sutra*, cited ibid., pp. 64–5.
87 Ibid., p. 65.
88 Ibid., p. 66.
89 *Lankavatara Sutra*, cited in *Religious Vegetarianism*, pp. 73–4.
90 Ibid., p. 70.
91 Ibid., p. 72.
92 Har Dayal, in *Buddhist Sanskrit Literature* (London, 1931), p. 199; cited in Chapple, *Nonviolence to Animals, Earth, and Self in Asian Traditions*, p. 29.
93 Dayal, *The Bodhisattva Doctrine*, p. 175.
94 *The Buddha Speaks the Brahma Net Sutra*, trans. Dharma Realm Buddhist University (Talmage, CA, 1981), p. 130.
95 *The Mahaparinirvana Sutra*, trans. Kosho Yamamoto (Obe City, 1973–5), p. 91, cited in Phelps, *The Great Compassion*, p. 65.
96 *Jivaka Sutta*, Majjhima Nikaya 55.3, in *The Middle Length Discourses of the Buddha*, trans. Bhikkhu Nanamoli and Bhikkhu Bodhi (Somerville, MA, 1995), p. 474.
97 Jivaka Sutta 55.12, ibid., p. 476.
98 Phelps, *The Great Compassion*, p. 130.
99 'Nowhere in the sutras or the teachings of the ancient sages do we find the notion that animals killed for food by ordinary beings benefit karmically from their misfortune. What we do find is the warning that those who participate – even indirectly – in the killing of innocent animals will suffer in future lives because of the negative karma they incur.' Ibid., p. 131.
100 Roshi Philip Kapleau, cited in Walters and Portmess, *Religious Vegetarianism*, p. 85.
101 Janet Gyatso, *Apparitions of the Self: The Secret Autobiographies of a Tibetan Visionary* (Princeton, NJ, 1998), p. 137.
102 Ibid.
103 Shabkar (Shabkar Tsogdruk Rangdrol), *The Life of Shabkar: The Autobiography of a Tibetan Yogin*, trans. Matthew Ricard (Ithaca, NY, 2001), p. 232. Phelps notes that the Jowo Rinpoche is a famous statue of the Buddha. Buddhists are instructed to show an image of the Buddha the same respect that they would to the living Buddha – hence this was a serious vow (*The Great Compassion*, p. 149).
104 Shabkar, *The Life of Shabkar*, p. 349.

105 Patrul Rinpoche, *The Words of My Perfect Teacher* (Boston, MA, 1994), p. 207.
106 Dalai Lama, *Freedom in Exile* (London, 1990), cited in Walters and Portmess, *Religious Vegetarianism*, p. 87. He did not eat the chicken.
107 Owing to health reasons, on his doctor's advice.
108 Dalai Lama and Fabien Ouaki, *Imagine All the People: A Conversation with the Dalai Lama on Money, Politics, and Life as It Could Be* (Somerville, MA, 1999), p. 30.
109 Michael Freeman, 'Sung', in *Food in Chinese Culture: Anthropological and Historical Perspectives*, ed. K. C. Chang (New Haven, CT, 1977), p. 164.
110 Donald S. Lopez, *Buddhist Scriptures* (London, 2004), p. 402.
111 Ibid., p. 403.
112 Ibid.
113 Ibid.
114 Ibid., p. 404.
115 Zhu Hong, *Jiesha wen*, from a longer tract known as *Jiesha fansheng wen*, in Lianchi dashi [Zhu Hong], *Lianchi dashi quanji*, trans. Daniel Stevenson (Taipei, 1992), pp. 3345–54; cited in Lopez, *Buddhist Scriptures*, p. 409.
116 Ibid., p. 410.
117 Ibid., pp. 411–12.
118 Ibid., p. 412.
119 Ibid., pp. 413–14.
120 Ibid., pp. 414–15.
121 Keeping, feeding and fattening sheep for profit and sale; buying and killing sheep for profit; raising, fattening and killing pigs for profit; buying and killing pigs for profit; raising, fattening and killing calves for profit; buying and raising calves for profit; raising hens for profit, and killing them when fully grown; buying hens for profit and killing them; fishing; hunting; selling fish; catching birds by net; charming snakes; Phelps, *The Great Compassion*, pp. 85–6.
122 Harris, '"A Vast Unsupervised Recycling Plant"', in *A Communion of Subjects*, ed. Waldau and Patton, p. 210.
123 Samyutta Nikaya i.224, cited ibid.
124 Saratthappakasini 2.112, cited ibid.
125 Lopez, *Buddhist Scriptures*, p. 395.
126 Ibid.
127 Zhu Hong, *Fangsheng yi*, in *Lianchi dashi quanji*, pp. 3333–42, cited in Lopez, *Buddhist Scriptures*, p. 396.
128 Ibid., p. 397.
129 Taking refuge in the Three Jewels is generally considered to make one officially a Buddhist, which makes the following liturgy even more startling.
130 Lopez, *Buddhist Scriptures*, p. 395.
131 A community of ordained Buddhist monks and nuns. It may also refer to a Buddhist congregation, or to those who have attained enlightenment.
132 Cited in Lopez, *Buddhist Scriptures*, p. 398.
133 Phelps, *The Great Compassion*, p. 107.

134 'Animal Liberation Report', *Vajrayana News* (March 2002), p. 4.
135 M. W. de Visser, *Ancient Buddhism in Japan: Sutras and Ceremonies in Use in the Seventh and Eighth Centuries AD and their History in Later Times* (Leiden, 1935), p. 198, cited in Chapple, *Nonviolence to Animals, Earth, and Self in Asian Traditions*, p. 29.
136 Ibid., p. 30.
137 Ibid.
138 Pure Land Buddhism is a broad branch of Mahayana Buddhism, and one of the most widely practised traditions of Buddhism in East Asia. It is also known as Shin Buddhism and Amidism, and is based on the Pure Land sutras that were first brought to China around 150 CE.
139 Zhu Hong, cited in Walters and Portmess, *Religious Vegetarianism*, p. 81. Zhu Hong also wrote: 'As a man values his life,/ So do animals love theirs./ Releasing life accords with the mind of heaven;/ Releasing life agrees with the teaching of the Buddha . . ./ Releasing life is the compassion of Kuan-yin;/ Releasing life is the deed of P'u-hsien./ By releasing life one comes to realize the truth of no birth./ By releasing life one ends transmigration.' Zhu Hong, cited ibid., p. 82. Kuan-yin (Guanyin) and P'u-hsien are bodhisattvas of compassion.
140 Chapple, *Nonviolence to Animals, Earth, and Self in Asian Traditions*, p. 30.
141 Ibid., p. 39.
142 Kyoko Motomochi Nakamura, trans. and ed., *Miraculous Stories from the Japanese Buddhist Tradition: The 'Nihon Ryoiki' of the Monk Kyokai* (Cambridge, MA, 1973), p. 117.
143 Ibid., p. 127. In another story, narrated by a monk, a wealthy man becomes ill due to his sacrificial killing of an ox each year for the past seven years. He then dedicates himself to buying animals and releasing them. At the end of seven virtuous years, he dies, but after nine days comes back to life. He then tells his family what had happened. He had been judged by seven oxen who were going to kill him and eat him, but then ten million men, who had been the creatures he had had released, came to his rescue and saved him and then restored him to life. Ibid., pp. 164–6.
144 Ivette Vargas, 'Snake-Kings, Boars' Heads, Deer-parks, Monkey Talk: Animals as Transmitters and Transformers in Indian and Tibetan Buddhist Narratives', in *A Communion of Subjects*, ed. Waldau and Patton, p. 231. The source of Tibetans' physical strength and courage is attributed to the demoness.
145 Ibid., p. 220.
146 Dhammapada Atthakatha 1.58ff, cited in de Silva, 'The Hills Wherein my Soul Delights', in *Buddhism and Ecology*, ed. Batchelor and Brown, p. 23.
147 Vinaya Pitaka 11.194–5, cited ibid. Indra is the Indian sky god whose herds of elephants are seen as clouds.
148 Vargas, 'Snake-kings, Boars' Heads, Deer-parks, Monkey Talk', p. 219.
149 Ibid.
150 Ibid.
151 Ibid., p. 223.
152 Ibid.

153 Written on the information card outside its enclosure at the Amsterdam Zoo. This is similar to the legend regarding the markings on the tabby cat, made by Muhammad as he blessed the feline (see Chapter Six n. 18).
154 Vargas, 'Snake-kings, Boars' Heads, Deer-parks, Monkey Talk'.
155 Ibid., p. 224.
156 Ibid.
157 As is also the case in Hinduism (see Chapter Seven).
158 Vargas, 'Snake-kings, Boars' Heads, Deer-parks, Monkey Talk', p. 229.
159 Ibid.
160 Ibid.
161 Ibid., p. 232.
162 Ibid.
163 Ibid.
164 Statement by Tenzin Gyatso, fourteenth Dalai Lama. Martin Palmer, Anne Nah and Ivan Hattingh, eds, *Faith and Nature* (London, 1988).
165 Tenzin Gyatso, fourteenth Dalai Lama, *Universal Responsibility and the Good Heart* (Dharamsala, 1980), p. 78.
166 Harris, '"A Vast Unsupervised Recycling Plant"', in *A Communion of Subjects*, ed. Waldau and Patton, p. 213.
167 Phelps, *The Great Compassion*, p. 93.
168 McGinnis, *Buddhist Animal Wisdom Stories*, p. 81.

TEN: Animals in Religion in China and Japan

1 Roel Sterckx, '"Of a Tawny Bull We Make Offering": Animals in Early Chinese Religion', in *A Communion of Subjects: Animals in Religion, Science and Ethics,* ed. Paul Waldau and Kimberley Patton (New York, 2006), p. 260.
2 Ibid.
3 For example, in Chinese cosmology there were ten suns. The *Shan Hai Jing* says that the suns were carried by birds, whereas the *Huainanzi* says that the birds are in the suns. This was a time of peace. Then the ten suns appeared at once in the time of Yao, destroying the grain. Yao ordered Archer Yi to shoot at the suns. Nine of the birds died, dropping their feathers; only one sun survived. Anthony Christie, *Chinese Mythology* (London, 1996), p. 62.
4 This story arose from texts from the third and sixth centuries CE involving the cosmic egg, but it was probably nor incorporated into Chinese tradition until later.
5 Rachel Storm, *Mythology of Asia and the Far East* (London, 2006), p. 57.
6 Christie, *Chinese Mythology*, p. 56.
7 Ibid., p. 36.
8 Ibid., p. 52.
9 Because dragons represented the *yang* principle, they were often accompanied by water or clouds, which were *yin*.
10 Storm, *Mythology of Asia and the Far East*, p. 58.
11 Though its origins are unknown, the dragon incorporated aspects of the Indian *naga* or snake gods, which are still worshipped as nature deities in

Hinduism as the snake goddess Manasa and in Buddhism as the snake king Mucalinda; Janet Westwood, ed., *The Cricket and the Dragon: Animals in Asian Art* (Melbourne, 2008), p. 5.
12 Christie, *Chinese Mythology*, p. 42.
13 Storm, *Mythology of Asia and the Far East*, p. 59.
14 Ibid.
15 Julia Ching, *Chinese Religions* (Maryknoll, NY, 1993), p. 19.
16 Christie, *Chinese Mythology*, p. 125.
17 Sterckx, '"Of a Tawny Bull We Make Offering"', in *A Communion of Subjects*, ed. Waldau and Patton, p. 263.
18 Ching, *Chinese Religions*, p. 19.
19 Sterckx, '"Of a Tawny Bull We Make Offering"', in *A Communion of Subjects*, ed. Waldau and Patton, p. 262.
20 Christie, *Chinese Mythology*, p. 131.
21 Ibid., p. 132.
22 Ching, *Chinese Religions*, p. 23.
23 Ibid., p. 24.
24 Ibid.
25 Ibid., p. 25.
26 Westwood, ed., *The Cricket and the Dragon*, p. 17.
27 Ching, *Chinese Religions*, p. 26.
28 Christie, *Chinese Mythology*, p. 15. Shang is also known as the Yin period. The *Shiji*, the first history of China, was completed around 109 BCE by Sima Qian.
29 Ching, *Chinese Religions*, p. 35.
30 Ibid.
31 John Berthrong, 'Sages and Immortals: Chinese Religions', in *The World's Religions*, ed. Pat Alexander (London, 1994), p. 245.
32 Ching, *Chinese Religions*, p. 15.
33 Ibid., p. 28.
34 Ibid., p. 16. Engraved inscriptions of what were referred to as 'dragon bones' (tortoise shells and animal bones) led to the discovery of ruins of the ancient Shang capital at Anyang, Henan Province, in 1911. 'Dragon bones' is a term used in Chinese pharmacology.
35 Sterckx, '"Of a Tawny Bull We Make Offering"', in *A Communion of Subjects*, ed. Waldau and Patton, p. 265.
36 Ibid., p. 266.
37 Ibid., p. 262.
38 Ching, *Chinese Religions*, p. 36.
39 Ibid.
40 In later centuries these developed into fully formed, three-dimensional figures such as cows, goats, birds, dragons and lions. Perhaps the animal features indicated the particular flesh they contained as a sacrificial offering.
41 Ching, *Chinese Religions*, p. 62.
42 Sterckx, '"Of a Tawny Bull We Make Offering"', in *A Communion of Subjects*, ed. Waldau and Patton, p. 262. The 'horse walk demon' was a spirit that had to be appeased to save horses from being injured on the road.

43 Ibid.
44 Western Zhou: *c.* 1050–771 BCE; Eastern Zhou: 770–256 BCE.
45 Edward Shaughnessy, trans., *Sources of Western Zhou History* (Berkeley, CA, 1991), pp. 197–8.
46 Arthur Waley, trans., *The Book of Songs* (New York, 1996), p. 315.
47 Western Han: 206 BCE–9 CE; Eastern Han: 25–220 CE.
48 Sterckx, '"Of a Tawny Bull We Make Offering"', in *A Communion of Subjects*, ed. Waldau and Patton, p. 267.
49 One record from 565 BCE notes that priests had failed to obtain a favourable response after three separate divination sessions, so the sacrificial bull was set free; ibid.
50 Ibid.
51 Ibid. Wang Mang, founder of the short-lived Xin dynasty (9–23 CE), was also known for his prolific sacrificial cults. At more than 1,700 cult centres he had more than 3,000 birds and beasts sacrificed. When it turned out to be too expensive, Wang substituted other animals – chickens in place of ducks and geese, and dogs instead of deer.
52 Ibid., p. 268.
53 Ibid.
54 Ibid.
55 The animals found there have been mainly sheep, with the occasional horse or ox; ibid.
56 Ibid., p. 264.
57 Ibid., p. 268.
58 Ibid., p. 262.
59 Roy Willis, ed., *World Mythology: The Illustrated Guide* (London, 1993), p. 101.
60 In the myth of Zhi nu the weaver maid, she marries an oxherd. They were so in love that her weaving was neglected. She was ordered back to her loom and they were only allowed to meet as a couple every seventh night of the seventh month. Zhi nu would meet him, crossing a bridge made of birds. This story was remembered in an annual event, for on the seventh night of the seventh month, girls would hold competitions in needlework: 'It was hoped that the Maid herself would honour the occasion in the form of a spider and weave a web across an opened gourd . . . The ladies of the Tang emperor Xuan Zong used, we are told, on this night to shut a spider in a box. In the morning the tension of the web which the spider had woven was inspected and the tightness or otherwise of the weave was taken as a judgement on the weaving skill of its captor.' Christie, *Chinese Mythology*, p. 68.
61 Ibid., p. 93.
62 Sterckx, '"Of a Tawny Bull We Make Offering"', in *A Communion of Subjects*, ed. Waldau and Patton, p. 269.
63 Ibid.
64 Christie, *Chinese Mythology*, p. 48.
65 E. N. Anderson and Lisa Raphals, 'Daoism and Animals', in *A Communion of Subjects*, ed. Waldau and Patton, p. 276.
66 Burton Watson, *The Complete Works of Chuang Tzu* (New York, 1968), p. 33.

67 Anderson and Raphals, 'Daoism and Animals', in *A Communion of Subjects*, ed. Waldau and Patton, p. 276.
68 Ibid., p. 277. The crane is still viewed as sacred in Korea and Japan.
69 Edward Werner, *Animal Tales and Folklore of China* (London, 1986), p. 149.
70 Manchu, one of the Tungusic languages originally from Eastern Siberia and Manchuria, was spoken by two Chinese dynasties, the Jin (1115–1234) and the Qing (1644–1911); Anderson and Raphals, 'Daoism and Animals', in *A Communion of Subjects*, ed. Waldau and Patton, p. 278.
71 Ibid., p. 279.
72 Ibid.
73 Ibid., p. 280.
74 Sterckx, '"Of a Tawny Bull We Make Offering"', in *A Communion of Subjects,* ed. Waldau and Patton, p. 264.
75 Anderson and Raphals, 'Daoism and Animals', in *A Communion of Subjects*, ed. Waldau and Patton, p. 281.
76 Ibid., p. 288. 'The bizarre imaginary animals of the *Shan Hai Jing* ("Classic of Mountains and Seas") are almost certainly the visionary experiences of shamans traveling to the unreal "mountains and seas" in question, but the *Shan Hai Jing* never became a canonical Daoist text.' Ibid., p. 281.
77 *Liexian Zhuan* 19, 36 and 47; ibid., p. 283.
78 *Liexian Zhuan* 60; ibid.
79 *A Gallery of Chinese Immortals*, trans. Lionel Giles (London, 1948; reprinted New York, 1979).
80 Christie, *Chinese Mythology*, p. 72.
81 Michael Loewe, *Ways to Paradise: The Chinese Quest for Immortality* (London, 1979), p. 200; this is a translation from the back of a bronze mirror, itself a cosmic symbol.
82 For the Chinese, the white hare of the moon grinds the elixir of life. This idea comes from the story of Chang-O, the beautiful wife of the archer King Ho Yi. The Queen Mother of Heaven gave Ho Yi a pill containing the elixir of immortality. The King drank too much wine so gave it to Chang'e for safe keeping. She swallowed it and discovered the gift of flight. When Ho Yi awoke, he asked for the pill. She flew away to the moon, coughed it up, and the pill changed into a white hare. She demanded that the hare restore the elixir, and gave it a mortar and pestle to grind it, but she was now ageing and Chang'e turned into a three-legged toad. Boria Sax, *The Mythical Zoo: An Encyclopedia of Animals in World Myth, Legend, and Literature* (Santa Barbara, CA, 2001), p. 136.
83 Christie, *Chinese Mythology*, p. 80.
84 Sax, *The Mythical Zoo*, p. 22.
85 Rodney Taylor, 'Of Animals and Humans: The Confucian Perspective', in *A Communion of Subjects*, ed. Waldau and Patton, p. 293.
86 Ibid., p. 294.
87 *Lunyu* (Analects of Confucius) 3.17; Arthur Waley, trans., *The Analects of Confucius* (New York, 1938), p. 98.
88 Han Yu (768–824), poet and prose master, was a leading Tang Confucianist and anti-Buddhist.

89 Eliot Weinberger, 'Han Yu's Address to the Crocodiles', in *The Language of the Birds: Tales, Texts, and Poems of Interspecies Communication*, ed. David M. Guss (San Francisco, CA, 1985), pp. 268–70.
90 Christie, *Chinese Mythology*, p. 56.
91 In the *Liezi*, Nugua cut off the feet of a tortoise to fix in place the cardinal points; ibid., p. 69. In Hinduism the tortoise supports the churn stick when the gods and the demons churn the ocean (see Chapter Seven).
92 Ibid., p. 70.
93 Ibid., p. 71.
94 Ibid., p. 114.
95 Ibid.
96 Ibid.
97 Ibid., p. 99. This story also explains why the Bodhisattva is ruler of hell and indicates how Buddhist deities are subordinate to 'native' China ones.
98 Ibid.
99 Ibid.
100 Another important crop, salt, was thought to have been discovered by observing the ways of the phoenix. A peasant noticed a phoenix perched on a mound near the edge of the sea. After the bird had flown away, he went to dig up the mound, for it was thought that treasure was buried underneath a phoenix. He dug up the earth, which was later found to contain a tasty element known as salt. Ibid., p. 101.
101 Ibid., p. 120.
102 Ibid.
103 Ibid., p. 126.
104 Ibid., pp. 126–30.
105 Ibid., p. 35.
106 Sterckx, '"Of a Tawny Bull we Make Offering"', in *A Communion of Subjects*, ed. Waldau and Patton, p. 261.
107 Christie, *Chinese Mythology*, p. 119.
108 Ibid., p. 119.
109 Xiaofei Kang, *The Cult of the Fox: Power, Gender, and Popular Religion in Late Imperial and Modern China* (New York, 2006), p. 1.
110 Ibid., p. 3.
111 A nine-tailed fox is mentioned in the Brothers Grimm story 'The Wedding of Mrs Fox'.
112 Kang, *The Cult of the Fox*, p. 15.
113 Ibid., p. 16.
114 Ibid., p. 17.
115 Ibid.
116 Ibid., p. 21.
117 Ibid., p. 23.
118 Ibid., p. 47.
119 Ibid., p. 48.
120 Ibid., p. 137.
121 Ibid., p. 71.
122 Ibid.
123 Although this section could have been included in Chapter One, I have

chosen to insert it here as it highlights another dimension in Japanese culture and religion.
124 Barbara C. Sproul, *Primal Myths: Creating the World* (London, 1980), p. 215.
125 Retold in Maria Leach, *The Beginning* (New York, 1956), p. 205. Based on material in G. Batchelor, *The Ainu and their Folklore* (London, 1901), pp. 582–3, and from 'Notes on the Ainu', *Transactions of the Asiatic Society of Japan*, x (1882), pp. 206–19.
126 David Leeming, *The Oxford Illustrated Companion to World Mythology* (New York, 2008), p. 11.
127 Donald L. Philippi, 'Inter-species Communication and the Ainu Way of Life', in *The Language of the Birds: Tales, Texts, and Poems of Interspecies Communication*, ed. David M. Guss (San Francisco, CA, 1985), p. 186.
128 Shigeru Kayano, *The Ainu and the Fox*, trans. Deborah Davidson and Noriyoshi Owaki (Tokyo, 2001), p. 32.
129 Philippi, 'Inter-species Communication and the Ainu Way of Life', in *The Language of the Birds*, ed. Guss, p. 187.
130 Ibid.
131 Ibid, p. 188. For the Ainu, other animals wear costumes of the gods; the squirrel quite literally, for the squirrel 'represented the discarded sandals of the god Aioina, which would never rot, perhaps because squirrels move in spurts that are like footsteps.' Sax, *The Mythical Zoo*, p. 66.
132 Philippi, 'Inter-species Communication and the Ainu Way of Life', in *The Language of the Birds*, ed. Guss, p. 189.
133 Ibid., p. 190.
134 Ibid.
135 In Sakhalin there were both male and female shamans, but in Hokkaido shamans were exclusively female.
136 Philippi, 'Inter-species Communication and the Ainu Way of Life', in *The Language of the Birds*, ed. Guss, p. 191.
137 The Ainu refer to the bear as 'Divine One Who Rules the Mountains'.
138 Philippi, 'Inter-species Communication and the Ainu Way of Life', in *The Language of the Birds*, ed. Guss, p. 197; the footnote next to this line reads: 'On the second day of the bear festival, the bear-cub is led out of his cage and is paraded around several times before the spectators, who bid farewell to him just before he is slain. This is called "letting the bear play".'
139 Donald L. Philippi, *Songs of Gods, Songs of Humans: The Epic Tradition of the Ainu* (Tokyo, 1979), pp. 115–25.
140 Gilbert Waldhauer, *Fireflies, Honey and Silk* (Berkeley, CA, 2009), p. 13.
141 Stephen Addiss, with Fumiko Yamamoto and Akira Yamamoto, *A Haiku Menagerie: Living Creatures in Poems and Prints* (New York, 1992), p. 7.
142 Seven popular Japanese deities, the Shichi Fukujin, were considered to bring good luck and happiness. Although they were included in the Shinto pantheon, only two of them, Daikoku and Ebisu, were indigenous Japanese gods.
143 Storm, *Mythology of Asia and the Far East*, p. 23.
144 Also known as Shōten (sacred/noble god) or Daishō Kangiten (great noble god).

145 Storm, *Mythology of Asia and the Far East*, p. 56.
146 Michael Pye, 'A Tapestry of Traditions: Japanese Religions', in *The World's Religions*, ed. Alexander, p. 257.
147 From 1872 until 1945 Shinto was the state religion of Japan.
148 Ibid., p. 258.
149 Addiss et al., *A Haiku Menagerie*, p. 15.
150 Storm, *Mythology of Asia and the Far East*, p. 55.
151 The Japanese white snow dogs went out of fashion, even though 'The samurai believed the snow country dogs possessed a special instinct for martial arts, as well as a unique temperament that could be emulated.' Martha Sherrill, *Dog Man* (Melbourne, 2008), p. 161.
152 Ibid., p. 105.
153 For further information, see Chapter Nine.
154 Addiss et al., *A Haiku Menagerie*, p. 7.
155 Lafcadio Hearn, 'Buddhist Names of Plants and Animals', in Kenneth Rexroth, *The Buddhist Writings of Lafcadio Hearn* (Santa Barbara, CA, 1977), pp. 202–13.
156 Addiss et al., *A Haiku Menagerie*, p. 9. A haiku is traditionally composed of seventeen syllables in three unrhymed lines of five–seven–five syllables, often describing nature or a season.
157 Ibid., p. 79.
158 Ibid., p. 82.
159 Ibid., p. 39.
160 Ibid., p. 56.
161 Ibid., p. 75.
162 Westwood, ed., *The Cricket and the Dragon: Animals in Asian Art*, p. 18. Obon's starting date varies in different parts of Japan: in eastern Japan, it will start around 15 July, while in other regions it is closer to 15 August.
163 Kang, *The Cult of the Fox*, p. 199.
164 Ibid., p. 200.
165 Lafcadio Hearn, *Kwaidan: Stories and Studies of Strange Things* (Rutland, VT, 1971), n.p.; cited in Sax, *The Mythical Zoo*, p. 54.
166 Iraphne Childs, *The Badger Woods and Other Tales* (Richmond, Vic., 1977), pp. 1–12.

Conclusion

1 Henry Beston, *The Outermost House: A Year of Life on the Great Beach of Cape Cod* (Harmondsworth, 1928), p. 25.
2 Carol Newsom, 'Common Ground: An Ecological Reading of Genesis 2–3', in *The Earth Bible*, vol. II: *The Earth Story in Genesis*, ed. Norman C. Habel and Shirley Wurst (Sheffield, 2000), p. 66.
3 I was a participant in a volunteer programme, collecting data for the organization Biosphere. One of the daily activities was listing numbers and types of species that came to drink at different waterholes.
4 Simone Weil, 'Attention and Will', in *Gravity and Grace*, trans. Emma Craufurd (London, 1995), p. 106.
5 Jay McDaniel, 'Practicing the Presence of God: A Christian Approach to

Animals', in *A Communion of Subjects: Animals in Religion, Science and Ethics*, ed. Paul Waldau and Kimberley Patton (New York, 2006), p. 143.
6 In the story, the Creator puts Giraffe in charge of looking after the sun; as a gift of thanks, the Creator honours Giraffe by rearranging several stars in a giraffe shape (known as Tutwa, 'Giraffe'). English-speakers call this constellation the Southern Cross.
7 'Wolf Clan Lesson', in Teresa Pijoan, *White Wolf Woman and Other Native American Transformation Myths* (Little Rock, AR, 1992), pp. 128–30. Pijoan, writing about the teller of the tale, Colie Flatblanket, says: 'At the telling of the salmon with the burning pitch, she cried. The fire and the lava from the high volcano brought more tears. The ending of the story brought a strong anger. Her story doesn't end, so she said, for the salmon are still trying to gain their freedom and rise to the surface.' Ibid., p. 165.

Bibliography

Adams, David, *The Cry of the Deer* (London, 1987)
Addiss, Stephen, with Fumiko Yamamoto and Akira Yamamoto, *A Haiku Menagerie: Living Creatures in Poems and Prints* (New York, 1992)
Alexander, Pat, ed., *The World's Religions* (Oxford, 1994)
Allan, Tony, Charles Phillips and Michael Kerrigan, *Arctic Myth and Mankind: Spirits of the Snow* (London, 1999)
Allan, Tony, Fergus Fleming and Charles Phillips, *Voices of the Ancestors: African Myth* (London, 1999)
Allen, Barbara, *Pigeon* (London, 2009)
Babbitt, Ellen C., *More Jataka Tales* (Varanasi, 2003)
Bahti, Mark, *Spirit in the Stone: A Handbook of Southwest Indian Animal Carvings and Fetishes* (Tucson, AZ, 1999)
Barber, Richard, *Bestiary* (Woodbridge, 1993)
Batchelor, Martine, and Kerry Brown, eds, *Buddhism and Ecology* (London, 1992)
Bauckham, Richard, 'Jesus and Animals I: What did He Teach?' and 'Jesus and Animals II: What did He Practice?', in *Animals on the Agenda*, ed. Andrew Linzey and Dorothy Yamamoto (London, 1998), pp. 33–48, 49–60
Beswick, Ethel, *Jataka Tales: Birth Stories of Buddha* (New Delhi, 1999)
Birch, Charles, and Lukas Vischer, *Living with the Animals: The Community of God's Creatures* (Geneva, 1997)
Birkhead, Tim, *The Wisdom of Birds* (New York, 2008)
Blech, Rabbi Benjamin, *The Complete Idiot's Guide to Judaism* (New York, 1999)
Bodkin, Frances, and Lorraine Robertson, *D'harawal: Seasons and Climatic Cycles* (Canberra, 2008)
Borges, Jorge Luis, *The Book of Imaginary Beings* (London, 2002)
Bough, Jill, *Donkey* (London, 2011)
Brasch, R., *The Star of David: The Story of Judaism, Its Teachings, Philosophy and Symbols* (Sydney, 1999)
Breuilly, Elizabeth, and Martin Palmer, eds, *Christianity and Ecology* (London, 1992)
Brewer's Dictionary of Phase and Fable: Millennium Edition, revd Adrian Room (London, 2001)
Buck, William, (retold by), *Ramayana* (New York, 1976)
Caduto, Michael J., and Joseph Bruchac, *The Native Stories from Keepers of the Earth* (Saskatoon, SK, 1991)

Cameron, Anne, *Dzelarhons: Myths of the Northwest Coast* (Madeira Park, BC, 1986)
Campbell, Alistair, *Maori Legends* (Paraparaumu, 1969)
Campbell, Joseph, *The Way of the Animal Powers: Historical Atlas of World Mythology* (London, 1984)
Carey, Margret, *Myths and Legends of Africa* (London, 1970)
Caswell, Helen (retold by), *Eskimo Folk Tales: Shadows from the Singing House* (Tokyo, 1968)
Chapple, Christopher Key, *Nonviolence to Animals, Earth, and Self in Asian Traditions* (Delhi, 1993)
Charles, R. H., *The Testaments of the Twelve Patriarchs* (London, 1908)
Charlesworth, James H., ed., *The Old Testament Pseudepigrapha*, I: *Apocalyptic Literature and Testaments* (New York, 1983)
Chernak-McElroy, Susan, *Animals as Teachers and Healers* (London, 1996)
Chesterton, G. K., *Saint Francis of Assisi* (Peabody, MA, 2008)
Childs, Iraphne, *The Badger Woods and Other Tales* (Richmond, Victoria, 1977)
Ching, Julia, *Chinese Religions* (New York, 1993)
Christie, Anthony, *Chinese Mythology* (London, 1996)
Clark, Ella E., *Indian Legends of the Pacific Northwest* (1953) (Los Angeles, CA, 2003)
Cohlene, Terri, *Turquoise Boy: A Navajo Legend* (Mahwah, NJ, 1990)
Cohn-Sherbok, Dan, *The Wisdom of Judaism* (Oxford, 2000)
Coogan, Michael D., ed., *World Religions: The Illustrated Guide* (London, 2003)
Crowley, Vivianne, and Christopher Crowley, *Spirit of the Earth: Ancient Belief Systems in the Modern World* (London, 2004)
Dawood, N. J., trans., *The Koran* (London, 2006)
Dimont, Max I., *Jews, God and History* (New York, 1962)
Dosick, Rabbi Wayne, *Living Judaism: The Complete Guide to Jewish Belief, Tradition, and Practice* (San Francisco, CA, 1998)
Dowrick, Stephanie, *Seeking the Sacred* (Crows Nest, NSW, 2010)
Dunn, Philip, Manuela Dunn-Mascetti and R. A. Nicholson, *The Illustrated Rumi: A Treasury of Wisdom from the Poet of the Soul* (New York, 2000)
Epstein, Isidore, *Judaism* (Harmondsworth, 1959, repr. 1968)
Erdoes, Richard, and Alfonso Ortiz, *American Indian Myths and Legends* (New York, 1984)
Falcon, Ted, and David Blatner, *Judaism for Dummies* (New York, 2001)
Fitzpatrick Grippo, David, 'Albert Schweitzer: Be a Healing Presence in a Hurting World' (St Meinrad, IN, 2009)
Fleming, Fergus, Shahrukh Husain, C. Scott Littleton and Linda A. Malcor, *Heroes of the Dawn: Celtic Myth* (London, 1996)
Foltz, Richard C., *Animals in Islamic Tradition and Muslim Cultures* (Oxford, 2006)
Forty, Jo, *Mythology: A Visual Encyclopedia* (London, 2004)
Frielander, Gerald, *Jewish Fairy Tales* (New York, 1997)
Gahlin, Lucia, *Egypt: Gods, Myths and Religion* (London, 2001)
George, Thomas, *Coyote Tales of the Northwest* (Edmonton, 2010)
Gibson, Graeme, *The Bedside Book of Birds: An Avian Miscellany* (London, 2005)
——, *The Bedside Book of Beasts: A Wildlife Miscellany* (London, 2009)

Gilbert, Martin, *Letters to Auntie Fori: The 5,000 Year History of the Jewish People and their Faith* (London, 2002)
Ginzberg, Louis, *The Legends of the Jews*, 6 vols (Philadelphia, PA, 1988)
Goldman, Ari L., *Being Jewish: The Spiritual and Cultural Practice of Judaism Today* (New York, 2000)
Goldstein, David, *Jewish Mythology* (London, 1988)
Grant, Bruce, *Concise Encyclopedia of the American Indian* (New York, 2000)
Greaves, Nick, with Rod Clement, *When Hippo was Hairy, and Other Tales from Africa* (Cape Town, 2000)
The Green Bible (NRSV) (New York, 2008)
Grimm, Jacob and Wilhelm, *The Complete Illustrated Works of the Brothers Grimm* (London, 1984)
Grossman, Loyd, *The Dog's Tale: A History of Man's Best Friend* (London, 1993)
Grübel, Monika, *Judaism: An Illustrated Historical Overview* (New York, 1997)
Guss, David M., ed., *The Language of the Birds: Tales, Texts, and Poems of Interspecies Communication* (San Francisco, CA, 1985)
Habel, Norman, trans. and ed., with Jasmine Corowa, *The Rainbow Spirit in Creation: A Reading of Genesis 1* (Collegeville, MN, 2000)
Habel, Norman, and Shirley Wurst, eds, *The Earth Bible*, vol. II: *The Earth Story in Genesis* (Sheffield, 2000)
—, *The Earth Bible*, vol. III: *The Earth Story in Wisdom Traditions* (Sheffield, 2001)
Habel, Norman, ed., *The Earth Bible*, vol. IV: *The Earth Story in the Psalms and the Prophets* (Sheffield, 2001)
Hahn, Daniel, *The Tower Menagerie* (London, 2003)
Hart, Hilary, *Pearlie of Great Price* (Ropley, Hants, 1997)
Hexham, Irving, *Concise Dictionary of Religion* (Downers Grove, IL, 1993)
Hillman, James, with Margot McLean, *Dream Animals* (San Francisco, CA, 1997)
Hirschfelder, Arlene, and Pauline Molin, *Encyclopedia of Native American Religions* (New York, 2000)
Hobgood-Oster, Laura, *Holy Dogs and Asses: Animals in the Christian Tradition* (Urbana and Chicago, IL, 2008)
Hoffman, Edward, *The Hebrew Alphabet: A Mystical Journey* (San Francisco, CA, 1998)
Houston, Jean, *Mystical Dogs* (Makawao, 2002)
Hughes, Serge, trans., *The Little Flowers of St Francis and other Franciscan Writings* (New York, 1964)
Hyland, J. R., *God's Covenant with Animals: A Biblical Basis for the Humane Treatment of All Creatures* (New York, 2000)
Inayat, Noor, *Twenty Jataka Tales* (Varanasi, 2003)
Ions, Veronica, *The World's Mythology in Colour* (London, 1974)
Jacobson, David C., *Modern Midrash: The Retelling of Traditional Jewish Narratives by Twentieth Century Hebrew Writers* (Albany, NY, 1987)
Jagannathan, Shakunthala, *Hinduism: An Introduction* (Mumbai, 1984)
Johnson, Pauline E. [Tekahionwake], *Legends of Vancouver* (Vancouver, 1913)
Joy, Charles R., *The Animal World of Albert Schweitzer: Jungle Insights into Reverence for Life* (Boston, MA, 1950)
Kalechofsky, Roberta, *Haggadah for the Liberated Lamb*, 2nd edn (Marblehead, MA, 2002)

Kang, Xiaofei, *The Cult of the Fox: Power, Gender, and Popular Religion in Late Imperial and Modern China* (New York, 2006)
Kayano, Shigeru, *The Ainu and the Fox*, trans. Deborah Davidson and Noriyoshi Owaki (Tokyo, 2001)
Khalid, Fazlun, and Joanne O'Brien, eds, *Islam and Ecology* (London, 1992)
Kidd, Sue Monk, *The Secret Life of Bees* (New York, 2002)
Knappert, Jan, *African Mythology* (London, 1990)
Knudtson, Peter, and David Suzuki, *Wisdom of the Elders* (Toronto, 1992)
Kosofsky, Scott-Martin, *The Book of Customs: A Complete Handbook for the Jewish Year* (New York, 2004)
Kowalski, Gary, *The Souls of Animals*, 2nd edn (Walpole, NH, 1999)
Kugler, Robert A., *The Testaments of the Twelve Patriarchs* (Sheffield, 2001)
Kundera, Milan, *The Unbearable Lightness of Being* (New York, 1999)
Lange, Nicholas de, *Judaism* (Oxford, 1986)
Leeming, David, *The Oxford Illustrated Companion to World Mythology* (New York, 2008)
Linzey, Andrew, *Animal Gospel* (London, 1998)
——, and Tom Regan, eds, *Animals and Christianity: A Book of Readings* (London, 1989)
——, and Dorothy Yamamoto, eds, *Animals on the Agenda* (London, 1998)
Lopez, Donald, ed., *Buddhist Scriptures* (London, 2004)
Lowenstein, Tom, and Piers Vitebsky, *Native American Myth and Mankind: Mother Earth, Father Sky* (London, 1997)
McDaniel, Jay B., *Of God and Pelicans: A Theology of Reverence for Life*, (Louisville, KY, 1989)
——, *Earth, Sky, Gods and Mortals: Developing an Ecological Spirituality* (Mystic, CT, 1990)
McDonald, Angela, *Pocket Dictionary of Ancient Egyptian Animals* (London, 2004)
McGaa, Ed, *Nature's Way: Native Wisdom for Living in Balance with the Earth* (San Francisco, CA, 2004)
McGinnis, Mark W., *Buddhist Animal Wisdom Stories* (Boston, MA, 2004)
McLeish, Kenneth, *Myth: Myths and Legends of the World Explored* (London, 1996)
McLoughlin, Sean, *World Religions: An Illustrated Guide* (London, 2007)
Majupuria, Trilok Chandra, *Sacred Animals of Nepal and India* (Lashkar, 2000)
Malek, Jaromir, *The Cat in Ancient Egypt* (London, 1993)
Malka, Victor, ed., *The Wisdom of Judaism* (New York, 1996)
Masri, Al-Hafiz Basheer Ahmad, *Animal Welfare in Islam* (Markfield, 2007)
Masson, Jeffrey Moussaieff, *Dogs Never Lie About Love* (London, 1998)
——, *The Pig Who Sang to the Moon* (London, 2005)
Maxwell, Robyn, *Life, Death and Magic: 2,000 Years of Southeast Asian Ancestral Art* (Canberra, 2010)
Mercatante, Anthony S., *Encyclopedia of World Mythology and Legend* (Frenchs Forest, NSW, 1988)
Metford, J.C.J., *Dictionary of Christian Lore and Legend* (London, 1983)
Milgrom, Jacob, *Leviticus (A Continental Commentary)* (Minneapolis, MN, 2004)
Neuberger, Julia, *On Being Jewish* (London, 1996)

Nivedita, Sister, and Ananda K. Coomaraswamy, *Myths and Legends of the Hindus and Buddhists* (Kolkata, 2006)
O'Flaherty, Wendy, trans. and ed., *The Rig Veda* (London, 1981)
O'Meara, John, trans., *The Voyage of Saint Brendan* (Dublin, 1994)
Ouseley, Rev. G. J., *The Gospel of the Holy Twelve* (London, 1923)
Patrick, Richard, *All Colour Book of Egyptian Mythology* (London, 1972)
Perek Shirah: The Song of the Universe (New York, 2004)
Phelps, Norm, *The Great Compassion: Buddhism and Animal Rights* (New York, 2004)
Pijoan, Teresa, *White Wolf Woman and Other Native American Transformation Myths* (Little Rock, AR, 1992)
Pilkington, C. M., *Teach Yourself Judaism* (London, 2000)
Pohatu, Warren, *Māori Animal Myths* (Auckland, 2001)
Porter, J. R., *The Lost Bible: Forgotten Scriptures Revealed* (London, 2001)
Prime, Ranchor, ed., *Hinduism and Ecology: Seeds of Truth* (London, 1992)
Pritchard, Evan T., *Native American Stories of the Sacred* (Woodstock, VT, 2005)
Reed, A. W., *Aboriginal Legends: Animal Tales* (Sydney, 1978)
—, *Maori Myths and Legendary Tales* (Auckland, 1999)
Reed, Evelyn Dahl, *Coyote Tales from the Indian Pueblos* (Santa Fe, NM, 1988)
Reid, Bill, 'The Haida Legend of the Raven and the First Humans', Museum Note No. 8, UBC Museum of Anthropology
Rose, Aubrey, ed., *Judaism and Ecology* (London, 1992)
Rosenberg, Stuart E., *To Understand Jews* (New York, 1970)
Salwak, Dale, ed., *The Wisdom of Judaism* (Novato, CA, 1997)
Sanders, Erin Ladd, *In the Name of Peace* (London, 2010)
Saunders, Nicholas J., *Animal Spirits* (London, 1995)
Sawyer, John F. A., *The Fifth Gospel: Isaiah in the History of Christianity* (Cambridge, 1996)
Sax, Boria, *The Mythical Zoo: An Encyclopedia of Animals in World Myth, Legend, and Literature* (Santa Barbara, CA, 2001)
—, *The Serpent and the Swan: The Animal Bride in Folklore and Literature* (Blacksburg, VA, 1998)
Schneemelcher, Wilhelm, ed., *New Testament Apocrypha*, vol. I: *Gospels and Other Writings* (London, 1963)
—, *New Testament Apocrypha*, vol. II: *Writings Relating to the Apostles, Apocalypses and Related Subjects* (Cambridge, 1992)
Schwartz, Howard, *Gates to the New City: A Treasury of Modern Jewish Tales* (New York, 1983)
Scollay, Susan, ed., *Love and Devotion: From Persia and Beyond* (South Yarra, Vic., 2012)
Scully, Matthew, *Dominion* (New York, 2002)
Sears, David, *The Vision of Eden: Animal Welfare and Vegetarianism in Jewish Law and Mysticism* (Spring Valley, NY, 2003)
Seton, Ernest Thompson, with Julia M. Seton, *The Gospel of the Redman* (Bloomington, IN, 2005)
Seventh-Day Adventists Believe: A Biblical Exposition of 27 Fundamental Doctrines (Hagerstown, MD, 1988)

Shapiro, Rabbi Rami M., *Minyan: Ten Principles for Living a Life of Integrity* (New York, 1997)
Shearer, Alistair, and Peter Russell, trans., *The Upanishads* (London, 1978)
Silcock, Arnold, ed., *Verse and Worse: A Private Collection* (London, 1958)
Slifkin, Rabbi Natan, *Man and Beast: Our Relationship with Animals in Jewish Law and Thought* (New York, 2006)
Spence, Lewis, *North American Indians: Myths and Legends* (New York, 1985)
Sproul, Barbara C., *Primal Myths: Creating the World* (London, 1980)
Storm, Rachel, *Mythology of India: Myths and Legends of India, Tibet and Sri Lanka* (London, 2000)
——, *Mythology of Asia and the Far East* (London, 2006)
Streep, Peg, ed., *The Sacred Journey: Prayers and Songs of Native America* (Boston, MA, 1995)
Telushkin, Rabbi Joseph, *Jewish Literacy: The Most Important Things to Know about the Jewish Religion, its People and its History* (New York, 1991; revd 2001)
Tlili, Sarra, 'All Animals Are Equal, or Are They? The Ikhwān al-safā''s Animal Epistle and its Unhappy End' (unpublished article, 2011)
Tompkins, Ptolemy, *The Divine Life of Animals* (New York, 2010)
Toperoff, Shlomo Pesach, *The Animal Kingdom in Jewish Thought* (Northvale, NJ, 1995)
Unterman, Alan, *Dictionary of Jewish Lore and Legend* (London, 1997)
Waal, Esther De, ed., *The Celtic Vision: Prayers and Blessings from the Outer Hebrides* (London, 1988)
Waldau, Paul, and Kimberley Patton, eds, *A Communion of Subjects: Animals in Religion, Science and Ethics* (New York, 2006)
Waldbauer, Gilbert, *Fireflies, Honey and Silk* (Berkeley, CA, 2009)
Walters, Kerry S., and Lisa Portmess, *Religious Vegetarianism* (Albany, NY, 2001)
Waskow, Arthur, *Seasons of Our Joy: A Modern Guide to the Jewish Holidays* (Boston, MA, 1982)
Wepa, Matthew Eru, *Symbols of the Maori World* (Rotorua, n.d.)
Westwood, Janet, *The Cricket and the Dragon: Animals in Asian Art*, exh. cat., National Gallery of Victoria (Melbourne, 2008)
White, T. H., *The Book of Beasts: Being a Translation from a Latin Bestiary of the Twelfth Century* (New York, 1984)
Wiesel, Elie, *Sages and Dreamers* (New York, 1991)
Willis, Roy, ed., *World Mythology: The Illustrated Guide* (London, 1993)
Wouk, Herman, *This is My God* (London, 1976)
Wyatt, Gary, *Mythic Beings: Spirit Art of the Northwest Coast* (Seattle, WA, 1999)
Wylen, Stephen M., *Settings of Silver: An Introduction to Judaism* (New York, 2000)
Young, Richard Alan, *Is God a Vegetarian? Christianity, Vegetarianism, and Animal Rights* (Chicago and La Salle, IL, 1999)

Acknowledgements

I thank *Voiceless* (www.voiceless.org.au) for awarding a grant to assist the publication of *Animals in Religion*; you do fantastic work, raising awareness of animals suffering in factory farming. To my husband, for his unending patience, and for his artistic eye when visiting art galleries and museums – always on the 'look out' for things to help my research. To Michael Leaman and the staff at Reaktion, you are wonderful. A special thank you to the outstanding editorial team, especially David Rose, Aimee Selby and Kathleen Steeden, for your skill, and attention to detail; I value the care you have bestowed on this work.

This book is a combined effort, drawing on the work of many storytellers, writers, theologians and dreamers. I could not have written it without the ability to draw on previous research from scholars and writers past and present. I have tried to acknowledge all sources, but if I have overlooked anyone, my heartfelt apologies. Finally, I must acknowledge the animals. What a poorer world it would be without them! May this book help us to truly 'love one another'. I hope this book will prompt people of faith to work together to make this a better world for all creatures. To close with the words of Anna Sewell: 'There is no religion without love, and people may talk as much as they like about their religion, but if it does not teach them to be good and kind to other animals as well as humans, it is all a sham.'

Photo Acknowledgements

The author and publishers wish to express their thanks to the below sources of illustrative material and/or permission to reproduce it. Some locations of artworks are also given below.

Photo Adityamadhav83: p. 302 (this file is licensed under the Creative Commons Attribution-Share Alike 3.0 Unported license – any reader is free to share – to copy, distribute and transmit the work, or to remix – to adapt the work, under the following conditions: you must attribute the work in the manner specified by the author or licensor – but not in any way that suggests that they endorse you or your use of the work); photo Anishshah19: p. 349; Archaeological Museum of Thessaloniki: p. 125; photo Jan Arkesteijn: p. 145; Arni Magnusson Institute, Reykjavik: p. 130; Arthur Sackler Museum (Harvard Art Museums), Cambridge, MA: p. 185; photos author: pp. 22, 189, 191, 363, 382, 401, 458; photo BabelStone: p. 56 (this file is licensed under the Creative Commons Attribution-Share Alike 3.0 Unported license – any reader is free to share – to copy, distribute and transmit the work, or to remix – to adapt the work, under the following conditions: you must attribute the work in the manner specified by the author or licensor – but not in any way that suggests that they endorse you or your use of the work); Bibliothèque Nationale de France, Paris: p. 254; Bodleian Libraries, University of Oxford: p. 277; Boston Museum of Fine Art: p. 114; photo Brattarb: p. 211 (this file is licensed under the Creative Commons Attribution-Share Alike 3.0 Unported license – any reader is free to share – to copy, distribute and transmit the work, or to remix – to adapt the work, under the following conditions: you must attribute the work in the manner specified by the author or licensor – but not in any way that suggests that they endorse you or your use of the work); British Library, London: pp. 146, 271; British Museum, London: pp. 25, 56, 89, 94, 98, 100, 102, 108, 115, 366; Burke Museum of Natural History and Culture, Seattle: pp. 29, 38, 64, 83, 86; Canadian Museum of History, Gatineau, Québec: pp. 22, 53, 85; Chester Grosvenor Museum: p. 184; photo Asahel Curtis: p. 78; photo Daderot: p. 365; photos Jean-Pierre Dalbéra: pp. 53, 148 (these files are licensed under the Creative Commons Attribution 2.0 Generic license – any reader is free to share – to copy, distribute and transmit the work/s, or to remix – to adapt the work/s, under the following conditions: you must attribute the work/s in the manner specified by the author or licensor – but not in any way that suggests that they endorse you or your use of the work/s); photo Dauster: p. 144; photo Einsamer Schütze: p. 89 (this file is licensed under the Creative Commons Attribution-Share Alike

3.0 Unported, 2.5 Generic, 2.0 Generic and 1.0 Generic license – any reader is free to share – to copy, distribute and transmit the work, or to remix – to adapt the work, under the following conditions: you must attribute the work in the manner specified by the author or licensor – but not in any way that suggests that they endorse you or your use of the work); from *The Elder or Poetic Edda* [. . .] *edited and translated* [. . .] *by Olive Bray* . . . (London, 1908): p. 129; photo Eloquence: p. 127; photo Farm: p. 433 (this file is licensed under the Creative Commons Attribution-Share Alike 3.0 Unported, 2.5 Generic, 2.0 Generic and 1.0 Generic license – any reader is free to share – to copy, distribute and transmit the work, or to remix – to adapt the work, under the following conditions: you must attribute the work in the manner specified by the author or licensor – but not in any way that suggests that they endorse you or your use of the work); photo FullyFunctnlPhil: p. 447 (this file is licensed under the Creative Commons Attribution-Share Alike 2.0 Generic license – any reader is free to share – to copy, distribute and transmit the work, or to remix – to adapt the work, under the following conditions: you must attribute the work in the manner specified by the author or licensor – but not in any way that suggests that they endorse you or your use of the work); photo G41m8: p. 51 (this file is licensed under the Creative Commons Attribution-Share Alike 4.0 International license – any reader is free to share – to copy, distribute and transmit the work, or to remix – to adapt the work, under the following conditions: you must attribute the work in the manner specified by the author or licensor – but not in any way that suggests that they endorse you or your use of the work); photo Bernard Gagnon: p. 335 (this file is licensed under the Creative Commons Attribution-Share Alike 3.0 Unported, 2.5 Generic, 2.0 Generic and 1.0 Generic license – any reader is free to share – to copy, distribute and transmit the work, or to remix – to adapt the work, under the following conditions: you must attribute the work in the manner specified by the author or licensor – but not in any way that suggests that they endorse you or your use of the work); photo Haukurth: p. 129; photo Hohum: p. 193; photo Dariusz Jemielniak ('Pundit'): p. 450 (this file is licensed under the Creative Commons Attribution-Share Alike 3.0 Unported license – any reader is free to share – to copy, distribute and transmit the work, or to remix – to adapt the work, under the following conditions: you must attribute the work in the manner specified by the author or licensor – but not in any way that suggests that they endorse you or your use of the work); The Jewish Museum, New York: p. 144; photo Johnbod: p. 121 (this file is licensed under the Creative Commons Attribution-Share Alike 3.0 Unported license – any reader is free to share – to copy, distribute and transmit the work, or to remix – to adapt the work, under the following conditions: you must attribute the work in the manner specified by the author or licensor – but not in any way that suggests that they endorse you or your use of the work); photo kern8: p. 123; Los Angeles County Museum of Art: p. 345; photo Sharon Mellerus: p. 108 (this file is licensed under the Creative Commons Attribution 2.0 Generic license – any reader is free to share – to copy, distribute and transmit the work, or to remix – to adapt the work, under the following conditions: you must give appropriate credit, provide a link to the license, and indicate if changes were made – you may do so in any reasonable manner, but not in any way that suggests the licensor endorses you or your use – with no additional restrictions – you may not apply legal terms or technological measures that legally restrict others from doing anything the license permits); Metropolitan Museum of Art: pp. 15, 18, 106, 110, 163, 235, 245, 248, 270, 312, 368, 405, 431, 449, 452; Museum of the Americas, Madrid: p. 49; National Gallery of Art, Washington, DC: p. 193; National Gallery of Australia, Canberra: pp. 50, 316; National Museum and Research Centre of Altamira: p. 8; National Museum, Copenhagen: p. 123; National Museum of Scotland, Edinburgh: p. 121; Palace Museum, Beijing: p. 411; private collections: pp. 145, 147; photo QuartierLatin1968: p. 125 (this file is licensed under the Creative Commons Attribution-Share Alike 3.0 Unported license – any reader is free to share – to copy, distribute and transmit the work, or to remix – to adapt the work, under the following conditions: you must attribute the work in the manner specified by the author or licensor – but not in any way that suggests that they endorse you or your use of the work); photo Carole Raddato: p. 184 (this file is licensed under the Creative Commons Attribution 2.0 Generic license – any reader is free to share – to copy, distribute and transmit the work, or to remix – to adapt the work, under the following conditions: you must attribute the work in the manner specified by the author or licensor – but not in any way that suggests that they endorse you or your use of the work); photo Rama: p. 190; photo Rameessos: p. 8; photo Reinhardhauke: p. 149 (this file is licensed under the Creative Commons Attribution-Share Alike 3.0 Unported license – any reader is free to share – to copy, distribute and transmit the work, or to remix – to adapt the work, under the following conditions: you must attribute the work in the manner specified by the author or licensor – but not in any way that suggests that they endorse you or your use of the work); Royal Academy of Arts, London: p. 127; photo sailko: p. 345 (this file is licensed under the Creative Commons Attribution-Share Alike 3.0 Unported license – any reader is free to share – to copy, distribute and transmit the work, or to remix – to adapt the work, under the following conditions: you must attribute the work in the manner specified by the author or licensor – but not in any way that suggests that they endorse you or your use of the work); San Diego Museum of Art: p. 365; Seattle Art Museum: pp. 17, 57, 58, 65, 69, 75, 445; photo Shakko: p. 271; photo Ralph Süssbrich: p. 236 (this file is licensed under the Creative Commons Attribution-Share Alike 3.0 Unported license – any reader is free to share – to copy, distribute and transmit the work, or to remix – to adapt the work, under the following conditions: you must attribute the work in the manner specified by the author or licensor – but not in any way that suggests that they endorse you or your use of the work); photo Swamibu: p. 108 (this file is licensed under the Creative Commons Attribution 2.0 Generic license – any reader is free to share – to copy, distribute and transmit the work, or to remix – to adapt the work, under the following conditions: you must give appropriate credit, provide a link to the license, and indicate if changes were made – you may do so in any reasonable manner, but not in any way that suggests the licensor endorses you or your use – with no additional restrictions – you may not apply legal terms or technological measures that legally restrict others from doing anything the license permits); photo Szilas: p. 411; photo Takeaway: p. 402 (this file is licensed under the Creative Commons Attribution-Share Alike 3.0 Unported license – any reader is free to share – to copy, distribute and transmit the work, or to remix – to adapt the work, under the following conditions: you must attribute the work in the manner specified by the author or licensor – but not in any way that suggests that they endorse you or your use of the work); photos © the Trustees of the British Museum,

London: pp. 25, 94, 98, 100, 102; Victoria & Albert Museum, London: pp. 187, 217, 343, 414; Wellcome Library, London – photo Wellcome Images: p. 355 (this file is licensed under the Creative Commons Attribution-Share Alike 4.0 International license – any reader is free to share – to copy, distribute and transmit the work, or to remix – to adapt the work, under the following conditions: you must attribute the work in the manner specified by the author or licensor – but not in any way that suggests that they endorse you or your use of the work); photo Will: p. 300 (this file is licensed under the Creative Commons Attribution 2.0 Generic license – any reader is free to share – to copy, distribute and transmit the work, or to remix – to adapt the work, under the following conditions: you must attribute the work in the manner specified by the author or licensor – but not in any way that suggests that they endorse you or your use of the work); photo Yanajin33: p. 451 (this file is licensed under the Creative Commons Attribution-Share Alike 3.0 Unported license – any reader is free to share – to copy, distribute and transmit the work, or to remix – to adapt the work, under the following – conditions: you must attribute the work in the manner specified by the author or licensor – but not in any way that suggests that they endorse you or your use of the work).

The Nationalmuseet København, the copyright holder of the image on the back cover (a photograph taken by Roberto Fortuna and Kira Ursem), has published this online under conditions imposed by a Creative Commons Attribution-Share Alike 3.0 Unported license: readers are free to share – to copy, distribute and transmit this image alone, and to remix – to adapt this image alone – under the following conditions: attribution, readers must attribute either image in the manner specified by the author or licensor (but not in any way that suggests that these parties endorse them or their use of the work), and share alike (if readers alter, transform, or build upon this image, they may distribute the resulting work only under the same or similar license to this one).

Index

Abba Didymus 214
Acaranga Sutra 345, 350
African myths 16, 26, 27, 28, 31, 35, 36, 37, 41, 78, 79, 83
afterlife, animals in the 77, 81
    animal motifs on burial chambers (China) 433
    in Islam 285–6
aggadah 134
ahimsa 292, 293, 295, 329, 330, 331, 334, 339, 341, 343, 348–52, *349*, 355–6, 358–60, 361, 372, 399
    Gandhi and 356
Ainu 438–44
    bear cult 442
    belief that animals are gods in disguise 440
    Chikap Kamuy 62
    Chira-Mante-Kamui 442
    creation myth, wagtail 439
    descended from polar bear or bear god 439
    female shamans 439
    Iomante or 'Bear Festival' (*Kumamatsuri*) 442
Airavata (elephant) 311, 316
    with Indra 308
Ajanta Caves 403
Akbar, the Mughal emperor 355–6
akedah (Binding of Isaac) ram 150
Al-Jahiz, *Kitab al-Hayawan* (Book of Animals) 269
Ambika *345*
Ammit 103, 109, 111
Amun 93, 100, 112, *115*, 116

Anansi (Ananse) the Spider 33, 87
animal/animalis 52
animal cruelty/abuse, condemned in Buddhism 397
animals as bearers of culture 46
animals as believers (Islam) 287
animals as kin, relatives 45, 352, 376, 458
animism 55, 447
    Shintoism 447
Anthony, St 206–7, 209
    and his pig 209–10
anti-heretical literature, animals in 234–5
Anubis (Anpu) *110*, 111
Apep *see* serpent/snake
Apis bull 92, 113–15, *114*
    at Saqqara 115
Apocrypha 134, 135–6, 139, 196–205
Aristotle 222
Ark, Noah's 144–8, *144*, *145*, *146*, *147*, *148*
Arnobius of Sicca 221
Aryans 293
    animal sacrifice 293
Ashoka, 383, 386–8, 399
Atman 295, 319, 327
'Attar of Nishapur, *The Conference of the Birds* 276, 277, *277*
Atum (Re) 93, 96
Augustine 221, 222
Avalokiteshvara (Guanyin) 367
    incarnated as a monkey 400
Avatamsaka Sutra 381
Aztec 20–21, 82

ba ('soul') 111
Baal Shem Tov 133, 179
baboons 96, 99, 101
    mummified 113
bal tashchit ('thou shalt not destroy') 134
Bancroft, Hubert Howe 13
Barth, Karl 222
Basil, St 183
Bastet *see* feline goddesses in ancient Egypt
bat 426
bears 9, *38*, 75
    Bear Mother (Haida) 26
    in beliefs of the Ainu 63
    Inuit 53
    in Washoe creation myth 38
Bear Medicine 73–5, *75*
beaver 33, 34, 47, 61
    carving by Jim Hart *85*
Behemoth 137
Benedict, Rule of 217
Bentham, Jeremy 222
Benu bird 95, 96
bestiaries 233
Beston, Henry, 457
Bhagavad Gita 289, 301–3, 305, 330
    Golden Rule 331
Bhagavata Purana 327, 333
Bhairav (manifestation of Shiva) 315
Bhisma 333
birds
    associated with Chaos (China) 410
    bird masks 29, *83*, *86*
    and establishment of Shang dynasty 415
    Lightning Bird 29
    as mediators between heaven and earth 18, *18*
    on a Roman tombstone, Chester *184*
    Thunderbird 19, 29, 30, 77, *78*
Black Elk 76
blessings
    Blessing of the Animals 239
    Jewish 135

blood
    in Islam 259
    in Judaism, as life force 158
blood sports 156, 182, 228, 260
boars (and pigs)
    Celtic 122, 123
    in Fenian stories 123, 124
    Gollinborsti 129, 130
    magic boars and afterlife 124
    Saehrimnir 128
Bodhichitta 365
bodhisattvas 365, *366*, 367
Book of the Dead 109
Brahman 297
Brendan, St, *Navigatio sancti Brendani* 215–17
Brethren of Purity, *The Case of the Animals versus Man before the King of the Jinn* 263–8
Brigid 126
Brihadaranyaka Upanishad 289, 298, 305
Broome, Rev Arthur 230
Brueghel the Elder, Jan, *Paradise Landscape with the Animals Entering Noah's Ark 145*
Bubastis (site of temple cult of Bastet) 105
Buddha 314, *363*, *405*
Buddhism
    division concerning eating meat 11
    overview of 361–4
    world view 370
Buddhist texts and narratives, animals in 381–2
buffalo 59, 61, 62
    White Buffalo Calf Woman and the sacred pipe 75–6
Buglioni, Benedetto (workshop of), *Nativity 188*
bulls, in ancient Egypt
    Buchus 113
    Mnevis 113
    Ptah 114
    see also Apis bull
Buraq 270, *270*, 271
burial box carvings (Haida) *85*

Index

butterfly
    Zhuang Zhou, as a butterfly 423
    symbol of conjugal love and death 454

Calvin, John 227
camel 247–8, 251, 253, 263
canopic jars (Four Sons of Horus) 111–12
carp 452
cats
    cat cemeteries 107, 117
    the Cathars 223–4
    ceremonial killing of 224
    as the devil 223–4
    killing of temple cats 105, 107
    magic knives (ancient Egypt) 92, 117
    mummified 105, *108*, *116*
    serving in the underworld 111, 117
cave paintings 8–9, *8*
Celtic Christianity 219–20
    prayers for their animals 219–20
Celtic history 120
    funerals 124
cemeteries for mummified remains of sacred animals (ancient Egypt) 113, 116, 117
    necropolis of Saqqara 113
Ceridwen 123
Cernunnos 122, *123*
Chauvet 8
Chinese mythological creatures 412
    animals in Chinese folk culture 431
Chira-Mante-Kamui (Ainu mountain god) 442
Christianity
    Acts of Paul (lion being baptized) 196–7
    Acts of St Bartholomew (apocryphal Gnostic text) 212
    animals at Jesus' birth 186, *187*, *188*, 188, *189*, *190*
    animals in extra-canonical texts/apocryphal literature 196, 197–8
    animals in the New Testament 186–91
    Christian symbols/images of animals 235–7, *236*
    Gospel of the Ebionites 202, 203
    Gospel of Pseudo-Matthew 189, 197–8
    Infancy Gospel of Thomas 198–9
    Jesus moulded birds from clay 199
    Jesus resurrected a fish 198–9
Ciarán of Clonmacnoise 206
Ciarán of Saighir 206
cicadas 414
    Obon/Bon, Japanese festival of the dead 451
'Companion of the Caves' 281
clans and totems 23, 46
communities, animals belonging to (Islam) 244
companions, animals as, to gods and goddesses 306–7
Confucian world view 394, 426
    Confucian principles 427
constellations, animal 55
Cowherd, William 231–2
    Bible Christian Church (England's first vegetarian church) 231–2
cows 303, 332, *335*
    in ancient Egypt 104
    Audumbla, primeval cow 128
    and Brigid 126
    'The Cow who Observed the Sabbath' 154–5
    cow protection in Hinduism 336
    in Hinduism 294, 334–6
    Lakshmi 320
    Surabhi (Kamadhenu) divine cow 311, 334, *335*
coyote 19, 48
    as creator of the heavens 39
    as creator of the Pueblos 38
    and death 79, 84
    gift of grief 84
    power of resurrection 80
    and salmon 70, 71, 72
    Washoe creation myth 38
creation myths 16, 27–43
    ancient Egypt 95–7

cruelty in 33–5
element of sacrifice in 42
emergence myths 45
   of the Washoe people 37–8
Native American 28
crocodiles 102, 103
   Crocopolis 103
   Han Yu reads crocodiles their rights 427–8
   Sobek (Sebek) crocodile god 102
Cross, John, carved platter *69*

Da Tang Xiyu Ji (Great Tang Records on the Western Regions) 432
Dalai Lama (14th) 393–4
David (biblical king) 152–3, *153*
David, Joe, whaling sculpture *57*
death, animals associated with *50*
   bats 83
   birds 82, 83
   disposal of the body of the first dead human 177
   garbled communication about death 77–8
deer 401
   Celtic mythology 124
   in a Hadith 248–9
   in the *Jataka* 384
   as totem animal 49
Descartes, René 226
Dhammapada 363, 372, 381, 388, 397
dharma 329–40, 369
dietary laws
   in Islam: halal, tayyib 255, 256, 257, 259, 260
   in Judaism: kashrut, kosher, treif 161–9
disguise, animals in 21
divination, Celtic 121
divination, in China 408, 438
   Shang oracle bones 416, 420
   use of tortoise/turtle 408, 412
divine punishment for cruelty to animals 255, 287
dogs 251, 210
   in the Book of Tobit, as companion to Gabriel 143
   in Buddhism, introduction of rice crop 430

   in Celtic myth 124, 125
   in Christian art 240
   St Christopher as cynocephalic (having a dog's head) *211*, *212*
   in creation myth 37
   dog sacrifices (China) 419
   God/dog 223
   Guinefort 212
   in Hinduism 321–2, 324
   in Inuit myth (as ancestors) 40
   in Islam 272, 275, 280–84
   John Bosco 211
   in Judaism 142–3
   St Peter and talking dog 200–201
   St Roch 210
   Satan in shape of a dog 199
   in Sufi literature 282–4
   white dogs (Japan) 448
dominion 149, 218, 230
donkey
   Balaam's donkey 152, 175
   consecration 151
   cruelty to 199–200
Donne, John 227
dove 176, 233, *235*
dragonflies 444
   Japan, 'The Island of the Dragonfly' *445*
dragon
   Benzaiten, married a dragon 446
   in China 410–11, *411*, 412, 432
   dragon-shaped ewer, German *217*
   slaying of Fafnir 130
Dreamtime 24–5, *25*
druids 120–23
   'Bull-sleep' ritual 122
Durga
   associated with lions/tigers 317
   Durga Puja festival, sacrifices of goats and buffaloes 317

eagle 76, 166, 219, 236
   feathers 45, 67, 76, 79
   in Inuit myth 44
   St John 235, 237
   on Native American myth 30
   in Norse myth 128

in Pacific Northwest myth 21, 22, 23, 47, 78
earth diver myths 33–5
Ebisu 446
Eckhart, Meister 232
eglah arufah calf 157
Egyptian, ancient 92, 93
   animal cults 112, 118, 119
   cosmic egg 95, 96
   creation myths 95
   underworld 109
ekoi mask 58
eland 58, 59
elephant
   Airavata 308, 311, 316, 338
   born as prince Megha 355
   in Buddhism 400, 401
   Gajendra 320–21, 323
   Ganesha *see* Ganesha
   Shiva and Parvati 338
   white elephants 338, 362
elk, in Siberian creation myth 41
emergence myth (Hopi) 45
Enlightenment, the 222
Ennead, the 97
Epimetheus 15
Epona, horse goddess 124, *125*
equality 373–5
Essenes, the 190, 203
ethics 12, 182, 230–31, 291, 306, 323, 325, 372
Eucharist 186
Eustace, St 213
Eye of Ra 108

falcon 98, 99
   in Sufism 276
Fall, the (of man) 204
feline goddesses in ancient Egypt
   Bastet *89*, 105, *106*, 107, 108
   Mafdet 105
   Pakhet 107
   Sekhmet 98, 99, 105, 107, 108
fire 40, 41
   jaguar and the gift of fire 41
   stealing of fire/sun by elk 41
fish, as taboo/unclean in ancient Egypt 90–91

Five Great Xian (five sacred animals) 436
Five Precepts 372
flood myths
   animals included in the covenant after the Flood 150
   Caddo people 44
   the Flood and diet (vegetarianism and meat eating) 148
   in Hinduism 310
   Inuit 44
   in Judaism 143–50, *144*, *145*, *146*, *147*, *148*
   Noah's care of the animals 146
   rift between human and non-human 143
four cardinal directions (animals associated with) 409, 433
Four Evangelists, and four beasts *236*
foxes
   fox cults in China 434–8
   fox worship in Japan *451*, *452*, 452–4, *453*, *450*
   nine-tailed fox 435, 454
   as shamans 435
Francis of Assisi, St 206, *206*, 207–9
frog 65, 97
   in creation myth 30
Fukurokuju (Japanese god of longevity) 446
Fuseli, Henry (Johann Heinrich Füssli), *Thor Battering the Midgard Serpent* 127

Gabriel, Archangel *248*
Gajendra, the elephant 320–21, 23
Ganesha *302*, 306, 308, 316–17, 338
   first scribe of the *Mahabharata* 301
   Ganesha's vehicle/*vahana*, the mouse 317
   Kangiten 446, *447*
Garuda 309
Genesis 11, 136
Gertrude's bird (Peter and Jesus) 204–5
Glooskap 35, 70
Goloka 334–5
Gompertz, Lewis (animal welfare) 177

Good Shepherd, the 192
goshala (cow shelter) 336, 358
Gospel of the Holy Twelve 201, 202
Great Chain of Being 215–19, 263–4, 274
Great Spirit (Native American) 18, 28
Grimm brothers, *The Three Languages* 240–41
Guanyin, seated on a lion *368*
guardian spirits 19, 25, 48, 49, 51, 61, 64, 66
Gundestrup Cauldron, the 123, *123*

Hadiths 247–51
    Muhammad and the Imams conversing with animals 247–50
haiku 386, 449, 450–51
Hanuman *300*, 301, 306, 308
hare 452
    Shinto story of Okuninushi and the hare 448
Hart, Jim, carving of a beaver *85*
Hathor *94*, 99, 103, 104
Hayagriva 311, 403
Hearn, Lafcadio 449
Hebrew, animals and 175–6
Heitsi-Eibib 28
helpers, animals as, for humans 138
Herodotus 88, 91, 103, 108
Hicks, Edward 193, *193*
hieroglyphs 90, 93
Hinduism
    Hindu pantheon 306
    Hindu sacred texts 290
    history of 290–95
    idea of the world as a forest 305–6
Hiroshige, Utagawa, *New Year's Eve Foxfires at the Changing Tree* 452
Hirsch, Rabbi Samson Raphael 140
horses 403, *414*
    in Chinese myth of Can Nu, Lady Silkworm 420
    dedicating horses in Shinto shrines 447
    horse fertility spirits, China 417
    horse sacrifice, Celtic 124
    horse sacrifice, Hindu 294, 296

Norse horse cult 130
Sleipnir, Odin's eight-legged steed 130
Horus, falcon-god 93, 99, *100*, 109
    Eye of Horus 112
Hue Shen Hua Chi 380
human/animal separation or conflict 87
hunting 55–63
    avoidance of killing clan animals 24
    'gift' (Ainu) 441
    'Greedy Brothers' (Sioux story) 59
    in Islam 259, 262
    in Judaism 159, 178
    myths/songs/rituals 20
    prayers (Ainu) 441
    relationship between hunter and hunted 61
    ritual of thanksgiving 53, 54, 60
    souls, apologizing to hunted animal 60
    spiritual significance 20
    taboos and rites 61–3

Ibis 113
    Thoth 101
Ikxareyavs (and Coyote) 19
Imbolc 126
Inca astronomy 55
incarnations 347
Indus people/Indus Valley 292
interconnectedness 20, 50
intermarriage 61
Iomante (Ainu festival) 442
    in African myth 26, 37
    bears, buffalo, whale, dog 21
interrelatedness (in First Peoples story of Wolverine and Muskrat) 43
interspecies communication 65
inu/inua (soul), *inusia* 52
Isaac the Syrian, St 205
Isis 104, 109

jaguar 20, 21, 66
    gift of fire 41
Jainism 340–60, *357*
    animal laity 353, 354
    cosmology 342, 346, 347

diet 356
occupations and implements 357
overview of 341–3
and pets 358
see also ahimsa
Jataka 383–5, 397, 406–7
Jatayu 300, 313, 320
Jerome, St 206, 213
Jesus with the wild animals 192–3
Jigme Lingpa 392
jiva 347
Jivaka Sutta 391
John Chrysostom, St 218, 457
John the Baptist 202–3
Josephus, *The Jewish War* 203
Jubilees, Book of 139
Judah the Prince, Rabbi (Yehuda HaNasi) 154

Kalechofsky, Roberta 173
Kalpa Sutra 344
kami (Shinto) 447, 452
kamui (Ainu) 439–40, 441, 442
Kangiten 446, *447*
Kapparot 173–4
karma 318–19, 323, 347–8, 352–3, 358–9, 372, 374, 392, 398, 401
euthanasia and negative karma 358
Karni Mata 319–20
Karuk (Karok) people 19
Khnum 96, 116
kitsune (fox) 452–4, *453*
Kokopelli 45
Krishna 313, 314, 334
cowherd 303
spoke to birds in their own languages 314, 318

Lamb of God *191*, 192
lambs slaughtered 192
language/speech, given by animals
Cree 46
Dagon people, via the jackal 47
Lankavatara Sutra (concerning vegetarianism) 389
legal rights, of animals, in Islam 262
leopards 90
Leviathan, the 137, 178

Lewis, C. S., concerning animal resurrection 238
Lewis, Mary
Agnus Dei 191
The Joyful Mysteries 189
liberation, of animals (*fangsheng yi*, release) 397–9, 400
life force (*bla*, Tibetan) 404
lions, guarding tombs 432, *433*, 382
llamas 55, *56*
Loki 130
Luther, Martin 226, 227

maat 93–4, 109
McDaniel, Jay 7, 458
McFague, Sallie 183
Mahabharata (Great Epic of India) 299, 301, 303, 332, 333
Mahavira 341, 343–5, 349–52, 354
Mahayana 364, 365, 374, 348, 378, 388, 389, 390, 394
Maimonides 156, 162, *163*, 164, 168
mammoth, in Siberian creation myth 42
manas (thinking faculty) in Jain tradition 354
Manichaean dualism 203
Manjusri, riding on a lion *365*
mantis (or praying mantis) 58
Manusmriti 304, 326, 329, 332
Maori origin myth 36
Martin de Porres, St 213
Martyrology of Donegal, The (*Félire na Naomh Neerennach*) 215
legend of Mochaoi 215
Master or Mistress of the Animals 19, 57
Maudgalyayana 370
related to all creatures, 43
meat consumption
in Buddhism 364
controversy in Buddhism 391–7
in Hinduism 332–4
Mecca and Medina: animal sanctuaries during pilgrimage 262
Messianic Age
peace between wild animals and humans 193
vegetarian diet in the 167

metta (Buddhism, loving kindness) 370, 377
Middle Ages, late, animals in the 218
Midrash 134, 138, 169–71, 176
misericords *214*
moksha 304, 318, 321–2, 342, 348, 354
mongoose (or ichneumon) (protecting Ra) 98
monkeys 43, 49, 301
    Monkey King, Sun Wukong *431*, 432
Montluçon, Jacquelin de, *Adoration of the Child 190*
Moses
    compassion for his flock 151
    saves a pigeon 272
Mu-lien (Mulian) saves his mother 430–31
Mwuetsi 28
Myle, Simon de, *Noah's Ark on Mount Ararat 147*
myth 13
    definition, types 14–16
    difference between mythology and religion 13–14
    of transformation/change 19

nafs ('animal self' in Sufism) 275
nagas *see* serpent/snake
Nahmanides (Ramban) 169, 178
Nakhshabi, *Tutinama* (*Tales of a Parrot*) 270, 272
naming the animals 137, 457
Nandi 315, *316*
    guardian of four-legged creatures 315
    son of Surabhi 315
narwhal, in Inuit creation myth 42
Nativity 186, *187*, 188, 197, 208
Neith
    creator of Apep 103
    mother of Sobek 103
Nekhbet 93, 100, 101
Neoplatonism 264, 268
Nicholas of Tolentino, St 213–14
nightingale, in Sufism 276
nirvana 362, 375, 378, 381
Noah 144–50, *145*, *146*, *147*, *149*

Noach parsa 145
Noble Eightfold Path ('Middle Way') 372
Nursi, Bediüzzam Said 250, 279–80
Nut 97, 99
    represented as a sow devouring her piglets 97

Odin 128, 129, 130
    as eagle 128
    with wolves and ravens 129, *129*
Ogdoad, the 95, 96
oni (demons, Japan) 447
Origen 221
Osiris 91, 104, 109, 114
Ouseley, Rev. Gideon 201
oxen 116, 155, 189, 190, 197, 429–30

Pacific Northwest myth and cosmology *14*, 29–30, *29*, 47, 48, 64, 86
Pali Canon 364, 383, 391
Pangu 409
Parasparopagraho jivanam 12, 340, 352, 360
Pashupati 315
    see also Shiva
Passover 171–3, 174, 195
    feeding/keeping pets during 172
    Paschal (Passover) lamb 171, 195, 202
Patrul Rinpoche 393
Paul the Hermit, St 206–7, 209
    with the otter 217
Peaceable Kingdom, The (Edward Hicks) *193*, 194
peacock *185*, 432
Perek Shirah 134, 141, 142
Peter, St 204
pets in ancient Egypt 91
pigs 380
    in China, Zhu Wuneng (pig) 432
    in Christianity 192
    as family members in Papua New Guinea 26–7
    in Judaism 162–4
Phra men ma (animal-headed sorceresses of Tibetan Buddhism) 403

pinjrapole (animal hospital) 358
polar bear 67, 439
Popol Vuh 31–3
prana 298–9, 372
prayer
    animals praying and worshipping 135, 140, 141, 242, 245
    in the Qur'an 243–7
Prometheus 15
protection, of animals in Islam 251–3, 254–5
Protestant Reformation 226–7
punishment
    for butchers/hunters 378–9
    for killing or injuring an animal 380
    for meat eaters 379, 388–9

qilin 410, 413
Quakerism, and George Fox 228
    Anna Sewell 228
Quetzalcoatl 21, 29

Ra 96, 97, 99, 108
Rainbow Serpent 25, 26
Ramana Maharshi (Bhagavan) 330
Ramayana 299, 300
Rashi 168
raven 57, 66, 129, 177
    after the Flood 146, 147
    Celtic myth 124
    creator of the world (Chukchi and Inuit) 40
    Raven 22, 23–4, 30, 35
Ray, John, and physico-theology 225–6
rebirth 342, 362, 374
re'em 147
Regan, Tom 11
reincarnation 55, 295
religious narratives 10–11
repentance (*pratikramana*) 359–360
Rigveda 294, 296
Rosh Hashanah
    shofar (ram's horn) 174
    tashlikh 174
Rumi 273, 274, 282

sacred pipe (Lakota ritual) 75–6
sacrifice of animals 194, 195, 324, 325, 326, 327, 328, 331, 341, 385
    in China 415–17, 418, 419, 420, 421, 423
    in Islam 260–61
    in Judaism 165
    Kali 329
    Shakta sect of Hinduism 329
    Vedic period 326
sages 305
saints 205–18
    Caitanya (Bengali saint) 321
salmon 68
    Coyote and 70, 71, 72
    rituals 68–70, 71–2
    salmon people (Pacific Northwest myth) 68–9, *69*, 71
samsara 318, 362, 363, 401
    hierarchy of 374
Sanai, *Tasbih at-tuyur* (Rosary of the Birds) 275
scapegoat 157, 173
scarab beetle 96, 97, *98*
    Khepri 96
Schweitzer, Albert 230–31
seals 53–4
Sekhmet *see* feline goddesses in ancient Egypt
serpent/snake 79, 219
    Ananta, snake lord 311
    Apep (Apophis) 95, 98, 103, 111
    Celtic ram-headed serpent 122
    in Central American and Mexican mythology 29
    cobras Dharanendra and Padmavati 346
    in Dayak creation myth 42
    giant serpent Vasuki 310
    in Judaism 139, 151
    Midgard Serpent/Jörmungandr *127*, 128, 129
    nagas 51, *51*, 314, 337, 401–3, *402*, 410
    origin of death (python) (Worora myth) 80, 82
    Shiva and snakes 315, 337

Vishnu as primeval serpent
    Adishesha 309
Seth 91, 93, 103, 104, 109
    the Seth animal 104
    and pig taboo 91
Seventh Day Adventists 232
Shabkar Tsogdruk Rangdrol 392–3
shamans 61, 63–8, 419, 422, 423,
    424, 441
    female 439
    foxes as 435
    guardian/helping spirits 64
    shamanic objects *49, 64, 65*
    shamanic songs in *Chu Ci* (Songs
        of Chu) 422
    and shape-shifting 8–9, 21, 22,
        36, 47, 53, 57
    Tugtutsiak 67
Shan Hai Jing (Classic of Mountains
    and Seas) 428–9
Shantideva 378
shape-shifting 47, 49, 50, 54, 57, 66,
    86, 125, 130, 435–6
sharia 251–2
shechita 166, 167
Shigeru Kayano 440
Shijing (Classic of Poetry) 415, 418
Shiva 292
    Pashupati 315
shochet 167
Siddhartha Gautama (Buddha) 362
    saves a lamb 363
    with a swan 362
Sigurd, understanding the language of
    birds 131
Simorgh (Simurgh) 270, 276, 278,
    279
slaughter (ritual) in Islam 256, 257,
    259
Smart, Christopher, 'my cat Jeffrey'
    224–5
smriti 299
Solomon 153
    conversing with animals 272,
        278, 275
soul 20, 52, 53, 62, 228, 229–30, 285,
    319, 348, 351, 352
    Kabbalah 169–71
    soul-birds in Sufism, 275

Southeast Asian cosmology 30
    birds and reptiles in 30–31
spider 278, 279
spirituality, animal 320–21
squirrel 301
Star Carr 9
Sufism 273
    Sufi literature about animals 279
synagogue art, animals in 175–6

Takbir 259
Tantricism 328
tanuki (racoon dogs, Japan) *449*,
    454–6
Taoism 422–6
    animals have their own Tao 425
    mythical creatures of 425
Taweret *102*, 103, 104
Tezcatlipoca 20
Thamud, tribe of 253
Thebes 112
Theravada Buddhism 364
Thomas Aquinas 222, 225
Thoth 95, 97, 101, 108
Three Jewels, The (Jainism) 348–9,
    398
Thunderbird 19, 29, 30, 77, *78*
tigers 412–13, 431
tiracchanakatha 'animal talk' 376
tirthankara 342, 343, 346, 350
Tissot, Jacques, *The Animals Enter the
    Ark 144*
Tlili, Saara 246
totem poles 22, 23
totemism 21–7, 413
    personal totem 49
transformative dance/masks 24
transmigration (reincarnation)
    in Buddhism 375, 385, 404
    in China 429
    in Hinduism 318, 323–4, 325,
        339
    in Islam 286
    in Jainism 342, 348, 352
    in Judaism (the Kabbalah) 170,
        171, 179–81
    in Judaism (reincarnation as dove)
        178–9
trials, of animals 158

tricksters/culture heroes/power
    animals *17*, 31, 38–9, 47, 86
trimurti 292, 309
Tripitaka 365
turtle, creation myths 29
tza'ar ba'alei chayim (kindness and
    respect for all) 155, 156, 157

Underhill, Evelyn 238–9
unicorns 293
unity of all life 369
Upanishads 289
uraeus 100

vahana 306, 307, *343*, 403
Valkyries 130
Varuna 308
Vasudhaiva kutumbakam (one family)
    291
Vedas 293, 295, 323, 334, 341
    about animal sacrifice and meat
        consumption 295–7
vegetarianism
    in Christianity 204, 231–2
    in Hinduism 334
    Jesus as vegetarian 204
    in Judaism 168–9
    vegetarian sects in the early
        Church 203
Viking/Norse history 126
Vishnu 320–21
Vishnu, avatars of 309–10
    Balarama, the cowherd 313
    Kalki 314, 315
    Kurma, tortoise 311
    Matsya, fish 309
    Narasimha, 'man lion' 313
    Rama 313
    Varaha, boar 312, *312*
vivisection 406

Wadjet 93, 100
walrus 67
Wesley, John 229–30

whales 51, 57
    Jasconius (*Voyage of St Brendan*)
        216
    Jonah and the Whale, in the
        Compendium of Chronicles
        245
    Nalukataq (spring whaling
        festival) 56
    whaling rituals 56, 57, 63
Wicca 10, 120
Widmann, Joseph Victor, *Der Heilige
    und die Tiere* 237–8
wisdom 9–10
witchcraft 223
wolf 23
    Fenrir 130, *130*
World to Come (compensation for
    animals who have suffered) 178

Xi Wangmu, Queen Mother of the
    West 425–6, 433, 436
Xolotl 82
Xuanzang (Tang Sanzang) (*Journey to
    the West*) 432

Yggdrasil 128
Yom Kippur 157, 173
    prohibition on wearing leather
        174
Yoshitoshi, Tsukioka, *The Fire-woman
    Kuzunoha Leaving Her Child* 453
Yu-Li 380
Yupik bladder festival 53–4

Zhou vessels, inscriptions 417
Zhu Hong, *Tract Against Taking Life*
    395–7, 399
Zhu Wuneng 432
Zhuang Zhou, as a butterfly 423
Zhuangzi 420, 422
Zunshi, Ciyun, *Verses on Resolving
    Doubts and Replacing Blood
    Sacrifice with Vegetarian Feasts
    and Fasts* 394–5